Corporate Decision-Making in Canada

THE FINDINGS AND RECOMMENDATIONS assembled in this volume are mainly the result of work undertaken by outside independent researchers. As such, the studies ultimately remain the sole responsibility of each author and do not necessarily reflect the policies or opinions of Industry Canada or the Government of Canada.

GENERAL EDITORS:
RONALD J. DANIELS & RANDALL MORCK

Corporate Decision-Making in Canada

The Industry Canada Research Series

University of Calgary Press

© Minister of Supply and Services Canada 1995

ISBN 1-895176-76-X
ISSN 1188-0988

University of Calgary Press
2500 University Dr. N.W.
Calgary, Alberta, Canada T2N 1N4

Canadian Cataloguing in Publication Data
  Main entry under title:
  Corporate decision-making in Canada

  (Industry Canada research series, ISSN 1188-0988 ; V)
  Issued also in French under title: La prise de décision dans les entreprises au Canada.
  Conference held in Toronto on March 20-21, 1995
    Includes bibliographical references.
    ISBN 1-895176-76-X

    Cat. no. Id53-11/5-1995E

    1. Decision-making—Canada—Congresses.
    2. Corporate governance—Canada—Congresses.
    I. Daniels, Ronald J.   II. Morck, Randall
  III. Canada. Industry Canada.   IV. Series.

    HD30.23C67 1995   658.4'03   C95-980250-9

The University of Calgary Press appreciates the assistance of the Alberta Foundation for the Arts (a beneficiary of Alberta Lotteries) for its 1995 publishing program.

EDITORIAL & TYPESETTING SERVICES: Ampersand Communications Inc.
COVER & INTERIOR DESIGN: Brant Cowie/ArtPlus Limited

Printed and bound in Canada

∞   This book is printed on acid-free paper.

Table of Contents

PART IV INSTITUTIONAL INVESTORS

PART V   INTERNATIONAL ASPECTS OF CORPORATE GOVERNANCE

PART VI   CORPORATE GOVERNANCE
AND SOCIAL RESPONSIBILITY

Preface

IN AN ERA OF GLOBALIZATION and rapid technological advancement, investments, particularly those in technology and human capital accumulation, are key determinants of corporate and national economic success. The role of corporate governance and the behaviour of corporate institutions are critical in this setting because they are the primary factors influencing investment decisions. This view is exemplified by the economic difficulties of many large and well-known global companies, whose experiences over the course of the 1980s and 1990s highlight the importance of corporate decision-making in effectively managing the challenges of structural change and economic adjustment.

One of the striking features of the research on corporate decision-making in Canada is the extent to which it has remained largely uninformed by both quantitative and qualitative empirical data. The extent to which past research has concentrated narrowly on the role of the board of directors and the board's ability to ensure that stakeholders' interests do not supersede those of shareholders is a further problem. This narrow focus has neglected other equally important market and legal constraints that affect corporate behaviour. As a result, the policy debate surrounding corporate governance has been too narrowly conceived, and has not been sufficiently attentive to the distinctive features of the Canadian economic landscape.

The Micro-Economic Policy Analysis Branch of Industry Canada, in collaboration with the Financial Research Foundation of Canada, commissioned 18 research studies to broaden and deepen our understanding of several key issues related to corporate governance and decision-making: ownership and concentration; the Board; director liability; institutional investors; executive compensation; minority shareholder protection; and long-term investment decisions. These issues are addressed from both economic and legal perspectives. The studies were presented and their findings discussed at a conference on "Corporate Decision-Making in Canada", held in Toronto in March 1995. The final version of these studies appear in this research volume.

The research assembled here will contribute to government policy-making on two broad fronts: by contributing to efforts to improve the growth and productivity performance of the Canadian economy by bettering the understanding of the concepts and linkages outlined above; and by deepening the knowledge-base for ongoing major revisions to federal business legislation, notably the Phase II amendments to the *Canadian Business Corporations Act*.

Academic and private-sector organizations actively participate in the preparation of some of the Department's research documents. Occasionally, other organizations also contribute resources toward Industry Canada's research programs. For this volume, I would like to acknowledge the Financial Research Foundation of Canada which contributed both the time of its principals and other support toward the successful completion of this project.

Dean Ronald J. Daniels and Professor Randall Morck have overseen this project and served as General Editors for the research volume. I would like to thank them both, as well as all of the authors and discussants for their fine work. I know that this volume will be of interest to the business and policy-making community, as well as to the wider public interested in economic issues here in Canada.

JOHN MANLEY
MINISTER OF INDUSTRY

Part I   *The Importance of*
Corporate Governance

Ronald J. Daniels   &   Randall Morck
Dean of Law   Faculty of Business
University of Toronto   University of Alberta

1

Canadian Corporate Governance: The Challenge

No CRYSTAL BALL IS REQUIRED TO PREDICT that, in the coming decades, the Canadian economy will increasingly be subjected to the phenomenon the popular press has labelled "globalization". Some key effects of globalization on Canada are already evident. One of them is that consumers now have greater choice because products from all over the world are available in Canada at affordable prices. Another is that globalization constrains government in new ways. Investors, entrepreneurs and businesses who do not like Canadian government policy are free, as never before, to take their business elsewhere. Globalization has also opened world markets to Canadian businesses while at the same time subjecting many Canadian companies to competition from parts of the world almost unheard of a decade ago. In Canada, the combined effects of globalization have forced a rapid rationalization of the economy, which has disrupted the *status quo*. People of different ideological persuasions may view these effects in different lights, but there is no longer any doubt that the effects are real.

The purpose of this volume is to examine corporate decision-making in Canada and to clarify the factors that, in the past, have sometimes led to less than optimal corporate governance. In this context, poor corporate governance practices that might have been tolerable even recently are now untenable. Our ultimate goal is to clarify government policy options that are realistic in the new global economic environment and also likely to improve Canadian corporate governance.

GLOBALIZATION: THE ECONOMICS BEHIND THE SCENES

In 1930 the Austrian economist, Joseph Schumpeter, proposed that a process he termed "creative destruction" underlies the success of capitalism. Capitalism hugely, some would say obscenely, rewards people who *create* innovations that improve efficiency or better meet consumer demand. Capitalism also *destroys* firms, sometimes brutally, that fail in these dimensions. Creative destruction, Schumpeter argues, leads to unmatched improvements in both production efficiency and living standards. Increasingly, mainstream economists are accepting Schumpeter's ideas, and now widely agree that giving free reign to capitalist creativity is more important than avoiding transitory monopoly pricing or other economic distortions.

Over the last several decades, the role of markets has increased steadily in both the industrialized and developing world. In large part, this growth of market importance, and the consequent premium on competitiveness, is related to the global integration of product, capital, and labour markets. The source of this integration has been thoroughly canvassed elsewhere and is mainly the result of reductions in domestic trade-protection barriers, technological innovation, and the liberalization of the command-based economies. The premium on international competitiveness has been felt more acutely in Canada than in other countries, owing to this country's relative openness to foreign competition. Compared to other OECD countries, the Canadian economy exhibits high levels of export dependency and import penetration. Canada's export sector, for instance, constitutes 25.2 percent of the domestic economy – second only to Germany's among the G7 countries in terms of the importance of export trade to the overall economy.[1] Likewise, in 1970 Canada's import penetration rate was more than five times that of the United States, and was three times the U.S. rate in 1985.[2] Another indication of Canada's dependence on external markets is the high level of foreign direct investment. In 1990 for instance, Canada received 5 percent of the total foreign direct investment inflows to larger industrialized countries, whereas the United States, with an economy roughly 10 times as large, received only 29 percent.[3]

The increasing openness of industrialized economies to the pressures of external markets has spawned a number of different effects. One of the most important is a sharp increase in the pace of innovation. In 1992, 187,200 patent applications were filed in the United States, up from 105,300 in 1972 and 68,384 in 1952. There were also 3,107 new product introductions in the United States in 1992, up from 1,762 in 1982.[4] When less tangible innovations are included in areas such as human resources management, marketing strategy, etc., the rate of creativity may well be even greater. Continual innovation is expensive, so innovative firms need to be able to reach large numbers of customers quickly in order to earn maximum returns on their creativity. Access to global markets is therefore essential for Canada, and that means granting foreign firms reciprocal access to Canadian markets.

This stepped-up pace of innovation means firms that lag behind can be pushed into obsolescence, and their work forces left high and dry. An innovative new competitor from a remote corner of the world can grab market share with little warning. The bankruptcy rate tracks the downside of this creativity explosion. In 1993 in the United States, 85,982 businesses failed; in 1952 there were 8,862 business failures.[5] Of course, bankruptcy laws and practices have changed over the years, as has the distribution of company failures across industries. Also, the employees of failed companies do not always lose their jobs. Often in bankruptcy, the creditors sell off the assets of the defunct firm as a unit and the buyer retains many or most of the predecessor firm's employees. Nonetheless, this increased pace of bankruptcy has substantial social costs.

In Canada there appears to be a clear national interest in fostering innovation, in encouraging Canadian firms to get ahead and stay ahead, and in cushioning firms that fall behind. Yet, the globalization of the economy constrains government in new ways too.

Traditional government policies based on taxes and subsidies are in disrepute. Government subsidies and tax credits for R&D are perhaps more likely to foster innovative "mining" of the government than true innovation. Government industrial policies that have sought to pick winners and subsidize their growth have seldom succeeded. Even the one previously notable exception, Japan, is now known to be no exception at all. Beason & Weinstein (1994) collected hard data on how much money the Japanese industrial policy directed at whom; and show convincingly that subsidies in that country were directed mainly at losers. The recipients of the biggest subsidies in Japan were weak firms whose collective performance actually declined subsequently. Indeed, taxing winners to subsidize losers, or even potential winners, is particularly unwise in a global economy where individual nations must compete for mobile capital and, especially, for information (i.e., people with expertise). Both capital and people can go elsewhere if they are too heavily taxed. In this new environment, taxing winners heavily to cushion losers is likely to lead in short order to a country of losers.

In short, government itself has become a competitive business in the new global economy. In the past, governments were monopolies. Businesses and people who did not like the government of the day could work to change it, but rarely could they simply take their business elsewhere. Today they can, and do. Governments are therefore under pressure themselves to become "competitive". Competitive government is not necessarily small government; rather, it is government that provides services most people and businesses want at tax rates they are willing to pay. Understandably, selective subsidies financed by taxes levied on everyone are seldom seen to fit these categories.

How then is government, robbed of its traditional policy tools, to promote the public interest in this new economic reality? We devote the final study in this volume to a list of viable options. A central thrust of our analysis is that governments should focus on *framework policy*. That is to say, the state should focus on providing the legal and institutional environment in which markets and firms are able to thrive. As Michael Porter has observed[6]

> ...[g]overnment's proper role is as a *pusher and challenger*. There is a vital role for pressure even adversity in the process of creating national competitive advantage ... Sound government policy seeks to provide the tools necessary to

compete, through active efforts to bolster factor creation, while ensuring a certain discomfort and strong competitive pressure.

In our view, a core feature of an effective framework for competition is the nature and quality of the corporate governance system that obtains in a given country. Here, we refer to the legal and market institutions that make up a country's corporate governance system. Nevertheless, before we begin to think about the precise nature of an optimal corporate governance system, there is great need to sort out where exactly the public interest lies in issues of corporate governance.

CORPORATE GOVERNANCE AND THE PUBLIC INTEREST

THE STANDARD OF LIVING ENJOYED BY CANADIANS depends critically on the success of Canadian business, which in turn depends on the decisions made by its top managers. Those decisions are heavily influenced by the legal and institutional settings in which directors and corporate officers function. How should corporations be run? If we are to propose ways in which government might improve their management, we must consider how corporate decision-making can go awry in the first place. This depends critically on the nature of the firm in question.

WHY CARE ABOUT MAXIMIZING SHAREHOLDER VALUE?

A CORPORATION IS A LEGAL FICTION. It has the rights and responsibilities of a "legal person", yet it is owned by shareholders, and has complex contractual links to its employees, creditors, customers, suppliers and the community – collectively termed its "stakeholders". Often, the interests of a firm's shareholders and various stakeholders conflict with each other and with others' perceptions of the greater good. This begs the question of whose interests should be paramount?

It is conventional wisdom, as well as orthodox economic theory, that those who bear the costs should have the decision-making authority. Theoretically, at least, this avoids problems analogous to out-of-control medical bills that arise from authorizing physicians to order tests and obliging taxpayers to pay for them.

A normal, healthy corporation has well-defined, legally enforceable contractual commitments to its employees, creditors, customers, suppliers and community. It may not, in the normal course of business, default on wages, interest payments, promised shipments, promised payments, or taxes. However, the shareholders have no such contractual rights. Rather, they are residual claimants. Whatever money the firm has left over after paying off its contractual obligations can either be paid out to shareholders as dividends or reinvested to generate capital gains for shareholders. The firm can freely alter its dividend payments and investment policies with few legal consequences. Thus, when unwise business decisions are made in the boardroom, it is the shareholders who pay the price. For this reason, economic theory dictates, corporations should be controlled by their shareholders.

Economic theory, as with any theory, is a simplification of reality. When a firm does poorly, employees may be laid off without the firm actually going bankrupt. Some stakeholders may thus bear more of the costs of bad management than will the typical shareholder. But most stakeholders do not. Senior workers are usually well protected from layoffs. Of course, if a corporation is run extremely badly, it may default on its wages, interest payments, deliveries and bill payments too. But this will happen only when shareholder value sinks to zero and the firm is bankrupt. Under such circumstances, bankruptcy trustees must run the firm in the interests of the creditors and other former contractual claimants who have been made residual claimants. In any event, from a policy perspective it is important to focus on those stakeholders who suffer from certain contracting disabilities, and are thus unlikely to have been able to anticipate and so negotiate for effective protection from the firm (in the form of *ex ante* compensation or *ex post* severance benefits) against the risks of dislocation. For these stakeholders, strong policy arguments exist for some type of public intervention, although not through modifications to the traditional apparatus of corporate governance.[7]

Ultimately, the reason good corporate governance is important is that its absence would erode public confidence in Canada's financial markets and therefore depress share prices. Such a lack of confidence would make raising equity capital very difficult for Canadian companies, limiting their potential for growth. This, in turn, would slow economic growth and thus exacerbate problems such as unemployment and government deficits. Good corporate governance, therefore, is unquestionably in the public interest.

DIRECTORS ARE SHAREHOLDERS' REPRESENTATIVES

IN PRACTICE, IN FIRMS WITH MANY SHAREHOLDERS, it is difficult for all shareholders to be consulted on all business decisions. The solution is the board of directors. Directors are elected by the shareholders and paid to represent the interests of the shareholders in corporate decision-making. To emphasize the ultimate purpose of the board, the law makes directors personally liable to lawsuits by shareholders if they fail in this duty. Officers of the corporation, top managers such as the CEO, president and senior vice-presidents, are assigned a similar legal duty and liability. In the jargon of economics, this is a type of *principal-agent relationship*: the shareholders are the *principals* and the officers and directors are their *agents*. Corporate directors and officers are required to act in the best interests of the corporation, and that means the best interests of its legal owners – the shareholders.

SHAREHOLDERS AND STAKEHOLDERS: A PRACTICAL COMPROMISE

TO SOME, THIS DOCTRINE MAY SEEM TO BE EXCESSIVELY NARROW. There are, after all, others besides shareholders whose fates are interwoven with that of the firm: its employees, creditors, managers, customers, suppliers, and the communities that depend on it. To reiterate, these parties are the firm's *stakeholders*.[8] Would it not be better if top managers ran the firm in the best interests of society, or the community, or at a bare minimum the workers *and* the shareholders together?

The economist's response is based on two considerations. First, the legal system collapses all of these into the interests of shareholders alone. If a firm passes over top (well-qualified) job applicants because of racial or gender prejudice, firm performance is suboptimal and the shareholders lose. If a firm pollutes the environment and is sued, the shareholders lose. If it mistreats its workers and is subjected to strikes or other labour unrest, share prices and dividends fall and, again, the shareholders lose. Second, even when managers make patently foolish decisions, they can usually point to some resulting social good – for example, benefits to some group of workers. Clearly, assigning a manager such a multi-dimensional responsibility effectively erases all responsibility. In this context, responsibility to all means responsibility to none.

The law has evolved a workable compromise. Managers owe principal duties to shareholders, but the legislatures and the courts have developed a range of overriding duties (and corresponding sanctions) to ensure fidelity to broader social goals. As a consequence, a corporation cannot claim devotion to shareholder interests to justify its neglect of explicit occupational health and safety, environmental, or human rights obligations. Not only will a failure by the corporation's agents to meet those obligations subject them to individual sanctions, the law also imposes financial sanctions on the firm's shareholders in the form of penalties levied on the corporation. In this way, shareholders have powerful incentives to monitor and discipline corporate misconduct. This compromise has strong efficiency properties; but it is also overlaid with a thick layer of democratic theory. Instead of vesting an unelected and unrepresentative cadre of senior corporate managers with the task of determining how corporate resources should serve the public good, this model relies on accountable and elected legislatures to make those decisions. This means that the decisions as to when and how corporate externalities should be internalized are fully transparent and subject to full and proper public deliberation and accountability.

MYOPIA

ANOTHER WIDELY REPEATED CONCERN with focusing on shareholders' interests is that shareholders themselves are said to be myopic. It is alleged that they are concerned mainly with short-term performance, so excessive catering to the wishes of shareholders means forsaking long-term investments. As the study by Giammarino explains very convincingly, there is absolutely no credible evidence that this concern has any basis in fact. Statistical analyses of large numbers of U.S. firms show that firms' share prices rise when they announce long-term investment projects or large R&D programs. The apparent conclusion is that long-term investments please shareholders. This is supported by other studies that find a strong and sustained positive correlation between R&D spending and share value. If firms do have a short-term bias, there is strong evidence to suggest that the average shareholder would be pleased to see this change.

PRINCIPAL-AGENT DUTIES

A MORE LEGITIMATE CONCERN IS THAT under some conditions managers can ignore small, poorly informed shareholders. Thus, a board with a single large active shareholder may toady to that shareholder while small investors, who collectively own most of the firm, are effectively disenfranchised. In firms that do not have a large shareholder, such as the large chartered banks, there is a danger that managers may ignore shareholders entirely and run their firms as personal fiefdoms. Shareholder rights activists allege that managers can then pursue pet projects, adopt biased hiring policies, and otherwise waste the shareholders' money. Such breakdowns of the principal-agent relationship are termed *agency problems*. Mainstream economics recognizes that various sorts of agency problems are pervasive throughout both the public and private sectors. Indeed, some economists even go so far as to allege that agency problems are the chief cause of economic inefficiency in modern capitalist economies.

Although agency-cost nomenclature is relatively new, the concept of accountability which underlies it is not. Since the early part of the century, corporate scholars have worried about the accountability problems set in train by the delegation(s) of authority required to realize gains from specialization in the modern corporation. Berle & Means' (1932) seminal study of the American corporation was focused precisely on this issue. It was these scholars who coined the phrase "separation of ownership and control" to describe the American system of corporate governance. Berle & Means conceived corporate America as riven by pervasive accountability problems emanating from scattered, small-stakes shareholdings. With so many shareholders, there was no incentive on the part of any shareholder to assume responsibility for controlling the affairs of the corporation. The consequence was virtually unchecked power for American corporate managers and the resultant suppression of the profit motivation.

In retrospect, it is clear that the Berle & Means' account was overly bleak. While it is undoubtedly true that small-stakes shareholders exert very little, if any, direct control over directors and managers in large public corporations, it does not necessarily follow that managers are entirely unbridled and free to frolic on their own. As a number of law and economics scholars have demonstrated, a variety of legal and market devices work to align managerial and shareholder interests. Legal instruments (such as shareholders' rights to sue directors and officers) ensure managerial accountability by imposing *ex post* costs on self-dealing managers. Market instruments (such as the takeover or the "corporate control" market, the market for managers, and the capital market) typically focus on less malign sources of managerial misconduct, and operate either directly (through the threat of displacement or debased reputation) or indirectly (through provision of information on managerial misconduct to parties capable of taking direct action). The existence of these various legal and market instruments does not mean, however, that the problem of accountability is trivial in the modern corporation; some residual agency problems remain. Rather, the claim is that the legal and market arrangements that comprise the system of corporate governance are fairly robust and, thus, to the extent that improvements to that system can be made through institutional reconfiguration, these gains are on the margin.

THE ROLE FOR LAW

IF FIRMS ARE BASED ON VOLUNTARY ACTIVITY among well-informed deliberative stakeholders, and if markets play an important supporting role in disciplining managerial misconduct, what role is there for law and legal institutions? As mentioned earlier, if it can be demonstrated that certain stakeholders are being denied access to adequate information, that their bargaining with the corporation is beset by severe asymmetries in power, or that they are being coerced into certain commitments with the corporation, then a plausible case for some sort of government intervention can probably be made. Nonetheless, most commentators agree that, save for employees, claims of this sort are unpersuasive; and even in those cases where the claims are clearly legitimate, it is not altogether clear that the best form of state intervention is through corporate law – because corporate law is usually viewed as being devoted to shareholder and, to a lesser extent, creditor interests. Policy makers must therefore be very careful about overloading a single regulatory instrument with multiple and often conflicting goals. This would be the result if the interests of employees and other constituencies deserving of protection were to be protected through corporate law.

If corporate law is, indeed, primarily about shareholder interests, what form should it take? Early corporate statutes contained several mandatory elements that were clearly in support of a highly interventionist role for the state in ordering private arrangements. Today, however, the clear trend in corporate law is toward an enabling regime, which confers considerable latitude on parties to pick and choose among various background terms. This enabling role for corporate law is consistent with the belief that the interaction between a shareholder and the corporation is largely voluntary in nature, and the law should, as much as possible, defer to the wishes of contracting parties. Viewed in these terms, the role for corporate law is clear: lawmakers should develop and maintain a corporate law regime that facilitates contracting by private parties. One way to accomplish this is to supply background legal terms that economize on the costs of repeated negotiation for private parties. Another way to facilitate private contracts is through the supply of certain terms that private parties are unable to generate on their own because of high investment costs and risks of appropriation (the public goods problem). The elaborate system of fiduciary duties developed under corporate law is an example of such a public good.

CORPORATE GOVERNANCE PROBLEMS IN CANADA

THE ECONOMICS UNDERLYING THESE AGENCY PROBLEMS varies across types of firms. We examine each of the most common types of corporation in turn.

WIDELY HELD FIRMS: OTHER PEOPLE'S MONEY?

A FIRM IS WIDELY HELD WHEN IT IS OWNED by a large number of small share-holders, each of whom has no effective control over management decisions. Some of Canada's largest firms, and almost all large U.S. firms, fall into this category. All the major Canadian chartered banks are widely held. So are Bell Canada and Air Canada. Although these and a number of other prominent Canadian firms are widely held, this genre of ownership structure is not common in Canada. Morck & Stangeland place only 16 percent of the 550 largest Canadian corporations in this category in 1989.

It is commonly alleged that in widely held firms managers too easily forget their duties as shareholders' agents and govern their firms to benefit themselves. This agency problem impoverishes shareholders and undermines the economic logic that links optimal corporate policy to the common good. For example, suppose a manager gains status and social influence from an unprofitable film-making subsidiary. Closing it would benefit the firm by $5,000,000 but would cost him (personally) intangible losses he values at $50,000. If he owns one-half of one percent of the firm's outstanding shares (a situation not uncommon in many large widely-held firms) he will forego $25,000 of share value but keep $50,000 in intangible benefits. He thus comes out $25,000 ahead. The other shareholders lose the remaining $4,975,000, perhaps without ever knowing they might have had it. Private admissions by corporate insiders, as retold by Mace (1971) reveal such instances to be disturbingly common in large U.S. firms. We doubt that large Canadian firms are entirely innocent either.

Of course, most self-serving behaviour by managers is less transparent. It might involve a phenomenon economists have dubbed "managerialism": corporate empire building through unprofitable takeover binges that enhance only the top managers' egos. Another possibility is ethnicity or gender-biased hiring or promotion policies that keep things comfortable for the managers but cost shareholders the value the best candidates would have added to the firm. Yet another example of managers' self-serving behaviour is funnelling shareholders' money into economically questionable pet projects such as unviable subsidiaries in exotic places. Some managers actually find it so wrenching to pay out cash windfalls to shareholders through increased or extraordinary dividends that they invest in almost any project, no matter how unprofitable, to keep the money inside the firm and under their control. Unnecessary Lear jets and palatial head office buildings are almost a caricature of self-serving managerial behaviour.

Because widely held firms are characteristic of corporate America, both the mass media and the academic research literature have dealt extensively with instances of self-serving management in widely held firms. The hit movie "Other People's Money" and the high-profile attention newspapers now give to poison pills, greenmail, and other instances of managerial misbehaviour testify to the extensive public awareness (if not always understanding) of corporate governance issues in widely held firms.

CLOSELY HELD FIRMS: ENTRENCHED INSIDERS?

AS THE STUDY BY RAO AND LEE-SING SHOWS, most large Canadian firms are not widely held. In more than three-quarters of the Canadian corporations they examine, at least one large blockholder controls 20 percent or more of the voting shares, and in over half of the firms a single blockholder controls more than 50 percent of the voting shares. Large shareholdings by management often enable them to dominate shareholder meetings since most small shareholders do not attend. This allows management to control director appointments and thus indirectly control corporate decisions. Under these circumstances, it is unlikely that senior managers would ever forget about dominant shareholders' interests for long. Given this, one might think Canadians would rejoice that most of our large firms are free of American-style agency problems. Unfortunately, the ownership structure of Canadian firms does not entirely eliminate these problems, and it brings with it another set of agency problems.

In closely held firms, the fear is that directors and officers will toady excessively to the dominant shareholder and ignore smaller investors. Consequently, their fiduciary duty to act in the interests of the corporation is interpreted to mean acting in the interests of *all* the shareholders. The agency problem here is the possible conflict of interest between the dominant shareholder (supported by the officers and directors who are under the dominant shareholder's control) and the other shareholders.

There is considerable evidence from the United States that blockholders *do* extract private benefits from firms. Barclay & Holderness (1989, 1992) show that large blocks of stock are generally transferred at prices higher than those prevailing on the open market for the same shares. Presumably this is because large blocks of shares confer more benefits than small stakes. Barclay, Holderness & Pontiff (1993) make the further case that the prices of many closed end funds in the United States are depressed because controlling blockholders extract private benefits. There is no reason to assume Canadian blockholders are more altruistic than their American peers.

Dominant shareholders are perhaps less likely deliberately to push the firm toward non-value-maximizing activities of the sort described in connection with widely held firms. After all, the dominant shareholder pays a high percentage of the cost himself. However, it is not reasonable to rule out such behaviour entirely. Large blockholders often dominate shareholder meetings with 20 percent of the stock or less. A decision that costs the firm $5 million is clearly not in the interest of a 20 percent dominant blockholder unless it also generates private benefits she values at more than 20 percent of $5 million, or $1 million. Certainly, such situations are not impossible.

An additional set of potential problems in closely-held firms involves what financial economists call "entrenchment". Dominant blockholders who exert a detrimental influence over corporate policy are almost impossible to remove; they are largely immune to takeovers, proxy challenges and board rebellion. Unfortunately, some dominant shareholders who originally brought value to their companies may continue to exercise control long after they should have retired.

There is substantial evidence that managerial entrenchment is also common. Morck *et al.* (1988) show that in the United States firm performance rises with insider ownership for widely held firms, but then falls as ownership levels rise above a threshold that permits entrenchment. Johnson *et al.* (1985) show that sudden deaths of CEOs over the age of 70 cause their firms' share prices to rise on average. Often, the death of a firm's dominant blockholder leads to it becoming widely held as the heirs cash out. However, the inheritance of dominant blocks of stock can also put less competent heirs into positions of power they have not earned. Morck & Stangeland (1994) find that Canadian firms whose dominant shareholders are their founders' heirs perform significantly worse than other firms of the same age and size in the same industries.

FIRMS WITH DUAL-CLASS SHARES: THE WORST OF BOTH WORLDS?

CANADIAN LAW AND PRACTICE ALLOW COMPANIES free reign to issue multiple classes of shares with different voting rights. This, in theory, allows closely held firms to grow without the dominant blockholder losing control. In practice, many fear that it also opens Canadian firms to the worst of both worlds. By issuing themselves stock with many votes per share, while others hold shares with few or no votes, dominant shareholders can entrench themselves although they own only a tiny fraction of the firm.

Dual-class recapitalizations (*i.e.*, transformations of one-vote-per-share firms into firms with different classes of voting stock) can be coercive. For example, suppose small shareholders in a one-vote-per-share firm are given two weeks either to convert their common stock into class B common stock that will have no votes but will pay an extraordinary dividend, or to commit to retaining their existing common shares (renamed class A common) that do have votes. On the one hand, each small shareholder knows that if all the others convert and she retains her class A stock, she will miss out on the extraordinary dividend and be left with a vote that is essentially useless. Thus, she should convert. On the other hand, if all the other shareholders retain their class A shares, if she chooses to convert her share to class B, her action will not, by itself, allow management to become entrenched; so she might as well have the dividend. Thus, again, she should convert. In essence, each small shareholder is enticed to convert her stock to non-voting common, despite the fact that this course entrenches management and reduces the value of the firm. Jarrell & Poulson (1988) show empirically that dual-class recapitalizations tend to lead to entrenchment and depress firm values.

At present, there are two specific ways in which corporate and securities law constrain the scope for opportunistic recapitalizations. First, it is open to shareholders to undertake a derivation action or seek an oppression remedy on the grounds that such conduct is motivated by an improper purpose. Such a claim would be salient in the context of a share recapitalization effected in the context of a hostile takeover bid. Second, both corporate law (provisions respecting fundamental changes) and securities law (e.g., Ontario Securities Policy 1.3) require special shareholder votes when dual-class share structures are created. These votes enable dissident shareholders to object to opportunistic dual-class recapitalizations.

FIRMS WITH TAKEOVER DEFENCES: PROTECTING SHAREHOLDERS FROM THE TEMPTATIONS OF WEALTH?

HOSTILE CORPORATE TAKEOVERS ARE EVENTS that often pit incumbent managers and workers against shareholders. Takeover bids are always good for shareholders because tender offers to buy control are generally made at premia of more than 30 percent above previous stock market prices, and can be much higher. It is difficult to see why shareholders need to be protected from selling their stock on such favourable terms. Indeed, shareholder rights activists argue that takeover defences exist primarily to entrench top managers who have established comfortable positions for themselves.

This view may be excessive. In some circumstances it is in the interests of the shareholders to have a takeover delayed so alternate buyers can be found. If a bidding war can be started, the ultimate takeover price might be increased even more. With this justification, many large Canadian firms have constructed defences against hostile takeovers.

Poison Pills

These are amendments to corporate charters that penalize shareholders who acquire more than a certain amount of stock. For example, a flip-in poison pill might declare anyone who buys more than 15 percent of outstanding voting stock to be an "acquiring person", and then go on to say that in the event anyone becomes an acquiring person, all other shareholders except the acquiring person shall receive 10 free shares for each share held. This reduces both the value of the acquiror's position and its voting strength by 90 percent; the acquiror is virtually back where she started.

In Canada, shareholders must vote on (i.e., approve) poison pills. However, in some cases the vote is tied to other issues, such as increased dividends, which casts doubt on the extent to which shareholder approval is truly voluntary. Nevertheless, the Canadian strain of poison pills is much less virulent than its American counterpart, which suggests that the requirement to obtain shareholder approval has limited somewhat the scope for opportunism. Even more significantly, there have been several setbacks for poison pills in Canadian courts and securities commissions.[9] The general thrust of these decisions is that poison pills may buy time for managers to conjure up another offer for shareholders, but ultimately shareholders must be given the opportunity to decide whether or not they want to tender their shares to an offer.

Voting Caps

Many corporations that have been established by Acts of parliament, such as chartered banks and privatized Crown Corporations like Air Canada and PWA Corp., have legislative voting caps. These conditions, set out in the statutes that created the firms, make it illegal for any shareholder to own more than minimal amounts of the firms' shares. In the case of Air Canada, the limit is 4 percent. For the banks, the limit is 10 percent. Voting caps are merely extreme forms of poison pills.

Takeover Rules

Under Canadian securities laws, a takeover bid is defined as any offer to acquire an issuer's equity that would confer more than 20 percent ownership of a single class of shares on the offeror. Once a takeover is deemed to have occurred, the acquiror must comply with certain rules, including *pro rata* take-up of shares, minimum bid periods, information disclosure obligations, and so on. For purchases of control from dispersed shareholders, the rules of Canadian securities law do not operate much differently from those of the United States. The crucial difference is in the context of sale of control by an existing control holder. Whereas these transactions are subject to only selective *ex post* review for substantive fairness in the United States, in Canada, the entire takeover regime applies to these transactions, thereby entitling all shareholders to participate *pro rata* in the transaction. The effect of this rule is to raise the costs of a change in control transaction for an interested acquiror. Because an existing control blockholder is unlikely to want to part with only a portion of her holdings (minority status is an unattractive prospect for a controlling shareholder), the acquiror is forced to bid for 100 percent of the company's shares. Many financial analysts regard this as a thinly disguised anti-takeover rule. By striving to make takeovers utterly fair, we may have made many of them prohibitively expensive.

Do takeover defences ultimately benefit shareholders? The preliminary answer appears to be "no". Empirical evidence suggests that on average takeover defences do have an entrenchment component. Stangeland (1994) finds that firms with poison pills record performance levels below those of industry rivals without such anti-takeover defences. Other recent studies also find that the adoption of poison pills and other takeover defences is correlated with reduced share value. A recent study by Comment & Schwert (1995) appears to contradict this, however.

FIRMS WITH FREE CASH FLOW

HARVARD BUSINESS SCHOOL PROFESSOR MICHAEL JENSEN suggests that corporate financial policy is closely related to corporate governance issues. He theorizes that in mature industries, a firm's existing operations produce substantially more cash flow than is needed for profitable capital investments. This excess he calls "free cash flow". Firms should use cash flows they cannot profitably use internally to pay increased dividends. In firms with inadequate corporate governance, managers may seek to retain control over their firm's free cash flow by retaining it for suboptimal investments. According to Jensen (1986), a low dividend rate in a mature industry is strong evidence of poor corporate governance. He also suggests that, in order to prevent managers from mis-investing funds, firms in cash-rich, mature industries should be more highly levered. Thus, there is a high probability that cash-rich firms with low debt are also subject to poor corporate governance.

The study in this volume by Gagnon and St. Pierre takes a preliminary cut at Canadian data and finds no evidence of a systematic link between leverage or dividend policy and performance. More specific empirical tests, analogous to those undertaken in the United States, have not yet been performed for Canada.

CONGLOMERATES: A SHELL GAME?

IN CANADA, AS IN CONTINENTAL EUROPE, KOREA AND JAPAN, much corporate activity is undertaken by conglomerates that consist of numerous related firms that collectively own controlling blocks of each others' stock. Public shareholders own the remaining shares at each level.

There are many valid reasons in economic theory to explain the existence of conglomerates. It is costly for firms to raise external capital. Financing investment projects is simpler and cheaper if it can be done using internal funds. Conglomerates can serve as a sort of internal capital market for member firms. Excess cash from one firm can be invested in another if the return there is higher. If conglomerates are run by managers who understand and can control all its diverse parts, they *should* make considerable economic sense.

However, the performance of conglomerates in general has not lived up to such expectations. Lang & Stulz (1992) show that the performance of conglomerates lags behind that of focused firms. Also, the collapses of conglomerates like Argus, Olympia & York and the Hees-Edper group of firms have added to investors' doubts about the real economic value of conglomerates. In the United States, conglomerates constitute a disproportionate share of hostile takeover targets. Raiders there have found the share prices of some conglomerates to be so depressed that money can be made by buying the whole conglomerate, breaking it up, then selling all its parts separately. In these cases, at least, the parts are worth considerably more than the whole.

The underlying problem with conglomerates is widely perceived to be that they are much more difficult to manage than focused corporations. It is difficult, if not impossible, for the head-office managers in a conglomerate to understand each component business thoroughly enough to formulate strategies that are as effective as those of their more focused rivals. This undercuts the main advantage of a conglomerate – the alleged allocation of the group's capital to where it earns the highest return. But more than that, conglomerates open up a whole new type of agency problem.

By controlling interfirm dividends, by having companies within the conglomerate group lend to each other at non-market interest rates, by organizing intercorporate billing for goods or services at artificial prices, or by transferring assets at synthetic prices, conglomerate managers can reduce profits in one firm and increase them in another. The fear is that profits in firms where insiders own relatively less stock might be diverted to firms where they own most or all of the stock – a kind of corporate shell game. In such a case, the agency problem is the plural version of that in a closely held firm: that the insider shareholder who controls the conglomerate might enrich herself at the expense of the public shareholders in all its firms.

An analogous problem arises for tax authorities in other countries when money flows from profitable, and therefore taxable, firms to loss-making firms within a conglomerate. This is not a problem here in Canada because tax-free payment of dividends within a corporate group is entirely legal.

In fact, as the study by Daniels, Morck & Stangeland points out, there are numerous other features of the Canadian legal and institutional environment that also facilitate conglomerate formation. Canada's current *Investment Companies Act* is a less effective barrier to establishing conglomerates with large numbers of partially owned subsidiaries than is the *Investment Company*

Act of 1940, and its requirements can easily be avoided through provincial reincorporation. More liberal interest deductions in Canada subsidize debt, which provides favourable financing for acquisitions. The lack of a vigorous, privately enforced securities disclosure regime in Canada reduces the transparency of internal corporate transactions, and heightens the attractiveness of the conglomerate form of organization to opportunistic corporate insiders. Similarly, the lack of a clearly articulated corporate law fiduciary duty from majority to minority shareholders in Canada helps explain, at least historically, the attraction of conglomerates to opportunistic controlling shareholders. The absence of such fiduciary duties allows controlling shareholders greater scope for unfair self-dealing than would be possible in the United States.

Daniels *et al.* also argue that the mercantilistic industrial policies of successive Canadian governments encouraged conglomerate formation. Restrictions on foreign investment by Canadians, such as the foreign property rule in the *Income Tax Act*, reduce Canadian shareholders' investment opportunities. When they may disagree with the policies of corporate managers, shareholders here have fewer alternative places to put their money than would be the case if they could freely invest abroad. This may have allowed inefficient conglomerate holding structures to survive, and may thereby have prolonged wealth-reducing redistribution from investors to Canadian corporate insiders. Trade protectionism and favourable tax treatment of certain types of domestic equity investments also contribute to an inward looking industrial economy. Canadian corporations have focused on producing a broad range of goods and services for the protected Canadian market rather than on a narrow range of competitive products for the global market. In this setting, the diversified conglomerate serves as a natural vehicle for achieving corporate growth. Further supporting the formation of the conglomerate was, in sharp contrast to the United States, a more congenial political environment for the concentration of economic power. Whereas American political traditions embody a deep and abiding mistrust of concentrated economic power, the Canadian political environment is more sanguine. Here, the development and preservation of a fragile national identity easily overcame concerns about concentrated power. So, to the extent that economic concentration may be the inexorable result of nationalism, Canadian political leaders have regarded it as a price worth paying to promote collectivist goals.

MULTINATIONALS: A GLOBAL SHELL GAME?

MULTINATIONAL CORPORATIONS ARE MULTI-FIRM ORGANIZATIONS akin to conglomerates, but with a more convincing economic rationale. All the subsidiaries of a multinational are usually in the same line of business so the overall organization is easier for head-office management to run than is a cross-industry conglomerate. Moreover, multinationals have immediate access to markets in many countries. This can be critical in earning a quick high return on expensive investments like R&D. For investment in innovation, production and marketing costs are often minimal compared to upfront R&D costs. Thus, the larger the firm's market for its new product, the higher the return on its original R&D. For firms in R&D-intensive industries like pharmaceuticals, computers, telecommunications equipment, home electronics, etc., a multinational structure is almost essential. Foreign partners are often avoided in these industries because of a fear of reverse engineering or the theft of proprietary information. The same considerations apply in other industries with high up-front fixed promotion costs like music recording or films, although foreign partners are a more practical alternative there. Morck & Yeung (1991, 1992) present empirical evidence that foreign subsidiaries do, in fact, add value only for firms with high spending on R&D or advertising.

There is, however, another reason for a multinational structure: tax avoidance. By shifting profits between subsidiaries (employing the same methods used by conglomerates) multinationals can control which subsidiaries are the most profitable and hence the most taxable. Harris *et al.* (1993) provide empirical evidence that U.S. multinationals commonly shift income from highly taxed to less-taxed subsidiaries. Canada has higher taxes than many of the other countries in which multinationals operate. Given higher domestic tax rates, multinationals operating in the Canadian environment have strong incentives systematically to shift profits out of Canada through manipulation of transfer pricing schemes. Not only does such behaviour reduce the revenues flowing to the Canadian branch, it also reduces the wealth of Canadian investors who hold minority stakes in the multinationals' subsidiaries. This phenomenon illustrates poignantly the law of unintended consequences; the creation of partially owned foreign subsidiaries was encouraged by Canadian tax and foreign investment policy.[10]

COOPERATIVES: THE MEMBERS' MONEY?

A NUMBER OF INDUSTRIES THAT ARE MADE UP OF corporations in other countries contain cooperatives in Canada. These organizations are owned by their members but controlled by professional managers. Thus, in theory, they might share many of the problems of lack of managerial accountability that afflict widely held firms and firms with entrenched management.

CROWN CORPORATIONS: TAXPAYERS' MONEY?

DESPITE A SERIES OF PRIVATIZATIONS DURING THE 1980s, Crown Corporations are still very much a part of the Canadian business scene. Corporations like the CBC, Alberta Treasury Branches, Ontario Hydro, and BC Tel. are unlikely to face privatization any time soon. Universities and hospitals are likely to remain in the public sector too. Given the agency problems that pervert decisions in the private sector, is not public-sector ownership an attractive alternative?

The answer is an emphatic "no". Megginson, Nash & Van Randenborgh (1994) show that the performance of state-controlled enterprises, including those only partially owned by the state, is unambiguously worse than that of similar private sector firms. This begs the question, "why?".

The reason seems to be that state-owned enterprises have their own set of agency problems that are, in many ways, more intractable than those of private-sector firms. In principle, Crown Corporations are supposed to be run in the public interest. In practice, this often means they are run in the interests of politicians and political appointees who pay none of the substantial costs of poor investments, empire building, etc., compared to the small fraction of such costs incurred by the managers and dominant shareholders of private-sector firms. The overriding agency problem in public-sector firms is that politicians and political appointees tend to lose sight of their duty to the public. Moreover, dysfunctional corporate governance in private-sector companies is ultimately constrained by the firm's bottom line and the bankruptcy that its violation triggers. State-owned enterprises have what economists call "soft" budget constraints – their deficits are picked up by the taxpayers. State-owned enterprises can thus tolerate worse governance than can their private-sector counterparts. Furthermore, those mechanisms that limit agency problems in private firms, such as shareholder votes, takeovers, project-based capital market scrutiny etc., are not features of the governance of state-owned enterprises. The only restraining lever the public holds is the threat of electing politicians who will privatize, and this is being exercised increasingly often.

OTHER NONPROFIT ENTERPRISES: DONORS' MONEY?

THE LARGEST CHARITABLE ORGANIZATIONS CAN BE as big and complex as large corporations. Their top executives have responsibilities on a par with those of corporate executives, and make decisions involving as much money. Yet charitable organizations have nothing analogous to shareholder votes, annual reports, etc. To provide accountability, director liability rules do extend to charities, even small local organizations. Is this the best way of making sure the managers of the charity act as their donors expect?

THE STUDIES IN THIS VOLUME

IN THIS VOLUME, INDUSTRY CANADA and the Financial Research Foundation of Canada have gathered together the thoughts of leading Canadian business and legal academics on topics related to corporate governance in this country. The studies were presented at a two-day conference sponsored by Industry Canada and the Financial Research Foundation of Canada, held in Toronto in early 1995. A number of authorities were invited to comment on the presentations; their comments are also included in this volume.

PROBLEMS AND POTENTIAL IN THE GOVERNANCE OF CANADIAN CORPORATIONS

IN THE STUDY TITLED "Governance Structure, Corporate Decision-Making and Firm Performance in North America", P. Someshwar Rao and Clifton Lee-Sing, both of Industry Canada, present a thorough and exhaustive statistical analysis of this topic using several hundred firms from both Canada and the United States. They essentially correlate various indicators of corporate strategy, such as leverage, capital intensity, R&D spending, and foreign market penetration, with indicators of corporate governance such as whether a company is widely held or closely held and how its board is structured. All of these variables are measured relative to benchmarks for firms in a given size range and in a specific industry. They then perform a similar analysis correlating standard accounting performance measures such as return on equity, return on assets, and various growth and productivity measures, again measured relative to size and industry benchmarks.

Their results are quite interesting. They find no consistent effect of institutional (i.e., pension fund, etc.) ownership on either corporate strategy or performance in Canada, but do find positive effects on both in the United States. This begs questions as to why Canadian institutional investors are more reticent about pushing for better corporate governance than their American peers. Later studies in the volume try to answer these questions. They find little difference in either strategy or performance between widely held and closely held Canadian firms, but find positive effects of heightened insider ownership and negative effects of highly concentrated ownership for U.S. firms.

These findings are consistent with, and add to, other studies of both countries. Morck & Stangeland (1995) find that the critical difference in Canada is between subclasses of closely held firms. Closely held firms controlled by entrepreneurs outperform widely held firms, while closely held firms controlled by heirs lag them. Several studies of U.S. data, including Morck et al. (1988), McConnell & Servaes (1993), and others, find that increased insider ownership improves corporate performance up to a point but beyond that, highly concentrated ownership is associated with poorer performance.

Rao and Lee-Sing's results for their board structure variables are also interesting. They find that in Canada large boards are associated with less R&D, and poorer overall performance and productivity, whereas in the United States big boards seem to have little effect, either positive or negative. They find that foreign directors have weak positive effects on Canadian firms, as does having a CEO who is also chairman of the board. They find no real effect in the United States on performance for the average firm. This is consistent with other U.S. studies, e.g., Weisbach (1988) and Morck et al. (1989), and Hermalin & Weisbach (1990), that find that board structure seems unimportant for typical firms, but matters when performance is poor. The presence of outsiders on the board is correlated with poorer performance in both countries.

It is important to emphasize the limitations of statistical evidence. First, statistical correlation does not usually imply causation. For example, a correlation between insiders on the board and good performance could be due either to outside directors causing poor management or to poor management causing shareholders to demand more outside directors. Statistical evidence of the sort in this volume can be consistent or inconsistent with a given conclusion; it cannot provide definitive proof. Second, the results in this study are from a type of statistical analysis called multiple regression, which looks for effects of one variable above and beyond the effects of the other variables. Thus, the fact that the presence of inside directors is positively correlated with performance while inside ownership is not, means that inside ownership is not related to performance among firms that have the same proportion of inside directors. If having many inside directors is the result of having large blocks of insider ownership, obviously insider ownership is still important.

In the study titled "Control and Performance: Evidence from the TSE 300", Vijay Jog, a distinguished business scholar at Carleton University, and Ajit Tulpule of Corporate Renaissance Group (Ottawa), show that the percentage returns provided to shareholders between 1977 and 1991 by closely held and widely held Canadian firms are similar. Jog and Tulpule's results do not prove that ownership structure has no effect on share prices. Their result is consistent with the share prices of, say, widely held firms being depressed relative to the shares of closely held firms by the same amount throughout the time period they examine. However, their results do show that intensified competition due to freer international trade has neither helped nor harmed either closely held or widely held Canadian firms disproportionately. Jog and Tulpule also present comparisons of various accounting performance measures for closely held and widely held firms, and report that there is again no difference. This analysis is not strictly comparable to that of Rao and Lee-Sing, since they use performance measures relative to size and industry benchmarks, while the accounting performance measures used here by Jog and Tulpule are unadjusted.

Giovanni Barone-Adesi, the Peter Pocklington Professor of Free Enterprise at the University of Alberta, comments that he is not surprised that results found for the United States do not hold up in Canada. There are numerous institutional differences between the two countries. Canadian managers are free of class-action suits by shareholders; they can use dual-class shares to retain control despite issuing large amounts of equity; they are less at risk from hostile takeovers because of coattail provisions; etc. Because of these differences, Barone-Adesi argues that most Canadian managers are well protected from shareholders, regardless of the structure of their boards or the distribution of their companies' shares. He further argues that making it easier for shareholders to bring class-action suits would help remedy this. He also points out that France assigns special legal duties to dominant shareholders, and argues that this might be appropriate for Canada as well.

David Stangeland of the Drake School of Management at the University of Manitoba comments that Jog and Tulpule make an important contribution by emphasizing that relationships between corporate governance characteristics of firms and their performance may change over time as institutions evolve and as competitive pressures change. He also points out that ownership structure and other corporate-governance-related firm characteristics are very different in different industries, and he argues that studies in this area must measure these features relative to industry norms.

THE BOARD AND BEYOND

AS MENTIONED EARLIER, THE PRINCIPAL GOAL of any corporate governance system is to solve the problem of delegated power from shareholders to directors and managers. One of the striking features of the recent debate over corporate governance is the extent to which it has focussed narrowly on the board of directors at the expense of other instruments. While the board of directors is admittedly the legal command centre of the corporation, it is clear that there are other organizational and market mechanisms that can attenuate agency problems in the modern corporation. For instance, commencing with Henry Manne, there has been a growing recognition of the capacity of the market for corporate control to monitor and discipline managers in widely held corporations. More recently, corporate scholars have looked to nuanced executive compensation arrangements and selective intervention by institutional investors as means for aligning shareholder and managerial interests.

The study "Alternative Mechanisms for Corporate Governance and Board Composition" by Jean-Marie Gagnon of the Université Laval, and Josée St-Pierre of the Université du Québec, adopts a holistic view of the system of corporate control. The authors invoke a cost-benefit analysis to evaluate the efficacy of alternative mechanisms for ensuring accountability, then develop a taxonomy that links alternative systems of control with different underlying corporate structures. Motivating the analysis is the belief that shareholders will, within bounds, seek to adopt the most efficient means to control managerial behaviour. The results of the analysis by Gagnon and St-Pierre show that the distribution of voting rights in the corporation does affect the precise means selected for control. In particular, they find that in widely held corporations, the ratio of outside to inside board members increases with the stock holdings of important outside shareholders (suggesting directorial appointments as a means to monitor performance) and decreases with the holdings of inside directors (suggesting entrenchment).

One of the key implications of the Gagnon and St-Pierre study is to remind us that markets, albeit not always unerringly, are capable of devising systems of control that support a multitude of corporate activities without having to rely on external governmental intervention. In other words, so long as shareholders are able to access timely and accurate information about corporate structure and performance, they should be able to pressure managers and controlling shareholders to offer governance arrangements that are welfare enhancing, thereby reducing the need for potentially destabilizing government intervention. The propensity of markets to solve governance problems is instructive, and worth bearing in mind when the nature and scope for legislation in this area is contemplated.

The study "Executive Compensation and Firm Value" by University of Toronto management professors Ramy Elitzur and Paul Halpern, involves a systematic investigation of the compensation practices of public Canadian companies, drawing on data generated pursuant to the recently enacted amendments to the Regulations under the *Ontario Securities Act*. Elitzur and Halpern cite data from the United States which shows the existence of a small but positive relationship between the introduction of incentive-based compensation arrangements (both short- and long-term) and share price increases (Bhagat *et al.*, 1985; Brickley *et al.*, 1985; Larcker, 1983; and Tehranian & Waegelin, 1986). They also discuss studies that track a broader range of firm-performance measures after the introduction of incentive-based compensation arrangements, and find that a link exists between these schemes and firm-performance improvements (Abowd, 1990). Nevertheless, their research notes the existence of managerial earnings manipulation in cases where accounting-based rather than market-based financial criteria are used to undergird compensation schemes.

Elitzur and Halpern's empirical study focuses on the executive compensation practices of a sample of 180 companies from the TSE 300 Index. Their focus is on the difference in compensation practices between closely held and widely held Canadian firms. In the case of a closely held firm, where management already has a significant equity stake in the firm, conditioning compensation on share-price changes would be superfluous and may even subject managers to excessive levels of risk. However, the case for performance-based compensation is stronger where the manager holds less stock, for instance, where the company is widely held or where it is closely held but control is secured by a dual-class share structure.

Elitzur and Halpern find that, regardless of ownership concentration, both salary and total compensation are positively related to firm size. However, in contrast to earlier studies, they find that performance, measured either by accounting-, cash flow-, or market-based variables, has no effect on the level of bonus, salary or total compensation for either closely held or widely held firms. Further, their research did not find any relationship between the percentage change in compensation and firm performance variables, although they did find that compensation was positively influenced by the existence of a poison pill. This latter effect seems to be stronger in the case of closely held corporations, and suggests entrenchment. One final important difference between closely held and widely held firms is the extent to which compensation levels persist despite a change in performance; the persistence effect is greater in the closely held firms.

In the study titled "In High Gear: A Case Study of the Hees-Edper Firms", Ron Daniels, Dean of Law at the University of Toronto, Randall Morck of the Faculty of Business at the University of Alberta, and David Stangeland of 'the Drake School of Management at the University of Manitoba, point out that a conglomerate structure allows profitable subsidiaries to bail out troubled ones (within the conglomerate) and so makes high(er)-risk business strategies viable. They find that, while Hees-Edper companies performed no better than independent firms of similar size in the same industries, they were exposed to much higher risks. They find that this is due to both higher leverage and higher-risk business strategies. Higher leverage is desirable for a firm because interest payments are tax deductible while dividend payments are not, but may serve little social purpose. Higher-risk business strategies may serve the national interest if, as many critics argue, Canadian business is overly conservative. They argue that Canadian public policy should not aim to discourage the formation of conglomerates.

The study by Paul Halpern and Vijay Jog, "Bell Canada Enterprises: Wealth Creation or Destruction?", tracks the performance of BCE, Canada's largest conglomerate, since its establishment in 1983. The authors focus specifically on BCE's growth and strategic direction and its value creation performance. This inquiry is salient; BCE is insulated from the discipline of the takeover market by virtue of its sheer size (it had $37 billion in assets in 1993) and certain regulatory impediments that limit foreign ownership. Also, it is important to determine whether and how shareholders have controlled managerial accountability problems in the conglomerate, especially given the company's dispersed shareholdings. As mentioned earlier, there is an extensive body of literature that argues that financial diversification and other motivations for the conglomerate structure are suspect from a social welfare perspective, and that they may simply reflect entrenched management's desire to stabilize the firm by diversifying it, or to buy the growing industries, even though this is not valued by shareholders.

Using a variety of measurement criteria, Halpern and Jog find that BCE has demonstrated marginal performance over the period since its inception. During the first six years, BCE operated like a large conglomerate, purchasing and establishing companies, many of which were in areas unrelated to its core activities. The source of financing for these transactions was the firm's steady supply of cash, secured through mature product lines and a highly regulated telecommunications' franchise. These results seem to confirm the existence of entrenchment behaviour. Halpern and Jog do find, however, that BCE's performance in the post-1989 period has improved (involving a return to more focused corporate growth), and seems to have attracted some modest recognition by shareholders. Nevertheless, shareholder support for the conglomerate is not as great as it could be, and the authors argue that this discount reflects the market's concern that management will repeat the mistakes of the past, namely by diverting free cash flows (kicked off by the regulated telecommunications monopoly) to investments in wholly owned or portfolio companies in related and semi-related businesses across the world. Further exacerbating the company's problems is its strategic commitment to the management of assets, not businesses.

Clifford Holderness of Boston College, a leading expert on closely held firms in the United States, comments that closely held firms are more important in the United States than is commonly realized, although they are not nearly as pervasive as in Canada. He argues that dominant shareholders can and do extract private benefits from the firms they control, but there must be constraints on this. Otherwise, closely held firms would eventually disappear, and this is not happening, even in the United States.

Vikas Mehrotra of the Faculty of Business at the University of Alberta comments that sole federal jurisdiction in areas related to corporate governance is needed to prevent managers reincorporating their firms in provinces that provide comfortable protection for insiders. He advances the argument that disputes between dominant shareholders and small shareholders are the central issue in Canadian corporate governance.

INSTITUTIONAL INVESTORS

ONE OF THE MOST IMPORTANT CHANGES TO CANADIAN capital markets, and one which was frequently discussed during the conference, is the growing significance of institutional owners. Spurred on by the retirement needs of an aging population, large institutional investors (public and private pension funds, mutual funds, insurance companies and banks) are blessed with ample pools of capital that they have directed to investment in Canadian corporate equity. For many Canadian and American commentators, the growth of institutional ownership has profound implications for the control of managerial behaviour in both widely held and closely held corporations. The claim is simple. By virtue of their size, sophistication, and staying power, institutional investors are capable of monitoring and disciplining both managers and controlling shareholders. Nevertheless, the claim for institutional ownership is not without its detractors. Many, such as Lakonishok *et al.* (1992), argue that the scope for vigorous institutional activism is hobbled by a range of legal and organizational problems within institutional investors themselves.

The studies commissioned for this volume address the scope for, and prospects of, institutional activism from a number of different perspectives. "Do Institutional and Controlling Shareholders Increase Corporate Value?", the study by Jeffrey MacIntosh of the Faculty of Law, University of Toronto and Lawrence Schwartz, a consulting economist in the private sector, addresses the effects of both institutional and controlling shareholders on corporate value. In the case of the former, the authors suggest that institutional shareholders will increase corporate value, although they concede the possibility that institutional clout may be co-opted into being an unwitting ally of opportunistic management. In the case of the latter, MacIntosh and Schwartz are more agnostic; they predict that controlling shareholders will engage both in more effective monitoring of managers than non-control shareholders, and in redistributive transactions that shift wealth from non-controllers to controllers. Given the prospects of controlling shareholder opportunism in the form of wealth redistributive transactions, MacIntosh and Schwartz predict that institutional investors will make controlling shareholders, not just management, a target of their monitoring.

To test their hypotheses, MacIntosh and Schwartz examined several different performance measures for TSE 300 firms, which they correlate with data on Canadian patterns of institutional ownership. They find a positive and statistically significant relationship between both return on assets and return on equity and institutional holdings. They also find some support for the hypothesis that institutional monitoring tends to mitigate the danger of redistributive transactions engineered by controlling interests. While the presence of institutional investors is correlated with increased corporate value, the relationship between controlling shareholders and corporate value is more ambiguous. MacIntosh and Schwartz find that, although firms with controlling shareholders generate higher profits, these profits are siphoned off by controlling shareholders.

The study "Institutional Activism by Public Pension Funds: The CalPERS Model in Canada?" by Steven Foerster of the Business School at the University of Western Ontario considers the desirability of importing into Canada the highly interventionist pattern of shareholder activism used by the California Public Employees' Retirement System (CalPERS) in the United States. CalPERS is not only the largest public pension fund in the United States (assets of US$ 80 billion), but also the most activist. Over the last several years, CalPERS has trained its sights on the most poorly performing corporations in the United States. Each year, the fund identifies performance laggards, and subjects the management of those firms to increasing pressure (ranging from quiet, behind-the-scenes diplomacy to more public and stinging forms of intervention, such as "Just Vote 'No'" proxy campaigns). Foerster cites a recent study by Nesbitt (1994) that found that whereas the targets of CalPERS activism underperformed the S&P Index by 60 percent prior to CalPERS' involvement, post-intervention returns jumped dramatically – outperforming the index by 40 percent.

Given the returns alleged to derive from CalPERS' activism, Foerster considers why Canadian investors have yet to embrace this model of intervention. On the basis of extensive interviews conducted with Canadian public fund managers, Foerster traces the lack of enthusiasm for CalPERS' style intervention to differences in "style", rather than to any fundamental difference in the underlying regulatory structure of the two countries. That is, Canadian institutional investors systematically favour a less confrontational style of dealing with performance problems than is manifest in the United States. Another interesting point Foerster raises is that CalPERS systematically avoids closely held firms. Since most Canadian firms fall into this category, it may be that CalPERS' style of intervention is not well suited to dealing with managers who are also dominant shareholders. It is important not to overstate the commitment to tacit pressure and activism; even Foerster acknowledges the activism of Canadian institutions (spearheaded by Fairvest) in responding to unfair management initiated transactions.

In the study titled "Monitoring Incentives Facing Institutional Investors", Michel Patry of the École des Hautes Études Commerciales and Michel Poitevin of the Université de Montréal analyze the governance of institutional investors themselves, and note that employees usually have little influence on how their pension money is invested. They point out that in defined benefit pension funds, the sponsoring organization has an incentive to maximize the fund's return. However, that sponsor is often a corporation with its own governance problems. Where the sponsor is not a corporation, it is usually a government and therefore subject to the political favour trading that plagues the public sector in Canada.

Several studies in the United States agree that portfolios of corporate pension funds perform surprisingly poorly compared to both broad market indices and mutual funds. The portfolio performance of public pension funds is even worse.

In a summary of this evidence, Lakonishok et al. (1992) agree that corporate treasurers, usually responsible for managing corporate pension funds, are more likely to favour hiring outside portfolio managers than indexing. Hiring outside managers gives them someone to blame for poor performance, but still provides work for the corporate treasurer's department. Outside managers must be evaluated, hired and fired; indexing is too easy a way to earn higher returns, and would not justify a large bureaucracy in the corporate treasurer's office. Since neither plan beneficiaries nor public shareholders have any input, the interests of corporate treasurers take precedence.

Romano (1993) argues that similar circumstances prevail in public-sector pension funds, with neither beneficiaries nor taxpayers having any serious input into how their plans are managed. Hiring, firing, and evaluating outside managers gives inside managers the same advantages as those in corporate pension funds have. However, the additional complication of pressure to put money into politically favoured investments may reduce performance even further in public-sector funds.

Lakonishok et al. (1992) continue that outside portfolio managers for pension funds are usually compensated with a management fee similar to that charged by mutual funds. Thus, outside managers' incentives are to acquire and keep a large portfolio to manage; increasing its value is less important to them.

Lakonishok et al. (1992) discuss evidence that corporate treasurers use quarterly performance to evaluate the performance of outside portfolio managers.

However, stock prices are known to exhibit mean reversion, that is, unusually low stocks tend to go up and unusually high stocks tend to go down. Thus, corporate treasurers systematically buy high and sell low. Also, there is evidence that portfolio managers systematically sell "dog" stocks and replace them with "high flying" stocks at quarterly reporting times. Having a few good stocks in one's portfolio apparently impresses sponsors. Again, buying high and selling low is not a recommended formula for financial success. Overall, Lakonishok *et al.* (1992) conclude, poor governance within pension funds results in sponsors reallocating their funds' assets among portfolio managers too often, in portfolio managers trading too often, and in poor overall returns.

Patry and Poitevin suggest that few institutional investors have the expertise necessary to intervene in the management of firms whose shares they own. They also argue that the governance problems within pension funds must be resolved before pension funds can be expected to improve the governance of corporations.

Patry and Poitevin contend that the current provision in the *Income Tax Act* that restricts pension funds to investing no more than 20 percent of their portfolios abroad probably does not contribute to better corporate governance. A primary effect of this rule is to prevent pension funds from selling out of poorly performing Canadian firms for lack of better alternative investments. Although this might force the funds to voice their concerns to the managers of such firms, it also reduces the power of pension funds to affect such firms by dumping their stock. Patry and Poitevin consider mandatory indexing, a flip tax on capital gains, greater legal liability for pension-fund managers, professional monitors, relational investing, and better disclosure of pension-fund managers' compensation, and of pension funds' risk and comparative performance. They discuss the pros and cons of these proposals in detail.

Brian Smith and Ben Amoako-Adu of the Department of Finance at Wilfrid Laurier University, contribute the study on "Outside Financial Directors and Corporate Governance". They find no consistent pattern relating the performance of Canadian firms to the presence on their boards of directors affiliated with financial institutions. This study is actually more wide-ranging than its title suggests. The authors also examine insider ownership. Perhaps because of the paucity of widely held Canadian firms and the limited disclosure of their owners' stakes, no statistically discernable pattern is found in the data for firms with insider ownership below 20 percent. Among firms with more than 20 percent managerial ownership, they find a positive relationship with share value similar to that found by Morck *et al.* (1988) in U.S. data. They also find no statistically discernable relation between the number of outsiders on the board and firm performance. However, they advance the important point that Canadian disclosure rules fail to establish who really is an outsider. A firm's lawyers, executives of its advertising firm, and executives of companies that do business with it are not really outsiders, yet are so classified when they sit on its board. Their fear of losing business with the firm may deter such directors from challenging the CEO. Perhaps the rules defining outside directors should be more stringent.

Mark Huson of the Faculty of Business at the University of Alberta makes some perceptive comments on the studies in Part IV, pointing out that the defining theme of corporate governance in Canada is controlling shareholders, not unsupervised managers as in the United States. Huson suggests that Amoaku-Adu and Smith do not distinguish which directors are controlled by management and which are really independent. Because of such problems in most studies of outside directors, he argues that government ought to hold off from requiring certain numbers of outsiders on boards.

Huson adds, however, that Amoaku-Adu and Smith's results are consistent with dominant shareholders extracting disproportionate income from firms they control. Can institutional investors limit this? Huson points out some econometric problems in Foerster's analysis relating to the use of returns excluding dividends. He argues that the analysis by MacIntosh and Schwartz does not distinguish between the possibility that institutional investors improve share values and the possibility that improved share values attract institutions. But despite these problems, he contends that institutional investors probably do improve corporate governance in Canada. Huson does not support Patry and Poitevin's idea of flip taxes to reduce churning in pension funds. In his opinion funds should be free to divest themselves of investments in poorly run firms, and the thinness of Canadian markets already constitutes a barrier to this.

Huson advocates instead measures to reduce pension funds' costs in confronting corporate governance problems. He proposes that pension funds be allowed to communicate among themselves on corporate governance issues, that institutional investors not be classified as controlling shareholders, that valuation techniques in shareholder appraisal rights take into account value lost due to things like poison pill adoptions, that outside board members' pay be linked to share prices, and that pension funds be allowed to invest abroad with no restrictions.

Michael Weisbach of the University of Arizona, one of the foremost experts on boards of directors in the United States, suggests that Canadians should not be too quick to imitate practices south of the boarder. Weisbach suggests that activist U.S. pension funds like CalPERS are overrated, and he argues that their apparent success may be due to mean reversion in stock prices rather than to any real effect on corporate governance. He points out that studies finding a statistical link between good company performance and institutional investors as shareholders may not indicate a beneficial effect of these investors on corporate governance. Rather, they may just be detecting fund managers rushing to buy winners so their quarterly portfolio reports look good. He supports Patry and Poitevin's call for increased indexing of pension funds' portfolios, although he stops short of calling for mandatory indexing. Weisbach argues that the current rule forcing Canadian pension funds to invest in Canada prevents them from diversifying as much as they should. He points out that Canadian pension funds should invest very little in Canada in order to insulate themselves from the Canadian business cycle.

INTERNATIONAL ASPECTS OF CORPORATE GOVERNANCE

The study titled "The Corporate Governance of Multinationals", by Randall Morck of the Faculty of Business at the University of Alberta and Bernard Yeung of the School of Business Administration at the University of Michigan, argues for a minimalist approach to corporate governance legislation. Globalization is fast making heavy-handed legislation of business impractical. Canada is in competition with other countries for capital, knowledgeable workers, and high value-added operations of multinationals. If the Canadian government passes onerous laws, Canada will simply lose out to more friendly jurisdictions. For this reason, the subsidiaries of foreign multinationals should be treated like other Canadian companies with dominant shareholders.

The same globalization process means that Canadian companies will be exposed to more bracing competition from abroad in coming years, and poor corporate governance will therefore be more costly. Rather than attempt to micromanage boards of directors, the emphasis should be on empowering shareholders. Increasing shareholder power is a more flexible and more effective way to improve corporate governance and thereby make Canadian firms globally competitive.

The corporate governance issue being addressed here is the fair treatment of minority shareholders by the dominant shareholder – in this case, the foreign parent company. One way of achieving fair treatment is to require that the boards of all closely held firms, including foreign controlled subsidiaries, have conduct committees charged with monitoring non-arm's-length transactions. These committees must have a majority of outside directors. If there is a political necessity, they could also be required to be Canadian citizens, although there is little economic rationale for this as long as they are sueable in Canada. It would also make sense that all closely held firms, including partially owned subsidiaries, disclose the details of all their non-arm's-length transactions, and that their small shareholders have the right to launch class-action suits against the dominant shareholder in cases of oppression.

The study by Lewis Johnson and Ted Neave of the School of Business at Queen's University, "Corporate Governance and Supervision of the Financial System", systematically links the governance structures of financial and market intermediaries with the asset and liability mix of various institutions. The authors do so by drawing on a transaction cost framework developed by Oliver Williamson. They demonstrate a linkage between the nature of assets and liabilities and the complexity and transparency of the monitoring arrangements that obtain across different financial and market intermediaries. To strengthen the performance of intermediaries, Johnson and Neave recommend greater reliance on mandatory production of information where asset valuations, liability valuations, or contingent risks are now opaque. Furthermore, they endorse the value of continuing information release, rather than sudden announcements of dramatic change.

"Banks and Corporate Governance in Canada", by Randall Morck of the Faculty of Business at the University of Alberta and Masao Nakamura of the Faculty of Commerce and Business Administration at the University of British Columbia, describes the somewhat checkered history of the German and Japanese banking systems. They argue that the alleged benefits of banks as major shareholders are unlikely to materialize in Canada; indeed, they suggest that the benefits are far from clear even in Germany and Japan. The authors point out that Canadian banks are a poor choice for a watchdog as they, almost alone among Canadian firms, are widely held and subject to all the inefficiencies that implies. They recommend no move toward increasing the role of Canadian banks in the corporate governance of non-financial firms.

Roberta Romano of Yale Law School, a leading expert in corporate governance issues, comments that individuals have been remarkably creative throughout history in structuring institutions to evade regulation. Although she is concerned about the distribution effects of subsidies to higher education and university research, which mainly benefit the upper middle class, she agrees with Morck and Yeung that excessive regulation is to be avoided, especially in an increasingly global economy. She points to the beginnings of the Eurobond market as an example. The United States imposed taxes on foreign bonds in the early 1960s with the result that the market simply moved abroad. Overly heavy-handed corporate governance regulations would simply fuel the search for administrative and legal structures that evade them. She agrees with Morck and Nakamura that the Japanese and German banking systems are probably not to be imitated. She points out that the banking systems were in place long before the rapid post-war growth of these two countries, and argues that a latecomer advantage (learning from others' mistakes), and perhaps things like good education and a high savings rate, were more important than corporate governance to that growth. She argues that German banking was more an effect than a cause of that country's rapid growth. Germany industrialized late, when the logistics of large-scale manufacturing had been worked out by others. The optimal scale for German industry was therefore larger than it had been during the period of industrialization in England and France. The need for large blocks of capital may have built the banks, and not the reverse. Romano points out that co-determination in Germany assigns half the seats on a firm's supervisory board or *Aufsichtsrat* to labour representatives. With half the board definitely not representing shareholders and the other half doing so weakly at best, widely held ownership is unlikely to be optimal in Germany, so another system had to be developed. This, she argues, shows that corporate governance must be thought of in the context of a country's overall economic system. German- and

Japanese-style banking makes little sense here, given the rest of Canada's economic system.

In his comments Adrian Tschoegl, a noted expert on the Japanese economy who teaches at the University of Pennsylvania's Wharton School, emphasizes that small countries can be home bases for global companies, and suggests that this is a feasible future for Canada. He then considers the roles of debt and equity, and how they differ across countries, and argues that these considerations might supplement the analysis in Johnson and Neave's study. Tschoegl points to the work of Allen (1993), who argues that debt financing is acceptable to investors in mature industries, where monitoring is easy. In newer, less well-understood industries, where monitoring is difficult, equity is predominant. He then provides insightful summaries of recent work on the roles of markets and intermediaries, and again connects them to Johnson and Neave's study. Finally, he comments at length on the study by Morck and Nakamura, pointing out that Japanese *keiretsu* are unique among conglomerates for their mutual cross holding. Firms own stock in each other collectively, and no single firm may dominate. Japanese banks are owned by other *keiretsu* firms. He adds that vertical monitoring is important in Japan: that firms monitor the governance of their suppliers. In a discussion of the history of Japanese banking, he notes that in the late 19th century Japan copied U.S. banking regulations, but was dissatisfied with the results. A series of modifications modelled on Belgian, British, and French laws and institutions followed, and led to the present system. Thus, the current similarities of the Japanese and German systems result from both retaining aspects of earlier practice that was once common to much of Europe.

CORPORATE GOVERNANCE AND SOCIAL RESPONSIBILITY

ALTHOUGH A CONSIDERABLE AMOUNT OF INK HAS BEEN SPILLED on the issue of the social responsibilities of directors, specifically the extent to which directors owe duties to non-shareholder constituencies, the fact remains that public concern with corporate misconduct typically involves a failure on the part of the corporation to adhere to explicitly legislated duties and responsibilities. In other words, the only question is how to ensure board compliance with legislatively prescribed goals, not whether these goals should be pursued in the first place.

The study by Ronald Daniels and Robert Howse of the Faculty of Law at the University of Toronto, "Rewarding Whistleblowers: The Costs and Benefits of an Incentive-Based Compliance Strategy", focuses on one relatively under-utilized (in the Canadian context) instrument for achieving corporate compliance with social responsibilities: whistleblower bounties. Daniels and Howse argue that whistleblower bounties have considerable potential to become a cost-effective means to enforce legislated responsibilities. The authors provide two principal arguments in favour of such bounties. First, whistleblower bounties increase the effectiveness of sanctions by raising the probability that misconduct will be detected, which means that the state will not have to use excessive sanctions to secure social optimal penalties (the product of both probability of detection and quantum of penalty). Second, whistleblower bounties take advantage of existing information and control systems within the corporation, thereby reducing the need for the state to establish more costly and, ultimately, less effective external monitoring systems.

Nevertheless, despite the arguments in their favour, state reliance on whistleblower bounties has proved to be extremely controversial. In the United States, for instance, there has been intense criticism of the bounties provided by the federal government under the *False Claims Act*. Critics allege that the existence of such bounties distorts internal information flows, causes managers to make lower-level employees over-invest in firm-specific capital so as to magnify the downside costs of whistleblowing, and subverts the ability of managers to create durable commitments to firm culture and team-work. Daniels and Howse find these concerns overstated, and argue that careful design and enforcement of whistleblower incentives can correct for many of these problems.

The comment on the Daniels and Howse study by Jennifer Arlen of the University of Southern California Law Center is sympathetic to enhanced reliance on whistleblower bounties in the control of corporate crime. However, she stresses that bounty provisions should not be enacted unless accompanied by a thorough reform of criminal law. Arlen is concerned with the interrelationship between bounties and the background system of criminal and quasi-criminal sanctions. Specifically, if bounty awards are employed in circumstances where corporations are in essence absolutely liable for agents' crimes, the awards may result in increased corporate crime because they may reduce the corporation's own efforts to reduce crime. Arlen thus argues for the adoption of alternative corporate liability rules, such as mitigation rules, negligence-based corporate liability or an evidentiary privilege.

The study, "Patient Capital? R&D Investment in Canada", by Ron Giammarino of the Faculty of Commerce and Business Administration at the University of British Columbia, is a thorough summary of recent research on links between R&D spending and firms' share values. Corporate managers often complain that focusing on maximizing share value necessitates adopting a short-term planning horizon and forsaking long-term investments like R&D. The inescapable conclusion of this study is that this complaint is bunk! High R&D spending is statistically significantly related to above-average market-to-book ratios (*i.e.*, high share prices). We know increased R&D spending causes share prices to rise and not the reverse; stock prices have been found to rise significantly immediately upon announcements by high-tech firms of increased R&D. Interestingly, this is true even when the firms in question have quarterly operating losses. (However, in older industries, R&D – which might rationally be seen as less valuable – does not increase, and may even reduce, share value.) Still, in general, shareholders like long-term investments and would like to see more.

Why then do firms not make their shareholders happier and richer by spending more on R&D than they do? Perhaps managers skimp on R&D because long-term investments invite takeovers? If this were true, we should expect to find higher R&D in firms protected by poison pills and other anti-takeover defences. In fact, after firms adopt such defences, R&D tends to fall significantly. Moreover, leveraged buyouts (LBOs), the type of takeover most likely to divert earnings away from long-term investments, are extraordinarily rare in industries where R&D spending is important. This suggests that raiders usually stay away from high-R&D firms. When two R&D-intensive firms merge, the R&D spending of the resulting firm is often lower than the combined R&D of the two merged firms. But this is not evidence of inefficiency. In fact, the motive for such mergers is often the savings attainable by rationalizing activities like R&D.

The answer, Giammarino argues, may lie in how firms make investment decisions. A recent survey by Jog & Srivastava shows that many Canadian firms use out-of-date data and conceptually flawed capital budgeting decision criteria in evaluating long-term projects. Accounting rates of return and pay-back periods fall into this category. Even firms that use conceptually valid methods such as net present values or internal rates of return often do not employ them correctly. For example, an R&D investment typically involves high risk in the early stages, but much greater certainty as the project develops. This means a high discount rate should be used for the first cash flows, but a lower rate is appropriate for cash flows in the more distant future. Failing to do this is likely to bias firms against R&D spending. Also, it is important to recognize that R&D investments have many of the characteristics of options. There is a small chance of a big payoff, as in a call option. Valuation techniques for options are complex, but evaluating R&D projects as options would tend to give them higher values than standard net-present-value analyses would assign. Managers' understandable aversion to high-risk investments like R&D perhaps encourages them not to question the negative verdicts simpler decision criteria produce.

Overall, the best way to increase R&D spending may be to educate managers how to value R&D properly. Improve corporate governance in this dimension, and firms' R&D spending will then take care of itself.

The study "Corporate Governance and Worker Education: An Alternative View" by Alice Nakamura, of the Faculty of Business at the University of Alberta, John Cragg, of the Faculty of Arts at the University of British Columbia and Kathleen Sayers of International Wordsmiths, points out that businesses may be loath to invest in worker training because of cost considerations. For example, employees whose training firms pay for may leave for highly paid jobs elsewhere, thus denying the firms a return on their invest-ment in training. Yet in the new global economy, as Morck and Yeung point out, continuous innovation is critical to success. This requires that highly educated employees create innovations and continuous education for other employees to apply innovations. The solution to this under-investment in training by employers is either to require workers to pay for their own training or to provide public education. For egalitarian and other reasons, Canada has focused on the latter. Because of the fiscal problems now facing all levels of government in Canada, this decision is being re-evaluated.

Can firms be encouraged to invest more in training through changes in corporate governance – for example by requiring worker representation on boards? The answer given by Nakamura, Cragg and Sayers is "perhaps, but other approaches would be much preferred". First, requiring workers on boards might drive investment out of Canada. Second, employee representatives on boards would protect the interests of existing employees, especially senior employees, but would see little point in encouraging firms to spend money training those who are now unemployed. Yet this is where the greatest social need is. We add a third reason; worker representation on boards might also simply marginalize boards. In Germany, which has mandatory labour representation on the *Aufsichtsrat*, or supervisory board, major decision-making has been transplanted to the *Vorstand*, or management board, which consists of directors who are also top executives. The *Aufsichtsrat* has become an ornament.

Nakamura, Cragg and Sayers argue that focusing on an alleged training deficit detracts from other problems underlying many of Canada's social ills. One such problem is the structure of Unemployment Insurance. They argue for UI reforms that would allow employers who commit to job security to pay lower UI taxes. Another underlying problem is the promotion of students who are illiterate from grade to grade through primary and secondary schools. The costs of correcting 12 wasted years are immense. Better monitoring of both student achievements and teacher performance are imperative. A third underlying problem is the prohibitive expense of lengthy post-secondary education for students from poor families and for students supporting families. Some type of government subsidy would seem reasonable here. Finally, students often have little information about what particular training would make them most employable. To correct this, the authors argue that information on the employment and average earnings of graduates of various post secondary programs should be made available to the public.

Although Michael Trebilcock of the Faculty of Law at the University of Toronto shares the skepticism of Nakamura *et al.* surrounding the scope for worker-based governance structures to address job training objectives, he is less sympathetic to the various alternative policy initiatives they prescribe. Trebilcock believes the instruments suggested by Nakamura *et al.* are not in themselves sufficient to address the need for job training or retraining. As a starting point for policy reform, Trebilcock stresses the need to disaggregate the potential demanders of job training or retraining services on the grounds that the appropriate policy mix for each constituency can vary dramatically. In determining the desired policy response for each group, Trebilcock argues for more supply-side competition in training programmes. Trebilcock worries about the excessive amount of centralized control exerted by the federal government (through, for instance, the purchase of seats in community colleges). Ultimately, Trebilcock believes that the most effective way to encourage competition is through a demand-side scheme, such as that associated with school voucher programmes.

Consulting economist Ron Hirshhorn's study, "The Governance of Nonprofits", is useful in identifying the scope for governance problems in the third or not-for-profit sector. The analysis is salient, given the growing reliance of the state on nonprofit organizations to deliver a range of public goods and services. Hirshhorn's analysis draws on a well-developed literature of organizational theory that explains the nonprofit organization as a response to market failures that are too costly to solve by either for-profit or state providers. In particular, Hirshhorn focuses on the perverse incentives that for-profit delivery introduces in areas where outputs are difficult to measure. Hirshhorn stresses the need to evaluate the rationale for nonprofit delivery on a case-by-case basis, having regard to the elaborate criteria that he develops. Hirshhorn cautions that mere evidence of some gap in the operation of private and political markets does not support reliance on non-profit modes of delivery. The calculus boils down to one of balancing the transaction cost savings in some areas against the increases in enforcement costs in other areas.

To illustrate this analysis, Hirshhorn examines three case studies involving community health care, local airport authorities and universities. Whereas Hirshhorn regards the case for nonprofit delivery to be relatively robust for community health care, he is skeptical of its value in the airport context (given monopoly properties) and universities (given the complexity of defining and measuring outputs).

Hirshhorn proposes several different avenues of policy reform designed to strengthen the operation of no-profits. He argues generally for independent management reviews of nonprofit performance and for the imposition of stringent reporting requirements. Hirshhorn acknowledges that securing performance improvements through the adoption of these measures will not be easy. The difficulty is that many nonprofit services cannot be precisely defined and are even more difficult to monitor. Indeed, it is often the case that these very properties are the reason why for-profit providers eschew provision of these services. Nevertheless, Hirshhorn is optimistic that precise performance measurements can be created for a number of nonprofit services, improving significantly the degree of product market pressure that can be directed at these providers. In any event, Hirshhorn's focus on the role of the state in providing information on nonprofits is well-placed. It is clear that in the globalized economy of the next millennium, the role of the state will increasingly shift from that of a direct producer of goods and services to that of an external monitor of, and a supplier of information on, goods and services produced by others, particularly nonprofits.

One particularly interesting set of recommendations favoured by Hirshhorn relates to the paucity of effective governance provisions in the *Canada Corporations Act*, Part II (CCA), which applies to Canadian nonprofits. In contrast to the relatively crisp lines of accountability set out in standard corporate legislation, Hirshhorn stresses the failure of nonprofit legislation to specify comparable duties. He argues that "reasonable rules could be established to determine those who qualify as significant stakeholders based on their contributions to the organization".

Bruce Chapman's comment on Hirshhorn's study concentrates on the charitable component of the non-profit sector. He develops a rationale for non-profit delivery of charitable services that draws on a supply-side analysis, rather than the demand-side analysis emphasized by Hirshhorn. Chapman argues that charitable non-profits can be used to supply public goods in a way that avoids the problematic and destabilizing political conflict that might occur were the goods provided in the public sector. Chapman also claims that the non-profit form not only prevents contract failure, but also permits donors and investors on the supply side to control the specific nature of the in-kind transfers that frequently characterize charitable non-profits. This rationale supports the use of a disbursement obligation on charities that forces managers of nonprofits to go back to their benefactors regularly for further funding, thereby limiting the scope for agency drift. Chapman also argues in favour of "line of activity" restrictions that limit the capacity of nonprofit managers to stray from benefactor objectives.

ENDNOTES

1 M. Porter, *Canada At the Crossroads: The Reality of a New Competitive Environment*, Ottawa: Business Council on National Issues/Supply and Services Canada, 1991, pp. 10-12.

2 T. Hatzichronoglou, "Indications of Industrial Competitiveness: Results and Limitations," in *Technology and National Competitiveness*, edited by J. Niosi, Montreal: McGill-Queen's University Press, 1991, p. 191 (citing OECD data).

3 Data from International Monetary Fund, reported in *The Economist*, World Economy Survey, September 19-25, 1992, p. 17.

4 Statistical Abstract of the United States, various years.

5 Statistical Abstract of the United States, various years.

6 Michael Porter, *The Competitive Advantage of Nations*, New York: The Free Press, 1990, p. 681.

7 R. J. Daniels, "Can Contractarianism be Compassionate?: Stakeholders and Takeovers," *University of Toronto Law Journal*, 1994.

8   The issue of the objective function of the firm is thoroughly canvassed in a symposium issue of the *University of Toronto Law Journal* devoted to Stakeholders and Corporate Governance.

9   *347883 Alberta Ltd. v. Producers Pipelines Ltd.* (1991), 80 D.L.R. (4th) 359 (Sask. C.A.); *Remington Energy Ltd. v. Joss Energy Ltd.*, unreported, Alberta Court of Queen's Bench, per Fraser J., Dec. 17, 1993; Re *MDC Corporation and Regal Greetings & Gifts Inc.* (1994) 17 OSCB 4971; and Re *Lac Minerals Ltd. and Royal Oak Mines Inc.* (1994) 17 OSCB 4963.

10 Several examples can be cited. The tax incentives contained in the 1963 federal budget which lowered withholding taxes on dividends from 15 percent to 10 percent for companies beneficially owned by Canadians to the extent of at least 25 percent of their voting stock, and also where the parent company and its associates held no more than 75 percent of the voting shares and the stock of the subsidiary was listed on a Canadian exchange; the establishment of the Foreign Investment Review Agency in 1974 and its attention to Canadian share ownership as one of the criteria necessary for entry into Canada; and the incentives set out in the Trudeau government's National Energy Program for Canadian ownership.

BIBLIOGRAPHY

Allen, F. "Strategic Management and Financial Markets." *Strategic Management Journal*, 14 (1993):11-22.

Barclay, M. and C. Holderness. "Private Benefits from Control of Public Corporations." *Journal of Financial Economics*, 25 (1989):371-97.

_____. "The Law and Large Block Trades." *Journal of Law and Economics*, 35 (1992):265-94.

Barclay, M., C. Holderness and J. Pontiff. "Private Benefits from Block Ownership and Discounts on Closed End Funds." *Journal of Finance*, 33 (1993):263-91.

Beason, M. and H. Weinstein. "Growth, Targeting and Economies of Scale in Japan: 1960-1990." *Review of Economics and Statistics*. 1994.

Berle, A. and G. Means. *The Modern Corporation and Private Property*. New York: Macmillan Inc., 1932.

Bhagat, S., J. Brickley and R. Lease. "Incentive Effects of Stock Purchase Plans." *Journal of Accounting and Economics*, 7 (1985):195-215.

Brickley, J., S. Bhagat and R. Lease. "The Impact of Long Range Managerial Compensation Plans on Shareholder Wealth." *Journal of Accounting and Economics*, 7 (1985):115-29.

Comment, R. and G. Schwert. "Poison or Placebo? Evidence on the Deterence and Wealth Effects of Modern Antitakover Measures." *Journal of Financial Economics*, 39, 1 (1995):3-4.

Daniels, R. "Can Contractarianism be Compassionate?: Stakeholders and Takeovers." *University of Toronto Law Journal*, 1994.

Harris, D., R. Morck, J. Slemrod and B. Yeung. "Income Shifting in U.S. Multinational Corporations." In *Studies in International Taxation*. Edited by A. Giovannini, G. Hubbard and J. Slemrod. Chicago: University of Chicago Press, 1993.

Hermalin, B. and M. Weisbach. "The Effects of Board Composition and Direct Incentives on Firm Performance." *Financial Management*, 4 (1991):101-12.

Jarrell, G. and A. Poulson. "Dual Class Recapitalizations as Antitakeover Mechanisms: The Recent Evidence." *Journal of Financial Economics*, 20, 1/2 (1988):129-52.

Jensen, Michael. "The Agency Costs of Free Cash Flow." *American Economic Review*, 76 (1986):323-29.

Johnson, W., R. Magee, J. Nandu, J. Nagarakam, and H. Newman. "An Analysis of the Stock Price Reactions to Sudden Executive Deaths." *Journal of Accounting and Economics*, 7 (1985):151-74.

Lakonishok, J., A. Shleifer and R. Vishny. The Structure and Performance of the Money Management Industry." *Brookings Papers on Economic Activity and Microeconomics*. (1992):339-91.

Lang, L. and R. Stulz. "Does Corporate Diversification Create Value?" Unpublished manuscript, 1992.

Larcker, D. "The Association Between Performance Plan Adoption and Corporate Capital Investment." *Journal of Accounting and Economics*, 7 (1983):3-30.

Mace, M. *Directors: Myth and Reality*. Cambridge, MA: Harvard Business School Press, 1971.

McConnell, J. and H. Servaes. "Additional Evidence on Equity Ownership and Corporate Value." *Journal of Financial Economics*, 27, 2 (1990):595-610.

Megginson, W., R. Nash and M. Van Randenborgh. "The Financial and Operating Performance of Newly Privatized Firms." *Journal of Finance*, 49 (1994):403-52.

Morck, R., A. Shleifer and R. Vishny. "Management Ownership and Corporate Performance: An Empirical Analysis." *Journal of Financial Economics*, 20 (1988):293-316.

_____. "Alternative Mechanisms for Corporate Control." *American Economic Review*, 79, 4 (1989):842-52.

Morck, R. and D. Stangeland. "Large Shareholders and Corporate Performance in Canada." Unpublished manuscript, 1994.

Morck, R. and B. Yeung. "Why Investors Value Multinationality," *Journal of Business*, 64, 2 (1991):165-88.

_____. "Internalization: An Event Study." *Journal of International Economics*, 33 (1992):41-56.

Nesbitt, S. L. *Rewards from Corporate Governance*. California Public Employees Retirement System. (Feb. 12, 1992):1-5.

Romano, R. "Public Pension Fund Activism in Corporate Governance Reconsidered." *Columbia Law Review*, 4 (1993).

Stangeland, D. "Issues in Corporate Control and the Performance of the Corporation." Ph.D. Thesis, University of Alberta, 1994.

Tehranian, H. and J. Waegelin. "Market Reaction to Short Term Executive Compensation Plan Adoption." *Journal of Accounting and Economics*, 7 (1985):131-44.

Weisbach, M. "Outside Directors and CEO Turnover." *Journal of Financial Economics*, 20 (1988):431-61.

Part II   The Governance of
            Canadian Corporations

P. Someshwar Rao & Clifton R. Lee-Sing
Industry and Science Policy Sector, Strategic Investment Analysis
Industry Canada

2

Governance Structure, Corporate Decision-Making and Firm Performance in North America

INTRODUCTION

FOR THE PAST DECADE, a number of inter-related global trends have been changing the world economy in a remarkable and fundamental way. The enormity of these changes has been paralleled only by those experienced during the nineteenth century Industrial Revolution. These developments include rapid product, process and organizational innovations; shorter product cycles; increased pace of business globalization; marked shifts in the comparative advantage and competitive position of firms and nations; fierce competition among firms and nations for markets, technology, capital and skilled employees; the revolution in information technologies; dramatic reduction in transportation and communication costs; and the emergence of the Asia-Pacific Region as a major player in the world economy.

These global developments have made it necessary for all countries to become more flexible and to accelerate the pace of structural adjustment. A nation's economic performance – absolute as well as relative – therefore, depends on the willingness and ability of its firms to adapt to the constantly changing environment. Slow economic growth, poor productivity performance, stagnant real incomes and high unemployment in Canada and other industrialized countries are attributed to the inability of firms to make necessary modifications to their strategies and activities, and governments to adjust quickly and decisively to these global changes.

The poor economic performance of the global economy, especially the OECD countries, and the serious economic difficulties of many large and well-known global companies such as GM, IBM and Eastman Kodak during the 1980s and the early 1990s, strongly suggest that corporate internal control (corporate governance) systems have failed to deal effectively with the challenges of structural changes and adjustment. Since all the above-mentioned structural trends are expected to continue, if not intensify, in the future. The challenge of adaptation and structural adjustment for Western firms and political systems, therefore, is likely to continue for several decades.

Reactions and feedback from capital, product and factor markets, and legal, political and regulatory systems, either individually or collectively, could effectively address the problems of inadequate, ineffective and inefficient management. However, as Jensen (1993) has eloquently argued, these control mechanisms are either too blunt as instruments or too slow to act, resulting in very slow structural adjustment, waste of productive resources, serious economic difficulties for firms and employees, and poor overall economic performance. On the other hand, a system of effective corporate governance – including the active participation of shareholders in the direct and indirect management of the corporation through the board of directors, and an arrangement of productive checks and balances between the shareholders, board of directors and management of the corporation – should increase corporate dynamism and flexibility, minimize the overall costs of economic adjustment, and change and improve the global economic performance.

The recent upsurge of interest and research activity related to corporate governance in Canada and other industrial countries is a reflection of the growing recognition of the importance of corporate governance to the strong economic performance of firms and nations. For example, in Canada, the TSE report *"'Where Were the Directors?' Guidelines For Improving Corporate Governance in Canada"*[1] examines the role of the board of directors in corporate governance and decision-making in Canada and recommends 18 measures to improve current governance structures and practices.

To date, the corporate governance debate in Canada and elsewhere has concentrated mainly on the role of the board of directors in ensuring that shareholders' interests are met and agency costs are minimized. As a result, both the research and policy debates have been too narrowly focused. In addition, much of the past research on corporate governance in Canada is primarily qualitative and is not based on rigorous empirical analysis. Current policy and research efforts that focus simply on inter-country comparisons of corporate governance environments cannot resolve these problems. For example, most Canadian firms are closely held while the majority of American firms are widely held. Although the problem of managers ignoring shareholders is prominent in widely held U.S. firms, it is less of an issue in closely held Canadian firms. Therefore, research and, ultimately, public policy should focus on problems that are specific to the Canadian corporate governance environment.

The primary objective of this study is to conduct an in-depth, firm-specific empirical analysis of the interaction between corporate governance, corporate decision-making, and corporate performance in Canada. In particular, by using extensive company data on Canadian and American firms, we will examine empirically the role of corporate governance structure in corporate decision-making and performance in Canada and compare the Canadian results with our findings for the American companies. Our secondary objective is to provide a general empirical background to the other studies in this volume, especially the qualitative studies dealing with specific issues of corporate governance.

The governance variables include, among others, concentration of owner-ship (*e.g.*, widely held *versus* closely held); size and composition (*e.g.*, inside *versus* outside directors) of the board of directors; institutional ownership; inside ownership; and the role of the CEO on the board of directors. Decision variables include debt-to-asset ratio; capital-to-labour ratio; R&D intensity; and degree of outward orientation (measured by the importance of foreign assets and foreign sales in total assets and sales). Firm performance variables include accounting measures (such as capital and labour productivity); sales and asset growth; growth in earnings-per-share; and rates of return on assets and equity.[2]

Following this Introduction, we discuss corporate governance structure, disaggregated by firm size class (measured by sales), and by major industry groupings in the section on the Governance System in Canada and the United States. The section on the Analytical Framework describes in some detail the framework we use to examine empirically the role of corporate governance structure, corporate decision-making and corporate performance in Canada and the United States. The Empirical Results are analyzed in the next section, which discusses the importance of good corporate governance and decision-making for healthy and robust corporate economic performance in the two countries. Finally, we summarize the main findings of the study and discuss their implications for possible action by corporations, institutions and governments in the Conclusions.

Our findings suggest that corporate governance structures in Canada differ significantly from those in the United States, especially with respect to the nature and concentration of corporate ownership, institutional ownership, inside ownership, and the composition of the board of directors. For example, the concentration of corporate ownership is substantially higher in Canadian than in American companies, but the concentration of institutional owner-ship is considerably higher in American than in Canadian companies. More important, however, is that corporate governance variables, especially in the United States, appear to have a significant influence on the corporate perfor-mance variables – directly as well as indirectly – through their influence on corporate decision variables.

THE GOVERNANCE SYSTEMS IN CANADA AND THE UNITED STATES

THIS SECTION PROVIDES definitions of corporate governance variables and an examination of the governance structure in Canada, disaggregated by six major size classes and by 11 major industry groups. The Canadian results are then compared with the findings for the United States. The description of both the database and the characteristics of Canadian and American samples, especially industry and size distributions, appear in Appendix 1.

The corporate governance literature focuses on two major groups of corporate governance variables: characteristics and interactions between a firm's board of directors and management; and the composition of a firm's ownership. These two groups of variables are further characterized as either structures or practices.

Appendix 2 provides comparative summaries of the Canadian and American governance environment.[3] These summaries describe the role of both structure and practice variables in shaping the governance environment. However, the objective of this study is to set out an empirical analysis of the governance environments in Canada and the United States. Therefore, the summaries in Appendix 2 may best serve as a foundation for comparing the Canadian and American environments.

The structural characteristics of the board and the management of a firm include board size (Jensen, 1993 and Friedlaender, 1992), senior officer size (Friedlaender, 1992), the inside director ratio (Jensen, 1993 and Friedlaender, 1992), the foreign director ratio, whether or not the CEO is the Chairperson of the board of directors (Jensen, 1993), whether the CEO is on the board of directors (Jensen, 1993), and the level of inside ownership (Jensen, 1993).

Firm-specific practices related to the board and management include proxies of board culture (Jensen, 1993), financial expertise of the board (Jensen, 1993), the level of legal liability taken by board members (Jensen, 1993), personnel characteristics (such as age, education and experience) of the senior management (Friedlaender, 1992), corporate life cycle and age (Morck & Stangeland, 1994), and CEO interaction – such as information flow and decision-making – with inside directors (Baysinger, 1990).

The structure of the ownership composition includes variables such as institutional ownership/activism (Jensen, 1993), percentage held by the largest shareholders (Morck & Stangeland, 1994), and concentration of corporate ownership (Morck & Stangeland, 1994).

Firm-specific practices related to the composition of ownership include the effects of differential voting rights (Morck & Stangeland, 1994), and the founder/heir ownership relation (Morck & Stangeland, 1994).

Since it was very difficult to obtain reliable quantitative data on corporate governance practices variables, this study focuses exclusively on the following corporate governance structure variables.

- Concentration of Voting Shares and Ownership Control
- Level of Inside Ownership
- Institutional Ownership
- Number of Directors and Senior Officers
- Inside Director Ratio
- Foreign Director Ratio
- CEO on the Board or Chairperson of the Board of Directors

CONCENTRATION OF VOTING SHARES AND OWNERSHIP CONTROL

CONCENTRATION OF CORPORATE OWNERSHIP, the percentage of voting shares held by significant shareholders, and the number of significant shareholders all measure the concentration of voting shares.

Concentration of Corporate Ownership or Corporate Control

The level of concentration of corporate ownership or corporate control is measured by the number of voting shares held by one or a small group of shareholders. This variable focuses on the *de facto* control of the voting shares. There are three categories of ownership concentration: *widely held control* – in which companies have no shareholder or group of related shareholders that own, directly or indirectly, more than 20 percent of the voting shares; *effective control* – in which companies have one shareholder or a small group of shareholders owning, directly or indirectly, 20 percent to 49.9 percent of the voting shares; and *legal control* – in which one or a small group of shareholders owns, directly or indirectly, more than 50 percent of the voting shares of a company. These definitions follow those used by Daniels & MacIntosh (1991).

In the Canadian sample, 55.5 percent of the firms are legally controlled while 21.4 percent and 23.1 percent are effectively controlled and widely controlled, respectively (Figure 1). In contrast, less than 25 percent of the U.S. firms are legally controlled, while 35.1 percent are effectively controlled and 40.2 percent are widely held.

The majority of Canadian firms are legally controlled in all six size classes. The differences in ownership structure between the two countries is more pronounced for firms with over US$ 1 billion annual sales (see Appendix 3, Table A3-5). These results are similar to the findings of Morck & Stangeland (1994).

Unlike the size classes, the concentration of ownership differs significantly across the major Canadian industry groups. For instance, the share of legally controlled firms varies between a low of 32 percent in Mining to a high of 72 percent in Transportation and Public Utilities (Appendix 3, Table A3-6). The Mining and Technology-Intensive Manufacturing industries have the majority of firms in the widely held and effectively controlled categories, while the high level of legally controlled firms in the Transportation and Public Utilities industry might be simply a reflection of the provincial governments' ownership of public utilities.

The levels of ownership concentration in the U.S. industries also differ noticeably from those in Canada. The percent of legally controlled firms is substantially lower in all the major U.S. industries. In the Finance, Insurance and Real Estate industry, and in the Transportation and Public Utilities industry, the majority of U.S. firms are widely held. In sharp contrast, about 70 percent of Canadian firms in these two industries are legally controlled.

FIGURE 1

CONCENTRATION OF OWNERSHIP IN CANADA AND THE UNITED STATES

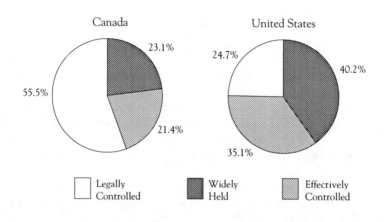

Source: Based on Table A3-5.

Percentage of Voting Shares Held by Significant Shareholders

A shareholder that owns at least 10 percent of the voting shares in a company is considered to be a "significant" shareholder. The percentage of voting shares held by all significant or "10 percent" shareholders focuses on the defacto control that may exist among these large block shareholders. This variable is directly related to the corporate concentration variable, discussed above, because the categorization of control – widely held, effective or legal – is based on the percentage of voting shares held by all significant shareholders.

On average, the majority (53.6 percent) of voting stock in the Canadian sample is held by one or more significant shareholders. The high concentration of ownership is consistent with the majority of legally controlled firms in Canada. The percentage of voting shares held by significant shareholders increases with the size of the firm except for firms with sales over US$ 2 billion (Appendix 3, Table A3-7). This result is consistent with the positive relationship between the proportion of legally controlled firms and firm size.

Unlike the similarities between the two concentration variables by size class, the concentration of ownership within industry groups differs from the percentage held by the significant shareholders. The percentage held by significant shareholders varies from a high of 80 percent in the Technology-Intensive Manufacturing industry to a low of 12 percent in the Agriculture, Forestry and Fishing industry (Appendix 3, Table A3-8). Although the Technology-Intensive Manufacturing industry has the highest level of significant shareholder ownership, it has a low number of legally controlled firms.

Number of Significant Shareholders

The number of significant shareholders is another measure of the concentration of voting shares within a firm. Although the number of 10 percent owners is not directly related to the total percentage of the voting shares held by the firms' significant shareholders, discussed above, it also indicates the concentration of ownership within a firm.

In the Canadian sample, unlike the percentage of voting shares held by significant shareholders, the number of significant shareholders tends to decline with the size of the firm, except for the smallest size class (Appendix 3, Table A3-9). This implies that the average dollar value of shares held by significant shareholders is considerably higher in larger firms. Canadian firms also have a higher number of significant shareholders across all size classes than American firms.

The average number of significant shareholders varies between different major industry groupings. Construction, Wholesale Trade, Services and Labour-Intensive Manufacturing tend to have more significant shareholders than the norm, while Agriculture, Finance and Mining have fewer significant shareholders. There is no systematic variation of the concentration of large shareholders across the industry groupings in the Canadian and the American samples (Appendix 3, Table A3-10).

LEVEL OF INSIDE OWNERSHIP

THE PERCENTAGE OF VOTING SHARES HELD BY "Insiders" follows the SEC's definition of inside shareholders (traders). Inside shareholders include directors, officers and affiliates of the firm.

In the Canadian sample, on average, over 21 percent of company shares are held by insiders, compared to less than 10 percent in the American sample. The percentage of voting shares held by insiders in Canadian firms declines from an average of 35 percent in the smallest size class to 13 percent for firms that are moderately sized and then increases to over 22 percent for the largest size class. Insider ownership in the United States, on the other hand, tends to decline systematically with the size of the firm (Figure 2).

Firms in the U.S. Retail Trade, Agriculture, Forestry and Fishing, Wholesale Trade, and Services industries tend to have higher than average levels of inside ownership (Appendix 3, Table A3-12). On the other hand, Mining, Transportation and Public Utilities, and Technology-Intensive Manufacturing tend to have lower than average levels of inside ownership. The lack of inside ownership information for several Canadian industries prevents Canada-U.S. comparisons by industry.

FIGURE 2

PERCENTAGE OF VOTING SHARES HELD BY INSIDERS, BY SIZE CLASS

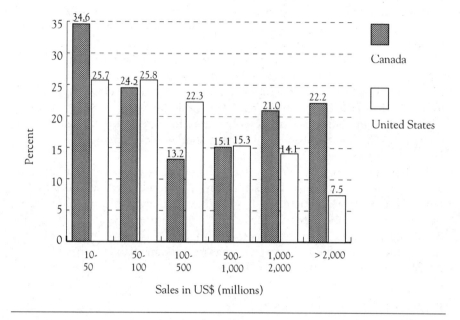

Source: Based on Table A3-11.

INSTITUTIONAL OWNERSHIP

INSTITUTIONAL OWNERSHIP IS THE PERCENTAGE of a firm's voting shares held by institutional investors. The term "institutional owners", as used in this study, is the same as that used by Disclosure Inc. Institutional owners include banks and other financial institutions, pension funds, mutual funds, and other corporations that own shares.

In the Canadian sample, institutional owners control about 38 percent of the dollar value of shares, compared to 53 percent in the U.S. sample. The apparent contradiction between the smaller proportion of legally controlled firms and the higher levels of institutional ownership in the American sample implies that there are a larger number of institutional holders in the United States, each controlling only a small block of corporate shares.

Institutional ownership in the Canadian sample increases systematically with firm size except for the largest size class. However, this increase is not nearly as prominent as in the American sample where the range of institutional ownership varies from a low of 16 percent in the smallest size class to over 55 percent in the largest size class. Canadian firms have higher levels of

FIGURE 3

PERCENTAGE OF VOTING SHARES HELD BY INSTITUTIONS, BY SIZE CLASS

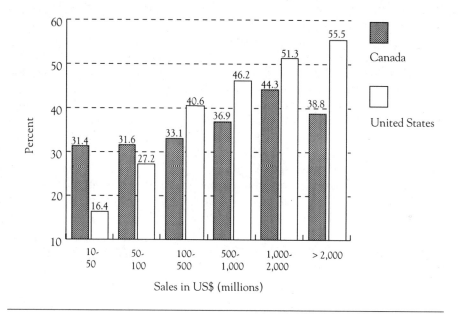

Source: Based on Table A3-13.

institutional ownership than their American counterparts in the two smallest size classes. On the other hand, in other size classes, Canadian firms tend to have significantly lower institutional ownership than similar size American firms (Figure 3).

The Agriculture, Forestry and Fishing industry has the lowest level of institutional ownership compared to the other Canadian industries (9.57 percent versus the Canadian weighted average of 38.24 percent). Finance, Resource-Intensive Manufacturing, Retail Trade and Wholesale Trade have lower than average levels of institutional ownership. On the other hand, Construction, Technology-Intensive Manufacturing, and Transportation and Public Utilities have high levels of institutional ownership.

Unlike Canada, the level of institutional ownership does not vary substantially across the major industry groups in the American sample. In the United States the level varies from a low of 49.4 percent in the Retail Trade industry to a high of 59.3 percent in the Finance, Insurance and Real Estate industry (Appendix 3, Table A3-14).

Number of Directors and Senior Officers

THE NUMBER OF DIRECTORS WHO SIT on a firm's board of directors is specified and available from the company's annual reports. Similarly, data on the number of senior officers (president, executive vice-presidents, senior vice-presidents, vice-presidents, chiefs, treasurer, secretary, controller, comptroller, and other comparable positions) is also available from the company's annual reports.

The average number of directors in Canadian firms is 9.25 while the average number for American firms is 9.87. The number of directors increases with firm size in both the Canadian and American samples. The number of directors in the four smallest size classes are similar in Canada and the United States. In the two largest size classes, however, the number of directors tends to be significantly higher in the American sample than in the Canadian sample. This discrepancy could be mainly a reflection of the larger size American firms in the largest two size classes (Figure 4).

The number of directors across the major industry groups in the Canadian sample tends to mirror that of the American sample. Construction and Services, on average, has the fewest number of directors, while Transportation and Public Utilities, and Resource-Intensive Manufacturing tend to have the largest number of directors (Appendix 3, Table A3-16). Like the number of directors, the num-

FIGURE 4

NUMBER OF DIRECTORS BY SIZE CLASS

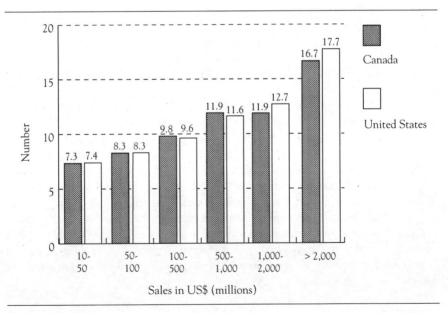

Sales in US$ (millions)

Source: Table A3-15.

ber of senior officers increases with the size of the firm on the two country samples (Appendix 3, Tables A3-17 and A3-18).

INSIDE DIRECTOR RATIO

THE INSIDE DIRECTOR RATIO REPRESENTS THE RATIO of inside directors (officers of the firm who also sit on the Board) to the total number of directors.[4]

The inside director ratio averages 20 percent in the Canadian sample compared to 22 percent in the American sample. In addition, the American insider ratio is higher than the Canadian ratio in all six size classes. The insider ratio declines with firm size in the two samples – *i.e.*, the larger firms tend to have the smaller insider director ratio (Figure 5).

In Canada, the inside director ratio tends to be higher in the Technology-Intensive Manufacturing, Wholesale Trade, Services, Mining, and Construction industries. On the other hand, the ratio is lower in the Finance, Insurance and Real Estate, and Transportation and Public Utilities industries. With few exceptions, the industrial structure of the Canadian insider ratio tends to be similar to the American (Appendix 3, Table A3-20).

FIGURE 5

INSIDE DIRECTOR RATIO BY SIZE CLASS

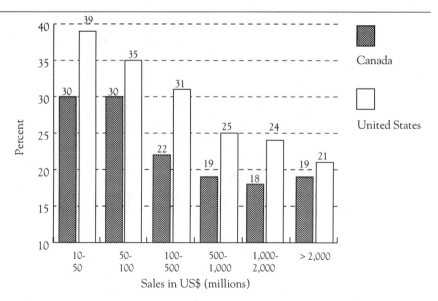

Source: Table A3-19.

FOREIGN DIRECTOR RATIO

THE FOREIGN DIRECTOR RATIO REPRESENTS the ratio of the number of directors that reside outside the nation where the firm is incorporated to the total number of directors.[5] This information is only available for the Canadian sample.

On average, only 15 percent of the directors of Canadian firms are residents of foreign countries. The foreign director ratio tends to remain constant for the first four size classes, between 18 percent and 19 percent. However, it increases to 24 percent for firms with sales between US$ 1 and US$ 2 billion. But, for the largest size class (sales over US$ 2 billion), the ratio averages only 11 percent (Figure 6).

Mining, Resource-Intensive Manufacturing, Services, and Wholesale Trade industries have an above-average foreign director ratio. On the other hand, the Labour-Intensive Manufacturing, Mining and Construction industries have a below-average ratio (Appendix 3, Table A3-22).

FIGURE 6

FOREIGN DIRECTOR RATIO IN CANADIAN FIRMS, BY SIZE CLASS

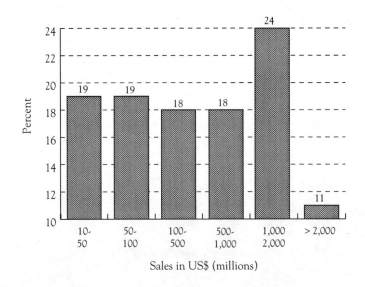

Sales in US$ (millions)

Source: Table A3-21.

CEO on the Board or Chairperson of Board of Directors

THIS VARIABLE INDICATES WHETHER the chief executive officer of the firm is also the chairman of the board of directors, as specified and available from the company's annual report.

On average, only 34.5 percent of Canadian firms have the CEO as the chairperson, compared to almost 60 percent in the American sample (Figure 7). In over 83 percent of Canadian firms, however, the CEO is also a member of the firm's board of directors (Appendix 3, Table A3-23). There appears to be no systematic relationship between whether or not the CEO is the chairperson and firm size in the Canadian sample. But there is a strong positive relationship between the CEO as chairperson and the size class. In contrast, the proportion of firms with the CEO as chairperson does not vary systematically across major industry groups (Appendix 3, Tables A3-24 and A3-26).

Summary

THE CONCENTRATION OF CORPORATE OWNERSHIP is substantially higher in Canada than in the United States. For instance, more than 55 percent of firms are legally controlled, compared to less than 25 percent in the United States. However, the institutional ownership is considerably higher in the United States. These two results imply that there are a large number of institutional investors in America each controlling only a small block of corporate shares.

FIGURE 7

CEO as Chairperson

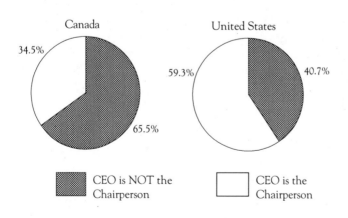

Canada

34.5%

65.5%

United States

59.3%

40.7%

CEO is NOT the Chairperson

CEO is the Chairperson

Source: Table A3-25.

The number of directors and officers increases with firm size in the two countries. The ratio of inside directors to total directors is higher in the United States in all six size classes. Similarly, the proportion of firms with the CEO as Chairperson of the Board of Directors is substantially higher in the American corporations.

There appears to be, on average, a significant systematic relationship between the corporate governance variables, firm size classes and major industry groups. Therefore, in empirically examining the effect of governance variables on corporate decision-making and corporate performance, the influence of size and industry characteristics of firms must be taken into account.

ANALYTICAL FRAMEWORK

IN THE PREVIOUS SECTION we examined seven main characteristics of the corporate governance structure in Canada and the United States. We now provide an empirical analysis of the influence of corporate governance on corporate decision-making and corporate performance in the two countries. This section will outline the analytical framework of the empirical (regression) analysis reported in the next two sections.

The corporate governance structure is expected to affect directly the corporate performance by having an effect on the managerial, technical and adjustment efficiencies of the firm. In addition, the corporate governance variables can indirectly influence the corporate performance through their influence on the firm's strategies and decisions with regard to inputs, outputs, innovations, markets, etc.

Therefore, the ability of corporate internal controls to deal effectively with the challenges of structural adjustment can be analyzed by studying the linkages between the three groups of variables: corporate governance structure variables, corporate decision-making variables, and corporate economic performance variables. The corporate governance structure variables used in the regression analysis are those defined in the previous section.

Corporate decision-making variables represent activities of firms resulting from both day-to-day and longer-term corporate strategies and decisions. They include leverage in the firm – measured by the debt-to-assets ratio; the capital-to-labour ratio – the ratio of assets to employees; the R&D intensity – measured by the ratio of R&D to total sales; and the firm's degree of outward orientation – measured in three ways: the ratio of foreign sales to total sales, the ratio of foreign assets to total assets, and a dummy variable based on the presence of foreign sales or assets.

Corporate economic performance variables measure the corporate performance in terms of productivity, profitability, and growth. These include the capital productivity ratio (sales to assets); labour productivity ratio (sales to employees); sales growth; asset growth; the growth in capital and labour productivity; return on equity; return on assets; and the growth in earnings-per-share. Table 1 includes and categorizes the variables used in the regression analysis.

TABLE 1

CORPORATE GOVERNANCE, DECISION MAKING AND PERFORMANCE VARIABLES

VARIABLE GROUP	MEASURE	VARIABLE
Governance	Concentration of Ownership	Widely Held
	Concentration of Ownership	Effectively Controlled
	Concentration of Ownership	Percentage of Voting Shares Held by all of the Significant Shareholders[1]
	Concentration of Ownership	Number of Significant Shareholders[1]
	Ownership Composition	Institutional Ownership
	Ownership Composition	Insider Ownership
	Composition of Board	Inside Director Ratio
	Composition of Board	Foreign Director Ratio
	Composition of Board	Board Size
	Composition of Board	Officer Size[1]
	Composition of Board	CEO is on the Board
	Composition of Board	CEO is the Chairperson
	Composition of Board	CEO is the Chairperson data not available[2]
Decision	Leverage	Debt-to-Asset Ratio
	R&D Intensity	R&D-to-Sales Ratio
	Capital Labour Ratio	Assets-to-Employee Ratio
	Outward Orientation	Foreign Sales to Total Sales
	Outward Orientation	Foreign Assets to Total Assets[1]
	Outward Orientation	Presence of either Foreign Assets or Sales[1]
Performance	Return	Return on Equity
	Return	Return on Assets
	Growth	Asset Growth
	Growth	Sales Growth
	Growth	Capital Productivity Growth
	Growth	Labour Productivity Growth
	Growth	Growth in Earnings-per-Share
	Productivity	Capital Productivity Ratio (Sales over Assets)
	Productivity	Labour Productivity Ratio (Sales over Employees)

Notes: This table contains a list of the variables described in the analytical framework section of the study. The variables, shown on the far right are categorized into three main groups: corporate governance variables, decision-making variables, and performance variables. These variables are further categorized into the various measures shown in the second column.

[1] Variables that were included in the empirical framework of our study but were not included in the regression outputs shown in Tables 5, 6, 7, and 8. These variables are highly correlated with other variables that represent similar measures and their inclusion would lead to problems of multicollinearity.

[2] This variable is used in the Canadian regressions because several firms did not report this information.

Two sets of dummy variables are included in the regression equations to control for the effects of firm size (sales) and type of industry on the corporate decision-making and corporate performance variables. Six size classes are represented by five dummy variables. Eleven major industry groupings are represented by ten dummy variables. Table 2 gives the neumonics of the dummy variables used in the regression analysis.

TABLE 2

REGRESSION DUMMY VARIABLES

VARIABLE GROUP	CLASS OR GROUP SIZE
SIZE (US$)	10 million to 50 million
	50 million to 100 million
	100 million to 500 million
	500 million to 1,000 million
	1,000 million to 2,000 million
	2,000 million and greater
MAJOR INDUSTRY	Agriculture, Forestry & Fishing
	Construction
	Finance, Insurance & Real Estate
	Labour-Intensive Manufacturing
	Mining
	Resource-Intensive Manufacturing
	Retail Trade
	Services
	Technology-Intensive Manufacturing
	Transportation & Public Utilities
	Wholesale Trade

Note: This table contains a list of the size and industry dummy variables used in the regression analysis. Five sizes of dummy variables and ten industry dummy variables were created using the indicator coding method. The two control groups were "US$ 2,000 million and greater" and "Wholesale Trade".

The linkages between the three sets of variables can be analyzed with the two models. The first formulation (Figure 8) analyzes the relationship between the corporate governance structure and corporate decision-making sets of variables, controlling for both the size and industry effects.

The second model (Figure 9) depicts the influences of the corporate governance and decision-making variables on the performance variables, controlling for industry and size effects.

Two sets of regression equations are used to generate the above models. The first set of equations (Regression Equations, Set 1) are used to test for the significance of the influence of corporate governance variables on decision-making variables. The two sets of regressions are estimated for both the Canadian and American samples.

FIGURE 8

**LINKAGES BETWEEN CORPORATE GOVERNANCE STRUCTURE
AND DECISION-MAKING**

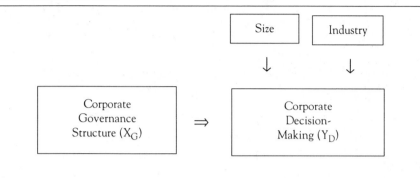

FIGURE 9

**LINKAGES BETWEEN CORPORATE GOVERNANCE STRUCTURE,
DECISION-MAKING AND PERFORMANCE VARIABLES**

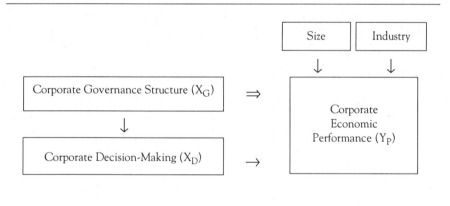

REGRESSION EQUATIONS, SET 1

$$Y_{D1} = f(X_{G1}, \ldots, X_{GN}, SIZ, MI)$$

$$\ldots$$

$$Y_{DN} = f(X_{G1}, \ldots, X_{GN}, SIZ, MI)$$

where

$X_{G1}, \ldots, X_{GN}$ are the corporate governance structure variables,

$Y_{D1}, \ldots, Y_{DN}$ are the corporate decision variables,

SIZ are the size class dummy variables, and

MI are the major industry group dummy variables.

The second set of equations (Regression Equations, Set 2) is used to analyze the relationship between the corporate governance structure variables, corporate decision-making and corporate performance variables, again, controlling for size and industry effects.

In this model, the total effect of a corporate governance variable on a corporate performance variable is the sum of the two effects: the direct effect and the indirect effect. The indirect effect measures the influence of the governance variable on the performance variable operating through its impact on the decision-making variable.

REGRESSION EQUATIONS, SET 2

$$Y_{P1} = f(X_{G1}, \ldots, X_{GN}, X_{D1}, \ldots, X_{DN}, SIZ, MI)$$

$$\ldots$$

$$Y_{PN} = f(X_{G1}, \ldots, X_{GN}, X_{D1}, \ldots, X_{DN}, SIZ, MI)$$

where

$X_{G1}, \ldots, X_{GN}$ are the corporate governance structure variables,

$X_{D1}, \ldots, X_{DN}$ are the corporate decision variables,

$Y_{P1}, \ldots, Y_{PN}$ are the corporate performance variables,

SIZ are the size class dummy variables, and

MI are the major industry group dummy variables.

POSSIBLE EFFECTS OF CORPORATE GOVERNANCE VARIABLES

THE REGRESSION RESULTS ARE DISCUSSED IN THE NEXT SECTION. First, however, we will review from the corporate governance literature *a priori* relationships among the governance structure, decision-making and performance variables. However, as described below, these relationships are confounded by many interactions.

Concentration of Ownership

Morck & Stangeland (1994) examined the relationship between concentration of ownership and firm performance in Canada and the United States. The managers of widely held firms can be neither effectively monitored nor controlled by the widely dispersed and often unsophisticated shareholders who hold only a small number of shares ("small" shareholders). Therefore, the decisions and performance of widely held firms could be adversely influenced by the divergence of interests of the managers and shareholders. On the other hand, sophisticated shareholders who own large numbers of shares ("large" shareholders) will have the ability and incentive to monitor effectively the decisions and performance of managers. But the concentration of corporate ownership could result in an unhealthy and undemocratic concentration of economic power.[6]

In addition, the effect of corporate ownership on firm performance could be significantly influenced by the nature or composition of the ownership concentration – the proportion of voting shares held by institutional investors and insiders, the number of significant shareholders, etc. Therefore, it is difficult to predict *a priori* the relationship between the level of concentration of ownership and its effect on decision-making and performance.

In an attempt to reach a better understanding of the relationship between the level of concentration of ownership and firm decision-making and performance, we disaggregated the two country samples into the three groups: widely held, effectively controlled and legally controlled. The averages of governance, decision and performance variables for the three groups are displayed in Appendix 4, Table A4-1.

There appears to be a systematic negative relationship between the rate of return on assets and equity and the level of ownership concentration in the United States. The relationship between rate of return and concentration of ownership is not as clear for the Canadian firms because the average rates of return on equity and the average return on assets are the same for widely held firms as for legally controlled firms.

On the other hand, growth of sales and assets in American firms appears to be positively related to ownership concentration. In the Canadian sample, legally controlled firms, on average, have much lower sales and asset growth than the other two groups (Appendix 4, Figure A4-2).

It is important to note that these are partial results because they do not take into account the size and industry effects or the interactions between the governance and decision-making variables. Therefore, these provide only a cursory glimpse of the relationship between performance and ownership concentration.[7]

Institutional Investors

According to several commentators, American institutional investor activism (for example, the California Public Employees Retirement System [CalPERS], Corporate Partners, Allied Investment Partners, etc) has a significant positive effect on firm performance because these well-informed investors can assess firm management strategies and activities in an unbiased way and can therefore exert pressure on the board for change and dynamism through either voting or selling mechanisms. In addition, institutional investors could take a more active role in the management of the firm by obtaining a seat on the board.

However, the effectiveness of institutional investors could be severely limited by the legal, tax and regulatory constraints (Jensen, 1993). Furthermore, institutional investors, such as public pension funds, may be risk-averse and shy away from activism for enhancing the firm performance. Nevertheless, the cost of a proxy fight has fallen from US$ 1 million to less than US$ 5,000[8] (*The Economist*, 1994) thereby minimizing the constraints on institutional activism.

Insider Ownership

A high degree of ownership by managers and directors could well align their interests in the firm with those of the shareholders. Managers and directors, whose remuneration and personal wealth are closely tied to the firm's performance, would prefer to emphasize firm performance over other objectives. But, as the level of inside ownership increases, management could become more entrenched and fail to act in the interests of other shareholders. Thus, the relationship between inside ownership and firm performance is confounded by the interaction of these two effects. The interaction between the entrenchment and the incentive alignment effects has been analyzed by Morck (1994).

Inside Directors

Baysinger & Hoskisson (1990) reviewed the body of literature that focuses on inside directors. They argue that insiders have access to information that is relevant to assessing both the managerial competence and the strategic desirability of initiatives. They also state that outside directors, although they are more open and objective, lack the amount and quality information needed to perform their roles. Hence, the inside directors ratio can improve the effectiveness of a firm's decision-making. Moreover, agency theory states that inside directors should perform just as well or better than outside directors because their reputations and economic well-being are tied directly to the performance of the firm.

On the other hand, inside directors may not be as objective as outside directors if the CEO is a member and/or the chairperson of the board. Also, outside directors may bring insight and objectivity to the decision-making process from their involvement and association with other organizations and outside sources. It is uncertain whether the positive effects of inside directors outweighs the negative effects; thus, the relationship between inside directors and decision-making and firm performance cannot be predicted unambiguously *a priori*.

CEO as Chairperson

Proponents of separating the offices of CEO and chairperson argue that the ability of the board to function independently and effectively will be compromised when the CEO is also the chairperson of the board. Separation of CEO and chairperson positions could improve the decision-making process and performance of the firm in three ways (Bacon, 1993). First, the relationship between the board (the overseer of management) and management will become clear. Second, with an independent leader the board will become more effective and better organized. Third, the board's responsibility to look after shareholders' interests will come to the forefront.

Conversely, a combined CEO/chairperson role would enhance the information flow between the Board and management and improve the cooperation and co-ordination between the two bodies. It is not clear whether the advantages of separation of the two positions dominate the disadvantages.

Board Size

The TSE report on Corporate Governance (1994) and Jensen (1993) looked into the debate of board size and its influence on the effectiveness of the board. Large boards bring a diversity of views and experience, increase the opportunity for a broad geographic representation, and provide extensive director resources for constituting board committees to deal effectively with complex issues. However, beyond a certain threshold of board size, the information flow and decision-making could become more difficult and cumbersome, and the directors might lose their sense of responsibility and accountability. Again, it is unclear whether board size has a positive or negative effect on the decision and performance variables.

SUMMARY

IN SHORT, IT IS DIFFICULT TO PREDICT, *a priori*, the relationship among the governance, decision and performance variables. Against this background, the regression results are discussed in the next section.

EMPIRICAL RESULTS

T HIS SECTION BEGINS WITH a discussion of the degree of empirical association between the corporate governance structure and decision-making variables, after controlling for the effects of size and industry characteristics. We then examine the degree of association between the governance structure and firm performance variables, discussing the roles of governance structure and decision-making on performance, along with the size and industry effects. Finally, we discuss the direct and indirect effects of the governance structure on the firm performance through its impact on the decision-making variables.[9]

CORPORATE GOVERNANCE AND DECISION-MAKING

Tables 3 and 4 display the Canadian and American regression results of Model 1 as shown in Figure 8, described in the previous section. The size of the F-statistics indicates significant associations among the decision, governance, size and industry variables in Canada and the United States. However, in general, the American results are much stronger than the Canadian regressions.

TABLE 3

CANADIAN CORPORATE GOVERNANCE AND DECISION-MAKING REGRESSION RESULTS

	DEBT / ASSETS	ASSETS / EMPLOYEE	R&D / SALES	FOREIGN SALES / TOTAL SALES[1]
(Constant)	0.3293^a	-3360297^a	0.3156^c	0.0843
Board Size	-0.0100^a	101307^a	-0.0195^b	-0.0021
CEO is Chair	0.0494	-75628	-0.0349	0.2095^a
CEO is Chair n/a	-0.0052	-149821	-0.0456	0.1568^a
Foreign Director Ratio	-0.0488	404900	-0.1678	0.4290^a
Inside Director Ratio	-0.0685	-1428028^c	-0.0451	0.0082
Inside Ownership	0.0000	15161^c	0.0008	-0.0007
Institutional Ownership	-0.0002	32952^a	-0.0002	-0.0009^c
Widely Held	-0.0272	967610^c	-0.0026	-0.0419
Effectively Controlled	0.0298	405216	-0.0188	-0.0234
F	4.2963	10.1254	1.0894	3.6924
r^2	0.1603	0.2862	0.2664	0.1485
n	566	631	89	533

a = 1%   b = 5%   c = 10%   t - statistic significance

Notes: This table summarizes the Canadian regression results illustrated in Figure 8, Model 1. Each column represents one of the equations depicted in Regression Equations Set 1. The contents of each cell indicate the coefficient value and it's significance in the regression equation. Industry and Size dummy variables, described in Table 2, have been included in the regressions as control variables but are omitted from this summary table.

[1] The ratio of Foreign Sales to Total Sales, a measure of the firm's outward orientation, was chosen for this Table. The other two measures of outward orientation, the ratio of Foreign Assets to Total Assets and the Presence of Foreign Sales or Assets, have very similar regression results.

TABLE 4

AMERICAN CORPORATE GOVERNANCE AND DECISION MAKING REGRESSION RESULTS

	DEBT ASSETS	ASSETS EMPLOYEE	R&D SALES	FOREIGN SALES TOTAL SALES[1]
(Constant)	0.2985^a	427934^a	0.4813^a	0.1418^a
Board Size	−0.0003	−4628	−0.0011	0.0004
CEO is Chair	0.0147^c	−8903	0.0085	−0.0152^c
Inside Director Ratio	−0.0129	−80081	−0.0703	−0.0168
Inside Ownership	−0.0005^b	−1402	−0.0001	−0.0002
Institutional Ownership	−0.0006^a	1475	−0.0006	0.0003
Widely Held	−0.0507^a	−57818	0.0056	0.0019
Effectively Controlled	−0.0279^b	−35763	0.0162	0.0063
F	17.5080	72.6868	3.3642	23.3684
r^2	0.2221	0.3541	0.0921	0.2544
n	1372	2940	753	1530

a = 1%   b = 5%   c = 10%   t - statistic significance

Notes: This table summarizes the American regression results illustrated in Figure 8, Model 1. Each column represents one of the equations depicted in Regression Equations Set 1. The contents of each cell indicate the coefficient value and its significance in the regression equation. Industry and Size dummy variables, described in Table 2, have been included in the regressions as control variables but are omitted from this summary table.

[1] The ratio of Foreign Sales over Total Sales, a measure of the firm's outward orientation, was chosen for this Table. The other two measures of outward orientation, the ratio of Foreign Assets to Total Assets and the presence of Foreign Sales or Assets, have very similar regression results.

The debt-to-asset ratio, a measure of leverage or riskiness of the firm, is significantly negatively related to institutional ownership and insider ownership, and positively related with the concentration of ownership. In addition, firms in the smallest size class have lower debt-to-asset ratios than firms in the largest size class.

The Canadian debt-to-asset ratio regression results are considerably weaker than the U.S. findings. The leverage of firms in Canada is significantly related to only one governance variable. The debt-to-asset ratio and board size are negatively related. Firms in the three smallest size classes have significantly lower leverage than firms in the largest size class.

Unlike the results on the debt-to-asset ratio, the governance variables have a stronger influence on capital intensity in Canada than in the United States. In Canada, board size, institutional ownership and insider ownership are positively related to capital intensity. In contrast, corporate ownership concentration and the inside director ratio are weakly negatively related to the capital-labour ratio. Firms in the three smallest size classes have higher capital intensity than firms in the largest size class.

None of the governance variables is significantly related to capital intensity in the American sample. In addition, unlike Canada, firms in the two smallest size classes have slightly lower capital intensity than firms in the largest size class. On the other hand, the capital-to-labour ratio and the industry characteristics are strongly related in the American sample.

The research and development intensity, measured by the ratio of R&D to sales, is not significantly related to any of the governance structure variables in the American sample. The R&D intensity of firms with sales between US$ 1 billion and US$ 2 billion is significantly higher than firms in the largest size class with sales over US$ 2 billion.

In the Canadian sample, only board size is significantly negatively related to the R&D-to-sales ratio. There is a weak positive relationship between the R&D intensity and firm size.

In the United States, firms that have a combined CEO-chairperson have significantly lower outward orientation, measured by the ratio of foreign sales to total sales, than firms that do not combine the two positions. Not surprisingly, firms in the smallest five size classes have lower outward orientation than firms in the largest size class.

In Canada, the outward orientation is strongly positively related to firms with the CEO as the chairperson of the board. Also, as expected, there is a strong positive relationship between the foreign director ratio and the outward orientation of the firm. The outward orientation of medium-size Canadian firms is not significantly different from that of the largest firms. However, the outward orientation of firms in the smallest size class (with sales less than US$ 50 million) have significantly lower outward orientation than firms in the largest size class.

Institutional ownership seems to have a much more positive influence on corporate decision-making in the United States than in Canada. On the other hand, the relationship between the inside director ratio and the decision variables is similar in the two countries. Firms with a higher inside director ratio, other things remaining constant, seem to have lower leverage, lower capital intensity, lower R&D intensity and lower outward orientation.

American firms with high levels of inside ownership tend to have low leverage. Inside ownership in Canadian firms is significantly positively related to capital intensity. In American firms, leverage increases with the concentration of ownership. That is, legally controlled firms tend to have higher debt-to-asset ratios compared to the effectively controlled and widely held firms. In Canada, the capital intensity of the widely held firms is somewhat higher than in the legally controlled group firms.

In both countries, a CEO-chairperson is associated with high levels of leverage. In Canada, outward orientation of firms with CEO as the chairperson tends to be higher than in the firms with the two positions separated.

The relationships between the size of the board of directors and the decision variables are stronger in Canada than they are in the United States.

In Canada, the size of the board is negatively related to both the degree of leverage and the R&D intensity. Board size in Canada is positively related to the capital intensity of the firm.

In the two countries, firms in the two smallest size classes have lower leverage and lower outward orientation than firms in the largest size class. In Canada, however, smaller firms tend to have higher capital intensity than the larger firms.

CORPORATE PERFORMANCE AND GOVERNANCE STRUCTURE

TABLES 5 AND 6 DISPLAY THE CANADIAN AND AMERICAN regression results for the corporate performance variables depicted in Figure 9 (Model 2). The size of the F-statistics suggests that the equations explain the inter-firm variation in the corporate performance variables fairly clearly. But, like the equations for corporate decision variables, the Canadian results are not as robust as the American results.

Profitability

For the U.S. sample, both the ROE and the ROA are significantly positively related to institutional ownership, inside ownership, and inside director ratio. Widely held and effectively controlled firms exhibit significantly higher profitability than the legally controlled firms. Similarly, the profitability of firms in the largest size class (sales over US$ 2 billion) is significantly better than firms in the two smallest size classes (firms with less than US$ 100 million).

In the case of Canadian firms, only one of the governance variables (inside director ratio) is significantly positively related to profitability. Like the U.S. results, the profitability of firms in the two smallest size classes is significantly inferior to that of firms with sales over US$ 2 billion.

Growth

The relationship between the two growth measures and the governance variables for American firms is very similar to the findings for the two profitability measures described above. The growth of sales and assets are significantly positively related to institutional ownership, inside ownership, and the inside director ratio. Similarly, the growth performance of firms in the two smallest size classes is significantly weaker than firms with sales over US$ 2 billion. However, the growth performance of firms with sales between US$ 500 million and US$ 1 billion is significantly better than firms in the largest size class.

In the Canadian sample, the asset growth is significantly positively correlated with the CEO as the Chairperson of the Board, the foreign director ratio, the inside director ratio, and size of the Board. However, sales growth is somewhat positively related to only the size of the Board. Unlike the U.S. results, the growth performance of firms with sales under US$ 100 million is somewhat better than the performance of firms with sales over US$ 2 billion.

TABLE 5

CANADIAN CORPORATE PERFORMANCE AND CORPORATE DECISION-MAKING REGRESSION RESULTS

	RETURN ON EQUITY	RETURN ON ASSETS	SALES GROWTH	ASSET GROWTH	SALES EMPLOYEE	SALES ASSETS	LABOUR PROD. GROWTH	CAPITAL PROD. GROWTH	EPS GROWTH
(Constant)	0.1765b	0.0391	0.0419	-0.0733	1077695a	2.4883a	0.0680	0.1152c	0.9702
Assets/Employee	0.0000	0.0000	0.0000b	0.0000	0a	0.0000a	0.0000b	0.0000	0.0000
Debt/Assets	-0.1997a	-0.0532b	-0.0234	-0.0485	139295	-0.7129a	-0.0349	0.0250	-1.1762b
Board Size	-0.0040	0.0003	0.0005	0.0047c	-20842a	-0.0301a	0.0000	-0.0042c	-0.0380
CEO is Chair	-0.0025	0.0108	0.0955c	0.1203b	101535	-0.2206	0.0669	-0.0247	0.0819
CEO is Chair n/a	-0.0444	-0.0033	-0.0342	-0.0331	-60893	-0.0092	-0.0384	-0.0011	0.2190
Foreign Director Ratio	0.0558	-0.0044	0.0733	0.2960a	-440007	-0.2477	0.0876	-0.2227b	0.9288
Inside Director Ratio	0.2112a	0.0691b	0.0422	0.1112c	8906	0.1922	0.0232	-0.0690	0.4137
Inside Ownership	-0.0004	0.0002	-0.0003	-0.0004	-672	0.0014	-0.0004	0.0001	0.0014
Institutional Ownership	-0.0001	0.0000	-0.0005	-0.0005	-211	0.0003	-0.0006	-0.0001	-0.0058
Widely Held	-0.0045	-0.0050	-0.0018	0.0203	-13106	-0.1585	-0.0209	-0.0221	-0.3349
Effectively Controlled	0.0095	-0.0139	0.0069	0.0210	-22336	-0.0453	-0.0007	-0.0141	-0.2455
F	2.3287	1.7335	2.5521	2.8663	9.2013	13.4619	2.3230	1.2780	1.2529
r²	0.1219	0.0937	0.1307	0.1460	20.3543	0.4453	0.1217	0.0708	0.0695
n	463	463	463	463	463	463	463	463	463

a = 1%   b = 5%   c = 10%   t - statistic significance

Notes: This table summarizes the Canadian regression results illustrated in Figure 9, Model 2. Each column represents one of the equations depicted in Regression Equations Set 2. The contents of each cell indicate the coefficient value and its significance in the regression equation. Industry and Size dummy variables, described in Table 2, have been included in the regressions as control variables but have been omitted from this summary table.

TABLE 6

AMERICAN CORPORATE PERFORMANCE AND CORPORATE DECISION-MAKING REGRESSION RESULTS

	RETURN ON EQUITY	RETURN ON ASSETS	SALES GROWTH	ASSET GROWTH	SALES/EMPLOYEE	SALES/ASSETS	LABOUR PROD. GROWTH	CAPITAL PROD. GROWTH	EPS GROWTH
(Constant)	0.0187	0.0296[b]	0.0435	0.0743[b]	547177[a]	2.1237[a]	0.1054[a]	-0.0307	-0.0657
Assets/Employee	0.0000[b]	0.0000[b]	0.0000[b]	0.0000[a]	0[a]	0.0000[a]	0.0000[b]	0.0000	0.0000
Debt/Assets	-0.1904[a]	-0.0500[a]	-0.0521[b]	-0.1541[a]	-69544	-0.4930[a]	-0.0235	0.1020[a]	-0.1348
Board Size	-0.0001	-0.0003	0.0001	0.0001	-947	-0.0042	-0.0005	0.0000	0.0068
CEO is Chair	-0.0011	-0.0014	-0.0060	0.0023	3613	-0.0058	-0.0067	-0.0083	0.0128
Inside Director Ratio	0.0975[a]	0.0263[b]	0.0500[b]	0.0487[b]	63148	0.0784	-0.0173	0.0012	0.4879[a]
Inside Ownership	0.0008[a]	0.0002[b]	0.0004[b]	0.0005[b]	649[c]	0.0021[b]	0.0002	0.0000	0.0004
Institutional Ownership	0.0012[a]	0.0005[a]	0.0007[a]	0.0007[a]	176	-0.0016[a]	0.0001	0.0000	0.0035[b]
Widely Held	0.0427[a]	0.0111[b]	0.0110	0.0082	-26840	-0.0591	-0.0076	0.0028	-0.0832
Effectively Controlled	0.0201	0.0036	0.0149	0.0051	-22908	0.0740	-0.0072	0.0097	-0.2321[a]
F	10.4983	7.0906	4.3160	5.9267	28.4526	46.9150	1.6636	2.8886	2.2912
r²	0.1591	0.1133	0.0722	0.0965	0.3389	0.4581	0.0291	0.0495	0.0397
n	1357	1357	1357	1357	1357	1357	1357	1357	1357

a = 1%   b = 5%   c = 10%   t - statistic significance

Notes: This table summarizes the American regression results illustrated in Figure 9, Model 2. Each column represents one of the equations depicted in Regression Equations, Set 2. The contents of each cell indicate the coefficient's value and it's significance in the regression equation. Industry and Size dummy variables, described in Table 2, have been included in the regressions as control variables but are omitted from this summary table.

Productivity

Both labour and capital productivity of American firms are significantly positively related to the inside ownership ratio. Like profitability and growth, productivity levels of firms in the two smallest size classes are significantly lower than the levels of firms in the largest size class. Labour and capital productivity of Canadian firms are significantly negatively correlated with the size of the Board. Productivity levels of Canadian firms with less than US$ 100 million are also significantly lower than the firms with sales over US$ 2 billion.

CORPORATE PERFORMANCE AND CORPORATE DECISION-MAKING

PROFITABILITY AND THE GROWTH PERFORMANCE of American firms are significantly negatively related to the degree of leverage (Tables 5 and 6). Although the profitability measures are also significantly negatively related to leverage in Canada, sales and asset growth of Canadian firms are only weakly related to leverage. In both the Canadian and American samples, leverage has a strong negative effect on capital productivity. However, leverage does not have a significant effect on labour productivity in the two countries.

The capital-to-labour ratio has a strong negative relationship with both profitability and growth in the American equations. Canadian firms' profitability and growth, however, are weakly (negatively) correlated with capital intensity. But, as expected, labour productivity of both American and Canadian firms is strongly positively related to the capital-to-labour ratio.

TOTAL EFFECT OF GOVERNANCE VARIABLES ON CORPORATE PERFORMANCE

HERE, WE WILL SUMMARIZE THE DIRECT AND INDIRECT impact of governance variables. Recall that the model in Figure 8 investigates the relationship between corporate decision-making and corporate governance structure variables, controlling for size and industry effects. Also recall that the model in Figure 9 investigates the direct relationship between corporate performance and corporate governance structure variables, controlling for size, industry and corporate decision-making variables. These two models are depicted by the first two columns that appear under each country in Table 7. The third column, direct and indirect performance, summarizes the two effects (net impact of direct and indirect) on performance. These total effects are very similar to the results obtained by the reduced form equations.[10]

In Table 7, the label in each cell corresponds to the signs and levels of significance found for the corporate governance variable (row). For example, the association between decision-making and institutional ownership in Canada is labelled "mixed". "Mixed" means that the number of times the governance variable is significantly positively related to the decision-making and/or performance variables is similar to the number of times that it is

TABLE 7

SUMMARY OF REGRESSION ANALYSIS

	CANADA			UNITED STATES		
	DECISION-MAKING	PERFORMANCE		DECISION-MAKING	PERFORMANCE	
	Indirect	Direct	Direct & Indirect	Indirect	Direct	Direct & Indirect
Institutional Ownership	Mixed	No Impact	No Impact	Weak Positive	Strong Positive	Strong Positive
Inside Ownership	Weak Positive	No Impact	No Impact	Weak Positive	Strong Positive	Strong Positive
Concentration of Ownership	No Impact	No Impact	No Impact	Weak Negative	Negative	Weak Negative
Board Size	Positive	Negative	Weak Negative	No Impact	No Impact	No Impact
Foreign Director Ratio	Weak Positive	Mixed	Weak Positive	n/a	n/a	n/a
Inside Director Ratio	Weak Negative	Positive	Positive	Weak Negative	Strong Positive	Positive
CEO/Chairman	Weak Positive	Weak Positive	Weak Positive	Weak Negative	No Impact	No Impact

significantly negatively related. The institutional ownership variable is found to be both significantly positively and negatively related to decision-making variables in the model's set of regression equations – *i.e.*, institutional ownership is significantly positively related to the capital-to-labour ratio and significantly negatively related to outward orientation. "No impact" means that the corporate governance variable in question was not found to be significant, either positively or negatively, in the two sets of regression equations. "Weak positive" or "weak negative" means that the governance variable was significant in one of the equations in the two sets of regression equations. "Positive" or "negative" and "strong positive" or "strong negative" means that the governance variable was significant in two and more than two of the regression equations, respectively.

SUMMARY

IN GENERAL, THE CORPORATE PERFORMANCE OF AMERICAN FIRMS is positively correlated (both directly and indirectly) by institutional ownership, the inside director ratio, and inside ownership, and negatively correlated with corporate ownership concentration. The Canadian results are not as strong and robust as the American findings.

The inside director ratio and the foreign director ratio seem to have a positive influence on the performance of Canadian firms. Similarly, the size of the Board seems to exert a positive influence (mainly indirectly via leverage and capital formation) on the economic performance of Canadian firms. The growth performance of Canadian firms is also significantly positively related to the foreign director ratio. Likewise, the growth performance of companies where the CEO is also the Chairperson of the Board is significantly better than companies where the two positions are not held by one person.

In general, the economic performance (productivity, growth and profitability) of both Canadian and American firms with sales under US$ 100 million is considerably inferior to the performance in the largest size class (sales over US$ 2 billion).

CONCLUSIONS

THE MAJOR OBJECTIVE OF THIS STUDY has been to examine the corporate governance structure in Canada and the United States, and to provide an empirical analysis of the degree of association between the governance, corporate decision, and performance variables in the two countries. Toward this goal, drawing from three major sources of company data, a large database on governance, decision and performance variables for 766 Canadian and 3,000 American firms was created. Some of the major findings of our study follow.

- The majority of Canadian firms in all size classes and in most industry groups is legally controlled (one or a small group of shareholders owning, directly or indirectly, more than 50 percent of the voting shares of the company). On average, 55 percent of Canadian firms are legally controlled, compared to less than 25 percent of American firms.

- Differences in the ownership structure of American and Canadian companies are more pronounced for very large firms.

- In the Canadian sample, on average, over 20 percent of company shares are held by insiders (directors or officers of the firm), compared to less than 10 percent in the United States.

- On the other hand, U.S. firms, on average, exhibit a much higher level of institutional ownership (percentage of shares held by institutional investors) than Canadian firms (53.3 percent *versus* 38.2 percent).

- In the two samples, the number of directors and senior officers increases with firm size (measured by total sales).

- On average, the inside director ratio (the number of directors who are also officers of the firm over the total number of directors) in the Canadian sample (20 percent) is lower than in the U.S. sample (22 percent).

- The foreign director ratio averages 15 percent for Canadian firms.

- On average, only 34.5 percent of Canadian firms have the CEO as the Chairperson of the Board, compared to over 60 percent for U.S. firms.

- Profitability, productivity and growth performance of American firms are significantly positively correlated (both directly and indirectly) by institutional ownership, the inside ownership ratio, and the inside director ratio.

- The economic performance of widely held and effectively controlled American firms is significantly better than the performance of legally controlled firms.

- In Canada, the inside director ratio has a positive effect on corporate performance.

- The growth performance of Canadian firms, especially asset growth, is positively related to the foreign director ratio.

- The size of the Board, and whether the CEO is the Chairperson of the Board, do not seem to matter much for corporate performance in the two countries.

In short, our findings indicate that the governance structure variables are not strongly correlated with the corporate decision-making and performance variables. However, the governance variables related to ownership – institutional ownership, inside ownership, and concentration of ownership – are strongly correlated with performance variables in the United States.

These results imply the need for different policy approaches in the two countries. In the United States, governments and corporate actions aimed at improving institutional activism, increasing the inside ownership and reducing the ownership concentration would improve corporate performance. In Canada, on the other hand, government and corporate efforts to improve corporate governance *practices* such as reducing executive entrenchment and differential voting rights, enacting minority shareholder provisions, enforcing director liability, and enhancing disclosure requirements might be more relevant for improving corporate performance.

Efforts to develop data on corporate governance practices would be very helpful in shedding further light on the importance of corporate governance for firms' adaptability, flexibility and dynamism. Future Industry Canada research in this area may focus on this effort.

ENDNOTES

1 The Toronto Stock Exchange Committee on Corporate Governance in Canada, "'Where Were The Directors?' Guidelines For Improved Corporate Governance in Canada," Draft Report (May 1994).

2 This study uses accounting-based, rather than market-based, measures of firm performance. Market-based performance measures are both easy to compute and reliable. However, they cannot be used to evaluate a firm's decision-making and performance in absolute terms, but only in relation to market expectations of the firm. The expected performance of a well-managed firm will be built into the firm's current stock price and only unexpected deviations will be picked up by the future stock performance.

3 The Canadian and American Corporate Governance Environment Summaries are from Framework Conditions for Industry Draft Agenda, OECD, 1994.

4 The definition of inside directors used in this study differs from that used by Amoako-Adu and Smith (1995). Their definition also includes the directors appointed from employees of parent companies, subsidiaries and affiliates. Therefore, our estimate of the inside director ratio will be biased downward, compared to the estimates of Amoako-Adu and Smith (1995). However, it is difficult to determine, a priori, which of the two measures captures better the independence of directors.

5 The Canadian Business Corporations Act (CBCA) uses country of citizenship to distinguish between domestic and foreign directors. Because the Compact Disclosure data sources used in this study do not include citizenship information, we use the country of residency to estimate the foreign director ratio.

6 The concentration of economic power in Canadian and American firms should also take into account executive entrenchment. However, like concentration, executive entrenchment is significantly higher in Canada. Canadian executives are much more entrenched than their American counterparts for several reasons: the absence of class actions by shareholders in the Canadian legal system; the consequent difficulty of dismantling poison pills and other takeover defenses in Canada; and the coattails provisions in Canadian corporate acquisitions that, while benefiting small shareholders, make the transfer of corporate control more expensive. The

widespread use of multiple classes of shares in Canada adds further to the entrenchment of Canadian executives.

7   The relationship between firm performance and ownership concentration, taking into account size, industry, governance structure, and corporate decision-making variables, is discussed later in this section.

8   Patricia Lipton, Head of the Wisconsin State Retirement System.

9   In the section on the Analytical Framework of this study, we assume that the relationships among the governance, decision-making, and performance variables are linear. However, we tested for the presence of non-linear relationships among the variables, but did not include the results. In general, the non-linear regression results are very similar to the results from the linear model. Nevertheless, the rate of return and growth performance variables are found to be somewhat non-linearly related to the Inside Director ratio.

10 The reduced form equations regress the performance variables only on the governance, industry and size variables. However, a Table summarizing the results of the reduced equations, which would be similar to Tables 5 and 6, is not included.

APPENDIX 1

SOURCES AND CHARACTERISTICS OF THE DATABASE

THIS APPENDIX BRIEFLY DESCRIBES the data sources, data grouping, and the characteristics of sample companies in the two countries.

SOURCES OF MICRO DATA

THE DATABASE FOR THIS STUDY IS DEVELOPED FROM three main sources of company financial data: Compact Disclosure Canada, Compact Disclosure SEC, and Compact Disclosure Worldscope. All three databases are provided in CD-ROM format by Disclosure Incorporated.[1] When necessary, information was supplemented by Moody's International Company Database provided by Moody's Investors Services.

The Compact Disclosure Canada database consists of over 8,500 Canadian public and private companies and Crown corporations. Companies included in the database are those that are incorporated in Canada, either federally or in one of the provinces or territories, and that trade on a Canadian exchange. Company records include annual financial statement data, interim financial statement detail, stock issue data, legal and company status indicators, and textual data.

The Compact Disclosure SEC database consists of over 12,000 public companies that file reports with the U.S. Securities and Exchange Commission. Company data is extracted from the company's 10K or 20F statements.

The Compact Disclosure Worldscope database consists of over 11,000 public companies from 40 countries. Company data is obtained from annual and periodic reports filed with each of the national stock exchange commissions.

Two criteria were used to select the firms that comprise the database for this study. First, only those firms that disclosed a full set of corporate governance variables are included. Second, only those firms that had sales and assets values greater than US$ 10 million are included. The final database consists of 766 Canadian firms and 3,000 American firms.

The two country samples refer to December 1993, or the latest reported date. However, data related to both level and growth values of the firms' corporate decision and corporate performance variables are based on five-year averages for the period 1988 to 1993.[2]

Each firm in the sample is categorized by a size class and a major industry group. The size of the firm is measured by the total dollar value of sales. The firm's major industry group is based on the firm's primary business activity. Individual firm data is aggregated into these size classes or major industry groupings using the weighted average method, which permits the major industry or size averages to capture the relative importance of the firms within the grouping.[3]

CHARACTERISTICS OF SAMPLE FIRMS

Size Distribution

The firms in our study vary in size from a minimum of US$ 10 million in sales and assets to US$ 138 billion in sales and US$ 219 billion in assets for the United States sample and US$ 16.5 billion in sales and US$ 102 billion in assets for the Canadian sample. Total sales and assets of the Canadian firms are US$ 397 billion and US$ 1.2 trillion while total sales and assets for the American sample are US $3.6 trillion and US $7.0 trillion.

In an effort to examine the differences in governance structure between firms of different sizes, both the Canadian and the American firms are grouped into six size classes based on the dollar value of their total sales. Table A1-1 displays the size classes used in this study.

Although the size groupings are chosen somewhat arbitrarily, they seem to capture adequately the differences in governance variables by the size of sales. In general, the Canadian sample is dominated by more smaller firms than the American sample. Over 80 percent of the Canadian firms have sales less than US$ 500 million while only just over 70 percent of the American firms fall into the same category. On the other hand, the American sample is dominated by extremely large firms – almost 19 percent of the American firms have sales over US$ 1 billion compared to only about 11 percent of the Canadian firms (Figure A1-1). However, the average size of sales and assets for Canadian firms with sales below US$ 2 billion compares very favourably with those of their U.S. counterparts (Table A3-1).

The most striking feature of the sample firms is that although large firms (sales over US$ 1 billion) account for a small proportion (less than 20 percent) of total firms, they contribute to over 70 percent of sales and assets in the two samples (Table A3-2).

TABLE A1-1

SIZE CLASSES DETERMINED BY SALES VOLUME

SIZE CLASS	SALES CRITERIA (US$ MILLIONS)
1	10 to 50
2	50 to 100
3	100 to 500
4	500 to 1,000
5	1,000 to 2,000
6	> 2,000

FIGURE A1-1

SAMPLE DISTRIBUTION OF CANADIAN AND AMERICAN FIRMS BY SIZE CLASS

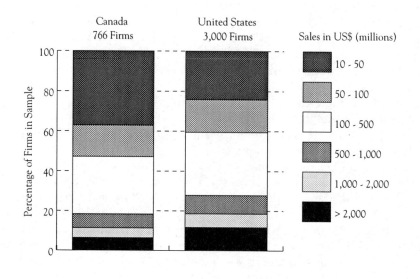

Source: Based on Table A3-1.

Industry Distribution

In order to capture the differences in governance structure and practices across industrial activities, the 3766 companies are grouped into three digit industry groups based on their U.S. Standard Industrial Classification 1986 (SIC) code as determined by the companies' primary business activity. These industries are further aggregated into 11 major industry groups.[4] Table A1-2 describes the major industry groupings used in this study.

Table A3-3 depicts the average sales and asset value of firms in the 11 major industries. Unlike the size classes, the average sales size of American firms tend to be at least twice as large as their Canadian counterparts in all the major industry groups except in the Agriculture, Forestry and Fishing industries, and the Finance, Insurance and Real Estate industries. The higher ratios of average sales to average assets for the U.S. firms implies that, on average, capital productivity of the American firms is significantly higher than the productivity of Canadian firms.[5]

TABLE A1-2

COMPONENTS OF THE MAJOR INDUSTRY GROUPINGS

MAJOR INDUSTRY GROUPING	INDUSTRY
Agriculture, Forestry and Fishing	—
Construction	—
Finance, Insurance and Real Estate	Depository Institutions Non-depository Institutions Securities and Brokers Insurance Other Financial Services
Labour-Intensive Manufacturing	Clothing Furniture and Fixtures Leather and Products Miscellaneous Manufactured Goods Printing and Publishing Textiles
Mining	—
Resource-Intensive Manufacturing	Fabricated Metals Food and Products Lumber and Wood Non-Metallic Minerals Paper and Allied Petroleum Refining Primary Metals Tobacco
Retail Trade	—
Services	Commercial Services Health Services Other Services
Technology-Intensive Manufacturing	Aircraft and Parts Chemicals and Allied Communications Equipment Computer and Office Electrical Products Light Machinery Machinery, excluding Electrical Miscellaneous Electrical Products Motor Vehicles and Equipment Other Transportation Equipment Rubber and Products
Transportation and Public Utilities	—
Wholesale Trade	—

FIGURE A1-2

SAMPLE DISTRIBUTION OF CANADIAN AND AMERICAN FIRMS BY INDUSTRY GROUPING

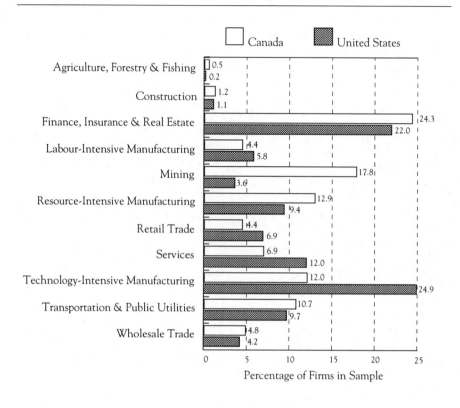

Source: Based on Table A3-4.

Over three-quarters of the Canadian firms are from just five major industries: Finance, Insurance and Real Estate; Mining; Resource-Intensive Manufacturing; Technology-Intensive Manufacturing; and Transportation and Public Utilities. In addition, these five major industries account for 85 percent of the total sales and over 95 percent of the total assets in the Canadian sample (Appendix 3, Table A3-4). The Finance, Insurance and Real Estate industry, alone, represents close to one-quarter of all Canadian firms and accounts for nearly three-quarters of the total assets of the Canadian sample.

The Finance, Insurance and Real Estate industry also plays an important role in the American sample with just over 20 percent of the number of firms and just over half of the total assets. The Technology-Intensive Manufacturing and Services industries are better represented in the American sample, while the Mining industry has a higher proportion of firms, sales and assets in the Canadian sample (Figure A1-2).

Although the sample selection method did not appear to have introduced any systematic bias toward any major industry in the two countries, it is interesting to note that the Canadian sample has a higher proportion of firms in Finance, Insurance and Real Estate, the Mining, and the Resource-Intensive Manufacturing industries than in the United States. On the other hand, the American sample has a higher proportion of Technology-Intensive Manufacturing and Services industries. The industrial distribution of firms in the two samples reflects the comparative advantage position of the two countries (Eden,1994, and the Industry Canada Working Paper Number 1).

ENDNOTES TO APPENDIX 1

1 Disclosure Incorporated, 5161 River Road, Bethesda, MD 20816.

2 Although accounting-based measures are ideally suited to measure the effectiveness of managers' decision-making and firm performance, the numerous conventions that are necessary in implementing an accounting system often leave us perplexed about accounting measures. To overcome both these ambiguities (which tend to be resolved over extended time periods) and short-term fluctuations, our analysis includes a five-year average of accounting variables.

3 The weights used in the averaging process are the value of the variables in the denominators of the ratios being averaged. For instance, employment values are used as weights in calculating the average value of the Asset/Employment ratio.

4 This industry grouping is consistent with the commonly used practices of the (former) Economic Council of Canada and the OECD.

5 The average value of capital productivity, the ratio of average sales to average assets, is 0.3416 for Canada and 0.5139 for the United States. The capital productivity, excluding the Mining industry, averages 0.3326 and 0.5023 for Canada and the United States, respectively, implying that the lower average value in Canada is not due to the inclusion of the Mining industry.

APPENDIX 2

GOVERNANCE ENVIRONMENT IN NORTH AMERICA

(See Table A2-1 and Table A2-2 on the following pages.)

TABLE A2-1
CANADIAN GOVERNANCE ENVIRONMENT

	CONCENTRATION OF OWNERSHIP AND CONTROL	STRATEGIC ROLE OF BOARDS	STRATEGIC INFORMATION OF OWNERS	USE OF TAKE-OVERS AS RESTRUCTURING TOOLS	CONCENTRATION OF CREDITORS	COMBINATION OF EQUITY AND CREDIT BY "UNIVERSAL" INVESTORS	USE OF BANKRUPTCY AS EXIT TOOLS	RATE OF RETURN OF INVESTMENT
Laws and Regulations	Competition and certain financial and investment legislation regulate the concentration of ownership and control.	Directors are to manage or supervise the management of corporations. Directors must retain ultimate control over the corporation.	Corporate and securities laws ensure widespread information available to the public. Strategic information is protected.	Takeovers usually allowed as governance tools. Minority shareholders generally protected.	Guidelines with respect to federal deposit-taking institutions (DTIs) discourage concentration of credit positions.	DTIs are not restricted in combining debt and equity. Limits are imposed on the amount of equity DTIs provide for non-financial firms.	Comprehensive exit procedures provided for corporations and financial institutions. Procedures aimed at survival.	Corporate law stresses maximization of shareholder value as key objective.
Standard Practices	High level of corporate ownership concentration. Approval required for certain mergers and acquisitions.	Directors manage or supervise the management of corporations. Institutional investors are increasing their influence.	Detailed annual, quarterly information on public companies is provided. Analytical information available from securities industry.	Corporate and corporation articles generally do not discourage take-overs. Few anti-takeover devices upheld by courts.	Standard practice for larger firms is small-size bank loans and dispersed bond ownership.	Equity and debt are separate instruments. Financial non-DTIs are increasing their equity holdings substantially.	Creditor or debtor may invoke both exit and reorganization processes.	Equity securities values are traded according to returns.

TABLE A2-1 (CONT'D)

	CONCENTRATION OF OWNERSHIP AND CONTROL	STRATEGIC ROLE OF BOARDS	STRATEGIC INFORMATION OF OWNERS	USE OF TAKE-OVERS AS RESTRUCTURING TOOLS	CONCENTRATION OF CREDITORS	COMBINATION OF EQUITY AND CREDIT BY "UNIVERSAL" INVESTORS	USE OF BANKRUPTCY AS EXIT TOOLS	RATE OF RETURN OF INVESTMENT
Implicit Rules	Corporations aiming at concentrated ownership generally go private.	Boards work closely with senior management. They are increasingly independent.	Widespread use of financial information. Aggregate statistical information available.	General acceptance of takeovers as part of adjustment process.	DTIs and bondholders keep arm's-length relations with borrowing companies.	Ownership and creditorship entail different rights and responsibilities.	Bankruptcy recognized as a risk of business. Process seen as providing an orderly, efficient and fair reallocation of assets.	Corporations recognized as profit maximizing organization.
Observed Outcomes	Vast majority of Canadian corporations are privately held. Over 80% of public corporations have a dominant shareholder.	Boards are increasing management and supervision of corporations to avoid potential liabilities.	Public information widely used. Strategic information generally not available.	Increasing number of takeovers. Poison pills often disallowed by courts.	Highly dispersed credit positions with respect to large firms.	Financial non-DTIs have increased their involvement in corporate governance.	Liquidations outnumber reorganizations. Recent legislation promotes more reorganizations and survivals of existing entities.	Average Return on Capital 1933 = 16.2% 1992 = 16.0%

Source: Corporate Governance Branch, Industry Canada.

Table A2-2

UNITED STATES GOVERNANCE ENVIRONMENT

	CONCENTRATION OF OWNERSHIP AND CONTROL	STRATEGIC ROLE OF BOARDS	STRATEGIC INFORMATION OF OWNERS	USE OF TAKE-OVERS AS RESTRUCTURING TOOLS	CONCENTRATION OF CREDITORS	COMBINATION OF EQUITY AND CREDIT BY "UNIVERSAL" INVESTORS	USE OF BANKRUPTCY AS EXIT TOOLS	RATE OF RETURN OF INVESTMENT
Laws and Regulations	Securities and investment legislation contains, and discourages, the concentration of ownership and control.	Regulatory rules discourage shareholders entering the boards. But legally the board rules and fiduciary duties of directors were recently strengthened.	Company and securities law prescribe widespread public financial information. Strategic and prospective information from within firms is classified.	Legal recognition of take-overs as governance tool, recent state anti-take-over legislation.	Banking legislation discourages concentration of credit positions.	Combination of equity and debt forbidden by law.	Elaborated bankruptcy legislation. In bankruptcy, creditor claims may be subordinated to company survival.	Company law stresses profitability as key corporate objective.
Standard Practices	(Private stock exchange rules discourage concentration of ownership.) Dispersed owners do not usually exercise their proxy rights.	Standard corporate charters and practice do not provide for strategic/ operational role for boards.	Detailed quarterly financial information, additional analytical information by securities firms. "Price sensitive" insider information not diffused.	Corporate charters designed to permit take-overs; recent toleration of anti-takeover devices.	Standard practice is small-size bank loans and dispersed bond ownership.	Equity and debts are stringently separated instruments but recent rise in the use of hybrids.	Standard bankruptcy procedures are available. Creditors are incited to use them rather than negotiate out-of-court rescue arrangements.	Equity securities valued and ownership trade according to returns.

TABLE A2-2 (CONT'D)

	CONCENTRATION OF OWNERSHIP AND CONTROL	STRATEGIC ROLE OF BOARDS	STRATEGIC INFORMATION OF OWNERS	USE OF TAKE-OVERS AS RESTRUCTURING TOOLS	CONCENTRATION OF CREDITORS	COMBINATION OF EQUITY AND CREDIT BY "UNIVERSAL" INVESTORS	USE OF BANKRUPTCY AS EXIT TOOLS	RATE OF RETURN OF INVESTMENT
Implicit Rules	Corporations aiming at concentrated ownership and control are expected to go "private" (no public issuance of securities).	The board needs to function as an amicable and advisory body to the CEO. But this understanding is changing for a more independent role.	Widespread credibility and use of financial information. Other more strategic information should be made available only if evenly available to all investors.	Perceived legitimacy and acceptance of take-overs as part of adjustment process.	Banks and bondholders keeps arm's-length relations with borrowing companies.	Ownership and creditorship entail essentially different rights and responsibilities.	Bankruptcy risks are recognized and accepted.	Companies recognized as profit-maximizing organizations.
Observed Outcomes	Dispersed ownership in industry, but some recent consolidation through institutional ownership.	Large majority of boards dominated by management, but recent cases of reversals.	Excellent diffusion of public information, containment of insider strategic information	Large number of take-overs but recent curbs in several states.	Highly dispersed credit positions.	Very few investors have an owner and creditor perspective.	Large number of exits settled via bankruptcies. Possible excess in the number of bankruptcies.	US-BW 1000 companies, return on equity 1993 = 18.4% 1992 = 14.9%

Source: OECD Framework Conditions for Industry, Draft.

APPENDIX 3

CORPORATE GOVERNANCE STRUCTURE: DETAILED TABULATIONS

TABLE A3-1

DATABASE SUMMARY - NUMBER OF FIRMS, AVERAGE SALES AND AVERAGE ASSETS BY SIZE CLASS (US$ MILLIONS)

	CANADA			UNITED STATES		
SALES CLASS	# OF FIRMS	AVERAGE SALES	AVERAGE ASSETS	# OF FIRMS	AVERAGE SALES	AVERAGE ASSETS
10 to 50	284	25,808	92,733	725	28,066	117,643
50 to 100	120	72,422	228,667	491	71,760	186,368
100 to 500	221	238,012	439,353	948	237,393	464,385
500 to 1,000	54	708,941	3,548,411	279	681,204	1,385,208
1,000 to 2,000	37	1,375,530	2,567,314	204	1,411,930	2,454,547
> 2,000,000	50	4,796,452	14,532,434	353	8,064,429	15,614,259

TABLE A3-2

DATABASE DISTRIBUTION - FIRMS, SALES AND ASSETS BY SIZE CLASS (US$ MILLIONS)

	CANADA			UNITED STATES		
SALES CLASS	% OF FIRMS	% OF TOTAL SALES IN SAMPLE	% OF TOTAL ASSETS IN SAMPLE	% OF FIRMS	% OF TOTAL SALES IN SAMPLE	% OF TOTAL ASSETS IN SAMPLE
10 to 50	37.1	2	2	24.2	1	1
50 to 100	15.7	2	2	16.4	1	1
100 to 500	28.9	13	8	31.6	6	6
500 to 1,000	7.0	10	16	9.3	5	6
1,000 to 2,000	4.8	13	8	6.8	8	7
> 2,000,000	6.5	60	62	11.8	79	79

TABLE A3-3

DATABASE SUMMARY - NUMBER OF FIRMS, AVERAGE SALES AND AVERAGE ASSETS
BY MAJOR INDUSTRY GROUPING (US$ MILLIONS)

MAJOR INDUSTRY GROUPING	CANADA			UNITED STATES		
	TOTAL NO. OF FIRMS	AVERAGE SALES	AVERAGE ASSETS	TOTAL NO. OF FIRMS	AVERAGE SALES	AVERAGE ASSETS
Agriculture, Forestry & Fishing	4	219,492	115,817	7	108,216	113,009
Construction	9	102,962	90,279	34	659,264	596,291
Finance, Insurance & Real Estate	186	749,953	4,650,208	660	767,971	5,590,339
Labour-Intensive Manufacturing	34	298,532	254,979	175	526,732	388,407
Mining	136	232,421	469,695	108	1,492,697	1,473,019
Resource-Intensive Manufacturing	99	509,715	580,386	281	2,090,011	1,956,505
Retail Trade	34	818,165	333,030	208	1,850,427	1,104,318
Services	53	106,200	109,232	361	347,574	373,289
Technology-Intensive Manufacturing	92	682,665	316,210	747	1,474,520	1,682,977
Transportation & Public Utilities	82	610,032	1,399,244	292	1,731,911	2,977,955
Wholesale Trade	37	481,884	187,504	127	922,843	294,044
Simple Average	766	519,087	1,519,712	3,000	1,201,821	2,338,690

TABLE A3-4

DATABASE DISTRIBUTION - FIRMS, SALES AND ASSETS BY MAJOR INDUSTRY GROUPING

MAJOR INDUSTRY GROUPING	CANADA			UNITED STATES		
	% OF FIRMS	% OF TOTAL SALES	% OF TOTAL ASSETS	% OF FIRMS	% OF TOTAL SALES	% OF TOTAL ASSETS
Agriculture, Forestry & Fishing	0.5	0	0	0.2	0	0
Construction	1.2	0	0	1.1	1	0
Finance, Insurance & Real Estate	24.3	35	74	22.0	14	53
Labour-Intensive Manufacturing	4.4	3	1	5.8	3	1
Mining	17.8	8	5	3.6	4	2
Resource-Intensive Manufacturing	12.9	13	5	9.4	16	8
Retail Trade	4.4	7	1	6.9	11	3
Services	6.9	1	0	12.0	3	2
Technology-Intensive Manufacturing	12.0	16	2	24.9	31	18
Transportation & Public Utilities	10.7	13	10	9.7	14	12
Wholesale Trade	4.8	4	1	4.2	3	1

TABLE A3-5

CONCENTRATION OF OWNERSHIP BY SIZE CLASS

	CANADA - % OF FIRMS			UNITED STATES - % OF FIRMS		
SALES (US$ MILLIONS)	WIDELY HELD	EFFECTIVE CONTROL	LEGAL CONTROL	WIDELY HELD	EFFECTIVE CONTROL	LEGAL CONTROL
10 to 50	23.9	23.6	52.5	45.6	31.0	23.4
50 to 100	20.8	24.2	55.0	30.1	39.3	30.6
100 to 500	22.6	20.4	57.0	31.8	37.2	31.0
500 to 1,000	20.4	25.9	53.7	39.4	39.4	20.8
1,000 to 2,000	21.6	8.1	70.3	47.6	34.8	17.6
> 2,000	30.0	12.0	58.0	62.3	28.6	9.1
Average of All Classes	**23.1**	**21.4**	**55.5**	**40.2**	**35.1**	**24.7**

TABLE A3-6

CONCENTRATION OF OWNERSHIP BY MAJOR INDUSTRY GROUPING

	CANADA - % OF FIRMS			UNITED STATES - % OF FIRMS		
MAJOR INDUSTRY GROUPING	WIDELY HELD	EFFECTIVE CONTROL	LEGAL CONTROL	WIDELY HELD	EFFECTIVE CONTROL	LEGAL CONTROL
Agriculture, Forestry & Fishing	50.0	0.0	50.0	28.6	42.8	28.6
Construction	22.2	11.1	66.7	26.5	17.6	55.9
Finance, Insurance & Real Estate	15.1	15.6	69.3	58.2	29.5	12.3
Labour-Intensive Manufacturing	17.6	20.6	61.8	33.1	29.7	37.2
Mining	42.6	25.0	32.4	31.5	32.4	36.1
Resource-Intensive Manufacturing	21.2	15.2	63.6	36.7	40.2	23.1
Retail Trade	11.8	26.4	61.8	31.7	33.2	35.1
Services	15.1	37.7	47.2	21.6	44.6	33.8
Technology-Intensive Manufacturing	24.0	38.0	38.0	35.3	41.9	22.8
Transportation & Public Utilities	17.0	11.0	72.0	56.5	20.5	23.0
Wholesale Trade	32.4	13.5	54.1	33.9	37.0	29.1
Average of All Groups	**23.1**	**21.4**	**55.5**	**40.2**	**35.1**	**24.7**

TABLE A3-7

PERCENTAGE HELD BY ALL OF THE SIGNIFICANT SHAREHOLDERS, BY SIZE CLASS

SALES (US$ MILLIONS)	CANADA - WEIGHTED AVERAGE
10 to 50	50.07
50 to 100	52.65
100 to 500	51.71
500 to 1,000	52.32
1,000 to 2,000	58.19
> 2,000,000	53.30
Weighted Average of All Classes	**53.55**

TABLE A3-8

PERCENTAGE HELD BY ALL OF THE SIGNIFICANT SHAREHOLDERS
BY MAJOR INDUSTRY GROUPING

MAJOR INDUSTRY GROUPING	CANADA - WEIGHTED AVERAGE
Agriculture, Forestry & Fishing	12.26
Construction	54.75
Finance, Insurance & Real Estate	42.25
Labour-Intensive Manufacturing	51.49
Mining	53.98
Resource-Intensive Manufacturing	37.27
Retail Trade	58.69
Services	44.40
Technology-Intensive Manufacturing	80.63
Transportation & Public Utilities	63.77
Wholesale Trade	61.31
Weighted Average of All Groups	**53.55**

TABLE A3-9

NUMBER OF SIGNIFICANT SHAREHOLDERS WITH AT LEAST 10 PERCENT OWNERSHIP BY SIZE CLASS

SALES (US$ MILLIONS)	CANADA - WEIGHTED AVERAGE	UNITED STATES - WEIGHTED AVERAGE
10 to 50	1.37	0.91
50 to 100	1.52	1.13
100 to 500	1.20	1.02
500 to 1,000	1.18	0.89
1,000 to 2,000	1.12	0.72
> 2,000	0.93	0.44
Weighted Average of All Classes	1.03	0.54

TABLE A3-10

NUMBER OF SIGNIFICANT SHAREHOLDERS WITH AT LEAST 10 PERCENT OWNERSHIP BY MAJOR INDUSTRY GROUPING

MAJOR INDUSTRY GROUPING	CANADA - WEIGHTED AVERAGE	UNITED STATES - WEIGHTED AVERAGE
Agriculture, Forestry & Fishing	1.60	2.44
Construction	3.30	1.76
Finance, Insurance & Real Estate	1.75	1.38
Labour-Intensive Manufacturing	2.45	2.18
Mining	1.76	1.23
Resource-Intensive Manufacturing	2.23	1.68
Retail Trade	2.31	1.97
Services	2.67	1.81
Technology-Intensive Manufacturing	2.06	1.41
Transportation & Public Utilities	1.88	1.31
Wholesale Trade	3.62	1.63
Weighted Average of All Groups	1.03	0.54

TABLE A3-11

PERCENTAGE OF VOTING SHARES HELD BY INSIDERS, BY SIZE CLASS

SALES (US$ MILLIONS)	CANADA - WEIGHTED AVERAGE	UNITED STATES - WEIGHTED AVERAGE
10 to 50	34.58	25.71
50 to 100	24.52	25.77
100 to 500	13.18	22.30
500 to 1,000	15.13	15.31
1,000 to 2,000	20.98	14.13
> 2,000	22.18	7.46
Weighted Average of All Classes	21.49	9.60

TABLE A3-12

PERCENTAGE OF VOTING SHARES HELD BY INSIDERS, BY MAJOR INDUSTRY GROUPING

MAJOR INDUSTRY GROUPING	CANADA - WEIGHTED AVERAGE	UNITED STATES - WEIGHTED AVERAGE
Agriculture, Forestry & Fishing	n/a	17.88
Construction	n/a	10.58
Finance, Insurance & Real Estate	2.69	10.76
Labour-Intensive Manufacturing	9.97	13.90
Mining	54.14	3.05
Resource-Intensive Manufacturing	26.82	9.50
Retail Trade	n/a	19.52
Services	24.13	14.99
Technology-Intensive Manufacturing	1.99	6.99
Transportation & Public Utilities	22.15	5.18
Wholesale Trade	n/a	16.27
Weighted Average of All Groups	21.49	9.60

Note: n/a = data not available

TABLE A3-13

INSTITUTIONAL OWNERSHIP BY SIZE CLASS

SALES (US$ MILLIONS)	CANADA - WEIGHTED AVERAGE	UNITED STATES - WEIGHTED AVERAGE
10 to 50	31.36	16.36
50 to 100	31.59	27.23
100 to 500	33.05	40.58
500 to 1,000	36.86	46.22
1,000 to 2,000	44.26	51.34
> 2,000	38.78	55.53
Weighted Average of All Classes	38.24	53.27

TABLE A3-14

INSTITUTIONAL OWNERSHIP BY MAJOR INDUSTRY GROUPING

MAJOR INDUSTRY GROUPING	CANADA - WEIGHTED AVERAGE	UNITED STATES - WEIGHTED AVERAGE
Agriculture, Forestry & Fishing	9.57	56.19
Construction	44.20	56.28
Finance, Insurance & Real Estate	28.75	59.28
Labour-Intensive Manufacturing	39.58	51.02
Mining	40.27	55.68
Resource-Intensive Manufacturing	26.70	51.52
Retail Trade	24.16	49.40
Services	22.98	51.69
Technology-Intensive Manufacturing	68.73	56.56
Transportation & Public Utilities	52.82	44.72
Wholesale Trade	20.31	54.46
Weighted Average of All Groups	38.24	53.27

TABLE A3-15

NUMBER OF DIRECTORS BY SIZE CLASS

SALES (US$ MILLIONS)	CANADA - WEIGHTED AVERAGE	UNITED STATES - WEIGHTED AVERAGE
10 to 50	7.34	7.38
50 to 100	8.27	8.29
100 to 500	9.81	9.62
500 to 1,000	11.92	11.62
1,000 to 2,000	11.89	12.70
> 2,000	16.66	17.74
Weighted Average of All Classes	**14.33**	**16.36**

TABLE A3-16

NUMBER OF DIRECTORS BY MAJOR INDUSTRY GROUPING

MAJOR INDUSTRY GROUPING	CANADA - WEIGHTED AVERAGE	UNITED STATES - WEIGHTED AVERAGE
Agriculture, Forestry & Fishing	12.28	14.73
Construction	8.93	10.15
Finance, Insurance & Real Estate	10.79	15.41
Labour-Intensive Manufacturing	11.28	13.43
Mining	10.54	15.15
Resource-Intensive Manufacturing	12.51	18.42
Retail Trade	11.83	13.54
Services	9.60	12.51
Technology-Intensive Manufacturing	11.24	18.89
Transportation & Public Utilities	13.70	14.71
Wholesale Trade	11.40	12.05
Weighted Average of All Groups	**14.33**	**16.36**

TABLE A3-17

NUMBER OF OFFICERS BY SIZE CLASS

SALES (US$ MILLIONS)	CANADA - WEIGHTED AVERAGE	UNITED STATES - WEIGHTED AVERAGE
10 to 50	5.24	9.02
50 to 100	6.51	8.96
100 to 500	8.47	9.76
500 to 1,000	10.39	11.48
1,000 to 2,000	10.05	12.03
> 2,000	16.25	15.86
Weighted Average of All Classes	**13.45**	**14.84**

TABLE A3-18

NUMBER OF OFFICERS BY MAJOR INDUSTRY GROUPING

MAJOR INDUSTRY GROUPING	CANADA - WEIGHTED AVERAGE	UNITED STATES - WEIGHTED AVERAGE
Agriculture, Forestry & Fishing	10.14	13.79
Construction	4.43	12.31
Finance, Insurance & Real Estate	17.80	18.27
Labour-Intensive Manufacturing	10.92	12.31
Mining	9.05	14.24
Resource-Intensive Manufacturing	10.45	16.57
Retail Trade	11.43	12.23
Services	11.29	12.61
Technology-Intensive Manufacturing	10.94	14.21
Transportation & Public Utilities	13.05	14.87
Wholesale Trade	11.38	11.35
Weighted Average of All Groups	**13.45**	**14.84**

95

TABLE A3-19

INSIDE DIRECTOR RATIO BY SIZE CLASS

SALES (US$ MILLIONS)	CANADA - WEIGHTED AVERAGE	UNITED STATES - WEIGHTED AVERAGE
10 to 50	0.30	0.39
50 to 100	0.30	0.35
100 to 500	0.22	0.31
500 to 1,000	0.19	0.25
1,000 to 2,000	0.18	0.24
> 2,000	0.19	0.21
Weighted Average of All Classes	**0.20**	**0.22**

TABLE A3-20

INSIDE DIRECTOR RATIO BY MAJOR INDUSTRY GROUPING

MAJOR INDUSTRY GROUPING	CANADA - WEIGHTED AVERAGE	UNITED STATES - WEIGHTED AVERAGE
Agriculture, Forestry & Fishing	0.23	0.13
Construction	0.25	0.28
Finance, Insurance & Real Estate	0.14	0.23
Labour-Intensive Manufacturing	0.21	0.27
Mining	0.27	0.31
Resource-Intensive Manufacturing	0.21	0.19
Retail Trade	0.18	0.24
Services	0.29	0.27
Technology-Intensive Manufacturing	0.30	0.20
Transportation & Public Utilities	0.14	0.19
Wholesale Trade	0.29	0.32
Weighted Average of All Groups	**0.20**	**0.22**

TABLE A3-21

FOREIGN DIRECTOR RATIO IN CANADIAN FIRMS BY SIZE CLASS

SALES (US$ MILLIONS)	CANADA - WEIGHTED AVERAGE
10 to 50	0.19
50 to 100	0.19
100 to 500	0.18
500 to 1,000	0.18
1,000 to 2,000	0.24
> 2,000	0.11
Weighted Average of All Classes	**0.15**

TABLE A3-22

FOREIGN DIRECTOR RATIO IN CANADIAN FIRMS BY MAJOR INDUSTRY GROUPING

MAJOR INDUSTRY GROUPING	CANADA - WEIGHTED AVERAGE
Agriculture, Forestry & Fishing	n/a
Construction	0.14
Finance, Insurance & Real Estate	0.13
Labour-Intensive Manufacturing	0.10
Mining	0.17
Resource-Intensive Manufacturing	0.19
Retail Trade	n/a
Services	0.23
Technology-Intensive Manufacturing	0.15
Transportation & Public Utilities	0.17
Wholesale Trade	0.24
Weighted Average of All Groups	**0.15**

Note: n/a = data not available

TABLE A3-23

CEO IS ON THE BOARD OF DIRECTORS BY SIZE CLASS

SALES (US$ MILLIONS)	CANADA - % OF FIRMS	
	No	YES
10 to 50	23.7	76.3
50 to 100	19.2	80.8
100 to 500	12.3	87.7
500 to 1,000	7.4	92.6
1,000 to 2,000	11.1	88.9
> 2,000	10.2	89.8
Average of All Classes	**17.0**	**83.0**

TABLE A3-24

CEO IS ON THE BOARD OF DIRECTORS BY MAJOR INDUSTRY GROUPING

MAJOR INDUSTRY GROUPING	CANADA - % OF FIRMS	
	No	YES
Agriculture, Forestry & Fishing	25.0	75.0
Construction	22.2	77.8
Finance, Insurance & Real Estate	18.8	81.2
Labour-Intensive Manufacturing	18.2	81.8
Mining	20.6	79.4
Resource-Intensive Manufacturing	16.3	83.7
Retail Trade	14.7	85.3
Services	14.0	86.0
Technology-Intensive Manufacturing	16.7	83.3
Transportation & Public Utilities	9.9	90.1
Wholesale Trade	16.2	83.8
Average of All Groups	**17.0**	**83.0**

TABLE A3-25

CEO IS CHAIRPERSON OF THE BOARD BY SIZE CLASS

SALES (US$ MILLIONS)	CANADA - % OF FIRMS		UNITED STATES - % OF FIRMS	
	NO	YES	NO	YES
10 to 50	73.3	26.6	55.3	44.7
50 to 100	100.0	0.0	46.2	53.8
100 to 500	53.3	46.6	40.1	59.9
500 to 1,000	71.4	28.6	31.7	68.3
1,000 to 2,000	83.3	16.7	29.4	70.6
> 2,000	50.0	50.0	18.2	81.8
Average of All Classes	**65.5**	**34.5**	**40.7**	**59.3**

TABLE A3-26

CEO IS CHAIRPERSON OF THE BOARD BY MAJOR INDUSTRY GROUPING

MAJOR INDUSTRY GROUPING	CANADA - % OF FIRMS		UNITED STATES - % OF FIRMS	
	NO	YES	NO	YES
Agriculture, Forestry & Fishing	n/a	n/a	50.0	50.0
Construction	n/a	n/a	38.2	61.8
Finance, Insurance & Real Estate	30.0	70.0	45.7	54.3
Labour-Intensive Manufacturing	100.0	0.0	36.0	64.0
Mining	81.2	18.8	37.0	63.0
Resource-Intensive Manufacturing	75.0	25.0	39.9	60.1
Retail Trade	n/a	n/a	33.2	66.8
Services	100.0	0.0	38.2	61.8
Technology-Intensive Manufacturing	83.3	16.7	43.4	56.6
Transportation & Public Utilities	25.0	75.0	34.7	65.3
Wholesale Trade	n/a	n/a	44.1	55.9
Average of All Groups	**65.5**	**34.5**	**40.7**	**59.3**

Note: n/a = data not available.

APPENDIX 4

(See TableA4-1, Figure A4-1 and Figure A4-2 on following pages.)

TABLE A4-1

CONCENTRATION OF OWNERSHIP TABULATIONS

VARIABLE	CANADA				UNITED STATES			
	WIDELY HELD	EFFECTIVELY CONTROLLED	LEGALLY CONTROLLED	ALL FIRMS	WIDELY HELD	EFFECTIVELY CONTROLLED	LEGALLY CONTROLLED	ALL FIRMS
Number of Firms	177	164	425	766	1206	1054	740	3000
Return on Equity	0.06	0.08	0.06	0.07	0.06	0.04	0.02	0.05
Return on Assets	0.03	0.02	0.03	0.03	0.03	0.03	0.02	0.03
Sales Growth	0.15	0.14	0.08	0.11	0.08	0.12	0.13	0.11
Asset Growth	0.14	0.13	0.07	0.10	0.11	0.13	0.14	0.13
Sales/Employee ($)	449,484	398,493	412,880	418,908	233,417	219,865	248,713	232,420
Sales/Asset	0.78	1.08	1.00	0.97	0.90	1.15	1.25	1.07
Labour Prod. Growth	0.14	0.14	0.08	0.11	0.07	0.11	0.13	0.10
Capital Prod. Growth	0.01	0.01	0.01	0.01	-0.02	-0.01	-0.01	-0.02
EPS Growth	-0.13	-0.08	-0.16	-0.14	-0.02	-0.09	-0.02	-0.05
Debt/Assets	0.21	0.27	0.26	0.25	0.20	0.20	0.23	0.21
Assets/Employee ($)	888,503	646,944	1,761,103	1,324,969	796,027	544,701	415,791	613,140
Presence of Foreign Sales or Assets	0.23	0.17	0.12	0.16	0.36	0.46	0.36	0.40
Institutional Ownership	6.18	18.75	48.33	32.26	31.69	41.18	30.37	34.70
Inside Ownership	4.18	17.83	26.24	19.34	11.59	18.90	36.04	20.19
Board Size	9.61	8.70	9.31	9.25	10.45	9.85	8.96	9.87
Inside Director Ratio	0.24	0.28	0.26	0.26	0.30	0.30	0.33	0.31
Foreign Director Ratio	0.03	0.03	0.04	0.04	n/a	n/a	n/a	n/a
CEO is Chairperson of the Board	0.26	0.29	0.50	0.35	0.61	0.58	0.59	0.59

Note: n/a = not available.

FIGURE A4-1

RETURN PERFORMANCE GROUPED BY CONCENTRATION OF OWNERSHIP

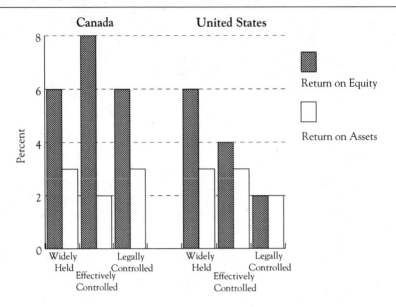

FIGURE A4-2

GROWTH PERFORMANCE GROUPED BY CONCENTRATION OF OWNERSHIP

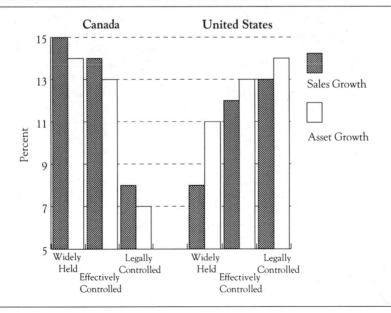

Source: Table A4-1 for both Figures.

ACKNOWLEDGEMENTS

W E ARE GRATEFUL TO Ross Preston and Denis Gauthier for their encouragement and support on this project, and to Ron Daniels and Randall Morck for their comments and suggestions at various stages of the study. We would also like to thank David Stangeland, Giovanni Barone-Adesi and Lee Gill for their many useful comments on the draft paper. Thanks are also due to Ashfaq Ahmad and Marc Legault for their assistance throughout.

BIBLIOGRAPHY

Amoako-Adu, B. and B. F. Smith. "Outside Financial Directors and Corporate Governance - Draft," 1995.

Bacon, J. "Corporate Boards and Corporate Governance." The Conference Board, Number 1036 (1993).

Baysinger, B. D. and H. N. Butler. "Corporate Governance and the Board of Directors: Performance Effects of Changes in Board Composition," *Journal of Law, Economics and Organization*, 1, 1 (1985):101-24.

Baysinger, B. D. and R. E. Hoskisson. "The Composition of Boards of Directors and Strategic Control: Effects on Corporate Strategy," *Academy of Management Review*, 15, 1 (1990):72-87.

Beck, S. "The Corporation and Canadian Society," presented at the Canadian Corporate Governance: A Multi-Disciplinary Perspective Conference held at the C.D. Howe Institute. (February 1994).

Clarkson, M. B. E. and M. C. Deck. "'Straddling Fences Makes it Difficult to Walk in a Straight Line': A Commentary Prepared in Response to "'Where Were The Directors?' The Draft Report of the TSE Committee on Corporate Governance in Canada May 1994." The Centre for Corporate Social Performance and Ethics, (July 1994).

Dalton, D. R., I. F. Kesner, and P. L. Rechner. "Corporate Governance and Boards of Directors: An International, Comparative Perspective." *Advances in International Comparative Management*, 3 (1988):95-105.

Daniels, R. and P. Halpern. "The Canadian Quandary: Accounting for the Survival of the Closely Held Corporation." Draft presented at the Canadian Corporate Governance: A Multi-Disciplinary Perspective Conference held at the C.D. Howe Institute. (February 1994).

Daniels, R. and J. MacIntosh. "Towards a Distinctive Canadian Corporate Law Regime." *Osgoode Hall Law Journal*, 29, 4 (Winter 1991):864-933.

Densetz, H. and K. Lehn. "The Structure of Corporate Ownership: Causes and Consequences." *Journal of Political Economy*, 93, 6 (1985).

Dey, P. *et al.* "Where Were The Directors?", The TSE Committee on Corporate Governance in Canada. (May 1994).

Donaldson, G. "Voluntary Restructuring: The Case of General Mills." *Journal of Financial Economics*, 27 (1990):117-141.

The Economist. "A Survey of Corporate Governance." (January 29th, 1994).

Eden, L., *Multinationals in North America*, The Industry Canada Research Series. Calgary: University of Calgary Press, 1994.

Friedlander, A. F., E. R. Berndt and G. McCullough. "Governance Structure, Managerial Characteristics, and Firm Performance in the Deregulated Rail Industry." Brookings Papers: Microeconomics. 1992.

Herzel, L. "Corporate Governance Through Statistical Eyes." *Journal of Financial Economics*, 27 (1990):581-93.

Industry Canada, Institutional Activism in Canada (Draft), Corporate Governance Branch, September 1994.

Industry Canada. *Economic Integration in North America: Trends in Foreign Direct Investment and the Top 1,000 Firms*, Working Paper Number 1. (January 1994).

Jensen, M. C. "The Modern Industrial Revolution, Exit, and the Failure of Internal Control Systems." *Journal of Finance*, 48, 3 (July 1993):831-80.

Jensen, M. C. and W. Meckling. "Theory of the Firm: Managerial Behaviour, Agency Costs and Ownership Structure." *Journal of Financial Economics*, 3 (October 1976):305-60.

MacIntosh, J. G. "The Role of Institutional and Retail Investors in Canadian Capital Markets." *Osgoode Hall Law Journal*, 31, 2 (1993).

Morck, R. K. and D.A. Stangeland. "Corporate Performance and Large Shareholders" (Working Paper No. 4-94). Institute for Financial Research, Faculty of Business, University of Alberta, 1994.

Morck, R. K. "On the Economics of Concentrated Ownership," Draft presented at the Canadian Corporate Governance: A Multi-Disciplinary Perspective Conference held at the C.D. Howe Institute, February 1994.

Neave, E. H., "Organizational Economics and Directors' Control (Draft presented at the Canadian Corporate Governance: A Multi-Disciplinary Perspective Conference held at the C. D. Howe Institute)," February 1994.

Porter, M. E. "Capital Disadvantage: America's Failing Capital Investment System." *Harvard Business Review*. (September-October 1992):65-82.

_____. "Capital Choices: Changing the Way America Invests in Industry." The Council on Competitiveness and The Harvard Business School. 1992.

Roe, M. J. "Political and Legal Restraints on Ownership and Control of Public Companies." *Journal of Financial Economics*, 27 (1990):117-41.

Romano, R. "A Cautionary Note on Drawing Lessons from Comparative Corporate Law." *Yale Law Journal*, 102 (1993): 2021-37.

_____. "Public Pension Fund Activism in Corporate Governance Reconsidered." *Columbia Law Review*, 93, 4 (May 1993).

Roth, C. W. "Concentration of Ownership and the Composition of the Board: An Examination of Canadian Publicly-Listed Corporations " (Draft). Industry Canada, 1994.

Vijay Jog   &   Ajit Tulpule
School of Business   Corporate Renaissance Group
Carleton University   Ottawa

3

Control and Performance: Evidence from the TSE 300

INTRODUCTION

SINCE THE PUBLICATION OF the Jensen & Meckling (1976) study on agency theory, a great deal of attention has been given to the potential for conflict between owners and managers and the effect of that conflict on firm performance. The existing empirical evidence has focused on the investigation of the determinants and consequences of ownership structure, as well as on the relationship between ownership structure and firm characteristics such as size, leverage, and expenditure on research and development. The increasing number of mergers and takeovers, and leverage and management buyouts in the 1980s added impetus to this empirical research.

The relationship between ownership concentration and corporate performance continues to be a debatable issue. The existing empirical evidence consists mainly of U.S. studies, which test the cross-sectional relationship between ownership and corporate performance, the latter measured either by accounting criteria or by Tobin's Q, with little emphasis on the temporal stability of results.

Summarizing their empirical research, Jensen & Warner (1988) conclude that "the precise effects of stock holdings by managers, outside shareholders, and institutions are not well understood, and the inter-relationships between ownership, firm characteristics, and corporate performance require further investigation". Similarly, Jog & Schaller (1989) assert that "... a lot needs to be known before any direct connection can be made between the ownership structure and the market value of equity".

The purpose of this study is to examine the possible relationship between corporate control (as measured by the controlled ownership of the firm) and the accounting and stock market performance of Canadian firms listed on the Toronto Stock Exchange (TSE). The study focuses on the Canadian companies that belonged to the TSE 300 Composite Index in the 14 years between 1978 and 1991 inclusive.

The study is organized as follows: a review of the research to date is followed by sections that present the main thesis of the study, describe the data employed, and discuss the methodology used. The last section presents results and conclusions.

PREVIOUS RESEARCH

THE EXISTING RESEARCH can be reviewed broadly under two headings: theoretical and empirical.

THEORETICAL RESEARCH

MOST OF THE BASIC TENETS OF THE AGENCY THEORY are well described in Berle & Means (1932) and Jensen & Meckling (1976). In effect, there are at least four sources of conflict that can arise between management (agents) and external shareholders (principals).

- Management's tendency to consume some of the firm's resources by way of perquisites.

- Managers have a greater incentive to shirk their responsibilities as their equity interest in a firm falls.

- Managers may forgo profitable but risky projects, as they bear the cost of failure more than the widely diversified shareholders.

- Managers may misrepresent the quality of future investment projects, thereby causing the outside investors to demand a higher risk premium.

In order to ensure that agents (management) act in the best interest of the principals, the principals (owners) incur certain costs. These may include payment of incentives to the manager, as well as monitoring costs to "limit the aberrant activities of the [managers]". Jensen & Meckling (1976) identify three components of these agency costs: the monitoring expenditures by the principals, the bonding expenditure by the agent[1] and the residual loss.[2]

It is these agency costs, resulting from the conflict between ownership and managerial performance, that provide an explanation of the relationship between corporate ownership and firm performance. It is argued that one way to reduce this conflict, and thereby the agency costs, would be to have managers own a substantial portion of the company's shares, thus automatically aligning the managers' interests with those of the owners, and ensuring that the managers act in the best interests of the owners. The higher the proportion of managerial ownership, the lower the agency costs would be, and the better the performance of the firm.[3] Similar arguments can be extended to cases where a significant block of shares is owned by a small number of investors who can, in turn, exert

exert a higher degree of monitoring on managers, thereby improving performance. If this is true in either case, then one would expect to find a positive relationship between corporate control and managerial performance: the higher the stake in the ownership of the firm by either management or a significant owner, the better the performance is likely to be.

On the other hand, Stulz (1988) argues that firm value increases as managerial ownership increases, but firm value would decrease if insiders own a large portion of the shareholders' equity. In the context of a possible tender offer, Stulz shows that managerial ownership affects both the probability of a takeover bid and the premium. When managers do not own any equity in the firm, the offer premium is small. As managerial ownership increases from zero, the premium offered also increases. However, a very high percentage of managerial ownership will, in fact, be an impediment to a takeover attempt, thereby reducing the firm's value. Stulz thus predicts a convex relationship between firm value and managerial ownership, implying that a certain level of insider ownership may exist, at which firm value is maximized.

Other theories, however, contend that the ownership of a firm and its performance are unrelated. Although conflict between owners and managers may indeed exist, there are other mechanisms that effectively resolve the conflict and align the interests of the owners and managers. Such alternative mechanisms include external monitors (auditors, bankers, institutional investors), performance-related compensation schemes, choice of managers with aligned and similar interests (Demsetz, 1983), the existence of an efficient labour market (Fama, 1980), a competitive product market (Hart, 1983), large shareholder blocks (Stiglitz, 1985; Shleifer & Vishny, 1986), and an increase in corporate disclosure demanded by government regulators (e.g., the *Canada Business Act*) or by securities legislators (e.g., the Ontario Securities Commission). According to these theories, alternative mechanisms will effectively counter the agency problem, and so the performance of a firm will be unrelated to its ownership structure.

In contrast to the above-mentioned theories which suggest a positive or no relationship, Muellar (1986) postulates that corporate ownership and performance are negatively related. He argues that even if its ownership is fairly large, management may still divert funds for its personal use, provided the benefits of such diversion are greater than the cost of receiving less return from its ownership of the firm. Figure 1 shows a graphical representation of the existing theoretical work.

EMPIRICAL RESEARCH

TABLE 1 SHOWS THE STATE OF EMPIRICAL RESEARCH in the area of corporate performance and managerial ownership. Five conclusions emerge from a review of this work. First, the findings are mixed, although there is some evidence that performance is positively related to insider/manager ownership.

FIGURE 1

RELATIONSHIP BETWEEN FIRM PERFORMANCE AND OWNERSHIP STRUCTURE AS SUGGESTED BY THEORETICAL RESEARCH

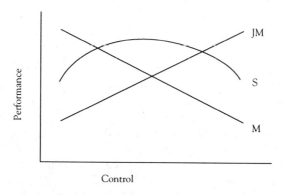

JM	Jensen & Meckling (1976)
S	Stulz (1988)
M	Muellar (1986)

FIGURE 2

RELATIONSHIP BETWEEN FIRM PERFORMANCE AND OWNERSHIP STRUCTURE AS EVIDENCED BY EMPIRICAL RESEARCH

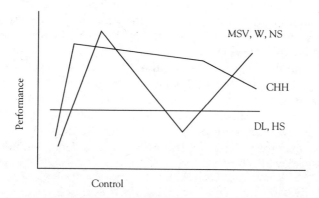

MSV	Morck, Shleifer & Vishny (1988)	DL	Demsetz & Lehn (1985)
CHH	Chen, Hexter & Hue (1990)	NS	Neun & Santerre (1986
W	Wruck (1989)	HS	Holderness & Sheehan (1991)

TABLE 1

SUMMARY OF EMPIRICAL RESEARCH

AUTHORS	YEAR	PERFORMANCE	OWNERSHIP	FINDING
Vance	1964	Net Income	Directors' Share-holding	Positive Relationship
Pfeffer	1972	Profit Margin, ROE	Managerial Share-holding	Positive Relationship
Demsetz & Lehn	1985	ARR / BV	Top 5 Share-holders' holdings	No Relationship
Neun & Samterre	1986	Net Profit Margin	Dominant Stock Ownership	S-shaped Relationship
Morck, Shleifer & Vishny	1988	Tobin's Q	Directors' Share-holdings	Increase, Fall, Increase
Holderness & Sheehan	1991	ARR, Tobin's Q	Majority Share-holding	No Conclusions
Kim & Lyn	1988	Tobin's Q	Insider Ownership	Positive Relationship
Wruck	1989	Firm Value	Insider Ownership	Increase, Fall, Increase
Chen, Hexter, & Hue	1990	Tobin's Q	Managerial Ownership	Large Firms: Positive Relationship Small Firms: No Relationship
Oswald & Jahera	1991	Excess Stock Returns	Directors' & Officers' Share-holdings	Positive Relationship

Second, in a majority of the studies, performance is measured based on Tobin's Q and is considered only for a specific year or two; the studies have not attempted to show temporal stability of these results. This makes generalizations about the relationship suspect. Third, there is some evidence of curvilinearity, which is consistent with both the alignment and entrenchment hypotheses. Fourth, there is some evidence (Oswald & Jahera, 1991) that both size and ownership are statistically significant factors in explaining the performance of a firm, an observation that seems also to corroborate those of Vance (1964), Pfeffer (1972), and Kim & Lyn (1988).[4] Finally, the definition of control varies significantly across studies, thereby making the task of comparison quite difficult. Figure 2 summarizes the existing empirical evidence from the U.S.-based studies.

SUMMARY

IN SUMMARIZING THE THEORETICAL ARGUMENTS and the empirical evidence, it can be said that the performance of a firm may depend upon its ownership structure (as a manifestation of the agency problem), but no unambiguous statements can be made about either the importance or the nature of the dependency. It depends upon the efficacy of alternate mechanisms, including disclosure and business rules imposed by regulators and government policies. Another observation about the existing empirical research is that the use of varied performance measures makes it difficult to draw unambiguous conclusions. In addition, most studies are cross-sectional in nature and provide only a snapshot analysis (at a specific point in time). Such analyses do not show how strongly the results would hold over a longer period of time or how robust they are.

The empirical research presented in this section also reveals that all these studies have been conducted using U.S. data. It is not clear whether these results are applicable to the Canadian situation. The only other empirical study in the Canadian context is by Morck & Stangeland (1994), who comment on some of the conspicuous differences between American and Canadian companies.[5] Thus, it would be of considerable interest to know more, not only about the relationship between performance and ownership, but also about the Canadian context, especially where there is a significant difference of ownership percentage between Canadian and American publicly traded firms.

TERMS OF REFERENCE

THIS STUDY ASKS the following questions: do companies that are closely held perform better than those that are widely held? And, if so, does the degree of ownership provide any indication of differential performance? This relationship between corporate ownership and performance is examined, using the ownership and performance data of Canadian companies listed on the TSE 300 Composite Index, spanning the years from 1978 to 1991 inclusive.

MEASURES OF PERFORMANCE AND CONTROL

ALTHOUGH TOBIN'S Q, AS A MEASURE OF PERFORMANCE, appears to dominate the U.S. studies, a lack of readily available replacement values for the sample companies makes it virtually impossible to use this ratio in this study. Instead, we follow two methods for evaluating firm performance. First, we use the stock market returns as a measure of performance, as they reflect long-term performance from an investor's viewpoint. Second, for a subset of the sample firms (manufacturing sector), we employ widely used accounting-based performance measures. This subset includes market-to-book ratio of equity as a proxy for the Tobin's Q.

Control – *i.e.*, how closely held (concentrated) or widely held (diffused) within a company – is measured by the percentage of the outstanding equity of the firm which is tradeable on the stock exchange. A firm whose entire outstanding equity is tradeable on the stock exchange is considered to have very diffused control (widely held), while a firm that has only a very small portion of its outstanding equity tradeable on the stock exchange is considered to be highly controlled (closely held). In addition, in order to account for obvious differences in the degree of "assets in place" between manufacturing and non-manufacturing firms, we evaluate firm performance in two separate groups, based on their industry classification.[6]

THE DATA

THE SAMPLE COMPANIES IN THIS STUDY include only those companies that were included in the Toronto Stock Exchange 300 Composite Index (TSE 300) between 1978 and 1991 inclusive. Control is measured using "float" percentages. These indicate the percentage of shares available for outside ownership and are used to calculate relative weights in the index, and can also be used to estimate the degree of control. The data are obtained from the index listing published in the *TSE Review*. The values are those at December 31 each year. The industry groupings used here are based on the TSE 300 groupings.

In contrast with the United States, where there are a large number of small banks, the Canadian banking industry is characterized by a small number of large banks. Because of government-imposed ownership restrictions, all of these banks are widely held. Also, utility companies in Canada are largely regulated by the federal and provincial governments. For these reasons, the sample used in this study excludes both banks and utility companies from the data set.

To calculate stock market performance, monthly returns for individual companies were drawn from the Toronto Stock Exchange/University of Western Ontario (TSE/Western) database, which is modeled after the University of Chicago Center for Research in Security Prices (CRSP) database, spanning a period of 14 years from 1978 to 1991. The accounting data on individual firms is gathered from the Stock Guide database maintained by Stock Guide Publications Ltd. Due to the unavailability of such data on a consistent basis prior to 1988, analysis based on the accounting measures is restricted to the years 1988 to 1991.

The data set is comprised of information on a total of 613 companies, over the 14-year period between 1978 and 1991. Table 2 shows the breakdown by industry of the 613 companies, as classified according to the Industry Codes used by the index. Due to the listing-delisting feature of the TSE 300 Index, the constituency of the index is fluid. Table 3 shows the number of companies forming part of the data set each year. The rows represent the "from" year and the columns indicate the "to" year. The numbers along the principal diagonal

TABLE 2

FIRMS IN DATA SET: BREAKDOWN BY INDUSTRY

INDUSTRY NUMBER	INDUSTRY	NUMBER	% OF GROUP	% OF TOTAL
	MANUFACTURING			
1	Metals and Minerals	63	18.10	13.58
3	Oil and Gas	113	32.47	24.35
4	Paper and Forest Products	24	6.90	5.17
5	Consumer Products	44	12.64	9.48
6	Industrial Products	71	20.40	15.30
7	Construction	23	6.61	4.96
8	Transportation	10	2.87	2.16
	Manufacturing Sub-Total	348	100.00	75.00
	NON MANUFACTURING			
9	Pipelines	6	5.17	1.29
11	Communications	30	25.86	6.47
12	Merchandising	57	49.14	12.28
14	Management Companies	23	19.83	4.96
	Non-Manufacturing Sub-Total	116	100.00	25.00
	Manufacturing & Non-Manufacturing Total	**464**		**100.00**
	EXCLUDED FROM ANALYSIS			
2	Gold	59		
10	Utilities	25		
13	Financial Services (Banks)	65		
	Total Sample	**613**		

thus indicate the number of companies forming part of the data set in the given year. The figure in cell C (i, j) indicates the number of companies forming part of the data set, which were listed in year i, and continued to be listed through year j. Table 3 also reveals that the data set includes at least 236 companies and at the most 264 companies (see the diagonal numbers) for any given year.

TABLE 3

THE NUMBER OF COMPANIES IN THE DATA SET (1978 - 1991)

YEAR[a]	1978	1979	1980	1981	1982	1983	1984	1985	1986	1987	1988	1989	1990	1991
1978	240	216	204	185	180	176	165	155	141	126	114	112	107	101
1979		236	218	196	190	183	172	162	148	132	120	117	112	106
1980			241	215	207	197	182	169	153	138	124	121	117	111
1981				249	234	218	200	182	161	144	129	125	121	116
1982					247	228	208	188	167	148	129	124	120	115
1983						247	225	198	176	156	137	129	124	120
1984							250	219	194	173	152	142	137	131
1985								243	210	189	166	156	150	141
1986									249	223	194	183	173	159
1987										254	220	206	195	176
1988											257	237	221	196
1989												262	245	218
1990													260	232
1991														264

Note: [a] Horizontal rows indicate the "from" year; vertical columns indicate the "to" year.

TABLE 4			
PORTFOLIO FORMATION AND RETURN CALCULATION PROCEDURE			
PORTFOLIO FORMATION VARIABLE	WEIGHT VARIABLE 1 FOR PORTFOLIO RETURNS	WEIGHT VARIABLE 2 FOR PORTFOLIO RETURNS	SECTOR GROUPS
Control	Equal	Size	Manufacturing, Non-manufacturing

METHODOLOGY

SINCE THIS STUDY USES both accounting and stock-market data, we adopt two distinctly different approaches in our enquiry into firm performance.

STOCK-MARKET-BASED PERFORMANCE

TO ANALYZE THE PERFORMANCE OF FIRMS that differ in their degree of control, we employ a portfolio-grouping approach. Specifically, at the beginning of each period all firms are first ranked in ascending order of control based on their year-end value of the previous year. They are then placed in four groups representing the four quartiles. Within each group, the portfolio return is calculated in two ways – first by equally weighting the returns and then by weighting the returns based on the market capitalization of the firms.[7] In each case, the portfolios are revised annually using the ownership and market capitalization data as of December 31st each year, and calculated separately for the manufacturing and non-manufacturing sectors. Table 4 shows this portfolio-grouping procedure.

Since the portfolio approach is used to analyze the relationship between control and performance, we use the well-known Sharpe measure for comparing the relative performance. The Sharpe measure uses the ratio of average returns and the corresponding standard deviation as a measure of performance. The significance of the Sharpe portfolio performance measure, is calculated using the Jobson & Korkie (1986) test.[8] In addition, non-parametric and parametric tests are also performed to test for the number of months and the relative amount by which a particular portfolio outperformed another.

ACCOUNTING-BASED PERFORMANCE MEASURES

AS NOTED EARLIER IN TABLE 1, many of the previous studies concentrate on accounting-based performance measures. To facilitate comparisons, we attempt to evaluate performance of our sample firms based on the eight most commonly used measures: asset turnover, gross margin, return on assets, return on equity, debt equity, capital expenditure-to-net fixed assets, interest coverage and market-to-book-value ratio. The last can serve as a proxy for Tobin's Q. Due to data availability constraints, and in order to ensure within-group homogeneity, we conduct this analysis only for the years 1988 through 1991 and only for our manufacturing firm sub-sample.[9]

RESULTS

AGGREGATE PORTFOLIO RESULTS - STOCK MARKET DATA

IN ORDER TO PROVIDE AN OVERVIEW of the potential differences between the two sectors, the overall results of the sectoral portfolios are shown in Table 5, before displaying the detailed breakdowns. Panel A of the table shows cumulative wealth based on annual revisions for each of the three portfolio-weighting schemes: equally weighted, control weighted and size weighted. The last column shows the comparable annual values for the TSE 300.[10]

These results indicate that the two sectors had significantly different performance: the non-manufacturing sector portfolio, irrespective of the weighting scheme, generated higher wealth than the manufacturing sector portfolio. Moreover, the systematic risk of the non-manufacturing portfolio is lower than that of the manufacturing portfolio. Panel C of the table (based on average return percentage) indicates that the higher overall performance of the non-manufacturing firms is due to the significantly higher performance during the middle period, 1982-1986. Investigating the within-sector returns shows the effect of the weighting variable. In the manufacturing sector, the size weighted portfolio dominates the equally weighted portfolio indicating that, based on the entire 1978-1991 period, large firms performed better than small firms in this sector. However, the reverse is true for the non-manufacturing sector. A comparison of the control weighted portfolio for the manufacturing sector with the equally weighted portfolio shows that the former under-performed the latter, indicating that a portfolio strategy of investing in manufacturing companies based on the percentage of control would have generated lower returns than either the equally weighted or the size weighted strategy. The results for the non-manufacturing sector are exactly the opposite. These results, shown without any statistical tests, indicate that if there is a positive relationship between control and performance, it is likely to exist in non-manufacturing-sector firms and not in manufacturing-sector firms. However, it should also be noted that, based on the sub-period analysis in Panel C of Table 5, the relationship is not constant in all periods. Therefore, if anything can be concluded from these overall results, it is that there appears to be a (temporally) positive, unstable, relationship between control and performance in the non-manufacturing sector only.

TABLE 5

CUMULATIVE WEALTH AGGREGATES

PANEL A

Growth of $1 cumulative investment in aggregate portfolios of manufacturing and non-manufacturing firms, revised annually. Growth of $1 cumulative investment in the TSE 300 Index.

YEAR	EQUALLY WEIGHTED		CONTROL WEIGHTED		SIZE WEIGHTED		COMPARABLE VALUES FOR TSE 300
	MFR	NON	MFR	NON	MFR	NON	
1977	1.00	1.00	1.00	1.00	1.00	1.00	1.00
1978	1.39	1.39	1.42	1.43	1.35	1.31	1.29
1979	2.28	1.61	2.28	1.59	2.20	1.53	1.88
1980	3.20	2.32	3.17	2.19	2.90	2.13	2.44
1981	2.71	2.12	2.90	1.89	2.80	1.95	2.20
1982	2.66	2.57	2.79	2.33	2.57	2.23	2.32
1983	3.46	4.21	3.72	3.83	3.50	3.68	3.14
1984	3.08	4.29	3.26	3.83	3.22	3.65	3.06
1985	3.47	6.57	3.73	5.96	3.75	5.29	3.83
1986	3.50	7.71	3.70	7.24	4.11	6.44	4.17
1987	3.83	7.57	4.00	7.44	4.41	6.21	4.41
1988	4.28	9.97	4.72	9.78	4.90	7.90	4.90
1989	4.71	10.64	5.18	10.30	5.64	8.73	5.95
1990	3.55	6.87	3.89	6.21	4.75	6.50	5.07
1991	3.70	7.76	4.14	7.11	5.15	7.11	5.68

PANEL B

Average monthly returns and their standard deviations, average monthly excess returns and their standard deviation, Sharpe measure and JK-Z test (H_0: $Sh_{PTF} = Sh_{TSE\ 300}$), portfolio beta.

Average Return (%)	0.97	1.36	1.01	1.34	1.23	1.33	1.17
Standard Deviation (%)	6.07	5.38	6.12	5.94	6.12	5.66	5.07
Excess Return (%)	0.05	0.44	0.09	0.42	0.34	0.41	0.25
Standard Deviation (%)	6.11	5.44	6.17	5.99	6.16	5.71	5.13
Sharpe Measure	0.01	0.08	0.01	0.07	0.06	0.07	0.05
JK-Z Test	0.09	1.37	-0.82	0.38	1.36	0.43	0.00
Beta	1.07	0.80	1.02	0.83	1.09	0.87	1.00

Note: ** Statistically significant at the 1% level.

TABLE 5 (CONT'D)

PANEL C

Average monthly returns and their standard deviations, average monthly excess returns and their standard deviations, Sharpe measure and JK-Z test (H_0: $Sh_{PTF} = Sh_{TSE\ 300}$), portfolio beta.

	EQUALLY WEIGHTED MFR	NON	CONTROL WEIGHTED MFR	NON	SIZE WEIGHTED MFR	NON	COMPARABLE VALUES FOR TSE 300
(1978-1981)							
Average Return (%)	2.33	1.69	2.45	1.45	2.38	1.53	1.83
Standard Deviation (%)	6.88	5.08	6.68	5.41	7.38	5.61	5.92
Excess Return (%)	1.27	0.63	1.39	0.39	1.32	0.47	0.77
Standard Deviation (%)	6.99	5.21	6.79	5.53	7.46	5.72	6.03
Sharpe Measure	0.18	0.12	0.20	0.07	0.18	0.08	0.13
JK-Z Test	2.25**	−0.11	2.41**	−0.26	1.52	−0.93	0.00
Beta	1.11	0.68	1.03	0.69	1.13	0.76	1.00
(1982-1986)							
Average Return (%)	0.49	2.26	0.47	2.36	0.83	2.14	1.18
Standard Deviation (%)	5.74	5.09	5.88	5.56	5.93	5.55	4.69
Excess Return (%)	−0.38	1.39	−0.39	1.48	−0.04	1.27	0.31
Standard Deviation (%)	5.78	5.13	5.91	5.68	5.97	5.58	4.70
Sharpe Measure	−0.07	0.27	−0.07	0.26	−0.01	0.23	0.07
JK-Z Test	−3.13**	3.37**	−2.73**	3.06**	−1.71	2.74	0.00
Beta	1.05	0.76	1.01	0.80	1.08	0.85	1.00
(1987-1991)							
Average Return (%)	0.35	0.21	0.38	0.24	0.49	0.35	0.64
Standard Deviation (%)	5.52	6.00	5.72	6.44	5.58	5.70	4.74
Excess Return (%)	−0.50	−0.64	−0.46	−0.61	−0.37	−0.50	−0.22
Standard Deviation (%)	5.55	6.03	5.75	6.48	5.60	5.72	4.76
Sharpe Measure	−0.09	−0.11	−0.08	−0.09	−0.07	0.09	−0.05
JK-Z Test	−1.18	−1.16	−0.78	−0.91	−0.58	−0.9	30.00
Beta	1.02	0.98	1.00	1.03	1.06	1.00	1.00

Note: ** Statistically significant at the 1% level.

TABLE 6

RELATIONSHIP OF VARIOUS PORTFOLIO STRATEGIES AS SHOWN IN TABLES 7 - 10

PORTFOLIO FORMATION VARIABLE	WEIGHT VARIABLE 1 FOR PORTFOLIO RETURNS	WEIGHT VARIABLE 2 FOR PORTFOLIO RETURNS
Control	Equal Manufacturing (Table 7) Non-manufacturing (Table 9)	Size Manufacturing (Table 8) Non-manufacturing (Table 10)

Panel B of Table 5 shows the statistical significance of the differences between portfolio returns and the TSE 300. Panel C shows mean return, standard deviation and the values of the Sharpe measure and the corresponding JK-Z tests based on the monthly returns for each portfolio compared to the TSE 300 Index for each of the sub-periods. Although there is no significantly superior performance by any of the portfolios over the TSE 300 based on the entire period (Panel B), the performance in selected sub-periods (Panel C) is in some cases superior (or inferior) to the TSE 300.

CONTROL-BASED PORTFOLIO RESULTS – STOCK MARKET DATA

TABLE 6 SHOWS THE TABLE REFERENCES corresponding to the procedure set out in Table 4. Tables 7 through 10 present the information for various portfolio formation strategies in the same format as Table 5.

Table 7 displays the results of portfolios created through annual revision (1YR), for the companies classified as belonging to the manufacturing sector (MFR), where portfolios are formed using control as the portfolio formation variable (CTRL) with portfolio returns created using equally weighted returns. All the tables thus represent results organized as per the periodicity of the revision for the sector under consideration, followed by the portfolio formation variable and the variable used to weight the individual firm returns. Also, each table has three panels identical to the pattern set out in Table 5. These outline the annual wealth index values for each of the four portfolios (panel A); the results of the JK-Z tests for the entire period (panel B); followed by the sub-period results (panel C). Collectively, Tables 7 through 10 enable us to make inferences about the relationship between corporate control and shareholder performance.

Manufacturing Firms

Tables 7 and 8 show the performance results for the control-based portfolios formed from firms belonging to the manufacturing sector. From panel A of these tables, It can be seen that as control increases, performance initially decreases, attains a peak, and then stays almost the same (for equally weighted) or declines slightly (size-weighted). Thus, a strategy of investing in manufacturing firms with larger control but with equal weights would have generated higher wealth for the investor; average monthly returns are highest for Portfolio 3 which, in fact, outperforms the TSE 300. Panel B of the tables indicates that Portfolio 3 outperformed all the other portfolios based on the JK-Z test over the entire period. Unfortunately, as seen from panel C of the tables, the under- or over-performance of the portfolios is sub-period dependent. Similar to the aggregate results, most of the over-performance in this sector occurred during the period from 1978 to 1981. However, Portfolio 3 was still the best performer of those under consideration.

Non-manufacturing Firms

Tables 9 and 10 show the relationship between control and performance of non-manufacturing firms. Here again, similar results are obtained: Portfolio 3 show superior performance but Portfolio 1 shows equally superior performance. Thus, the relationship here is less linear than that found in the manufacturing sector. Casual observation of these tables indicates that, as control is reduced (moves from widely held to some), performance decreases in this sector; it then increases as control increases, but declines or stays the same at higher levels of control. Similar to the non-manufacturing sector, relative performance also varies across sub-periods.

Figure 3 plots the cumulative wealth of each of the portfolios in Tables 7 through 10 for the entire period as well as for the three sub-periods. The difference between the two sectors, based on the entire period evaluation can also be seen in Figure 3. It is interesting to compare the shape of the lines in Figure 3 for the four graphs. Although the individual shapes vary, casual observation indicates that the third-quartile portfolio generally outperforms the other quartiles, and that the second and fourth quartile portfolios underperform the first and the third quartile in relative terms. This pattern is more pronounced in the non-manufacturing sector than in the manufacturing sector. These results contradict the typical relationships shown by "snap-shot" analysis of accounting performance and ownership structure. Figure 4 shows the shape of our overall relationship for the entire period in comparison to those found by others (as shown in Figure 2). Although our definitions of both ownership and performance are quite different from previous studies, our results cast some doubt on the validity of snap-shot analysis of the relationship between performance and control-related variables. If anything, our results indicate that, from an investor perspective, it is better to invest in a diversified portfolio of either widely held firms or high control firms and avoid investing in low control or very high control firms. There is only a slight re-affirmation of the Chen, Hexter & Hue results, where a slight decline in performance in the "highest ownership" portfolio of firms was found.

TABLE 7

MANUFACTURING FIRM SAMPLE – EQUAL WEIGHTING
(1 YEAR, MFR, CTRL, EQL)

PANEL A

Growth of $1 cumulative investment in aggregate portfolios of manufacturing and non-manufacturing firms, revised annually. Growth of $1 cumulative investment in the TSE 300 Index.

YEAR	PORTFOLIO 1	PORTFOLIO 2	PORTFOLIO 3	PORTFOLIO 4	MANUFACTURING
1977	1.00	1.00	1.00	1.00	1.00
1978	1.35	1.42	1.45	1.38	1.39
1979	2.19	2.35	2.37	2.20	2.28
1980	3.01	3.33	3.32	2.96	3.20
1981	2.28	2.54	3.09	2.98	2.71
1982	2.17	2.25	3.05	2.92	2.66
1983	2.61	2.90	4.21	4.04	3.46
1984	2.07	2.53	3.61	3.69	3.08
1985	2.37	3.08	4.36	4.03	3.47
1986	2.30	2.60	4.96	3.96	3.50
1987	2.35	2.73	5.72	4.30	3.83
1988	2.71	3.05	6.76	5.32	4.28
1989	2.97	3.40	7.80	5.56	4.71
1990	2.61	2.51	5.94	4.01	3.55
1991	2.79	2.32	6.36	4.56	3.70

PANEL B

Average monthly returns and their standard deviations, average monthly excess returns and their standard deviations, Sharpe measure and JK-Z test (H_0: Sh_{PTF} = $Sh_{TSE\ 300}$), portfolio beta.

	PORTFOLIO 1	PORTFOLIO 2	PORTFOLIO 3	PORTFOLIO 4	MANUFACTURING
Average Return (%)	0.82	0.71	1.28	1.07	0.97
Standard Deviation (%)	6.46	6.34	5.86	5.61	6.07
Average Excess Return (%)	−0.10	−0.21	0.36	0.15	0.05
Standard Deviation (%)	6.51	6.39	5.91	5.66	6.11
Sharpe Measure	−0.01	−0.03	0.06	0.03	0.01
JK-Z Test	−0.60	−1.09	1.78**	0.55	0.08
Beta	1.15	1.11	1.05	0.96	1.07

Note: ** Statistically significant at the 1% level.

TABLE 7 (CONT'D)

PANEL C

Average monthly returns and their standard deviations, average monthly excess returns and their standard deviations, Sharpe measure and JK-Z test (H_0: Sh_{PTF} = $Sh_{TSE\ 300}$), portfolio beta.

1978-1981	PORTFOLIO 1	PORTFOLIO 2	PORTFOLIO 3	PORTFOLIO 4	MANUFACTURING
Average Return (%)	2.03	2.24	2.58	2.49	2.33
Standard Deviation (%)	7.70	7.41	6.43	6.06	6.97
Average Excess Return (%)	0.96	1.17	1.52	1.42	1.27
Standard Deviation (%)	7.81	7.54	6.55	6.16	7.07
Sharpe Measure	.0.12	0.16	0.23	0.23	0.18
JK-Z Test	−0.15	1.34	4.41**	4.06**	1.95**
Beta	1.24	1.20	1.03	0.96	1.11
1982-1986					
Average Return (%)	0.20	0.21	0.96	0.61	0.49
Standard Deviation (%)	6.11	5.83	5.88	5.20	5.74
Average Excess Return (%)	−0.68	−0.66	0.08	−0.27	−0.38
Standard Deviation (%)	6.14	5.87	5.93	5.24	5.78
Sharpe Measure	−0.11	−0.11	0.01	−0.05	−0.07
JK-Z Test	−4.00**	−4.37**	−1.46	−2.52**	−3.13**
Beta	1.09	1.07	1.12	0.91	1.05
1987-1991					
Average Return (%)	0.49	−0.02	0.56	0.39	0.34
Standard Deviation (%)	5.66	5.76	5.24	5.53	5.66
Average Excess Return (%)	−0.37	−0.88	−0.30	−0.47	−0.51
Standard Deviation (%)	5.68	5.79	5.27	5.57	5.69
Sharpe Measure	−0.06	−0.15	−0.06	−0.08	−0.09
JK-Z Test	−0.60	−2.42**	−0.30	−0.95	−1.08
Beta	1.08	1.01	0.99	1.00	1.02

Note: ** Statistically significant at the 1% level.

TABLE 8

MANUFACTURING FIRM SAMPLE – SIZE WEIGHTING
(1 YEAR, MFR, CTRL, SIZE)

PANEL A

Growth of $1 cumulative investment in size-weighted portfolios of manufacturing firms, revised annually by ranking firms by control.

YEAR	PORTFOLIO 1	PORTFOLIO 2	PORTFOLIO 3	PORTFOLIO 4	MANUFACTURING
1977	1.00	1.00	1.00	1.00	1.00
1978	1.33	1.42	1.42	1.24	1.35
1979	1.98	2.34	2.38	2.10	2.20
1980	2.47	3.51	3.37	2.26	2.90
1981	1.93	3.44	3.42	2.41	2.80
1982	1.94	2.10	3.67	2.55	2.57
1983	2.67	3.01	4.75	3.57	3.50
1984	2.39	2.90	4.17	3.40	3.22
1985	2.89	3.66	4.64	3.79	3.75
1986	3.11	3.99	5.22	4.10	4.11
1987	3.84	3.67	5.90	4.24	4.41
1988	4.57	4.05	6.05	4.94	4.90
1989	5.16	5.15	7.20	5.03	5.64
1990	4.51	4.52	6.40	3.57	4.75
1991	4.26	4.85	7.96	3.54	5.15

PANEL B

Average monthly returns and their standard deviations, average monthly excess returns and their standard deviations, Sharpe measure and JK-Z test (H_0: Sh_{PTF} = $Sh_{TSE\ 300}$), portfolio beta.

	PORTFOLIO 1	PORTFOLIO 2	PORTFOLIO 3	PORTFOLIO 4	MANUFACTURING
Average Return (%)	1.06	1.16	1.45	0.93	1.23
Standard Deviation (%)	6.27	6.50	6.52	5.95	6.12
Average Excess Return (%)	0.14	0.24	0.53	0.01	0.34
Standard Deviation (%)	6.32	6.54	6.55	5.97	6.16
Sharpe Measure	0.02	0.04	0.08	0.00	0.06
JK Z Test	0.63	0.82	2.27**	0.00	1.36
Beta	1.15	1.11	1.06	0.97	1.09

Note: ** Statistically significant at the 1% level.

TABLE 8 (CONT'D)

PANEL C

Average monthly portfolio returns and their standard deviations, average monthly portfolio excess returns and their standard deviations, Sharpe measure and JK-Z Test (H_0: Sh_{PTF} = $SH_{TSE\ 300}$), portfolio beta.

1978-1981	PORTFOLIO 1	PORTFOLIO 2	PORTFOLIO 3	PORTFOLIO 4	MANUFACTURING
Average Return (%)	1.63	2.93	2.87	2.08	2.38
Standard Deviation (%)	7.14	8.07	7.55	6.83	7.38
Average Excess Return (%)	0.57	1.87	1.81	1.02	1.32
Standard Deviation (%)	7.26	8.15	7.64	6.89	7.46
Sharpe Measure	0.08	0.23	0.24	0.15	0.18
JK-Z Test	−2.12**	3.88**	3.06**	0.51	1.52
Beta	1.15	1.27	1.13	0.98	1.13
1982-1986					
Average Return (%)	0.96	0.43	0.89	1.05	0.83
Standard Deviation (%)	5.71	6.12	6.23	5.77	5.93
Average Excess Return (%)	0.08	−0.44	0.02	0.18	−0.04
Standard Deviation (%)	5.74	6.19	6.26	5.80	5.97
Sharpe Measure	0.01	−0.07	0.00	0.03	−0.01
JK-Z Test	−1.67**	−2.59**	−1.72**	−0.78	−1.71**
Beta	1.11	1.00	1.17	1.02	1.08
1987-1991					
Average Return (%)	0.72	0.47	0.88	−0.10	0.49
Standard Deviation (%)	6.15	5.16	5.81	5.23	5.58
Average Excess Return (%)	−0.14	−0.39	0.03	−0.96	−0.37
Standard Deviation (%)	6.17	5.16	5.84	5.26	5.60
Sharpe Measure	−0.02	−0.08	0.00	−0.18	−0.07
JK-Z Test	0.77	−0.97	−1.95**	−3.24**	−0.58
Beta	1.18	0.99	1.15	0.94	1.06

Note: ** Statistically significant at the 1% level.

TABLE 9

NON-MANUFACTURING FIRM SAMPLE – EQUAL WEIGHTING (1 YEAR, NON-MFR, CTRL, SIZE)

PANEL A

Growth of $1 cumulative investment in equally weighted portfolios of non-manufacturing firms, revised annually by ranking firms by control.

YEAR	PORTFOLIO 1	PORTFOLIO 2	PORTFOLIO 3	PORTFOLIO 4	NON-MANUFACTURING
1977	1.00	1.00	1.00	1.00	1.00
1978	1.42	1.20	1.55	1.38	1.39
1979	1.73	1.39	1.86	1.45	1.61
1980	2.59	2.32	2.39	1.93	2.32
1981	2.76	1.95	2.17	1.60	2.12
1982	3.34	2.20	2.58	2.15	2.57
1983	5.42	3.34	4.70	3.33	4.21
1984	5.73	3.66	4.38	3.24	4.29
1985	8.39	5.92	6.89	4.80	6.57
1986	9.34	6.43	9.50	5.29	7.71
1987	8.17	6.00	10.64	5.24	7.57
1988	11.32	7.42	14.19	6.72	9.97
1989	13.29	7.51	14.07	7.45	10.64
1990	9.04	4.61	8.98	5.30	6.87
1991	9.66	5.92	9.24	6.34	7.76

PANEL B

Average monthly returns and their standard deviations, average monthly excess returns and their standard deviations, Sharpe measure and JK-Z test (H_0: $Sh_{PTF} = Sh_{TSE\ 300}$), portfolio beta.

	PORTFOLIO 1	PORTFOLIO 2	PORTFOLIO 3	PORTFOLIO 4	NON-MANUFACTURING
Average Return (%)	1.49	1.21	1.50	1.25	1.36
Standard Deviation (%)	5.09	5.33	5.78	5.35	5.38
Average Excess Return (%)	0.57	0.29	0.58	0.33	0.44
Standard Deviation (%)	5.13	5.39	5.85	5.40	5.44
Sharpe Measure	0.11	0.05	0.10	0.06	0.08
JK-Z Test	1.83**	0.90	1.81**	1.08	1.37
Beta	0.65	0.71	0.88	0.88	0.80

Note: ** Statistically significant at the 1% level.

TABLE 9 (CONT'D)

PANEL C

Average monthly portfolio returns and their standard deviations, average monthly portfolio excess returns and their standard deviations, Sharpe measure and JK-Z Test (H_0: $Sh_{PTF} = SH_{TSE\ 300}$), portfolio beta.

1978-1981	PORTFOLIO 1	PORTFOLIO 2	PORTFOLIO 3	PORTFOLIO 4	NON-MANUFACTURING
Average Return (%)	2.26	1.52	1.76	1.13	1.69
Standard Deviation (%)	4.87	5.03	5.13	5.41	5.08
Average Excess Return (%)	1.19	0.46	0.70	0.07	0.63
Standard Deviation (%)	4.98	5.15	5.27	5.53	5.21
Sharpe Measure	0.24	0.09	0.13	0.01	0.12
JK-Z Test	1.96**	−0.76	0.11	−2.49**	−0.11
Beta	0.60	0.67	0.69	0.76	0.68
1982-1986					
Average Return (%)	2.15	2.13	2.64	2.11	2.16
Standard Deviation (%)	4.62	4.93	5.62	4.56	5.09
Average Excess Return (%)	1.28	1.25	1.77	1.24	1.39
Standard Deviation (%)	4.66	4.96	5.69	4.58	5.13
Sharpe Measure	0.27	0.25	0.31	0.27	0.27
JK-Z Test	3.40**	3.55**	4.30**	3.09**	3.37**
Beta	0.68	0.81	0.89	0.62	0.76
1987-1991					
Average Return (%)	0.21	0.03	0.15	0.49	0.21
Standard Deviation (%)	5.53	5.80	6.22	5.96	6.00
Average Excess Return (%)	−0.64	−0.82	−0.70	−0.37	−0.64
Standard Deviation (%)	5.55	5.85	6.26	5.99	6.03
Sharpe Measure	−0.12	−0.14	−0.11	−0.06	−0.11
JK-Z Test	−1.30	−1.75**	−1.46	−0.36	−1.16
Beta	0.88	0.92	1.08	1.06	0.98

Note: ** Statistically significant at the 1% level.

TABLE 10

NON-MANUFACTURING FIRM SAMPLE – SIZE WEIGHTING
(1 YEAR, NON-MFR, CTRL, SIZE)

PANEL A

Growth of $1 cumulative investment in size-weighted portfolios of non-manufacturing firms, revised annually by ranking firms by control.

YEAR	PORTFOLIO 1	PORTFOLIO 2	PORTFOLIO 3	PORTFOLIO 4	NON-MANUFACTURING
1977	1.00	1.00	1.00	1.00	1.00
1978	1.24	1.11	1.48	1.40	1.31
1979	1.54	1.29	1.84	1.43	1.53
1980	2.22	2.25	2.11	1.92	2.13
1981	2.27	2.03	1.97	1.51	1.95
1982	2.71	2.41	2.10	1.67	2.23
1983	4.19	3.58	4.35	2.61	3.68
1984	3.89	4.02	3.98	3.71	3.65
1985	5.33	6.20	5.83	3.79	5.29
1986	6.25	7.02	8.12	4.36	6.44
1987	5.53	6.29	9.00	4.03	6.21
1988	7.27	8.65	10.65	5.04	7.90
1989	9.29	8.66	11.14	5.84	8.73
1990	6.92	6.27	8.05	4.76	6.50
1991	7.53	7.41	8.25	5.25	7.11

PANEL B

Average monthly returns and their standard deviations, average monthly excess returns and their standard deviations, Sharpe measure and JK-Z test (H_0: $Sh_{PTF} = Sh_{TSE\ 300}$), portfolio beta.

	PORTFOLIO 1	PORTFOLIO 2	PORTFOLIO 3	PORTFOLIO 4	NON-MANUFACTURING
Average Return (%)	1.34	1.35	1.46	1.15	1.33
Standard Deviation (%)	5.28	5.55	6.24	5.55	5.66
Average Excess Return (%)	0.42	0.43	0.53	0.22	0.41
Standard Deviation (%)	5.32	5.60	6.31	5.61	5.71
Sharpe Measure	0.08	0.08	0.09	0.04	0.07
JK-Z Test	0.53	0.55	0.80	-0.17	0.43
Beta	0.73	0.84	1.01	0.87	0.87

Note: ** Statistically significant at the 1% level.

TABLE 10 (CONT'D)

PANEL C

Average monthly portfolio returns and their standard deviations, average monthly portfolio excess returns and their standard deviations, Sharpe measure and JK-Z Test (H_0: $Sh_{PTF} = SH_{TSE\ 300}$), Portfolio Beta.

1978-1981	PORTFOLIO 1	PORTFOLIO 2	PORTFOLIO 3	PORTFOLIO 4	NON-MANUFACTURING
Average Return (%)	1.86	1.63	1.59	1.02	1.53
Standard Deviation (%)	5.33	5.59	5.86	5.80	5.61
Average Excess Return (%)	0.80	0.57	0.53	−0.04	0.47
Standard Deviation (%)	5.42	5.69	5.97	5.93	5.72
Sharpe Measure	0.15	0.10	0.09	−0.01	0.08
JK-Z Test	0.39	−0.48	−0.88	−3.11**	−0.93
Beta	0.68	0.70	0.83	0.83	0.76
1982-1986					
Average Return (%)	1.84	2.21	2.60	1.92	2.14
Standard Deviation (%)	5.38	4.94	6.67	5.14	5.55
Average Excess Return (%)	0.96	1.33	1.73	1.04	1.27
Standard Deviation (%)	5.41	4.95	6.73	5.18	5.58
Sharpe Measure	0.18	0.27	0.26	0.20	0.23
JK-Z Test	1.62	3.88**	3.58**	2.38**	2.74**
Beta	0.68	0.81	1.09	0.80	0.85
1987-1991					
Average Return (%)	0.44	0.28	0.21	0.48	0.35
Standard Deviation (%)	5.12	6.01	5.98	5.76	5.70
Average Excess Return (%)	−0.41	−0.58	−0.64	−0.37	−0.50
Standard Deviation (%)	5.14	6.05	6.01	5.78	5.72
Sharpe Measure	−0.08	−0.10	−0.11	−0.06	−0.09
JK-Z Test	−0.65	−1.06	−1.88**	−0.40	−0.93
Beta	0.83	1.03	1.14	1.00	1.00

Note: ** Statistically significant at the 1% level.

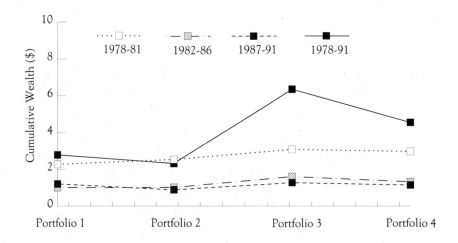

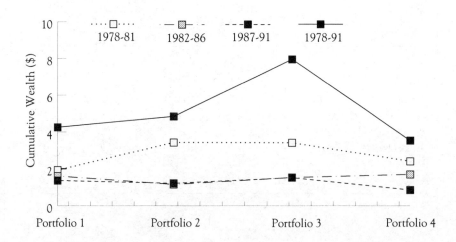

FIGURE 3 (CONT'D)

NON-MANUFACTURING, CONTROL, EQUALLY WEIGHTED

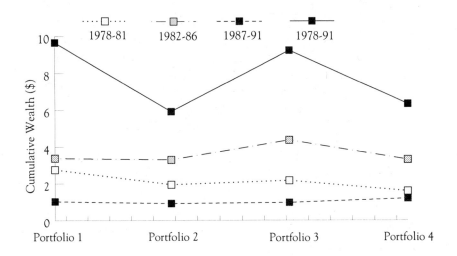

NON-MANUFACTURING, CONTROL, WEIGHTED

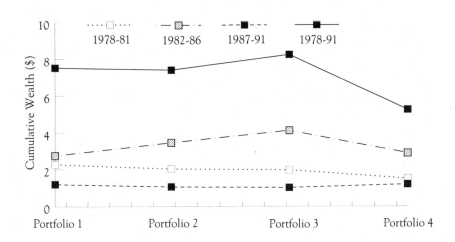

FIGURE 4

RELATIONSHIP BETWEEN PERFORMANCE AND CONTROL/OWNERSHIP

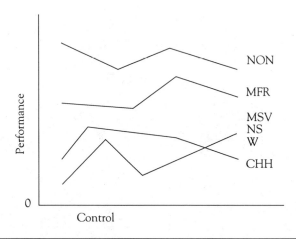

Notes: Information documented by previous studies and as observed in the present study.
         CHH   Chen, Hexter & Hue (1990)
         MSV   Morck, Shleifer & Vishny (1988)
         NS   Neun & Santerre (1986)
         W   Wruck (1989)
         MFR   Manufacturing firms
         NON   Non-manufacturing firms

NON-PARAMETRIC AND THE PAIRED DIFFERENCE TESTS

IN ADDITION TO THE JK-Z TESTS, we conducted two tests based on the differences in return across portfolios. First, the non-parametric test (test of proportions) compares the number of times the monthly returns of portfolio i was greater than that of portfolio j. Although not testing for economic significance, this test does provide additional information about the nature of the relationship. Second, the parametric test of differences simply subtracts, in a pairwise comparison, returns for portfolio j from those of portfolio i for each month, and determines whether these differences are statistically significant. Table 11 shows the results of these tests for the portfolios described in Tables 7 through 10. The results are mixed at best. Both non-parametric and parametric tests indicate that, on a month-by-month basis, no portfolio consistently dominates the adjacent portfolio. These results indicate not only that the number of times any portfolio dominates the other is almost random, but also that the difference in returns is random. The direction (i.e., the sign) is consistent with the results shown in Tables 7 through 10.

TABLE 11

FURTHER PARAMETRIC AND NON-PARAMETRIC RESULTS

Non-parametric Results: the proportion (p) of the number of times the monthly return of $R_{it} > R_{jt}$ over the period January 1978 to December 1991 (N = 168), the proportion q being equal to 1 - p, and the t-statistic for the null hypothesis H_0: $p_i > p_j$.

H0:	P2 > P1	P3 > P2	P4 > P3	H0:	P2 > P1	P3 > P2	P4 > P3
MFR, CTRL, EQL				**MFR, CTRL, SIZE WTD**			
p	0.48	0.57	0.47	p	0.59	0.52	0.45
q	0.52	0.43	0.53	q	0.41	0.48	0.55
t	-0.61	1.71**	-0.77	t	2.35**	0.30	-1.39
NON, CTRL, EQL				**NON, CTRL, SIZE WTD**			
p	0.46	0.50	0.49	p	0.52	0.53	0.49
q	0.54	0.50	0.51	q	0.48	0.47	0.51
t	-1.08	0.00	-0.30	t	0.31	0.77	-0.15

Parametric Results: the difference between the mean returns ($\mu_i - \mu_j$) of two portfolios (P_i, and P_j), the standard error (σ) of the difference between mean portfolio returns, and the t statistic for the hypothesis $H_0 : \mu_i = \mu_j$.

	P2 , P1	P3 , P2	P4 , P3		P2 , P1	P3 , P2	P4 , P3
MFR, CTRL, EQL				**MFR, CTRL, SIZE WTD**			
$\mu_i-\mu_j$	-0.11	0.57	-0.21	$\mu_i-\mu_j$	0.09	0.29	-0.52
σ	0.69	0.66	0.62	σ	0.69	0.71	0.68
t	-0.16	0.86	-0.34	t	0.13	0.41	-0.76
NON, CTRL, EQL				**NON, CTRL, SIZE WTD**			
$\mu_i-\mu_j$	-0.28	0.29	-0.24	$\mu_i-\mu_j$	0.00	0.10	-0.31
σ	0.56	0.60	0.60	σ	0.59	0.64	0.64
t	-0.49	0.48	-0.41	t	0.00	0.16	-0.48

Note: ** Statistically significant at the 1% level.

TABLE 12

ACCOUNTING-BASED PERFORMANCE MEASURES

		PORTFOLIO 1 – LOW CONTROL PORTFOLIO 4 – HIGH CONTROL MEAN VALUES				PORTFOLIO 1 – LOW CONTROL PORTFOLIO 4 – HIGH CONTROL MEDIAN VALUES			
YEAR	PERFORMANCE MEASURE	PORTFOLIO 1	PORTFOLIO 2	PORTFOLIO 3	PORTFOLIO 4	PORTFOLIO 1	PORTFOLIO 2	PORTFOLIO 3	PORTFOLIO 4
1991	Asset Turnover	0.78	0.85	0.71	0.84	0.69	0.53	0.60	0.71
	Gross Margin	0.11	0.06	0.02	0.04	0.04	0.03	0.06	0.02
	Return on Assets	-0.02	0.03	0.00	0.03	0.02	0.04	0.02	0.02
	Return on Equity	-0.17	-0.19	-0.15	0.00	-0.01	0.01	-0.01	0.00
	Debt Equity	1.15	1.61	0.92	1.39	0.72	0.69	0.68	0.38
	Capital Expenditure / Net Fixed Assets	-0.25	-0.12	-0.11	-0.14	0.17	0.11	0.09	0.12
	Interest Coverage	1.20	1.43	2.24	6.11	1.14	1.18	1.18	0.91
	Market Value / Book Value	1.51	1.28	1.35	1.60	1.45	1.24	1.17	1.15
1990	Asset Turnover	0.72	0.90	0.81	0.91	0.77	0.69	0.65	0.71
	Gross Margin	-0.10	0.10	0.07	0.09	0.10	0.09	0.09	0.08
	Return on Assets	0.02	0.06	0.04	0.06	0.06	0.07	0.05	0.04
	Return on Equity	-0.01	0.11	0.04	0.08	0.10	0.14	0.08	0.04
	Debt Equity	0.77	1.13	0.89	1.75	0.60	0.56	0.40	0.41
	Capital Expenditure / Net Fixed Assets	-0.29	-0.16	-0.15	-0.15	0.20	0.15	0.15	0.14
	Interest Coverage	1.82	2.57	1.08	7.21	2.32	2.39	1.78	1.12
	Market Value / Book Value	1.29	1.12	1.14	1.35	1.30	1.16	1.06	1.22

TABLE 12 (CONT'D)

		MEAN VALUES	PORTFOLIO 1 – LOW CONTROL PORTFOLIO 4 – HIGH CONTROL			MEDIAN VALUES	PORTFOLIO 1 – LOW CONTROL PORTFOLIO 4 – HIGH CONTROL	
YEAR	PERFORMANCE MEASURE	PORTFOLIO 1	PORTFOLIO 2	PORTFOLIO 3	PORTFOLIO 4	PORTFOLIO 1	PORTFOLIO 2	PORTFOLIO 3	PORTFOLIO 4
1989	Asset Turnover	0.70	0.87	0.89	0.85	0.64	0.64	0.78	0.65
	Gross Margin	0.15	0.15	0.12	0.17	0.15	0.11	0.11	0.14
	Return on Assets	0.08	0.08	0.08	0.10	0.07	0.07	0.08	0.08
	Return on Equity	0.18	0.22	0.18	0.27	0.17	0.18	0.24	0.20
	Debt Equity	0.60	1.00	0.86	1.64	0.42	0.73	0.41	0.36
	Capital Expenditure / Net Fixed Assets	-0.17	-0.16	-0.21	-0.19	0.17	0.15	0.16	0.18
	Interest Coverage	5.00	7.90	6.34	10.84	2.94	3.79	4.47	3.82
	Market Value / Book Value	1.54	1.42	1.39	1.54	1.40	1.25	1.24	1.54
1988	Asset Turnover	0.95	0.75	0.92	0.94	0.88	0.65	0.79	0.74
	Gross Margin	0.13	0.16	0.05	0.20	0.09	0.13	0.14	0.17
	Return on Assets	0.10	0.10	0.08	0.13	0.09	0.07	0.09	0.11
	Return on Equity	0.35	0.27	0.19	0.36	0.24	0.19	0.22	0.30
	Debt Equity	0.77	0.83	0.64	2.02	0.43	0.74	0.44	0.29
	Capital Expenditure / Net Fixed Assets	-0.20	-0.21	-0.18	-0.17	0.17	0.20	0.16	0.19
	Interest Coverage	6.14	15.48	8.31	12.85	3.64	4.32	6.17	8.87
	Market Value / Book Value	1.76	1.51	1.54	1.76	1.59	1.40	1.33	1.62

TABLE 13

RANKING FOR ACCOUNTING-BASED PERFORMANCE MEASURES:
PORTFOLIOS 1 (LOW CONTROL) AND 4 (HIGH CONTROL)

YEAR	PERFORMANCE MEASURE	MEAN RANK PORTFOLIO 1	MEAN RANK PORTFOLIO 4	MANN-WHITNEY Z	K-S Z
1991	Asset Turnover	27.48	28.5	-0.23	0.72
	Gross Margin	28.89	27.14	-0.40	0.58
	Return on Assets	28.00	28.00	0.00	0.51
	Return on Equity	28.26	27.75	-0.11	0.65
	Debt Equity	23.91	31.95	-1.86	1.55
	Capital Expenditure / Net Fixed Assets	31.46	23.82	-1.78	0.92
	Interest Coverage	24.74	26.15	-0.34	0.62
	Market Value / Book Value	27.59	28.39	-0.18	0.75
1990	Asset Turnover	27.39	25.79	-0.37	0.56
	Gross Margin	25.26	27.48	-0.52	0.61
	Return on Assets	26.13	26.79	-0.15	0.84
	Return on Equity	26.96	26.14	-0.19	0.81
	Debt Equity	24.65	27.97	-0.78	0.69
	Capital Expenditure / Net Fixed Assets	31.86	21.55	-2.45	1.55
	Interest Coverage	24.68	25.26	-0.14	0.78
	Market Value / Book Value	26.61	26.41	-0.04	0.76
1989	Asset Turnover	22.72	24	-0.31	0.57
	Gross Margin	24.56	22.82	-0.46	0.81
	Return on Assets	24.72	22.71	-0.49	0.7
	Return on Equity	26.33	21.68	-1.14	0.76
	Debt Equity	21.78	24.61	-0.69	0.56
	Capital Expenditure / Net Fixed Assets	22.76	23.14	-0.09	0.38
	Interest Coverage	25.47	20.63	-1.21	0.71
	Market Value / Book Value	23.89	23.25	-0.15	0.59
1988	Asset Turnover	18.75	20.87	-0.57	0.56
	Gross Margin	23.44	17.61	-1.57	0.11
	Return on Assets	22.38	18.35	-1.08	0.27
	Return on Equity	22	18.61	-0.91	0.36
	Debt Equity	15.91	22.85	-1.87	0.06
	Capital Expenditure / Net Fixed Assets	21.67	18.09	-0.97	0.33
	Interest Coverage	21.07	17.59	-0.95	0.33
	Market Value / Book Value	21.06	19.26	-0.48	0.62

ACCOUNTING-BASED PERFORMANCE RESULTS IN THE MANUFACTURING SECTOR

THIS SECTION HAS TWO PURPOSES: first, to supplement the results obtained from the stock market analysis and, second, to provide a basis for comparison with other accounting-based studies.[11] As noted earlier, eight commonly used accounting measures are used to perform comparisons between firms with differential degrees of control. Table 12 shows the corresponding values of means and medians for each of these eight measures for the four quartiles for the years 1988 through 1991.

Several observations are in order here. First, there is a noticeable difference between means and medians for each of the ratios; therefore, one must be careful about drawing strong conclusions based on these results. Second, although the mean values signify that these values are uniformly higher for Portfolio 1 compared to Portfolio 4, no consistently increasing or decreasing patterns can be seen for firms belonging to Portfolio 2 or Portfolio 3. For the firms of Portfolio 1 and 4, moreover, the median values lead us to conclusions opposite to those indicated by means. Based on median value results, there is really no pattern which can be considered as consistent across each of the four years and across the portfolios. These casual observations are also confirmed through further statistical analysis. Table 13 shows the mean ranks for each of the measures and for each of the years for the two extreme portfolios (1 and 4), the values of the Mann-Whitney Z for detecting the differences in ranking and the Kolmogorov-Smirnov Z for detecting differences in distribution of each. The only performance measure showing a statistically different difference was capital expenditure-to-net fixed asset ratio and that only for the year 1990. Thus, these results are consistent with the results based on stock market performance as shown earlier. The absence of any statistically significant differences between firms based on the market-to-book-value ratio also indicates that similar conclusions could have been drawn using the Tobin's Q values. Thus, we can conclude that, based on these accounting measures, there is no consistent relationship between firm performance and the associated degree of control.

SUMMARY, LIMITATIONS AND CONCLUSIONS

THE MAIN PURPOSE OF THIS STUDY is to provide a Canadian empirical perspective on the issue of control and performance, using both stock-market-based and accounting-based performance measures.

A valid criticism of our use of the stock market performance measure and our conclusions based on the results generated by it would be that stock market returns may not be an accurate representation of performance. The argument is that the differences in the firm-specific environment in corporate governance may have already been capitalized in the stock prices at the beginning of our time period. After this capitalization, shareholders earn the normal returns affected only by new information or surprises. Only if the rate of arrival of information and surprises affects one group of firms (widely held) differently from the other (closely held), would we be able to detect differences in stock-market-based performance measures. And even if the difference were found, it could not be attributed to the issue of control and performance.[12]

There are two reasons why this criticism may not be entirely appropriate. First, in addition to analyzing stock market performance, we also analyzed accounting-based performance measures (for a subset of firms), including a measure which closely resembles the Tobin's Q ratio. These results were in line with the stock-market-based results for the period studied. Second, it is difficult to believe that during such a long period, the stock market would show no preference to the corporate governance structure and not adjust expected returns accordingly, if the governance structure were deemed important for differential performance. Our results are consistent with the notion that alternative mechanisms are in place to mitigate agency problems. The differences in control are of less importance due to the efficacy of disclosure rules and other mechanisms. As a result, differences in ownership need not be related to differential performance; individual differences in operating procedures and other factors may of more importance.

This analysis allows us to draw some reasonably robust conclusions based on the overall results and associated statistical tests. First, it is clear that the relationship between control and stock market performance is sector-specific, with the non-manufacturing sector being more sensitive to the effects of control than the manufacturing sector. In the manufacturing sector, an investor would have been better off simply investing in large Canadian manufacturing firms – which did better than the overall manufacturing sector portfolio. There was little, if any, use in investing in securities, based on the degree of control of a firm within that sector or within a specific size group. However, in the non-manufacturing sector, investment based on control does have performance implications. Second, the relationship between control and stock market performance is inconsistent with that shown in previous snap-shot-type U.S.-based research. For example, the third quartile firms outperform other firms in the non-manufacturing sector.[13] Third, accounting-based measures fail to detect any differences in firm performance based on the associated degree of control, either for a given year or over the entire time period. Overall, from a statistical perspective, none of our results shows any consistent differences between widely held firms and closely held firms belonging to the TSE 300.

There are several limitations to our research design which clearly affect both the comparability of our results with those of previous studies, and our conclusions. These include issues about the definition of control, the choice of our sample (since it is restricted to only TSE 300 companies), the empirical methodology and its robustness, our *ad hoc* method of classifying stocks into two sector groups, the nature of institutional ownership in Canada, our inattention to the identity of the controlling owner (foreign, *versus* founder *versus* corporate *versus* family) and our somewhat arbitrary partition of the sample into quartiles.

It is possible that a more powerful research methodology – using more precise definitions of control, or enlarging the sample to non-TSE 300 firms – may lead to different conclusions. It is also possible that a better definition of control or ownership, or a "quantified" measure of corporate governance (based, for example, on the ratio of independent to insider directors on the Board) may be required to assess the effect of governance on firm performance. It is also possible that the governance structure (through the Board of Directors) is such that the ownership characteristic of the firm is irrelevant. One option we are now considering is to evaluate the performance of firms that have either a dual-class voting structure or only the restricted voting class of shares in the public hands.[14]

Notwithstanding these limitations, our results indicate that much more longitudinal research is necessary before any definitive conclusions about the general relationship between control, corporate governance and firm performance can be drawn. Moreover, any categorical statement made about the relationship between control and performance, based on the conclusions of existing empirical research, must be viewed with great caution.

These results may also suggest that the corporate governance environment in Canada has performed remarkably well; using control as the only distinguishing feature across firms does not seem to matter for firm performance. Given an environment which can be characterized by better monitoring, increased (but cost-effective) disclosure rules for publicly traded companies, a vigilant institutional and investment research presence, a well-functioning board of directors for each corporation, and a policy framework which ensures that timely and relevant information is available to investors, then the actual degree of control of a publicly traded firm by inside owner/managers may cease to be a matter of public debate. From a policy perspective, the focus should shift away from a concern over the degree of ownership of publicly traded corporations and toward ensuring that the overall corporate governance environment provides the necessary mechanisms for inside owner/manager discipline.

ENDNOTES

1 Costs paid by the agent in order to guarantee the principal that the agent will not take certain actions which would be detrimental to the principal's interests.
2 The dollar equivalent of the reduction in welfare experienced by the principal due to the divergence between the agent's decision and those decisions which would maximize the principal's interests.
3 As Jensen & Ruback (1983) point out, ownership of shares is not the only way to align manager's interests with those of shareholders. A less than

adequate performance by a management team results either in its replacement by a better performing team, or in a takeover bid which will eventually replace the management. This notion of external discipline induces managers always to act in the best interest of the owners.

4 Vance found that net income was positively related to the directors' shareholdings (of companies listed on the NYSE and AMEX). Similarly, Pfeffer reports a positive relationship between managerial shareholding and the Return on Equity as well as the Net Profit margin. Using the ANOVA approach, Kim & Lyn (1988) investigate the relationship between a firm's insider ownership and its Tobin's Q. They find that Q increases with insider ownership.

5 The Morck & Stangeland study compares the profitability performance differences between U.S. and Canadian firms, as well as differences between the type of control (heir-controlled versus professional management-controlled). They do not investigate the performance of Canadian firms from a shareholder viewpoint. They classify firms into two groupings: closely held (defined as those firms with 20 percent or more shares held by a dominant shareholder) and widely held (all other firms).

6 There is no real justification for such an *ad-hoc* grouping, except for the conjecture that outside investors may be in a better position to value the hard assets found in a manufacturing firm than the soft assets (which leave the premises at 5 p.m.) of a non-manufacturing firm. Thus, the degree of asymmetric information may be different in these two groups, and therefore a different relationship between control and performance might be expected.

7 In an earlier version of this study, we also used a control-based weighting within a size-based weighting scheme. Since the main focus of the current study is on control and ownership-related issues and since the results from that complex weighting scheme do not result in any new insights, we do not report these findings here in the interest of brevity.

8 See Kryzanowski & Zhang (1992). The Sharpe measure is given by $\phi_i = \mu_i/\sigma_i$ where μ_i is the mean excess return on portfolio i, and σ_i is the estimated standard error of the excess return of portfolio i. The Jobson-Korkie test statistic for the Sharpe measure is given by $Z_{iv} = \hat{A}_{iv} / \sqrt{\theta_{iv}}$ where $\hat{A}_{iv}$ is the sample estimate of the transformed difference between the Sharpe measures of portfolios i and v, and θ_{iv} is the estimate of the variance of $\hat{A}_{iv}$.

9 The diversity of firms within our non-manufacturing sample makes it impossible to make valid comparisons across the sample. Hence, we report only the results in the manufacturing sector. It should also be noted that our "accounting" sample contains a slightly lower number of companies than our "stock-market" sample, due mainly to unavailability of data.

10 Note that the TSE 300 also includes sectors which are classified as neither manufacturing nor non-manufacturing; namely banks and utilities.

11 It could be argued that stock-market based measures account mainly for differences, rather than level of value. If this is so, then the accounting-based performance measures may be able to detect any systematic differences in levels, based on measures like the market-to-book-value ratio.

12 We thank Randall Morck for encouraging us to think about this issue. We have made liberal use of his very helpful suggestions.

13 This conclusion must be viewed with caution. In most of the U.S. studies, the highly controlled firm may have only a 30 percent insider ownership; this is not the case in Canada. Thus, our results cover a much wider span of control than the U.S. studies do.

14 There are at least 40 firms with dual-class ownership structure, and a further 100 firms which have only restricted voting shares traded on the Toronto Stock Exchange. At present we are in the process of analyzing their performance in relation to their peers in the industry.

ACKNOWLEDGEMENTS

WE WOULD LIKE TO THANK A. Srivastava, W. Lawson, P. Halpern and R. Morck for valuable comments and both the Social Sciences and Humanities Research Council and the Financial Research Foundation of Canada for providing financial support. This study is partially based on Tulpule's thesis for a Masters degree in Management Studies at the School of Business, Carleton University.

BIBLIOGRAPHY

Berle, A. and G. Means. *The Modern Corporation and Private Property*. New York: Macmillan, 1932.

Chen, H., L. Hexter and M. Hue. "Ownership Structure and Firm Performance: Some New Evidence." Second Northern Finance Association Meeting, Montreal, Canada, 1990.

Demsetz, H. "The Structure of Ownership and the Theory of the Firm." *Journal of Law and Economics*, 26 (1983):375-90.

Demsetz, H. and K. Lehn. "The Structure of Corporate Ownership: Causes and Consequences." *Journal of Political Economy*, 93 (1985):1155-77.

Fama, E. "Agency Problems and the Theory of the Firm." *Journal of Political Economy*, 88 (1980):288-307.

Hart, O. "The Market Mechanism as an Incentive Scheme." *The Bell Journal of Economics*, 14 (1983):366-82.

Holderness, C. G. and D. P. Sheehan. "Monitoring an Owner: The Case of Turner Broadcasting." *Journal of Financial Economics*, 30 (1991):325-46.

Jensen, M. and W. Meckling. "Theory of the Firm : Managerial Behaviour, Agency Costs and Ownership Structure." *Journal of Financial Economics*, 3 (1976):305-60.

Jensen, M. and R. Ruback. "The Market for Corporate Control." *Journal of Financial Economics*, 11 (1983):5-50.

Jensen, M. and J. Warner. "The Distribution of Power Among Corporate Managers, Shareholders, and Directors." *Journal of Financial Economics*, 20 (1988):3-24.

Jobson, J. D. and B. M. Korkie. "Performance Hypothesis Testing with the Sharpe & Treynor Measure." *Journal of Finance*. (1986):889-908.

Jog, V. and H. Schaller. "Concentrated Ownership and Market Value of the Firm." Working Paper - Carleton University, 1989.

Kim, W. and E. Lyn. "Excess Market Value, Market Power, and Inside Ownership Structure." *Review of Industrial Organization*, 3 (1988):1-25.

Kryzanowski, L. and H. Zhang. "The Contrarian Investment Strategy does not Work in Canadian Markets." *Journal of Financial and Quantitative Analysis*, 27 (1992):383-96.

McConnell, J. and H. Servaes. "Additional Evidence on Equity Ownership and Corporate Value." *Journal of Financial Economics*, 27, (1990):595-610.

Morck, R., A. Shleifer and R. Vishny. "Management Ownership and Market Valuation : An Empirical Analysis." *Journal of Financial Economics*, 20 (1988):293-315.

Morck, R. and D. Stangeland. "Corporate Performance and Large Shareholders." Paper presented at the sixth Northern Finance Association Conference, Vancouver, September 1994.

Muellar, D. *Profits in the Long Run.* Cambridge: Cambridge University Press, 1986.

Neun, S. and R. Santerre. "Dominant Stock ownership and Profitability." *Managerial and Decision Economics*, 7, (1986):207-10.

Oswald, S. and J. Jahera. "The Influence of Ownership on Performance: An Empirical Study." *Strategic Management Journal*, 12 (1991):321-26.

Pfeffer, J. "Size and Composition of Corporate Boards of Directors: The Organization and its Environment." *Administrative Science Quarterly*, 17 (1972):218-28.

Shleifer, A. and R. Vishny. "Large Shareholders and Corporate Control." *Journal of Political Economy*, 94 (1986):461-88.

Stiglitz, J. "Credit Markets and the Control of Capital." *Journal of Money, Credit and Banking*, 17 # 2 (1985):133-52.

Stulz R. "Managerial Control of Voting Rights: Financing Policies and the Market for Corporate Control." *Journal of Financial Economics*, 20, (1988):25-54.

Vance S.C. *Board of Directors: Structure and Performance.* Portland: University of Oregon Press, 1964.

Wruck K. "Equity Ownership Concentration and Private Value: Evidence from Private Equity Financing." *Journal of Financial Economics*, 23, (1989):3-28.

David A. Stangeland
Faculty of Management
University of Manitoba

Commentary on Part II

Governance Structure, Corporate Decision-Making and Firm Performance in North America

T HE STUDY BY RAO AND LEE-SING is essentially a broad compilation of several measures of corporate governance structure, corporate decision-making, and corporate performance. It is important in two ways. First, it identifies many of the characteristics that are basic to Canadian firms and contrasts them with those of U.S. firms. Second, it represents a first pass at assessing some of the relationships between these characteristics and thus provides a valuable background for the studies that follow.

Of the characteristics identified for Canadian firms that are different from those for American firms, three stand out. Two of them relate to general firm attributes: size and industry. The third is a difference in governance structure – concentration of ownership.

In terms of size, American firms are generally larger than Canadian firms. Both absolute values and relative proportions show there are more U.S. firms than Canadian firms in the largest size category. More firms (by proportion) fall into the smallest size category in Canada than in the United States. Total sales of U.S. companies amount to nearly ten times the total sales of Canadian companies during the time period studied. All of these results are consistent with an economy that is roughly ten times the size of the Canadian economy.

The distribution of firms across industries is also different when comparing Canada to the United States. Both countries have similar proportions of firms in wholesale trade, transportation, labour-intensive manufacturing, construction, agriculture, forestry, fishing, and finance. There are large differences, however, in mining, service industries, and technology intensive manufacturing. Relative to their U.S. counterparts, there are few Canadian firms in service industries and high-technology manufacturing, but many in basic mining.

Probably the most striking difference between the characteristics of Canadian and American firms is the level of ownership concentration. More than 75 percent of the Canadian sample have a dominant shareholder (or a small group of shareholders) who control(s) 20 percent or more of the firm's stock. The comparable figure in the United States is less than 60 percent. Over 50 percent of the firms in the Canadian sample have a majority share-holder compared to less than 25 percent of the American sample. Differences in ownership structures between Canadian and American firms are also more pronounced for the largest-size category of firms.

What makes these differences so important is that if they are ignored, then spurious relationships between other variables may be observed and, perhaps, interpreted inappropriately as causal. For example, Rao and Lee-Sing show that the concentration of ownership variable is quite different depending on the industry and size class to which a firm belongs. They also show significant differences in industry distribution and size of Canadian firms relative to U.S. firms. With respect to the latter, if these facts are ignored there is a risk of attributing operating decision-making and performance effects to differences in ownership structure whereas they are attributable to nothing more than size and industry characteristics. Using differences in ownership structure to explain differences in profitability between Canadian and U.S. firms is one example of this problem. If industry effects are ignored, then Canadian firms in more cyclical industries may appear to have performance differences related to their different ownership structures even though there is nothing more than a profitability-industry relationship. A similar problem occurs with research and development. Since there are fewer Canadian firms in high-technology industries, Canadian firms spend less on R&D. By ignoring the industry differences, however, one may conclude that it is a different corporate governance system that determines the difference in R&D spending.

The implication of spurious relationships is serious for policy makers. If policy is based on false relationships, then the effect of that policy is not likely to be what policy makers had intended. For instance, continuing with the example of research and development, if Canadian corporate governance is seen to be responsible for unacceptably low R&D levels, it may be argued that a policy of R&D tax breaks can correct the problem. If, however, the low R&D level derives from Canadian firms being in non-R&D-intensive industries, such a policy may actually precipitate a two-fold problem. On the one hand it will reduce the tax revenue of the government; on the other, it will promote over-investment in R&D projects whose costs are unlikely to be recovered (that is, negative net present value research and development). To conclude the example, such R&D tax breaks should only be targeted at those industries where R&D is truly too low. If U.S. firms are to be used as a benchmark, then a comparison of same-industry, same-size companies across the two countries must be conducted to determine which particular Canadian industries have this problem.

In conducting their analysis of the relationships between corporate governance and corporate operations, Rao and Lee-Sing do control for size and industry and they find these controls to be quite important. The relationships between governance and performance are less clear. Some of the governance variables show significant correlation with the performance variables for American firms, but the results are weaker for Canadian firms. An interesting extension to their work might be to match firms by industry and size and then test whether the Canadian governance variables are important in explaining the differences. In a recent working paper ("Large Shareholders and Corporate

Performance in Canada", March 23, 1995), Morck & Stangeland do such an analysis (using industry matches) on a different set of governance variables with some success. In their study they also find firm age to be an important control.

To conclude, Rao and Lee-Sing provide valuable background information on the characteristics of Canadian firms and how they differ from U.S. firms. These differences must be addressed and taken into account in future studies that attempt to relate governance to aspects of corporate operations. Finally, this study provides a first pass at analyzing some of these relationships and can be used as a benchmark by other researchers.

Commentary on Part II
Control and Performance: Evidence from the TSE 300

IN THEIR STUDY, JOG AND TULPULE evaluate corporate control and industry type for the period from 1978 to 1991. They analyze how differences in these characteristics are related to stock returns and accounting-based measures of performance.

The relationship between their control variable and performance is of main concern. Control is defined as the percentage of outstanding equity of a firm that is tradable on the stock exchange. This measure gives an indication of ownership concentration. The more stock that is tradable, the less concentrated is ownership; the less stock that is tradable, the more concentrated is ownership. Ownership concentration is thought to have an important influence on management-shareholder agency conflicts. With low ownership concentration (such as in a very widely held firm) management owns few or no shares and thus has little incentive to act in shareholders' interests. As ownership concentration increases, either management owns more of a significant block of shares or some other party does. In either case, management is more likely to act more in the shareholders' interests because of its personal shareholdings or because of monitoring by a powerful blockholder. The positive effects of increased ownership concentration can be offset if a high ownership concentration enables management to become entrenched.

Jog and Tulpule's justification for including an industry-type characteristic is that some industries are easier to evaluate and therefore problems of asymmetric information are less severe. They break down their sample into manufacturing and non-manufacturing firms. They propose that manufacturing firms have more "hard" assets in place, and thus investors will have an easier time valuing them than the "soft" assets (such as human capital) of non-manufacturing firms. Because of fewer information asymmetry problems with manufacturing firms, there is less chance for management to get away with suboptimal behaviour.

What are the empirical findings of Jog and Tulpule's study? First, no significant relationships are observed between the accounting-based measures and the different firm characteristics. They do, however, present some interesting observations on stock returns. They find higher stock returns for moderately high levels of ownership concentration, a stronger effect for non-manufacturing firms, and temporally unstable relationships.

Jog and Tulpule conclude that their results for Canadian firms are inconsistent with previous research that does a "snapshot" (one time period) analysis. In addition, they state that a one-time-period analysis must be viewed with caution as their evidence shows the relationships to be unstable over time.

The conclusion of potentially unstable relationships over time appears to be justified. As agents in the economy learn about the cause and effect nature of relationships, they may develop various types of contracts to improve efficiency. The nature of those new contracts may not be evident in summary measures like ownership concentration.

It may be premature to discount previous studies based on this study's analysis. First, Jog and Tulpule use different measures of both ownership and performance. Second, the interpretations to be drawn from their abnormal-return performance variable are unclear. Jog and Tulpule assert that stock market returns reflect long-term performance from an investor's viewpoint. This is true. However, if markets are somewhat efficient, then the effects of ownership concentration are already capitalized in the stock price and return. Only unexpected changes in ownership concentration should cause abnormal returns. If a particular constant ownership structure resulted in long-run abnormal returns, this would be powerful evidence that the market is not semi-strong form efficient. Jog and Tulpule do not address the efficiency issue and they do not examine changes in ownership. At best, the abnormal-return evidence for their different portfolios can be interpreted as evidence that some portfolios had more positive surprises while others had more negative surprises over the time period studied. Given that surprises are unexpected (otherwise they are not surprises) a recurring pattern would not be expected. This is consistent with the temporal instability of Jog and Tulpule's result. To restate the point, this study's return evidence does not refute evidence from other studies because it does not test the relationship between control and performance. To test whether such a relationship exists, Jog and Tulpule must examine changes in control and determine how those changes affect the returns.

To conclude, Jog and Tulpule state that they find no consistent differences between widely held and closely held firms belonging to the TSE 300. Much of the research on the relationships between control and performance uses a single-period cross-sectional methodology. Jog and Tulpule highlight the fact that these relationships may indeed change over time. This is an important consideration for policy makers who are often required to make decisions based on dated studies.

Giovanni Barone-Adesi
The Wharton School
University of Pennsylvania

Commentary on Part II

THE STUDIES IN THIS SESSION HIGHLIGHT the differences between Canadian and American corporations along the lines commonly associated with corporate governance and performance. Most current academic research on the subject attempts to explain empirical regularities observed in the United States. It is not surprising, therefore, that the authors generally find little support for current theories in the Canadian markets. Differences in the regulatory and legal framework in the two countries contribute much to the explanation of these results.

On the governance side, Canadian firms are more frequently controlled by one large shareholder than American firms. However, using a simple comparison of the percentage holdings of Canadian and American large shareholders to measure the degree of control exercised by Canadian executives may be too restrictive. In fact, Canadian executives are much more entrenched than their American counterparts for several reasons: the absence of class actions by shareholders in the Canadian legal system; the consequent difficulty of dismantling poison pills and other takeover defences in Canada; and the coattails provisions in Canadian corporate acquisitions that tend to benefit small shareholders but that also make the transfer of corporate control more expensive. The widespread use of multiple classes of shares in Canada adds further to the entrenchment of Canadian executives. Advocates of shareholders' rights are occasionally vocal even in Canada, but they do not appear to have a widespread influence on corporate decision-making.

Moving to the measurement of performance, it is necessary to distinguish between accounting-based and market-based measures of corporate performance. Accounting-based measures of performance are intended to keep track of invested capital. If accounting were an exact science, accounting measures would be ideally suited to measure managers' effectiveness in choosing profitable projects. Unfortunately, the number of conventions necessary to implement an ideal accounting system would still leave us with perplexities about accounting measures – although accounting ambiguities do tend to be resolved over extended time periods.

Performance measures based on stock prices are easy to compute and are also reliable. Unfortunately, they cannot be used to measure managers' performance in absolute terms; they can be used only in terms relative to market expectations. The expected performance of a very good manager will be built into his/her firm's current stock price and only unexpected deviations will be picked up by the future stock performance.

In practice, stock-based performance measures are ideally suited to reveal the value of new information (such as takeover offers), and to shed some light on related issues, such as the value of corporate control. However, stock-based measures do not allow us to determine unequivocally whether a firm is over-investing or underinvesting, whether managers are shirking, or whether changes in strategy are called for.

To answer all of these questions, accounting measures are often the only meaningful ones. The choice of performance measures is therefore tied to the question being asked. However, in order to ask meaningful questions, we must be willing to move beyond corporate statistics and be prepared to focus on the different legal and regulatory frameworks that shape corporate decisions. In this connection, multilateral comparisons across countries would be useful, although different accounting and legal standards require caution in the interpretation of results. In an accounting context, the secret reserves allowed under German accounting rules is a typical example. The special responsibility given to the controlling shareholder in France, in recognition of his/her influence is an example in a legal context.

Before all the difficulties and ambiguities of performance evaluation discourage us from further research, I would like to mention that the ongoing process of integration in international capital markets may make most of these worries obsolete. The fact is that, in a competitive international market, Canadian firms will have to demonstrate good performance in order to attract investors. This simple reality should provide Canadian managers with the necessary incentives to perform – otherwise Canadian investors will buy foreign securities.

At present, there are still some barriers to capital market integration, mostly in the insurance and pension industries. However, the continuing relaxation of these barriers through amended regulation and the extensive use of derivative securities in portfolio management, is eliminating the shelters that managers in many countries have hitherto enjoyed; everyone is now being forced to play by similar rules. This trend will not last forever but, for as long as it lasts, it will provide effective performance monitoring and ensure the competitiveness of Canadian industry.

ACKNOWLEDGEMENTS

I WISH TO EXPRESS MY THANKS to the University of Alberta and the Wharton School, University of Pennsylvania.

Part III   The Board and Beyond

Jean-Marie Gagnon   &   Josée St-Pierre
Faculty of Administrative Studies   Department of Business and Economics
Université Laval   Université du Québec à Trois-Rivières

4

Alternative Mechanisms for Corporate Governance and Board Composition

THE GROWING BODY OF LITERATURE on corporate governance now includes a number of studies that take into account the role of the board of directors. The main themes in these studies focus on the relationship between board composition and corporate performance or behaviour and the board seen as a complement or substitute for other mechanisms. In this study, we examine empirically the determinants of board composition, drawing on a sample of 258 Canadian firms partitioned by type of ownership. Our results suggest that board composition is a function of the distribution of voting rights. However, the same statistical model does not apply to all three types of ownership. Under diffuse ownership, the ratio of outside to inside members of the board increases with the stock holdings of the important outside shareholders, and decreases with the holdings of the inside directors. These results are consistent with monitoring and entrenchment behaviour, respectively. We find no evidence of substitution between board composition and financial variables or regulation. Using a system of simultaneous equations, we explore the association between board composition and overall performance, but we do not detect a statistically significant relationship.

The organization of this study is that we first compile an inventory of the various mechanisms that are available and examine the process for selecting a subset of those mechanisms adapted to the peculiar circumstances of the firm (taking into account their interactions). We then discuss a number of behavioural hypotheses, and examine board composition. Presentation of the data is then followed by tests of models of board composition and monitoring and of board composition and performance. Following a discussion of the implications for public policy, the study ends with a brief summary.

MECHANISMS FOR CORPORATE GOVERNANCE

MECHANISMS

THE MECHANISMS CONSIDERED IN THIS STUDY are: board composition, executive compensation, debt policy, dividend policy and takeover defences (poison pills and charter, statutory and litigious defences). These appear as column headings in Table 1. We examine the mechanisms themselves, their cost and the probability of their use.

Board Composition

Corporate governance deals with "the distribution of power among corporate managers, shareholders and directors".[1] Board composition, which is discussed at length below, refers to the distribution of members according to their primary allegiance, which may be either to the shareholders or to the managers. The former are called "outsiders" (or outside directors) and the latter, "insiders". Ultimately, all directors are responsible to the shareholders. However, one would not expect an inside director (employee) with no stock ownership, for example, always to favour the same business strategies as an outside director who is also an important shareholder. The optimal composition of the board is likely to depend on specific circumstances within the firm, including the other mechanisms for corporate governance.

Executive Compensation

Executive compensation is one type of contract that can be designed to align efficiently the interests of managers and shareholders. This alignment is achieved by relating the value of the compensation package to the market value of the shares, either directly or indirectly, through earnings. A manager's remuneration has two parts – variable and fixed. The variable component comprises all types of compensation tied to earnings or to the market value of the shares (such as stock options). The fixed component is made up of salaries, retainers and directors' fees.

Debt Policy

There are several reasons why debt policy can be seen as a mechanism for corporate governance. First, it implies a style of governance that emphasizes rules over discretion. Increasing debt means that a larger part of the firm's cash flow is being returned to the bondholders and is therefore being removed from the control of the managers: the larger the debt, the smaller the discretionary power of the managers. Second, given the size of the firm, debt financing allows voting rights to be concentrated more in the hands of the remaining shareholders. Third, a relatively high debt-to-assets ratio tends to make the firm less attractive as a takeover target, and may therefore be used as a substitute for takeover defences.

Dividend Policy

Dividend policy, *i.e.*, the target ratio of dividends-to-earnings, can also be seen as a mechanism for corporate governance. The higher the payout ratio, the smaller the amount of free cash flows. As an instrument it operates just like debt policy, but it imposes much less severe constraints because the payment of dividends is not mandatory.

Takeover Defences

The remaining mechanisms are direct substitutes as takeover defences. The four categories we use are borrowed from Malatesta (1992): poison pills, charter defences, statutory defences and litigious defences.[2]

Poison pills include shareholder rights plans,[3] as well as voting and preferred stock plans. They are pre-emptive defences *par excellence* and transfer substantial power from the shareholders to the managers, in the event that a prospective bidder be interested in the firm. Charter defences include super-majority and fair-price clauses as well as board schemes. They must be approved by the shareholders but, in practice, this is also true of poison pills in Canada.[4] Statutory defences (control share laws, fair-price and freeze-out laws) imply that those controlling the firm can enroll the members of the legislature to fend off the bid. Finally, litigious defences include, besides litigation, sale of assets, share repurchases and greenmail or standstill agreements. Although Malatesta (1992) classifies bond issues as litigious defences, we do not.

This concludes our list of mechanisms for corporate governance. In a competitive market we would expect each firm to select a subset adapted to its own circumstances. The most important of the latter is the distribution of ownership rights, which appear under the column heading "Distribution of Voting Rights" and make up the second dimension of Table 1. We return to this shortly.

SELECTION OF A SUBSET OF MECHANISMS FOR CORPORATE GOVERNANCE

BOTH MANAGERS AND SHAREHOLDERS PARTICIPATE in selecting a set of tools for corporate governance. The cost/benefit analysis of each group should take three factors into account: the cost of each mechanism, its effectiveness and the probability of its use.

Cost of Mechanisms

Table 2 shows the various mechanisms for corporate governance, according to the nature of the costs involved (opportunity or out-of-pocket costs) and ranked by ascending order of importance, the smaller ones appearing at the top of the list. We assume these costs to be borne by the organization and therefore out of the shareholders' resources.

Board composition is the least costly mechanism for corporate governance. Appointments to the board of directors may generally be changed at negligible marginal cost. However, the cost of changing board composition is

TABLE 1

CROSS CLASSIFICATION OF THE DISTRIBUTION OF VOTING RIGHTS AND MECHANISMS FOR CORPORATE GOVERNANCE[a]

DISTRIBUTION OF VOTING RIGHTS	BOARD COMPOSITION: ratio of outside to inside members	EXECUTIVE COMPENSATION: ratio of variable to fixed remuneration	DEBT POLICY: ratio of debt to assets	DIVIDEND POLICY: ratio of dividends to earnings	TAKEOVER DEFENCES			
					POISON PILLS	CHARTER DEFENCES	STATUTORY DEFENCES	LITIGIOUS DEFENCES
Inside Concentrated Ownership	Low ratio	Low ratio for directors (may be high for second-level managers)	Low ratio	Unstable ratio	Light use	Intensive use	Intensive use	Light use
Outside Concentrated Ownership	High ratio	High ratio	Low ratio	Unstable ratio	Light use	Light use	Light use	Light use
Diffuse Ownership	High ratio (in non complex organizations)	High ratio	High ratio	Stable ratio	Intensive use	Intensive use	Intensive use	Intensive use

Note: [a] Expected level (high or low) or behaviour (stable or unstable) or intensity of use of mechanism (intensive or light) is indicated in each cell.

likely to be affected by the distribution of voting rights, *i.e.*, as we consider different lines in Table 1. Mounting a proxy fight under diffuse ownership may involve a substantial and risky investment, but may be hopeless under concentrated ownership.

Executive compensation is the next mechanism. Again, using the compensation package as a corporate governance mechanism may involve only a small or even zero opportunity cost. The amount involved is the excess of whatever remuneration the shareholders are willing to offer over the amount that would be optimal if agency problems were negligible.

Charter defences as corporate governance mechanisms may involve only small out-of-pockets costs, at least when used pre-emptively or initially (as when the corporation is first organized). Subsequent modifications to the distribution of voting rights may require the approval of shareholders.[5]

Poison pills are potentially a very costly mechanism of corporate governance, since they give the board the power to veto a takeover. The opportunity cost resides in the reduction of the expected value of a possible takeover premium. Although the amount of an eventual premium is likely to increase when the board has veto power, the probability that an offer will be extended decreases.

Statutory defences imply enlisting the coercive power of the State. This may be an involved and disruptive undertaking and, therefore, is not used frequently.[6] So far, the stock market has generally reacted to the adoption of poison pills (and other takeover defences) as if they are reducing the shareholders' wealth,[7] but the Canadian evidence is inconclusive.[8]

The dividend-to-earnings ratio may be increased to return so-called "free cash flows" to the shareholders. Such a policy may prevent takeovers, but costs may be incurred in the process. First, changes in dividend policy may affect the investors' expectations of future cash flows. Second, different payout ratios will tend to attract clienteles with different tax and consumption preferences. These investors may be deceived by unexpected policy changes, implying portfolio rebalancing costs. The costs attached to changes in dividend policy are also related to the distribution of ownership. For instance, one would expect the announcement effects mentioned above to be severe with diffuse ownership, but not with concentrated ownership.

Use of the debt-to-assets ratio as a governance mechanism generates costs similar to those of dividend policy. Assuming, for instance, that individual investors in the top tax brackets tend to buy shares of lightly leveraged companies because they prefer to capture the tax benefit of debt financing on personal account, increasing the debt-to-assets ratio for defence purposes is likely to impose more financial risk on them than they are willing to bear. The opportunity cost to the firm may also be significant if there is some validity to Williamson's (1988) conjecture that some types of assets cannot be financed through debt because of their low value as collateral. As a consequence, the strategy of changing the debt-to-assets ratio might entail constraints on asset selection and imply a suboptimal risk-return combination for the firm and

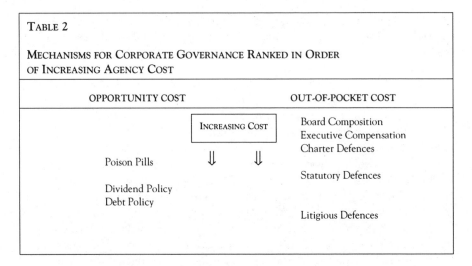

TABLE 2

MECHANISMS FOR CORPORATE GOVERNANCE RANKED IN ORDER
OF INCREASING AGENCY COST

OPPORTUNITY COST		OUT-OF-POCKET COST
	INCREASING COST	Board Composition
		Executive Compensation
	⇓ ⇓	Charter Defences
Poison Pills		
		Statutory Defences
Dividend Policy		
Debt Policy		
		Litigious Defences

portfolio rebalancing costs for the shareholders. Under concentrated ownership, for control considerations, the latter already bears unsystematic risk and may be reluctant to increase the debt-to-assets ratio. We suggest, therefore, that changes in the structure of liabilities may be a costly mechanism for corporate governance.

Finally, litigious defences appear to be a mechanism of last resort: court proceedings are disruptive and also entail direct costs. Furthermore, they are remedial, not pre-emptive. We doubt that management would propose *ex ante* to use them.

Effectiveness of Mechanisms

If effectiveness is defined as a relationship between the means to an end and the achievement of that end, then shareholders and managers do not rank mechanisms in the same order. They have conflicting interests: the managers want to maximize the private benefits they draw from control while the owners wish to maximize the present value of the residual cash flows. (These hypotheses are discussed further in the next section.)

For instance, shareholders may consider that connecting managers' remuneration packages with the market value of the firm's shares is an effective way to align the managers' interests with theirs. The managers may readily accept or choose that type of contract, but it does not reduce their risk of losing control, unless it provides them with a significant proportion of the voting rights, which is not generally the effect being sought. Therefore, although executive compensation can be an effective mechanism for corporate governance for the shareholders, it is not for the managers. We conjecture the opposite holds true for poison pills. They provide the managers with powers the shareholders could retain for themselves.[9]

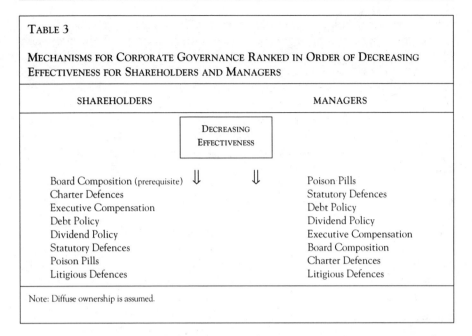

TABLE 3

MECHANISMS FOR CORPORATE GOVERNANCE RANKED IN ORDER OF DECREASING
EFFECTIVENESS FOR SHAREHOLDERS AND MANAGERS

SHAREHOLDERS	MANAGERS
DECREASING EFFECTIVENESS	
Board Composition (prerequisite) ⇓ ⇓	Poison Pills
Charter Defences	Statutory Defences
Executive Compensation	Debt Policy
Debt Policy	Dividend Policy
Dividend Policy	Executive Compensation
Statutory Defences	Board Composition
Poison Pills	Charter Defences
Litigious Defences	Litigious Defences

Note: Diffuse ownership is assumed.

In Table 3, we list the mechanisms for corporate governance according
to decreasing effectiveness for the shareholders and the directors: the rankings
are not identical.

Board composition appears as the first item on the shareholders' side
because it is a prerequisite condition to using any of the other mechanisms on
the list. Policy decisions can be implemented only through the board.

From the shareholders' point of view, charter defences appear to be quite
effective. The initial owners may have the statutes written and modified
eventually according to their preferences. Subsequent investors for whom control
considerations are important may select companies according to the jurisdiction
under which they have been created. This provides them with control over
policy decisions and the distribution of the wealth created by the firm.

We have already suggested that poison pills are not very effective from
the shareholders' point of view because shareholders tend to defend their position
by surrendering it to the managers. That is why they appear so close to the
bottom of the list on the left of Table 3, but at the top of the list on the right.

The role and effectiveness of statutory defences, from the managers'
point of view is ambiguous. As a preventive measure a statutory defence is
generally presented as a device to protect the shareholders. For instance, the
law may require a minimum number of directors to be independent,[10] or it may
stipulate that no shareholder may hold more than a given percentage of the
votes.[11] However, the *actual* effect may differ from the *intended* effect.
Restricting the exercise of voting rights may favour managerial entrenchment.
Furthermore, a number of empirical studies[12] suggest that, in the United

States, changes in the legislation designed to increase their effectiveness have tended to reduce the market value of the affected firms. Therefore, such changes were interpreted as effectively protecting the managers rather than the shareholders. Consequently, we see statutory defences as rather effective, if infrequent, mechanisms for corporate governance when employed by the managers.

We then list debt and dividend policy on the managers' side. By accepting more or less severe constraints as to the distribution of its cash flows, the firm becomes less or more susceptible to a change in control and, therefore, the risk of the managers of losing private benefits is reduced or increased.

Were it not for golden parachutes (one of its components), executive compensation would appear at the bottom of the list, on the managers' side. However, golden parachutes and similar contracts guarantee some monetary compensation in the event that private benefits are transferred to another group.

Board composition is a mechanism that managers cannot use directly but only through their influence on the shareholders, who may change it at will. Therefore, it receives a rather low rank on the managers' (right) side of Table 3.

Probability of Use

The expected value of a mechanism for corporate governance is a function of its cost, effectiveness and probability of use. We now consider this third aspect.

We suggest that the main factor affecting the probability of use is the distribution of ownership rights. Table 1 presents three cases horizontally.

A simple (albeit an extreme) case is that of the owner-managed firm, used as a starting point by Jensen & Meckling (1976). A manager who owns all the voting rights, has no need of a takeover defence. Debt and dividend policies can be selected according to portfolio-consumption needs, and executive compensation is not relevant for the owner-manager, only for subordinates. Finally, the directors are all insiders or affiliated outsiders selected according to the owner's preferences, unless nominations dictated by some debt covenant have been accepted. Specifically, it has been observed that owner-managers prefer lower debt-to-assets ratios.[13] Therefore, in this case, all the constraints on the selection of mechanisms for governance are likely to be based on operating and consumption, as opposed to control, considerations. In this regard, for the owner-managed firms, which would be part of the first line of Table 1, we would expect the observed mechanisms for governance to be combined randomly because there is a very low probability that they will be useful. This should remain so at least as long as one individual or a group of closely related individuals owns more than 50 percent of the voting rights of the firm.

In this regard, the opposite extreme is shown at the bottom of Table 1. We assume that shares have been sold to a broad spectrum of outside investors and there is no controlling shareholder. Such business entities might be expected to be relatively large and to be found mostly in the so-called transparent industries. In this case the shareholders hire professional managers who capture private benefits from control, at the owners' expense, and are motivated to exert influence on the selection of corporate governance mechanisms because they may affect their own wealth. Several consequences follow from this action. More resources should be allocated to selecting the mechanisms because two parties with conflicting interests are involved and the probability that any instrument shall be used is increased. For instance, some mechanisms, such as takeover defences, which are not useful to the owner-manager, may be seen as effective risk-reducing devices for the managers, who will negotiate their adoption by the shareholders. The behaviour of the shareholders is also likely to be affected: they now need to control and monitor the agents. Board composition and the compensation package acquire additional importance. As the shares are now owned through diversified portfolios, financial risk (*i.e.*, higher debt-to-assets ratios) may become acceptable. Finally, dividend policy should be tailored for a specific clientele and therefore remain stable. The bottom line of Table 1 summarizes the new situation.

Outside concentrated ownership represents an intermediate situation.

Behavioural Hypotheses

As we have already suggested, corporate governance inter-relates professional managers, shareholders and directors, whereas agency theory is concerned primarily with the conflicts of interests between the agents (the professional managers) and the principal (the common shareholders) who hired them to manage the firm for his benefit. Plausible assumptions can readily be made about managers and shareholders, but the directors' position is ambivalent. They cannot be classified as agents or principals unless additional information is available. We examine these questions briefly in this section. All of the players are assumed to behave opportunistically: each attempting to maximize his own utility function, subject to the constraints imposed by the other parties.

The principal maximizes his own wealth, part of which is represented by the present value of the residual cash flows derived from the firm. To achieve that objective, he attempts to monitor the managers and align their interests with his own. Various mechanisms are available to him. He may seek membership on the board of directors; he may prefer relatively high debt-to-assets and dividend payout ratios, in order to minimize the free cash flows; or he may allow the managers to increase their personal wealth by allowing or encouraging them to invest in the firm. However, none of these mechanisms is without cost. For instance, being an important shareholder increases the likelihood of that principal being appointed to the board of directors, but it also implies that otherwise diversifiable risk must be borne. Increasing the proportion of equity held by the managers may, at some level, entail entrenchment and excessive private benefits for the managers. Therefore, we expect the principal to substitute some mechanisms for others, until the desired equilibrium between monitoring and control is reached.

Agents want to maximize the private benefits they can draw from the firm. They seek retrenchment in it. Control of some voting rights, as suggested by Stulz (1988), representation on the board and adoption of takeover defences may enable them to achieve that objective. But, again, costs are involved. For instance, assuming that takeover bids can hurt the managers, but not the shareholders, the latter may object to takeover defences and "vote with their feet", i.e., sell their shares and reduce the value of the firm. Similarly, the relationship between managerial ownership and firm value need not be monotonic. It has been observed empirically[14] that, at some levels, increasing the managers' ownership may reduce firm value. Managers might also be expected to substitute mechanisms for corporate governance up to the point where their control over the free cash flows produced by the firm is still acceptable to the shareholders.

As mentioned earlier, the directors are members of a third group, whose allegiance is somewhat ambiguous. In order to classify one as an agent or a principal, two characteristics must be known: his status and the proportion of voting rights he controls. Status refers to being an inside (employee) or outside (independent) director. The former is assumed to have a larger proportion of his human capital than the latter invested in the firm. (This classification is further refined below.) In principle, an outside director owes his undivided allegiance to the shareholders and is assumed to be more likely than the inside directors to challenge a controversial decision by the CEO. However, an inside director with a significant proportion of his own financial wealth (which may nonetheless represent a negligible proportion of the total value of the firm) invested in the firm is more likely to play that role than an outside member who owns only qualifying shares. Therefore, to assess the motives of a director properly, those two characteristics must be taken into account.

With respect to the determinants of board composition, again, two propositions derive from these considerations. First, two characteristics of the distribution of voting rights are important: the *proportion* held by the directors themselves, and the *concentration* of voting rights among the remaining shareholders. An increase in the proportion owned by the directors might be expected to entail an increase in the proportion of inside members of the board, while an increase in the concentration of shares held by non-members should entail an increase in the proportion of outside directors. In this study, we assume the distribution of ownership to be exogenously determined.

Second, given the distribution of ownership (i.e., given a *line* in Table 1), substitution might be expected to occur among the various mechanisms for corporate governance. Alternatively, given a *column* in Table 1, the numerical values on each line might be expected to differ markedly. While monitoring and entrenchment represent behaviours attributed to outside shareholders and managers, respectively, substitution should characterize both groups. The outcome is that the so-called substitution hypothesis may, in principle, be held in two extreme forms.

The firms will select the combinations of mechanisms that enable them to survive and prosper, given their peculiar circumstances. If the mechanisms are literally perfect substitutes, all the possible combinations are equally effective. To the observer of a cross-section of surviving firms, they would appear as having been randomly selected. Alternatively, the mechanisms may be very imperfect substitutes, being related only as complements. If the optimal combination for each firm is unique, then, again, in a cross-section study of surviving firms, they would appear as having been randomly assembled.

The actual universe of firms is probably best described by propositions located between these two extremes; corporate control mechanisms are neither perfect substitutes nor complements. Although economic Darwinism (to use Weisbach's phrase) is felt gradually, there must be some broad generalization to be made about them. Firms in similar circumstances should have similar combinations of corporate governance mechanisms. Given that those common traits or factors have been correctly identified, their effects should be discernible empirically. The rest of this study presents such an effort with regard to the composition of the boards of directors.

BOARD COMPOSITION

THE RELEVANCE OF BOARD COMPOSITION

A LARGE PART OF THE LITERATURE dealing with board composition is focused on the cause-and-effect relationship illustrated below.

Each of the three links must be examined.

The proportion of outside[15] to inside directors is generally used as the indicator of board composition. The outsiders are seen as professional referees who assess the managers' performance, determine their remuneration and replace them if necessary. They are assumed to be loyal to the shareholders.

The mere existence of professional or outside directors provides evidence of a desire to monitor managers. However, it does not *per se* indicate that such monitoring is actually carried out or conducted efficiently. Persistence of a relatively high proportion of independent directors is consistent with at least four (not mutually exclusive) hypotheses. First, it may be a harmless practice that can persist for some time after it has become obsolete. However, one would expect it eventually to disappear and be replaced by some other mechanism for governance, unless it is actually beneficial to some of the organization's stakeholders. Second, the presence of outside directors may be useful to the shareholders who have selected, or at least accepted, them as monitors. This is the hypothesis tested by most researchers and implicitly held by the lawmakers. Third, the outside directors may, paradoxically, play a role that is useful to the managers, who account for their presence as part of the bonding costs they incur to guarantee they are not bound to expropriate the shareholders. In other words, the professional directors might first exist as creatures of the managers and continue to exist, provided their role is seen by the shareholders as indifferent. Fourth, the presence of at least some outside directors may be required by the regulatory authorities.

There is some empirical evidence in the United States that outside directors are seen by the market as monitors of the managers. The correlation between poor performance and CEO resignations is stronger with outsider-dominated boards.[16] In addition, the number of outside directors tends to increase after unsatisfactory performance.[17] Other results suggest that outside directors help control managerial consumption of perquisites and monitor banking acquisitions and are also associated with lower costs in the insurance industry.[18] Furthermore, the market also recognizes that the quality of monitoring is not constant. The senior executives of companies that reduce their dividends are less likely to receive additional outside directorships than the senior executives of companies that do not.[19] In this context, there appears to be a positive correlation between holding fewer additional outside directorships and the likelihood of being the target of a hostile takeover.[20] However, there is no evidence in Canada that board composition is related to the board's reaction to a takeover bid.[21] Another study has concluded that attention to board structure may be misplaced because managerial incentives, such as compensation, may be more efficient mechanisms for monitoring.[22]

Establishing a link between board composition and monitoring is an intermediate objective, which is interesting only to the extent that it enables us ultimately to relate board composition to overall performance. This second undertaking is more difficult because of the problem of endogeneity. It is conceivable that board composition determines performance to some extent, but it is also possible that performance is one of the determinants of board composition. First, outside directors may be drafted to improve unsatisfactory performance, as suggested above, which would be the source of measurement problems (to which we shall return). But, fundamentally, potential agents such as prestigious outside directors can minimize their professional nondiversifiable risk by accepting more readily appointments to the boards of the most profitable firms. Admittedly, on the supply side, the number of candidates for board seats is relatively large, but we expect them to display opportunistic behaviour, as do all other agents. The simultaneous relationship is suggested by the arrows in the illustration above.

These problems may explain why there is precious little empirical evidence concerning the relationship between board composition and overall performance. One study concludes that there is no relation;[23] another cautiously suggests there are some fragile nonmonotonic effects.[24] A positive relation has been detected in cross-country comparisons, not taking into account the endogeneity problem.[25]

To summarize, there is some evidence that independent directors do monitor managers (*i.e.*, the intermediate relation), but research efforts have not shown convincingly that they succeed in improving overall performance (*i.e.*, the ultimate and interesting relation). In this study, we consider both aspects.

Board composition is multidimensional. Researchers have studied the proportion of outside members, the number of directorships in other companies held by the members, the membership of the committees of the board, and the separation of the positions of CEO and Chairman of the Board. We take the first three dimensions into account. Furthermore, as suggested in Table 1, the distribution of ownership among the directors and the remaining shareholders is a determinant of board composition and its role.[26] We examine the determinants of board composition under diffuse ownership, which is our base case, and then make whatever adjustments are necessary to take into account concentrated inside and outside ownership.

DIFFUSE OWNERSHIP

Ratio of Outside to Inside Members

This dimension of board composition may be seen as a proxy for the level of monitoring of the managers by the shareholders. The concept has found its way into Canadian corporate law and several studies[27] have attempted to uncover its determinants.

We partition the board into four groups: inside, outside affiliated, group representatives and independent.

Inside directors are employees or ex-employees of the firm or of one of its subsidiaries. Following Shivdasani (1993), we define *outside affiliated* directors as members who, although not employees, have substantial business relationships with the incumbent managers.[28] Lawyers, underwriters, accountants and consultants, as well as relatives of inside directors among others, are included in this subgroup. The inside and outside affiliated members are collectively designated as "insiders". The third subgroup comprises *group representatives*. It so happens that companies having shareholders in common also tend to have interlocking directors. We classify as "group directors" board members holding directorships in other companies of the same group.[29] Finally, we classify *independent* directors as those who appear to have no relationship with the firm except for their membership on the board. The group representatives and independent directors are collectively designated as "outsiders".[30]

The level of monitoring provided by outsiders is often estimated through the sheer proportion of their membership on the board. However, their own personal characteristics are also important. The professional directors have their reputation (human capital) at risk, and the number of directorships[31] they already hold in other companies may be seen as an indicator of the value of that capital.

As the probability of their obtaining additional directorships is a function of their performance as perceived by the shareholders, it is a plausible hypothesis that outside "prestigious" directors are more likely to challenge a manager's decision because they have more to lose from unsatisfactory orientations than non-prestigious members. They offer high-quality monitoring. Weighting each director by the number of additional directorships he holds may provide a better proxy for his importance.

In the same vein, any director may have more or less influence on the board. Weighting each of them by the number of committees on which he sits may also provide a better estimator of his influence on corporate decisions.

Taking the ratio of outsiders to insiders as the dependent variable, what are the explanatory variables? We hypothesize that board composition is determined by three factors: complexity of the organization, important shareholders, and operating conditions.

Complexity of the Organization

Following Fama & Jensen (1983), we qualify as complex those organizations where the transfer of information from agents to principal (or even between agents) is costly. The more costly the transfer, the more complex the organization, and so it is more likely that decision management is separated from decision control. Such a situation calls for a high level of monitoring and, therefore, a high ratio of outsiders to insiders.

The notion of the board as a meeting place where the inside and outside directors trade information implies that the optimal board cannot be made up exclusively of insiders, even though the latter include the affiliates that small firms may find expedient to have on the board. Neither can it be composed exclusively of outsiders: at least, the CEO will be a board member, even though he may be the sole insider.[32] Furthermore, it is plausible that the marginal contribution of the outside monitors decreases, especially after their proportion exceeds 50 percent.

We assume that the determinants of complexity are the type of technology and the size of the firm. Highly developed and rapidly changing technologies make it more difficult for the shareholders to monitor the strategic decisions of managers. This opacity increases with the level of R&D activity, or the ratio of scientific and professional employees to total employees.

Complexity is also a (nonlinear) function of corporate size. Large firms are more likely to have diffuse ownership and offer "independent" monitors to

FIGURE 1

RELATIONSHIP BETWEEN THE PROPORTION OF OUTSIDE DIRECTORS
AND FIRM SIZE OR COMPLEXITY

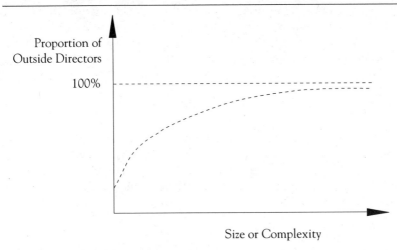

Size or Complexity

the capital market, as part of their bonding costs. To summarize, we expect the relationship between the proportion of outside board members and size or complexity to be as depicted in Figure 1.

Large Shareholders

Even under diffuse ownership, a firm may have large non-controlling shareholders other than its own directors: families, institutional investors or some other firm (hereafter referred to as blockholders). It is efficient for such investors to have their preferences known. As they have to bear some unsystematic risk, they are likely to require a relatively high level of monitoring, especially by directors who meet with their approval. The larger the number of important blockholders and their holdings, the higher the ratio of outside to inside members of the board.

Shareholdings by the inside directors are also relevant. The entrenchment hypothesis suggests that as they acquire additional shares, inside directors will seek additional seats on the board, thereby causing the ratio of outside to inside directors to fall.

Regulated firms, such as financial institutions and public utilities, represent a special case. Part of the monitoring function is taken over by the State, usually through a regulatory agency, which then plays the role of a large shareholder and explicitly or implicitly imposes a relatively large number of independent directors.[33] Given the coercive powers of the regulators, one should expect an even stronger effect than with "ordinary" important shareholders.

There is an alternative political reason why regulated firms may enroll prestigious outside directors: they may carry weight with the regulators and other representatives of the State. This is in the nature of a bonding cost incurred by the organization. Again, this reasoning suggests that regulated firms should be expected to retain the services of more outside directors. However, this effect would play in the opposite direction under the substitution hypothesis as envisioned by Demsetz & Lehn (1985). They suggest that as the monitoring function is largely taken over by the State, there is less need for outside directors.

Operating Conditions

The phrase "operating conditions" is meant to include both the return on assets and the financial policies with respect to indebtedness and dividends.

We have already suggested that the relationship between board composition and financial performance is not necessarily one-sided. However, we ignore the reciprocal character of the relationship for the moment. Even if such a restrictive assumption allows a workable description of firm behaviour, it may be difficult, empirically, to detect a relationship between firm performance and board composition. For instance, assume that firms tend to replace inside with outside directors when financial performance deteriorates. Depending upon the length of time it takes for the firm to react and the length of time it takes for the effects of the reaction to be felt, one may observe in cross-section studies that, contrary to expectations, increases in the proportion of outsiders are associated with deteriorating performance and that no relationship between the proportion of insiders and performance is detected. Panel data would be required to provide evidence on this mechanism.[34]

Nevertheless, we still expect our preliminary tests to detect a positive association between the rate of return on assets and the ratio of outside to inside directors. To abstract from industry effects, we compute relative rates of return (i.e., rates of return in excess of industry averages).

Financial policies with respect to debt and dividends may be seen as part of the operating conditions under which board composition has to be determined. On the one hand, we assume that outsiders are less likely to resist a takeover bid because it generally includes a premium for the shareholders. On the other hand, relatively high debt-to-assets[35] and dividend payout ratios will contribute to a reduced probability of a takeover offer. Therefore, under the substitution hypothesis, higher debt-to-assets and payout ratios would allow managers and inside directors to accept a higher proportion of outside directors. However, from the shareholders' point of view, the predicted association would be negative: the smaller the free cash flows, the less useful the outside directors' monitoring. But then, as the debt level rises, they might also prefer more monitoring. In addition, managers may see the various anti-takeover devices as complements rather than substitutes and tend to increase the debt-to-assets and payout ratios when they believe they are vulnerable to a takeover bid. At that point, they may also prefer to acquire additional protection[36] by reducing, or at least not increasing, the proportion of independent directors. This suggests that the relationship we are considering is ambiguous.

To summarize, under diffuse ownership we expect board composition to be explained statistically in the following manner:

Board Composition = weighted or unweighted ratio of
outsiders to insiders

= f (complexity, size, independent blockholdings, voting rights held by inside
directors, voting rights held by outside
directors, regulation, return on assets,
debt-to-assets ratio, and dividend
payout ratio) (1)

The signs in equation (1) are predicted to be positive, except for the sign attached to voting rights held by the inside directors, which should be negative; the signs attached to the financial variables are indeterminate.

CONCENTRATED INSIDE OWNERSHIP

IN THIS INSTANCE, THE CONTROL OF THE FIRM is assumed to be securely held by the managers and the inside directors. Control considerations are not important: there is little need, for instance, for takeover defences and substitution between the various mechanisms for corporate governance. The selection of board members is expected to be dictated entirely by the operating conditions. This leads one to expect the mean ratio of outsiders over insiders to be low under concentrated inside ownership. First, one would expect the inside directors to select as directors individuals with the technical skills required by the firm. For smaller firms, it may be more efficient to have some consultants as members of the board rather than to hire them on a part-time basis. The number of affiliated outside directors should then increase. Because we classify them as insiders, the ratio of outsiders over insiders would decrease. Second, we expect the firms in that group to be, on average, smaller in size. This entails a smaller proportion of outsiders on the board and also a stronger size effect, as suggested by Figure 1. Except for size and blockholders, the explanatory variables complexity, debt-to-assets ratio[37] and dividend payout discussed under diffuse ownership should not be statistically significant under concentrated inside ownership.

Under concentrated ownership, the behaviour of two explanatory variables may be especially interesting: regulation, and the rate of return on assets. If the ratio of outside to inside members is increased in response to explicit or implicit requirements of the regulatory authority, the variable regulation is expected to be statistically significant for the three types of ownership. But if it is a bonding cost incurred to satisfy the shareholders, it is expected to be significant only under diffuse ownership. Under concentrated ownership, the large shareholders are more likely to rely on their own monitoring.

A similar proposition applies to the rate of return on assets. If the outside directors "explain" the latter to some extent, this effect must be observed under the three types of ownership. Otherwise, the data are consistent with the competing hypothesis that it is the profitable firms that tend to attract the prestigious directors, whose usefulness is then greater under diffuse than under concentrated ownership.

CONCENTRATED OUTSIDE OWNERSHIP

UNDER CONCENTRATED OUTSIDE OWNERSHIP, one would expect the presence of group directors, who we have classified as outsiders, because they owe their primary allegiance to the group as a whole. That is also why the other block-holders might insist on being able to rely on their own independent outside directors. This entails a higher ratio of outsiders to insiders. Except for this consideration, the relevant statistical model should be similar to the one proposed under concentrated inside ownership.

DATA

THE EMPIRICAL PART OF THIS STUDY is based on a sample of 258 Canadian firms drawn from two sets of data.

The first set is made up of 151 observations used in a previous study of boards' reactions to takeover bids (St-Pierre et al., 1994). The data were extracted from the files of the Commission des valeurs mobilières du Québec (QSC) for the period 1978-91.[38] The shareholders of those firms all received takeover offers, 51 of which were contested by the boards of directors. We define these as hostile or disciplinary bids and classify the firms as targets. Following Morck et al. (1988a), we assume the remaining 100 observations to have no special characteristic worthy of mention. In fact, when we compared targets and non-targets with regard to all the variables used in this study, we found they were not statistically different except for the distribution of voting rights. The inside directors of target firms own a significantly lower proportion of voting rights than the directors of non-target firms.

The second set is a control sample of 107 observations drawn from the *Financial Post* (FP) files. First, a random sample of 500 firms on FP cards was examined in order to remove those subject to takeover offers, mergers or major restructuring during the five-year period ending with 1992. The analysis was based on the events as reported in the "History" section of the FP cards. A firm was discarded if there is no information concerning the members of its board of directors. The 1986 to 1988 financial statements were collected for the remaining 107 firms and added to the data bank.

BOARDS OF DIRECTORS

FOR BOTH SETS OF DATA, we examine the corporate proxy circulars, the *Financial Post's Directory of Directors* and Kofmel's *Who's Who in Canadian Business* to trace individual information about the directors. Each one is classified as:

- an *inside* director, if he is an employee or ex-employee of the firm or of one of its subsidiaries;
- an *affiliated outside* director, if he appears to be a relative of some inside director or is referred to as having some business relationship with the firm;
- a *group* director, if he owns an additional directorship in a firm of the same group, as identified by Statistics Canada;
- an *outside (independent)* director, otherwise.

The first two subgroups were designated as insiders; the last two as outsiders. We noted the number of board committees the director may sit on, the number of voting rights he and his family own or control, as well as the total number of directorships he may hold in other companies quoted on a stock exchange. (When restricted voting shares are outstanding, we took into account voting rather than ownership rights.)

COMPANIES

FOR COMPANIES, WE ALSO SEARCHED the proxy circulars, the FP cards and Statistics Canada to uncover the distribution of voting rights among the shareholders. A company was then classified as to its type of ownership:

- *inside concentrated* ownership: directors own 20 percent or more of the voting rights;
- *outside concentrated* ownership: three or fewer of the main shareholders own 20 percent or more of the voting rights;
- *diffuse* ownership: three or fewer of the main shareholders or directors do not own 20 percent or more of the voting rights.

The financial ratios and other data were computed as follows:

Dividends — ratio of ordinary dividends over book value of common shares.[39]

ROA — "excess rate of return" equal to the difference between the accounting rate of return on assets of the firm i and that of its industry j, divided by the absolute value of industry j's average rate. The averages are computed over the two fiscal years preceding the observation date.

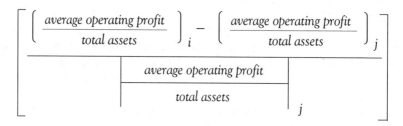

Assets   Total assets of company *i*, in Canadian 1992 dollars (*i.e.*, inflated with the Consumers' price index).

Industry   Standard industrial classification code of firm *i*, according to Statistics Canada.

Target   Dummy variable equal to one for firms having received takeover bids contested by the board, equal to zero otherwise.

D/A   Total debt-to-total assets ratio, using book values.

Managers' compensation   Ratio of variable to fixed compensation.

$$: \quad \frac{VS + VOp}{SB + DF + DC + OC}$$

where:

VS = Market value of the shares owned by the managers and their relatives

VOp = Market value of stock options that may be exercised and owned by the managers and their relatives

SB = Salary and bonus

DF = Directors' fees

DC = Deferred compensation such as fringe benefits and the firm's contributions to management savings plans

OC = Other compensations such as financial benefits from interest-free loans to managers.

The industry to which firm *i* belongs is also characterized by:

Knowledge ratio   Ratio of scientific, technical and professional to total personnel, as provided by Beck (1992).

Regulated   Dummy variable equal to one for the firms in: public utilities, communications, storage, transportation and financial services except holding companies, equal to zero otherwise.

DESCRIPTIVE STATISTICS

IN TABLES 4 AND 5 WE PRESENT SOME DESCRIPTIVE STATISTICS of the main characteristics of the 258 boards of directors we examined.

TABLE 4

**FREQUENCY DISTRIBUTION OF THE PROPORTION OF OUTSIDERS[a]
ON THE BOARD OF DIRECTORS**

	NUMBER OF COMPANIES			
PERCENT	FULL SAMPLE	DIFFUSE OWNERSHIP[b]	CONCENTRATED INSIDE OWNERSHIP[c]	CONCENTRATED OUTSIDE OWNERSHIP[d]
0 - 10	8	3	4	1
11 - 15	7	3	3	1
16 - 20	8	2	5	1
21 - 25	7	0	5	2
26 - 30	17	4	8	5
31 - 35	11	2	6	3
36 - 40	28	7	8	13
41 - 45	19	8	8	7
46 - 50	22	4	8	6
51 - 55	9	2	4	3
56 - 60	33	11	6	16
61 - 65	17	6	8	3
66 - 70	25	9	6	10
71 - 75	18	10	4	4
76 - 80	12	5	5	2
81 - 85	7	6	0	1
86 - 90	6	1	3	2
91 - 95	3	1	0	2
96 - 100	1	0	0	1
TOTAL	258	84	91	83
MEAN (%)	51	55	45	53
MEDIAN (%)	54	58	44	55

Notes: [a] Includes both the group representatives and the independent directors with no connection with the firm except for their board seats.
[b] Neither the directors nor the three main shareholders own 20% or more of the voting rights.
[c] The directors own 20% or more of the voting rights.
[d] The three main shareholders own 20% or more of the voting rights.

First, we note the numerical importance of the outsiders (Table 4). Although our definition of an outsider is somewhat restrictive, even under concentrated inside ownership only 13 percent of the firms have a ratio of outsiders to insiders equal to or smaller than 25 percent. The median is higher than 50 percent, the absolute majority, under both diffuse and concentrated outside ownership. Second, the choice of operational definitions for the four subsets of directors is important (Table 5). Some characteristics that appear to be statistically different between the three types of ownership are, however, not statistically different when the inside and outside affiliated directors are subsumed under the caption "insiders", and group and outside directors are subsumed under "outsiders", and *vice versa*.

TABLE 5

MAIN CHARACTERISTICS OF THE BOARDS OF DIRECTORS

	DIFFUSE OWNERSHIP GR 1 N=84	CONCENTRATED INSIDE OWNERSHIP GR 2 N=91	CONCENTRATED OUTSIDE OWNERSHIP GR 3 N=83	GR 1 vs GR 2 |T|	T TEST PROB.	GR 1 vs GR 3 |T|	T TEST PROB.	GR 2 vs GR 3 |T|	T TEST PROB.	OVERALL SAMPLE WILCOXON TEST X2	PROB.
Average Number on Board:											
Inside Directors	3.08	3.99	3.60	3.25	0.0014	1.66	0.1010	1.15	0.2537	8.43	0.0148
Outside Affiliated Directors	1.20	1.15	0.99	0.27	0.7868	1.23	0.2213	1.01	0.3156	1.28	0.5272
Insiders: Subtotal	4.29	5.14	4.59	2.60	0.0100	0.89	0.3730	1.50	0.1345	5.15	0.0762
Outside "Group" Directors	2.15	1.36	1.48	1.84	0.0689	1.82	0.0712	0.35	0.7247	7.06	0.0293
Independent Directors	3.80	3.56	3.81	0.55	0.5831	0.02	0.9822	0.67	0.5063	0.91	0.6337
Outsiders: Subtotal	5.95	4.92	5.29	1.83	0.0688	1.29	0.1974	0.78	0.4374	4.64	0.0981
Average Number of Positions on Board Committees by:											
Inside Directors	1.56	1.86	1.95	1.05	0.2949	1.25	0.2118	0.28	0.7763	0.42	0.8090
Outside Affiliated Directors	0.73	0.56	0.61	0.96	0.3425	0.60	0.5489	0.36	0.7189	0.12	0.9439
Insiders: Subtotal	2.29	2.42	2.57	0.36	0.7212	0.72	0.4702	0.38	0.7037	0.36	0.8348
Outside "Group" Directors	1.62	0.98	0.89	1.43	0.1550	1.95	0.0530	0.25	0.8004	7.33	0.0256
Independent Directors	2.39	1.76	2.30	1.24	0.2168	0.16	0.8720	1.29	0.1994	1.17	0.5584
Outsiders: Subtotal	4.01	2.74	3.19	1.92	0.0562	1.24	0.2167	0.83	0.4094	3.60	0.1652
Average Number of Directorships in Other Corporations by:											
Inside Directors	1.67	1.25	1.28	1.42	0.1589	1.33	0.1867	0.11	0.9107	3.25	0.1970
Outside Affiliated Directors	2.20	1.37	2.42	1.85	0.0670	0.44	0.6614	2.49	0.0147	7.19	0.0274
Insiders: Subtotal	1.87	1.34	1.46	1.80	0.0732	1.45	0.1481	0.50	0.6198	5.58	0.0613

TABLE 5 (CONT'D)

Outside "Group" Directors	3.68	3.37	2.59	0.54	0.5905	2.14	C.0350	1.67	0.0991	4.97	0.0832
Independent Directors	2.09	1.19	1.60	3.55	0.0005	1.73	C.0851	1.96	0.0522	6.78	0.0336
Outsiders: Subtotal	2.62	1.73	2.05	2.91	0.0041	1.76	0.0778	1.34	0.1813	7.61	0.0223
Average tenure on board (in years) by:											
Inside Directors	8.23	11.58	8.21	3.75	0.0002	0.02	C.9867	3.79	0.0002	17.07	0.0002
Outside Affiliated Directors	6.13	5.62	4.50	0.53	0.5984	1.68	C.0950	1.24	0.2150	2.85	0.2411
Insiders: Subtotal	10.26	9.76	9.30	0.38	0.7027	0.68	0.4979	0.35	0.7279	0.47	0.7904
Outside "Group" Directors	4.47	2.85	4.94	2.09	0.0380	0.45	0.6545	2.43	0.0163	4.77	0.0919
Independent Directors	6.87	6.24	6.36	0.80	0.4227	0.71	0.4816	0.18	0.8610	0.74	0.6893
Outsiders: Subtotal	7.44	6.59	7.36	0.64	0.5316	0.05	0.9591	0.51	0.6090	0.20	0.9052
Percentage of voting rights held by:											
Inside Directors	1.57	46.46	2.13	15.23	0.0000	0.86	C.3904	14.83	0.0000	153.37	0.0001
Outside Affiliated Directors	0.16	0.91	0.11	1.74	0.0845	0.42	C.6741	1.86	0.0644	7.89	0.0194
Insiders: Subtotal	1.73	47.37	2.24	15.80	0.0000	0.77	0.4408	15.41	0.0000	8.60	0.0136
Outside "Group" Directors	0.39	5.52	0.41	3.07	0.0025	0.07	0.9482	3.04	0.0027	2.05	0.3586
Independent Directors	0.67	3.71	0.49	3.21	0.0016	0.54	0.5895	3.46	0.0007	18.72	0.0001
Outsiders: Subtotal	1.06	9.23	0.90	4.33	0.0000	0.34	0.7349	4.39	0.0000	3.31	0.1912

Notes: Inside directors – employees or ex-employees of the company or of one of its subsidiaries.
Outside affiliated directors – relatives of inside directors and directors having some business relationship with the firm.
Outside group directors – directors holding an additional directorship in a firm of the same group.
Independent directors – all other directors.
Diffuse ownership – neither the directors nor the three main shareholders own 20% or more of the voting rights.
Concentrated inside ownership – the directors own 20% or more of the voting rights.
Concentrated outside ownership – the three main shareholders own 20% or more of the voting rights.

Not only are the outside directors more numerous under diffuse ownership, but also they occupy more positions on their boards' committees and have received more directorships in other corporations. By contrast, the inside directors enjoy longer tenures on their boards, which is related to their controlling a relatively high proportion of the voting rights. This is attributable to our partitioning our sample on that basis.

In most respects (except for percentage of voting rights held) the two groups under concentrated ownership appear not to differ significantly.

Board Composition and Monitoring

WE FIRST PROPOSE TO USE the ratio of outsiders to insiders as an indicator of the level of monitoring or the distribution of power in the firm. In other words, we suggest that, knowing the determinants of that ratio, we can infer what groups wish to monitor the managers. Equation (1) is based on the hypothesis that (holding some control variables constant) the ratio is determined by the distribution of property rights.

Preliminary Test

WE FIRST ESTIMATE OVER ALL OUR OBSERVATIONS a regression equation similar to the one presented in some contributions (probabilities in parentheses).[40]

$$
\begin{aligned}
\text{Ratio of outsiders/insiders} = {}& -1.1080 + 0.2377 \times \text{Log. assets} \\
& (0.1933)\ (0.0003) \\
& + 0.0816 \times \text{Regulated firms} \\
& (0.7632) \\
& - 0.0101 \times \text{Tenure of insiders} \\
& (0.5780) \\
& - 1.3016 \times \text{Voting rights held by inside directors} \\
& (0.0026) \\
& + 2.9065 \times \text{Voting rights held by outside directors} \\
& (0.0024) \\
& - 0.3655 \times \text{Blockholdings by non-members} \\
& (0.3647)
\end{aligned}
$$

Adjusted R^2 = 0.1179
(N = 255)

This result compares with those we have just quoted and suggests that our data are probably not substantially different from those that have been collected in the United States. The negative sign attached to the inside directors' voting rights variable is consistent with the entrenchment hypothesis, while the positive one for the outside directors' is consistent with the monitoring hypothesis. But, surprisingly, the coefficient of the blockholdings by non-members is not significant: this is not consistent with that hypothesis. One would expect the large shareholders, although they are not directly represented on the board, to prefer a relatively high ratio of outsiders to insiders. However, the equation is estimated across heterogeneous groups (*i.e.*, across three different types of ownership) and it may capture differences between groups rather than differences between firms. One possible technique that would take this effect into account is to partition the data according to the type of ownership.

Ownership and the Ratio of Outsiders to Insiders

In Table 6, we present measures of central tendency for the dependent and independent variables to be included in the regression equations. There are some significant differences between the three groups. The firms under diffuse ownership do display, on average, a higher ratio of outside to inside directors. However, they are also the largest firms, in terms of total assets, and include the highest proportion of takeover targets. In these respects, the firms with concentrated inside ownership tend to be located at the opposite end of the frequency distribution. They have, on average, lower outsider to insider ratios: companies under managerial control prefer inside directors.

In Table 7, we present a multivariate test of the model designed to explain monitoring of the managers through board composition.

First, we note that the ratio of outsiders to insiders is significantly higher for the regulated firms under diffuse ownership, regulation being represented by a dummy variable. This, however, does not apply to either type of concentrated ownership. Such a combination of results suggest that this effect is not attributable to the regulators. It is consistent with the hypothesis that the regulated firms under diffuse ownership take the initiative in composing their boards with a relatively large proportion of outsiders in response to a perceived preference of their shareholders.

The distribution of voting rights is represented by three proxies: block-holdings of non-members of the board, voting rights of the inside directors, and voting rights of the outside directors. The important shareholders who are not members of the board exert influence on board composition in the direction of increasing the ratio of outsiders to insiders. This is the effect predicted by the monitoring hypothesis. As for the inside directors, their blockholdings are negatively correlated with the dependent variable for the subset of firms with diffuse ownership. However, that regression coefficient is not significant under concentrated ownership. These results suggest that the inside directors may seek entrenchment under diffuse ownership, but have already achieved it under concentrated inside ownership and cannot achieve it under concentrated outside ownership. The voting rights held by the outside directors appear to play a significant and positive role only under concentrated inside ownership.

Size, as represented by the logarithm of total assets, has an estimated positive and significant regression coefficient, but only under concentrated

TABLE 6

MEAN VALUES OF DEPENDENT AND INDEPENDENT VARIABLES TO BE USED IN THE REGRESSION EQUATIONS OF TABLES 7, 8 AND 9

	DIFFUSE OWNERSHIP (N=84)	CONCENTRATED INSIDE OWNERSHIP (N=91)	CONCENTRATED OUTSIDE OWNERSHIP (N=83)	KRUSKAL-WALLIS TEST	
				X²	PROB.
[Outsiders / Insiders]	1.8786	1.2952	1.6529	10.471	0.0053
[Outsiders * Other Directorships]/ [Insiders * Other Directorships]	3.7701	3.3801	3.2797	0.765	0.6823
[Outsiders * Board Committees]/ [Insiders * Board Committees]	2.3287	1.6011	1.7330	3.994	0.1392
Ratio of Technical and Professional to Total Personnel, for Industry[a]	25.0083	24.9879	26.6277	2.909	0.2335
Regulated Firms (%)[b]	19.0476	18.6813	19.2771	0.01C	0.9949
Blockholdings Non-members (%)[c]	0.0339	0.0496	0.5705	187.77C	0.0001
Hostile Takeover Targets (%)[b]	32.1429	14.2857	13.2530	12.01C	0.0025
Debt-to-Assets Ratio	0.5553	0.5522	0.5198	1.476	0.4780
Total Assets (1992) ($000)	1,779,946	690,703	1,065,061	8.653	0.0132
Dividends over Book Value of Common Equity[d]	0.0241	0.1376	0.0232	0.392	0.8221
Excess Rate of Return on Assets	1.2533	2.4838	1.1094	1.824	0.4018

DEFINITIONS AND NOTES TO TABLE 6

Definitions	Diffuse ownership – neither the directors nor the three main shareholders own 20% or more of the voting rights.
	Concentrated inside ownership – the directors own 20% or more of the voting rights.
	Concentrated outside ownership – the three main shareholders own 20% or more of the voting rights.
	Outsiders – includes both the group representatives and the independent directors.
	Insiders – includes employees and ex-employees of the firm and its subsidiaries and affiliated outside directors.
	Excess rate of return on assets – difference between the firm's average rate of return on assets and its industry's, divided by the absolute value of the industry's average rate.
Notes:	a As provided by Beck (1992).
	b As a percentage of the number of firms.
	c Held by the three largest shareholders non-members of the board, as a percentage of total voting rights outstanding.
	d The median values for the three groups are 0.0262, 0.0263 and 0.0241, respectively.

inside ownership. This is consistent with the relationship summarized in Figure 1. The firms classified under diffuse ownership are the largest, on average, and occupy the top flat section of the curve. To a lesser extent, this is also true for the corporations with concentrated outside ownership, while those with concentrated inside ownership are on the rising portion of the curve and still at the stage of increasing their ratio(s) of outsiders to insiders.

The excess of the firm's average rate of return on assets to that of the firm's industry appears to be significant and positive under diffuse ownership, but not under either type of concentrated ownership. This is not consistent with the hypothesis that outside directors have a discernible favourable effect on performance, because we would then expect that regression coefficient to be positive and significant under all three types of ownership. Rather, it is consistent with the joint hypotheses that relatively profitable firms find it easier to attract professional directors and that the latter represent some form of bonding cost incurred under diffuse ownership.

Finally, we note that our tests provide no evidence in favour of some substitution between the proportion of outsiders on the board and financial control devices such as the debt-to-assets and dividend ratios. Negative signs for those coefficients would have been implied by the substitution hypothesis.

The ratio of technical and professional to total personnel (knowledge ratio) designed as a proxy for complexity is not significant. This may be due to measurement errors: the ratio is computed for the industry, not the firm. It is also tenable that this effect may have been captured by the size variable.

Under concentrated outside ownership, the regression equation has no explanatory power. This is consistent with the hypothesis that ownership is so concentrated that board composition can be adapted precisely to the shareholders' preferences and opportunities. Therefore, no empirically detectable regularities exist.[41]

TABLE 7

REGRESSION OF THE RATIO OF THE NUMBER OF OUTSIDERS
TO THE NUMBER OF INSIDERS[a]

INDEPENDENT VARIABLES	DIFFUSE OWNERSHIP (N=81)	CONCENTRATED INSIDE OWNERSHIP (N=89)	CONCENTRATED OUTSIDE OWNERSHIP (N=79)
Intercept	−1.6663 (0.3106)	−1.7815 (0.1333)	4.4529 (0.0693)
Ratio of Technical and Professional to Total Personnel, for Industry	0.0211 (0.1768)	−0.0219 (0.0246)	−0.0141 (0.4359)
Regulation: Dummy =1 if Regulated, = 0 Otherwise	1.1413 (0.0326)	−0.5579 (0.1397)	−0.2796 (0.6390)
Blockholdings, Non-members of Board (%)	9.1052 (0.0040)	2.6494 (0.0522)	−2.1819 (0.0704)
Voting Rights of Inside Directors (%)	−12.0389 (0.0307)	−0.5394 (0.3710)	−2.5981 (0.5593)
Voting Rights of Outside Directors (%)	−5.7211 (0.4076)	4.3219 (0.0001)	−5.2642 (0.4910)
Target: Dummy = 1 if Target of Hostile Takeover, = 0 Otherwise	0.0881 (0.8278)	0.2591 (0.4742)	−0.5911 (0.3577)
Debt-to-Assets Ratio	0.7210 (0.3383)	0.7465 (0.2458)	−0.6783 (0.5760)
Log (Total Assets)	0.1511 (0.2423)	0.2476 (0.0075)	−0.0386 (0.8109)
Dividends over Book Value of Common Equity	−0.0727 (0.9720)	−0.0789 (0.5210)	−3.0291 (0.2114)
Excess Rate of Return on Assets	0.3031 (0.0018)	−0.0008 (0.9675)	0.0087 (0.8475)
R^2	0.3983	0.4636	0.1078
F-value	4.700 (0.0001)	6.828 (0.0001)	0.834 (0.5978)

Notes: [a] Probabilities in parentheses.
For definitions, see Definitions and Notes to Table 6.

Tentatively, the main lesson to be drawn from Table 7 is that, under diffuse and concentrated inside ownership, board composition is determined by the distribution of property rights as represented by blockholdings. As the most interested parties persist in appointing directors of their own kind, they must believe they are deriving net benefits from that course of action.[42] However, this does not necessarily imply that such perceived advantages can induce a detectable positive correlation between the rate of return on assets and board composition. We now turn to that question.

BOARD COMPOSITION AND PERFORMANCE

THE QUESTION OF INTEREST IS: can corporate performance, as measured by the rate of return on assets, be explained partially by its governance mechanisms in general and board composition in particular? To answer this question, we use the excess rate of return on assets as our dependent variable.

ONE-EQUATION MODEL

WE FIRST HYPOTHESIZE THAT THE excess rate of return is associated statistically with three factors: corporate governance mechanisms, financial variables and a number of control variables. All the variables already appear in Table 1.

The first governance mechanism we consider is the distribution of ownership. We expect large shareholders to be involved in monitoring activities (in addition to influencing board composition) that result in improved financial performance. On the other hand, managers or inside shareholders are expected to capture private benefits that depress performance as seen by the residual owners. In the same vein, the regulatory authorities are seen as monitors whose allegiance is to the consumers, rather than to the owners, unless they are captured by the industry. Whether or not regulation improves performance is a moot point. The type of managerial compensation is expected to be a powerful tool to improve performance because it is designed to tie the managers' interests to the shareholders' interests. Board composition is the last element of the governance mechanisms.

The second factor includes financial variables. The negative relationship between the debt-to-assets ratio and the accounting rate of return is well documented:[43] the larger the earnings, the more likely the firm is to reduce its debt. Therefore, we need the debt-to-assets ratio as a control variable and expect a negative sign. However, the notion of indebtedness as a mechanism for governance suggests that the managers left with smaller free cash flows are forced to concentrate on capital expenditures whose net present value is positive. This would imply a positive relation between the excess rate of return and the debt-to-assets ratio. By similar reasoning, one also expects a positive relation between the excess rate of return and the ratio of dividends to the book value of common equity.

TABLE 8

REGRESSION OF THE RATIO OF THE FIRM'S RATE OF RETURN ON ASSETS [a]

INDEPENDENT VARIABLES	DIFFUSE OWNERSHIP (N=81)	CONCENTRATED INSIDE OWNERSHIP (N=89)	CONCENTRATED OUTSIDE OWNERSHIP (N=79)
Intercept	−1.6282 (0.3671)	9.4191 (0.1871)	−3.9241 (0.5316)
Ratio of Technical and Professional to total Personnel, for Industry	0.0032 (0.8649)	0.0784 (0.1808)	0.0177 (0.7107)
Regulation: Dummy = 1 if Regulated, = 0 Otherwise	−0.0222 (0.9724)	2.9404 (0.1792)	−1.1286 (0.4829)
Blockholdings, Non-members of Board (%)	−6.1296 (0.0943)	−19.0639 (0.0183)	3.0404 (0.3395)
Voting Rights of Inside Directors (%)	0.5631 (0.9323)	0.0355 (0.9913)	−6.7114 (0.6157)
Target: Dummy = 1 if Target of a Hostile Takeover, = 0 Otherwise	−0.1755 (0.7032)	1.0836 (0.6157)	−0.5079 (0.7703)
Debt-to-Assets Ratio	−0.2254 (0.7967)	−1.2302 (0.7492)	−1.7163 (0.5919)
Log (Total Assets)	−0.0609 (0.6648)	−0.6819 (0.2529)	0.2785 (0.5061)
Dividends Over Book Value of Common Equity	0.3658 (0.8806)	−0.3334 (0.6505)	13.4372 (0.0599)
Board Composition: Ratio of Outsiders to Insiders	0.3888 (0.0043)	0.4452 (0.4688)	0.0678 (0.8314)
Managers' Compensation: Ratio of Variable to Fixed Compensation	0.0003 (0.1575)	−0.0046 (0.7748)	0.0933 (0.1645)
R^2	0.1836	0.1228	0.1144
F-value	1.597 (0.1253)	1.105 (0.3686)	0.879 (0.5572)

Notes: [a] Probabilities in parentheses.
For definitions, see Definitions and Notes to Table 6.

The third factor controls for operating conditions and complexity, as represented by size and the knowledge ratio, and vulnerability to takeovers. One expects the firms with lower accounting rates of return to be more likely to become targets of hostile takeovers.

To summarize, we propose to test the following statistical model:

Excess rate of return = f (insiders' blockholdings, outsiders' block holdings, type of managers' compensation, board composition, regulation, debt-to-assets ratio, dividend-to-book-value ratio, size, knowledge ratio, and takeover target) (2)

The results of this regression, by type of ownership, are presented in Table 8.

As in some recent studies,[44] this ordinary least squares estimate suggests a significant relation between board composition and performance, albeit for only the diffuse ownership case. This is consistent with the proposition that the role played by the outside directors is a function of the type of ownership. However, if the outsiders did explain performance, we would also expect board composition to be significant under concentrated outside ownership. In fact, we may not be observing a cause-and-effect relationship because ownership and board composition may be endogenous to performance. That problem is considered in Table 9.

SIMULTANEOUS-EQUATIONS MODEL

IN TABLE 9, WE ESTIMATE SIMULTANEOUSLY EQUATIONS (1) AND (2). Using the two-stage least squares method, we estimate simultaneously the determinants of board composition and of the excess rate of return. The results are as follows.

Again, we find that board composition, under diffuse ownership, is determined by the distribution of voting rights: the ratio of outsiders to insiders rises with the blockholdings of non-members and falls with those of the directors. Such behaviour is consistent with the monitoring and entrenchment hypotheses, respectively. However, the excess rate of return on assets variable becomes non-significant. Moreover, board composition also becomes a non-significant explanatory variable of the return on assets. These new figures provide no reason to alter the tenor of our earlier conclusions. Our data suggest that board composition is seen as important to the large shareholders, who attempt to monitor the managers, but do not display any detectable association between performance[45] and board composition.

TABLE 9

SIMULTANEOUS (DOUBLE-STAGE LEAST SQUARES) REGRESSIONS OF THE RATIO OF OUTSIDERS TO INSIDERS AND THE EXCESS RATE OF RETURN ON ASSETS[a]

INDEPENDENT VARIABLES	DIFFUSE OWNERSHIP (N=81)		CONCENTRATED INSIDE OWNERSHIP (N=89)		CONCENTRATED OUTSIDE OWNERSHIP (N=78)	
	RATIO OF OUTSIDERS TO INSIDERS ON BOARD	EXCESS RATE OF RETURN ON ASSETS	RATIO OF OUTSIDERS TO INSIDERS ON BOARD	EXCESS RATE OF RETURN ON ASSETS	RATIO OF OUTSIDERS TO INSIDERS ON BOARD	EXCESS RATE OF RETURN ON ASSETS
Intercept	-1.7024 (0.3356)	-2.9421 (0.7888)	3.9958 (0.7992)	10.0311 (0.1807)	4.4566 (0.1198)	-7.0268 (0.6704)
Ratio of Technical and Professional to Total Personnel, for Industry	0.0171 (0.3395)	0.0625 (0.6520)	0.0272 (0.8376)	0.1038 (0.1076)	-0.0143 (0.4435)	0.0279 (0.6921)
Regulation: Dummy = 1 if Regulated, = 0 Otherwise	1.0012 (0.1012)	3.1212 (0.6611)	0.9769 (0.8190)	3.2788 (0.1556)	-0.2709 (0.6736)	-0.8965 (0.6585)
Blockholdings, Non-members of Boards (%)	10.2764 (0.0078)	11.7309 (0.7717)	-10.1524 (0.7613)	-23.3915 (0.0104)	-2.1846 (0.1225)	4.7040 (0.5921)
Voting Rights of Inside Directors (%)	-10.7583 (0.0866)	-30.4106 (0.6654)	0.9208 (0.8404)	3.4416 (0.4238)	-2.5750 (0.5687)	-4.5890 (0.7921)
Voting Rights of Outside Directors (%)	-8.1186 (0.3286)	—	10.2022 (.5147)	—	-5.2470 (.4980)	—
Target: Dummy = 1 if Target of a Hostile Takeover, = 0 Otherwise	0.2050 (0.6640)	-0.2642 (0.8134)	0.9220 (0.6909)	0.3377 (0.8847)	-0.5869 (0.3658)	-0.0647 (0.9817)
Debt-to-Assets Ratio	0.7851 (0.3360)	1.3229 (0.7417)	0.6263 (0.8231)	-2.2451 (0.5845)	-0.6781 (0.5977)	-1.0792 (0.8134)

TABLE 9 (CONT'D)

INDEPENDENT VARIABLE	DIFFUSE OWNERSHIP (N=81)		CONCENTRATED INSIDE OWNERSHIP (N=89)		CONCENTRATED OUTSIDE OWNERSHIP (N=78)	
	RATIO OF OUTSIDERS TO INSIDERS ON BOARD	EXCESS RATE OF RETURN ON ASSETS	RATIO OF OUTSIDERS TO INSIDERS ON BOARD	EXCESS RATE OF RETURN ON ASSETS	RATIO OF OUTSIDERS TO INSIDERS ON BOARD	EXCESS RATE OF RETURN ON ASSETS
Log (Total Assets)	0.1236 (0.3942)	0.4104 (0.7079)	-0.2525 (0.8510)	-0.9935 (0.1384)	-0.0388 (0.8454)	0.2760 (0.5294)
Dividends over Book Value of Common Equity	-0.2274 (0.9192)	0.8971 (0.8800)	-0.3021 (0.6999)	-0.2171 (0.7796)	-3.1733 (0.4919)	15.8957 (0.2613)
Excess Rate of Return on Assets	0.6154 (0.2133)	—	-0.7181 (0.6973)	—	0.0108 (0.9681)	—
Board Composition: Ratio of Outsiders to Insiders	—	-2.0234 (0.7050)	—	2.1401 (0.1403)	—	0.8846 (0.8249)
Managers' Compensation: Ratio of Variable to Fixed Compensation	—	0.0010 (0.5220)	—	-0.0158 (0.4022)	—	0.0933 (0.1844)
R^2	0.3182	0.0195	0.0455	0.1301	0.1046	0.1054
F-value	3.313 (0.0014)	0.141 (0.9990)	0.377 (0.9533)	1.181 (0.3162)	0.794 (0.6343)	0.801 (0.6278)

Notes: [a] Probabilities in parentheses.
For Definitions, see Notes to Table 6.

PUBLIC POLICY

WHAT LESSONS CAN WE LEARN from this discussion? To determine that, compare the objectives of the *Canada Business Corporations Act* (CBCA) with the empirical evidence assembled here.

We take it that the objective of the Act is to create an environment such that efficient governance mechanisms are available and corporate resources are allocated to the best alternative use. As we have been unable to uncover a strong association between overall performance and board composition, we cannot suggest stringent regulation in that area.[46] However, we do have evidence that under diffuse ownership, both inside and outside blockholders seek to secure representation on the boards of the companies in which they have invested. That is evidence of a desire to monitor managers on the part of those who are best motivated to do so efficiently. We suggest that lawmakers might facilitate this in two ways.

First, we have observed that the apparent ratio of outside to inside directors may differ markedly depending on the more-or-less-restrictive definition of an outside director. The objective being that at least some members of the board be truly independent of the managers, we suggest that the definitions and regulations of the insurance legislation[47] be also made part of the CBCA: that affiliated outside directors not be counted as independent directors. Second, our empirical work takes into account the distribution of voting, as opposed to ownership, rights. Those two distributions differ to the extent that restricted voting shares have been issued. In order to increase the owners' monitoring ability, it would be desirable for cumulative voting to become mandatory when some outstanding shares have restricted voting rights.

On a purely intuitive basis, it might be considered desirable that the proportion of outside directors be increased, and that the directors' remuneration be tied more closely to the value of the firm and to the directors' attendance at board meetings. As trends in these directions have already been observed in the United States,[48] there is probably little risk and equally little gain in putting them on the statute books. Finally, one effective but controversial rule would be to require directors to have a non-negligible part of their personal wealth invested in the firm they monitor. Such a measure would have to be based on the *a priori* belief that self-interest provides powerful incentives. This would not necessarily be seen as a feasible or even desirable piece of legislation, however.

CONCLUSIONS

THE EMPIRICAL RESULTS OF THIS STUDY can be summarized as follows. Our data are consistent with the proposition that board composition is a function of the distribution of voting rights. First, our simple statistical model partly explains the differences in board composition under diffuse and concentrated inside ownership, but not under concentrated outside ownership. Second, the influence of the blockholders who are not members of the board moves in the direction of increasing the ratio of outsiders to insiders. This is consistent with the hypothesis of a desire to monitor the managers. The influence of the block-holders who are also inside directors moves in the opposite direction, suggesting that they seek entrenchment.

These results also suggest that board composition is perceived as important and that large shareholders attempt to monitor managers – but they do not necessarily succeed in doing so efficiently. However, to the extent that it is not costless, such behaviour would not have persisted unless it is of some benefit to those who engage in it. In that sense, our data provide some indirect evidence of a relationship between board composition and performance, but we have been unable to uncover any direct evidence of that relationship.

Our statistical model does not explain board composition under concentrated outside ownership. The firms in our subsample behave as if the combination of mechanisms for corporate governance were unique to each one of them, or, paradoxically, as if they are unimportant.

Only under diffuse ownership is the ratio of outsiders to insiders higher for the regulated firms. This is not consistent with the hypothesis of substitution between regulation and board composition, but rather suggests that managers seek the services of outside directors as a bonding expenditure to assure the shareholders that they are bound not to expropriate them.

We find no evidence that debt and dividend policies are substitutes for board composition, or that the latter is an effective takeover defence.

Overall, the evidence provided in this study suggests that both *monitoring* and *entrenchment* forces are at work in this sample.

ENDNOTES

1 Title of an essay by Jensen & Warner (1988).
2 See Stangeland (n.d., Appendix) for a description of 11 anti-takeover devices.
3 The behaviour of Inco Limited (1988) is a good example of the simultaneous use of several governance mechanisms. In 1988, after an especially profitable year, it adopted a shareholder rights plan (poison pill), paid a special dividend of $10.00 (as opposed to a regular dividend of $0.20) and almost doubled its long-term debt. However, this restored it only to its former level, where it remained afterwards. The out-of-pocket cost of the operation was $10 million.
4 Not all takeover defences have to be approved by the shareholders (see Stangeland).

5 If the plan calls for a special resolution, under the *Canada Business Corporations Act*, it must be passed by a majority of not less than two-thirds of the votes cast (Canada, 1985).

6 The best-known case in Canada is Bill C-131 drafted by the federal government to prevent accumulation of shares of Canadian Pacific Company.

7 Malatesta (1992, p. 636).

8 Halpern (1990).

9 In the Inco case, summarized in note 3, the Caisse de dépôt et placement du Québec, a large institutional investor, went to court to have the shareholders cast two, rather than one, vote: one on the special dividend and one on the poison pill. In at least one other case, the regulation was eventually diluted (Alcan). In another case (John Labatt) the resolution was defeated by the shareholders.

10 For instance, the *Canada Business Corporations Act* requires corporations with shares issued to the public to have at least two outside directors. (See Canada 1985, par. 23-427.)

11 For instance, the *Canada Bank Act* sets to 10 percent the upper limit of the proportion of voting rights that may be held by any given shareholder in a Schedule A bank.

12 See Brickley *et al.* (1988), Pound (1992), Wahal *et al.* (1993).

13 Friend & Lang (1988).

14 Morck *et al.* (1988b) and McConnell & Servaes (1990).

15 The operational notion of outside director is discussed below.

16 Weisbach (1988).

17 Hermalin & Weisbach (1988).

18 Brickley & James (1987) for the banking, and Mayers *et al.* (n.d.) for the insurance industries.

19 Kaplan & Reishus (1990).

20 Shivdasani (1993).

21 St-Pierre *et al.* (1994).

22 Beatty & Zajac (1994).

23 Hermalin & Weisbach (1991).

24 Barnhart *et al.* (1994).

25 Li (1994).

26 Thain & Leighton (1991).

27 For this section, the most useful papers have been: Baysinger & Butler (1985), Brickley & James (1987); Weisbach (1988); Morck, Shleifer & Vishny (1988b); Beatty & Zajac (1994); and Occasio (1994).

28 The notion of affiliated members has also been retained in laws such as those legislating insurance companies. Teolis *et al.* (1992; section 172 relates to inside directors, who may represent no more than 15 percent of the directors, and section 171 relates to affiliated persons, who may represent no more than two-thirds).

29 Groups are identified in Statistics Canada, *Inter-Corporate Ownership*, cat. 61-517.

30 In several studies, "grey" directors include all the board members who could not be classified as inside or independent directors. Amoako-Adu & Smith in their study of Canadian boards (n.d.) make use of the concept of outside financial directors.

31 See, for instance, Cotter *et al.* (1994), and Kaplan & Reishus (1990).

32 Jensen (1993) argues that the only inside board member should be the CEO and that boards should not get beyond seven or eight people.

33 Compare note 10 with note 28, for instance.

34 Hermalin & Weisbach (1988), and Weisbach (1988).

35 Chenchuramaiah *et al.* (1994) have examined the inverse relationship between debt and managerial ownership.

36 For evidence that firms may adopt that behaviour, see Pound (1992) and Wahal *et al.* (1993).

37 We do mean to imply that debt-to-assets and dividend payout ratios are independent of the distribution of ownership. Empirical studies suggest that both are lower under concentrated inside ownership (Friend & Lang, 1988, and Eckbo & Verma, 1994). For tax reasons, the payout ratio should be higher when the main shareholder is a taxable Canadian corporation.

38 Note that these files cover all the firms that have sold securities to Quebec investors and are not restricted to firms based in Quebec.

39 We use as the denominator the book value of the common stocks rather than current earnings in order to remove the random component of the latter. (Book value of common stock includes the cumulative value of reinvested earnings. The ratio we use is an accounting estimate of dividend return.)

40 See Weisbach (1988, p. 448) or Beatty & Zajac (1994, p. 328).

41 We also ran the regressions using the ratio of outsiders to insiders weighted by the number of committees or directorships in other corporations as the dependent variables. Under diffuse ownership, total assets and block-holdings, but not regulation, remain as statistically significant explanatory variables. These variables are not significant for the two groups with concentrated ownership. As the models appear to have no explanatory power, they are not presented here.

42 Not only do the main shareholders persist in nominating outsiders, panel data suggest that the trend is increasing over time (SpencerStuart, 1993). Admittedly, this evidence from the United States is relevant to the diffuse ownership case.

43 Harris & Raviv (1991), Gagnon *et al.* (1987). Harris & Raviv argue that there is no relation between debt and control.

44 See Li (1994).

45 This statement also applies to alternative measures of performance, such as Tobin's Q, with which we have experimented.

46 For a similar conclusion, see Baysinger & Butler (1985).

47 The relevant sections are referred to in note 28.

48 SpencerStuart (1993).

ACKNOWLEDGEMENTS

WE HAVE RECEIVED MOST USEFUL COMMENTS from Randall Morck, Lee Gill and an anonymous referee. However, they cannot be held responsible for whatever shortcomings that remain.

BIBLIOGRAPHY

Amoako-Adu, B. and B. F. Smith. "Outside Financial Directors and Corporate Performance: An Aspect of Corporate Governance." Manuscript, Wilfrid Laurier University, undated.

Barnhart, S. W., M. W. Marr and S. Rosenstein. "Firm Performance and Board Composition: Some New Evidence." *Managerial and Decision Economics*, 15 (1994):329-40.

Baysinger, B. D. and H. N. Butler. "Corporate Governance and the Board of Directors: Performance Effects of Changes in Board Composition." *The Journal of Law, Economics and Organizations*, 1,1 (Fall 1985):101-24.

Beatty, R. W. and E. J. Zajac. "Managerial Incentives, Monitoring and Risk Bearing: A Study of Executive Compensation, Ownership, and Board Structure in Initial Public Offerings." *Administrative Science Quarterly*, 39 (June 1994):313-35.

Beck, N. *Shifting Gears: Thriving in the New Economy*. Toronto: Harper Collins Publishers Ltd., 1992.

Brickley, J. A. and C. M. James. "The Takeover Market, Corporate Board Composition, and Ownership Structure: The Case of Banking." *Journal of Law and Economics*, 30, 1 (April 1987):161-80.

Brickley, J., R. Lease and C. W. Smith. "Ownership Structure and Voting on Antitakeover Amendments." *Journal of Financial Economics*, 20 (1988):267-91.

Canada. *Business Corporations Act with Regulations*. Don Mills, ON: CCH Canadian Limited, 1985 6th ed.

Chenchuramaiah, T. B., K. P. Moon and R. P. Rao. "Managerial Ownership, Debt Policy, and the Impact of Institutional Holdings: An Agency Perspective." *Financial Management*, 23, 3 (Autumn 1994):38-50.

Commission des valeurs mobilières du Québec. *Bulletin de statistiques*. Montreal, biannual.

Cotter, J. F., A. Shivdasani and M. Zenner. "The Effect of Board Composition and Incentives on the Tender Offer Process." University of Iowa, March 1994.

Demsetz, H. and K. Lehn. "The Structure of Corporate Ownership: Causes and Consequences." *Journal of Political Economy*, 93 (1985):1155-77.

Eckbo, B. E. and S. Verma. "Managerial Shareownership, Voting Power, and Cash Dividend Policy." *Journal of Corporate Finance*, 1, 1 (1994):33-62.

Fama, E. and M. C. Jensen. "Separation of Ownership and Control." *Journal of Law and Economics*, 26 (June 1983):301-25.

Financial Post Directory of Directors, The Financial Post Information Service, Toronto, updated annually.

Financial Post Survey of Industrials (on cards), The Financial Post Information Service, Toronto, updated continually.

Friend, I. and L. H. P. Lang. "An Empirical Test of the Impact of Managerial Self-Interest on Corporate Capital Structure." *The Journal of Finance*, 43, 2 (June 1988):271-81.

Gagnon, J-M., Suret, J-M. and J. St-Pierre. "Asymétrie de l'information, fiscalité et endettement au Canada." *Finance*, 8, 1 (1987):75-103.

Halpern, P. "Poison Pills: Whose Interests Do They Serve?" *Canadian Investment Review*, 3, 1 (Spring 1990):57-66.

Harris, M. and A. Raviv. "The Theory of Capital Structure." *The Journal of Finance*, 46, 1 (March 1991):297-355.

Hermalin, B. E. and M. S. Weisbach."The Determinants of Board Composition." *The Rand Journal of Economics*, 19, 4 (Winter 1988):589-606.

_____. "The Effects of Board Composition and Direct Incentives on Firm Performance." *Financial Management*, 20, 4 (Winter 1991):101-12.

Inco Limited. "Notice of Special Meeting." Toronto, November 7, 1988.

Jensen, M. C. "The Modern Industrial Revolution, Exit and the Failure of Internal Control Systems." *The Journal of Finance*, 48, 3 (July 1993): 831-80.

Jensen, M. C. and W. H. Meckling. "Theory of the Firm: Managerial Behavior, Agency Costs and Ownership Structure." *Journal of Financial Economics*, 3, 4 (1976):305-60.

Jensen, M. and J. B. Warner. "The Distribution of Power Among Corporate Managers, Shareholders and Directors." *Journal of Financial Economics*, 20 (1988):3-24.

Kaplan, S. N. and D. Reishus. "Outside Directorships and Corporate Performance." *Journal of Financial Economics*, 27 (1990):389-410.

Kofmel, K. G. (ed.). *Who's Who in Canadian Business*. Toronto: Trans-Canada Press, Toronto, updated annually.

Leighton, D. and D. Thain. "The Role of the Corporate Director." *Business Quarterly* (Autumn 1990):20-24.

Li, J. "Ownership Structure and Board Composition: A Multi-Country Test of Agency Theory Predictions." *Managerial and Decision Economics*, 15 (1994):359-68.

Malatesta, P. "Takeover Defences," in *The New Palgrave Dictionary of Money and Finance*. Edited by P. Newman, M. Milgate and J. Eatwell. New York: The Stockton Press, 1992, Vol. III, pp. 633-36.

Mayers, D., A. Shivdasani and C. W. Smith. "Board Composition in the Life Insurance Industry", undated manuscript.

McConnell, J. J. and H. Servaes. "Additional Evidence on Equity Ownership and Corporate Value." *Journal of Financial Economics*, 27 (1990):595-612.

Morck, R., A. Shleifer and R. W. Vishny. "Characteristics of Targets of Hostile and Friendly Takeovers," in *Corporate Takeovers: Causes and Consequences*. Edited by A. J. Auerback. Chicago: The University of Chicago Press, 1988a.

_____. "Management Ownership and Market Valuation, an Empirical Analysis." *Journal of Financial Economics*, 20 (1988b):293-315.

Occasio, W. "Political Dynamics and the Circulation of Power: CEO Succession in U.S. Industrial Corporations, 1960-1990." *Administrative Science Quarterly*, 39, (June 1994): 285-312.

Pound, J. "On the Motives for Choosing a Corporate Governance Structure: A Study of Corporate Reaction to the Pennsylvania Takeover Law." *Journal of Law, Economics and Organization*, 8, 3 (1992):656-72.

Rosenstein, S. and J. G. Wyatt. "Outside directors, Board Independence, and Shareholder Wealth." *Journal of Financial Economics*, 26 (1990):175-91.

Salant, R. "Board Expansions: Inside vs Outside Directors Firm Size and Market Reaction", Manuscript, Mankato State University, March 1993.

Shivdasani, A. "Board Composition, Ownership Structure and Hostile Takeovers." *Journal of Accounting and Economics*, 16 (1993):167-98.

SpencerStuart. *SpencerStuart Board Index, 1993 Proxy Report*. Board trends and practices at 100 major companies, Montreal, 1993.

St-Pierre, J., J-M. Gagnon and J. Saint-Pierre. "Takeover Bids, Structure of Ownership and Board Composition," Working Paper #DAE-1994-02, Université du Québec à Trois-Rivières.

Stangeland, D. A. "Issues in Corporate Control and the Performance of Corporations", Unpublished Ph.D. dissertation, University of Alberta, Edmonton, Alberta.

Statistics Canada. *Inter-Corporate Ownership*. Ottawa: Supply and Services Canada, cat. 61-517, occasional.

Stulz, R. M. "Managerial Control of Voting Rights." *Journal of Financial Economics*, 20 (1988):25-54.

Teolis, J. W., J. S. Graham and J-P. Bernier. *Financial Institutions Reform Package: Phase Three, New Insurance Legislation Annotated*. Don Mills: CCH Canadian Limited, 1992.

Thain, D. H. and D. S. R. Leighton. "Ownership Structure and The Board." *Canadian Investment Review*, 4, 2 (Fall 1991):61-65.

Wahal, S., K. W. Wiles and M. Zenner. "Who Opts Out of State Antitakeover Protection." University of North Carolina at Chapel Hill, October 1993.

Weisbach, M. S. "Outside Directors and CEO Turnover." *Journal of Financial Economics*, 20 (1988):431-60.

Williamson, O.E. "Corporate Finance and Corporate Governance." *The Journal of Finance*, 43, 3 (July 1988):588-91.

Ramy Elitzur & Paul Halpern*
Faculty of Management
University of Toronto

5

Executive Compensation and Firm Value

INTRODUCTION

THE NEW REGULATION REQUIRING REPORTING of dollar compensation for CEOs has become a catalyst for discussions about the extravagance of corporations and at some social gatherings a subject for lively conversation. However, on its own, this development is not very useful in understanding the role of compensation in corporate activity. The issue is usually framed in the context of U.S. capital markets in which the widely held corporation is the norm. In that scenario, the growth of U.S. corporations has led in many cases to a separation of managers and owners and to difficulties in the effective monitoring of managers by owners and their representatives, including boards of directors. It is also argued that employees, executives, directors and owners usually do not share the same goals. This conflict of interest occurs when the interests of the managers of a firm (who are interested in their own compensation) are not aligned with the interests of the owners (who are interested in the value of their investment); this is referred to as the "agency problem". Compensation systems in which managers' rewards are related to performance (which, in turn, is of value to shareholders) can be used to ameliorate the agency problem. If the system for executive compensation is not well designed, it will cause the corporation to deviate from its shareholder value-maximization goals and subsequently reduce the value of the company. The debate in the U.S. literature does not argue with the use of compensation incentives to elicit appropriate performance. Rather, it questions whether executive compensation is sufficiently sensitive to changes in shareholder wealth to elicit the correct behaviour by management.

The debate in the United States, and its framing in the context of the widely held corporation, leaves a Canadian audience bemused because in Canada, the widely held corporation is the exception rather than the rule. Many have commented on the number of widely held companies in Canada. A company is defined as widely held if there are no blocks of voting shares in excess of 15 percent of the outstanding equity.[1] In 1993 there were 90 companies defined as widely held on the TSE 300 Composite Index.

In fact, the typical Canadian company can be described as closely held. At one extreme, the owner of a firm has a significant equity interest in the company, either directly or indirectly. In some cases, the majority owner is a member of the founding family of the company. In these circumstances the owner may have direct managerial input as the CEO or indirect control though his or her position on the board of directors. In either case, management is entrenched. Although it could be argued that their large equity interest will lead these individuals to maximize share value and that compensation schemes to align interests are unnecessary, there is empirical evidence consistent with entrenched management making decisions that will maximize personal utility, not share value.[2]

Another more serious form of entrenchment is the dual-class share structure in which an individual or group of individuals, most frequently the members of the founding family, have a majority of the voting (or superior voting) shares and a small number of the non-voting (or restricted voting) shares. This share structure usually arises when the founder wishes to cash out a major portion of his or her position yet still maintain control. The resulting structure, where the individual has a controlling position in the voting equity but a small percentage of the overall equity of the firm, has the potential for serious agency costs of equity and protection from the discipline of the takeover market. The agency cost of equity arises when management can undertake non-wealth-maximizing decisions for which they bear only a small part of the cost through the effect on the share price.

Unlike the case of the widely held company, entrenched management may have a very different view of executive compensation, its form as cash or share-price related, and its role in generating wealth for investors. For example, in a closely held company, in which management already has a large proportion of the total equity, decisions affecting the value of the equity will be reflected in personal wealth. Thus, compensation schemes that are based on share-price performance may not be necessary; a scheme using more cash through salaries and even less cash through bonus payments related to performance, could be more beneficial to these individuals. Similarly, in the dual-class share structure, owners may have a small stake in the overall equity of the firm. By providing more compensation linked to equity, appropriate incentives may be provided to maximize share price. However, since owners control the firm through their control of the voting shares, there is no incentive for them to introduce these equity-based schemes, since this would reduce their ability to gain through the agency cost of equity based on their small holdings.

The importance of the relationship between compensation and firm performance, as well as the amount of compensation to the CEO and top management, recently became an important issue in Canada with the amendment to the *Ontario Securities Act* governing disclosure of executive compensation for Ontario issuers. The new disclosure requirements increase both the breadth and the depth of the disclosure obligation. Under the new disclosure rules, the issuer must disclose compensation in detailed form for the CEO and the four most highly paid executives, in addition to the CEO. This disclosure must include annual compensation (salary, bonus, and other forms of short-term rewards) and long-term compensation (options, stock appreciation rights, restricted shares, etc.). However, for a number of years, companies interlisted on U.S. exchanges have been required to provide similar disclosure on executive compensation. When the Multi-Jurisdiction Disclosure System (MJDS) was implemented in 1990, Canadian interlisted companies could choose to continue reporting under U.S. regulations or to use their home-country documents, which had fewer onerous executive compensation disclosure requirements.[3] With the new Ontario regulations, those companies choosing to use their home-country documents will now have generally to satisfy the same disclosure requirements concerning executive compensation as found in U.S. jurisdictions.

Since the change in Ontario is quite recent, there is limited scope to undertake empirical research on the relationship between compensation and firm-specific variables, and compensation and wealth creation. Based on our analysis of cash compensation and firm-specific variables, however, our results are similar to those found in other studies with respect to the influence of company size but they differ significantly when the focus is on the influence of firm-specific performance variables. Unlike other studies, we have broken the sample into two sub-samples based on ownership concentration; a sample of companies that are widely held and a sample of companies that are closely held. Regardless of the ownership concentration, there is a strong positive relationship between salary and total compensation and firm size. However, contrary to findings in other studies, performance measured either by accounting-, cash-flow- or market-based variables has no effect on the level of bonus, salary or total compensation for either closely held or widely held firms. We also investigated the determinants of the percentage change in compensation and found no relationship to performance variables.

Compensation was positively influenced by the existence of a poison pill variable and the interlisting status of the firm. There is some evidence that the effect of these variables is stronger for the closely held sample. Finally, a persistent difference in the relationship of closely held and widely held firms is the importance of persistence in the percentage change in cash compensation. For the closely held companies, the constant term is positive and significant for both bonus and salary, whereas for the widely held firms, it is significant for only the salary component.

In the first two sections of this study we review the effects of executive compensation on the incentives of managers with particular emphasis on the incentive effects associated with different compensation practices. The linkage between the theory and testable hypotheses is presented in the next section. Then we identify the actual compensation practices of the sample of Canadian companies with respect to cash compensation – salary and bonus.[4]

The relationships among cash compensation, total and bonus and salary components, and firm-specific characteristics are presented in the next section, followed by our conclusions.

THE EFFECTS OF COMPENSATION PLANS ON MANAGERS' INCENTIVES

THE LITERATURE IN THIS AREA has expanded greatly since the early 1980s, coinciding with the growth in the takeover market and the recognition that these transactions are a way to discipline management whose interests are not aligned with those of shareholders.[5] There are a number of studies that identify a positive relationship between the introduction of short- and long-term incentive-based compensation schemes and announcement period share-price increases (Bhagat et al., 1985; Brickley et al., 1985; Larcker, 1983; and Tehranian & Waegelin, 1986). The firm-specific performance measures used are both accounting- and market-based.

Of particular interest for the present study is the relationship between compensation and the financial performance of companies. The existence and strength of this relationship provides information on the managerial incentives in place to assist in the alignment of shareholder and manager interests. The literature identifies two general questions related to compensation and performance. The first considers the relationship of compensation to underlying financial characteristics of the firm, with "compensation" defined as cash compensation, including salary and bonus, plus deferred compensation, such as options, (although many of the articles consider only the cash compensation). The financial characteristics are related to size of company and performance, measured from both accounting- and market-based perspectives. These papers find that compensation is related to both size and market-based performance of the equity of the firm. Some researchers (Murphy, 1984; Gibbons & Murphy, 1990; and Kaplan, 1994) investigate compensation for upper level executives of the firm, either the CEO alone or the top executives. Other researchers, such as Leonard (1990) and Abowd (1990), consider a larger group of managers, and different factors have been introduced to explain executive compensation such as equity ownership by executives and the existence of major blockholders, including institutional holdings (Mehran, 1995). In addition, if the definition of compensation is broadened sufficiently to include top executive turnover, many studies have noted that turnover is significantly related to return on assets, stock returns, and operating income, and this relationship exists across a number of countries (Gibbons & Murphy, 1990; Kaplan, 1994; and Kang et al., 1995).

The second set of studies considers the effect of incentive compensation schemes on management behaviour. At one extreme, the studies consider the influence of incentive compensation on firm performance in subsequent periods.

If incentive compensation is intended to align the interests of shareholders and managers, the performance of the firm should be related to incentives introduced in the compensation scheme. The research to this point is consistent with a positive relationship between incentive compensation and future firm performance. Abowd (1990) identifies in a large sample of managers the sensitivity of compensation to specific performance measures and determines the relationship between this sensitivity and the future period performance of the particular variable. He finds that accounting-based performance measures yield weaker results than performance measures based on the ratio of cash flow to replacement cost of assets and on stock rate of return. Mehran (1995) finds that firm performance, measured as either Tobin's Q or return on assets, is related to the percentage of compensation that is equity based and inversely to cash compensation.

At the other extreme there are studies that examine the relationship between incentive compensation plans and non-shareholder value maximizing managerial behaviour to improve their wealth. Watts (1977) and Watts & Zimmerman (1978) argue that bonus schemes create an incentive for managers to select accounting policies that boost the present value of their awards. Examples of this behaviour are noted by Dhaliwal *et al.* (1982) with respect to the choice of depreciation accounting, and by Hunt (1985) in the choice of inventory valuation models when considering owner-managed firms compared to non-owner-managed firms. Healy (1985) detects a strong association between accruals and managers' income-based incentives under a bonus contract. Kamin & Ronen (1978) report that owner-managers are less likely to smooth income than non-owner-managers. Finally, Elitzur & Yaari (1994) suggest that the choice of an executive incentive compensation plan by owners affects earnings manipulation undertaken by managers.

Based on the literature on incentive compensation, such plans should meet the following objectives.

- Enhance goal congruence between shareholders and executives, leading to the enhancement of shareholder wealth.

- Reinforce informative reporting, i.e, ameliorate earnings manipulation.

- Strike a balance between the long-range strategy and the short-term goals of the firm.

The pay instruments commonly used in the design of incentive compensation plans are as follows:

- **Cash Bonuses** These take four forms: profit sharing, profit sharing with a hurdle, target plans, and target plans with a threshold.

Under a profit-sharing plan the bonus is a percentage of divisional profit after a deduction of a capital charge. Sometimes the cash bonus is calculated as a percentage of divisional profit in excess of the budgeted income, denoted as profit sharing with a hurdle. Under a target plan the executive is paid cash as a function of pre-set targets; under a target plan with a threshold, the cash is paid only in a certain interval of the performance measure.

- **Stock Options** A stock option is a right to buy a number of shares in the company at a given price at some future period.

- **Stock Purchase Plans** A very popular form of incentive compensation in which executives can buy shares in the company at a discount.

- **Phantom Shares** Sometimes the company awards executives shares for bookkeeping purposes only, *i.e.*, the executives do not actually own shares, but for the purpose of calculation of incentive payments they are viewed as if they do. At the end of a specified period of time the executive is paid on the basis of stock performance. This payment can be in cash, in shares, or a combination of both.

- **Performance Shares** Shares are awarded to executives when specific long-term goals have been attained. The goals can be either corporate, divisional, or individual. Performance shares are rarely observed in Canada.

- **Performance Unit Plan** An arrangement similar to performance shares, except that, on achievement of given targets, the executive receives specially valued units and not shares. Consequently, this manner of compensation has the same advantages and drawbacks as performance shares.

- **Formula Value Stock Plan** Under this alternative, the executive receives some shares that are not traded publicly, the value of which is calculated according to a formula. This formula can be based on accounting variables or other long-term measures of performance. In this way, a formula value stock plan very much resembles performance shares or a performance unit plan.

- **Restricted Stock** In this case, the executive receives shares in the company at a discount or, sometimes, at no cost. The shares awarded cannot be transferred until certain conditions are met.

When the conditions are met, the restrictions are lifted and executives can do with the shares whatever they please. (For example, an executive can transfer these shares only after a specific period of continuous employment with the company.) Restricted stocks are not common in Canada because they are not tax effective (for either the company or the executive), and they are restricted by the Toronto Stock Exchange (TSE).

- **Stock Appreciation Rights (SARs)** With SARs, the executive is paid based on the appreciation of a specified number of shares. SARs have characteristics similar to phantom shares.

The attributes of these incentive-based compensation instruments are summarized in Table 1.[6]

THE THEORY OF EXECUTIVE INCENTIVE COMPENSATION DESIGN

THE DESIGN OF THE OPTIMAL incentive compensation scheme stems from the Principal-Agent model (see Appendix 1 for a description of the theory behind optimal compensation schemes).

Under this model a principal hires an agent to run the firm. The principal's payoff is a function of some outcome less the cost of compensating the agent. The outcome and, in turn, the principal's payoff, depend on the agent's effort and some random state of nature (which can describe, for example, exogenous economic conditions). According to the model, the observation of both outcome and the state of nature is not enough to reveal how much effort the agent has expended.

In the model the agent's payoff is derived from compensation less the disutility of effort. In this sense, effort is costly from the agent's viewpoint because it involves the opportunity cost due to the sacrifice of leisure time and so forth. The choice of effort is made in a manner that optimizes the agent's payoff.

The principal decision on the optimal compensation scheme must take into account both the agent's choice of effort, as described in the paragraph above, and the motivation of the agent to stay with the firm.

The model implies that optimal compensation should follow this formula:

Compensation = Fixed Compensation + Variable Compensation

The fixed component of compensation should depend on the agent's reservation payoff, *i.e.*, how much the agent can receive elsewhere. The variable component of compensation should be non-decreasing in outcome. If the agent is risk-neutral the variable component of compensation is a constant multiplied by outcome, *i.e.*, compensation becomes a linear equation.

Table 1
Attributes of Various Pay Instruments

Instrument	Pay for Performance	Informative Reporting	Aligning Interests of Executives with Shareholders	Lead to Short-term Orientation	Cash Outflow for the Company	Dilution of Equity	Tax Effectiveness
Cash Bonus	+	–	+	–	–	++	–
Stock Options	+/–	+/–	+	++	++	–	+
Stock Purchase Plan	–	+	+	++	++	–	+
Phantom Shares	+/–	+/–	+	++	–	++	–
Performance Shares	++	0	++	++	+	+	0
Performance Unit Plan	++	0	++	++	+	+	0
Formula Value Stock Plan	++	0	++	++	+	+	0
Restricted Stock	+/–	0	+	++	+	–	–
Stock Appreciation Rights	+/–	+/–	+	++	–	++	–

Note: ++ Effective
         +   Somewhat Effective
         0   Unclear
         /   In-between
         –   Weak

LINKING THE THEORY OF EXECUTIVE COMPENSATION DESIGN TO TESTABLE HYPOTHESES

THE THEORY OF EXECUTIVE COMPENSATION DESIGN provides some interesting insights. First, it implies that there should be a positive correlation between compensation and outcome. Hence, it follows that compensation should increase with performance. Second, the theory implies that optimal compensation in the setting above involves a constant, **w**, which relates to the manager's reservation utility.

While quite elegant and providing many intuitive implications for compensation, the theory is remarkably silent on the definition of compensation and how performance is to be measured. Considering compensation, the possibilities include salary, cash bonus, and equity awards as described in the previous section. Mehran (1995) presents evidence that is consistent with the board of directors taking into consideration executives' total incentives in designing pay packages. Thus, executives who have large holdings of the equity of the company that they manage (more frequently the case in Canada than in the United States), will likely have less equity-based compensation and more cash compensation. Therefore, all forms of compensation should be used. By omitting equity-based compensation, an observation that cash compensation is unrelated to performance does not lead to the conclusion that compensation is unrelated to firm performance, since the influence may be found in the omitted variable. However, data restrictions are often particularly important in determining the measure of compensation actually used. In this study we use cash compensation, in total and separately for bonus and salary, and do not use option-related compensation (due to data problems).

There are a great many definitions of performance, based on both market and accounting information. The measures can be based on various forms of reported income (net income, operating income and so forth), sales, assets, cash flow (operating cash flow, for example) in either levels, changes, or ratios. Also, stock market returns can be used. In this study we use both accounting- and market-based performance measures, since one of our purposes is to identify the variables that appear to be relevant in the Canadian context. The choice of variables used in this study is conditioned by the variables used in the literature.

According to the theory of optimal incentive contracts, **w** is related to a manager's reservation utility. We would therefore expect that heads of large companies make a high marginal contribution to production. Their ascent to the top echelons of the firm as successful winners of an internal corporate labour-market competition, suggests that top executives will demonstrate clearly the talents necessary to direct a large corporation and that these scarce talents are best utilized by having them near the top of the organization. The talent of senior managers is magnified by spreading their responsibility and control over long chains of command and scales of operation.

The existence of this scarce factor suggests a high reservation utility to top executives and with this high opportunity cost comes a high wage. Also, since the success of a top executive can be readily observed in the performance of the company, it is possible that competing companies may be willing to pay the executive based on the company's current performance. Thus, not only should cash (salary) compensation be related to the size of the organization but also there may be a standard to which the reservation payoff, **w**, is related.

This standard could be related to whether or not the company is interlisted on U.S. markets. Since we control for industry and size, any effect of interlisting could reflect the added responsibility of managing a company which trades securities in the United States. Alternatively, managers (and their compensation consultants) may use U.S. firms as their comparison group and thus have higher salaries on average. The interlisting effect is measured by using a dummy variable, which takes on the value of unity if the company is interlisted over the period of consideration and zero otherwise.

We also control for other exogenous factors that relate to the existence of entrenchment. The first variable identifies whether the company had a poison pill over the period of interest and takes the value of unity if a poison pill is in existence and zero otherwise. Typically, a poison pill is introduced into firms in which shares are widely held and management ownership in the equity of the firm is small. The result of the poison pill, although open to debate (Comment & Schwert, 1993), is to provide management with the power to decide on the success of a takeover bid, thus leading to potential entrenchment. In our sample, a number of firms that meet the closely held definition also have poison pills. This reflects the fact that, although technically closely held, the ownership structure does not eliminate the threat of a takeover. In terms of compensation, there can be offsetting effects. If the poison pill is not an entrenchment device and managers' interests are to be aligned with share-holders' interests, the low levels of managerial equity ownership suggest that total compensation would be composed of greater equity linked instruments. If, on the other hand, the pill does result in entrenchment, management can increase its salary and bonus without undue concern to the incentive effects. This influence would lead to a positive influence in the relationship of cash compensation and poison pills. Unfortunately, without the equity linked compensation, we cannot test for the first implication of the poison pill.

The second entrenchment influence is the dual-class share structure, and this is identified as a dummy variable with the value of unity if dual-class shares are present. This variable is found in the closely held sample. The typical company with dual-class shares is one in which the founder retains some equity ownership through voting shares, but need not be active in the management of the firm. If the founder/controlling shareholder, along with other members of the family, is in the top management team, there may be no need to provide incentives through equity-based compensation since management already has equity ownership, although this conclusion will depend upon the size of management's equity position. However, holders of superior class voting shares may not want to increase their equity exposure. Also, with entrenchment, the cash part of compensation will be higher. The result would be an increase in cash compensation in the presence of dual-class shares.

EXECUTIVE COMPENSATION IN PRACTICE

THIS SECTION CONSIDERS the current compensation practices of Canadian companies based on a sample of 180 companies on the TSE 300 Index. The period of analysis relates to the companies' fiscal year which occurred between January 1993 and March 1994. The description of the database and the data sources are presented below; the characteristics of the compensation information follow; and the section ends with the regression results and analysis.

DATA

UNDER THE 1993 REVISION to the *Ontario Securities Act* (OSA), companies with securities traded in Ontario must complete Form 40, "Statement of Executive Compensation", which requires the company to report the compensation for the CEO and for each of the company's four executive officers (other than the CEO) who receive the highest compensation. The only exception to the reporting requirement is for an executive officer whose cash compensation, both salary and bonus, does not exceed $100,000. The company must supply information on the salary, bonus and long-term and deferred compensation for each of the company's last three financial years. The compensation covered includes options, stock appreciation rights and long-term incentive plans.

In addition, the executive compensation report requires filing the five-year rate of return on the common equity of the company, with dividends reinvested and the rate of return on a broad index, with dividends included, over the same period.

Finally, and probably most interesting, there is the requirement under Item *ix* that the policies used by the compensation committee to determine the compensation of executive officers must be described for the most recent financial year. The report must include a discussion of the specific relationship of corporate performance to executive compensation. Also, if an award was made to an executive officer whose compensation must be reported under a performance-based plan, despite failure to meet the relevant performance criteria, the company must disclose the bases for the decision to waive or adjust the relevant performance criteria.

While these disclosures identify a company's rationale for compensation payments, they are not required for any compensation decisions prior to January 1, 1994. This covers the bulk of our sample of 180 companies. Also, there is some evidence that these disclosures are not very helpful. The same disclosure requirements must be met by companies listed in the United States.

Form 40 is included in the proxy material that is released approximately three months after the fiscal year end. The basic data was provided to us by KPMG who entered the numerical contents of the proxy statements they received. In addition we obtained balance-sheet and income-statement data from the *Financial Post* files and share-price and dividend data from both the *Toronto Stock Exchange Review* and the *Financial Post* files.

We calculated the average value of compensation for the top five executives for each company in the sample for the two most recent financial years. If the company did not report compensation for five executives we removed it from the sample. The companies covered 14 industries, but one industry was removed since it had only one company. Consequently, we were left with 180 companies in 13 industries.

Our data set includes cash compensation, salary and bonus, and does not at this time include the deferred compensation and long-term incentive plans. As noted above there are some problems with the quality of the reported deferred compensation numbers, but as this data is improved it will be used in future research. Certainly, the omission of this part of executive compensation results in an incomplete picture of a company's compensation philosophy and of the tradeoffs that may be made between cash and deferred compensation. The use of the cash component of compensation is not unique to this study (see Abowd, 1990; Gibbons & Murphy, 1990; and Leonard, 1990, among others).

In order to take into consideration the unique characteristics of the Canadian market, we break the sample into two parts: companies that are widely held and all others. To be widely held, a company should not have any blocks of shares owned that are greater than 15 percent of the outstanding equity. In the case of dual-class shares, we look at the concentration of holdings of the voting shares. Using this definition we obtain 131 companies that were not widely held and 49 that were widely held. The former group is called "closely held" in our study, but there need not be a control position in place. Table 2 presents some comparative statistics for the two groups of companies.

Table 2 shows that, as a percentage of the number of companies in each group, widely held companies are interlisted and have poison pills more often than the closely held companies. In addition, except in one case, dual-class share structures are found in closely held companies. In our sample, of the 131 companies in the closely held sample, 24 percent had dual-class share structures. There was no difference in the existence of negative earnings in the prior fiscal year, which was 24 percent of the sample for both groups.

Compensation Characteristics

In Table 3, Panel A, we show summary statistics on the levels and changes in cash compensation by bonus and salary and the sum of the two elements for the total sample, the closely held and the widely held sub-samples separately. Considering levels first, it is clear that for the total sample, cash compensation

TABLE 2

CHARACTERISTICS OF CLOSELY HELD AND WIDELY HELD COMPANIES

	CLOSELY HELD (131 COMPANIES)		WIDELY HELD (49 COMPANIES)	
	NUMBER	PERCENTAGE	NUMBER	PERCENTAGE
Negative Earnings	31	24	12	24
Interlisted	36	27	21	72
Poison Pill	8	6	10	20
Dual-Class Shares	31	24	1	2

through salary is higher and has less variability than compensation through bonus. The average value for salaries is $258,000 whereas the average value for bonus is $87,000. We also observe that the distribution for bonus is more highly skewed than the distribution for salaries. These observations are consistent with the use of salaries to reflect reservation utility and bonus to be related in some way to performance, although salaries may be related to longer-term performance. We also compare the two sub-samples and observe that the means and standard deviations for all compensation categories are greater for the closely held sample than for the widely held sample. Also, the distributions for all compensation forms are more skewed for the closely held companies.

The changes in the components of cash compensation are presented in Panel B of Table 3 and show a consistent pattern. While the average value of the changes in bonus and salary for the total sample is approximately the same, roughly $19,000, the variability in the distribution of changes is much larger for the bonus than for the salary categories. Also, the cash bonus distribution is negatively skewed, whereas for the change in salaries it is positively skewed. These observations are again consistent with the bonus reflecting some element of performance whereas salaries appear to be less sensitive to this effect.

Looking at the two sub-samples, there are some interesting differences between the changes for the closely held and widely held sub-samples. For the former, the pattern of means, standard deviations, and skew is very similar to the total sample results. However, the widely held sample is different. The mean change for bonus is less than the mean change for salary. The standard deviation for change in bonus is greater than the standard deviation of the change in salary just as in the closely held sample, but the values of the standard deviations for both compensation categories are smaller. Also, there is positive skewness in the change in the bonus, unlike the case of the closely held company in which the skew is negative.

TABLE 3

SUMMARY STATISTICS FOR CASH COMPENSATION BY COMPONENT FOR TOTAL SAMPLE AND TWO SUB-SAMPLES

PANEL A - LEVELS					
	MEAN (000)	STANDARD DEVIATION (000)	SKEW	MINIMUM (000)	MAXIMUM (000)
TOTAL SAMPLE					
Bonus	86.7	143.0	4.98	0	1,312.0
Salary	258.4	129.9	2.21	100.0	956.1
Total Compensation	345.1	220.0	2.72	107.5	1,541.0
CLOSELY HELD					
Bonus	93.3	158.0	4.86	0	1,312.0
Salary	261.9	138.0	2.34	100.0	956.1
Total Compensation	355.2	236.0	2.77	107.5	1,541.0
WIDELY HELD					
Bonus	69.1	90.7	2.08	0	388.9
Salary	249.3	106.0	0.96	109.9	516.9
Total Compensation	318.4	170.4	1.494	109.9	886.5

PANEL B - CHANGES					
TOTAL SAMPLE					
Bonus	18.9	103.7	−0.20	−484.5	531.0
Salary	19.0	34.6	6.86	−16.8	376.0
Total Compensation	37.9	112.1	0.34	−465.0	551.5
CLOSELY HELD					
Bonus	22.2	110.0	−0.44	−484.5	531.0
Salary	21.0	39.0	6.26	−16.8	376.0
Total Compensation	43.2	119.0	0.14	−465.5	551.5
WIDELY HELD					
Bonus	10.1	84.8	1.03	−270.8	360.1
Salary	13.7	15.1	1.10	−13.1	61.7
Total Compensation	23.9	89.2	1.19	−239.6	389.3

Table 4 presents the means and standard deviations of the cash compensation elements by industry class. The industry classification with the largest number of companies in our sample is Oil and Gas with 39 firms, and the classifications with the smallest number of firms are Transportation and Environmental Services and Real Estate, with three firms each. For every industry classification, the average salary in the industry was greater than the average bonus value. The ratio of average salary to bonus ranged from a high value of 8.8 times for the

TABLE 4

SUMMARY STATISTICS FOR CASH COMPENSATION BY INDUSTRY CATEGORY

INDUSTRY (TSE 300 CATEGORY)		MEAN COMPENSATION (STANDARD DEVIATION IN BRACKETS)			
	NUMBER OF FIRMS	BONUS ($000)	SALARY ($000)	RATIO (Salary/Bonus)	TOTAL ($000)
1. Metals & Minerals	7	75.2 (111.2)	259.2 (99.1)	3.4	334.4 (165.6)
2. Gold & Silver	13	80.9 (103.8)	225.8 (110.0)	2.8	306.7 (163.4)
3. Oil & Gas	39	39.4 (47.6)	191.4 (67.7)	4.9	230.8 (94.1)
4. Paper & Forest Products	13	73.5 (97.8)	240.3 (97.8)	3.3	313.8 (97.8)
5. Consumer Products	16	118.0 (215.1)	258.3 (150.8)	2.2	376.3 (356.3)
6. Industrial Products	28	75.0 (79.1)	250.7 (86.5)	3.3	325.7 (123.6)
7. Real Estate	3	33.1 (39.9)	289.8 (86.4)	8.8	322.9 (125.5)
8. Transportation & Environmental Services	3	82.4 (35.3)	255.8 (33.6)	3.1	338.1 (62.4)
9. Utilities	14	84.1 (59.6)	214.8 (84.7)	2.6	298.9 (138.8)
10. Communications & Media	18	102.9 (54.9)	452.1 (277.7)	4.4	555.0 (305.2)
11. Merchandising	12	75.1 (73.4)	320.1 (153.4)	4.3	395.2 (164.9)
12. Financial Services	18	170.8 (315.1)	302.7 (114.2)	1.8	473.5 (328.6)
13. Conglomerates	6	204.6 (236.6)	413.4 (165.0)	2.0	618.0 (345.4)

Real Estate industry to a low of 1.8 times for the Financial Services industry. Since Real Estate has few observations, the next highest ratio is 4.9 times for the Oil and Gas industry. This ratio could depend upon a number of factors, including the viability of the industry (e.g., Real Estate) and the extent to which there are other forms of performance-related compensation such as

SARs, and options and top management ownership of equity securities, which would result in a low ratio. In this study we have not controlled for these factors.

Average total cash compensation by industry ranges from a low of $230,000 in the Oil and Gas Industry to a high of $618,000 in the Conglomerate segment. Next we investigate the relationship of compensation to size and performance variables.

RELATIONSHIP OF COMPENSATION AND FIRM-SPECIFIC VARIABLES

COMPENSATION SHOULD BE RELATED to many factors, such as responsibility, size of firm and company performance, among others. As we have noted, managerial talent and productivity and the ability to manage a large organization are scarce factors which should receive compensation related to the size of the organization. This compensation is typically in the form of salaries. However, top executives should also be compensated through incentive schemes, since their decisions have an effect throughout the organization. This implies that cash bonuses will be related not to size but to company performance. This relationship is confused somewhat when the ownership structure of the firm is taken into consideration. For example, when a firm is widely held the normal relationship between performance and compensation is as described. However, if the firm is closely held and the owner/manager has substantial personal holdings in the equity of the firm, the salary compensation may be higher to reflect the fact that incentives based on share-price performance are not needed and may, in fact, increase the owner/manager's exposure to stock price variability, thereby generating more risk-averse behaviour.

We now consider the relationship of cash compensation, measured as bonus, salary and total compensation, with both performance and firm-size variables, along with other firm-specific variables including entrenchment variables such as the existence of poison pills and dual-class share structures. Since this is the first analysis of Canadian data, we will relate our observations to those observed in studies using data from other countries.

COMPENSATION AND FIRM SIZE

GIVEN THE DIFFERENCES IN OWNERSHIP STRUCTURE found in the sample of firms, the analysis will consider closely held and widely held firms separately; the results of the widely held sample will be most relevant in comparisons with studies undertaken on U.S. data.

Table 5 presents the results of regressing the components of compensation and total compensation on corporate size variables, measured by assets and sales and other firm-specific variables, both for widely held and closely held samples. In the regressions all dollar variables are measured as the natural logarithm of the specific variable. With this specification, the regression coefficient on the size variable is interpreted as an elasticity measure where an increase of, say, ten percent in the size variable is associated with a specific percentage increase in compensation.

We also consider the influence of additional firm-specific variables on cash compensation. If the bonus is related to performance, we would expect the size of the bonus to be related to the existence of negative earnings measured as net income during the fiscal year. This variable is measured as a dummy variable, taking the value 1 if net income is negative and zero otherwise. There are 12 companies in the widely held sample and 31 in the closely held sample with negative net income in the fiscal year. If salaries reflect opportunity cost of managers or long-term (not short-term) performance, there should be no significant relationship with this variable. We also include dummy variables to identify interlisting status, the existence of a poison pill, and the existence of dual class shares in the closely held company sample. The dummy variables take the value of 1 if the company has the particular characteristic and zero otherwise.

A number of studies have investigated the relationship between compensation and size and the results are summarized in Rosen (1990) and in Milgrom & Roberts (1992). These studies find that the elasticity for total cash compensation ranges in the small interval .2 to .25, using sales as the size variable. This result is sufficiently robust over countries and different samples that the result has been called a compensation "constant". In Table 5, Panel A, the elasticity of total compensation for widely held companies is .164 when size is measured by sales and .161 when size is measured by assets. This result is slightly lower than noted in other studies and is statistically significant. Thus for a 10 percent increase in size in our sample, measured either as sales or assets, there is an increase of approximately 1.6 percent in total compensation. For the closely held sample in Panel B, the elasticity measure is higher at .19 for sales and .17 for assets.

We also consider the effect of firm size on the components of total cash compensation. If, as noted above, the salary component is related to the opportunity cost of managing large firms, then the coefficient on the size variable for salary compensation should be positive. Considering the bonus, if there is a performance-based element, then the relationship to firm size may still be positive – a successful firm based on shareholder value criteria may have growth in sales and/or assets – but it is likely to be an indirect and hence less significant effect. In columns 2 and 5 of Panel A in Table 5, we observe that for widely held companies, salary is positively and significantly related to firm size with a coefficient of approximately .14. Notice that the constant term is statistically significant, suggesting that there is a fixed element in the salary relationship which is independent of size effects. The observed relationship with bonus found in rows (1) and (4) while positive, is not statistically significant using either assets or sales as the measure of firm size. For the closely held firms in Panel B, the elasticity of salary with respect to firm size is greater than that observed in the widely held sample; the values range between .17 and .18. The constant term remains positive and statistically significant. For the bonus

TABLE 5

COMPENSATION RELATED TO SIZE AND OTHER FIRM-SPECIFIC VARIABLES

PANEL A - WIDELY HELD COMPANIES

	(1) BONUS	(2) SALARY	(3) TOTAL COMPENSATION	(4) BONUS	(5) SALARY	(6) TOTAL COMPENSATION
Constant	2.370 (0.550)	10.485[a] (39.827)	10.363[a] (32.046)	7.686 (1.633)	10.204[a] (40.220)	10.199[a] (29.739)
Sales	0.462 (1.425)	0.138[a] (6.984)	0.164[a] (6.745)	—	—	—
Assets	—	—	—	0.047 (0.147)	0.145[a] (8.354)	0.161[a] (6.829)
Negative Earnings	−3.119[b] (−1.974)	0.077 (0.802)	−0.027 (−0.230)	−2.619[c] (−1.653)	0.140 (1.639)	0.055 (0.475)
Interlisted	1.111 (0.814)	0.056 (0.667)	0.106 (1.039)	0.866 (0.623)	0.039 (0.518)	0.081 (0.804)
Poison Pill	1.472 (0.880)	0.000 (0.001)	−0.023 (−0.182)	1.781 (1.050)	0.082 (0.900)	0.076 (0.611)
$\bar{R}^2$	0.046	0.521	0.479	0.003	0.610	0.486

PANEL B - CLOSELY HELD COMPANIES

	BONUS	SALARY	TOTAL COMPENSATION	BONUS	SALARY	TOTAL COMPENSATION
Constant	3.783 (1.124)	9.921[a] (36.957)	10.098[a] (29.557)	4.840 (1.259)	10.003[a] (30.122)	10.280[a] (24.710)
Sales	0.424[c] (1.705)	0.181[a] (9.145)	0.189[a] (7.479)	—	—	—
Assets	—	—	—	0.334 (1.212)	0.169[a] (7.128)	0.169[a] (5.688)
Negative Earnings	−1.376 (−1.560)	0.059 (0.833)	−0.076 (−0.845)	−1.488[c] (−1.682)	0.012 (0.151)	−0.125 (−1.304)
Interlisted	0.026 (0.031)	0.133[b] (1.991)	0.165[b] (1.937)	−0.048 (−0.057)	0.104 (1.433)	0.134 (1.472)
Poison Pill	2.293 (1.489)	0.031 (0.251)	0.146 (0.932)	2.271 (1.464)	0.033 (0.243)	0.145 (0.862)
$\bar{R}^2$	0.031	0.386	0.300	0.021	0.271	0.196

Notes: [a] Statistically significant at 1% level.
        [b] Statistically significant at 5% level.
        [c] Statistically significant at 10% level.

relationship, the elasticity measures for sales (while approximately the same as in the widely held firm) are significant at the 10 percent level. However, using assets, the coefficient relationship is not statistically significant. A statistical test could not reject the hypothesis that the overall relationship for compensation for the closely held and widely held samples were the same.[7]

The regressions also present information on the effect of other firm-specific information on the level of compensation. For the widely held sample, neither the interlisted dummy variable nor the existence of a poison pill has an effect on the level of cash compensation measured as salary, bonus, and the sum of the two. As expected, the existence of negative earnings has a statistically significant negative effect on the bonus relationship but no effect on salary or total compensation when size is measured by sales. When size is measured by assets, the coefficient of the negative earnings variable is negative but only marginally significant in the bonus relationship.

In Panel B of Table 5 the relationship for the closely held firms presents a somewhat different picture. When size is measured by sales, the interlisted dummy variable is positive and significant for salaries; thus, closely held firms which are interlisted have higher salaries; this relationship is also found in total cash compensation but not for the bonus. The result for salaries in the closely held company is consistent with the opportunity cost argument and perhaps the added skills necessary to manage a firm which has shares listed on U.S. exchanges. However, this latter argument is muted since the interlisted variable is not significant for the widely held shares. The relationship for the interlisted variable (when size is measured by assets) while positive for salaries and total compensation, is not significant. For bonus compensation, while the relationship with the presence of negative earnings is negative as found in the widely held sample, it is marginally significant. Finally, entrenchment as measured by the poison pill variable has a positive influence, as observed in the widely held sample, but it is not significant. The interpretation of this last variable is difficult for the closely held sample because it includes companies in which the ownership of the voting shares is greater than 15 percent. Thus there will be some companies for which control is precarious and the poison pill is an entrenchment tool. In other firms there may be dual-class shares which act as a very effective entrenchment device and a poison pill is not needed. The effect of dual-class shares on the relationship of compensation and firm-specific variables is considered in the following section.

Therefore, for the widely held sample we observe bonuses to be related to the existence of negative earnings and salaries to be influenced only by size and having a significant fixed element. For the closely held sample, there is evidence that salaries, along with a significant fixed element, are influenced by size and interlisted status and bonuses are marginally negatively affected by the existence of negative earnings.

As noted above, the closely held sample includes companies with very different ownership characteristics, but we do not know the actual equity ownership of the CEO and top executives. However, we do know whether the firm had a dual-class share structure. This share structure typically can induce two types of behaviour. First, the major shareholder owns a large proportion of the voting shares but not of the total equity since the voting shares are typically a small proportion of the total equity. This can result in agency costs of equity since owner/managers bear only a small proportion of the cost of opportunistic, non-shareholder wealth maximization. Second, the dual class shares are an effective anti-takeover device that could result in poor decision-making and compensation payments unrelated to performance. Further, it could also lead to poor performance not followed by disciplinary action through the takeover market. To investigate the effect of dual-class shares, we have re-estimated the regression for the closely held sample, introducing a dummy variable with a value of unity if the company has dual-class shares. The regression results are found in Table 6 where the results for firm size measured by sales are presented. When size is measured by assets the results are unchanged in terms of signs and significance of the variables.

Considering salaries first, we observe that both interlisted status and dual-class share structures have a positive and significant effect. The result for the dual-class variable is consistent with the entrenchment/agency cost argument presented earlier. A counter argument to this conclusion is that in closely held companies the owner/manager already has a large equity interest, and cash compensation (whether in bonus or in salary) is needed more than performance-related compensation. While this may be true, with dual-class shares, it is not necessarily the case that the owner/manager owns a large portion of the total equity. Thus, the observation of higher salary in dual-class shares still appears to be an entrenchment problem. Looking at the bonus relationship, dual-class shares do not have a significant effect and the poison pill variable is positive and almost significant at the 10 percent level. If the poison pill is introduced in those companies in which owners do not have a large ownership position or dual-class shares, then the observation of higher bonus compensation is consistent with an entrenchment story.

Therefore, it appears that for these relationships, unlike the situation in widely held companies, salary and bonus compensation are both related to some entrenchment variables, either poison pill or the existence of dual-class share structures. This is different from the widely held companies where the poison pill variable is not significant and where negative earnings have a significantly negative effect on bonus compensation.

The relationships identified to this point reflect cross-sectional dispersion across firms but do not take into consideration the effect of changes in variables over time. The compensation decision may be framed in terms of changes in compensation in relation to certain firm-specific variables. We introduce this aspect by considering the effect on the percentage change in cash compensation, measured as the change in the natural logarithm of these variables over two adjacent fiscal year ends, based on changes in firm size and the other firm-

TABLE 6

THE RELATIONSHIPS BETWEEN COMPENSATION AND SALES, FIRM-SPECIFIC VARIABLES
AND DUAL-CLASS VARIABLES IN THE CLOSELY HELD SAMPLE

	CLOSELY HELD COMPANIES		
	BONUS	SALARIES	TOTAL COMPENSATION
Constant	3.673	9.899[a]	10.074[a]
	(1.090)	(37.514)	(29.857)
Sales	0.414[c]	0.179[a]	0.187[a]
	(1.663)	(9.200)	(7.482)
Negative Earnings	-1.344	0.065	-0.068
	(-1.522)	(0.940)	(-0.773)
Interlisted	0.122	0.152[b]	0.1865[b]
	(0.144)	(2.298)	(2.202)
Poison Pill	2.490	0.070	0.190
	(1.600)	(0.573)	(1.219)
Dual Class Shares	0.819	0.1627[b]	0.184[b]
	(.930)	(2.358)	(2.085)
Adjusted R^2	.030	.407	.318

Notes: [a]   Statistically significant at 1% level.
       [b]   Statistically significant at 5% level.
       [c]   Statistically significant at 10% level.

specific variables identified in the previous section. The change in firm size is
measured using the same formula as the change in compensation. Table 6 presents
the relationships of change in cash compensation to change in firm size and
other firm-specific variables. Panel A shows the results for widely held firms
and Panel B shows the results for closely held firms. Based on the observed
performance of the dual-class variable in Table 6, we show the set of regressions
for closely held firms including the dual-class variable so that the results in
Panel B of Table 7 are not exactly comparable with those in Panel A.
However, the introduction of the dual-class variable does not have an important
effect on the sign or significance of the regression coefficients of the other
firm-specific variables in the closely held sample.[8]

For widely held companies (Panel A) with the size variable measured by
change in sales, the only significant variables for the change in bonus compensation are the existence of negative earnings and the poison pill; both variables are positive and significant at the 10 percent level. The negative earnings result is difficult to interpret since it suggests that the change in bonus is

TABLE 7

CHANGES IN COMPENSATION RELATED TO CHANGES IN SIZE AND
OTHER FIRM-SPECIFIC VARIABLES

PANEL A - WIDELY HELD COMPANIES

CHANGE IN

	(1) BONUS	(2) SALARY	(3) TOTAL COMPENSATION	(4) BONUS	(5) SALARY	(6) TOTAL COMPENSATION
Constant	−0.720 (−0.702)	0.048[a] (2.845)	0.019 (0.419)	−0.474 (−0.429)	0.033[c] (1.861)	0.000 (0.016)
Change in Sales	1.733 (0.896)	−0.004 (−0.121)	0.051 (0.597)	—	—	—
Change in Assets	—	—	—	0.293 (0.123)	0.069[c] (1.833)	0.124 (1.215)
Negative Earnings	2.752[c] (1.650)	−0.002 (−0.061)	0.095 (1.240)	2.279 (1.368)	0.016 (0.603)	0.104 (1.458)
Interlisted	−0.385 (−0.280)	0.049[b] (2.168)	0.026 (0.426)	−0.509 (−0.364)	0.044[b] (1.967)	0.012 (0.198)
Poison Pill	2.866[c] (1.707)	−0.027 (−0.981)	0.088 (1.202)	2.932[c] (1.711)	−0.020 (−0.727)	0.103 (1.403)
Adjusted R^2	0.042	0.024	−0.007	0.024	0.093	0.018

greater for companies in which there are negative earnings. The poison pill variable is consistent with the entrenchment argument. Considering change in salaries, the interlisted variable is positive and significant suggesting that changes in salaries are greater if the firm is interlisted. This may be a result of compensation practices in the United States or the difficulty of dealing with shareholders in both countries. Finally, the constant term for change in salary is positive and statistically significant. The interpretation of this result is that there is some persistence in salary compensation. When we use assets to measure size, the results are similar. The persistence effect is observed for salaries only and the percentage change in salaries is positively and significantly related to the percentage increase in assets over the fiscal year. This result is consistent with the span of control argument in which the increasing asset size suggests more responsibility and hence more compensation. Note that increases in sales can occur without increases in assets, and thus the results for the two size variables can be different. Finally, there are no significant variables in the change in total compensation relationships.

TABLE 7 (CONT'D)

PANEL B - CLOSELY HELD COMPANIES

CHANGE IN

	(1) BONUS	(2) SALARY	(3) TOTAL COMPENSATION	(4) BONUS	(5) SALARY	(6) TOTAL COMPENSATION
Constant	1.177[b] (2.259)	0.090[a] (4.641)	0.152[a] (4.382)	1.332[a] (2.780)	0.099[a] (5.471)	0.159[a] (4.986)
Change in Sales	0.332 (0.254)	0.071 (1.455)	0.095 (1.091)	—	—	—
Change in Assets	—	—	—	−1.493 (−1.492)	.032 (0.853)	0.108 (1.619)
Negative Earnings	−1.264 (−1.581)	−0.017 (−0.556)	−0.086 (−1.630)	−1.084[b] (−2.060)	−0.017 (−0.548)	−0.070 (−1.295)
Interlisted	−1.266[c] (−1.679)	−0.002 (−0.079)	−0.069 (−1.378)	−1.058 (−1.402)	−0.002 (−0.080)	−0.077 (−1.538)
Poison Pill	2.867[b] (2.075)	−0.019 (−0.362)	0.206[b] (2.249)	3.111[b] (2.255)	−0.024 (−0.461)	0.188[b] (2.051)
Dual Class	0.298 (0.381)	−0.033 (−1.145)	−0.032 (−0.621)	0.369 (0.474)	−0.035 (−1.207)	−0.038 (−0.738)
Adjusted $\bar{R}^2$	0.048	−0.007	0.061	0.064	−0.018	0.071

Notes: [a] Statistically significant at 1% level.
[b] Statistically significant at 5% level.
[c] Statistically significant at 10% level.

Panel B of Table 7 presents the closely held sample results, including a dual-class share variable. Using the change in sales variable, for the change in bonus compensation relationship, the constant and poison pill variables are significant. The negative earnings and interlisted status variables have a negative coefficient and the latter is marginally significant. When assets are used, the negative earnings variable has a negative and significant coefficient and the poison pill remains positive and significant. Therefore, the bonus relationship shows a persistence effect, an entrenchment effect through the poison pill relationship, and a performance effect in the wrong direction observed in the negative earnings variable. When salaries are considered, regardless of whether assets or sales are used, the constant is the only significant variable. (Recall that for the widely held sample, the interlisted variable has a positive and significant effect as does change in assets.) Finally, for total compensation, in the closely held sample the two significant variables are the constant and the poison pill, and the change in assets is almost significant at the 10 percent level. However, it may be incorrect to infer some relationships from total compensation since we observe that the significance of this variable in total compensation comes from the bonus relationship.

There are some important observations in these results. First, in both the widely held and closely held samples there is an entrenchment effect noted in the bonus relationship through the significance of the poison pill variable. Thus, the change in bonus payments is higher for firms that have poison pill plans in place. Second, in both samples there is a persistence effect in the change in salary relationship. There are some important differences in the two samples, as well. First, closely held firms have a persistence effect in the change in bonus. Thus, managers in these firms will have a bias toward positive changes in bonus payments compared to managers in widely held firms. Second, there is no effect on salary of interlisted status in the closely held firms, although this relationship does exist in the widely held sample. Third, the closely held firm sample displays a significant relationship between change in bonus and the existence of negative earnings. Unlike the result for the widely held sample, the performance relationship is in the correct direction; the presence of negative earnings is related to a smaller change in the bonus.

COMPENSATION AND PERFORMANCE

IF COMPENSATION CONTRACTS are designed to motivate executive officers to make decisions consistent with shareholder value, then the performance variables on which compensation is based should be related to shareholder wealth. We consider two sets of performance measures: accounting-based and market-based. The former relates to conventional financial ratios measured over the most recent fiscal year. The accounting ratios include return on equity defined as net income divided by book equity, and return on assets defined as operating income divided by the book value of total assets; all variables are measured at the end of the fiscal year. These variables do not reflect actual cash flows, so we also included the ratio of cash flows from operations divided by the book value of total assets. The market-based performance measure is the rate of return on the common equity over the fiscal year and is measured as the natural logarithm of the value relative of the equity security including dividends.

Compensation by component and its total value is measured first by the log of the compensation value and second by the change in the logarithm. Many studies have considered the relationship of levels of compensation and performance. By and large the semi-elasticity of compensation with accounting performance measures is positive. As noted by Rosen (1990), the semi-elasticity is estimated to be about 1.0 to 1.25 and statistically significant. These result hold in the United States as well as in Britain. Other studies estimate the

TABLE 8

INFLUENCE OF MARKET-BASED PERFORMANCE ON LEVELS OF COMPENSATION

	WIDELY HELD			CLOSELY HELD		
	BONUS	SALARY	TOTAL COMPENSATION	BONUS	SALARY	TOTAL COMPENSATION
Constant	10.158[b]	10.284[a]	10.314[a]	4.715	9.925[a]	10.118[a]
	(1.946)	(36.221)	(26.892)	(1.201)	(30.322)	(24.329)
Assets	−0.072	0.142[a]	0.155[a]	0.343	0.173[a]	0.175[a]
	(−0.212)	(7.643)	(6.201)	(1.239)	(7.493)	(5.975)
Stock Return	−1.687	−0.054	−0.078	−0.813	−0.104	0.027
	(−1.084)	(−0.643)	(−0.686)	(−0.776)	(−1.189)	(0.246)
Negative Earnings	−2.279	0.151[c]	0.071	−1.621[c]	−0.001	−0.108
	(−1.413)	(1.722)	(0.597)	(−1.773)	(−0.012)	(−1.115)
Interlisted	0.928	0.041	0.084	0.099	0.136[c]	0.164[c]
	(0.669)	(0.541)	(0.827)	(0.116)	(1.915)	(1.816)
Poison Pill	1.952	0.088	0.084	2.681[c]	0.112	0.202
	(1.148)	(0.950)	(0.669)	(1.693)	(0.846)	(1.207)
Dual Class	—	—	—	0.990	0.232[a]	0.249[a]
				(1.114)	(3.128)	(2.648)
Adjusted R^2	0.007	0.604	0.480	0.019	0.319	0.227

Notes: [a] Statistically significant at 1% level.
[b] Statistically significant at 5% level.
[c] Statistically significant at 10% level.

semi-elasticity with respect to market rate of return and find the values positive and range between .10 and .16. The implication of these findings is that compensation is based on performance, measured either by accounting returns or market returns. The influence of accounting performance measures should not surprise anyone, even if they can be manipulated by managers, since accounting information is readily available, typically audited, and does provide some information on the performance of the firm and ultimately on the performance of the share price. It would be comforting to those who believe that incentive compensation should maximize shareholder value if accounting performance measures were related to cash flow.

Table 8 presents the results of the regressions of the level of compensation on market performance, measured as the annual rate of return on equity including reinvestment of dividends, and other firm-specific variables for both widely held and closely held companies. The size variable used is assets since this provides slightly higher adjusted R^2 values, but the size, sign and significance of the individual regression coefficients are not affected dramatically if sales are used instead. For widely held companies, the only significant variable in the bonus relationship is the constant; the stock return performance variable is negative and not significant. The salary and total compensation relationships also do not show any relationship to share-price performance; the only significant variables are the constant and the size of the firm and, for the salary component, an anomalous positive relationship of negative earnings and salary. For the closely held sample, compensation is also not related to any form of performance. As observed in similar regressions in previous sections, the dual-class and interlisted variables are positive and significant for salaries and total compensation and the poison pill is positive and significant for the bonus relationship.[9]

However, instead of levels, the change in compensation may be related to firm performance over the period. To investigate this possibility, the relationship of the percentage change in cash compensation, bonus, and total is related to the percentage change in sales, the stock market performance variable, and other firm-specific variables. The results are presented in Table 9 for both widely held and closely held companies. Looking first at the widely held sample, for the percentage change in bonus relationship the poison pill variable is positive and almost significant at the 10 percent level, and the stock return performance variable has an insignificant influence on bonus as does the existence of negative earnings. The poison pill relationship is consistent with entrenchment by existing management. For the change in salary variable, the interlisted variable is positive, reflecting a greater responsibility and hence higher salaries. Also, the stock-return variable has a positive and significant effect. This is somewhat puzzling since the salary and the relationship should be related to long-term and not to short-term performance; the one-year stock return reflects the latter.

Considering the closely held companies, performance does not affect either the bonus or the salary relationship. For the bonus relationship, interlisting status is negative and marginally significant and the poison pill, just as in the widely held sample, is positive but is now statistically significant. The negative interlisting effect is puzzling and may reflect the fact that interlisted companies were reporting executive compensation before the requirement was imposed in Ontario and this may have had a constraining effect on the bonus payments. For the salary equation, only the constant is positive and significant. The dual-class variable has no significant effect in any of the regressions. Finally, stock market performance has a positive and statistically significant effect on total compensation. This strong and positive effect is surprising, given the poor performance observed in the bonus and salary regressions and the weak influence of stock-market performance in the widely held sample.

The major difference between the widely held and closely held firms is the significance of the constant for the closely held sample. This reflects a

TABLE 9

CHANGE IN COMPENSATION RELATED TO CHANGE IN SIZE, STOCK PRICE
PERFORMANCE, AND FIRM-SPECIFIC VARIABLES

| | WIDELY HELD | | | CLOSELY HELD | | |
	BONUS	SALARY	TOTAL COMPENSATION	BONUS	SALARY	TOTAL COMPENSATION
Constant	−0.986	0.030	−0.026	0.956	0.078	0.073
	(−0.802)	(1.528)	(−0.487)	(1.762)	(3.697)	(2.044)
Sales	1.717	−0.005	0.048	0.220	0.070	0.069
	(0.878)	(−0.159)	(0.574)	(0.168)	(1.436)	(0.829)
Stock Return	0.591	0.040	0.099	0.831	0.007	0.206
	(.401)	(1.706)	(1.569)	(0.899)	(0.215)	(3.494)
Negative Earnings	2.655	−0.088	0.074	−1.110	−0.014	−0.044
	(1.561)	(−0.304)	(1.026)	(−1.358)	(−0.441)	(−0.841)
Interlisted	−0.426	0.047	0.019	−1.323	0.002	−0.071
	(−0.300)	(2.084)	(0.317)	(−1.772)	(0.055)	(−1.485)
Poison Pill	2.810	−0.031	0.079	2.626	−0.012	0.173
	(1.652)	(−1.140)	(1.088)	(1.906)	(−0.231)	(1.970)
Dual Class	—	—	—	0.335	−0.036	−0.046
				(0.430)	(−1.218)	(−0.934)
Adjusted R^2	0.023	0.065	0.025	0.053	−0.017	0.151

Notes: [a] Statistically significant at 1% level.
[b] Statistically significant at 5% level.
[c] Statistically significant at 10% level.

persistence element that was observed in previous regressions using change in compensation. Also, the poison pill effect is stronger in the closely held sample, while the interlisted variable gives different signs in the two samples – positive and significant in the salary equation and negative and marginally significant in the bonus equation for the closely held sample.

Since accounting numbers are so pervasive, perhaps the limited success we observe in relating levels and/or changes in compensation to market-based performance will be improved by introducing accounting performance measures since compensation committees may actually use these numbers. Table 10 summarizes the relationships of compensation to accounting performance variables. In estimating the relationships, we have removed the variable identifying the existence of negative income since it would likely be highly

TABLE 10

RELATIONSHIP OF COMPENSATION TO ACCOUNTING-BASED PERFORMANCE VARIABLES

| ACCOUNTING PERFORMANCE VARIABLE | COMPENSATION | | | | | |
| | WIDELY HELD | | | CLOSELY HELD | | |
	BONUS	SALARY	TOTAL	BONUS	SALARY	TOTAL
Return on Equity	> 0 n.s.	< 0 n.s.	> 0 n.s.	> 0 n.s.	< 0 significant	< 0 n.s.
Return on Assets	> 0 significant	< 0 n.s.	> 0 n.s.	> 0 n.s.	< 0 significant	< 0 n.s.
Cash Flow Divided by Assets	< 0 n.s.	< 0 significant	< 0 significant	< 0 n.s.	< 0 significant	< 0 n.s.

Notes: Accounting performance is measured by Return on Equity, Return on Assets and Cash Flow Divided by Assets. The entries identify the sign of the regression coefficient and its significance in a relationship of compensation to accounting performance. Size variable in regression is Sales.
n.s. = not significant
significant - statistical significance at least at 5% level
marginal = statistical significance at 10% level

correlated with the accounting-based performance variable. The accounting-based performance variables include the return on equity and return on assets, both of which reflect accounting profits and not cash flows. The third performance variable attempts to remedy this problem by using cash flow divided by assets. For the widely held sample, only return on asset for bonus is significant and positive. For the closely held sample, both accounting-based performance variables are significant only for salaries but the sign is in the wrong direction. Although not reported in the table, when assets are used as the size variable the coefficients on the salary relationships remain negative but become insignificant. This result is consistent with that found for the annual stock return. Note that although not presented, the sign and significance of the dual-class, poison pill and interlisted variables remain unchanged under all specifications of the performance variables and generally similar to the results found when performance is measured by rate of return on equity in the market. For salaries, cash flow divided by assets is significant in both samples, but the sign is in the wrong direction.

Finally, a similar analysis is undertaken using change in cash compensation and performance variables; the results are presented in Table 11. In the closely held sample, there is no significant relationship of compensation in any of its forms with accounting performance. For the widely held sample, the return on equity has a negative and significant effect on the change in bonus and total compensation. This is counter to our expectations of a positive sign. The other

TABLE 11

RELATIONSHIP OF CHANGE IN COMPENSATION TO
ACCOUNTING-BASED PERFORMANCE VARIABLES

| ACCOUNTING PERFORMANCE VARIABLE | WIDELY HELD | | | CLOSELY HELD | | |
	BONUS	SALARY	TOTAL COMPENSATION	BONUS	SALARY	TOTAL COMPENSATION
Return on Equity	< 0 significant	< 0 n.s.	< 0 significant	> 0 n.s.	> 0 n.s.	> 0 n.s.
Return on Assets	< 0 n.s.	> 0 n.s.	< 0 n.s.	> 0 n.s.	> 0 n.s.	> 0 n.s.
Cash Flow Divided by Assets	< 0 n.s.	< 0 marginal	< 0 n.s.	> 0 n.s.	> 0 n.s.	> 0 n.s.

Notes: Accounting performance is measured by Return on Equity, Return on Assets and Cash Flow Divided by Assets. The entries identify the sign of the regression coefficient and its significance in a relationship of change in compensation to accounting performance. Size variable in regression is Sales.
n.s. = not significant
significant = statistical significance at least at 5% level
marginal = statistical significance at 10% level

performance variables, although also having a negative sign (except return on assets for salaries), provide no significant relationships. For total compensation, return on equity is negative and significant.

Although not shown in Table 11, we have investigated the effect of other variables on the compensation relationship. For the widely held sample, regardless of the accounting performance variable, the bonus equation displays a positive and significant effect for the poison pill variable. Using change in salary, the constant and the interlisting variables are positive and significant. These results are somewhat different from those found in the closely held sample. Here, regardless of the accounting-based performance measure, the constant is positive and significant, interlisted status is negative and significant, and the poison pill remains positive and significant. For the change in salary, the constant is the only significant variable. The results using the performance-based variables suggest that there is an entrenchment effect through the poison pill influence on bonuses. The differences between closely and widely held companies arise in the influence of the interlisted variable in the bonus relationship where it is insignificant for the widely held companies and negative and significant for the closely held companies. Also, the interlisted variable is positive and significant for the salary relationship only in the widely held sample.

CONCLUSIONS

THE PURPOSE OF THIS STUDY HAS BEEN TO IDENTIFY the factors that are important in the determination of executive compensation in Canada and to ascertain whether these variables are consistent with shareholder wealth maximization. Also, we are interested in determining whether the ownership structure and direct entrenchment variables such as poison pills and dual-class shares have any effect on compensation.

The results of our analysis are not very encouraging when the effect of firm performance on compensation is considered. When performance is measured by stock-market return, regardless of the ownership structure, there is no relationship between it and the level of compensation either in terms of components or in total. With *changes* in compensation, salaries are positively related to stock return for the widely held (sample) and total compensation in the closely held companies. The results using the accounting-based performance variables are confusing. Regardless of the ownership structure of the firms and the form of compensation, most of the performance variables are insignificant and, where they are significant, they have the wrong sign. When performance is considered as the presence of negative earnings, the effect is to have lower bonus compensation for both widely held and closely held companies. Thus, there appears to be some performance-related effect on the bonus payments through the negative earnings influence.

Finally, we consider the effect of entrenchment variables on compensation. Regardless of the ownership structure, the poison pill variable has no effect on the salary equation. However, it is positive and significant for the bonus relationship for both widely held and closely held companies when both the change in bonus and (in some instances) total compensation are considered. Thus entrenchment seems to have a positive effect on the change in bonus. The dual-class share variables are significant only in the levels equation for salary and total compensation. Therefore, there appears to be some entrenchment behaviour in compensation for both widely held and closely held companies.

The final difference is the importance of the constant term in the relationships, especially in the *changes* relationships. For the levels, while the salary relationship always has a positive and significant constant term, it is most likely that for closely held companies, the bonus relationship tends to have a positive and significant constant term. Therefore, they have a bias toward positive compensation. This observation, however, is probably consistent with the high ownership proportions of managers and their desire to obtain compensation through salaries and bonuses which are independent of performance since they already own a substantial portion of the equity.

The results, while disheartening in some respects, should be interpreted with two important caveats. First, we did not measure non-cash compensation and the performance-related aspects that may be found in these areas. Second, the reporting of compensation for non-interlisted companies is relatively new in Canada. As the compensation information becomes more accessible and information on the relationship (or the lack thereof) between compensation and performance is recognized, there will be changes in compensation practices in firms in which the takeover and capital markets can have an influence. Thus, companies with entrenched owners/managers, closely held companies, and those with dual-class shares and, to a lesser extent, those with poison pills, may lag behind other companies which must make changes in compensation or in management due to market pressures. It is our expectation that, using data for future periods, subsequent studies of compensation and performance will find stronger relationships than we observed, at least for the widely held companies.

ENDNOTES

1 Daniels & MacIntosh (1991) report that in 1990 only 14 percent of the companies in the TSE 300 were widely held, compared to 63 percent of the companies in the American *Fortune 500*. Of the remainder, 60.3 percent are owned by a single shareholder with legal control, 25.4 percent by one shareholder with effective control (20 percent to 49.9 percent of voting shares) or by two or three shareholders having the ability to combine and establish joint legal or effective control. As of the end of 1993, approximately 38 percent of the companies on the TSE 300 were widely held, based on the 15 percent holding of voting shares definition.

2 For a summary of the literature in this area see Daniels & Halpern (1995).

3 An analysis of the costs and benefits of these instruments is found in Elitzur (1995).

4 Although the database does include deferred compensation such as stock options, we do not use it in this study since the reliability of the data is questionable and there are inconsistencies within the data. For a discussion of problems with the reporting of Long Term Incentive Plans see OSC *Staff Report*, February 1995.

5 We are in the process of collecting data on deferred compensation and intend to include this variable in subsequent research.

6 For formal analysis of the optimal incentive scheme see Varian, 1992, Ch. 25, pp. 448-452; Kreps, 1990, Ch. 16, pp. 586-608; and Laffont, 1990, Ch. 10, pp. 159-164.

7 We used a Chow test in which regressions are run separately for the widely held and closely held samples and for the two samples combined. The calculated test statistic has an F distribution.

8 We also tested whether the widely held firms could be as different from the specification for the closely held firms. The Chow test found that the null

hypothesis (which assumed) that the widely held firms had the same relationship as the closely held firms could not be rejected.

9 We also ran the regressions eliminating the negative earnings dummy variable in case there was multicollinearity between this variable and the share return variable. The regression fit is slightly poorer only for the bonus relationship in the widely held sample and the results for the other variables are unchanged.

APPENDIX 1

THE THEORY OF EXECUTIVE COMPENSATION SCHEMES

THE MODEL FOR THE DESIGN of executive compensation packages is the Principal-Agent model. This Appendix utilizes such a model which combines features of models from Rasmusen (1989, Ch. 6), Kreps (1990, Ch. 16), Laffont (1990, Ch. 11) and Varian (1992, Ch. 25). In this model an agent is hired by a principal to run a firm. The principal's value function, V, depends on some outcome, x, and the cost of compensation to the agent. The outcome, x, is a function of effort, e, and a state of nature, θ, occurring according to a probability density, $f(\theta)$. The agent's utility, U, depends on compensation, s, which, in turn, is a function of x. The agent chooses an effort level that optimizes her payoff. In addition, the agent must be paid enough to take the job. The minimal utility of the agent which will induce the agent to stay is denoted as U_0. Denoting by E the expectations operator, the following program depicts the principal's problem:

$$\underset{\tilde{e}}{Max}\ EV\ (\ x\ (\tilde{e},\ \theta) - C\ (\tilde{e})\ ) \tag{1}$$

$$\text{where } C\ (\tilde{e})\ =\ \underset{s(.)}{Min}\ Es(x(\tilde{e},\ \theta)\ ) \tag{2}$$

subject to

$$\tilde{e} = \underset{e}{ArgMax}\ EU(e,s(x(e,\theta))) \tag{2.1}$$

$$EU(.) \geq U_0 \tag{2.2}$$

Constraints (2.1) and (2.2) are known as the *Incentive Compatibility Constraint* and the *Participation Constraint* respectively.

This problem is solved through the "two steps approach" based on Grossman & Hart (1983). The solution procedure is as follows:

Step 1 Find for each level of effort, e, the cheapest contract to induce the agent to (a) take the job and (b) choose that effort level.

Step 2 Find the optimal level of effort for the principal.

Step 1 is achieved through the solution of Program (2) to (2.2). Step 2 is obtained by maximizing problem (1), given our solution to Step 1.

From this model, the optimal compensation is of the following form:

$$s(.)^* = w + g(x) \; : g'(x) \geq 0 \tag{3}$$

w is a constant and related to the *Participation Constraint* and, thus, depends on U_0, the agent's reservation utility (which is exogenous). $g(x)$ denotes a function which is nondecreasing in outcome, **x**. If the agent is risk-neutral, the optimal compensation package will take the following form:

$$s(.) = w + bx \tag{4}$$

b is a constant and, thus, Equation (4) describes a linear incentive scheme.

ACKNOWLEDGEMENTS

WE WISH TO THANK KPMG for access to their executive compensation database, and Frans Harts and Steven Hadjiyannakis for data collection and database construction.

BIBLIOGRAPHY

Abowd, J. "Does Performance-Based Managerial Compensation Affect Corporate Performance." *Industrial & Labor Relations Review*, Supplement (1990):52S-73S.
Bhagat, S., J. A. Brickley and R. Lease. "Incentive Effects of Stock Purchase Plans." *Journal of Accounting and Economics*. (1983):195-215.
Brickley, J. A., S. Bhagat and R. Lease. "The Impact of Long-range Managerial Compensation Plans on Shareholder Wealth." *Journal of Accounting and Economics*. (1985):115-29.

Daniels, R. and J. MacIntosh. "Toward a Distinctive Canadian Corporate Law Regime." *Osgoode Hall Law Journal.* (1991).

Daniels, R. and P. Halpern. "Too Close for Comfort: The Role of The Closely Held Public Corporation in the Canadian Economy and the Implications for Public Policy." *Canadian Business Law Journal.* (Forthcoming, Fall 1995).

Elitzur, R., and Yaari. "Executive Incentive Compensation and Earnings Manipulation in a Multi-period Setting." *Journal of Economic Behavior and Organization.* (Forthcoming).

Gibbons, R. and K. Murphy. "Relative Performance Evaluation for Chief Executive Officers." *Industrial & Labor Relations Review,* Supplement (1990):30S-51S.

Jensen M. and K. Murphy. "Performance Pay and Top-Management Incentives." *Journal of Political Economy.* (1990):225-64.

Kang, J. and A. Shivdasani. "Firm performance, corporate governance, and top executive turnover in Japan." Manuscript, University of Rhode Island, 1994.

Kaplan, S. "Top Executive Rewards and Firm Performance: A Comparison of Japan and the United States." *Journal of Political Economy.* (1994):510-45.

_____. "Top Executives,Turnover, and Firm Performance in Germany." *Journal of Law, Economics and Organizations.* (1994):142-59.

Kostiuk, P. "Firm Size and Executive Compensation." *The Journal of Human Resources.* (1989):90-105.

Kreps, D. M. *A Course in Microeconomic Theory.* Princeton, N J: Princeton University Press, 1990.

Lambert, R., D. Larcker, and K. Weigelt. "The Structure of Organizational Incentives." *Administrative Sciences Quarterly.* (1993):438-61.

Laffont, J. J. *The Economics of Uncertainty and Information.* Cambridge, MA: The MIT Press, Second Printing, 1990.

Larcker, D. F. "The Association Between Performance Plan Adoption and Corporate Capital Investment." *Journal of Accounting and Economics.* (1983):3-30.

Leonard, J. "Executive Pay and Firm Performance." *Industrial & Labor Relations Review,* Supplement. (1990):13S-29S.

Mehran, H. "Executive Compensation Structure, Ownership and Firm Performance." *Journal of Financial Economics.* (Forthcoming 1995).

Milgrom, P. and J. Roberts. *Economics, Organization, and Management.* Englewood Cliffs, N.J.: Prentice Hall, 1992.

Murphy, K. "Corporate Performance and Managerial Remuneration." *Journal of Accounting and Economics.* (1985):11-42.

Rasmusen, E. *Games and Information: An Introduction to Game Theory.* London: Basil Blackwell Ltd., 1989.

Staff Report. "Executive Compensation and Indebtedness Disclosure." Ontario Securities Commission. February 17, 1995, 1-86 to 1-95.

Rosen S. "Contracts and the Market for Executives," NBER, Working Paper 3542, December 1990.

Tehranian, H. and J. Waegelin "Short Term Bonus Plan Adoption and Stock Market Performance - Proxy and Industry Effects: A Note." *Financial Review.* (1986):345-53.

Tosi, H. and L. Gomez-Mejia. "The Decoupling of CEO Pay and Performance: An Agency Theory Perspective." *Administrative Sciences Quarterly.* (1989):169-89.

Varian, H. R. *Microeconomic Analysis.* New York: Norton, Third Edition, 1992.

Zenger, T. "Why Do Employers Only Reward Extreme Performance? Examining the Relationships among Performance, Pay and Turnover." *Administrative Sciences Quarterly.* (1992):198-219.

David Stangeland
Faculty of Management
University of Manitoba

Ronald J. Daniels
Dean of Law
University of Toronto

Randall Morck
Faculty of Business
University of Alberta

6

In High Gear: A Case Study of the Hees-Edper Corporate Group

INTRODUCTION

THIS STUDY COMPARES FIRMS IN THE HEES-EDPER GROUP with a number of other independent firms of similar size and in the same industries over a four-year period from 1988 to 1992, just prior to the first release of news that the Hees-Edper group was in financial trouble. During that period, Hees-Edper firms recorded profitability levels comparable to (or below) those of the matched firms. The Hees-Edper firms were also shown to have been much higher risk investments well before the group's financial position began to deteriorate. They were more highly levered, but even after risk levels are adjusted for this, the risk levels of Hees-Edper firms remain much higher.

Our study shows that the extreme incentive-based compensation schemes used by Hees-Edper firms encouraged managers to adopt high-risk strategies, and that the intercorporate co-insurance (allowed by the interlocking ownership structure of the firms) made this possible by increasing the group's apparent debt capacity. Since this higher risk did not improve overall performance, it was arguably at an economically inefficient higher level. The higher leverage of Hees-Edper companies should have produced a sizable tax advantage because of the deductibility of interest at the corporate level. The mediocre performance of the companies thus raises the possibility that abnormally poor performance was masked by tax breaks.

THE ECONOMICS OF CONGLOMERATES

DURING THE 1960S AND 1970S CONGLOMERATES WERE "the glamour investment on the stock market" (Firth, 1980) and financial markets reacted to the news of diversifying acquisitions by sending stock prices of acquiring firms skyward (Matsusaki, 1993). The resulting mob psychology infected managers and investors alike, and diversifying acquisitions did enormous damage to many firms that would otherwise have remained healthy and prosperous. Eventually, the corporate world realized the diversification was excessive and there was a return to "core" lines of business. Today, the conglomerate merger wave of the 1960s seems like a mania.

IN DEFENCE OF CONGLOMERATES

ARE THESE JUDGEMENTS PRECIPITOUS? There are arguments in favour of conglomerates that make economic sense. Indeed, some of them are reasonably persuasive, at least superficially.

First, Caves (1982) and Rugman (1994) argue that certain intangible assets have higher returns when used on a larger scale. These are thought to include R&D, marketing expertise, and good management. The intuition is that a new product or advertising campaign has fixed up-front costs, but its return depends on the size of the operation to which it is applied. Similarly, a good manager in charge of a large operation generates more wealth than the same good manager in charge of a small operation. The implication is that good managers should be put in charge of operations that are as large in scope and scale as possible.

These arguments are a widely accepted justification for international horizontal expansion, but they also appear to have some applicability to domestic firms. Montgomery & Wernerfelt (1988) and Panzar & Willig (1981) utilize them analogously to explain why the wave of corporate diversification made by conglomerates in the '60s and '70s make sense.

Second, to some extent a conglomerate structure is a substitute for capital markets. If capital markets were hopelessly myopic or otherwise grossly inefficient, it would make sense to circumvent them. However, most of the academic work on this issue suggests that markets are not that inefficient and those, including Keynes (1933), who do argue for such a degree of inefficiency also argue frequently that corporate managers are afflicted by the same mood swings that affect investors. Nonetheless, even in an economy with efficient capital markets, there are reasons to circumvent them. Two such reasons (that also dovetail into an argument in support of conglomerates) are the "lemon" problem and the "free-cash" problem.

The lemon problem is characterized by a firm that has good investment projects but no spare cash; it must therefore raise funds by issuing securities. Myers & Majluf (1984) point out that this is not costless. Firms should issue new shares when their outstanding shares are overpriced. Securities, like used cars, are difficult to value, and buyers are always inclined to suspect that there is something wrong with the product – otherwise, (they ask) why is it for sale now? Is it a lemon? Investors might rationally view the news of a new securities issues as a signal that outstanding securities are overvalued. In fact, share prices do tend to fall when firms announce they are issuing more shares. Lesser analogous effects are also observed for bond issues. This lemon problem in capital markets means that firms should use a "pecking order" approach when financing new projects – that is, they should use funds obtained from internal cash flow whenever possible, and raise external capital only when internal funds are not available and when the benefits of the new project outweigh the cost of depressing the prices of the firm's outstanding securities. By transferring funds between divisions, a conglomerate structure side-steps the lemon problem; it can act like a financial intermediary in the sense of Diamond (1991).

Jensen (1986) argues that firms in stable, low-growth industries often invest in money-losing projects. The free-cash problem is characterized by a firm in a low-growth industry with no profitable investment projects; it should pay out its free cash to shareholders as dividends. But, retaining funds within the firm often serves managers in other ways; it enables firms to expand and thus to build up the size of managers' empires and/or it allows for labour peace or it cements ties with politicians. Such "over-investment" by cash cows is called the free-cash problem. Conglomerates that span both low-growth cash-rich industries and high-growth cash-starved industries neatly solve both the free-cash problem and the lemon problem in one easy step. A conglomerate can invest internal funds in the best of all its divisions' projects, and thus better serve shareholders.

Third, diversification reduces risk at the corporate level (Gahlon & Stover, 1979). Financial academics never tire of arguing that diversification brings no benefits to shareholders because shareholders could achieve the same risk reduction by holding a more diversified portfolio themselves. This argument is suspect because it assumes that diversification at the corporate level and at the individual investor's portfolio level are perfect substitutes. They are not. Reducing risk at the corporate level might allow for more credible long-term commitments to workers, suppliers and customers. It might also reduce the need to forego a return on part of the firm's capital in order to maintain the financial slack necessary to insure liquidity. Lower level corporate risk might also attract better workers and managers at lower wages, since a risk premium need not accompany any investment in firm-specific skills (Aron, 1988). It might also encourage managers to undertake more risky corporate investments than their innate aversion to risk would otherwise preclude, thereby encouraging a greater alignment of managers' interests with those of shareholders. Diversification at the corporate level may well not benefit shareholders, but the case is not as open-and-shut as many believe.

Fourth, diversification reduces corporate taxes by making a more highly levered capital structure optimal. By insuring each other through intercorporate transfers of earnings, the divisions of a conglomerate each lower the other's probability of defaulting on its debt relative to that of a free-standing one-industry firm. This makes a higher over-all leverage more feasible for a conglomerate than for a portfolio of independent one-industry firms. Of course, if the firm elects to lever up in order to take advantage of the co-insurance to increase its debt-related tax deductions, the risk reduction that corporate diversification can provide is limited. The benefits of lower corporate taxes to investors as a whole are mitigated by the higher personal taxes on debt, but in a world where tax-free investors – like pension funds – are playing an ever greater role, it is not clear that there would be a wash in securities prices in general. Moreover, shareholders are paying for bailouts they would otherwise walk away from because of the limited liability granted the owners of stock. The size of this reduction in dividends, in the absence of tax gains, would exactly compensate for the better terms the firm could get from creditors and it would be a wash. The tax deductibility of interest, but not dividends, shifts the balance in favour of diversification.

THE FAILURE OF THE CONGLOMERATE FORM

THE POOR PERFORMANCE OF CONGLOMERATES casts doubt on the universal validity of the arguments noted above. Berger & Ofek (1995) find a 13 percent to 15 percent discount in the values of conglomerates relative to comparable portfolios of stand-alone firms. Comment & Jarrell (1995) find a positive link between firm focus increases and stock returns. John & Ofek (1995) find that asset sales improve firm performance when they also increase the firm's focus. In the 1980s, firms that announced acquisitions in their own lines of business saw their stock prices rise, while those that announced takeovers in other industries saw their stock prices decline (Morck et al., 1990). Wernerfelt & Montgomery (1988) find a "positive focus effect" in an empirical study of the determinants of firms' values. Many firms that diversified aggressively in earlier years spent the 1980s shedding unrelated operations and re-establishing their commitments to core businesses (Donaldson, 1990).

WHY DID CONGLOMERATES FALL SO FAR OUT OF FAVOUR?

FIRST, THE IDEA THAT CONGLOMERATES COULD EXPLOIT the intangible assets of their component firms on a large(r) scale was always more strained than the analogous theory justifying multinationals. Arguably, R&D and marketing skills are considerably less transferable to operations in unrelated industries than they are to operations in the same industry but in another country. Thus, attention was centred on management skills as the intangible asset that would increase the values of all the assets combined with the conglomerate. Conglomerates, it was believed, had "... dynamic, entrepreneurial management ... [which were] injected into firms which were taken over, [and] greatly increased efficiency and profits ... which would be reflected in higher share price performance" (Firth, 1980). Management skills are now viewed as much less portable; today, managers who are acknowledged experts at finding oil are not as likely to be considered to have an advantage in running a brewery too. Moreover, even good managers can be guilty of *hubris*.

Second, conglomerates were seen as being plagued by corporate governance problems. They were over-centralized (Baker, 1992). Many degenerated into little more than exercises in empire-building. Shareholders who would have had considerably more influence and better information about the financial decisions being made in smaller, one-industry firms were unable to monitor or discipline the managers of large complex conglomerates who had more opportunity to run amok. Amihud & Lev (1981) find that manager-run firms are much more likely to establish diversified conglomerate structures than owner-run firms; they argue that conglomerates themselves may be a manifestation of corporate governance problems.[1] Certainly, the reduced risk in a conglomerate should be attractive to managers. Rose & Shepard (1994) find that salaries of managers of conglomerates are 10 percent to 12 percent higher and total compensation is 13 percent to 17 percent greater than that of their peers in otherwise comparable one-industry firms of similar size. However, they also find that this premium is not related to tenure and argue that this implies it might be due to the fact that a higher level of skill may be required to manage a conglomerate.

Although the gains to be made through better use of internal funds, lower corporate risk, and higher debt capacity may be real, it appears they are largely swamped by the corporate governance problems that emerge in conglomerates.

AN AMALGAM OF CONGLOMERATES AND FREE-STANDING FIRMS?

DESPITE THESE FINDINGS, CONGLOMERATES MIGHT STILL be a valid corporate form, useful in some circumstances. Roe (1994) makes the case that the failure of the U.S. conglomerate, despite its potential advantages, was due (in part) to the fact that in conglomerates owning 100 percent of their subsidiaries, managers were deprived of market signals that provided valuable feedback to managers in free-standing companies. Instead, conglomerate managers received feedback through a command-and-control system based mainly on accounting information. Roe goes on to say that "an amalgam of partial control, market signalling and partial integration of finance and industry (or of different levels of Industry)" might have been superior to both the conglomerate form and the market-disciplined free-standing firms.

However, in the United States, conglomerates with large numbers of partially owned subsidiaries are discouraged by the *Investment Company Act* of 1940.[2] Once 40 percent of the portfolio of a U.S. conglomerate is devoted to the partial ownership of other firms, the company is presumed to be an investment company and must therefore pay taxes on dividends it receives from its partially owned subsidiaries. Since one of the main reasons underlying the existence of a conglomerate is its ability to reallocate capital efficiently, this is a serious barrier. The only escape is for the conglomerate to become a mutual fund, but this entails restrictions on portfolio composition and on intercompany dealings.

In Canada, the federal *Investment Companies Act*[3] does not constitute a barrier to conglomerate formulation comparable to that posed by the U.S. legislation. This act requires federally incorporated companies that use debt capital to finance equity or debt investments to comply with certain reporting obligations (administered by the Office of Superintendent of Financial Institutions – the regulator of federal financial institutions). The Act also requires companies to comply with restrictions on sundry related-party trans-actions. The embrace of this statute can be easily avoided through provincial incorporation or reincorporation, because there are no comparable legislative schemes in the provinces.

Federal tax legislation has a more important regulatory influence on the structure and performance of Canadian conglomerates. In contrast to the United States, Canada permits tax-free dividends to be paid within a corporate group, thereby permitting internal capital transfers to be effected on a more tax-efficient basis. However, the comparative benefits of this difference in dividend treatment should not be overstated. In contrast to the scope permitted by consolidated reporting of conglomerate earnings in the United States, the Canadian tax statute does not allow consolidation. Presumably, this makes it more difficult for Canadian conglomerates to maximize the tax-avoidance value of losses incurred by member corporations. The more liberal availability of the deduction for interest payments in Canada further complicates matters, particularly in respect of debt incurred on foreign assets. Interest deductibility provides an implicit subsidy for debt, and this encourages corporate managers to use high levels of debt to finance asset acquisitions. Thus, in tandem, a cursory review of tax legislation in Canada and the United States does not supply unequivocal evidence that the size and durability of the Canadian conglomerate is necessarily related to differential taxation standards. Which effects dominate is an empirical question.

Looking beyond tax policy, however, there is a range of distinctive regulatory policies in Canada that, while not providing targeted incentives for conglomerate formation, create scope for Canadian controlling shareholders and their appointed managers to engage in opportunistic behaviour *via* the conglomerate vehicle. For instance, it is arguable, generally, that the commit-ment of successive Canadian governments to mercantilist industrial policies has reduced the bargaining power of Canadian shareholders who invest(ed) in securities of Canadian corporations. The foreign-property rule of the *Income Tax Act* is an example. This rule caps the permissible level of tax favoured retirement investments at 20 percent of the value of the portfolio (10 percent until recently). Thus, Canadian investors have fewer alternative investments to choose from when they wish to move their money because they disagree with the policies of corporate managers. This may have allowed inefficient conglomerate holding structures to survive, and may also have prolonged wealth-reducing redistribution from investors to Canadian corporate insiders.[4]

The same arguments can be made in the context of Canadian corporate and securities law. Here it is arguable that the lack of a vigorous, privately enforced securities disclosure regime in Canada reduces the transparency of internal corporate transactions to external shareholders and heightens the attractiveness of the conglomerate form of organization to opportunistic corporate insiders.[5] Similarly, the lack of a clearly articulated corporate law fiduciary duty from majority to minority shareholders in Canada is also significant – at least historically – in explaining the attraction of conglomerates to opportunistic managers and shareholders (Daniels & MacIntosh, 1991). In the absence of legislated fiduciary duties, controlling shareholders in Canada and their appointed management enjoy much greater scope for unfair self-dealing transactions than if their companies were incorporated in the United States.[6]

We also believe that the mercantalist industrial policies adopted by successive Canadian governments encouraged conglomerate formation. High levels of external trade protection, restrictions on the export of domestic capital, and favourable tax treatment of certain types of domestic equity investment all contributed to an inward-looking industrial economy in which Canadian corporations focused on producing a broad range of goods and services for the protected Canadian market rather than on a narrow range of competitive products for the international market. In this setting, the diversified conglomerate served as a natural vehicle to achieve corporate growth.

In sharp contrast to the United States, in Canada a more congenial political environment for the concentration of economic power provided further support for the formation of conglomerates. Whereas American political traditions have coalesced around a deep and abiding mistrust of concentrated economic power, the Canadian political environment has been much more sanguine. In Canada, the development and preservation of a fragile national identity easily outweighs concerns over the concentration of corporate power. So, to the extent that economic concentration is the inexorable result of state protectionism, Canadians regard this as a price worth paying to promote collectivist goals (Benidickson, 1993).

A respectable case can be made, therefore, that Canadian laws and customs do encourage just the sort of amalgam Roe (1994) visualizes. The largest example of corporate concentration in recent years is the Hees-Edper group, controlled by Edward and Peter Bronfman, to which we now turn.

THE HEES-EDPER GROUP

IN 1952 SAM BRONFMAN, THE ENTREPRENEUR WHO BUILT Seagram's into a liquor empire during Prohibition in the United States, informed his nephews, Edward and Peter, that, while his sons would inherit the family business, a trust would be established to provide for them. By the early 1990s, with the help of South African financial strategist Jack Cockwell and ignoring the trend against diversification, that trust – the brothers' nest egg – had grown into a corporate empire of more than 100 companies spanning industries from merchant banking to forestry. At its apex, the group of Bronfman companies made up 15 percent of the total capitalization of the Toronto Stock Exchange. When it was eventually liquidated the trust yielded more than C$ 100 million in Seagram's stock.

Cockwell's strategy was based on pyramids of control. A privately held company would own a controlling stake in a firm that would hold a controlling stake in another firm that would hold a controlling stake in yet another firm, and so on. Using this strategy, control could be leveraged. The Bronfmans could fully control a firm in which they held only 51 percent of 51 percent of ... of 51 percent of the stock. By crossing the layers of the pyramid and liberally using restricted-voting or non-voting shares for outsiders and super-voting shares for Bronfman insiders, the equity stakes needed to exert control were further reduced.

This pyramid ownership structure meant that publicly traded rumps of stock existed throughout the group. Thus, the group's organizational structure was an amalgam of a conglomerate (with decisions coordinated by the central, privately held companies) and public ownership (with traded stock, shareholder meetings, boards of directors, financial statements, and institutional ownership).

A number of the Hees-Edper companies were added to the group *via* workouts organized by the brothers' merchant bank, Hees International Bancorp Inc. A typical example was the takeover by Hees of Versatile Corporation in May 1987. Versatile, a farm equipment maker, had expanded into the energy sector, and then into ship building through the purchase of Davie in 1985. By 1987 the firm was bankrupt and Hees assumed control in a workout, eventually holding an equity stake of over 40 percent. Another example is the 1989 workout of National Business Systems, in which Hees bought $80 million of the failed firm's debt from U.S. institutional investors and assumed control. Critics may now refer to this as "vulture capital", but Hees was arguably acquiring an expertise in organizing the affairs of troubled firms. This falls into the category of special management skills similar to those claimed for the managers of U.S. conglomerates in the 1960s and 1970s.

In other cases, the Hees-Edper group expanded by acquiring major players in specific industries, such as Noranda Forests and MacMillan Bloedel. The group's real estate firms, Carena Development and Bramalea, the energy firm Norcen, and the publishing company Pagurian, all played dominant roles in their respective industries throughout the 1980s.

Another feature of the Hees-Edper group that deserves comment is its practice of using exaggerated incentive-based compensation schemes to pay managers and (in some cases) employees. Top managers received salaries that were low by industry standards, often in the neighbourhood of only $100,000 per year, but were allowed (and expected) to borrow up to ten times their annual salary from the group – interest free – to buy stock in its member firms.[7] However, based on anecdotal information describing the compensation arrangements used in one group firm, Royal Trust, it appears that there was asymmetric sharing of risk and return by management and shareholders; implicit promises were allegedly made to key managers that they would be protected from any downside losses resulting from leveraged equity investments, but that they would retain all upside gains. This system was in place for the better part of a decade. Certainly, these arrangements provided strong incentives for conglomerate managers to take risks. However, the existence of incentive-based compensation does not in itself mean that agency problems in the design of these schemes were obviated.

How did the Hees-Edper group take advantage of its hybrid structure? Did it reduce risk by setting up a network of co-insurance between group firms? Or did it use this co-insurance to lever up to a higher debt level and convert the risk reduction into a tax advantage? Did the publicly traded rumps of stock lead to better corporate governance than would have been the case in a pure conglomerate? We now turn to these issues by comparing various financial measures for Hees-Edper group firms with those for comparable independent firms.

DATA AND METHODOLOGY

PUBLICLY TRADED COMPANIES IN THE HEES-EDPER GROUP were identified each year using Statistics Canada's *Directory of Intercorporate Ownership*. The period from 1988 through 1991 was selected because these years saw the group's largest extent. The sample period begins with 1988 to avoid including the October 1987 crash in the data; the end of the sample period just predates the real estate problems that triggered the decline of the Bronfman group.

Total debt and total assets were taken from the CD-ROM *Canadian Compustat*. Daily stock returns were taken from the TSE-Western CD-ROM. Companies are classified by industry using three- and four-digit standard industrial classification (SIC) codes. Size is measured using 1990 total assets.

Each Bronfman company is matched with an independent control company in the same industry and of roughly the same size. However, because of the lack of suitable control companies (*i.e.*, companies that are not member firms of other corporate groups such as the Reichmann brothers' Olympia and York), most large real estate companies and some financial firms had to be dropped from the study. This left 19 companies spanning four years – a total of 76 firm-year observations. Six firm-year observations were deleted as outliers, defined as having beta (ß) or variance estimates more than three standard errors from the mean estimates for that company or its control match, or having a debt-to-assets ratio greater than one. This left 70 firm-year observations. The distribution of the data over time is as follows: 19 observations in 1988, 19 in 1989, 17 in 1990 and 15 in 1991.

FINDINGS

THE MAIN RESULTS ARE DISPLAYED IN TABLE 1. Tables 2 through 5 contain statistical test results that determine the reliability of the differences between the results obtained for the Hees-Edper firms and those obtained for the control firms shown in Table 1.

TABLE 1

UNIVARIATE STATISTICS FOR ALL VARIABLES FOR ALL FIRM-YEARS STUDIED

ROW VARIABLE	SAMPLE	MEAN	MEDIAN	MINIMUM	MAXIMUM	STANDARD DEVIATION
1) Operating	Edper Firms	7.1	8.7	−95.0	22.5	14.7
2) Income/Assets (%)	Control Firms	7.7	9.5	−49.7	25.7	9.9
3) Levered Equity	Edper Firms	0.694	0.645	−0.22	2.03	0.454
4) Beta	Control Firms	0.303	0.043	−0.048	1.35	0.402
5) Leverage (%)	Edper Firms	33.1	32.6	0 .	70.8	17.2
6)	Control Firms	26.3	18.5	0	95.1	24.6
7) Unlevered Asset	Edper Firms	0.473	0.436	−0.129	1.74	0.337
8) Beta	Control Firms	0.215	0.025	−0.005	1.07	0.293

Note: Sample size is 70 Bronfman firm-years and 70 control firm-years, except for operating income, where data are only available for 65 firm-year pairs.

Rows 1) and 2) of Table 1 give a measure of overall corporate profitability, operating income-per-dollar of assets, expressed as a percentage return. Hees-Edper firms have slightly worse performance by this measure than do comparable independent firms. However, these differences are not sufficiently clear-cut to pass the statistical tests shown in Table 2. Analogous tests using other accounting-performance ratios yield similar results. We conclude that Hees-Edper firms did not perform better than comparable independent firms. Their performance was, at best, comparable to that of the matched control firms.

Rows 3) and 4) of Table 1 compare levered equity ßs for the two groups of firms. A firm's ß is a standard measure of risk used by portfolio managers.[8] A high ß indicates a high-risk investment, while a low ß indicates a relatively safe investment. The ßs for Bronfman firms are substantially higher than those of the control firms. Table 3 shows that these differences are statistically highly significant. We conclude that the stock of Bronfman firms is much riskier than that of comparable independent firms.

Rows 5) and 6) of Table 1 compare the leverage of Hees-Edper firms with those of the matched control firms. Bronfman firms have much higher financial leverage than comparable independent firms, and Table 4 shows that this difference is statistically highly significant. We conclude that Bronfman firms have taken on much higher debt loads than comparable independent firms.

Rows 7) and 8) of Table 1 show a comparison of unlevered ßs. Unlevered asset ßs are theoretical ßs that companies would have if they had no debt.[9] This risk measure is used by financial economists as a measure of the underlying risk in the firm's operations. Even after making this adjustment, Hees-Edper companies continue to have higher risk levels than the control firms. We conclude that the higher risk of the Bronfman companies is not due solely to

TABLE 2

STATISTICAL TESTS COMPARING OPERATING INCOME PER DOLLAR OF ASSETS OF
BRONFMAN FIRMS (DEBT/ASSETS) TO THAT OF MATCHED CONTROL FIRMS

	MEAN	MEDIAN
Bronfman Companies (%)	7.11	8.72
Industry/Size-Match Companies (%)	7.74	9.48
Difference between Bronfman and Matching Companies (%)	0.63	0.100
p-Value for Differences (t-Test for Means, Wilcoxon Signed Rank Test for Medians)	0.468	0.811
Number of Observations (Firm Years)	65	65

TABLE 3

STATISTICAL TESTS COMPARING LEVERED EQUITY BETAS OF BRONFMAN FIRMS WITH
THOSE OF MATCHED CONTROL FIRMS

	MEAN	MEDIAN
Bronfman Companies	0.694	0.645
Industry/Size-Match Companies	0.303	0.043
Difference between Bronfman and Matching Companies	0.391	0.360
p-Value for Differences (t-Test for Means, Wilcoxon Signed Rank Test for Medians)	0.0001	0.0001
p-Value for Weighted t-Test	0.0001	
Number of Observations (Firm Years)	70	70

high debt loads. The underlying business operations of the Hees-Edper firms appear to entail more risk than other Canadian companies of similar size in the same industries. They have higher operating leverage as well as higher financial leverage.

Missing from Table 1 are stock market performance measures. A proper analysis of stock price performance is complicated for firms like the Hees-Edper group. Their involved and interlocking ownership structure with multiple classes of differential voting stock, some privately held, make it difficult to apply the standard tools of firm valuation and stock return measurement. We are pursuing further research in this area, examining a broader range of performance measures, including some that are market-value based.

TABLE 4

STATISTICAL TESTS COMPARING LEVERAGE IN BRONFMAN FIRMS (DEBT/ASSETS) TO
LEVERAGE IN MATCHED CONTROL FIRMS

	MEAN	MEDIAN
Bronfman Companies (%)	33.1	32.6
Industry/Size-Match Companies (%)	26.3	18.5
Difference between Bronfman and Matching Companies (%)	6.8	6.6
p-Value for Differences (t-Test for Means, Wilcoxon Signed Rank Test for Medians)	.0033	.0009
Number of Observations (Firm Years)	70	70

TABLE 5

STATISTICAL TESTS COMPARING UNLEVERED ASSET BETAS OF BRONFMAN FIRMS
WITH THOSE OF MATCHED CONTROL FIRMS

	MEAN	MEDIAN
Bronfman Companies	.473	.436
Industry/Size-Match Companies	.215	.025
Difference between Bronfman and Matching Companies	.259	.261
p-Value for Differences (t-Test for Means, Wilcoxon Signed Rank Test for Medians)	.0001	.0001
p-Value for Weighted t-Test	.0001	
Number of Observations (Firm Years)	70	70

CONCLUSIONS

OUR OVERALL RESULTS SUPPORT THE FOLLOWING CONCLUSIONS. First, our data show no clearly superior performance in terms of average return on assets for Hees-Edper firms over comparable independent firms. This suggests that the conglomerate structure did not improve overall economic efficiency by enabling member firms to exploit each other's intangible assets and thereby achieve new synergies. For example, employing superior management techniques developed at one firm to invigorate another should have produced higher performance. Therefore Canadian public policy that directly or indirectly encourages the formation of conglomerates cannot be justified on the grounds of increased economies of scale or scope in applying such assets, at least in this case, or if such advantages were achieved, they were offset by other negative factors.

Second, our data do not provide evidence that the Hees-Edper group allocated capital internally in ways superior to those accomplished by financial markets or financial institutions. This should also have produced evidence of better performance in group firms than in comparable independent firms. The fact that it did not casts doubt on the benefits of centralized managerial control over a diverse range of industries. Quite simply, senior Hees-Edper managers failed to confer tangible economic gains on member firms through superior capital allocation. Indeed, quite the opposite may be true. Hees-Edper management may have used a small stable of cash cows to support earlier investments in chronically under-performing firms. In this respect, the lack of vigorous market pressure may have allowed the conglomerate's management systematically to persist in maintaining irrational and idiosyncratic commitments to dog companies.

Third, Hees-Edper management did not use the co-insurance their conglomerate structure allowed to reduce overall risk levels in the corporation. Instead, they used the group's risk-sharing potential to increase overall levels of risk beyond what would have been permitted by debt markets for comparable independent firms. This was accomplished in part through increased financial leverage, and in part it appears to stem from higher operating leverage, *i.e.*, riskier overall business practices. To the extent that Canadian business is hampered by excessive innate risk aversion on the part of Canadian managers, encouraging conglomerates may have an invigorating effect.

This line of argument is valid only if the managers of the conglomerate use the risk-sharing potential of intercorporate co-insurance to justify investments that would otherwise be regarded as too speculative. The riskier management decisions made in the Hees-Edper group were facilitated by the group's conglomerate structure, but they might not have occurred without the extreme incentive-based compensation schemes Bronfman managers and employees were given. Furthermore, high relative levels of firm risk should have been accompanied by higher levels of relative returns if the risk-taking was of an economically efficient sort. Perhaps the incentive-based compensation scheme the group used actually encouraged excessive and overly speculative risk-taking.

Fourth, Hees-Edper companies were more highly levered than comparable independent firms, and this likely produced a tax advantage. The fact that this is not reflected in higher earnings casts a somewhat harsher light on the mediocre accounting performance of the firms in the group. Also, since the higher debt in group firms was accompanied by risk-sharing, there need be no improvement in managerial incentives of the sort Jensen (1989) envisions.

Jensen essentially argues that an imminent threat of bankruptcy encourages better management in highly levered firms. Thus, to the extent that the group used the increased debt capacity created by its intercorporate risk sharing to avoid taxes, its social benefits are more questionable.

Public Policy Implications

How can public policy accentuate the desirable features of corporate groups like Hees-Edper and mitigate their undesirable features? As argued elsewhere, vibrant and open capital and product markets are probably the strongest antidote against the growth of seemingly perverse organizational structures (Morck, 1995; Daniels & Halpern, 1995). With vigorous markets, the ability of managers to devise and maintain inefficient organizational forms is constrained. In this respect, we believe that further relaxation of the foreign property rule, a continued liberalization of external trade barriers, and reduced protectionism of domestic capital market suppliers are all necessary steps. However, we believe that other policy instruments are also in order.

Nuanced reforms to securities regulations that give private investors both the ability and the incentive to prosecute alleged breaches of disclosure obligations would be useful, particularly at a time when resources for public enforcement are so limited. Reforms to corporate and securities proxy rules that impair institutional shareholders' voices (such as the shareholder communication rules that require shareholders to bear the costs of a dissident proxy circular in the event of a disagreement with management) would also be useful (Pound, 1991). Both of these reforms would bolster the capability of shareholders to monitor and to intervene as required, with the result that less reliance would be placed on the putative superiority of internal *versus* external systems of capital allocation. Also, federal regulators should recognize that some variation on section 9.1 of the Ontario Securities Commission Regulations (which forces disclosure about intercorporate transactions in such groups) is critically important in preventing abuse in groups like Hees-Edper. A regulation of this nature should be a key part of any federal securities law if Ottawa asserts its jurisdiction in that area.

Another set of reforms to securities regulation focuses on tax distortions that implicitly favour debt over equity instruments by allowing the deduction of interest. Removing the interest subsidy on debt would remove an incentive to share risk across companies in a corporate group like Hees-Edper solely in order to to reduce corporate taxes. The effect of the change would be to reduce the desirability of strained capital structures such as those in levered buyouts (LBOs). On the whole, such a change could also be expected to reduce the general corporate tax rate. If it is desirable to subsidize debt because high leverage encourages more careful management decisions (as Jensen, 1989, argues) it should be recognized that conglomerates can and do circumvent this. Intercorporate risk-sharing in such groups allows for higher leverage without a perspective-enhancing increased chance of bankruptcy. Perhaps intercorporate dividends should therefore be taxed more vigorously, and overall corporate tax rates be reduced.

Finally, although more amorphous in character, we believe that changes to the political climate in which Canadian corporations operate are appropriate. It is perplexing that the substantial concentration of economic power that was amassed in the Hees-Edper group received so little attention from the regulators and the financial community. It strikes us as odd that a single group was able to assemble control over more than 15 percent of the market capitalization of the country's premier stock exchange with scarcely a hint of criticism by regulators, politicians or the press. In this respect, we suggest that increased scrutiny, more analysis and, indeed, reform of the economic and political institutions that could accept such potentially destabilizing economic power are in order. However, concerns about vertical equity should not be used to thwart the creation of optimal organizational arrangements. Specifically, we fear that deep-seated concerns about vertical equity will limit the capacity of shareholders to devise workable incentive-based compensation arrangements that could, in turn, spawn incentives for managers to use firm-level diversification rather than explicit pay differentials to guard their firm-specific human capital investments. The Hees-Edper group provides solid evidence of the ability of strong incentive schemes to increase risk taking. It would be a pity if such incentives were disallowed simply because of concern that successful managers might earn too much.

ENDNOTES

1 A third concern raised at the time was that conglomerates could engage in predatory pricing in one market by diverting profits from another (see, e.g., Bradburd, 1980; Greening, 1980). But this should increase, not decrease, the relative financial performance of conglomerates.

2 *Investment Company Act* of 1940 §3(1)(3), 15 U.S.C. §80a-3(a)(3) 1988. See also Roe (1994), p. 260.

3 R.S.C. 1985, c. I-22.

4 These policies are discussed more fully in Daniels & Halpern, "The Role of the Closely Held Public Corporation in the Canadian Economy and the Implications for Public Policy," *Canadian Business Law Journal*, forthcoming.

5 In contrast to the United States, Canada does not have clearly articulated civil liability standards for certain disclosure documents. Moreover, the incentives for private enforcement of existing statutory and common law disclosure standards is subverted by the prohibitions on contingency fees and class actions.

6 The recent (and growing) receptivity of Canadian courts to imposing fiduciary duties from majority to minority shareholders under the rubric of oppression, combined with the Ontario Securities Commission's 1990 enactment of its policy on related party transactions (O.S.C. Policy 9.1), has greatly restricted the scope for majority opportunism.

7 *Financial Post*, August 7, 1990.

8 Betas here are estimated using the market model $r = \alpha + \beta r_M + \varepsilon$. The TSE 300 index is used as the market return r_M. A different regression is done using daily data for each firm in each year.

9 A firm's unlevered beta, denoted β_U, is calculated as $\beta_U = \beta \times$ (value of equity/value of firm), where the value of equity over the value of the firm is approximated by one minus debt over assets. This construction under-states β_U if the firm's debt is sufficiently risky that it carries a hefty risk premium. Thus, it may understate the level of risk in some Bronfman companies at some times.

Bibliography

Amihud, Yakov and Baruch Lev."Risk Reduction as Managerial Motive for Conglomerate Mergers." *Bell Journal of Economics*, 12, 2 (1981):605-17.

Aron, Debra J. "Ability, Moral Hazard, Firm Size, and Diversification." *Rand Journal of Economics*, 19, 1 (1988):72-87.

Baker, George P. "Beatrice: A Study in the Creation and Destruction of Value." *Journal of Finance*, 47, 3 (1992):1081-119.

Benidickson, Jamie. "The Combines Problem in Canadian Legal Thought, 1867-1920." *University of Toronto Law Journal*, 43 (1993):799.

Brenner, Menachen and David H. Downes. "A Critical Evaluation of the Measurement of Conglomerate Performance Using the Capital Asset Pricing Model." *Review of Economics and Statistics*, 61, 2 (1979):292-96.

Berger, Philip and Eli Ofek. "Diversification's Effect on Firm Value." *Journal of Financial Economics*, 37 (1995):39.

Caves, Richard. *Multinational Firms, Competition and the Productivity in Host Country Markets*. Cambridge: Cambridge University Press, 1982.

Comment, Robert and Gregg Jarrell. "Corporate Focus and Stock Returns." *Journal of Financial Economics*, 37 (1995):67.

Daniels, Ronald and Paul Halpern. "Too Close For Comfort: The Role of the Closely Held Public Corporation in the Canadian Economy and the Implications for Public Policy." *Canadian Business Law Journal* (Forthcoming, 1995).

Daniels, Ronald and Jeffrey MacIntosh. "Toward a Distinctive Canadian Corporate Law Regime." *Osgoode Hall Law Journal*. (1991):884.

Diamond, Douglas. "Monitoring and Reputation: The Choice Between Bank Loans and Directly Placed Debt." *Journal of Political Economy*, 99 (1991):689.

Donaldson, Gordon. "Voluntary Restructuring: The Case of General Mills." *Journal of Financial Economics*, 27, 1 (1990):117-41.

Firth, Michael. "Takeovers, Shareholder Returns and the Theory of the Firm." *Quarterly Journal of Economics*, 94 (1980):235.

Gahlon, James M. and Roger D. Stover. "Diversification, Financial Leverage and Conglomerate Systematic Risk." *Journal of Financial & Quantitative Analysis*, 14, 5 (1979):999-1013.

Jensen, Michael. "Agency Costs of Free Cash Flow, Corporate Finance, and Takeovers." *American Economic Review*, 5 (1986):323.

———. "Eclipse of the Public Corporation." *Harvard Business Review*, 61, 5 (1989).

John, Kose and Eli Ofek. "Asset Sales and Increase in Focus." *Journal of Financial Economics*, 37 (1995):105.

Keynes, John Maynard. *The Means to Prosperity*. London: Macmillan, 1933.

Matsusaki, John G. "Takeover Motives during the Conglomerate Merger Wave." *Rand Journal of Economics*, 24, 3 (1993):357-79.

Montgomery, Cynthia A. and Birger Wernerfelt. "Diversification, Ricardian Rents, and Tobin's q." *Rand Journal of Economics*, 19, 4 (1988):623-32.

Morck, Randall. "On the Economics of Concentrated Ownership." *Canadian Business Law Journal*, (Forthcoming, 1995).

Morck, Randall, Andrei Shleifer and Robert Vishny. "Do Managerial Objectives Drive Bad Acquisitions?" *Journal of Finance*, 45 (1990):31.

Myers, Stewart and Nicholas Majluf. "Corporate Financing and Investment Decisions When Firms Have Information That Investors Do Not Have." *Journal of Financial Economics*, 13 (1984):187.

Panzar, John C. and Robert D. Willig. "Economies of Scope." *American Economic Review*, 71, 2 (1981):268-72.

Pound, John. "Proxy Voting and the SEC: Investor Protection Versus Market Efficiency." *Journal of Financial Economics*, 29 (1991):241.

Roe, Mark. *Strong Managers, Weak Owners: The Political Roots of American Corporate Finance*. Princeton, N.J.: Princeton University Press, 1994.

Rose, Nancy and Andrea Shepard. "Firm Diversification and C.E.O. Compensation: Managerial Ability on Executive Entrenchment?" Unpublished manuscript, 1994.

Rugman, Alan. "The Comparative Performance of U.S. and European Multinational Enterprises, 1970-79." *Management International Review*, 23, 2 (1994):4.

Wernerfelt, Birger and Cynthia A. Montgomery. "Tobin's q and the Importance of Focus in Firm Performance." *American Economic Review*, 78, 1 (1988):246-50.

Paul Halpern,   &   Vijay Jog,
Faculty of Management   School of Business
University of Toronto   Carleton University

7

Bell Canada Enterprises:
Wealth Creation or Destruction?

INTRODUCTION

ON APRIL 28, 1983 BELL CANADA ENTERPRISES INC. (hereafter BCE) succeeded Bell Canada as the parent corporation of a group of companies with interests in telecommunications services, telecommunications equipment manufacturing, energy and printing. At the time of the reorganization the new management holding company claimed to have the largest number of share-holders of any Canadian corporation. In the decade between 1983 and 1993, BCE's asset base grew from $15 billion to $37 billion.

This study analyzes BCE's growth, its strategic directions, and its value-creation performance in a number of ways, all within the context of agency costs and the role of corporate governance. To this end we describe the nature and size of BCE, evaluate the effectiveness of its corporate governance structure, and analyze the potential for the principal-agent problems that can lead to agency costs of equity.[1] We also investigate the agency cost associated with free cash flow, given the use of BCE's conglomerate structure as an internal capital market; and we document changes to its strategic directions as gleaned from its annual reports. We then emphasize BCE's acquisition-divestiture strategies and its financial performance over the ten years since its inception. Finally, we evaluate the market's assessment of BCE over this period by investigating the market value of BCE equity as compared to its value estimated as the sum of the market value of its constituent parts.

Our analysis indicates that BCE has displayed marginal performance over its initial ten years. During the first six years, BCE operated much like a large conglomerate, both purchasing and establishing companies, many of which were in areas unrelated to its core activities. The financing of those trans-actions was based on the steady cash flows derived from its regulated telecom-munications business. Its many acquisitions, however, do not appear to have increased shareholder value. A change in strategic direction occurred in the post-1989 period, which appears to have been recognized by shareholders. However, even with this change in strategic direction, it is apparent that BCE management still sees itself as a manager of assets, rather than of businesses.

From our analysis we conclude that BCE is an under-valued company exhibiting the classic characteristics of the "adverse selection" problem. Its past performance appears to have led investors to place a high discount on its underlying assets, reflecting the previous poor performance of its acquisition activities. It also appears that the diversified nature of the firm and its agency problems have had negative consequences for the valuation and performance of BCE. One way to unlock this under-valuation would be to re-shape BCE as a more focused firm – possibly with an arm's-length and minority relationship with its regulated subsidiary, Bell Canada.

WHY BCE?

BCE PROVIDES A UNIQUE OPPORTUNITY to assess the effects of agency costs and corporate governance. It is the largest company in Canada, and its shares are held by many individual and institutional investors, both domestically and internationally. The company is well-known outside Canada, and is interlisted on the New York Stock Exchange (NYSE). In addition, the governance structure of the company is consistent with the agency cost model. There are small managerial equity holdings; and although many institutions own large numbers of BCE shares, none of them is represented on the board. BCE is also insulated from the discipline of the takeover market for two reasons. The first is the sheer size of the company; although higher valued transactions (takeovers) have occurred in the United States, there have been none of this (potential) magnitude in Canada. The second reason is that there are foreign ownership restrictions on Canadian telecommunications companies and these preclude a foreign firm from acquiring an economically significant position in BCE. Moreover, because of BCE's large market capitalization, institutional investors in Canada, almost by default, have to hold shares of BCE, since it commands such a large weighting in the TSE 300 Index.

Finally, as a regulated utility Bell Canada, BCE's largest subsidiary, has historically contributed a large and relatively stable cash flow to the BCE entity. While providing a check on spending and investment by Bell Canada, the regulatory process has no oversight of the operating, investment and financing decisions of BCE Inc.[2]

The diversified nature of BCE and its size in relation to the rest of the Canadian corporate sector raises issues that have interesting implications for how we view corporate governance. These issues relate to agency costs arising from relatively small managerial stakes (simply because the size of the corporation prevents any individual from having a large stake); the issues of free cash flow; and, due to its large size, entrenchment behaviour.[3] While we can identify closely held Canadian companies to investigate the effect of entrenchment, they may not reflect the effect of free cash flow and the agency costs of equity through low managerial stakes.

Some Theoretical Background and BCE-specific Data

THE CONFLICT BETWEEN MANAGEMENT and shareholders, often referred to as the principal-agent problem, underlies the analysis in this study. The severity of the difficulties associated with agency issues is related to ineffective monitoring of management and to the existence of managerial compensation contracts that do not align the interests of management and shareholders. In addition, other markets, such as the takeover and product markets, which normally assist in reducing the severity of agency issues, may not be effective in the case of BCE.

This study considers a number of agency issues. First, there is the agency cost associated with low levels of managerial share ownership. In this case, managers consume excessive perquisites since the cost of this consumption to them is much lower given their small ownership stake. This perquisite consumption relates not only to lavish offices, for example, but also to low levels of effort. In addition, managers can strive to increase the size of the firm based on their desire for greater prestige and visibility, their wish to leave a legacy, and their anticipation of the increased compensation, which is generally related to the growth of both sales and assets of the firm.[4] In addition to excessive perquisite consumption, low levels of share ownership by management can lead to an adverse selection problem which has a negative effect on share prices. The intuition behind the adverse selection problem is the same as for the classic Akerlof lemon's premium in the market for used cars. This refers to a case where potential shareholders may find it difficult to reach a correct value of the firm due to their inability to separate "good" firms from "bad" ones; this inability, in turn, arises from the possibility that some firms will misrepresent firm information. If this is so, outside investors may demand a higher risk premium from all firms, thus producing a wedge between the cost of internal and external financing.

The second agency cost issue relates to the dollar investment by managers in the firm. Even though their proportionate ownership interest may be small, their dollar investment in the firm may represent a substantial proportion of their personal wealth. Since these managers may have poorly diversified personal portfolios, they may forgo projects that are profitable but may be risky since they are affected by the cost of failure to a greater extent than widely diversified shareholders. In addition, these managers may have an incentive to engage in risk-reducing investments through a conglomerate corporate structure.

The existence of free cash flow(s), defined as the amount of internally generated cash flow available over and above the funds needed to take all value-maximizing investment decisions, can also lead to an agency cost that reduces the share price. In this case, management uses the free cash flows to invest in unprofitable projects that increase the size of the firm, and hence their compensation and influence. This problem is particularly acute in companies with steady cash flows from operations. The conglomerate structure can lead to an internal capital market where cash flows from various parts of the conglomerate firm are used by management to invest in new businesses. In such companies, managers typically believe they can make better use of corporate cash flows than can individual shareholders. In this organizational form, the divisions of the firm share a common general office whose functions are to allocate the internally generated funds, monitor the performance of individual divisions and engage in strategic planning. However, the monitoring by investors of the executives who are responsible for these central office functions is blunted, since the firm's reliance on outside capital markets is relatively minor. These considerations imply that, in companies with certain character-istics – such as low managerial equity stakes, conglomerate structure, free cash flows and entrenched management – the share price will be depressed to reflect the agency costs and the inability to control these costs through effective monitoring, external market oversight, or increasing managerial equity stakes.

To provide a perspective on BCE in the context of the agency issues mentioned here, we present some statistics on BCE common equity securities. As can be seen in Table 1, the total number of shareholders for BCE has decreased over time, and the average share holding has increased from 740 shares per shareholder in 1985 to 1,278 shares in 1993. To some extent, this may reflect the growth of institutional-investor holdings in BCE stock. As suggested in a number of articles (including that by Holderness & Sheehan, 1988), the presence of institutional investors may overcome the free-rider problem caused by the cost of monitoring by individuals, and provide an effective control of agency costs in corporations.[5] A similar pattern can be seen when the number of shareholders and the average holding per shareholder are grouped by foreign and Canadian ownership. A striking feature of this representation is the larger average holding per shareholder for foreign owner-ship compared to Canadian ownership; this is consistent with the larger role played by institutions as investors in the United States, compared to Canada.

Since BCE is extremely large, it is also clear that a typical shareholder is not in a position to impose any capital market discipline. If it is assumed that control of at least a 5 percent block is required to have a credible influence; this would represent a holding of $700 million in 1993, an amount large enough to rule out even some of the country's largest institutional investors.

As an indication of the sheer size of BCE, the market value of the corpo-ration's equity increased from approximately $10.4 billion in 1985, equal to 9 percent of the total market value of shares on the TSE 300, to $14.2 billion in 1993, or 5.42 percent of the TSE 300 value. Despite its loss of relative weight on TSE 300 between 1985 and 1993, BCE had the largest market value of equity of all companies in Canada for all the years shown in Table 1.

As noted earlier, the ownership of shares of a company by management, and the monitoring activity of investors and the board of directors, are important elements in agency costs. In Table 2 we present some information directed at the potential for agency costs. We first note the size of the board of

TABLE 1
BCE SHARE STATISTICS

	1985	1986	1987	1988	1989	1990	1991	1992	1993
Total Shareholders	332,440	338,528	318,675	319,202	288,619	277,295	260,747	254,521	241,078
Average Shareholdings	740	783	859	907	1,046	1,101	1,190	1,200	1,278
No. of Cdn Shareholders	325,877	331,623	311,847	312,320	282,008	270,805	255,532	249,431	233,846
No. of Common Shares Owned (000s)	231,332	250,695	251,986	266,385	269,214	273,734	282,366	280,918	261,937
Average Shareholdings	710	756	808	853	955	1,011	1,105	1,126	1,120
No. of Other Shareholders	6,563	6,905	6,828	6,882	6,611	6,490	5,215	5,090	7,232
No. of Common Shares Owned (000s)	14,714	14,580	21,881	23,160	32,837	31,676	27,926	24,427	46,224
Average Shareholdings	2,242	2,112	3,205	3,365	4,967	4,881	5,355	4,799	6,392
Cdn-Owned Shares (000s)	231,332	250,695	251,986	266,385	269,214	273,734	282,366	280,918	261,937
Cdn-Owned Shares (%)	94.02	94.50	92.01	92.00	89.13	89.63	91.00	92.00	85.00
Foreign-Owned Shares (%)	5.98	5.50	7.99	8.00	10.87	10.37	9.00	8.00	15.00
Relative Weight on TSE 300 (%)	9.01	7.93	7.21	7.14	7.66	7.97	8.51	6.96	5.42
Market Value of Equity ($ millions)	10,365	9,850	10,169	10,786	13,783	12,064	14,779	12,672	14,252

TABLE 2

GOVERNANCE STRUCTURE

	1983	1984	1985	1986	1987	1988	1989	1990	1991	1992	1993
Percentage Ownership											
Board	0.0014	0.0014	0.0007	0.0008	0.0008	0.0010	0.0011	0.0012	0.0005	0.0005	0.0003
No. of Directors	21	22	19	21	20	20	19	20	20	19	15
No. of Corporate Insiders	7	10	7	7	6	6	5	6	7	6	4
No. of Directors - Other Companies	9	9	9	10	9	1C	10	10	9	9	7
No. of Directors - Other	5	3	3	4	5	4	4	4	4	4	4
Percentage Ownership											
Corporate Insider	67.80	76.12	51.31	61.20	72.63	86.25	87.03	88.13	70.86	71.99	56.01
Other Company	30.59	22.62	46.21	36.60	23.27	6.75	6.73	6.66	13.69	13.99	12.69
Law Firm	0.81	0.63	1.18	0.94	0.83	0.82	0.85	0.85	1.04	1.18	0.58
Financial Institution	0.68	0.48	0.94	0.95	0.84	0.72	0.00	0.00	0.00	0.00	0.00
Investment House	0.00	0.00	0.00	0.00	2.16	5.26	5.20	4.14	13.77	12.15	29.58
Individual	0.12	0.14	0.36	0.31	0.28	0.19	0.19	0.21	0.63	0.69	1.14

directors. As seen in Table 2, the number of board members declined from 21 in 1983 to 15 in 1993; the most striking decrease occurred in 1993 with the change in CEO. While there is no theory that suggests the optimal size of a board to promote effective monitoring, one senses intuitively that the larger the board the less effective it is likely to be. This is particularly true if there are many "inside" members on the board. The relative importance of inside directors to outside directors is also shown in Table 2. Over the sample period, the ratio of inside directors to all directors ranged from a high of .45 in 1984 to a low of .26 in both 1989 and 1993. The outside directors were composed primarily of individuals from other companies. There were also a few directors from investment houses, financial institutions and law firms. Finally, there were no directors from either pension or mutual funds. This board structure is not dramatically different from that of many other large Canadian companies and suggests that the monitoring role of the board is not very strong.

The existence and continuation of agency problems are affected by the board of directors and its role in monitoring the management. If we assume that membership on the board is suggested by the incumbent management, that information is provided to the board by the same incumbent manage-ment, and that the members of the board have no (or very little) equity in the firm, then we can infer that the board of directors is unlikely to discipline management to act in the best interests of its shareholders. Thus, the role of the board is crucial in resolving agency problems.

Our analysis shows that BCE has followed the standard practice of nominating a majority of outside members to the various required sub-committees of the board. Although not shown here, outsiders do represent a majority on the sub-committees on Management Resources, Pension Fund Policy, Investments, and Audit. Unfortunately, we know very little about the role(s) played by members of the BCE board, especially by the outside members. This does not imply that boards of directors generally (or the BCE board specifically) are necessarily captive to incumbent management; there is some empirical evidence that boards can and do occasionally engage in disciplinary behaviour. However, the evidence is not rich enough to indicate any pattern of intensity and success with respect to a board's monitoring when the firm's management is performing in a "satisfying" mode as opposed to a "wealth-maximization" role.[6]

The other element of agency costs derives from the percentage of shares owned by management. The higher this proportion, the better the alignment of the interests of managers and shareholders. In their survey paper, Jensen & Warner (1988) state:

> Share ownership can be an important source of incentives for management, boards of directors, and outside block holders. The pattern and amount of stock ownership influence managerial behaviour, corporate performance, and stockholder voting patterns in election contests. In addition, a firm's

characteristics can influence its ownership structure. The data suggest that for some firms the amount of ownership by inside or outside block holders is economically significant. The precise effects of stock holdings by managers, outside shareholders, and institutions are not well understood, however, and the interrelations between ownership, firm characteristics, and corporate performance require further investigation.

In the case of BCE, the percentage of BCE shares owned by insiders who are members of the board ranges from .0003 percent to a high of .0014 percent (see Table 2). Such small percentages are not at all surprising considering the size of BCE. Although not shown, some insiders held large numbers of BCE shares (during the sample period) and therefore had large dollar investments in the corporation. The effect of substantial dollar holdings by insiders is ambiguous. If the total investment in BCE is a large proportion of the insider's wealth, an insider could, conceivably, try to reduce the company's risk (thereby reducing any risk to his or her personal portfolio) by being overly conservative with respect to board decisions. On the other hand, if the amount invested in the company is a small proportion of a board member's overall wealth, then any risk-reducing behaviour will not be as important – although the agency issue will still be present. In the case of BCE, since it is so large, it is unlikely that any attempt by management to reduce risk through investment policy would be effective because so many assets would have to be shifted to have an effect on the company's risk. However, significant changes in assets and in risk exposure can be achieved by large diversification investments and/or divestitures. Such risk-reduction behaviour can be a significant factor in the decisions undertaken by management and may influence the value of the firm.

It is also interesting to note how the ownership percentages of the board members changed between 1983 and 1993. In the early years of the sample period, there was relatively little equity owned by members of the board who could be considered as truly "outsider" – *i.e.*, not even associated with BCE-related subsidiaries. However, in the last three years of the period, the relative ownership of BCE shares shows that outsiders held a proportionately larger number of shares. Nonetheless, this is unlikely to lead to any attempt to influence BCE's management. As will be seen later, this increase in ownership by outsiders coincides with some significant strategic changes announced by BCE.

Another interesting characteristic of BCE is its somewhat larger degree of immunity from product-market discipline. BCE has as its base Bell Canada, which is a regulated telecommunications company. Although there is now competition in the long-distance market and competition in local markets is on the horizon, Bell Canada has a strong brand name and remains large and financially strong. These factors ensure that even with these changes in the marketplace, Bell Canada will continue as a significant player, generating cash flows for the parent. This does not imply that Bell Canada will not restructure its operations to improve internal cash flows. However, the important issue is how these cash flows will be used.

Finally, the traditional disciplinary constraints on agency costs are not applicable to the BCE case. The takeover market has little relevance since the acquisition of a controlling interest would require such a substantial investment in a hostile takeover – an amount that is not likely to be available even in today's setting of globalized capital markets.[7]

This brief review of BCE suggests that the company has been substantially immune from the elements of the typical market-discipline environment with which other public corporations must cope. Its management holds a relatively small stake in the company, with outsiders owning relatively higher percentage(s) only in recent years. Thus, BCE has the elements consistent with high agency costs of equity. In addition, the holding company structure with large numbers of subsidiaries also introduces an agency cost of free cash flows.

BCE: FORMATION AND GROWTH

GENERAL

IT IS IN THE CONTEXT OF FORMATION AND GROWTH that a review of BCE is most relevant and necessary. Since the reorganization of BCE in 1983 was a crucial development in its future growth (and had been long sought by Bell Canada's management), our review of BCE starts in that year.

Prior to the 1983 reorganization, Bell Canada was a regulated company, subject to regulatory review and the determinations by the regulatory authority (the CRTC) with respect to rates that were "fair and reasonable". To allow for reasonable rates, the CRTC determined a revenue requirement based on the expected costs to be incurred by Bell plus an allowed return on capital projected over a period called the "test year". The total amount of this revenue requirement was then compared to forecast revenues based on existing rates; and rate adjustments were then approved by the CRTC. Crucial in determining the allowed return on capital was an estimate of the cost of equity capital, which was applied to the dollar book value of the equity of the consolidated company. Clearly, expected net income to Bell depended upon the allowed return to equity capital; the actual return on equity, and hence net income, depended on actual revenues earned and costs incurred over the period. Since there was no distinction made between regulated and unregulated operations under this form of regulation, there was *de facto* regulation of all of Bell Canada's operations. Thus, if a subsidiary such as Northern Telecom had a good year, its profits would be included in the regulatory process and would contribute to a lowering of telephone rates. If other subsidiaries' financial results were poor, telephone rates could be adversely affected. Whether or not the regulators would treat these outcomes symmetrically was always a matter of concern to Bell management. In any case, the process did not provide Bell with any incentive to engage in profitable competitive services or non-telephone operations.

The regulatory changes associated with the reorganization in 1983 were very important to BCE, particularly with respect to the growth of its non-regulated operations. Apart from ventures that were defined as integral to the provision of telecommunications services, such as the company that prints the telephone directories, BCE could now start companies and make investments free from the implicit regulation that was the hallmark of the previous regulatory regime. This new structure therefore provided an incentive to engage in these competitive operations. The change was also accomplished by a redefinition of corporate assets, some of which were regulated while others were not. An allowed rate of return was applied to the regulated assets which required the determination of a capital structure for the company's regulated operations. These operations had been a subset of the previous Bell Canada.

Prior to the reorganization, Bell Canada had both wholly-owned subsidiaries and majority control of a number of companies. However, the reorganization provided an incentive to expand both through acquisition and internal growth funded by Bell Canada's substantial cash flows. A review of the 1984 composition of BCE shows that it owned 15 major subsidiaries.[8] In 1987, this number increased to 20, further increasing to 29 in 1990, 33 in 1992 and then declining to 26 in 1994. If all of the subsidiaries of these major subsidiaries are included, the numbers of companies that were directly and indirectly controlled by BCE management were 64 in 1984, 105 in 1987, 198 in 1990, 178 in 1992, and 148 in 1994. The number(s) of subsidiaries and the increase over time are a clear indication of the expansion strategy followed by management.

BUSINESS SEGMENTS

BCE INC. HAS OPERATIONS IN MANY AREAS that are both related and unrelated to telecommunications. Table 3 shows the sectoral breakdown of BCE *Revenue, Assets* and *Earnings* by business segment.[9] The two major segments are telephone-related: Telecommunications and Equipment Manufacturing. For *Revenue* and *Earnings* a third segment, denoted as "Other", includes operations that are non-telecommunications related, such as financial services and pipelines, among others. For the *Assets* category, there are two additional segments, "Investments" and "Corporate". The former reflects investments in financial assets and investments in non-telephone related companies; the latter is the dollar amount, at book value, for BCE headquarters.

For *Revenue*, growth occurred in the two major segments, with Equipment Manufacturing growing at a faster rate than Telecommunications. The "Other" segment increased steadily through 1987, dipped in 1988, increased again (to its maximum) in 1990, then decreased quickly thereafter. The pattern for the two major segments in the *Assets* category again displays growth over the period, with Telecommunications growing more rapidly than Equipment Manufacturing. The "Investments" and "Other" segments in this category display growth up to 1990, at the end of which there was a significant reduction, signifying the change in strategy we address below. There was also a dramatic increase in the "Other" segment in 1989, followed by another large increase in 1990. This reflects significant investments by BCE. Beginning in 1991, the dramatic reduction is a result of the changes in operating strategy discussed below. The Corporate segment decreased in the period from 1987 to 1989, increased from 1990 to 1992, then fell again in 1993.

For *Earnings*, which we define as *earnings before interest and taxes*, we provide data for each of the three major segments. The data for 1993 are not presented since they are not available using a consistent definition, making any comparison with previous years virtually impossible. Earnings for the Telecommunications segment have continued to grow, reflecting the stable nature of the regulated operations. The Equipment Manufacturing segment is more volatile but, apart from 1988, showed positive growth over the period ending in 1992.[10] The "Other" segment was extremely volatile, reflecting not only the uneven operations of the entities in this segment but also the divestiture and closing of some of the companies.

Figures 1, 2 and 3 illustrate the breakdowns for Table 3 in percentage terms. For *Revenue* (Figure 1), the "Other" segment accounts for a very small percentage of the total, while the Telecommunications segment provides a slightly diminishing proportion over time. Beginning in 1991, the percentage of revenue from Equipment Manufacturing exceeded the percentage from Telecommunications. In the analysis of the *Assets* category (Figure 2) the three non-telecommunications segments are accumulated into "Other". In *Assets*, the Telecommunications segment continues to account for the largest component; and the "Other" segment increases until 1990 (with a small retrenchment in 1988); from 1991 onward, the proportion is small. Figure 3 shows clearly that the Telecommunications segment has been a consistent source of earnings for BCE.

In all three sectors, assets grew at a higher rate than revenue and earnings. The Equipment Manufacturing segment now has 34 percent of assets and generates 53 percent of revenue, but produces only 30 percent of earnings. Despite the fact that revenues from the Telecommunications segment fell from 57 percent in 1983 to 43 percent in 1992, this sector still contributes over two-thirds of earnings. It can also be seen that the Telecommunications segment has been a steady performer, with operating margins averaging 28 percent and return on assets in the 12 percent range. On the other hand, both the Equipment Manufacturing and "Other" segments have had low and volatile margins. Clearly, the corporation's foray into non-telecommunications businesses was not accompanied by attractive and steady performance; BCE's overall performance has clearly been supported by the regulated side of its business.

TABLE 3
SECTORAL BREAKDOWN OF BCE – REVENUE, ASSETS AND EARNINGS ($ MILLIONS)

	1983	1984	1985	1986	1987	1988	1989	1990	1991	1992	1993
Revenue											
Telecommunications	5,076	5,541	5,966	6,390	6,758	7,092	8,011	8,468	8,151	8,415	8,614
Equipment Manufacture	3,276	4,359	5,829	6,114	6,471	6,598	7,161	7,851	9,379	10,222	10,550
Other	550	715	1,051	1,063	1,092	755	1,509	2,054	964	935	663
Total	8,902	10,615	12,846	13,567	14,321	14,445	16,681	18,373	18,494	19,572	19,827
Assets											
Telecommunications	10,571	11,213	11,882	12,704	13,830	15,981	17,334	18,326	19,595	21,106	22,079
Equipment Manufacture	2,213	3,356	3,867	3,926	3,849	5,428	5,861	6,229	11,066	11,895	12,608
Other	337	423	1,918	3,589	3,815	236	11,797	12,980	(120)	599	851
Investments	1,183	1,423	1,802	2,190	3,577	3,291	3,640	3,286	0	0	0
Corporate	636	1,072	1,114	1,305	954	645	629	1,166	2,992	,056	1,170
Total	14,940	17,486	20,583	23,714	26,025	25,581	39,261	41,987	33,652	36,656	36,708
Earnings											
Telecommunications	1,436	1,586	1,735	1,843	1,772	1,838	2,035	2,259	2,358	2,495	n/a
Equipment Manufacture	297	470	581	583	606	250	623	820	1,067	1,178	n/a
Other	77	112	178	197	194	40	76	(3)	146	39	n/a
Total	1,810	2,167	2,494	2,623	2,572	2,128	2,734	3,076	3,571	3,712	n/a

TABLE 3 (CONT'D)

PERCENTAGES

	1983	1984	1985	1986	1987	1988	1989	1990	1991	1992	1993
Revenue											
Telecommunications	57.02	52.20	46.44	47.10	47.19	49.10	48.02	46.09	44.07	43.00	43.45
Equipment Manufacture	36.80	41.06	45.38	45.07	45.19	45.68	42.93	42.73	50.71	52.23	53.21
Other	6.18	6.74	8.18	7.84	7.63	5.23	9.05	11.18	5.21	4.78	3.34
Total	100.00	100.00	100.00	100.00	100.00	100.00	100.00	100.00	100.00	100.00	100.00
Assets											
Telecommunications	70.76	64.12	57.73	53.57	53.14	62.47	44.15	43.65	58.23	57.58	60.15
Equipment Manufacture	14.81	19.19	18.79	16.56	14.79	21.22	14.93	14.84	32.88	32.45	34.35
Other	14.43	16.69	23.49	29.87	32.07	16.31	40.92	41.52	8.89	9.97	5.51
Total	100.00	100.00	100.00	100.00	100.00	100.00	100.00	100.00	100.00	100.00	100.00
Earnings											
Telecommunications	79.35	73.16	69.57	70.26	68.90	86.37	74.43	73.44	66.03	67.21	n/a
Equipment Manufacture	16.41	21.67	23.30	22.23	23.56	11.75	22.79	26.76	29.88	31.73	n/a
Other	4.24	5.16	7.14	7.51	7.54	1.88	2.78	0.00	9.00	1.05	n/a
Total	100.00	100.00	100.00	100.00	100.00	100.00	100.00	100.20	100.00	100.00	n/a

Note: n/a = not available.

FIGURE 1

BCE REVENUE: SECTOR BREAKDOWN

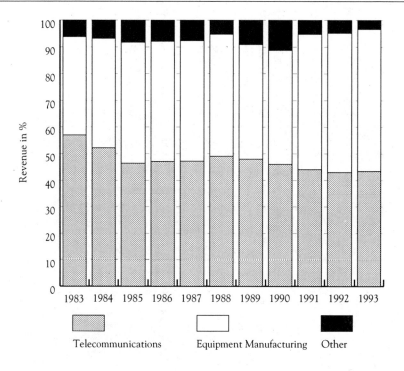

STRATEGIC DIRECTIONS

IN LIGHT OF THE UNEVEN AND GENERALLY UNATTRACTIVE performance in its non-regulated business sectors, it is worthwhile to evaluate BCE's changes in strategic direction over the ten-year period under review. There appear to have been two distinct phases in the evolution of BCE strategic philosophy. The first phase, from 1983 to approximately 1989, reflects diversification and growth through acquisitions directly by BCE or through subsidiary companies. This strategy is closely associated with the CEO, Jean de Grandpré. The second phase, from 1990 to 1993, reflects the corporation's return to its core activities – by divesting non-telecommunications assets and purchasing telecommunications-related assets both in Canada and abroad. Growth in the second phase was accomplished both by acquiring majority positions and by making non-majority investments. Clearly, the latter are portfolio investments and, in this sense, the company did not change from the holding company philosophy that it followed during the first phase. Throughout both phases (periods), the

FIGURE 2

BCE ASSETS: SECTOR BREAKDOWN

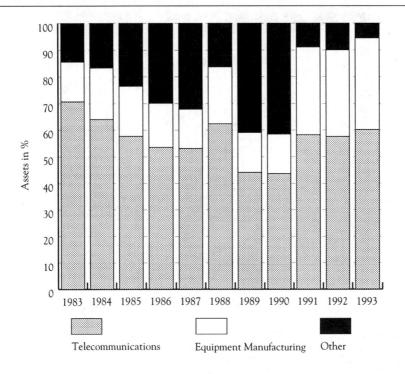

corporation's regulated telecommunications activities in Canada have provided significant cash flows.

Phase 1 - The Diversification Years

Beginning in 1983 with the acquisition of TransCanada Pipeline (TCPL), BCE entered its diversification phase funded by its available pool of internal capital. As noted in the 1983 annual report,

> BCE will avoid large investments in businesses which have financial characteristics fundamentally different from those of the existing businesses – for example, companies which experience severe fluctuations in earnings through an economic cycle... .

> TCPL was attractive because of the growth and stability of its income stream and asset base.

FIGURE 3

BCE EARNINGS: SECTOR BREAKDOWN

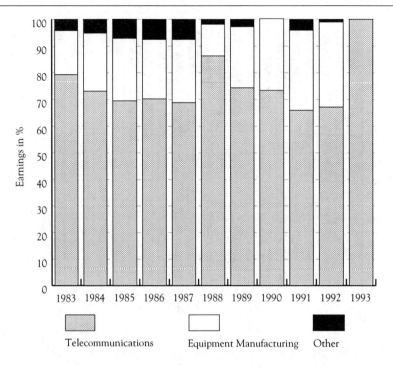

In considering the supply of funds during this acquisition phase, the following was noted in the annual report:

> We have a large and growing pool of capital; and BCE will continue to study opportunities for investment and diversification, either directly or through subsidiary companies.

BCE's diversification strategy was continued in 1984 with the purchase of a number of large real estate assets. The diversification approach was affirmed in the following statement in the annual report.

> An important aspect of BCE's management activities is to encourage entry into new businesses which may not fall naturally within the business plans, experience or resources of a particular business within the group.

The importance of the telecommunications segment in the BCE organization was reinforced in 1986, when severely depressed energy prices combined with weaknesses in parts of the real-estate markets had a negative impact on BCE earnings. As noted in the annual report, "The negative impacts of some of these conditions on some of our investments were *more than offset by strong growth in other operations, especially telecommunications*"(italics added). The company also extended its diversification activities to additional markets. As the annual report noted, "the security provided by the diversity of our positions in various industries is now fully reinforced by the additional security of diverse markets for each company's products and services". During 1986, the company raised $300 million of equity of which $200 million was used to maintain its percentage holding in BCE Development Corporation (BCED), its real estate operation.

In 1988, while affirming their strategy of diversification, management noted a change in its previous policy – of generally seeking a "strong voting position" in companies in which BCE invested.

> Recent transactions do, in effect, signal a more flexible attitude towards control in situations where we have strong confidence both in management and in the fundamental soundness of the business prospects.

Finally, in 1989, the company's corporate strategy began to be questioned openly. That year, the company entered the financial services business with the purchase of Montreal Trust Inc. from Power Financial Corporation. A selection of quotes from the 1989 annual report illustrate these questions and the beginning of the shift in emphasis.

> We have reassessed what sort of businesses are best suited to our corporate strategies, and how these investments should fit together.

> We intend to continue our investments in telecommunications. We have also entered into financial services and we expect the future will see growth in this area. In addition, BCE will maintain certain other long term investments, such as natural gas transportation, but will not hesitate to review and alter other holdings in the light of changing circumstances.

> In view of what happened in 1989, when disastrous results from one subsidiary, BCED, had the effect of wiping out the contribution to BCE's consolidated net income of several well-performing companies, some shareholders may question the whole notion of a diversified holding company, or retain some nostalgia for earlier, more simple times.

> BCE assets outside of telecommunications must meet the criteria of financial compatibility. Financial services and natural gas pipelines, although different from our core telecommunications business, fit this corporate strategy.

TABLE 4

BCE ACQUISITIONS 1983 - 1989

COMPANY	DATE OF ANNOUNCEMENT	COMMENT
TransCanada Pipelines	December 5, 1983	Bell acquires 5.3 million shares from Dome, valued at $168 million, tenders an offer for all shares outstanding at $31.5 per share; approximate value of $670 million, or an 8.34% premium.
Esso Bank Note	September 21, 1984	Offers 0.85 Bell shares for 2.6 million shares. Approximately $71 million – a 27% premium.
Daon Development Corporation	January 21, 1985	First move into real estate. Approximate value $160 million. General tender offer for shares outstanding at $3, representing a 13.33% premium.
Encor	November 16, 1987	TCPL announces bid for Encor to expand oil and gas base and offers $8.75/share. Approximate value $980 million.
Kinburn	February 9, 1988	BCE gives Kinburn a loan of $190 million.
Northwest Tel	August 29, 1988	Pays CNR $200 million for all shares of Northwest Tel, giving Northwest Tel a monopoly over Northern BC, Yukon, and NWT.
Montreal Trust Inc.	March 8, 1989	Package of $875 million in cash and shares. Purchased from Power Financial Corporation, representing a premium of $4.38/share, 2.5 times book value.
Encor	January 5, 1989	TCPL proposes spinning off Encor to BCE to raise cash and reduce debt. TCPL to get $570 million in cash to pay down debt.

Table 4 sets out the list of major diversification acquisitions undertaken during this period (Phase 1, as referred to earlier) when management saw its role as managers of assets, not as managers of businesses. In 1987 the annual report stated:

> Asset growth is a particularly relevant measure of BCE's performance, because the role of BCE's management is primarily one of managing assets rather than business.
>
> Five essential ways asset management can enhance BCE's performance:
>
> 1. Acquisition
> 2. Divestiture
> 3. Re-grouping of existing units
> 4. Creation of new operating units
> 5. Public equity participation.

The management of BCE is committed to using all the options available to it to pursue the ultimate objective of increasing the company's value to its shareholders.

This emphasis on asset growth is consistent with agency costs of equity and free cash flow rather than shareholder value maximization through efficient operation of companies.

Phase 2 - Returning to Core Activities

In 1990 a new CEO took over from de Grandpré. Raymond Cyr began a process which attempted to refocus the operations of BCE. The company concentrated on the telecommunications business both in Canada and internationally, where there were perceived to be many growth opportunities. The result was a decided improvement in the financial results of the company. In addition, the company reduced its investment in Encor and TCPL and announced its intention to divest the remainder of its energy-related assets by the end of 1992. BCE also wrote down the value of loans made to Kinburn and wrote off BCED. However, as part of an assistance plan for BCED, the company invested $250 million in a joint venture with Carena Developments, which acted as the manager of the rescue attempt. Tables 5A and 5B list the major acquisitions and divestitures during these years. This focus continued through 1991.

BCE's strategy in the immediate future is to continue refining our corporate focus, divesting non-core interests and improving profitability. In a longer perspective, we will expand our role on the international market, with the goal of becoming a strong global competitor.

The final year of Cyr's tenure as CEO was marked by a continuation of the return to BCE's core businesses. As noted in the annual report, there was a divestment of $1.1 billion of non-core assets.

BCE's major goal will be to continue to improve our earnings by focusing closely on telecommunications, asserting our competitive strengths in Canada and expanding our international business through alliances, joint ventures, and investments.

Thus the company continued to make acquisitions during this period, including the acquisition of 20 percent of Mercury Communications Limited, a British provider of telecommunications services, and a majority interest in a U.K.-based cable TV and telecommunications company. This international focus was also reflected in the telephone directory business, with the acquisition of the Caribbean Publishing Company and the formation of a joint venture to publish directories in India.

In 1993 a new CEO took over and the refocusing on core activities, both domestically and internationally, continued. The company completed the

TABLE 5A

BCE ACQUISITIONS 1990 - 1993

COMPANY	DATE OF ANNOUNCEMENT	COMMENT
BF Realty	January 24, 1990	Assets transferred into BF Realty with a $500-million loan from BCE and Carena.
Kinburn/SHL Systemhouse	April 17, 1990	BCE seized 5.1 million shares of SHL as part of a Kinburn loan covenant. Kinburn failed to pay $350 million of a $400-million loan.
Telemax	September 27, 1990	Joint bid for 20.4% of Mexican government Telephones with an approximate value of $400 million.
SHL Systemhouse	February 3, 1992	SHL strategic partnership issues 32.5 million shares at $12.75, valued at $414 million.
SHL Systemhouse	June 10, 1992	Alliance deal falls apart.
Mercury Communications	November 11, 1992	British cable investment, valued at $960 million. This gives BCE a 20% stake in Mercury.
Talisman	March 10, 1993	Exchange of Encor shares for Talisman shares. BCE to hold 19% of Talisman shares, worth $234 million. This is considered a more liquid investment.
Talisman/Encor	April 15, 1993	Share offer enhanced by $17.7 million.
Jones Intercable	December 2, 1993	30% stake in U.S. cable company, valued at $330 million. BCE Telecom International also paid $55 million for an option to buy control, as well as invest $100 million in expansion plans.

divestiture of its non-telecommunications assets, acquired non-controlling positions in foreign companies and engaged in the formation of a number of joint ventures. As noted in the 1993 annual report, "BCE will continue to invest in rapidly growing telecom markets in Canada and abroad".

However, even with its redefined focus on core activities, senior BCE management continued to view its role as that of a manager of assets. The shareholders, while viewing the divestiture of the diversification activities positively, need not be satisfied with the continuation of the asset management philosophy and the holding company approach. BCE shareholders do not need BCE to make partial investments in publicly traded corporations; if they want to make such investments, they can make them on their own.

TABLE 5B

BCE DIVESTITURES 1989 - 1993

COMPANY	DATE OF ANNOUNCEMENT	COMMENT
BCED	June 27, 1989	O&Y offers to buy BCED for $557 million.
BCED	August 11, 1989	O&Y deal fails. Analysts believe they backed out of the deal.
BCED	January 24, 1990	Closed out BCED. BCED takes $610 million write-down. BCE took a $400 million write-down for its share of BCED.
Encor	June 27, 1990	Unloading 48.9% of Encor in share issue. Valued at $100 million. $7 for 3 shares and 2 warrants. Shares trading at $2.
TransCanada Pipelines	September 10, 1990	Issues warrants to sell 48.9% stake in TCPL for approximately 1.3 billion. $119 million after tax gain.
Kinburn	October 24, 1990	BCE takes $224 million write-down due to loan default.
Montreal Trust Co.	December 2, 1993	Sold to Bank of Nova Scotia for $290 million with a $400 million write-down. Some analysts believe price $100 million less than expected.
BF Reality and Brookfield	December 2, 1993	Sold to Carena Development Corp., taking a $350 million write-down.

EVALUATION OF THE OPERATING STRATEGIES

ACQUISITIONS, DIVESTITURES AND WRITE-DOWNS

TO IDENTIFY THE MAJOR ACQUISITIONS and divestitures for which dollar values are reported, we reviewed the *Financial Post* cards and BCE annual reports, considering only acquisitions made by BCE and not those made by wholly owned subsidiaries such as Bell Canada or partially owned companies such as Northern Telecom. There are a number of acquisitions and divestitures in every year, some of which may be relatively small individually but, depending on whether BCE is in a net acquiring or divesting mode, may be large in the aggregate. Also, there are some transactions for which dollar values are not available. The total amount of investments in other companies and subsidiaries can therefore be substantial. Further, BCE's capital expenditures are extremely large. From the consolidated statements we observe that capital expenditures in every year from 1987 to 1993 were never less than $3.2 billion.

TABLE 6

ACQUISITIONS & DIVESTITURES ($ MILLIONS)

		ACQUISITIONS			
	DATE	ORIGINAL $	1994 $	CAR (-5, +5)	T-STAT
TCPL	Dec. 5/83	838.00	1,218.14	−0.0376	−2.27
Esso Bank Note	Sept. 21/84	71.00	100.38	−0.0121	−1.19
Daon	Jan. 21/85	160.00	223.39	0.0661	6.51
Encor	Nov. 16/87	980.00	1,213.76	−0.0075	−0.82
Kinburn	Feb. 2/88	263.00	299.30	0.0290	1.79
Northwest Tel	Aug. 29/88	200.00	240.01	0.0032	0.32
Montreal Trust	Mar. 8/89	875.00	1,024.60	−0.0044	−0.43
Encor	Jan. 5/89	570.00	675.19	−0.0055	0.52
BF Realty	Jan. 24/90	500.00	561.30	−0.0493	−6.86
Telemax	Sept. 27/90	400.00	436.94	−0.0078	−0.99
Mercury	Mar. 11/93	960.00	977.88	0.0072	0.86
Talisman	April 10/93	251.70	254.04	0.0092	1.06
Jones Intercable	Dec. 2/93	330.00	329.26	0.0097	1.17
		DIVESTITURES			
BCED	Jan. 24/90	400.00	449.04	−0.0493	−6.86
Encor	June 27/90	100.00	112.26	−0.0166	−2.34
TCPL	Sept. 10/90	1,300.00	1,420.05	−0.0032	−0.43
Kinburn	Oct. 24/90	224.00	242.67	0.0670	7.84
Montreal Trust Co.	Dec. 2/93	290.00	289.35	0.0097	1.17
Montreal Trust Co.	Dec. 2/93	400.00	399.10	0.0097	1.17
BF Realty	Dec. 2/93	350.00	349.21	0.0097	1.17

Except for 1991 and 1992, the value of acquisitions was generally large in all the years (between $1.0 billion and $1.9 billion). Finally, disposal of investments began in 1990 and ranged from $400 million to $1.3 billion. In our analysis, we consider only those transactions that were in excess of $200 million.

FIGURE 4

BCE ACQUISITIONS 1983 - 1993

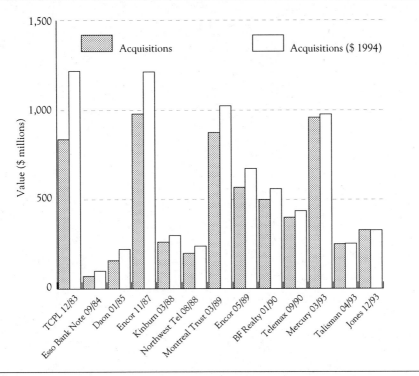

Note: Acquisitions made before 08/89 were made with Grandpré as CEO. Between 08/89 and 04/93,
        Cyr was CEO. Also note that Encor was purchased initially by TCPL and was spun off to BCE.

Table 6 and Figures 4 and 5 summarize these major acquisitions and divestitures in original dollars as well as in 1994 dollars. Table 6 also shows the reaction of capital markets to the corresponding announcement of these events, as reflected in the BCE share price. The first series of transactions is concerned with the acquisition and ultimately the sale of TCPL. December 1983 registered the first of a series of transactions in which BCE acquired a significant portion of TCPL shares; by 1987, BCE had invested approximately $1 billion in TCPL. In 1987 TCPL purchased Encor and, in 1989 under a reorganization, all of TCPL's oil and gas assets were consolidated into the newly formed Encor Inc., with BCE receiving shares in this newly created company. In addition, BCE purchased $227 million of Encor preferred shares, which were convertible into Encor equity. Beginning in 1990 BCE began to sell off the Encor and TCPL assets, and by 1993 all TCPL shares had been sold for a total of approximately

FIGURE 5

FIGURE 5

BCE DIVESTITURES 1990 - 1993

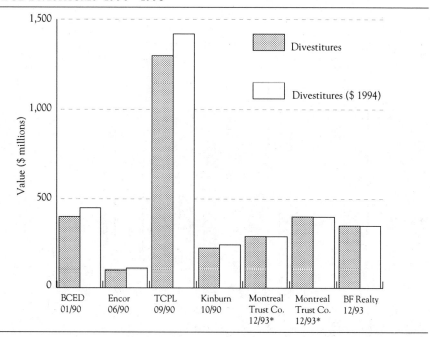

Note: * Montreal Trust was sold in two blocks.

$1.3 billion. In 1993, Encor shares were sold to Talisman for $275 million worth of Talisman shares. BCE received approximately $100 million in 1990 for the sale of some Encor shares. The cost of the combined TCPL and Encor transaction was approximately $1.2 billion. BCE received approximately $1.6 billion over the ten years that the corporation held equity in these companies. This total transaction was nominally profitable.

The second series of transactions, which relate to BCE's foray into real estate, was not as profitable. In 1985 BCE purchased approximately 69 percent of the shares of Daon for approximately $160 million. The real estate market faltered badly and, in mid-to-late 1989, Olympia and York offered to purchase Daon, but the deal fell through. At the beginning of 1990, BCE wrote down its investment in Daon, renaming it BCED. BCE then entered a joint venture with Carena in which Carena would manage the BCED assets. BCE agreed to advance up to $250 million to the joint venture. The real estate market failed to improve, however, and in 1994 BCE sold its interests in BCED, renamed BF Realty, to Carena in exchange for an agreement that Carena would provide financial support to a subsidiary of BF Realty in order to enable the subsidiary to complete its restructuring. These acquisitions and divestitures were extremely unprofitable for BCE, and did little to generate confidence in the ability of management to engage in a profitable diversification strategy under a holding company structure.

The third set of transactions centred on another diversification thrust, this one into the financial services industry, with the acquisition of Montreal Trust from Power Corporation for $875 million in shares and cash. The deal was originally transacted in 1989. In December 1993 BCE agreed to sell Montreal Trust to the Bank of Nova Scotia in exchange for (bank) common shares valued at approximately $290 million. BCE took a $400 million charge against its investment in Montreal Trust.

In 1988 the company sold its interests in certain subsidiary companies to Kinburn for notes valued at approximately $190 million. In 1990 Kinburn defaulted on its loan. BCE then wrote down the loans and seized 5.1 million shares of SHL Systemhouse as a part of a Kinburn loan covenant. BCE had previously held a small interest in SHL. Early in 1993 the company sold its equity investment in SHL, but the terms were not disclosed. There had been previous attempts to sell this interest.

During this period BCE continued to acquire companies that were in the telecommunications area. In 1988 the company acquired Northwest Tel for $200 million. Some of the international diversification transactions include the acquisition of an interest in the equity of Telemax, the Mexican government telephone system, for approximately $400 million; the acquisition of a 20 percent equity interest in Mercury Communications, a British cable company, for approximately $1 billion; and the acquisition of a 30 percent interest in the equity of Jones Intercable, a U.S. cable company, for approximately $330 million.

ABNORMAL RETURNS ON ANNOUNCEMENTS

TO DETERMINE THE REACTIONS OF INVESTORS to announcements of acquisitions and divestitures, we estimated the cumulative abnormal returns (CAR) and the corresponding t-statistics for a period of 11 days, centring on the date of each announcement. Although not shown here, most of the observed reactions to BCE's acquisition-divestiture program, as indicated by the CARs, were found to be small and statistically insignificant.[11] These findings of no meaningful reaction by BCE's shareholders to BCE's divestiture and acquisitions are not surprising for two reasons. First, while some of the transactions were large in terms of absolute dollar amounts, they were still small relative to the size of BCE, and thus market reaction, if any, would be difficult to detect. Second, for the events associated with write-downs there should be no abnormal return, since this is not a cash flow item and these write-downs reflect the economic realities that should already be reflected in the share price of BCE. A significant share price reaction would be observed only if the write-down provided new information to the market. For example, the BF Realty/BCED transactions in January 1990 could reflect the disappearance of the Olympia and York bid and the formation of a joint venture, which could lead to continuing losses. However, no meaningful statistically significant reactions were observed.

FIGURE 6

CUMULATIVE WEALTH INDEX, BCE vs TSE 300

Even in the absence of statistically significant reactions, one of the note-worthy features of these acquisition-divestiture phases at BCE is that, in most instances, these acquisitions resulted in significant value destruction for BCE shareholders. Except for a nominal gain recorded for the TCPL divestiture, BCE's investments in the realty, energy, financial services and software integration areas suffered major losses. Its current portfolio of acquisitions is relatively new, and whether these acquisitions ultimately prove to create value awaits the verdict of time. Moreover, from the reaction of the security market to the announcements of these acquisitions, investors did not interpret them as wealth-enhancing.

Mercury Communications and Jones Intercable reflect minority positions and their impact on BCE's cash flows will depend upon activities and manage-ment decisions unaffected by BCE management. As straight portfolio invest-ments, the insignificant abnormal returns associated with these transactions are to be expected.[12]

FIGURE 7

BCE CUMULATIVE EXCESS RETURNS

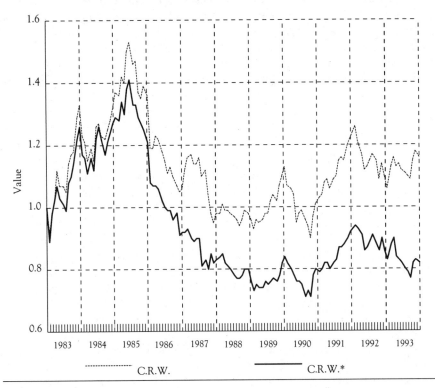

Notes: CRW is calculated with Ri – Rf.
CRW* is calculated with standard market model.
Both omit October 1987.

PERFORMANCE OF COMPANY RETURNS

AN IMPORTANT PERSPECTIVE OF BCE PERFORMANCE has to do with the impact of operating, financing, and investment decisions on its shareholders. Figure 6 shows the cumulative wealth index based on monthly returns for BCE and the TSE 300 Index for the period from 1983 to 1994. The cumulative excess returns shown in Figure 7 are measured using the risk-free rate as well as the standard market model over the same period.[13] Figure 6 shows that BCE stock outperformed the TSE 300 Index especially in the post-1990 period, a period consistent with the change in corporate strategy. Similar conclusions can be drawn from Figure 7, which shows positive cumulative excess returns in that latter period. Over the period from 1985 to 1990 the cumulative excess wealth falls. This is consistent with almost continuously negative excess returns, implying that during this period BCE's shareholders experienced negative risk-adjusted returns. The cumulative excess returns have yet to reach the relative performance of BCE in its early years.

Viewing BCE as a portfolio of investments suggests another way to observe the wealth effects of investments made by BCE management. As a portfolio, the excess return over an investment horizon should also provide another indication of the success of the investments made by BCE. The Jensen performance measure is used to identify any wealth gains or losses. It is the estimated value of the intercept from a regression of the excess monthly return on BCE equity on the excess monthly return on the TSE 300 Index. The excess return is defined as the rate of return on equity for month t, less the corresponding monthly yield on a Government of Canada Treasury bill.

Table 7 sets out the values of the intercept and summary statistics for the regressions over various time periods. We first consider the effect of the diversification activities on the performance of the company. Looking over the period from 1983 to 1989 when all of the diversification activities occurred, the Jensen measure was very small (.076 percent) and not significantly different from zero. What can we say about the period when the new strategy emerged in 1990 to refocus and return to the core activities by concentrating on the telecommunications business? The Jensen measure for this period is .024 percent and, again, is not significant. This is probably due to the fact that this period was still affected by the continued presence of Montreal Trust, which was not sold until the end of 1993. The poor performance of this subsidiary would have affected the performance of the overall company. Therefore, it may be too early to evaluate the effect of the new strategy. Using the four three-year non-overlapping periods to evaluate the performance of BCE, beginning in 1983, we also see that none of the intercepts is statistically significant, and the values of the Jensen measure are small. Clearly, the overall performance of the corporation during this period does not indicate that BCE created shareholder wealth from a risk-adjusted perspective.

Valuation of BCE

The Holding Company Discount

ANOTHER WAY TO IDENTIFY THE EFFECTS of the potential agency costs from small managerial equity stakes and free cash flows on value creation in the context of a holding company is to compare the market value of the equity of BCE with the sum of the values of its constituent parts. If the market value of the equity of the total entity were found to be less than the sum of the market values of the component parts, this finding would be consistent with the presence of agency costs and what is often referred to as the "holding company discount". In general, the BCE share price will be affected by three factors.

TABLE 7

JENSEN REGRESSIONS

PERIOD	ALPHA	T STAT
1983 - 1985	0.01076	0.24
1984 - 1986	0.00044	0.01
1985 - 1987	−0.00245	−0.08
1986 - 1988	−0.00494	−0.18
1987 - 1989	0.00076	0.03
1988 - 1990	−0.00046	−0.02
1989 - 1991	0.00292	0.10
1990 - 1992	0.00363	0.13
1991 - 1993	0.00165	0.06
1983 - 1989	0.00076	0.02
1990 - 1993	0.00024	0.01

- Growth opportunities generated both by the management of the individual entities in the BCE structure and by the ability of BCE management to develop or acquire profitable subsidiaries or portfolio investments.

- The negative impact of agency costs.

- A negative impact due to the "holding company discount".

The holding company discount is often referred to as discount observed on closed-end investment funds, where such funds usually have a market price lower than the net asset value of their holdings. The size of the discount is variable and, at times, the closed-end fund sells at a premium to its net asset value. As noted earlier, BCE management is not involved in the management of the businesses, but rather in the management of the assets of the overall firm and the investment of the cash flows generated by the constituent parts. To the extent that shareholders view BCE's management as a manager of the assets of the individual companies similar to a portfolio investment, there is an analogy to the closed-end fund.

Can the effect of growth opportunities and the presence of agency costs exist simultaneously? While the two components can co-exist, it is the net result of the two factors that is important. For example, at the BCE (i.e., holding company) level, the agency cost argument suggests that management consumes a large amount of perquisites and its investment decisions need not be optimal. The free cash flow theory proposes that investment in diversification activities or other areas will be excessive and beyond the optimal amount. Therefore, even if some of the investments do follow the net present value rule and generate above-normal profits, the possible use of free cash flow to finance non-value-maximizing investments and the expectation by the market of continued future behaviour of this type will have a negative effect on the market value of the equity. The net result in such circumstances could be a negative impact on share prices.

Is the holding company discount a factor separate from the influence of agency costs? It is difficult to explain the perception that a closed-end investment fund – issuing equity claims and purchasing a set of securities – results in a loss of wealth. The fact that many of these funds have not been "opened", even though doing so would improve investors' wealth, suggests either that the market value of the fund does not reflect its true value (if a sale of the underlying securities were undertaken) or that there may be constraints to removing the existing management. In the latter case, it could be that management is entrenched and making decisions which are either reducing wealth through excessive perquisite consumption or not investing the cash flows from the securities in an optimal way. Barclay *et al.* (1993) find that the larger the managerial (or managerial affiliated) blocks in closed-end funds, the larger the discounts to net asset value tend to be. They observe that the average discount over their sample period for closed-end equity funds with management affiliated blocks is 15 percent, and for those without blocks the discount is 8.2 percent. They only include blocks which have not been accumulated for the purpose of opening the fund.

Our search for equivalent Canadian closed-end investment funds has been disappointing. We could find only one closed-end fund, that can be truly defined as a fund, which holds primarily Canadian common stocks. For 1993 this fund had a discount of 17 percent.[14]

Barclay *et al.* (1993) attribute this discount to an agency cost that is based on benefits accruing to managers of these funds who, by having large blocks, can entrench themselves and receive private benefits. These benefits include the earning of management fees, fees for purchasing research, commissions on securities transactions, acquisition of services from related companies and the employment of relatives and friends.[15] In the holding company context, the discount, if it exists, can be associated with the agency costs that we have identified. As noted previously, the holding company provides an internal capital market due to the generation of cash flows; to the extent that these cash flows are stable, the company is able to issue debt to finance its activities. Freed from direct equity market monitoring, management can engage in diversionary behaviour leading to a reduction in value. There is, however, no literature that documents the size of holding company discounts and whether they change over time. Although we believe that the holding company discount is really a manifestation of the agency cost issue, we include it in our analysis as a separate variable.

The Valuation of Components and the Discount

The task of valuing individual subsidiaries of BCE and the comparison of their aggregate value to the overall BCE value is not easy for a variety of reasons. To provide a perspective on this difficult task, it should be noted that there are a large number of companies in the BCE structure, including wholly owned subsidiaries, majority owned subsidiaries, and portfolio investments both in Canada and abroad. For example, in 1993 there were 142 subsidiaries, of which 94 had BCE ownership greater than 90 percent, 20 were majority owned, and 28 were portfolio investments. This compares with the 1983 total of 73 subsidiaries, of which 46 were wholly owned, 7 majority owned, and 20 portfolio investments.[16]

In addition, both the assets and revenues of these subsidiaries and portfolio investments have changed dramatically, since they are affected by BCE's acquisitions and divestitures. The assets increased dramatically in 1989 and fell in 1993, reflecting the Montreal Trust purchase and divestiture, respectively. Prior to 1988, wholly owned assets, as a proportion of total telecommunications and other assets, ranged from approximately 3 percent to 11 percent of total BCE assets. From 1989 to 1992, the proportion increased to approximately 42 percent, reaching a maximum of 47 percent in 1992. The value in 1993 fell to 18 percent following the major diversifications of that year. Although the wholly owned non-financial subsidiaries have generated approximately $1 billion in revenue and now have over $4 billion in assets, they have generated only small or negative earnings.

BCE also has some significant holdings in wholly owned subsidiaries. Some of the subsidiaries are actually larger than many medium-size Canadian companies. For example, Tele-Direct had a revenue of $497 million in 1993 and employed 2,700 people worldwide. There are also a variety of minority investment holdings of BCE such as Jones Intercable, Mercury Communications, Encom and Videotran, among others.

To estimate the value of the components of BCE, we have grouped these subsidiaries and portfolio investments into three major classes – Bell Canada, subsidiaries with publicly traded equity in Canada, and all other wholly owned subsidiaries. Since Bell Canada is wholly owned, an estimate of value must be inferred by examining companies that are comparable in terms of risk. Since the companies in the second class are publicly traded, the market value of this class equals the price per share of each of the publicly traded subsidiaries multiplied by the number of shares of each company owned by BCE. These subsidiaries, along with BCE's interest in them and their estimated market values, are shown in Table 8. Apart from Bell Canada, we have not valued any of the wholly owned subsidiaries belonging in the third class, but assume initially that their values are zero. However, given the poor performance of the diversification activities described thus far, it is possible that the wholly owned subsidiaries have had a negative influence on the share value of BCE, or that the market,

TABLE 8

BCE's PUBLICLY TRADED SUBSIDIARIES

	PERCENTAGE OWNED							
	1983	1984	1985	1986	1987	1988	1989	1990
BCE Development Co.	–	–	67.9	65.8	67.0	67.0	67.0	67.0
BCE Mobile Communications	–	–	–	–	–	80.6	73.0	69.7
BF Realty Holdings	–	–	–	–	–	–	–	–
Bruncor Telephone Co.	–	–	30.7	31.2	31.0	31.2	31.2	31.4
Encor	–	–	–	–	–	–	48.9	67.0
Maritime Telegraph	32.5	31.4	31.4	32.0	32.5	33.1	33.7	33.8
Memotech Data	–	–	–	–	–	31.6	30.8	31.5
New Brunswick Telephone Co.	32.5	31.3	–	–	–	–	–	–
Newfoundland Telephone Co.	54.4	53.3	–	–	–	–	–	–
NewTel Enterprises	–	–	53.4	54.2	54.9	55.5	56.0	55.7
Northern Telecom	51.9	51.9	52.0	52.3	52.5	52.8	53.1	53.1
Quebecor Inc.	–	–	–	–	–	21.2	21.2	21.6
TransCanada PipeLines	42.3	47.2	47.8	48.5	49.3	49.1	48.9	24.4

with limited information on these subsidiaries, has placed a discount on the implied value of the non-traded subsidiaries.[17] The approach, then, is to compare the overall value of the BCE as reflected in its market price to the estimated value of the first two classes of subsidiaries, assigning a zero value to all other wholly-owned subsidiaries except Bell Canada. Since both the market value of the publicly-traded subsidiaries and BCE's ownership of them is known, the main challenge is to estimate the value of Bell Canada.

In order to estimate the implied value of Bell Canada, we identified a set of comparable companies that are in a similar business to Bell Canada, although they are certainly smaller. Recently, the introduction of long distance competition has affected all of the companies, but not equally, since they do not have the same ratios of long-distance to local exposure. The former influence may result in a lower discount rate if size is inversely related to risk; while the latter influence results in higher risk and hence a higher

TABLE 8 (CONT'D)

BCE'S SHARE OF SUBSIDIARY MARKET VALUE ($ MILLIONS)

	1983	1984	1985	1986	1987	1988	1989	1990
BCE Development Co.	–	–	236	271	252	345	135	14
BCE Mobile Communications	–	–	–	–	–	1,002	1,493	832
BF Realty Holdings	–	–	–	–	–	–	–	–
Bruncor Telephone Co.	–	–	102	100	102	104	105	108
Encor	–	–	–	–	–	0	234	187
Maritime Telegraph	73	90	101	108	114	123	163	164
Memotech Data	–	–	–	–	–	112	115	93
New Brunswick Telephone Co.	74	80	–	–	–	–	–	–
Newfoundland Telephone Co.	73	76	–	–	–	–	–	–
NewTel Enterprises	–	–	93	94	100	108	136	127
Northern Telecom	2,864	2,702	2,950	2,679	2,747	2,502	3,444	4,197
Quebecor Inc.	–	–	–	–	–	66	49	51
TransCanada PipeLines	595	968	1,008	980	999	1,107	1,269	640
Total	3,680	3,916	4,489	4,231	4,313	5,467	7,143	6,414
BCE Market Value ($millions)	7,204	8,289	10,365	9,850	10,169	10,786	13,783	12,084
% of BCE Market Value	51.08	47.24	43.31	42.95	42.41	50.69	51.82	53.08

discount rate. How these two influences affect the value of Bell Canada is difficult to determine; and so we assume that they net out.

Table 9 shows valuation ratios for five telecommunications companies – BC Telecom, Bruncor, Maritime Tel&Tel, Newtel Enterprises, and Telus. For each of these companies the following three ratios are calculated for the years 1985 to 1993: market value of equity to earnings, market value of equity to revenue, market value of equity to assets. By applying the ratio for the average of these companies (and excluding some obvious outliers due to write-offs and highly unusual items) to the appropriate Bell Canada financial variable for

TABLE 9

ESTIMATION OF IMPLIED BELL CANADA MARKET VALUES 1985 - 1993

	1985	1986	1987	1988	1989	1990	1991	1992	1993
MARKET-VALUE-TO-EARNINGS RATIO									
BC Telecom	10.2	10.1	8.66	8.88	10.5	10.5	12.4	10.7	13.6
Bruncor	12.5	10.9	10.4	10.5	61.8	10.9	11.0	11.2	55.8
Maritime Tel & Tel	9.59	10.5	9.08	8.98	10.0	8.65	9.9	9.25	11.5
Newtel Enterprises	9.86	9.79	9.51	9.5	9.51	11.4	11.7	10.1	12.5
Telus Corporation	0	0	0	0	0	25.4	11.9	10.2	12.3
Average	**10.5**	**10.3**	**9.42**	**9.46**	**10**	**10.4**	**11.4**	**10.3**	**12.5**
MARKET-VALUE-TO-SALES RATIO									
BC Telecom	0.95	0.98	0.88	0.87	1.11	1.1	1.29	1.08	1.32
Bruncor Inc.	1.38	1.27	1.21	1.14	1.07	1.02	1.07	1.2	1.42
Maritime Tel & Tel	1.05	1.02	0.99	0.98	1.08	1.0	1.11	1.09	1.26
Newtel Enterprises	1.27	1.16	1.1	1.04	0.95	0.88	1.1	1.1	1.34
Telus Corporation	0	0	0	0	0	1.52	1.76	1.52	1.76
Average	**1.16**	**1.11**	**1.04**	**1.01**	**1.05**	**1.11**	**1.27**	**1.2**	**1.42**
MARKET-VALUE-TO-ASSETS RATIO									
BC Telecom	0.39	0.42	0.42	0.44	0.54	0.57	0.67	0.56	0.71
Bruncor Inc.	0.6	0.55	0.54	0.49	0.46	0.42	0.43	0.48	0.58
Maritime Tel & Tel	0.47	0.45	0.43	0.41	0.43	0.4	0.45	0.43	0.48
Newtel Enterprises	0.55	0.48	0.47	0.33	0.39	0.35	0.44	0.43	0.55
Telus Corporation	0	0	0	0	0	0.58	0.72	0.57	0.69
Average	**0.5**	**0.47**	**0.46**	**0.42**	**0.45**	**0.46**	**0.54**	**0.49**	**0.6**

TABLE 9 (CONT'D)								
VALUES FOR BELL CANADA ($ MILLIONS)								
1985	1986	1987	1988	1989	1990	1991	1992	1993
Operating Revenue								
5,769	6,255	6,378	6,624	7,273	7,655	7,729	7,863	7,957
Net Income (after extra-ordinary items)								
652	711	731	793	875	966	986	1,006	871
Total Assets								
11,941	12,693	13,508	14,512	15,699	16,605	17,163	18,414	18,945
IMPLIED BELL CANADA VALUE BASED ON:								
Market Value-to-Earnings Ratio								
6,868	7,346	6,886	7,502	8,758	10,007	11,213	10,352	10,869
Market Value-to-Sales Ratio								
6,712	6,930	6,651	6,669	7,650	8,465	9,787	9,414	11,305
Market Value-to-Assets Ratio								
6,024	6,024	6,274	6,065	7,125	7,695	9,267	9,090	11,364
Average 6,535	6,776	6,603	6,745	7,844	8,722	10,089	9,619	11,179

each year from 1985 to 1993, we obtain three estimates of the implied value of Bell Canada. These values are shown at the bottom of Table 9. The implied value for Bell Canada for any year is equal to the average of the three estimated values for Bell Canada, using the different valuation ratios.

In Table 10, the implied equity values for Bell, publicly traded subsidiaries, and the sum of these two values are presented for the years 1985 to 1993. The sum of these two values is the implied value of BCE, assuming that the non-traded, wholly owned subsidiaries of BCE have no value. The corresponding actual market values of BCE equity are shown in column 5 of the table. To determine if the actual market value is above or below the implied value we calculate the discount, defined as the actual market value minus the implied value, both in dollar terms and as a percent of the implied value. As can be seen in the table, the dollar discount is always negative and ranges from a low in 1985 of $675 million to a high in 1992 of $6.09 billion. The percent discount had its lowest value of 6 percent in 1985 and its highest value of 32 percent in 1992. The discount value for 1993 is 25 percent.

TABLE 10

ESTIMATE OF THE UNDERLYING BCE MARKET VALUES AND DISCOUNTS ($ MILLIONS)

YEAR	ESTIMATED VALUE OF BELL	VALUE OF PUBLICLY TRADED SUBSIDIARIES	BCE IMPLIED VALUE	BCE ACTUAL MARKET VALUE	DISCOUNT (ACTUAL IMPLIED)	DISCOUNT (%)	REDUCTION IN BELL IMPLIED VALUE FOR BREAKEVEN (%)
1985	6,535	4,505	11,040	10,365	−675	−6.11	10.33
1986	6,767	4,263	11,030	9,850	−1,180	−10.70	17.44
1987	6,604	4,368	10,972	10,169	−803	−7.32	12.16
1988	6,746	5,480	12,226	10,786	−1,440	−11.78	21.35
1989	7,845	7,154	14,998	13,783	−1,216	−8.11	15.50
1990	8,723	6,425	15,147	12,064	−3,084	−20.36	35.35
1991	10,090	8,596	18,686	14,779	−3,907	−20.91	38.72
1992	9,620	9,141	18,761	12,672	−6,089	−32.46	63.30
1993	11,180	7,895	19,075	14,252	−4,822	−25.28	43.14

Obviously, one possible explanation of the discount is that the value of Bell Canada has been incorrectly calculated and is too high. If this were true, we consider the size of the estimation error that would be necessary in order to make the implied and actual market values of BCE the same. In the last column of Table 10, the overestimate of the implied Bell value is calculated as a proportion of the implied value. In order to break even, the value of the implied Bell market value would have to be reduced by approximately 43 percent in 1993 and 64 percent in 1992: the lowest value is 10 percent in 1985. While it is possible that we may have overestimated the value of Bell, it is unlikely that the differences would be as large as are required to achieve the breakeven value. In addition, we have assumed a zero value for the wholly owned subsidiaries – which is clearly incorrect. In 1993, these subsidiaries accounted for almost $800 million in revenue and $4 billion in assets. This assumption therefore reduces the implied value of BCE; the result should be a premium, not a discount, when the actual and implied market values are compared.

In contrast to some evidence consistent with improved value-creation performance noted in the previous section, the size of the implied discount indicates that the discount has actually increased over time. Some of it may be the result of (our) undervaluation of Bell Canada. However, it should be emphasized that in Table 10 we have assigned absolutely no value to the wholly owned subsidiaries of BCE. If there is any value in these subsidiaries, then our analysis would indicate an even higher discount associated with BCE shares –

an observation consistent with the agency cost arguments of free cash flow, small managerial stakes, entrenchment, and internal capital markets through the holding company structure.

SUMMARY AND CONCLUSIONS

THE UNDERLYING PURPOSE OF THIS STUDY is to provide an analysis of the effects of agency costs and corporate governance on corporate value. BCE was used as an example in our analysis because it represents the stereotype of a widely held large firm where monitoring by the board of directors and shareholders is unlikely to be effective. In addition, entrenchment of management exists because of the large size of the company and constraints on foreign ownership of Bell Canada. Another interesting aspect of BCE is the importance of free cash flow and the holding company structure of the company with respect to agency costs.

Our analysis of BCE is consistent with the intuitive implications of the agency costs argument: if managers have a very small equity stake in the company, there is a greater chance that dispersed external shareholders may place a lower value on the firm. Although the board of directors is expected to monitor management performance and reduce any misalignment of interests, it is very likely that the board's efforts in this connection may not be effective.

Our analysis also indicates that the performance of BCE is not as stellar as it could be in the light of its changing corporate strategy, its historical propensity to make diversification investments in unrelated areas, and its continued holding-company mentality of managing assets and not maximizing shareholder value. Although a return to its core business has been evident since 1990, our analysis also indicates that the market continues to place a substantial discount on BCE shares. This discount can be explained by the market's expectation of management investment of free cash flows generated primarily from the regulated telecommunications company into wholly owned and portfolio investments in related and quasi-related businesses across the world.

What changes are necessary to increase the value of BCE and thereby reduce the discount we have observed? In order for changes to have any effect on the discount, the market must anticipate that those changes will reduce the agency costs and improve the efficiency of BCE. One approach is to improve the monitoring of management by having a more active board on which there are outside representatives. This is the crux of the TSE guidelines on the composition of the board, although we would require that "independent" directors not be so defined if they are associated with any subsidiary and/or affiliated BCE company. However, while this change in board structure is necessary, it is not sufficient to generate the changes that may be required. Even with the best structured board, its effect on operations will still depend upon the strength it shows in its interactions with the CEO and inside directors. A strong CEO can control even the strongest and best intentioned group of outside board members. Also, without a direct linkage between the outside directors' compensation to shareholder wealth, the influence of the board may well be muted.

A second approach to unlocking this discount would be to reduce BCE's ownership in wholly owned subsidiaries. This action may generate a more transparent method for valuing individual components within the BCE structure. However, this is unlikely to reduce the discount dramatically for two reasons. First, we have measured the discount by assuming that the subsidiary values are zero. If the subsidiary values were positive, however, the discount would actually be larger, not smaller. Second, the conversion of wholly owned subsidiaries to partially owned subsidiaries with publicly traded equity will not remove the holding company discount, since BCE will still be valued at a discount similar to a closed-end investment fund.

A third approach would be to sit back and wait for the discipline of the product market to take effect in the markets in which BCE subsidiaries and investments sell their goods and services. Some of the subsidiaries and partially owned companies are in competitive industries and the product market will have an effect here. However, as long as cash flows are generated from other parts of the holding company, BCE can subsidize money-losing operations in competitive markets.

At present, Bell Canada is BCE's major subsidiary and under the current regulatory structure it is a regulated monopoly which has only modest incentives to become more efficient and large incentives to acquire assets and increase the size of its rate base. With the arrival of competition in supplying long distance telecommunications services, there has been a push to improve the efficiency of some operations. The most recent action is the elimination of a large number of jobs. Further, if price-cap regulation is introduced as an alternative to the current rate-base, rate-of-return form of regulation, there will be an added incentive for Bell Canada to improve its efficiency and hence its cash flows. However, those larger cash flows will ultimately be channelled to BCE and we are left with the same problem we started with – dissipation of wealth through uneconomic investments.

We are caught in a dilemma. On the one hand we argue that BCE shareholders will have their share value maximized if BCE spins off or sells off its non-telecommunications assets and returns to a pure telecommunications company, which may or may not include the long-distance aspects of its business. This could be equivalent to the U.S. decision under which AT&T was broken into local and long-distance companies. However, in this case the impetus is shareholder maximization and not purported efficiencies due to competition. On the other hand, there may be economies of scope which arise from the operation of a number of related companies. This factor suggests a spin off/sell off of some companies, but retention of the telecommunications companies. Shareholder value would be maximized if the retained companies were managed more effectively and the emphasis on asset management were eliminated. However, the unanswered question is whether BCE management can manage this resulting company to create value, perhaps assisted by a more active board of directors. From our analysis, BCE management has historically been unsuccessful in coming even close to reaching this objective.

ENDNOTES

1   The popularity of the agency theory approach to analyzing firm value is generally attributed to the Jensen-Meckling paper in 1976, although similar arguments can be traced to Veblen (1924) and Manne (1965).

2   Technically, regulation is on the regulated operations of Bell Canada, thereby removing some of the competitive operations from regulatory control. The introduction of competition in long distance and proposed changes in regulation could have an effect on cash flows from Bell Canada.

3   Since there is voluminous literature in this area, we refer to it only briefly. The seminal papers are: Manne (1965), Jensen & Meckling (1976), Myers & Majluf (1984), Demsetz & Lehn (1985), Jensen (1986), and Hoshi et al. (1989).

4   See Jensen & Meckling (1976), Jensen (1986), and Elitzur & Halpern (1995).

5   However, Holderness & Sheehan (1988) also state on page 319,

> We note at the outset that in light of the current lack of knowledge about large-block shareholders and the paucity of precise hypotheses about them in the literature, this paper is as much a descriptive analysis as it is a test of specific hypotheses on the role of majority shareholders.

6   See Morck, Shleifer & Vishny (1989), Weisbach (1988), and Warner, Watts & Wruck (1988).

7   In light of the recent and very large leveraged buyouts (LBOs) and takeovers, it may be argued that no company is now immune from being taken over. However, BCE is quite different from many other large companies which have been taken over or have successfully completed an LBO transaction. Unlike these companies, in the case of BCE, there is a large degree of uncertainty about the potential response of the regulators of its telephone subsidiary, Bell Canada, and about its holdings of other regulated telephone companies. In addition, there is a legislated cap on the proportion of equity ownership of a telecommunications company by a foreign company. This would eliminate the incentive for a foreign firm, which could have access to capital markets to finance a takeover of BCE, to engage in such a takeover.

8   This number includes only those which are classified as a level 2 subsidiary by Statistics Canada in its Intercorporate Ownership Statistics. A level 2 subsidiary is defined as one on which the parent exerts (can exert) direct control. This number, therefore, excludes those companies which are in turn owned by these fifteen subsidiaries. We have also excluded "numbered" subsidiaries of BCE in this count.

9   Earnings are defined as operating earnings before interest and taxes.

10 For 1993 the after-tax net income contribution from the equipment manu-facturing segment is $-\$588$ million (loss), reflecting the serious problems faced by Northern Telecom.

11 These abnormal returns and their t-statistics are based on standard event methodology using mean returns estimated over 120 days, ending 30 days prior to the actual event date as the expected return for calculating the abnormal returns on the event date. Daily data is used in all cases and CARs are reported for the $(-5 +5)$ window with event date termed as day zero.

12 Note that BCE paid $400 million for a 20 percent stake in Telemax in 1990. The recent devaluation of the Mexican peso may imply a possibility of a write-down of this investment similar to the one recently announced by Labatt's.

13 The cumulative wealth index is defined as the net cumulative value of $1 invested net of the risk-free rate. Cumulative excess returns is calculated using the market model with the TSE 300 representing the index. The regression period used in these calculations is a 60-month moving period, updated monthly.

14 The discount is a sufficiently important problem that at least one manage-ment has tried to reduce it through innovative means. Canadian General Investment Ltd. decided to list its shares on the London Stock Exchange, where the average discounts are 7 percent and 12 percent for single country funds. The discount at the announcement date of February 13, 1995 was 28 percent. Management anticipated a reduction of the discount to 15 per-cent. As of February 25, 1995, the discount was 26 percent; and the shares will be listed in London at the end of February, 1995. See *Report on Business*, February 14, 1995, pp. B13.

15 For a discussion of the literature on agency costs associated with high owner-ship and its effect on equity value see Daniels & Halpern (forthcoming, 1995).

16 See Statistics Canada, Catalogue number 61-517, various years.

17 In its 1993 annual report, BCE lists the value of its investment in these wholly owned subsidiaries and its minority interests. These amount to approximately $2 billion.

ACKNOWLEDGEMENT

WE WOULD LIKE TO THANK the Financial Research Foundation of Canada and the Social Sciences and Humanities Research Council for providing partial funding for this study. We also wish to thank James Blake for his extremely valuable research assistance.

BIBLIOGRAPHY

Akerlof, G. A. "The Market for 'Lemons': Qualitative Uncertainty and the Market Mechanism." *Quarterly Journal of Economics*, 84 (August 1970):488-500.

Barclay, M., C. Holderness and J. Pontiff. "Private Benefits from Block Ownership and Discounts on Closed-end Funds." *Journal of Financial Economics.* (June, 1993):263-91.

Daniels, R. and P. Halpern. "The Role Of The Closely Held Public Corporation In the Canadian Economy and the Implications for Public Policy." *Canadian Business Law Journal.* (Forthcoming, 1995).

Demsetz, H. and K. Lehn. "The Structure of Corporate Ownership: Causes and Consequences." *Journal of Political Economy*, 93 (1985):1155-77.

Elitzur, R. and P. Halpern. "Executive Compensation and Firm Value." Paper presented at the Conference on Corporate Decision-making in Canada, March 20-21, 1995, Toronto, Canada.

Holderness, C. G. and D. P. Sheehan. "The Role of Majority Shareholders in Publicly Held Corporations." *Journal of Financial Economics*, 20 (1988):317-46.

Hoshi, T., A. Kashyap, and D. Scharfstein. "Corporate Structure, Liquidity, and Investment: Evidence from Japanese Industrial Groups." *Quarterly Journal of Economics*, CVI (1989): 33-60.

Jensen, M. C. "Agency Costs of Free Cash Flow, Corporate Finance, and Takeovers." *American Economic Review*, 76 (1986):323-29.

Jensen, M. C. and W. Meckling ."Theory of Firm: Managerial Behavior, Agency Costs and Ownership Structure." *Journal of Financial Economics*, 7 (1976):305-60.

Jensen, M. C. and J. B. Warner. "The Distribution of Power Among Corporate Managers, Shareholders, and Directors." *Journal of Financial Economics*, 20 (1988):3-24.

Manne, H. "Mergers and Market for Corporate Control." *Journal of Political Economy*, 73 (1965):110-20.

Morck, R., A. Shleifer, and R. W. Vishny. "Alternative Mechanisms for Corporate Control." *American Economic Review*, 79 (1989):842-52.

Myers, S. C. and N. S. Majluf . "Corporate Financing Decisions When Firms Have Investment Information that Investors Do Not." *Journal of Financial Economics*, 13 (1984):187-221.

Shleifer A., and R. W. Vishny. "Large Shareholders and Corporate Control." *Journal of Political Economy*, 94 (1986):461-88.

Veblen, T. *The Engineers and the Price System*, New York: Viking, 1924.

Warner, J. B., R. L. Watts, and K. H. Wruck. "Stock Prices and Top Management Changes." *Journal of Financial Economics*, 20 (1988):461-92.

Weisbach, M. S. "Outside Directors and CEO Turnover." *Journal of Financial Economics*, 20 (1988):431-60.

Clifford G. Holderness
Wallace E. Carroll School of Management
Boston College

Commentary on Part III

Large-Block Shareholders and Conglomerates: Sense or Nonsense?

INTRODUCTION

T HE PARADIGM THAT HAS DOMINATED RESEARCH in financial economics for over 60 years is that of the widely held corporation. Yet, we now know that most public corporations, even many large ones, have shareholders who own high-percentage blocks of common stock. For example, Mikkelson & Partch (1989) find that in a random sample of 240 NYSE and Amex industrial corporations, officers and directors on average control 20 percent of the votes (median 14 percent). Similarly, Holderness & Sheehan (1988) report that 11 percent of all NYSE and Amex corporations have majority shareholders who control at least 50 percent of the common shares.

Ownership of Canadian corporations is even more concentrated than that of American corporations. In their study elsewhere in this volume, Rao and Lee-Sing classify only 23 percent of Canadian corporations as being widely held, compared with 40 percent of American corporations. I believe the Canadian situation to be more "natural" than that in the United States because a series of populist laws passed by Congress in the 1930s disenfranchised natural large-block shareholders, specifically financial institutions (Roe, 1990). Despite (or perhaps because of) these laws, evidence shows that since the 1930s the ownership of American corporations has become significantly more concentrated.[1]

The relationship between blockholders and conglomerates is one that has been overlooked in the rapidly growing literature on ownership structure. This potentially important relationship is, however, addressed in two studies presented at this conference on Corporate Decision-Making in Canada: "In High Gear: A Case Study of the Hees-Edper Corporate Group" by Ron Daniels, Randall Morck and David Stangeland; and "Bell Canada Enterprises: Wealth Creation or Destruction?" by Paul Halpern and Vijay Jog. These studies address the role of blockholders in the context of two very different companies, albeit with some important similarities. The Hees-Edper Group is controlled by the Bronfman family. Hees-Edper, in turn, owns high-percentage blocks of stock in other corporations. BCE, the largest Canadian corporation, holds dozens (and at times hundreds) of high-percentage stakes in other companies.

Both Hees-Edper and BCE hold blocks in companies in diverse businesses. In short, both are conglomerates with blockholder features.

My comments here will focus on the relationship between blockholders and conglomerates generally, and on these two studies specifically.

CHANGING VIEWS OF ECONOMISTS ON CONGLOMERATES

ECONOMISTS' VIEWS OF CONGLOMERATES have changed significantly over the last 25 years.[2] In the 1960s and 1970s economists largely applauded the efforts of corporations to expand into unrelated fields. A number of arguments were advanced in support of such expansion. Conglomerates could allocate capital more efficiently than markets; conglomerates could do a better job of identifying and developing promising young managers; and conglomerates could take cash generated by mature industries and funnel it to promising growth areas, solving what has become known as the free-cash flow problem.

By the mid-1980s this attitude had changed, and conglomerates were not held in such high regard. In the United States several highly publicized hostile takeovers were aimed at companies that had diversified. Upon gaining control, the acquirer would often sell divisions unrelated to the company's core operations. At the same time, academic studies were appearing to confirm that a focused firm typically creates more value for its shareholders than does an unfocused conglomerate.[3]

Although the current opinion of academics and the financial press is anti-conglomerate, there are nonetheless some glaring exceptions, notably active large-block shareholders, such as Warren Buffett and Laurence Tisch. Although such individuals are almost universally classified as active investors (see Jensen,1993), they could also be classified as conglomerate investors. Buffett, for example, counts among his investments large blocks of stock in transportation (US Air), newspapers (Washington Post), financial services (Salomon Brothers), and food (See's Candy). Tisch controls an insurance company (CNA), a movie theater chain (Loews), and a television network (CBS).

Are these active investors to be praised for their conglomerates, while others are criticized? Are conglomerates somehow more effective when controlled by an active investor? To answer such questions – questions which are important both in Canada and the United States – we need a theory of conglomerates. The studies on Hees-Edper and BCE go beyond praise or criticism of conglomerates. Both studies seek to understand conglomerates in a deeper sense. My remaining comments offer suggestions for extending these studies and thus furthering our understanding of the relationship between conglomerates and blockholders.

TOWARD A THEORY OF CONGLOMERATES AND BLOCKHOLDERS

INCENTIVES OF TOP MANAGEMENT

INDIVIDUALS, NOT CORPORATIONS MAKE DECISIONS. Consequently, to understand any organizational form, we must examine the punishment and reward structure confronting top decision-makers. Both studies pursue this issue.

Halpern and Jog identify a major change in policy at BCE in the early 1990s to refocus operations. During the 1980s BCE had diversified into a large number of industries, many of which had little, if anything, to do with BCE's primary operations in communications. This policy changed in the early 1990s, coincidental with the arrival of a new CEO, Raymond Cyr. I would like to see this issue explored further. Why was there a change in CEO? Were both CEOs compensated in the same manner? How was their compensation structured? In particular, was the new CEO's compensation package more oriented toward incentive-based compensation (bonuses and stock options)? Was the change to a more focused operation at BCE actually the result of Cyr's efforts?

Daniels, Morck and Stangeland also explore the incentives of top executives. They claim that the Hees-Edper Group uses "extreme incentive-based compensation schemes ... to pay managers, and in some cases employees".[4] They further state that Hees-Edper's top managers faced asymmetric incentives: if their gambles paid off, the managers profited personally; if their gambles failed, on the other hand, the managers did not suffer the consequences. This sounds like the incentives confronting savings and loan executives in the United States during the 1980s: win with a risky investment and you get the upside; lose with a risky investment and the government (through its guarantee of deposits) is left with the loss.

The compensation scheme at Hees-Edper is worthy of additional investigation. The authors cite only one newspaper article as proof of the asymmetric compensation system. Stronger and more definite information about the precise nature of the compensation would be helpful. For both studies I would also like to see investigations of top management turnover. Is it related to firm performance? Is it related to the composition of the board of directors? Recent papers by Rose & Shepard (1994), Mehran (1995), and Dial & Murphy (1995) offer examples of how the authors of the BCE and Hees-Edper studies could expand upon their already-illuminating discussions of executive compensation.

THE ROLE AND INCENTIVES OF THE BOARD OF DIRECTORS

THE BOARD OF DIRECTORS IS CLOSELY RELATED to the top management team. The board has the legal power to manage the corporation, a right which it delegates, but does not transfer outright, to top managers. Halpern and Jog report that board membership at BCE fell from 21 in 1983 to 15 in 1993. This is interesting given that it has been argued that small boards are typically more effective than large boards. Some commentators maintain that a board with fewer than 10 members is optimal, even for the largest corporations. Halpern and Jog, however, do not explore why the reduction in board size at BCE took place, nor do they discuss the implications of the change on firm performance. Neither do Daniels et al. discuss boards within the Hees-Edper Group or at the Hees-Edper portfolio companies.

I would like to see both studies investigate the role of the board of directors. Boards need not be ineffective in the presence of a large-block, even majority, shareholder. For example, there is research that analyzes the serious constraints placed by a board of directors on a domineering majority shareholder – in this case, Ted Turner of Turner Broadcasting (Holderness & Sheehan, 1991). Do directors in the Hees-Edper Group have such powers? Similarly, do directors of companies in which BCE owns large blocks have such powers? What is the role of the Bronfman family on the Hees-Edper boards?

Similarly, it would be illuminating to determine the relationship between top executive turnover and firm performance. Here the work of Weisbach (1988) is potentially valuable. Investigations in this area should recognize the importance of a three-way classification of directors into insiders, grays (those who have business relations with the company, such as lawyers and investment bankers), and true outsiders. The traditional classification of insiders *versus* outsiders can miss important effects.

SHARED BENEFITS OF BLOCKHOLDER CONTROL OF CONGLOMERATES

THERE ARE TWO (NOT MUTUALLY EXCLUSIVE) REASONS why someone would hold a high-percentage block of stock. First, a blockholder can use voting power to improve management. The benefits related to this are often called "shared benefits" of control because they accrue to all shareholders. Second, a blockholder can use voting power to secure corporate benefits that do not accrue to other shareholders. The related benefits in this case are often called the "private benefits" of control.

There are several interesting research topics on the shared benefits of blockholder control of a conglomerate. For example, one could hypothesize that a blockholder would have a greater effect on the management of a conglomerate than on the management of a focused corporation. The explanation might take this form: blockholders are primarily monitors; monitors have generalized skills that are not limited to specific firms or industries; thus, blockholders are most effective in conglomerates. Certainly, Warren Buffett and Laurence Tisch seem to fit this profile.

Although this is a plausible explanation, I know of no supporting or, for that matter, contradicting empirical evidence. The two studies under discussion, however, touch upon potential shared benefits of blockholder control of a conglomerate. BCE, for example, often buys complete control of non-telecommunications companies but only buys minority control of companies in its primary business of telecommunications. This pattern could reflect regulatory constraints, or it could reflect the shared benefits of control.

The Daniels, Morck and Stangeland study offers little discussion of what types of block investments are made by Hees-Edper, much less why they are made. Development of this point could yield valuable insights.

Finally, it would be interesting to see how management in the target firms changes after either BCE or Hees-Edper makes a block investment. The authors could investigate the stock-price reaction when BCE or Hees-Edper initially announces a large block investment. Similarly, the authors could investigate operational changes and top management turnover following block investments.[5]

CONSTRAINING PRIVATE BENEFITS OF BLOCKHOLDER CONTROL OF CONGLOMERATES

MANAGEMENT IMPROVEMENTS ARE THE POTENTIAL shared benefits for minority shareholders of block investments. Consumption of certain types of private benefits by the blockholder represents the downside for minority shareholders of block investments.[6] Simply put, what prevents a controlling shareholder from maximizing expected cash flows and then expropriating those cash flows through excessive compensation, perquisites, and transactions with the corporation at non-market prices? There is evidence from several sources that blockholders typically consume private benefits. This appears to explain why, for example, trades of high-percentage blocks of stock are typically priced at substantial premiums to the post-announcement exchange price (Barclay & Holderness, 1989, 1992). Private benefits also appear to explain, at least in part, why closed-end funds in the United States often trade at a discount to net asset value (Barclay, Holderness & Pontiff, 1993).

There is also considerable empirical evidence that blockholders (at least in the United States) are constrained in their power to consume private benefits at the expense of minority shareholders. If this were not the case, blockholder-controlled firms would eventually cease to exist as minority investors realized the folly of investing in such firms. The evidence in the United States is that the law, as opposed to organizational factors, constitutes the primary constraint on dominant shareholders.[7]

Finally, it is important to know how, if at all, Canadian law constrains controlling shareholders such as BCE, the Hees-Edper Group, and the Bronfman family. A related point would be to determine how Canadian corporations adapt to controlling shareholders, perhaps by giving the board additional powers.

Conclusion

THE ESSENCE OF PRIVATE PROPERTY is the collocation of wealth effects and decision rights. The natural state of a market economy is to have owners manage. For this reason, and over time, more corporations will have large-block shareholders.

The relationship between blockholders and conglomerates is potentially important and has received little attention to date. Investigations such as those conducted by Halpern and Jog into BCE and by Daniels, Morck, and Stangeland into the Hees-Edper Group will help us better understand this intriguing relationship.

Endnotes

1 Preliminary research indicates that ownership of stock by directors and officers of a randomly chosen American corporation has approximately doubled in fractional terms since 1935. Holderness, Kroszner & Sheehan (1995).
2 This issue is reviewed at length by Daniels *et al.*
3 See the papers in the *Journal of Financial Economics*, Symposium on Corporate Focus (January 1995).
4 Daniels *et al.*, this volume.
5 For examples of specific types of investigations, see Barclay & Holderness (1991).
6 Only consumption of pecuniary private benefits will reduce the wealth of minority shareholders (Barclay & Holderness,1992).
7 See Holderness & Sheehan (forthcoming).

References

Barclay, Michael J. and Clifford G. Holderness. "Private Benefits from Control of Public Corporations." *Journal of Financial Economics*, 25, (1989):371-97.
_____. "Negotiated Block Trades and Corporate Control." *Journal of Finance*, 46, (1991):861-78.
_____. "The Law and Large-Block Trades." *Journal of Law & Economics*, 35 (1992):265-94.
Barclay, Michael J., Clifford G. Holderness and Jeffrey Pontiff. "Private Benefits from Block Ownership and Discounts on Closed-end Funds." *Journal of Financial Economics*, 33, (1993):263-91.
Dial, Jay and Kevin J. Murphy. "Incentives, Downsizing, and Value Creation at General Dynamics." *Journal of Financial Economics*, 37 (1995):261-314.
Holderness, Clifford G. and Dennis P. Sheehan. "Constraints on Active Investors," in *Relational Investing*. Edited by John C. Coffee, Jr. and Ronald Gilson. Oxford: Oxford University Press (Forthcoming).
_____. "Monitoring an Owner: The Case of Turner Broadcasting." *Journal of Financial Economics*, 30 (1991):325-46.

_____. "The Role of Majority Shareholders in Public Corporations: An Exploratory Analysis." *Journal of Financial Economics*, 20 (1988):317-46.

Holderness, Clifford G., Randall Kroszner, and Dennis P. Sheehan. "Were the Good Old Days Good? Changes in Managerial Stock Ownership since the Great Depression," unpublished working paper, Boston College, Chestnut Hill, MA, 1995.

Jensen, Michael C. "The Modern Industrial Revolution, Exit, and the Failure of Internal Control Systems." *Journal of Finance*, 48 (1993):831-80.

Symposium on Corporate Performance. *Journal of Financial Economics*, 37 (1995):1-126.

Mehran, Hamid. "Executive Compensation Structure, Ownership, and Firm Performance." *Journal of Financial Economics*, 38 (1995):163-84.

Mikkelson, Wayne H. and M. Megan Partch. "Managers' Voting Rights and Corporate Control." *Journal of Financial Economics*, 25 (1979):263-90.

Roe, Mark J. "Political and Legal Restraints on Ownership and Control of Public Companies." *Journal of Financial Economics*, 27 (1990):7-41.

Rose, Nancy L. and Andrea Shepard. "Firm Diversification and CEO Compensation: Managerial Ability or Executive Entrenchment?" Unpublished Working Paper, Massachusetts Institute of Technology, Cambridge, MA,1994.

Weisbach, Michael. "Outside Directors and CEO Turnover." *Journal of Financial Economics*, 20 (1988):431-60.

Vikas C. Mehrotra
Faculty of Business
University of Alberta

Commentary on Part III

BOARDS OF DIRECTORS ARE MORE THAN INTERFACES between managers of modern public corporations and their owners. In principle, they are the appointed monitors of corporate management put in place by shareholders to act in the latter's best interests. The reality of boards is quite different. Several corporate declines could have been arrested if boards had been more vigilant and assertive. Recent derivative-blamed losses at Metallgesellschaft and Procter and Gamble, and even at Barings, could have been prevented had the board(s) of those firms been more vigilant and in tune with the corporations' strategic objectives and follow-on activities.

To be sure, boards *are* goaded into action when matters get really out of hand. Witness the push at General Motors in 1992 that resulted in a major overhaul of the board itself. But such examples of board assertiveness are rare and tend to occur far too late. In GM's case, it was prolonged and mounting inaction in the face of lacklustre market and operating performance that led the board, studded with star directors, finally to replace the CEO. An ounce of prevention, as the old saying has it, would have avoided pounds of cure – in the form of real and opportunity losses at GM. Effective corporate governance is about prescribing the right dose of "prevention". Too much interference with line managers detracts from creative risk-taking; too little oversight leads to loss of accountability with value-damaging consequences.

If we are to see any material change in board behaviour, the incentives and controls that underlie its role will have to be overhauled. Modest steps in this direction have already been taken. The Dey report (1994) sponsored by the Toronto Stock Exchange (TSE), similar in spirit to the Cadbury report (1992) in the United Kingdom, has several useful recommendations aimed at improving board oversight and governing effectiveness. Appointing more "outside and independent" directors to the board and splitting the roles of the Chairperson (of the board) and the Chief Executive Officer (CEO) are two recurring themes in the Dey and Cadbury reports. However, including more outsiders on the board will not achieve the desired changes unless some additional measures (such as the use of federal *versus* provincial legislation to effect these changes) are considered. Whatever one's views of the efficacy of legislative changes, most would agree on the need for consistency and uniformity of legislation across different jurisdictions and over time. In this regard, replacing provincial securities legislation with a national jurisdiction deserves close scrutiny.

The Dey report falls short of recommending legislative changes to achieve most of its recommendations, relying instead on the coercive powers of the TSE to incorporate the changes. Again, this follows the spirit of the Cadbury report. Legislative changes, if adopted, must take into account corporate governance issues unique to Canadian corporations, in at least one important respect. In both of the other two major English-speaking economies, the United Kingdom and the United States, the ownership structure of companies is diffused throughout a large base of shareholders. Canadian companies, on the other hand, tend to be closely held or, at least closely controlled through pyramidal ownership arrangements. This has pointed up a different sort of conflict among a corporation's stakeholders, namely, the intra-shareholder conflict. Whereas in the United States a potential conflict exists between debt and equity claims on corporate cash flows, in Canada the issue is cast more in terms of dominant *versus* minority shareholders, presumably because dominant shareholders can extract private benefits from the corporation that are not available to minority shareholders with otherwise similar dividend rights.[1] Reallocation of private benefit consumption can be more than merely redistributive – to the extent that it reduces *ex ante* contracting costs with outside equity providers and thereby the cost of equity capital, it can lead to increased real investment and therefore benefit society.

What is needed is a mechanism to check the ability of controlling shareholders to transfer wealth to themselves. To be sure, safeguards to protect minority shareholders do exist – such as fairness-opinion legislation in the case of minority buy-outs and, in extreme cases, judicial injunctions – which can provide additional relief to minority shareholders. Furthermore, any change that restricts the ability of controlling shareholders to extract private benefits is likely to reduce the incentive of those shareholders to monitor management, precisely because the benefits of such monitoring can no longer be privately appropriated. Ultimately, the net benefit of imposing restrictions on the activities of controlling shareholders remains an open empirical issue. Having noted this *caveat*, one change that deserves scrutiny is board reform designed to induce additional external monitoring of the firm's management. The obvious question is who should take on this role?

Take the case of institutional shareholders, the one group that almost everyone agrees is in a position to provide, and benefit from, corporate oversight and monitoring. This is especially true in the Canadian context where corporate ownership structures, market size limitations, and foreign equity holding restrictions render "voting with one's feet" less effective. Legislation aimed at easing foreign-equity-holding restrictions may not directly increase institutional monitoring (access to U.S. equities may even reduce the incentive of Canadian institutions to engage in domestic monitoring), but it is likely to put pressure on Canadian boards to deliver shareholder returns more in line with those available internationally.

In addition, under current legislation, institutional investors face something of a "Catch-22" in terms of board representation. Getting truly independent institutions to sit on corporate boards and to wield real influence will not become a reality unless those institutions hold significant equity in the firms. But large equity holdings put the independent institutions in the dangerous position of being defined as controlling shareholders and hence as insiders on the board. Such branding puts restrictions on the trading behaviour and communicating abilities of institutions and detracts from the very purpose such holdings were intended to achieve. Legislative changes aimed at raising the ceiling used to define inside or controlling shareholders is a possible solution to the above problem. The definition of outside directors may, alternatively, be modified to accommodate the same result. Clearly, a 20 percent equity stake held by the family or heirs of the founding member is very different from a similar stake held by a pension fund. The pension fund should therefore be treated as an outsider subject to a stated purpose of investment.

The rest of this commentary deals with four studies that were part of the discussion group on The Board and Beyond. I have attempted to put the evidence presented in these studies in a policy perspective. Where appropriate, I have also taken the liberty of pointing out shortcomings and offering suggestions for strengthening the evidence. The studies discussed in this session were "Alternative Mechanisms for Corporate Governance and Board Composition" by Jean-Marie Gagnon and Josée St-Pierre; "Executive Compensation and Firm Value", by Ramy Elitzur and Paul Halpern; "In High Gear: A Case Study of the Hees-Edper Corporate Group", by Ron Daniels, Randall Morck and David Stangeland; and "Bell Canada Enterprises: Wealth Creation or Destruction", by Paul Halpern and Vijay Jog.

Halpern and Jog provide a case history of Bell Canada Enterprises, highlighting a failed diversification strategy, its ultimate abandonment, and the subsequent re-focusing. The market evidence appears to be consistent with value creation from increased corporate focus. A diversified company can trade at a discount to the sum of its divisional values due to cross-divisional subsidies, sheer valuation complexities arising from difficulties in separating aggregate cash flows, lack of proper incentives for divisional managers, diminishing returns to scope in management (this goes back to early Coasian views on the boundaries of a firm), or sub-optimal corporate capital structure for the several divisions of the firm. BCE was no exception to this holding company discount. Halpern and Jog show that the failed diversification strategy at BCE was accompanied by a reduction in the proportion of outside directors on the board since 1984, a period during which the implied discount on BCE assets increased. Such evidence is consistent with management entrenchment, aided further by foreign-equity-holding restrictions that all but force Canadian institutions to hold large capitalization stocks such as BCE in their portfolios.

Two alternative policy recommendations emerge, given the peculiarities of the BCE case. First, relaxing foreign-equity-holding restrictions would subject

BCE management to stricter capital market discipline by raising its cost of funding non-value maximizing assets. Second, regulatory pressure could be applied to make BCE shed Bell Canada, which might ultimately organize itself into smaller regional utilities à la the AT&T breakup in the United States in 1984. Shedding the crown jewel – Bell Canada – would, more importantly, force managers to rethink their diversification strategy on a stand-alone basis, free from complicated cross-subsidies that appear to be reflected in much of the discount in BCE shares today. Recent work by Daley, Mehrotra & Sivakumar (1995) at the University of Alberta shows that gains to spinning-off assets are primarily concentrated in firms that shed unrelated assets. *Prima facie*, BCE's spin-off of Bell Canada would likely create value by creating an independently viable spun-off unit. This would also force the remaining parent assets to strive for efficiency gains.

The role of boards is particularly important in large conglomerate-style companies where shareholders' interests and management actions often collide head on. To wit, managers desire diversification across industries for risk-reduction reasons since their human capital is inherently undiversifiable (forcing them to bear firm-specific risk). At the risk of over-simplification, to the extent there are diminishing returns to scope in management and/or complex cross-subsidies in the organization of conglomerates, shareholders prefer strictly "pure plays", assuming responsibility for diversification on their own by putting together portfolios of shares in firms across many industries. The board's task here is to harmonize the two objectives and to select an optimal level of diversification.

Daniels, Morck and Stangeland discuss the rationale of the conglomerate organizational form in their case study of the Hees-Edper group and show that the performance of this group is indistinguishable from other Canadian companies of a similar size, even though the Hees-Edper group carries a higher debt leverage and asset risk. They conclude that the alleged benefits of a conglomerate organizational form were absent at Hees-Edper. An excellent discussion on the merits and demerits of the conglomerate form provides the introduction to this study, and the subsequent empirical evidence sets a backdrop for several policy implications. The authors argue that more stringent disclosure requirements for conglomerates may reduce the monitoring cost of outside shareholders. Furthermore, they suggest that proxy solicitation rules should be modified so that dissident shareholders do not have to bear a disproportionate cost of proxy campaigns. In the end, they point out that capital- and product-market discipline is the best device to improve corporate governance in Canada. To this end, NAFTA and the increasing inter-provincial freeing of trade is a step in the right direction and should be encouraged.

Elitzur and Halpern examine the evidence of the relationship between salary, bonus, and total compensation to Canadian executives and various measures of corporate performance since the *Ontario Securities Act* was amended to require executive compensation disclosure for firms registered in Ontario.

As with the broader U.S. evidence, they find firm size to be positively related to all measures of compensation.

The more interesting findings have to do with changes in individual components of executive compensation and firm performance. The authors find no significant relation between compensation and market returns. Thus, from the shareholders' perspective, the evidence presented offers little hope that bonus-based incentive schemes create value for shareholders too. The preceding concern is somewhat mitigated by the fact that over suitably long intervals, stock returns and accounting performance measures do tend to converge. In the debate on corporate governance, it is important not to be distracted by the publicity surrounding high levels of managerial compensation that has been featured in the media recently and to focus instead on the marginal product of top managers. Thus, any effort to regulate managerial compensation is likely to miss the point with respect to effective corporate governance and may well lead to the best managers leaving for less regulated regimes (such as the United States).

Another interesting finding is that the existence of shareholders'-rights plans (poison pills) is positively related to changes in bonus and overall compensation, which raises the question of whether such bonuses are awarded by self-serving compensation committees. The recommendation of both the Cadbury report and the Dey report – that compensation committees be composed mainly of outside directors – is particularly germane here. Another conflict of interest arises when executives from companies that have a consulting relationship with the firm are placed on the board. Such directors should excuse themselves from auditing and compensation committees.

Gagnon and St-Pierre provide evidence on the determinants of outside *versus* inside directors on Canadian boards under various ownership structures. They view the board as one form of corporate governance and, as such, partially substitutable with other forms (of governance) such as executive compensation, debt policy, dividend policy, and anti-takeover devices adopted with or without shareholder approval. They point out that the actual frequency of use of these various forms depends on their effectiveness as well as on their cost of adoption. They assert that board changes are a low cost mechanism for improving corporate governance effectiveness. Such an assertion depends crucially on the ownership regime of the firm. Under diffuse ownership, board changes are often costly affairs – the out-of-pocket expense of a proxy battle is itself a substantial sum and may deter outsiders with insignificant ownership from attempting it. The free-rider problem associated with bringing about such changes is particularly acute under diffuse ownership regimes. Furthermore, political considerations may preclude institutional owners from overtly confronting management in some instances. In this regard, legislation to safeguard the confidentiality of proxy ballot-counting may be needed to elicit timely institutional responses free from political considerations.

An important contribution of the Gagnon and St-Pierre study is the view that different governance structures are substitutable at the margin, and thus in equilibrium we would expect to see varying degrees of usage for each of these mechanisms, depending on the circumstances and characteristics of the firm. For instance, they discuss the role of debt in corporate governance and point out that higher debt ratios relieve the need to supply additional monitoring. I believe that using debt as a tool of corporate governance requires a richer theory of debt *versus* investment opportunity set variables facing the firm than is currently available in the literature. What is needed is panel data relating debt use with corporate performance, adjusting for variables in the investment opportunity set facing the firm. Empirically, the evidence in Gagnon and St-Pierre is not surprising, given that they find a positive correlation between the voting rights of outsiders and their board presence, and a negative correlation between the voting rights of insiders and the presence of outsiders on the board. This is *expected*. The interesting result is with the return on assets variable, which is positively related to outsider presence on the board for diffusely held firms. Interpreting this result involves solving the age-old chicken and egg problem – and Gagnon and St-Pierre's methodology is not appropriate for such a task. We need panel data, with lead and lag variables, to understand such a relationship.

CONCLUSION

IN ORGANIZATIONAL FORMS CHARACTERIZED BY separation of ownership and control, the board of directors plays a central role in effective corporate governance. This commentary is based on the studies presented in the session on The Board and Beyond at the conference on corporate governance organized by Industry Canada. The key policy recommendations contained here are summarized below.

First, the establishment of a national securities law should provide consistency and uniformity of legislation across different jurisdictions and should be welcomed.

Second, any changes that are sought in an effort to improve Canadian corporate governance must address the peculiarities of Canadian corporate ownership. The presence of controlling shareholders is a mixed blessing in Canada. While controlling shareholders provide valuable monitoring of management, they also contribute to a conflict between controlling and minority shareholders. Laws that limit the ability of controlling shareholders to garner corporate resources for private use have the potential to reduce *ex ante* contracting costs between outside equity providers and controlling shareholders, thereby reducing the cost of equity capital and leading to a higher level of social investment. At the same time, regulators must take into account the above trade-off.

Third, the role of institutions requires special scrutiny. We are probably entering an era of increased institutional activism and, in general, regulators should encourage this trend. To this end, rules governing proxy ballots must be re-examined. In particular, the confidentiality of proxy ballots must be provided for, and the playing field with respect to proxy campaigns between management and outside shareholders has to be leveled.

Fourth, regulators must redefine "insiders" in the context of institutional owners, especially those who are clearly non-management oriented. Current rules discourage activist institutions from accumulating large blocks of a firm's shares.

Finally, while regulators should in general welcome the trend toward increased disclosure of corporate policies, such as those dealing with management compensation, such disclosure must not be used as a pretext for interfering with market-determined compensation packages.

ENDNOTE

1 Seagram's latest foray into Hollywood *via* its purchase of MCA is a case in point. It is not clear if the interests of Seagram's minority shareholders were best served in this acquisition. Whether the acquisition creates value for Seagram's shareholders in the long run remains to be seen; in the short span of the announcement week, however, financial markets lopped off approximately $2 billion from Seagram's equity value.

Lee Gill
Corporate Law Policy Directorate
Industry Canada

Commentary on Part III

Alternative Mechanisms for Corporate Governance and Board Composition

THE STUDY BY JEAN-MARIE GAGNON AND JOSÉE ST-PIERRE on alternative mechanisms for corporate governance and board composition presents a good summary of the mechanisms of corporate governance and an econometric analysis of the determinants of one of those mechanisms – the composition of the board of directors. The study also provides some useful insights into the possible ranking of these corporate governance mechanisms according to their cost, effectiveness (for both shareholders and managers), and probability of use.

The authors point out clearly that these rankings were made on a purely intuitive basis. However, they do not provide a full explanation of the intuition behind these rankings. The explanations underlying the "cost of mechanisms" are comprehensible, but more explanation and discussion of the rankings is required especially with respect to effectiveness. For example, they offer little to support the statement that executive compensation warrants being ranked as the third most effective mechanism for corporate governance behind board composition and charter defences, and ahead of debt policy.

Although the study goes on to provide some fairly convincing evidence as to the usefulness of debt policy, it is not clear why this policy is not as good as executive compensation. Is this result particular to a widely held corporation, or does it apply to all types of corporations? The study also points, in several places, to the value of poison pills to managers, and argues that they are not particularly valuable for shareholders. However, the authors offer little evidence to support their claim, nor do they explain why so many shareholders are inclined to vote for shareholder-rights plans if they are so bad for them.

In the course of the Phase II consultations to the proposed changes to the *Canada Business Corporations Act* (CBCA) some corporate executives told us that one of the main reasons poison pills have been implemented is that statutes such as the CBCA do not allow sufficient time for corporations to appraise proposals properly, solicit views from shareholders, and respond to bidders. We were informed by companies that have implemented poison pills that they did so primarily to ensure that sufficient time was available to respond adequately to a takeover bid. They also informed us that if we increased our allowed response period to between 45 and 60 days, there would be significantly less need for poison pills and fewer shareholders would continue to approve their use. If that is true, it suggests that these pills are now being implemented to the benefit of shareholders. Is that true?

More explanation could also be provided in the statistical part of the study. There is little explanation, for example, of Table 7, which sets out the results of one of the key groups of equations found in the study.

The variables used to explain the outside/inside director ratio in firms with diffuse ownership and concentrated inside ownership are significant. However, in the case of diffuse ownership the only significant variables are regulated enterprises, blockholdings which do not have members represented directly on the boards, return on assets, and voting rights of inside directors. The significance of these variables requires discussion.

It is not surprising to find that there are more outside directors in regulated enterprises. It is also not surprising that the ratio of outside to inside directors falls when the voting rights of inside directors are extended. It is interesting, however, that the ratio of outside to inside directors rises as a result of increased holdings by institutional and other blockholding investors that have direct representatives on the board. It would, perhaps, be even more interesting to know whether that result has evolved over time because the number of institutional investors and other blockholding investors has grown, or because the type of firm that is prone to hiring (more) outside directors attracts these types of investors.

Although it is not mentioned by the authors, Table 7 suggests that the outside/inside ratio is also positively related to the return on assets. What does this suggest – that the more outsiders there are, relatively speaking, on the boards of diffusely owned firms, the greater the return of the corporation? Or, might this also be related to the possibility that institutional investors are involved in surveying management and in ensuring an acceptable return on assets?

One thing the authors do not discuss in any detail is the non-significant results. For example, the authors find that the complexity of the organization (as represented by the knowledge and log-assets variables) has not induced a higher level of monitoring by way of outside directors. Why is this the case?

Under Concentrated Inside Ownership the authors indicate that the existence of blockholders continues to be a significant determinant of the outside/inside director ratio on the board. Inside directors, although important shareholders, accept (or may have to accept) monitoring by other large shareholders. The authors detect a significant size effect and indicate that this result is consistent with the hypothesis of a nonlinear relationship between corporate size and the ratio of outside/inside directors. It is not clear, however, why this result is not found in the diffuse ownership case. Was this result specific to certain industries which are not large factors in the diffuse ownership case?

The authors have certainly put together a good summary and analysis of the mechanisms of corporate governance. More work, however, has to be done to elaborate on the details of these preliminary results and to quantify more clearly the importance of corporate governance mechanisms.

Commentary on Part III
Executive Compensation and Firm Value

THIS STUDY BY RAMY ELITZUR AND PAUL HALPERN is a very good examination of the observed importance of firm-specific performance and size variables in the determination of executive compensation in Canada. I hope there will be more follow-up work undertaken in support of that which has already been done.

The authors indicate they found that the bonus received by an executive is positively related to net income, a form of short-term performance. They also found that the bonus received had a positive relationship with the return on assets. However, there was no relationship to other performance variables, such as return on equity or the ratio of cash flow from operations to assets.

In all cases, however, the adjusted R^2 seems very low. Actually, I had thought that none of these equations would be significant as the adjusted R^2 were all below one and in some cases they were negative. At least one case, however, appears to have a significant explanatory value. I carried out a rough calculation on the log bonus equation with respect to sales and other variables found in Table 5. By my calculation, the F-test indicated that the equation had a significant explanatory value at the 5 percent level, a surprising result that might deserve some explanation. On the whole, it would have been useful if the F statistics had been presented and discussed in the study.

Still, as the authors clearly indicate, in most cases the explanatory variables are not significant. Only in a few cases do the equations used satisfactorily describe the levels of executive compensation found in the sample.

The authors suggest some of the possible reasons for this lack of significance of the explanatory variables. First, they point out that they use cash compensation only; they do not use option-related compensation. The authors also acknowledge that all forms of compensation should be used. They note that an observation that cash performance is unrelated to firm performance does not lead to the conclusion that total compensation, including equity compensation, is unrelated to firm performance. That is indeed true and I feel that it is one of the major problems of the study. Having said this, the authors clearly note their continued work on collecting information on deferred compensation and that they intend to include this variable in future reports. Starting with this year much of this information should be available from Form 40 filed with the *Ontario Securities Commission* (OSC).

With respect to salary, as the authors point out, the equations had a better fit. Salary was found to be positively related to size: measured either as assets or sales, type of industry the firm is in, and whether the firm is interlisted on an American stock exchange. Of particular interest is the fact that salary was found to relate negatively to a five-year rate of return variable. This should be explained further in the study.

Another piece of information now available from the OSC is the breakdown of compensation among the top five executives in a firm. Some of the results might be more robust if the authors focused on the CEO or on individual rather than aggregate statistics.

As a final point, Elitzur and Halpern mentioned that one assumption in the model is that managers are risk-neutral. Substantiation for this assumption would be useful. Many feel that managers are, on average, risk-averse and that some of the agency problems would make them more risk-averse than the shareholders might like. How would the model change if risk aversion were assumed?

Part IV   *Institutional Investors*

Jeffrey G. MacIntosh   &   Lawrence P. Schwartz
Faculty of Law   Consulting Economist   8
University of Toronto   Toronto

Do Institutional and Controlling Shareholders Increase Corporate Value?

SHAREHOLDERS' INCENTIVES AND FIRM VALUE

DOES THE CONCENTRATION OF SHAREHOLDINGS make any difference to corporate value or behaviour? Ever since Berle & Means,[1] this has been perhaps the most important question confronting those with an interest in corporate governance. In a capitalist economy the corporation is the primary instrument for the generation of wealth. If, as Berle & Means suggested, corporations are run by managers in the interests of managers first, and shareholders second, then we might be inclined to regulate corporate and managerial behaviour rather more closely than if managers were entirely faithful to the goal of maximizing shareholder wealth. If the combination of market oversight (*i.e.*, product, capital, corporate control, and managerial labour markets) and direct shareholder monitoring of management were sufficient to align manager and shareholder interests, the role of the state in policing corporate governance would likely be much reduced.

Since Jensen & Meckling (1976),[2] most economists have agreed that there is indeed a relationship between the concentration of share ownership and corporate performance.[3] Jensen & Meckling suggested that there is a linear and monotonically increasing relationship between managerial ownership and corporate performance. The reason is that as managers acquire an increasing share of the equity, their share of the cost of perquisite consumption and bad management increases correspondingly. Jensen & Meckling therefore predicted that managerial consumption of perquisites and slack should diminish as managerial ownership increases.

While Jensen & Meckling started a revolution in modern thinking about concentration of share ownership, their view of the relationship between ownership concentration and corporate performance is insufficiently nuanced in a number of important respects. First, the evidence suggests that hostile takeovers serve an important disciplinary function, by removing inefficient (or high perquisite-consuming) managers.[4] However, increasing managerial ownership tends to make it easier for managers to fend off a hostile takeover bid.[5]

Thus, the increased degree of managerial entrenchment that accompanies increasing managerial share ownership may actually reduce corporate value in the mid-range between the ownership level at which managers have no power to defeat a hostile takeover, and the level at which they can absolutely defeat a hostile takeover.[6]

There is empirical evidence to support the proposition that there is a non-linear relationship between managerial ownership and corporate performance.[7] Morck, Shleifer & Vishny[8] found, for a sample of very large (*Fortune 500*) firms, that as managerial ownership increases from zero to 5 percent, the value of the firm also rises. However, between 5 percent and 25 percent ownership, firm value falls. After 25 percent, it rises once again. However, McConnell & Servaes found that there was an increase in value up to between 40 percent and 50 percent ownership, and a decrease thereafter.[9] Interestingly, the size of the average firm in the McConnell & Servaes sample is significantly smaller than that used in the Morck *et al.* sample.

Wruck found a relationship similar to that identified by Morck *et al.*, but in relation to non-managerial blockholdings in a sample of NYSE and AMEX firms.[10] This suggests that some caution should be exercised in interpreting the Morck *et al.* results as the product of managerial entrenchment, given that the blockholdings in Wruck's sample were *non-managerial* holdings. Unless the blockholders in Wruck's sample were associated (or were otherwise acting in concert) with the managers, it is not clear why increases in blockholdings would serve to further entrench managers. One would expect the opposite to be true.[11]

Indeed, Morck *et al.* find that the non-linear relationship between management ownership and firm value applies (with the same turning points) to outside directors, with nearly the same empirical robustness as it does to the two top officers. Given that outside directors have less capacity than inside directors to consume the perquisites of control, this too suggests that some care should be taken in interpreting the Morck *et al.* results.[12]

Moreover, if managerial entrenchment is the explanation of the Morck *et al.* results, the advent of wealth-reducing poison pills and (in the United States) state anti-takeover legislation may have substantially altered the relationship between managerial share ownership and firm value.[13] Both poison pills and state anti-takeover statutes give even those managers who hold very little (or none) of the firm's equity the power to defend against a hostile takeover. In the United States there is no requirement that shareholders must approve the adoption of a poison pill. Since both pills and anti-takeover statutes can be used as powerful entrenchment tools by managers,[14] it would be interesting to see if more recent data sets, spanning the era of poison pills and state anti-takeover legislation (*i.e.*, encompassing the mid to late 1980s) would yield similar results.

In Canada, there are five potentially significant differences that distinguish Canadian practices from those in the United States. First, poison pills must be approved by shareholders.[15] Managers are therefore less likely to entrench themselves by getting such measures passed. Second, there is no legislation in Canada comparable to state anti-takeover statutes. Third, Canadian courts and regulators have been tough on poison pills.[16] It is now generally thought that a poison pill may buy target management more time to find an alternate transaction, but it will not allow management to entrench itself. Thus, if there is the same non-linear relationship in Canada between managerial share ownership and firm value as that observed in the United States, the poison pill should have made fewer inroads into this relationship.

The fourth significant difference is perhaps the most important. While most public corporations in the United States do not have a controlling share-holder, most public corporations in Canada do. This is significant, because the Morck et al. study is based on U.S. data, and so was conducted in an environment in which there were few controlling shareholders to play a counterweight role to the managerial pursuit of self-interest. As discussed below, increasing managerial shareholdings is likely to have very different effects in corporations both with and without controlling shareholders.

Fifth, the largest firms in Canada tend to be much smaller than those in the Morck et al. sample.[17] This smaller size is undoubtedly an important reason why many of the largest Canadian corporations have controlling shareholders and the largest U.S. corporations do not. Because of wealth constraints in both countries, it is difficult for individuals or families to have large stakes in the largest corporations. The largest firms in Canada may correspond more closely with the sample used by McConnell & Servaes, and therefore we might have a greater expectation that the curvilinear relationship between ownership and control found in that study will apply in Canada.

In summary, there is good reason to be cautious in assuming that the Morck et al. results hold in Canada – less because of the effect of poison pills (for all the reasons noted above) than because controlling shareholders tend to prevent management entrenchment. Indeed, there is also good reason to be cautious in assuming that the findings of Morck et al. still hold in the United States, in this era of poison pills and state anti-takeover legislation.

Another important limitation on the Jensen & Meckling view of the relationship between managerial share ownership and firm value is that it fails to take into account the distribution of non-managerial shareholdings. Managers are much more likely to remain in control where there is no other significant blockholder to oppose them, given that a significant blockholder can supply a counterweight to management's power. An aggregate managerial holding of 20 percent, for example, means one thing where no other share-holder holds more than 1 percent. It means something else entirely where there is a single (non-managerial) 25 percent blockholder, or where there is a controlling (non-managerial) shareholder with a block of 51 percent.

Moreover, non-managerial shareholders (NMS) come in many varieties, and the incentives confronting different types of NMS, and hence their desire and ability to supply a counterweight to management, vary considerably. At the very least, there are four different types of non-managerial shareholder: retail shareholders; institutional shareholders; controlling (but non-management) shareholders; and individual, corporate, and other large, but non-controlling (and non-institutional) blockholders.[18] Retail shareholders are most subject to the collective-action problems first noted by Berle & Means. Typically, they hold small stakes, do not have the deep pockets needed to finance litigation aimed at holding managers accountable, have high coordination costs, and face daunting free-rider problems. Although the motivations of institutional shareholders vary, institutions generally have much larger stakes. They also tend to have the financial resources needed to sue management if necessary, lower coordination costs, and less daunting free-rider problems. While many factors tend to blunt institutional incentives to monitor,[19] large blockholders (particularly individuals, who are free from the internal agency problems that burden most institutions) often have potent incentives to monitor and discipline management. Controlling shareholders have not only the incentive but also the ability to ensure that managers do their bidding.

The ability to "entrench" presumes an ability to control. Morck *et al.* state that:

> ... we have recognized that pure voting power is probably not the main mechanism by which managers retain control. It is more likely that ownership is also positively correlated with status as a founder, tenure with the firm, preponderance of inside directors, ability to persuade shareholders, and other conditions that facilitate management control.[20]

The point can be broadened by noting that control not only derives from a variety of sources, but also (importantly) is not an indivisibility. The power to elect directors is an important manifestation of control, but even the power to elect *all* of the directors does not result in unencumbered power to direct financing and investment decisions. For example, in Canada, fundamental changes in the life of a corporation (such as amalgamation, sale of all or substantially all of the assets, reincorporation in another jurisdiction, changes to the articles, etc.) must typically be approved by a special resolution (requiring the approval of two-thirds of those shareholders voting). This passes a power of negative control (the power to obstruct a special resolution) to a blockholder or a coalition of blockholders holding one-third of the voted shares. Class and majority of the minority voting entitlements resulting from statutory, administrative, or judicial approval requirements cede further veto powers to particular classes or even to minority shareholders within a minority class. These veto powers substantially strengthen the ability of NMS to prevent managers from adopting wealth-transferring or wealth-reducing measures. This point is often overlooked by economists, who tend to assume that once the 50.1 percent ownership threshold is reached, further share acquisitions do not increase control.[21]

While the view that control is not an indivisibility has force in both the United States and Canada, it is of particular importance in the Canadian setting. While in the United States many corporate law statutes (including those of Delaware) require only simple majority approval for fundamental changes, the standard in Canada is approval by two-thirds of all shareholders voting. Moreover, there are more class and minority voting entitlements in Canada than in the United States. For example, under most Canadian corporate law statutes, restricted and non-voting shareholders must be given the right to vote on an equal footing with voting shareholders in respect of a number of different types of fundamental changes.[22] Perhaps more importantly, the corporate law requires that restricted and non-voting classes of shareholders *separately* approve a significant number of different types of transactions by a two-thirds majority.[23] These mandatory class voting entitlements give significant power to restricted and non-voting shareholders in the context of fundamental corporate changes.

In addition to these corporate law requirements, there are a number of statutory, stock exchange, and administrative requirements that a variety of transactions be approved by a majority of disinterested shareholders. For example, Policy 9.1 of the Ontario Securities Commission requires that all "going private" transactions, and transactions with related parties[24] be approved by a majority of the minority (*i.e.*, non-conflicted) shareholders. Policy 9.1 further requires that the company secure a valuation of the subject matter of the transaction (in the case of a related-party transaction) or of the firm itself (in the case of a "going private" transaction), and that a summary be sent to shareholders prior to the shareholder vote. In addition, approval by a committee of independent directors is recommended, but not required (although because of the policy, such approval is quickly becoming standard practice). Policy 9.1 also has valuation requirements (and recommends independent director approval) in the case of takeover bids effected by insiders ("insider bids") and the issuer itself ("issuer bids").[25] All of these requirements greatly add to the power of institutions holding restricted and non-voting blocks of shares.

In Canada, minority interests also have the power to sue the corporation and/or its directors, officers and controlling shareholders, on the grounds that their rights or interests have been disregarded. The corporate oppression remedy[26] (for which, in the case of public corporations, there is no direct analogue in the United States) greatly adds to the power of minority shareholders. In addition, under the so-called "public interest" powers,[27] Canadian securities regulators have much broader powers than their American counterparts to intervene in transactions that they find objectionable. On balance, therefore, there appears to be more opportunity in Canada than there is in the United States for minority interests to block redistributive transactions.

The distribution, size and identity of NMS will interact with the extent of managerial shareholdings to influence the degree of corporate monitoring and hence corporate value. Indeed, there will be many permutations and combinations, given that the interaction of various different types of NMS (and managerial shareholders) will affect the incentives of other NMS. For example, the presence of a large non-managerial blockholder may have a negative effect on the incentives of institutional shareholders to engage in monitoring. Each institution might reason that the blockholder will be an effective monitor, reducing the payoff from engaging in additional monitoring. Conversely, the absence of institutional or block shareholders will accentuate the incentives of retail investors to monitor management. Incentives to monitor are not independent of the size or distribution of other shareholdings, nor of the identity of the other shareholders.

It is also important to note that entrenchment results from a short-circuiting of the market for corporate control by management. There are, however, other market controls that tend to limit the ability of managers to engage in perquisite consumption or other forms of inefficient behaviour, even where they have effectively entrenched themselves. Managerial labour markets, capital markets, and product markets all supply some measure of discipline.[28] Indeed, if these markets operate with a high degree of rigour, the absence of an effective control market would, in theory, have an inconsequential effect on managerial incentives.

Take, for example, the case of a corporation with two classes of shares – one fully voting, the other non-voting. The use of a dual class structure may serve to entrench the managers, but it comes at a cost. As Morck argues,[29] and as supported by Morck & Stangeland,[30] the use of a dual class structure is likely to increase the corporation's cost of capital (in both current and subsequent rounds of financing). At least part of this cost is likely to be passed on to the managers, limiting to some extent their incentive to adopt such structures.

However, as argued by Daniels & Halpern,[31] the efficacy of at least one market – the managerial labour market – may also be partly short-circuited by management entrenchment.

Do Controlling Shareholders Increase or Decrease Firm Value?

A S THE ABOVE DISCUSSION MAKES CLEAR, both theory and evidence suggest that it would be naïve simply to assume that the presence of a controlling shareholder will have an unambiguous effect on firm profitability. Controlling shareholders can supply effective monitoring of managers; but they may also engage in value-reducing redistributive transactions. For example, a controlling shareholder might set up a transfer pricing arrangement on non-market terms with another controlled company for the purpose and effect of redistributing shareholder wealth to that other company.

Holderness & Sheehan suggest that a controlling shareholder might appoint herself manager, then pay herself an excessive salary, hire relatives at inflated salaries, negotiate favourable deals with other controlled companies, loot the corporation, or invest in negative net present value projects.[32] While this is not necessarily an exhaustive list of the ways in which controlling shareholders can cheat minority shareholders, it suggests that there are several ways to achieve this result.

Examining a sample of large public firms trading on the NYSE and AMEX, however, Holderness & Sheehan found little evidence that majority shareholders (holding 50 percent or more of the equity) exploit minority shareholders. When majority blocks were traded, the value of minority shares increased in price appreciably, and such trades were accompanied by significant changes in the composition of management and the board.[33] Majority share-holders who were CEOs earned only marginally more compensation on average than other CEOs. There were only a small number of cases involving the employment of relatives, and no suits at all alleging abuse of majority power. Finally, Holderness & Sheehan found that investment policies, the frequency of corporate control transactions, accounting rates of return, and Tobin's Q were not significantly different for either widely held or majority controlled firms.

These findings are of particular interest in the Canadian setting, (subject to differences in the legal régime as already described) in which the danger of the types of redistributive behaviour referred to above is heightened. The key factors that heighten the danger of predation are: the high concentration of share ownership within individual corporations, and the fact that common shareholders control many corporations – in extended corporate empires like that controlled by the Bronfman interests. In such settings, there are many more possibilities for redistributive behaviour.

It is our hypothesis that Canadian controlling shareholders engage in *both* more effective monitoring of managers than non-control shareholders, *and* redistributive transactions that shift wealth from non-controllers to controllers. There are four measures of profitability used to test this hypothesis: return on assets, return on sales, sales growth, and the ratio of share price to book value per share. Since the redistribution of wealth will have a minimal impact on return on assets, return on equity, and sales growth,[34] we hypothesize that the presence of a controlling shareholder (and the managerial monitoring that this brings) will have a positive effect on these three measures of profitability.

The effect on the price-to-book ratio is likely to be more ambiguous. It is probable that the price-to-book ratio will be positively affected by the more proficient monitoring of managers brought to bear by the presence of a controlling shareholder. However, it may also be negatively affected by the redistribution of wealth from minority interests to the controlling shareholder. We have no *a priori* way of knowing which effect will dominate. Thus, we simply hypothesize that neither effect will dominate, and that the price-to-book ratio will be unaffected by the presence of a controlling shareholder.

Note that we do not distinguish between controlling shareholders with different attributes. For the purposes of this study, we define a controlling shareholder as any non-institutional shareholder holding in excess of 10 percent of the total voting power in the corporation. We run a second set of regressions with the control threshold set at 20 percent. The test of whether the presence of a controlling shareholder affects firm value is therefore a somewhat crude one. Specifically, there is evidence that not all types of controlling shareholders have the same effect on firm value. For example, Morck & Stangeland present Canadian evidence suggesting that firms controlled by descendants of founding stockholders diminish firm value.[35] Morck & Stangeland also find that there are differences in corporate performance based on whether the controller is a foreign company, a Canadian-owned subsidiary, or an independent private-sector firm.[36] Looking at U.S. data, Holderness & Sheehan find evidence that individual controllers tend more toward entrenchment (and inefficient behaviour) than corporate controllers.[37]

Moreover, although controlling shareholders will ultimately *appoint* management[38] (indeed, that is what it means to be a controlling shareholder), the controlling shareholder (CS) may or may not be an officer or director of the corporation. A CS who is an officer or director (or both) may derive either pecuniary or non-pecuniary benefits from occupying the position of director/officer, and may wish to retain control for the purpose of maintaining the flow of these benefits, which are not shared by other shareholders.

In contrast, a CS who is not a manager will not participate in any special benefits flowing to management. The non-manager CS may still derive benefits from control that do not flow to other shareholders (such as the psychic benefit that goes with "pulling the strings"), or that are earned at the expense of the other shareholders (*e.g.*, the opportunity to indulge personal and non-optimal investment preferences). In such cases, however, the element of side benefits consumed *as manager* has been removed. Therefore, a non-manager CS can be expected to monitor managers more effectively than a manager CS.

It should be noted, however, that there is evidence that almost all majority (as distinct from merely controlling) shareholders are represented on the board of directors or in management.[39] Consequently, failing to distinguish between management and non-management controlling shareholders may not constitute a serious empirical failing.

Do Institutional Shareholders Increase or Decrease Corporate Value?

WE HYPOTHESIZE THAT FIRM VALUE IS POSITIVELY CORRELATED with the degree of institutional ownership, for the following reasons.

Many have argued that institutional shareholders are better able to resolve problems of collective action than retail shareholders.[40] Institutional shareholders typically hold much larger stakes than retail shareholders. Thus, they have more at stake in corporate decisions. They also have lower coordination costs, are better able to evaluate management's performance, and possess the resources to oppose management (whether in court or otherwise) in the event that management attempts to proceed with wealth-redistributing or wealth-reducing measures.

There is U.S. evidence that institutional shareholders are more likely to vote than retail investors, and are more likely to oppose as least some forms of wealth-reducing measures.[41] There is also evidence that the market reaction to the adoption of shark-repellent measures is negative for firms with low institutional ownership, but zero for firms with high institutional ownership.[42] Indeed, the incidence of such amendments appears to have decreased over time and also appears to be a result of the fact that institutional shareholders not only play an active role in preventing management from introducing such measures, but also tend to vote against such resolutions when they are presented for approval.[43] McConnell & Servaes also find evidence that increasing institutional ownership correlates with increasing firm value and profitability.[44]

In Canada, the growth of institutional holdings has tracked that in the United States.[45] As indicated by MacIntosh,[46] over the past two or three decades, the percentage of equity held in the portfolios of life insurance companies and public pension funds has greatly increased. However, the percentage of equity held in mutual fund portfolios appears to have shrunk over the past 25 years.[47]

Several commentators have argued that Canadian institutional investors have become increasingly important in matters of corporate governance.[48] As summarized by MacIntosh,[49] the influence of institutional investors has been felt in a number of ways, including (but not necessarily in order of importance):

- Voting against management (often in conjunction with other institutional investors).
- Threatening to exercise dissent rights.
- Suing to enjoin a transaction.
- Enlisting the support of securities regulators to stop a transaction.
- Publicly expressing dissatisfaction with management, or a particular course of action recommended by management.
- Mounting or participating in a proxy battle to unseat management (in rare cases).
- Supporting institutional organizations (such as the Pension Investment Association of Canada) and soft dollar brokers (like Fairvest Securities) which actively support institutional causes.
- Creating proxy voting guidelines, either individually or through representative organizations, dealing with matters like poison pills, executive compensation, blank cheque preferreds, etc.
- Meeting with management, either individually or collectively, to discuss matters of concern.

Anecdotal evidence suggests that the number of Canadian institutions willing to engage in public activism *vis-à-vis* corporate managers is small. Indeed, even some of the very largest institutional investors, such as the Ontario Municipal Retirement System (OMERS) have preferred to avoid activities that attract public attention.[50] However, anecdotal evidence also suggests that a good many institutions engage in "quiet diplomacy", chatting with management behind closed doors about matters of concern.

The increasing willingness of Canadian institutions to engage in such activities, and their commensurately decreasing propensity to sell their investments when dissatisfied with management,[51] suggests that institutions do, indeed, engage in useful monitoring that might be expected to enhance corporate value.

On the other side of the ledger, there are many problems that tend to blunt institutional incentives.[52]

- Institutional investors are not exempt from free-rider problems (increasing corporate value will benefit other, non-contributing shareholders, and in particular may benefit the institution's rivals).

- Institutions may be co-opted by management (*e.g.*, a bank might vote with management in the fear that if it does not, the bank will lose the corporation's deposit and/or loan business).

- Pension fund managers may follow a "golden rule" – a mutual back-scratching arrangement under which fund managers appointed by management from one corporation will refrain from engaging in activism in return for similar behaviour from other fund managers.

- Political pressures brought to bear on public pension funds.

- Limited monitoring capabilities, given large portfolios, limited staff, and limited ability to engage in active management activities.

- The need or desire to maintain liquid portfolios, which results in the acquisition of small blocks without significant voting power.

- Legal restraints on institutional monitoring activities.[53]

- Agency conflicts within institutional investors

- An institutional culture of "passivity".

- Fear of political reprisals for too direct involvement in corporate activities.

- Fear that approaching other shareholders with concerns about management, will trigger a "race to the exit" which will cause the share price to fall.

- Potential fiduciary conflicts between maximizing fund value and corporate value when fund managers become corporate directors.

- The proliferation of non-voting shares in Canada.
- Difficulties in identifying other shareholders.
- Poison pills.

Some researchers have suggested that institutional shareholders actually *diminish* corporate value. The co-option referred to above may not merely render institutions ineffective monitors, but may convert them into unwilling allies of management against other (non-co-opted) shareholders. There is evidence, for example, that institutions tend to vote with management in proxy contests,[54] and that institutions that are more subject to co-option are more likely than other institutions to vote with management.[55]

It has also been argued by some commentators that because the performance of investment managers is evaluated quarterly, such managers tend to have extremely short investment horizons and therefore undervalue long-term investment projects.[56] According to this view, long-term projects are systematically undervalued by the market, resulting in an inefficiently low level of expenditures in long-term projects such as research and development. However, there appears to be little evidence to support the view that the market undervalues long-term activities. In fact, the evidence supports the view that the market *does not* inappropriately discount long-term investment projects.[57]

On balance, both theory and U.S. data support the view that institutional shareholders increase corporate value. We thus feel comfortable with the hypothesis that the presence of institutional investors will have a positive effect on all four of our accounting measures of profitability. The measure of institutional ownership we use is described later in this study, in the Data section.

It is important to note, however, that institutional shareholders frequently play a somewhat different monitoring role in Canada than in the United States because the great majority of Canadian public corporations have a controlling shareholder. As elaborated above, we hypothesize that this results in better monitoring of management, thus diminishing the marginal value of institutional monitoring of managers. However, we also hypothesize that the presence of a controlling shareholder will result in a higher probability of redistributive transactions. Canadian institutions are therefore more likely to monitor controlling shareholders than management.

Initially, this might seem like an arid distinction, given that controlling shareholders will act through their appointed managers. Indeed, there is significant similarity in the characters of redistributive events for controlled and non-controlled corporations. For example, in a case where the controlling shareholder is also a manager, the firm may be just as prone (perhaps even more prone)[58] to overpay managers as in a case where the firm is widely held. However, it is virtually certain that a non-trivial class of redistributive events will occur more frequently in controlled corporations than in non-controlled corporations. For example, controlling shareholders can be expected to use their powers of control to engineer non-arm's-length transactions more often than the managers of a non-controlled corporation.

An interesting question is whether the marginal value of increased institutional ownership is greater or less when there is a controlling shareholder. When there is a controlling shareholder, the increasing presence of institutional shareholders should mitigate the incentive and/or ability of controlling shareholders to engage in redistributive transactions. It should not interfere with the controlling shareholder's superior capability to monitor management, but (assuming that controlling shareholders are good managerial monitors) neither will increasing institutional presence add much to managerial monitoring. When there is no controlling shareholder, increasing institutional presence should have a greater (positive) marginal effect on managerial monitoring, since dispersed shareholders are likely to supply much less effective monitoring of management than a controlling shareholder. However, because there is probably less danger of redistributive transactions, an increasing institutional presence will result in a smaller (positive) marginal influence in discouraging such transactions. It is therefore difficult to tell, *a priori*, whether an increasing institutional presence will have a greater effect when there is a controlling shareholder or when there is not.

To test which effect is dominant, we constructed an interaction term, which is the percentage of institutional ownership multiplied by a dummy variable, which is zero if there is no controlling shareholder, and 1 if there is a controlling shareholder. Because we cannot determine on an *a priori* basis which effect will dominate, we hypothesize that (randomly) the interaction variable will be positively related to our four measures of profitability. Note, however, that we have already suggested that the danger of redistribution by a controlling shareholder is most likely to show up in the form of a lower price-to-book ratio. If this is so, and if controlling shareholders are less likely to engage in redistributive transactions as institutional ownership rises, the interaction term is most likely to be positive when the dependent variable is the price-to-book ratio.

DATA

THE UNIVERSE OF FIRMS FROM WHICH the data set is drawn is the TSE 300 Composite Index, which consists of 292 firms, given that some firms have more than one class of common equity included in the TSE 300. Inclusion of an issuer in the data set required that data be available regarding institutional holdings, control holdings, assets, return on equity (ROE), return on assets (ROA), the ratio of price to book value, and sales growth.

The greatest difficulty we encountered was in assembling data relating to institutional holdings. To date, no data set has been assembled dealing with Canadian firms. Canadian data is simply not as readily available as U.S. data, given that Canadian shareholders are subject to public reporting requirements only at a 10 percent ownership level, compared to a 5 percent level in the United States. Many institutions have holdings of less than 10 percent. This is partly the result of a need to achieve prudent diversification, but it is also a consequence of the desire to keep the institution's holdings confidential.

Some institutional investors are expressly forbidden to cross the 10 percent ownership threshold. For example, banks are forbidden by the *Bank Act* (subject to limited exceptions) from holding more than 10 percent of a single issuer.[59] Thus, few bank holdings will be publicly reported. Mutual funds are similarly forbidden from holding more than 10 percent, although in this case by a National Policy statement[60] issued by the Canadian Securities Administrators rather than by a legislative requirement. The mutual fund policy, however, allows a mutual fund to hold a block that is larger than 10 percent with the permission of the regulators.

An additional difficulty in determining institutional holdings is the uneven reporting of 10 percent blocks. In many cases, one entity (a bank, for example) will market a number of mutual funds under common management. Many funds take the view that they need not aggregate such holdings for reporting purposes. In other cases, external managers will manage a variety of funds (such as pension and mutual funds) with diverse beneficial ownership. Many of these fund managers contend that they need not aggregate these diversely owned funds for reporting purposes.

Our data relating to institutional holdings is drawn from two sources. The first is *Vickers Institutional Holdings Guide*, a commercial service assembled by Vickers Stock Research Corporation (based in New York). While Vickers digests holdings of less than 10 percent, the service depends on voluntary disclosure by institutional investors and hence is unavoidably incomplete, due to the fact that some funds choose not to disclose their holdings. Our second source is a database graciously furnished by Fairvest Securities Corporation, a Toronto-based institutional broker that has been a champion of institutional causes (and whose activities are funded by soft dollar commissions). Fairvest maintains a list of all 10 percent or greater holdings in all TSE 300 corporations, and in some cases large institutional holdings of less than 10 percent. The information concerning these holdings is obtained from public filings, information circulars, prospectuses and other sources. We combined the Vickers and Fairvest databases to produce our own institutional ownership database.

The accuracy of the database is diminished by a number of factors. First, as noted above, we are certain that we do not have all holdings of less than 10 percent. Second, the Fairvest database is continually updated as new information is received, but no historical record is kept showing institutional ownership at specific points in time. Given that the database was provided to us in early November 1994, it speaks as of that date. The Vickers database, however, was compiled as of March 31, 1994. Combining the two databases thus results in a timing mis-match. While we would prefer that all our data speak as of the same date, since Fairvest does not keep historical records of share ownership, this was simply not possible.

Third, there is an additional timing mis-match between the institutional shareholder ownership data and the accounting information for our sample of firms. Given that our accounting data relates to the 1993 fiscal year, we are thus relying on data that describe institutional holdings *subsequent* to the reporting period as a proxy for institutional holdings throughout the reporting period. Ideally, when attempting to relate institutional ownership to flow variables such as return on assets or sales growth, the statistic on institutional ownership would be a weighted composite reflecting degrees of institutional ownership throughout the reporting period, given that institutional ownership can change over the course of a year. Once again, because of the unavailability of data on institutional holdings during the reporting period, we had little choice in this regard.

Subsequent to the conference for which this study was prepared (in March 1995), an attempt was made to obtain accounting data for the 1994 fiscal year. This was not possible, because as of June 1995, the *Financial Post* database from which our accounting data are drawn contained fiscal 1994 accounting data for only a fraction of the firms in our portfolio.

While we would have preferred that our database distinguish between voting and restricted or non-voting shareholdings, the Vickers database does not explicitly distinguish between voting and non-voting shares.[61] The Fairvest database, on the other hand, records the largest voting block of shares (as a percentage of *total* voting power) and the identity of the shareholder. Most such blocks are in excess of 10 percent. Our combined database therefore reflects institutional ownership of voting, restricted-voting, and non-voting equities.

Because we include non-voting and restricted-voting shares as well as voting shares, we implicitly make two important assumptions. First, institutions possess a lever over management even when they hold restricted- or non-voting shares.[62] Second, institutions also possess a lever over management when they hold a large share of a single class of equity, rather than a high percentage of the total equity.

While we would rather have worked with a more finely graded sample, we believe that both of our assumptions are defensible on theoretical grounds. While restricted voting shares confer limited voting power, and non-voting shares confer none at all, holdings of both classes of share may nonetheless give institutions both the incentive to monitor management and a lever over management. Arguably, holding a non-voting block gives institutional investors a *greater*, rather than a lesser, incentive to monitor management and controlling shareholders. Without a significant voice, institutional shareholders will perceive exit to be a more important source of self-protection. The value of the exit option will, in turn, depend on a reliable and accurate flow of information about the company – giving institutions an incentive to monitor on a regular basis.

Moreover, while there is a tendency in the literature to draw a clear line between exit and voice, the two are, in fact, related. The very fact that institutions can stampede for the exit and cause the firm's share price to fall, by itself provides them with a lever over management. In many cases, management compensation depends partly on share price. Managers will thus want to avoid any conduct that will cause the share price to fall. Indeed, many senior officers have a significant portion of their wealth invested in the firm's stock – an arrangement that further increases their incentive to avoid a substantial drop in share price.[63]

Further, predatory behaviour towards restricted or non-voting shareholders that causes a drop in the corporation's stock price will adversely affect the corporation's cost of capital in subsequent rounds of financing. This in turn will raise the probability of bankruptcy (which will almost certainly result in the managers losing their jobs), in addition to depreciating the value of the managers' human capital in the external labour market. Also, institutions holding restricted- or non-voting equity retain the power to embarrass management by going public with their concerns about management's intended course of action. Since many managers prefer to avoid negative publicity, the power to go public allows institutions to exert influence over management even when they do not hold voting stock. Thus, while we would have preferred to segregate the institutional ownership sample by voting power, we suggest that there is good theoretical justification for mixing voting, restricted-voting, and non-voting holdings in our database. Where a corporation had more than one common share class in the TSE 300 Composite Index, we determined institutional ownership only for the traded class with the largest public float.

The institutional ownership variable (% INST) represents the percentage of institutional ownership in the class selected for inclusion in the study, rather than the percentage which institutional holdings constituted of *all* common share classes. As indicated above, we assume that institutions possess a lever over management by virtue of holding large positions in a single class of common shares, rather than a large share of the total equity of the company. We contend that this assumption is theoretically defensible for the same reasons that inclusion of restricted- and non-voting shares is defensible. In addition, class and "majority of the minority" voting requirements (alluded to earlier) give those who hold large positions in a single class of shares an effective veto over many types of corporate fundamental changes (even though the constitution of the corporation may designate these shares as restricted-voting or non-voting). Given that many types of redistributive activities must be consummated as fundamental changes subject to these statutory, administrative, and judicial voting entitlements, this gives institutional blockholders a solid bargaining position *vis-à-vis* management.

Controlling shareholdings (CONTROL) were determined from the Fairvest database. We adopted mechanical cutoffs to determine who is a controlling shareholder, defined as any non-institutional shareholder (or where it appeared likely that shareholders were acting in concert, coalitions of share-holders) holding either 10 percent or more (in the first set of regressions) or 20 percent or more (in the second set) of total voting power.[64] These were identified from the Fairvest data base. In our final sample of 99 companies, there were 63 firms satisfying the first criterion, and 55 satisfying the second.

Accounting data for each issuer was compiled from the *Financial Post Surveys* for the fiscal year ending closest to March 31, 1994. In most cases, the fiscal year end was December 31, 1993. From this source, we obtained data on total assets, the ratio of share price to book value per share, sales growth for the 1993 reporting period, return on assets, and return on equity.

From the total of 292 TSE 300 firms, we collected complete data for 99 firms. These 99 firms are broadly representative of the industry structure of the TSE 300 Index.

METHODOLOGY

WE USE STANDARD OLS REGRESSION METHODOLOGY to determine if rising levels of institutional ownership and/or the existence of a controlling shareholder affect firm value. To this end, we define four independent variables. The first, % INST, as described above, is the percentage of institutional owner-ship of the firm's outstanding common shares that are listed in the TSE 300 index. The second, CONTROL, also described above, is a dummy variable that is 1 if there is a control shareholder, and 0 if there is no control shareholder. The third, ASSETS, is designed to control for possible size effects.[65] The fourth independent variable, INTERACTION, is an interaction term equal to institutional holdings multiplied by the CONTROL dummy. The theoretical basis for the interaction term arises from the earlier discussion about the manner in which interactions between different types of shareholders may affect corporate value.

Four dependent variables are regressed on the independent variables described above. These are: the ratio of share price to book value per share; return on assets; return on equity; and sales growth.

All of the accounting data were taken from the *Financial Post Surveys*, in which the price-to-book ratio is defined as the ratio of average share price to book value per share. In turn, the average price is equal to the sum of the high and low stock prices for the year divided by two, and book value is defined as the year-end book value per share (excluding preferred shares). Although the latter is defined to include any intangibles reflected on the balance sheet, the typical balance sheet does not place a value on intangibles. Thus, the price-to-book ratio is largely based on the book value of tangible assets.

The price-to-book ratio is a proxy for Tobin's Q, which is the ratio of the firm's market value of debt and equity to the replacement cost of its tangible assets.[66] As indicated by Ross & Westerfield, "... firms with high Q ratios tend to be those firms with attractive investment opportunities or a significant competitive advantage".[67] Tobin's Q has been extensively used in similar types of investigations in the United States. The other dependent variables are commonly accepted indicia of firm performance.

Note, however, that measuring profitability is as much art as science. No single measure can give an unambiguous signal as to firm performance. For example, sales growth may be associated with future profitability, but may also be a sign of managerial empire building undertaken at the expense of future profits. This is why we use four different measures of profitability.

In the first set of regressions, the four measures of profitability are regressed on ASSETS, % INST, and CONTROL, with the CONTROL threshold set at 10 percent. In a second set of regressions, the same four measures of profitability are regressed on the same independent variables, plus the INTERACTION variable. The third and fourth sets of regressions repeat the above with CONTROL set at 20 percent.

RESULTS

WE DESCRIBE OUR REGRESSION RESULTS BELOW. Note that in each table we first describe the results with the CONTROL threshold set at 10 percent. These results are described in each table as regression "A". We then describe the results when the CONTROL threshold is raised to 20 percent. This is described in each table as regression "B". In each case, "Model 1" refers to the regression without the interaction term as an independent variable, and "Model 2" refers to the regression with the interaction term.

PRICE-TO-BOOK RATIO

WHEN PRICE-TO-BOOK RATIO IS REGRESSED against ASSETS, % INST, and CONTROL, none of the independent variables is statistically significant (see Table 1(A), Model 1). When the interaction term is added as an independent variable, the results change somewhat (see Table 1(A), Model 2). In this case, the percentage of institutional holdings is statistically significant at the 10 percent level, although the sign of the coefficient is negative, counter to our hypothesis that increasing institutional holdings increases firm value. The CONTROL variable is statistically significant, but again the coefficient is negative. The INTERACTION coefficient is positive and statistically significant.

When the control threshold is raised to 20 percent and the regressions rerun without the INTERACTION term, the CONTROL variable is statistically significant at the 5 percent level, again with a negative coefficient (see Table 1(B), Model 1). When the INTERACTION term is introduced, again only the CONTROL variable is statistically significant, again with a negative coefficient (see Table 1(B), Model 2). The INTERACTION term is positive, but not quite significant at conventional levels. In none of the regressions is the ASSET variable either statistically or economically significant.

TABLE 1(A)

DETERMINANTS OF PRICE-BOOK RATIO - CONTROL 10%

INDEPENDENT VARIABLE	COEFFICIENT	STANDARD ERROR	T-STATISTIC
MODEL 1			
ASSETS	−0.0015980	0.00100208	−1.5947184
% INST	−0.0035428	0.00882972	−0.4012464
CONTROL (10%)	−0.2230006	0.27994731	−0.7965807
Constant	2.32191285		
Standard Error of Y est	1.32214303		
R^2	0.03019484		
No. of Observations	99		
Degrees of Freedom	95		
MODEL 2 (INCLUDES INTERACTION TERM)			
ASSETS	−0.0015103	0.00098566	−1.5322851
% INST	−0.0265151	0.01400213	−1.8936485 ***
CONTROL (10%)	−0.8412449	0.40392588	−2.0826714 **
INTERACTION	0.037277	0.0178324	2.0904018 **
Constant	2.72774422		
Standard Error of Y est	1.29929986		
R^2	0.07327550		
No. of Observations	99		
Degrees of Freedom	94		

Notes: ** Statistically significant at 5% level, 2-tailed test.
*** Statistically significant at 10% level, 2-tailed test.

These regressions supply some (weak) evidence that increases in institutional holdings result in a lower price-to-book ratio. They supply more robust evidence that the presence of a control shareholder results in a lower price-to-book ratio. There is also some evidence that when there is a controlling shareholder, increased institutional holdings result in an increase in the price-to-book ratio.

TABLE 1(B)

DETERMINANTS OF PRICE-BOOK RATIO - CONTROL 20%

INDEPENDENT VARIABLE	COEFFICIENT	STANDARD ERROR	T-STATISTIC
MODEL 1			
ASSETS	−0.0016572	0.00098005	−1.6910123[***]
% INST	−0.0046251	0.00867397	−0.5332189
CONTROL (20%)	−0.5322349	0.26504631	−2.0080828[**]
Constant	2.49518792		
Standard Error of Y est	1.29926333		
R^2	0.06346930		
No. of Observations	99		
Degrees of Freedom	95		
MODEL 2 (INCLUDES INTERACTION TERM)			
ASSETS	−0.0015594	0.00097043	−1.6069738
% INST	−0.0201169	0.01218708	−1.6506784
CONTROL (20%)	−1.0222615	0.37906480	−2.6967989[*]
INTERACTION	0.0306753	0.017147	1.7889563[***]
Constant	2.16252486		
Standard Error of Y est	1.28447317		
R^2	0.09430507		
No. of Observations	99		
Degrees of Freedom	94		

Notes: [*] Statistically significant at 1% level, 2-tailed test.
[**] Statistically significant at 5% level, 2-tailed test
[***] Statistically significant at 10% level, 2-tailed test.

TABLE 2(A)

DETERMINANTS OF RETURN ON ASSETS - CONTROL 10%

INDEPENDENT VARIABLE	COEFFICIENT	STANDARD ERROR	T-STATISTIC
		MODEL 1	
ASSETS	−0.0007253	0.00603769	−0.1201334
% INST	0.18195008	0.05319997	3.42011590*
CONTROL (10%)	4.62878708	1.68671135	2.74426781*
Constant	−1.7786128		
Standard Error of Y est	7.96604675		
R²	0.15773592		
No. of Observations	99		
Degrees of Freedom	95		
	MODEL 2 (INCLUDES INTERACTION TERM)		
ASSET	−0.0010586	0.00602131	−0.1758223
% INST	0.26924555	0.08553704	3.14770709*
CONTROL (10%)	6.97814216	2.46752544	2.82799197*
Interaction	−0.141654	0.108936	−1.300344
Constant	−3.3207895		
Standard Error of Y est	7.93723692		
R²	0.17261906		
No. of Observations	99		
Degrees of Freedom	94		

Note: * Statistically significant at 1% level, 2-tailed test.

RETURN ON ASSETS

THE RESULTS FOR RETURN ON ASSETS are quite different. Although once again the ASSET control variable is not statistically or economically significant in any of the regressions, the coefficients on % INST and CONTROL are both positive and statistically significant both with (Table 2(A), Model 2) and without (Table 2(A), Model 1) the INTERACTION variable present. The INTERACTION term is negative but not statistically significant.

TABLE 2(B)

DETERMINANTS OF RETURN ON ASSETS - CONTROL 20%

INDEPENDENT VARIABLE	COEFFICIENT	STANDARD ERROR	T-STATISTIC
		MODEL 1	
ASSETS	−0.0019615	0.00614657	−0.3191224
% INST	0.17597162	0.05440051	3.23474212*
CONTROL (20%)	2.87380689	1.66228982	1.72882420***
Constant	−0.2858958		
Standard Error of Y est	8.14858437		
R²	0.11869363		
No. of Observations	99		
Degrees of Freedom	95		
		MODEL 2 (INCLUDES INTERACTION TERM)	
ASSETS	−0.0025013	0.00610959	−0.4094200
% INST	0.26147897	0.07672653	3.40793405*
CONTROL (20%)	5.57851356	2.38648709	2.33754189**
INTERACTION	−0.169312	0.107953	−1.568392
Constant	−1.7614647		
Standard Error of Y est	8.08668768		
R²	0.14116810		
No. of Observations	99		
Degrees of Freedom	94		

Notes: * Statistically significant at 1% level, 2-tailed test.
** Statistically significant at 5% level, 2-tailed test.
*** Statistically significant at 10% level, 2-tailed test.

When the control threshold is raised to 20 percent, the results are broadly similar, except that the Control variable is not significant (Table 2(B), Model 1) unless the Interaction term is added to the regression (Table 2(B), Model 2). Otherwise, as with the 10 percent control definition, both the presence of a controlling shareholder and increasing institutional holdings appear to result in a higher return on assets.

TABLE 3(A)

DETERMINANTS OF RETURN ON EQUITY - CONTROL 10%

INDEPENDENT VARIABLE	COEFFICIENT	STANDARD ERROR	T-STATISTIC
	MODEL 1		
ASSETS	0.01610556	0.01781706	0.90394035
% INST	0.39340964	0.15699170	2.50592635**
CONTROL (10%)	12.0896625	4.97743918	2.42889206**
Constant	−11.778928		
Standard Error of Y est	23.5075896		
R^2	0.10554815		
No. of Observations	99		
Degrees of Freedom	95		
	MODEL 2 (INCLUDES INTERACTION TERM)		
ASSETS	0.01555183	0.01787758	0.86990699
% INST	0.53841534	0.25396371	2.12004835**
CONTROL (10%)	15.9921547	7.32620507	2.18287019**
INTERACTION	−0.2353	0.3234364	−0.727502
Constant	−14.340624		
Standard Error of Y est	23.5660489		
R^2	0.11055609		
No. of Observations	99		
Degrees of Freedom	94		

Note: ** Statistically significant at 5% level, 2-tailed test.

RETURN ON EQUITY

THE RESULTS FOR RETURN ON EQUITY are similar to those for return on assets. The ASSETS size control is not significant in any of the regressions. The coefficients on the % INST and CONTROL variables are positive and statistically significant with (Table 3(A), Model 2) or without (Table 3(A), Model 1) the INTERACTION TERM. The INTERACTION term itself is negative but not significant.

When the control threshold is raised to 20 percent, the CONTROL variable ceases to be statistically significant. The % INST variable, however, continues to be significant both with (Table 3(B), Model 2) and without (Table 3(B), Model 1) the INTERACTION term.

TABLE 3(B)

DETERMINANTS OF RETURN ON EQUITY - CONTROL 20%

INDEPENDENT VARIABLE	COEFFICIENT	STANDARD ERROR	T-STATISTIC
MODEL 1			
ASSETS	0.01312820	0.01799842	0.72940895
% INST	0.38069448	0.15929570	2.38986034**
CONTROL (20%)	8.33923236	4.86752102	1.71324013***
Constant	−8.3990426		
Standard Error of Y est	23.8607040		
R^2	0.07847468		
No. of Observations	99		
Degrees of Freedom	95		
MODEL 2 (INCLUDES INTERACTION TERM)			
ASSETS	0.12609538	0.01809779	0.69674427
% INST	0.46284288	0.22727892	2.03645318**
CONTROL (20%)	10.9376908	7.06923874	1.54722329
Interaction	−0.162661	0.319778	−0.50867
Constant	−9.8166472		
Standard Error of Y est	23.9543410		
R^2	0.08100432		
No. of Observations	99		
Degrees of Freedom	94		

Notes: ** Statistically significant at 5% level, 2-tailed test.
*** Statistically significant at 10% level, 2-tailed test.

To summarize, this suggests that the increasing presence of institutional shareholders raises return on equity. It also suggests, although somewhat more weakly, that the presence of a controlling shareholder also raises return on equity.

TABLE 4(A)

DETERMINANTS OF SALES GROWTH - CONTROL 10%

INDEPENDENT VARIABLE	COEFFICIENT	STANDARD ERROR	T-STATISTIC
MODEL 1			
ASSETS	−0.0276291	0.05109070	−0.5407869
% INST	−0.0224936	0.45017612	−0.0499693
CONTROL (10%)	13.6814696	14.2728834	0.95856381
Constant	17.1980469		
Standard Error of Y est	67.4083751		
R^2	0.01431223		
No. of Observations	99		
Degrees of Freedom	95		
MODEL 2 (INCLUDES INTERACTION TERM)			
ASSETS	−0.0286734	0.05134607	−0.5584345
% INST	0.25096130	0.72940737	0.34406191
CONTROL (10%)	21.0408758	21.0415419	0.99996834
INTERACTION	−0.443735	0.9289396	−0.477679
Constant	12.3671443		
Standard Error of Y est	67.6838828		
R^2	0.01669912		
No. of Observations	99		
Degrees of Freedom	94		

SALES GROWTH

THE % INST VARIABLE IS NEGATIVE WITHOUT the INTERACTION term (Table 4(A), Model 1), and positive with the INTERACTION term (Table 4(A), Model 2), but is not statistically significant in either regression. The CONTROL variable is positive without the INTERACTION term, and positive with the INTERACTION term, but again is not statistically significant in either regression. The INTERACTION term has a negative sign, but is not significant either.

When the CONTROL threshold is raised to 20 percent, the results are similar (Table 4(B), Model 1 and Model 2). In none of the regressions is the ASSETS control significant.

In our sample, sales growth does not appear to be affected by either the presence of a controlling shareholder, or by institutional holdings.

TABLE 4(B)

DETERMINANTS OF SALES GROWTH - CONTROL 20%

INDEPENDENT VARIABLE	COEFFICIENT	STANDARD ERROR	T-STATISTIC
		MODEL 1	
ASSETS	−0.0307057	0.05093946	−0.6027881
% INST	−0.0335046	0.45084163	−0.0743157
CONTROL (20%)	10.4081062	13.7761475	0.75551646
Constant	20.4184369		
Standard Error of Y est	67.5310039		
R^2	0.01072266		
No. of Observations	99		
Degrees of Freedom	95		
		MODEL 2 (INCLUDES INTERACTION TERM)	
ASSETS	−0.0331060	0.05110259	−0.6478353
% INST	0.34667099	0.64176543	0.54018333
CONTROL (20%)	22.4335455	19.9613456	1.12384936
INTERACTION	−0.752783	0.9029539	−0.83369
Constant	13.8578867		
Standard Error of Y est	67.6396566		
R^2	0.01798372		
No. of Observations	99		
Degrees of Freedom	94		

WINDOW DRESSING?

THERE IS SOME EVIDENCE THAT institutions engage in "window dressing" – that is, selling poor performers at the end of the year and buying stocks that are likely to be more superficially appealing to their sponsors.[68] Because of the timing mis-matches in our data noted earlier, we cannot be sure that some institutions are not purchasing stocks with a high return on equity and on assets at year's end. In other words, instead of institutional monitoring resulting in a higher return on assets and return on equity, it may be that a high return on assets and a high return on equity results in higher institutional ownership.

It should be noted, however, that some of our institutional sample (obtained from the Fairvest database) speaks as of early November 1994. This precedes most of the year ends in the sample. If window dressing does indeed occur in the fourth quarter (as the evidence suggests),[69] then the institutional holdings shown in Fairvest, which tend to be the largest holdings (*i.e.*, those in excess of 10 percent), will tend to be relatively unaffected by possible window dressing. It is precisely these institutional shareholdings that are most likely to supply useful monitoring.

Second, many of the reporting dates for institutions in the Vickers database also precede the year end. For example, of 243 institutional holders of Canadian Pacific, 101 (just under 42 percent) reported as of a date prior to the end of 1993. This reporting pattern appears to be broadly representative of the database as a whole. Thus, even for the Vickers database, many institutional holdings are reported prior to the end of the fourth quarter.

Perhaps most importantly, the literature offers only equivocal support for the view that all we have detected is window dressing. Lakonishok, Shleifer, Thaler & Vishny[70] investigated a large sample of (mostly private) U.S. pension funds to determine whether these institutions engaged in window dressing to curry favour with plan sponsors. The study found some evidence of window dressing by comparing fourth quarter selling and purchasing behaviour of the sample funds to their behaviour in the first three quarters. In the fourth quarter, there was evidence that funds were more likely to sell losers (stocks realizing returns in the previous year in the two lowest quintiles of the entire CRSP data sample, which consists of firms traded on the New York Stock Exchange, American Stock Exchange, and over-the-counter).[71]

However, the evidence that institutional investors tend to accelerate their selling of losers in the last quarter was strongly offset by the finding that, in general, institutional traders are contrarian in their trading strategies. After reviewing trading behaviour during the first three quarters, the authors concluded that:[72]

> ... when it comes to purchases, funds are clearly contrarian: relative to availability they overbuy losers... and underbuy winners. ... Second, when it comes to sales, funds oversell winners relative to their holdings ... but they also oversell losers. ...[73]

The Lakonishok *et al.* study found, however, that smaller funds had a stronger propensity to dump losers in the fourth quarter than larger funds.[74]

Although there was weak statistical evidence, as noted above, that the funds accelerated their *sales* of losers, there was robust evidence that the funds accelerated their *purchases* of losers. While initially this appears counter-intuitive, the authors suggest a plausible explanation: the continued holding of past losers may be difficult to defend to plan sponsors. However, it may not be difficult to defend the *buying* of stocks that were losers *before* they were held by the fund.

This evidence strengthens, rather than detracts from our results. In general, the funds in the sample were shown to be contrarian investors: they sold winners and bought losers. Assuming that ROE and ROA are correlated with stock returns (the basis for the study by Lakonishok *et al.*), then institutions engaging in contrarian trading will sell, rather than buy stock with high ROE and ROA. The Lakonishok *et al.* study suggests that the existence of window dressing should not affect this result, since the accelerated sales of losers in the fourth quarter were offset by the accelerated purchases of losers. The net effect on the balance of winners and losers in the overall portfolio should thus be minimal.

A second study by Lakonishok, Shleifer & Vishny, however, is also worthy of note. The second study used the same data sample, disaggregated by size, to determine if institutions engage in positive feedback trading. Positive feedback (PF) trading is the opposite of contrarian trading. It occurs when an institution buys last quarter's winners, and sells last quarter's losers. The study found robust evidence of PF trading in the two smallest quintiles of traded firms by size, but no evidence of such trading in the three largest quintiles.

These studies using American data are merely suggestive of what might occur in the Canadian market. On average, Canadian funds are smaller than their U.S. counterparts. Further, TSE stocks tend to correspond in size to those in the lowest two quintiles in the Lakonishok *et al.* sample. Obviously, we cannot rule out the possibility that window dressing or, more generally, PF trading strategies drive our results.

We note, however, that because institutional blocks tend to be large compared to retail holdings, and because it is time-consuming and expensive for brokers (and hence their institutional clients) to break up large blocks, much institutional trading is consummated with other institutions. Hence, it is not entirely clear that window dressing (or more generally PF trading strategies) will result in a large increase in the percentage of a particular firm that is institutionally held. For every institutional buyer/seller, there must be a seller/buyer on the other side of the transaction. If that trader is another institution engaging in a different trading strategy, then such trading will effect no change at all in the percentage of a given firm that is institutionally held.

It is also likely that some retail traders engage in PF trading strategies. In theory, retail PF trading might exceed institutional PF trading. If this is the case, then firm profitability will tend to lead to *decreased*, rather than increased, institutional ownership. We have no evidence that this is the case, but present it as a theoretical possibility. At the very least, it seems unrealistic to believe that all institutional purchases made for the purpose of window dressing (or PF trading) will be made by retail sellers. It is also unrealistic to believe that all institutions engage in window dressing (or PF trading).

Finally, we note that our regressions yield some support for the view that as institutional holdings rise, the price-to-book ratio falls. Window dressing, however, should create an artificial demand for certain stocks based on factors other than risk/return characteristics, since the only end in view is to make the portfolio holdings more superficially appealing to plan sponsors. It should thus create a price pressure effect, driving the price upward and increasing the price-to-book ratio. We do not observe this. In short, we think it is unlikely that window dressing or PF trading drive our results.

THE PRICE-TO-BOOK RATIO AND UNTRADED EQUITY

M ANY CANADIAN CORPORATIONS have more than one class of common shares. In some cases, one class of common shares is publicly traded, while the other is not. In calculating the price-to-book ratio as defined earlier, however, the *Financial Post* uses the book value for *all* common shares, but the price for only the traded class of equity. Where this is the case, the price-to-book ratio will be biased downward.

In fact, it is not uncommon for controlling shareholders to hold a class of superior voting equity, whether traded or non-traded. Where such equity is traded, it tends to trade at a premium to the restricted- or non-voting equity.[76]

This downward bias on the price-to-book ratio offers an alternative explanation for some of the regression results in which price-to-book ratio is the dependent variable. In particular, the regressions appear to show that the presence of a controlling shareholder has a negative effect on the price-to-book ratio. This may be an artifact of the manner in which the price-to-book ratio is computed.

SUMMARY AND CONCLUSIONS

THE ROLE OF INSTITUTIONAL SHAREHOLDERS

TAKEN AS A WHOLE, THESE RESULTS OFFER the first empirical support in Canada for the hypothesis that institutional investors increase firm value. There is a positive and statistically significant relationship between both return on assets and return on equity (two commonly used measures of profitability) and institutional holdings. Although in all regressions of price-to-book against institutional holdings, the coefficient on institutional holdings was wrongly signed to support the hypothesis that an increased institutional presence increases value, in none of these regressions was the coefficient statistically significant.

There is also some support for the hypothesis that institutional monitoring acts to reduce the danger of redistributive transactions engineered by controlling interests. The price-to-book ratio is the measure of profitability most likely to be affected by redistributive transactions effected by controlling shareholders. Thus, if institutional shareholders play a useful role in monitoring for redistributive events, the interaction term should have its strongest effect where the dependent variable is the price-to-book ratio. This is, in fact, the case. The interaction term was negatively signed and was not statistically significant in the regressions of ROA, ROE, and sales growth on the three independent variables – institutional holdings, control, and the interaction term. However, it was positive and statistically significant in one of two regressions in which price-to-book was the dependent variable, and nearly significant at conventional levels in the second. Thus, there is some support for the hypothesis that institutional shareholders monitor for redistributive events.

The evidence as a whole tends to confirm the hypothesis that increased institutional holdings result in a more profitable firm. This suggests that institutional investors do indeed perform useful monitoring of corporate managers and/or controlling shareholders, and that this monitoring is of benefit to other non-controlling shareholders.

That the percentage of institutional ownership achieved statistical significance in many of the regressions is particularly interesting given the "noisiness" of the institutional ownership database. Database errors are likely to reduce the chances of finding a statistically significant relationship. As indicated earlier, there are a number of database errors in our institutional ownership sample, stemming from the difficulties we encountered in identifying all institutional owners, the timing mis-match between the two sources of institutional ownership data, and the timing mis-match between the ownership data and the accounting data.

Given that the institutional ownership sample combined voting, restricted-voting, and non-voting shares, the results suggest that institutions derive a lever over management from sources other than voting power. Further investigation (through stratification of the sample into voting, restricted-voting, and non-voting shares) is in order.

Because the institutional ownership sample focused on the percentage of institutional ownership in single traded classes of equity (where in some cases the firm had two classes of equity), the results suggest that institutions derive power from holding large positions in single equity classes. This too deserves further investigation through further stratification of the sample.

One important caveat is in order. There is the possibility that our results are driven by "window dressing" or, more generally, positive feedback trading by institutional managers. For the reasons given earlier, we do not think that this is the case, but we cannot rule it out.

THE ROLE OF CONTROLLING SHAREHOLDERS

THE PRESENCE OF A CONTROLLING SHAREHOLDER had a somewhat more ambiguous effect on firm profitability. There is fairly strong support for the hypothesis that the presence of a controlling shareholder resulted in a lower price-to-book ratio. However, there is even stronger support for the hypothesis that the presence of a controlling shareholder resulted in higher returns on both assets and equity, although there was no discernible effect on sales growth.

Except for the absence of an effect on sales growth, these results are consistent with our hypotheses about the effect of a controlling shareholder on firm value. Earlier we hypothesized that the presence of a controlling shareholder should result in better monitoring of managers. This in turn should result in higher ROA and ROE (which we assume are not as likely to be affected by redistributive transactions as price-to-book). However, in an efficient market, where controlling shareholders regularly engage in some redistribution of profits at the expense of non-controlling interests, the price of firms with controlling shareholders will be discounted to reflect this risk. The fact that the price-to-book ratio is less when there is a controlling shareholder suggests that, even though such corporations generate higher profits, these profits are siphoned off by controlling shareholders.

Again, there is a caveat. Because of the way in which the price-to-book ratio is computed, there may be a built-in downward bias when there is a controlling shareholder. Our results in relation to the price-to-book ratio are therefore more tentative than in relation to ROA, ROE, and sales growth.

POLICY IMPLICATIONS

IF INSTITUTIONS DO, INDEED, PERFORM USEFUL MONITORING of both corporate managers and controlling shareholders, this lends weight to the arguments of Black,[77] Roe,[78] MacIntosh[79] and others that legal restraints on institutional activism tend to impede effective monitoring. In Canada, there are a variety of such restraints, many of which could be lessened or removed without adverse consequences.[80] There are also a number of ways in which regulation could be enhanced to promote institutional activism (such as introducing confidential voting), and to reduce the extent to which institutions can be co-opted into voting with management. Our results should encourage policy makers to consider both removing legal restraints that are not cost-effective, and introducing measures designed to facilitate the institutional role in corporate governance.

Do any policy implications derive from our results in relation to controlling shareholders? While the results appear to be consistent with our hypothesis that controlling shareholders both monitor managers and engage in redistribution, the evidence is far from conclusive. Moreover, as indicated above, Morck & Stangeland find evidence that not all types of controlling shareholders have the same effect on firm value. The controlling shareholder data must be further stratified to determine the effect of different types of controlling shareholders on value. Thus, we do not draw any specific policy conclusions.

However, supposing that controlling shareholders do indeed engage in redistribution of wealth from non-controlling interests, this is not necessarily a prescription for any particular market intervention (such as strict control of related-party transactions). As long as shareholders are fully cognizant of the danger of controlling shareholder predations, and stock prices are adjusted accordingly, shareholders of controlled companies should earn normal returns.

Arguably, there is a danger that a non-controlled firm may be acquired by a controlling shareholder, inflicting unanticipated losses on shareholders. There appear to be two mitigating factors, however. In an economy in which control is the rule rather than the exception, it is possible that a discount is built into the stock price of non-controlled companies to reflect this danger. Further, not all types of control transactions present the same risk to shareholders. An any-or-all takeover offer presents the least risk, given that shareholders can fully cash out at a premium if they choose, and avoid the risk of subsequent looting or expropriation.

A partial takeover apparently presents somewhat greater risks. The implicit back-end price (i.e., the market-trading price after the event) is almost invariably less than the front-end price. Some have argued that this effectively coerces shareholders into tendering.[81] If there is a danger of redistribution following the acquisition of control, this will magnify the extent of the coercion. The takeover may succeed, even though shareholders as a whole are worse off as a result, and the controlling shareholder may thus profit by purchasing control and adopting a strategy of redistributing assets in its favour. A private change of control, where redistribution ("looting") is the motive for the transaction, may similarly reduce shareholder wealth with no efficiency benefits.

We note, however, that the magnitude of the redistribution necessary to make a looting strategy profitable is necessarily large, and would likely attract legal (or administrative) intervention. We also note that the U.S. evidence casts doubt on the frequency with which control is purchased for the purpose of effecting redistribution. In addition to Holderness & Sheehan's evidence (above), Barclay & Holderness find that private changes in control tend to result in significant benefit to minority shareholders.[82] There is also evidence tending to refute the theory that partial takeovers are coercive.[83] Further investigation of the role of controlling shareholders in Canadian markets is clearly in order.

ENDNOTES

1 Adolf A. Berle, Jr. & Gardiner C. Means, *The Modern Corporation and Private Property*, New York: Macmillan Co., 1932.

2 Michael Jensen & William Meckling, "Theory of the Firm: Managerial Behaviour, Agency Costs, and Ownership Structure," *Journal of Financial Economics*, 3, 1976, p. 305.

3 A notable exception is Demsetz, who hypothesizes that the optimal ownership structure is determined endogenously by a variety of factors which may vary from firm to firm and from industry to industry. Consequently, in his view, there should be no relation between ownership structure and firm performance. See Harold Demsetz, "The Structure of Ownership and the Theory of the Firm," *Journal of Law & Economics*, 26, 1983, p. 375.

4 See, *e.g.*, Michael C. Jensen, "The Takeover Controversy: Analysis and Evidence", in *Knights, Raiders and Targets: The Impact of the Hostile Takeover*, edited by John C. Coffee, Jr. *et al.*, New York, Oxford University Press, 1988, p. 314.

5 Stulz provided the theoretical basis for the view that as managerial ownership increases, firm value will decrease owing to the diminished likelihood of a takeover bid. In Stulz' model, as management ownership increases, the premium that an acquirer must pay to purchase control increases, while the probability of an offer occurring decreases. At 50 percent managerial ownership, the probability of a hostile bid is reduced to zero, and a minimum firm value is achieved. See René Stulz, "Managerial Control of Voting Rights, Financial Policies, and the Market for Corporate Control," *Journal of Financial Economics*, 20, 1988, p. 25. Morck *et al.* hypothesize (as in Jensen & Meckling, *supra*, note 2) that increasing managerial ownership will align managerial and shareholder interests, while also (as in Stulz) reducing the probability of a takeover bid. See Randall Morck, Andrei Shleifer & Robert W. Vishny, "Management Ownership and Market Valuation," *Journal of Financial Economics*, 20, 1988, p. 293.

6 A pithy summary of the theory and evidence may be found in Randall K. Morck, "On the Economics of Concentrated Ownership", paper prepared for Canadian Corporate Governance: An Interdisciplinary Perspective, C.D. Howe Institute, February 10-11, 1994.

7 Studies on this point are conveniently summarized in Vijay Jog & Ajit Tulpule, "Control and Performance: Evidence from the TSE 300", in this volume.

8 Randall Morck, Andrei Shleifer & Robert W. Vishny, "Management Ownership and Market Valuation," *Journal of Financial Economics*, 20, 1988, 293.

9 J. J. McConnell & H. Servaes, "Additional Evidence on Equity Ownership and Corporate Value," *Journal of Financial Economics*, 27, 1990, p. 595.

10 Karen Hopper Wruck, "Equity Ownership Concentration and Firm Value," *Journal of Financial Economics*, 23, 1988, p. 3.

11 See, *e.g.*, Michael J. Barclay & Clifford G. Holderness, "Private Benefits From Control of Public Corporations" *Journal of Financial Economics*, 25, 1989, p. 371; Michael J. Barclay & Clifford G. Holderness, "Negotiated Block Trades and Corporate Control" *Journal of Financial Economics*, 46, 1991, p. 861.

12 Morck *et al. supra*, note 4, at 309-10 interpret this result in the following manner:

> It suggests that outside board members, like officers, respond to financial incentives and contribute more to corporate wealth as their ownership stakes rise. In addition, it suggests that outside board members are capable of becoming entrenched. Since outside board members are less likely than top officers to enjoy corporate perks, such entrenchment perhaps takes the form of unchecked deployment of corporate wealth into projects that the board, but not necessarily the market, considers desirable. Finally, this interpretation suggests that for outside board members, as well as for top officers, the convergence-of-interests effect again dominates at very high ownership levels.

13 The demise of the junk-bond market also had a significant effect on the ability of acquirors to complete hostile acquisitions successfully, although at the time of writing, this market is staging a powerful resurgence.

14 The use of poison pills is policed by the courts, limiting the managers' freedom to abuse the pill to entrench themselves. While pills are thus imperfect entrenchment devices, the evidence suggests that managers can indeed use poison pills to service their own, rather than shareholders' best interests. See Jeffrey G. MacIntosh, "Poison Pills in Canada: A Reply to Dey and Yalden," *Canadian Business Law Journal*, 17, 1991, p. 323; Jeffrey G. MacIntosh, "The Poison Pill: A Noxious Nostrum for Canadian Shareholders," *Canadian Business Law Journal*, 18, 1989, p. 276; Jeffrey G. MacIntosh, "Are Poison Pills Good for Shareholders? The Empirical Evidence," *Corporate Governance Review*, 6 (6), 1994, p. 2.

15 See those articles cited *ibid.*

16 See, *e.g.*, *347883 Alberta Ltd. v. Producers Pipelines Ltd.* (1991), 80 D.L.R. (4th) 359 (Sask. C.A.); *Remington Energy Ltd. v. Joss Energy Ltd.*, unreported, Alberta Court of Queen's Bench, per Fraser J., Dec. 17, 1993; *Re MDC Corporation and Regal Greetings & Gifts Inc.*, Ontario Securities Commission, Oct. 13, 1994; *Re Lac Minerals Ltd.*, Ontario Securities Commission, Oct. 13, 1994.

17 Randall Morck & David A. Stangeland, "Corporate Performance and Large Shareholders," Working Paper No. 4-94, Institute for Financial Research, Faculty of Business, University of Alberta.

18 Indeed, this classification is an oversimplification, since there will often be a divergence of incentives even within these classes. Public and private

pension funds, for example, face rather different incentives to get involved in matters of corporate governance.

19 These have been well developed in the extensive U.S. literature dealing with institutional shareholders, and are summarized in Jeffrey G. MacIntosh, "Institutional Investors and Corporate Governance in Canada", paper prepared for Canadian Corporate Governance: An Interdisciplinary Perspective, C.D. Howe Institute, February 10-11, 1994 (*Canadian Business Law Journal*, forthcoming).

20 Morck *et al.*, *supra*, note 5, at 310.

21 See, *e.g.*, Clifford P. Holderness & Dennis P. Sheehan, "The Role of Majority Shareholders in Publicly Held Corporations: An Exploratory Analysis," *Journal of Financial Economics*, 20, 1988, p. 317.

22 This is done in the *Canada Business Corporations Act*, R.S.C. 1985, c. C-44 (CBCA), for example, in connection with an amalgamation (s. 183(3)), sale of all or substantially all the assets of the corporation (s. 183(5)), and continuance in another jurisdiction (s. 188(4)).

23 This is done in the CBCA, for example (with some limitations), in connection with an amalgamation (s. 183(4)), sale of all or substantially all the assets of the corporation (s. 189(6)), and amendments to the articles of incorporation (s. 176).

24 Related parties include directors, officers, and significant shareholders.

25 See generally "Note on Statutory and Judicial Voting Entitlements," in *Cases and Materials on Partnerships and Canadian Business Corporations*, edited by Jacob S. Ziegel *et al.*, Toronto: Carswell, 1995, 3rd edition.

26 See generally Jeffrey G. MacIntosh, "Minority Shareholder Rights in Canada and England: 1860-1987," *Osgoode Hall Law Journal*, 27, 1989, p. 561.

27 See Philip Anisman, "The Commission as Protector of Minority Shareholders," in *Special Lectures of the Law Society of Upper Canada, 1989: Securities Law in the Modern Financial Marketplace*, Toronto: Richard De Boo, 1989, p. 451; Jeffrey G. MacIntosh, "Corporations," in *Law Society of Upper Canada, Special Lectures, 1990: Fiduciary Duties*,Toronto: Thomson Professional Publishing Canada, 1990, p.189.

28 See, *e.g.*, Ronald Gilson, "The Case Against Shark Repellant Amendments: Structural Limitations on the Enabling Concept," *Stanford Law Review*, 34, 1982, p. 775.

29 *Supra*, note 6.

30 *Supra*, note 17.

31 R. Daniels & P. Halpern, "The Canadian Quandary: Accounting for the Survival of the Closely Held Corporation", paper prepared for Canadian Corporate Governance: An Interdisciplinary Perspective, C.D. Howe Institute, February 10-11, 1994, (*Canadian Business Law Journal*, forthcoming).

32 Holderness & Sheehan, *supra*, note 21.

33 In a window beginning 20 days prior to the trade and ending ten days after

the trade, Holderness & Sheehan found a statistically significant increase in the value of market-traded equity of 12.8 percent. *Ibid.*

34 Controlling shareholders might use their powers of control to force managers to choose accounting procedures that reduce reported income, in order to reduce return on assets and return on equity. They might do so to conceal the true magnitude of the firm's profits, in order to facilitate redistribution to themselves from non-controlling interests. This suggests that the presence of a controlling shareholder may indeed negatively affect return on return on assets and return on equity. We think this unlikely, however. As an empirical matter, the market would appear to adjust in an unbiased manner to changes in accounting methods. If this is the case, then influencing the selection of accounting methods will not enable controlling shareholders to conceal their predations.

35 R. Morck & D. Stangeland, "Corporate Performance and Large Shareholders: An Empirical Analysis," *supra*, note 17; Morck, *et al. supra*, note 5. See also B. Johnson, R. Magee, N. Nagarajan, & H. Newman, "An Analysis of the Stock Price Reaction to Sudden Executive Deaths: Implications for the Managerial Labour Market," *Journal of Accounting & Economics*, 7, 1985, p. 151.

36 Morck & Stangeland, *supra*, note 17.

37 Holderness & Sheehan, *supra*, note 21.

38 A control shareholder "appoints" management indirectly, by virtue of the ability to elect a majority of directors. The directors formally appoint the officers.

39 Holderness & Sheehan, *supra*, note 21.

40 Bernard S. Black, "Shareholder Passivity Reexamined," *Michigan Law Review*, 89, 1990, p. 520. In the Canadian setting, see MacIntosh, "Institutional Investors and Corporate Governance in Canada," *supra*, note 19.

41 James A. Brickley, Ronald C. Lease, & Clifford W. Smith, Jr., "Ownership Structure and Voting on Anti-takeover Amendments," *Journal of Financial Economics*, 20, 1988, p. 267.

42 Agrawal & Mandelker, "Large Shareholders and the Monitoring of Managers: The Case of Antitakeover Charter Amendments," *Journal of Finance & Quantitative Analysis*, 25, 1990, p. 143.

43 *Ibid.*

44 McConnell & Servaes, *supra*, note 9. See generally Bernard S. Black, "The Value of Institutional Investor Monitoring: The Empirical Evidence," *U.C.L.A. Law Review*, 39, 1992, p. 986.

45 MacIntosh, *supra*, note 19.

46 *Ibid.*

47 *Ibid.* This may well be due to the movement of bank balances into money market mutual funds, rather than a movement of diversified mutual funds into non-equity instruments.

48 See MacIntosh, "Institutional Investors and Corporate Governance in Canada," supra, note 19; Jeffrey G. MacIntosh, "The Role of Institutional and Retail Shareholders in Canadian Capital Markets," *Osgoode Hall Law Journal*, 32, 1994, p. 371; R.J. Daniels & E.J. Waitzer, "Challenges to the Citadel: A Brief Overview of Recent Trends in Canadian Corporate Governance," *Canadian Business Law Journal*, 23, 1994, p. 23; K.E. Montgomery, "Survey of Institutional Shareholders," *Corporate Governance Review*, ("Survey") 4:4, 1992, p. 5; Kathryn E. Montgomery, "Shareholder Activism in Canada: A Survey of Institutional Shareholders," ("Shareholder Activism"), Working Paper Series No. NC 92-014-B, Western Business School, University of Western Ontario.

49 *Ibid.*

50 Public pension funds will wish to avoid the spotlight in order to avoid a political backlash. See, *e.g.*, Mark J. Roe, "A Political Theory of American Corporate Finance," *Columbia Law Review*, 91, 1991, p. 10.

51 See MacIntosh, *supra*, note 48.

52 See MacIntosh, *ibid.*

53 See MacIntosh, *supra*, note 48, for a number of proposals for reform of Canadian legislation to permit a more activist role.

54 John Pound, "Proxy Contests and the Efficiency of Shareholder Oversight," *Journal of Financial Economics*, 20, 1988, p. 237.

55 Brickley, Lease & Smith, *supra*, note 41.

56 See *e.g.*, Michael E. Porter, "Capital Choices: Changing the Way America Invests in Industry." *Journal of Applied Corporate Finance*, 5:2, (1992):4.

57 With respect to U.S. data see, *e.g.*, Office of the Chief Economist, Securities and Exchange Commission, "Institutional Ownership, Tender Offers, and Long-Term Investments," April 19, 1985. With respect to Canadian data, see Lewis D. Johnston & Bohumir Pazderka, "Firm Value and Investment in R&D," *Managerial and Decision Economics*, 14, 1993, p. 15.

58 See Morck & Stangeland, *supra*, note 17, although see also Holderness & Sheehan, *supra*, note 21.

59 MacIntosh, *supra*, note 48.

60 See National Policy 39.

61 The Vickers database lists the class of shares held, but does not indicate whether the class is voting or non-voting. Knowing the identity of the share class held by institutional investors, it was possible to determine the voting power of the shares. However, it was not feasible within the time and resource constraints of our study.

62 In future iterations of this study, we hope to segregate the sample according to the voting power of the institutional holdings, in order to determine which holdings supply institutions with the greatest leverage over management.

63 The greatest source of managerial sensitivity to share price comes not from options or bonuses, but from managerial shareholdings. See Michael C. Jensen & Kevin J. Murphy, "Performance Pay and Top Management

Incentives," *Journal of Political Economy*, 98, 1990, p. 225. While Jensen & Murphy demonstrate that management remuneration is not highly sensitive to firm performance, managerial share holdings may well give managers a good incentive to pay attention to share price.

64 In the case of *Canada Malting*, two corporate shareholders (John Labatt and Molson Brewing) each held just under 20 percent of the common shares. While there is evidence that these shareholders have in fact acted jointly in relation to some corporate decisions, we were not prepared to assume that they would always do so. Indeed, a disagreement between the two shareholders would result in the votes of one effectively cancelling the votes of the other. Thus, we classified this company as not controlled.

65 There is evidence suggesting that smaller firms have higher risk adjusted returns than larger firms (the "small firm effect"). There is also evidence that such firms have lower price-to-book ratios. See, *e.g.*, Avner Arbel, "Generic stocks: An old product in a new package." *Journal of Portfolio Management*, Summer 1985, p. 4. In turn, there is evidence that price-to-book ratios are predictive of shareholder returns. See generally Eugene F. Fama, "Efficient Capital Markets: II," *Journal of Finance*, 46, 1991, p. 1575. We thought it prudent to control for the effect of size on the various accounting measures of profitability discussed below.

66 See generally E. Lindenberg & S. Ross, "Tobin's Q Ratio and Industrial Organization," *Journal of Business*, 54, 1981, p. 1.

67 Stephen A. Ross & Randolph W. Westerfield, *Corporate Finance*, St. Louis: Times Mirror/Mosby College Publishing, 1988, p. 41.

68 See, *e.g.*, J. Lakonishok, A. Shleifer, R. Thaler & R. Vishny, "Window Dressing by Pension Fund Managers," *American Economic Review*, 81, 1991, p. 227.

69 Lakonishok, *ibid.*

70 *Ibid.*

71 Note, however, that the study was unable to reject the null hypothesis of no difference in the selling intensity of losers as between quarters 1 to 3 and quarter 4 (the t-statistic for difference in means was only 1.75). See *ibid.* at 230.

72 *Ibid.* at 230.

73 See J. Lakonishok, A. Shleifer & R.W. Vishny, "The Impact of Institutional Trading on Stock Prices," *Journal of Financial Economics*, 32, 1992, p. 23 (finding that institutional investors tend to engage in contrarian trading).

74 *Ibid.* at 231.

75 In this case, the t-statistic for the difference in means of a statistic reflecting purchasing intensity was 5.47, allowing rejection of the null hypothesis of no difference in means. It should also be noted that while there was some evidence that the funds slowed their sales of winners, this did not achieve statistical significance. *Ibid.* at 230.

76 Vijay M. Jog & Allan L. Riding, "Market Reactions of Return, Risk, and Liquidity to the Creation of Restricted Voting Shares," *Canadian Journal of Administrative Sciences*, March 1989, p. 62.
77 *Supra*, note 40.
78 *Supra*, note 50.
79 *Supra*, note 48.
80 *Ibid.*
81 See generally MacIntosh, "The Poison Pill: A Noxious Nostrum for Canadian Shareholders," *supra*, note 14.
82 "Negotiated Block Trades and Corporate Control," *supra*, note 11.
83 The evidence is summarized in MacIntosh, "The Poison Pill: A Noxious Nostrum for Canadian Shareholders," *supra*, note 14.

Michel Patry　　　　　　&　Michel Poitevin
Department of Economics　　Department of Economics
École des HEC and CIRANO　Université de Montréal, CRDE and CIRANO

9

Why Institutional Investors are not Better Shareholders

INTRODUCTION

THE GROWING INTEREST IN GOVERNANCE REGIMES and their effects on the performance of firms has generated a widespread and interesting debate – with institutional investors often at the centre of that debate. Voices are being heard that call for banks, mutual funds and pension funds to play a more active and effective role in monitoring managers, even to the point of guiding enterprises on some issues.

The apparent success of Japanese and German firms has fuelled this interest in governance regimes and firm performance and has led many observers to suggest that Canada and the United States should consider implementing changes to their system(s) of corporate governance that would encourage long-term partnerships at the price of liquidity. Many scholars[1] have argued that the weak role played by institutional investors in North America is attributable to legal and institutional barriers. Our approach is somewhat different in that we concentrate on two determinants of institutional investors' activism: their own governance and organizational structure.

Our focus is particularly on mutual funds and pension funds and we ask: do managers of mutual funds and pension fund managers have an incentive to monitor and influence the management of the firms in which they invest? Can they effectively monitor and influence corporate policy? What cost-benefit relationship supports their decisions? Finally, how can we make institutional investors more active partners?

To answer these questions, we first present an overview of the role and informational structure of financial contracts. We then examine how the exit and voice mechanisms function to control managerial behaviour. A brief outline of the importance of institutional investors follows. We continue with an examination of the governance and internal organization of mutual funds and pension funds and follow with an analysis of their consequences on the level of monitoring and influence on activities. Finally, we offer a critical assessment of some of the propositions designed to improve the governance of Canadian firms.

THE NEED FOR CORPORATE GOVERNANCE

THIS SECTION PROVIDES AN OVERVIEW OF THE ROLE and functions of financial markets in modern capitalistic economies. It has four parts. First, we examine the role played by financial markets in modern economies. The second part is devoted to financial market imperfections and presents some evidence suggesting these imperfections are real. The third part focuses on the "institutional" response to these imperfections, namely the emergence of contracts. The last part examines the governance of financial contracts and its related objectives and problems.

THE ROLE OF FINANCIAL MARKETS

FIRMS AND HOUSEHOLDS EVOLVE in an economic environment that is inherently uncertain. These agents have strong incentives to insure risks as well as to smooth fluctuations associated with their income. Insurance needs arise when unexpected losses are possible; smoothing needs arise when income is expected to fluctuate over time. For example, a firm may want some insurance against foreign exchange risk if it is doing business in a foreign country; it may also want to smooth its income if its line of business fluctuates seasonally. On a personal level, a household may wish to insure itself against potential losses related to accidents or unemployment, while at the same time seeking to smooth its income over the period when all members are working and into retirement.

In an economy with complete contingent markets, the demand for insurance and smoothing could be fully satisfied. Because of prohibitive transaction costs, however, many contingent markets do not exist. It can be argued, therefore, that financial markets have arisen as a substitute for absent contingent markets. If agents cannot transfer goods and services across all zones and states of the world, as they would with complete contingent markets, sophisticated financial securities will allow them to transfer income over time and throughout the world.

If financial markets merely provide insurance and income smoothing, why are they so often associated with growth and investment? It is easy to reconcile this view of financial markets with the view presented above. Suppose a firm wants to undertake a large and costly investment. Without financial markets, the firm would have to obtain its financing through entrepreneurial funds, or through credit from its suppliers. In both cases, this would impose large risks on the financing party. Well-functioning financial markets spread such risks across a large number of investors. This diversification effectively reduces the financial cost of the investment, and therefore promotes investment and growth. This explains why sophisticated financial markets are a primary source of growth and investment.

As with most markets, financial markets have developed a structure where a layer of intermediaries links the buyers and sellers of securities.

Traditional theories of financial intermediation argue that these intermediaries allow the matching of diverse term horizons (some buyers may prefer short-term securities, while sellers may be more interested in long-term securities); and pool a large number of small buyers to accommodate the needs of large sellers. We now argue that the role of financial intermediaries becomes crucial when financial markets are plagued with imperfections.

IMPERFECTIONS OF FINANCIAL MARKETS

A FINANCIAL SECURITY IS A PROMISE TO PAY some predetermined financial return in the future in exchange for an immediate payment. Some securities, like bonds or loans, promise a fixed specified return, while others, like shares, promise an unspecified dividend stream. Still others are more complicated and may promise to return combinations of these basic securities, and occasionally even returns based on these basic securities (derivatives).

What would constitute a reasonable expectation if financial markets were complete and perfect? If financial markets provide smoothing and insurance, agents' profits or consumption should be fairly constant over time, or at least should be perfectly correlated because all idiosyncratic risks would be diversified and aggregate risks would be shared by all agents. Yet, even a cursory examination of macro-economic data reveals that agents' idiosyncratic risks are not perfectly diversified.

Tables 1 and 2 show the sources and uses of funds of non-financial corporations in Canada and in the United States. Examination of the tables suggests that financial markets do not provide complete insurance or smoothing. Two features shown by the tables deserve comment. First, the reliance on internal funds for investment increases during recessions. Second, financial slack, measured by the change in marketable securities, increases during boom periods. We argue that such features should not arise in the presence of perfect financial markets.

Suppose that corporate profits are lower during recessions than during boom periods. Perfect financial markets should then direct the flow of funds toward firms during recessions, and toward investors during booms. The data clearly contradict this assumption. Firms use more internal funds during recessions and increase their financial slack during booms – exactly the opposite of what perfect financial markets should achieve. This shows that agents cannot fully insure themselves and smooth their consumption. They must rely on internal funds when money is tight, and build up financial slack in good times, rather than reimburse investors for the financing provided in bad times.

The sources of imperfections in financial markets are the investor's lack of information and the manager's lack of commitment to the investor. These problems arise as a result of the separation of ownership and control. Recent theory emphasizes three main problems: moral hazard, adverse selection, and imperfect commitment.

TABLE 1

SOURCES AND USES OF FUNDS OF NON-FINANCIAL CORPORATIONS IN CANADA

| YEAR | TOTAL ($ BILLIONS) | SOURCES | | USES | |
		INTERNAL (%)	EXTERNAL (%)	CAPITAL EXPENDITURES (%)	FINANCIAL ASSETS (%)
1969	11.1	60.7	39.3	87.4	12.6
1970*	10.3	68.3	31.7	91.5	8.5
1971	14.3	52.7	47.3	77.8	22.2
1972	14.8	58.8	41.2	83.6	16.4
1973	19.7	53.3	46.7	79.9	20.1
1974	28.1	42.4	57.6	73.0	27.0
1975	24.1	55.0	45.0	70.7	29.3
1976	27.6	60.8	39.2	76.9	23.1
1977	30.1	56.2	43.8	64.2	35.8
1978	42.0	43.9	56.1	52.5	47.5
1979	57.2	40.6	59.4	60.5	39.5
1980*	60.4	44.4	55.6	62.1	37.9
1981	75.2	29.7	70.3	59.1	40.9
1982*	32.1	58.3	41.7	79.2	20.8
1983	40.4	77.0	23.0	79.0	21.0
1984	59.9	64.5	35.5	69.3	30.7
1985	66.0	67.1	32.9	71.5	28.5
1986	72.7	56.7	43.3	68.0	32.0
1987	84.0	59.0	41.0	68.0	32.0
1988	93.2	55.5	44.5	74.8	25.2
1989	105.9	48.3	51.7	80.8	19.2
1990*	81.4	54.1	45.9	85.5	14.5
1991	69.8	58.9	41.1	88.4	11.6
1992	66.2	63.0	37.0	82.5	17.5

Note: * Trough of the recession.
Source: Tables A.213-2/04 and E.3-2/04 Sources and Uses of Funds of Non-Financial Corporations, OCDE *Financial Statistics* 1977 and 1994.

We highlight these information and commitment problems by means of the following simple example. A financial investor is looking for profit opportunities, and an entrepreneur possesses a project which is potentially lucrative. The entrepreneur has private information about the quality or profitability of his project, which depends on how much effort he will exert, among other things. In addition, the life of the project is long and the entrepreneur may need refinancing at some point in the future if initial profits are low.

MORAL HAZARD

SINCE MANAGERIAL EFFORT IS NOT DIRECTLY OBSERVABLE by the financier, the entrepreneur's compensation is necessarily based on a number of noisy signals

TABLE 2

SOURCES AND USES OF FUNDS OF NON-FINANCIAL CORPORATIONS
IN THE UNITED STATES

	SOURCES			USES		
YEAR	TOTAL ($ BILLIONS)	INTERNAL (%)	EXTERNAL (%)	TOTAL ($ BILLIONS)	CAPITAL EXPENDITURES (%)	FINANCIAL ASSETS (%)
1948	29.4	67.0	33.3	25.6	80.9	19.5
1949*	20.5	97.6	2.4	18.4	81.0	19.0
1950	42.6	43.4	56.3	40.4	59.4	40.6
1951	36.9	56.4	43.6	37.9	80.7	19.5
1952	30.2	74.5	25.8	30.0	84.7	15.3
1953	28.6	78.0	21.7	28.5	91.9	8.1
1954*	29.8	81.9	18.1	28.1	82.9	17.4
1955	53.4	56.0	43.8	49.1	66.2	33.6
1956	45.1	66.7	33.5	41.1	90.5	9.7
1957	43.5	73.6	26.4	40.0	89.3	10.5
1958*	42.2	72.7	27.5	38.5	72.2	28.1
1959	56.6	64.3	35.7	52.1	72.9	27.3
1960*	48.2	74.5	25.7	41.8	90.4	9.3
1961	55.8	66.1	33.9	50.7	72.0	28.0
1962	60.6	71.3	28.7	56.2	77.9	22.2
1963	68.5	68.6	31.5	60.3	73.8	26.0
1964	74.2	70.5	29.5	64.9	77.2	23.0
1965	92.7	63.8	36.2	83.4	73.9	26.1
1966	99.0	63.9	36.1	92.0	81.8	18.2
1967	94.9	67.7	32.3	87.6	81.3	18.7
1968	114.0	57.7	42.4	106.2	71.0	29.0
1969	116.0	56.2	43.8	115.0	72.4	27.6
1970*	101.8	61.7	38.3	97.9	80.9	19.1
1971	127.4	58.6	41.4	121.8	69.9	30.1
1972	153.4	56.3	43.7	145.1	65.5	34.5
1973	215.2	25.0	56.4	189.7	62.7	37.3
1974	179.0	49.9	47.9	191.1	72.5	27.5
1975*	155.3	80.4	19.6	153.4	73.2	26.8
1976	214.6	66.2	33.8	210.4	74.6	25.4
1977	259.3	63.7	36.3	242.2	74.2	25.8
1978	314.1	58.0	42.0	324.7	66.8	33.2
1979	326.0	60.6	39.4	368.1	64.7	35.3
1980*	324.8	61.6	38.4	342.1	71.2	26.8
1981	375.8	63.7	36.3	383.6	74.7	25.3
1982*	298.5	81.2	18.8	303.5	84.5	15.5
1983	420.3	68.0	32.0	385.8	70.2	29.8
1984	492.6	68.3	31.7	502.7	73.7	26.3
1985	459.2	76.7	23.3	435.3	78.6	21.4
1986	492.2	72.6	27.4	454.3	73.0	27.0
1987	474.1	74.4	25.6	436.6	82.7	17.3

Notes: * Trough of the recession.
Source: Data from the Board of Governors of the Federal Reserve System (1990).

of his effort, such as profits, sales, growth in sales or profits, output, market share, etc. This raises the problem of moral hazard, which flows from a deficient internal structure that fails to provide the manager with appropriate incentives to maximize the value of the assets under his control. As a result, the manager may pursue goals other than wealth-maximization, such as personal prestige or the accumulation of perquisites.

ADVERSE SELECTION

RECALL THAT THE INHERENT PROFITABILITY of a project, or the quality of an entrepreneur are not easily or directly observable. This is the source of an adverse selection problem, which arises when the firm's decision-makers have private information about the quality of different projects, their competitors, the technology, or even about their own ability to manage the assets they control. The manager's problem, then is to convince financial investors to provide the necessary funding to undertake production. The financier's problem is to offer a contract that will induce entrepreneurs to reveal their private information and to select valuable projects on this basis.

IMPERFECT COMMITMENT

A PERFECT RISK-SHARING OR SMOOTHING ARRANGEMENT between an entrepreneur and a financier requires the development of a long-term relationship between the two parties. The dynamics of such a relationship bring about some problems of their own. A perfect arrangement necessitates a strong commitment by both parties to co-operate during all future periods. Such co-operation requires that the firm reimburse financiers in good times and that financiers provide the firm with the funding it needs in bad times.

But a long-term, dynamic contract is complex and cannot cover all contingencies. Contracting parties are generally unable to describe explicitly all future contingencies, or even to anticipate all possible events. For these reasons, dynamic contracts are incomplete – and it is this incompleteness that makes the governance of the contract an important factor in the success of the relationship.

The incompleteness of contracts in dynamic relationships also generates the need for punctual or selective interventions by the financier. For the same reasons that contracts are incomplete, however, these interventions are far from trivial. For example, the financier may want to intervene when the firm is in genuine difficulty, or when the entrepreneur appears to be doing a poor job. But again, lack of information may preclude the financier from drawing the correct inference. Financial statements give at best a noisy and imperfect picture of a firm's financial health and of managerial performance.

THE GOVERNANCE OF FINANCIAL CONTRACTS

IF THE FINANCIER CANNOT RELY SOLELY on financial statements, what other tools may be used to draw the correct inference about managerial performance? One possibility is to monitor the firm's performance closely. Monitoring implies the gathering of information about the firm's external as well as its internal economic environment. The financier should learn about the firm's main competitors, the technology they use, the technologies that are available, the characteristics of customers, the future prospects of the industry, the research and development activities that are likely to affect the product market, the internal structure of decision-making, and the quality and competence of the firm's managers, among other things. Without precise information about these elements, the financier can hardly evaluate managerial performance.

Monitoring activities have the following characteristics. First, they are costly: to gain a good understanding of a firm's economic environment consumes resources. (Note, however, that monitoring activities are subject to economies of scale.) Second, the result of monitoring is noisy and almost never produces a precise answer to the question: is the firm performing as it should? Finally, the information gathered has a public-good aspect. Once produced, it is difficult to keep other investors from taking advantage of it. The decision to monitor or not depends on cost and expected benefits. Even when the costs of monitoring are easy to determine, the benefits still depend on what gain is expected from the information produced. There are two general mechanisms (or strategies) at an investor's disposal to discipline a non-performing firm: the investor can sell his/her shares (exit), or the investor can try to influence management (voice). We turn to a discussion of these two mechanisms in the next section.

Monitoring activities are further complicated by the "two-tier agency" problem, another aspect of financial markets that has not been discussed so far. In modern economies, financiers are often agents themselves, *i.e.*, they act as intermediaries between buyers and sellers of financial securities. Institutional investors are a perfect example of such intermediaries. In a two-tier agency structure, the incentive problems that exist between the intermediary and the firm's manager also exist between the primary financial investors and the intermediary. The contract between the intermediary and the investors should therefore provide the intermediary with the necessary incentives to behave in the investors' interests. We therefore ask: "Who shall monitor the monitor?".

Alternatively, a disgruntled financier could sell all shares in the entrepreneur's project, thus exiting the market. In both cases, the financier needs reliable information to determine a course of action.

CORPORATE GOVERNANCE: EXIT AND VOICE STRATEGIES

WE HAVE SO FAR ARGUED THAT AGENCY PROBLEMS in financial markets are the consequence of informational and commitment problems. The incompleteness of contracts draws our attention to their governance. This section surveys a number of corporate governance strategies.

EXIT MECHANISMS

AN EXIT STRATEGY CONSISTS OF SELLING THE SHARES of a non-performing firm and investing the proceeds elsewhere. Financially exiting a firm is often associated with having a short-run perspective, or behaving "myopically". We point out that this is not necessarily the case. Suppose a monitoring investor judges that a firm is not performing satisfactorily because of problems deriving from moral hazard or adverse selection. One obvious way of transmitting this information is to liquidate the firm's shares. This affects share prices and thereby transmits some information to the firm's board as well as to other potential investors.

Exit may therefore be a valid market response to agency problems if it triggers a response from the board, from other investors, or from a raider, that induces managers to return to a wealth-maximizing policy. However, this mechanism is not perfect. First, while share-price movements may communicate some information about a firm's under-performance, they do not inform other investors and board members about the *nature* of an agency problem. Second, share-price movements caused by factors unrelated to firm performance may trigger a market response when none is desirable. Managers are frequently heard to complain about the "short-run" bias of the market. Sometimes money managers also voice the same complaint.

One way in which an exit strategy can produce a corrective response, if adopted by a significant number of shareholders, is through a takeover: some investors exit while others enter. The incoming investors acquire relevant information about a firm's agency problems and decide to take it over. (They must have some private information as to the cause of under-performance in order to profit from their takeover.) If the incoming investors can induce incumbent shareholders to tender their shares at a price that leaves with them a portion of the gains from reorganizing the enterprise, they will proceed with the reorganization.

This strategy is not always successful, however. For one thing, it is plagued by a free-rider problem, as shown by Grossman & Hart (1980). Since each individual shareholder has an interest in being the last to sell, the initiator of a takeover may have difficulty convincing incumbent shareholders. This results in the "raider" having to offer a high price to all the firm's shareholders, thus reducing his own gain. The incentive to monitor and initiate takeovers is thus reduced.

According to this logic, there may be too few takeovers. But even when they occur, they may not be efficient. As Shleifer & Summers (1988) argue, a takeover may be profitable only because the raider breaks implicit contracts between the firm and its partners – workers, long-term suppliers, etc. Since implicit agreements may be *ex ante* efficient, takeovers may then have a lower social value than expected, because they create a commitment problem.

The ultimate desirability of a takeover rests on its ability to solve the moral hazard or adverse selection problems that are at the source of inefficiency. In the case of moral hazard, success depends on the extent to which the raider can restructure the incentives facing incumbent managers. Jensen (1988, 1989) argues that many management buyouts in the United States did just that by increasing the participation of management teams in equity. The same results can be obtained by reorganizing a company, by having it focus on its core business, and by divesting it of the units its management team cannot run competitively, thus changing the incentive structure facing managers. Bhagat, Shleifer & Vishny (1990) and Patry & Poitevin (1991) found evidence in both the United States and Canada that is consistent with that hypothesis. Conversely, a raider can alleviate adverse selection problems by replacing the management team. Notice, however, that in any case, a successful takeover requires an extensive monitoring operation.

Exiting customers are another indicator of a firm's poor performance. Although a declining market share is a reliable signal of poor performance, it does not provide information about the nature of the agency costs. Nevertheless, financiers often base their financing decisions on product market data.

The market for managers is more closely related to our analysis. An active market for managers provides incentives for managers to perform adequately in the expectation that they may raise their market value. However, we believe that this market does not work as efficiently as may be thought. It suffers from the same deficiencies as financial markets. If financiers must incur great costs to evaluate a firm's performance, it is likely that participants in the market for managers will have the same problem. Even though they constitute another potential group of monitors of the firm's performance, they are not likely to invest as much in monitoring activities as financiers since they are not likely to have as much at stake as financial investors.

Voice Mechanisms

VOICE MECHANISMS ACTIVELY SEEK TO INFLUENCE the actions of firms. Voice mechanisms can be informal, as when money managers discuss corporate strategy with a management team, or they can be very formal, as in a proxy fight.

Voice can be exercised through an active presence on the board of directors. Directors have access to privileged information about the firm and its economic environment and are required to take an active part in the firm's strategic planning. Through its compensation committee, the board is also responsible for structuring adequate compensation packages for corporate managers. The board is also a key instrument in solving moral hazard problems. A presence on the board therefore reduces monitoring costs by providing access to inside information.

On the negative side, board members are frequently "captured" by management. For example, certain directors may lean toward management's point of view more often than they should. This is particularly likely in Canada where ownership is fairly concentrated, the supply of potential directors relatively small, and the number of interlocking directorships important. Institutional investors also tend to be afraid that rules concerning insider trading and conflict of interest will limit their investment options. We return to this point later in our study.

A proxy fight is a more spectacular voice mechanism. The initiator of a proxy fight must gather sufficient votes to ensure his point gains a majority. If successful, a proxy fight can result in a significant change in the way in which a firm is run. A proxy fight is, however, a strenuous voice mechanism in which the investor begins at a clear disadvantage compared with the manager(s). The logistics of proxy fights are weighted in favour of management, which suggests that some reforms might be helpful here.

Although the benefits of voice mechanisms are relatively well understood, their costs are often understated. Both an active presence on the board, and a proxy fight can be fairly costly, in addition to the monitoring costs that we have already discussed. Indeed, some proxy fights have been shown to cost millions of dollars. Furthermore, an important element of voice mechanisms is that they have a strong public-good characteristic in that all shareholders benefit without having to pay any of the cost. This may be why we do not observe enough "voice". Another implicit cost related to proxy fights is the breach of trust that they may cause. For example, management may be reluctant to lay off a group of workers toward which it considers it has a responsibility based on a long-term relationship. A proxy fight can avoid this problem without implicating management. The cost of doing so is that it may be more difficult in the future to build the necessary trust for long-term relationships. A similar argument has been used in our discussion of takeovers.

Finally, we note another voice mechanism on the part of creditors which is often overlooked in the literature. Debt covenants are certainly part of the governance package which disciplines managers by placing limits on managerial discretion over sets of strategic decisions. These are useful to contain moral hazard problems, but are not especially helpful in cases of adverse selection where managerial quality is the real problem.

INSTITUTIONAL INVESTORS IN CANADA

CORPORATE AND PUBLIC PENSION FUNDS, mutual funds, banks and near banks, insurance companies, and public and private endowments are institutional investors. In the United States, at the end of 1990, these investors held over US$ 6 trillion, or 45 percent, of all financial assets. Comparing this figure with their 21 percent share in 1950 illustrates their indisputable rise. In the equity market, which is of particular importance to us, the share held by institutional investors rose from 23 percent in 1955 to 53 percent in 1992. American institutional investors own over US$ 1 trillion of the equity in the United States and 90 percent of this is held by corporate, public, and union pension funds (Lakonishok et al., 1992). This means that pension funds control 47 percent of all U.S. equity and explains why pension funds have been at the forefront of the movement toward institutional activism.

The position of Canadian institutional investors is similar. For instance, at the end of 1993, the book value of financial assets under the control of trustee-administered pension funds, mutual funds, insurance companies, banks and near banks had swollen to $1,283 billion, of which $142 billion was equity (Table 4). Canadian public and private pension funds together controlled book value assets of nearly $250 billion and book value stocks of $70 billion. Note that in Canada the share of institutional investors in total equity is only 35 percent, compared to 53 percent in the United States. Nevertheless, these institutional holdings are substantial.

This last figure appears more impressive, in fact, when the relative lack of liquidity of the Canadian equity market is taken into account. Fowler & Rorke (1988) estimate that a mere 5.3 percent of the stocks traded on the Toronto Stock Exchange can be said to be widely traded. Most stocks (59.4 percent) on the TSE are traded in thin markets, which increases the price of exit. Daniels & Waitzer (1994, p. 33), quoting The Globe and Mail, estimate that 50 percent to 60 percent of the shares of widely held companies that are traded in deep markets are held by institutional investors. Here, the size and power of institutional investors in the United States as well as in Canada have increased substantially over the past 30 years.

In the United States this increase has been accompanied by a call for a more active role for institutional investors in corporate governance issues. As in the United States, the growing importance of institutional investors in the equity market has been accompanied in Canada by an awareness of corporate governance problems and the potential benefits shareholders could derive from a louder institutional "voice". The wave of mergers and takeovers that swept Canada in the 1980s, and the ensuing attempts of corporate managers to adopt poison pill strategies, prompted an interest in corporate governance and in the protection of minority shareholders. Examination of the TSE Report on Corporate Governance, of the Corporate Governance Standards of the Pension

Investment Association of Canada and of the *Corporate Governance Guidelines* of some major institutions, like the Caisse de dépôt et placement du Québec, shows that the issues of managerial compensation and the independence and effectiveness of the board are receiving considerable attention. Fairvest Inc. has developed a score card that permits institutional investors to assess more precisely the corporate governance quality of Canadian corporations.

Nonetheless, few poison pill battles have been successfully fought by Canadian institutional investors. A remarkable exception is the battle over Labatt's poison pill. Generally, however, very little Canadian research has been done on compensation packages; even if the Caisse de dépôt et placement has at times been considered aggressive in its defense of minority shareholders (as in the battle over the adoption of a poison pill at Inco), no major institution in Canada is seen as the CalPERS of the North. As Daniels & Waitzer (1994) put it: "In many ways, institutional activism in Canada is still very much in a nascent stage." (p. 33). Should we ask them to do more?

The Berle & Means (1932) model of the corporation, in which control and ownership are divorced, has led many to believe that managers now effectively control America's corporations. Since someone must watch the managers, and since individual shareholders do not have the incentive to do the watching, then why not have the institutional shareholders do it? This is the claim we critically assess in this study.

The split between ownership and control in the large American and Canadian corporations is not necessarily a reality. For instance, Demsetz & Lehn (1985) compute the total percentage of stock controlled by the five most important shareholders of the *Fortune 500* corporations in the United States. This amounts, on average, to 25 percent (compared to 33 percent in Japan [Prowse,1991]). Whether such an ownership structure induces efficient oversight is one thing; arguing that no individual or coalition of shareholders has a focused interest in monitoring the managers is quite another. It does not ring true.

In Canada, any split between ownership and control is the exception rather than the rule because Canadian corporations are more tightly controlled than their American counterparts. Table 3 shows that, in 1994, 60 percent of the *Financial Post 500* largest Canadian non-financial corporations were wholly owned or effectively controlled by a single shareholder. Only 79 of the 500 companies in the *Financial Post 500* list, a mere 16 percent, could be considered widely held. The equivalent percentage for the *Fortune 500* firms is estimated at 63 percent (Daniels & MacIntosh, 1991)

The importance of family-controlled businesses in Canada and of wholly foreign-owned Canadian subsidiaries explains this characteristic of the Canadian corporate landscape. Another explanation is the relative size of Canadian firms. The median number of employees of the top 200 industrial firms in Canada was 4,938 in 1993, compared to 10,136 for the *Fortune 500* firms in the United States.[2] As a firm grows in size, concentration of owner-

TABLE 3

OWNERSHIP CONCENTRATION (BY SALES OR REVENUE) OF THE *FINANCIAL POST* 500

	PUBLIC CORPORATIONS		ALL	
	NUMBER	PERCENT	NUMBER	PERCENT
Wholly owned or 50%+ by one shareholder (or government)	93	36.6	300	60.6
Two largest owners together > 34%	60	23.6	67	13.5
One owner > 15% or two largest owners together own 20% < X < 34	36	14.2	36	7.3
Largest owner between 10% and 15% but second < 10%	11	4.3	13	2.6
Widely held (including cooperatives and memberships)	54	21.3	79	16.0
Total	254	100.0	495	100.0

Source: *The Financial Post 500*, 1994.

ship results in increased firm-specific risk for the investor (Demsetz, 1993). Hence, there is a tradeoff between the social benefit of concentrated ownership (which reduces the incidence of moral hazard) and the cost of bearing firm-specific risks.

Whatever the reasons, the fact is that ownership in Canadian corporations is much more concentrated than it is in U.S. corporations. Combined with the smaller percentage of equity in the hands of Canadian institutions (recall that the percentage of total equity owned by institutional investors in the United States is roughly twice that in Canada) this translates into a reduced potential for Canadian institutional investors.

Another singular aspect of the Canadian corporate landscape which has a bearing on the potential role of institutional investors is the high level of cross-ownership. Daniels & MacIntosh (1991) contend that of "... the top one hundred most profitable companies in Canada in 1987, close to 45 percent held 10 percent or more of the voting shares of another company on the list" (p. 888). Berkowitz, Kotowitz & Waverman (1977) find that the 361 largest enterprises in Canada had stakes in 4,944 other firms. Through cross-ownership and inter-linked directorships, a few large groups have spun an intricate web of relationships that allows these groups to exercise extensive control over the largest enterprises in Canada. Compared to the Japanese *keiretsu* system of cross-ownership, however, Canadian market ownership appears very diffused. Viner (1988) estimates that 65 percent of the stock of the companies listed on the Tokyo stock exchange is held by *keiretsu* members (cited in Coffee, 1991, p. 1,296).

This networking effect has many implications for the potential role of institutional investors. First, it is a source of the relative lack of liquidity in the equity market in Canada. This raises the cost of exit and might lead one to think that, as in Japan and Germany where liquidity is lower and intercon-nectedness higher than in the United States, Canadian institutional investors would be induced to play a more active role. Second, interlocking director-ships create circumstances in which managers can assist each other to entrench themselves further, which makes disciplining corporate managers much more difficult since no one wants to "rock the boat". Third, the extensive control and power wielded by a few large groups or families increases the severity of the penalty that a disgruntled management could impose on an unsettling institutional investor. (This last point is discussed more fully later in our study.)

THE GOVERNANCE OF MUTUAL FUNDS AND PENSION FUNDS

BANKS, MUTUAL FUNDS, CORPORATE AND PUBLIC PENSION FUNDS all tend to be large institutions with diffuse ownership. They should not be expected to behave like individual investors. Their internal structures and governance must be examined to understand the extent to which they might be expected to become involved in the governance activities of the firms in which they invest. If the managers of an institution are themselves engaging in wealth-reducing activities, or cannot motivate their employees and those (money managers) to whom they delegate the management of funds to monitor and discipline corporate managers, there is a moral hazard problem at the institu-tional investor level. In addition, if institutional investors cannot discriminate between good and bad money managers, there is an adverse selection problem. In other words, agency problems cannot be solved simply by allocating the respon-sibility for active monitoring of corporate managers to a class of agents (financial intermediaries) since they are themselves plagued with information problems. Hence, the classic question "Who shall monitor the monitor?" resurfaces.

We concentrate on two types of institutional investors in Canada – mutual funds and pension funds. Together, they own almost 25 percent of all equity in Canada (Table 4) and 69 percent of all the equity controlled by institutional investors. What incentives do they have to monitor and discipline corporate managers? How are they organized? Who does the monitoring?

THE GOVERNANCE OF MUTUAL FUNDS

SINCE MUTUAL FUNDS POOL FINANCIAL RESOURCES from hundreds of thousands of individual sources of capital, controlling fund managers poses many serious problems that are analogous to those of controlling corporate managers. First,

TABLE 4

INSTITUTIONAL FINANCIAL ASSETS AND CANADIAN SHARES

TYPE OF INSTITUTION	DECEMBER 31, 1993 ($ MILLIONS)		
	CANADIAN STOCKS (BOOK VALUE)	FINANCIAL ASSETS (BOOK VALUE)	ASSETS OF TOP TEN (MARKET VALUE)
Pension Funds [a]	68,864	249,542	116,988 [f]
Public	39,872 [b]	160,132	111,487 [f]
Private	28,992 [b]	101,226	36,411
Mutual Funds [c]	28,899	111,192	79,508 [g]
Insurance Companies [c]	21,430	158,219	147,388 [h]
Banks and Near-Banks [c, d]	12,731	722,582	—
Caisse de Dépôt et placement [e]	9,890	41,685	—
Institution-owned	141,814		
Total Shares Owned	**406,216** [i]		

Notes:
[a] Quarterly Estimates for Trusteed Pension Funds, Statistics Canada cat. 74-001 and Benefits Canada, April 1994 for Top 10 concentration.
[b] Canadian Stocks of all pension funds distributed at *pro rata* of total stock holdings.
[c] *System of National Accounts*, Statistics Canada cat. 13-214 and CANSIM Database.
[d] Includes Trust companies and Mortgage Loans.
[e] *Statistiques Financières 1993*, Caisse de dépôt et placement du Québec.
[f] Excludes pension funds under control of the Caisse de dépôt.
[g] Benefits Canada, April 1994.
[h] The Financial Post 500, 1994.
[i] To avoid double-counting, we have subtracted from 517,408 the shares issued by mutual funds.

there is the collective-action problem of monitoring the management: no single investor has the incentive to incur the full cost of assessing the quality of the job done by the specialists to whom the responsibility of managing the funds was delegated, while sharing the benefits of a better performance.

Second, what motivates the individual investor to delegate responsibility (the root of the agency problem at hand) is the fact that the agent-manager has (presumably) a superior ability to choose stocks. Therefore, if individual investors are to second-guess the experts and do the analytical work, they might as well do the investing themselves.

Third, the agency relationship gives rise to adverse selection and moral hazard complications. On the one hand, adverse selection shields poor management. On the other hand, moral hazard implies that money managers may increase the risk of their portfolio(s) in order to boost returns to the marginal investors (the so-called "bait and switch" tactic). The seriousness of this (moral hazard) problem depends on two factors: the relative ease with which investors can determine risk levels, and the predisposition of money managers not to engage in such behaviour (integrity).

As a result of these informational frictions, the problem of motivating the agent-manager for the individual investor is solved by observing the performance of the agent. Since it is difficult to separate good performance from good luck, an individual investor takes two steps: he chooses a fund based on its medium- to long-run performance (thus smoothing out streaks of good or bad luck) and he compares the performance of this fund to those of the other funds available on the market, presumably controlling for risk level. Using inter-temporal and inter-agent comparisons to assess the relative performance of an agent can be very efficient, particularly when there are many agents (Sappington, 1991).

Most Canadian mutual funds are open-ended, in which individual investors hold a *pro rata* ownership of the pooled resources. An individual investor in an open-ended mutual fund can insist at any time that the fund buy back his/her share in the fund at its net asset value. (No such obligation binds the closed-end mutual fund). As a result, a dissatisfied investor in an open-ended fund is likely to sell his/her shares. Even if the costs of exit are not nil (because of fees and search costs), exit is less costly than the influence costs the investor would have to bear in order to bring about a change in the fund's policy. When many investors flee, the managers of the fund must necessarily sell the stocks owned by the investors. Liquidity is therefore central to both the investors and the funds. Given the large number of competing funds in Canada, exit mechanisms should function well.[3]

Other mechanisms also constrain managers of mutual funds. Regulations with respect to information provided to investors, the assets the fund can invest in, and the role, composition, and fiduciary duties of the board also limit mutual fund managers. Conversely, the market for corporate control is ineffective and so certain forms of compensation for managers are also regulated.

THE GOVERNANCE OF PENSION FUNDS

PENSION FUNDS ARE STRIKINGLY DIFFERENT FROM mutual funds in one crucial respect. Workers have very little control over the financial resources they invest in pension funds. The main instrument of control is indirect and relies on the monitoring capability of the pension funds committee. This voice mechanism works in a very imperfect manner. In the first place, workers should delegate representatives, thus creating an agency relationship, to monitor the allocation of funds. Finally, individual workers are plagued by a collective action problem and, as a result, the disciplining potential of workers is seriously impaired.

The individuals who invest in pension funds are in a much more vulnerable position than those investing in mutual funds. Their voice is muted, their influence is weakened by a collective action problem, and exit is costly, if not impossible.

Under defined-benefits pension plans, which represent 90 percent[4] of Canadian pension plans (the remaining 10 percent are defined-contribution plans), the sponsor – a private corporation or the government – promises employees a stream of future benefits that do not depend on the fund's performance. Furthermore, the sponsor must compensate any shortfall, and this becomes the first claim on the corporation in the case of bankruptcy. (However, the sponsor is also entitled to any surplus above the actuary-calculated liabilities of the fund.) There is therefore a possibility that the sponsoring organization may have an intrinsic interest in maximizing the return on the funds and therefore in taking whatever action, including over-seeing corporate managers, that fosters that goal.

Unfortunately, the fact that the sponsor is the residual claimant for defined-benefits plans does not, in itself, guarantee that the sponsor will aim at maximizing the risk-adjusted return on the assets, nor does it signify that the sponsor will monitor corporate managers. For one thing, the property rights on the surplus are not well-defined, and so workers argue that in some circumstances they should share in the spoils. Also, in the private sector, a large surplus may increase the likelihood of a takeover – a prospect incumbent managers do not relish. In addition, the delegation of the fund's management to the treasurer's office and to external money managers is likely to give rise to other moral hazard, adverse selection, and commitment problems (see next section). Finally, Canadian corporate pension fund managers often find them-selves embroiled in serious conflicts of interest that pit their fiduciary duty against the business interests of the corporation that employs them.

Some Evidence on Performance

Do money managers pursue wealth maximization? There is a growing body of evidence that returns on the assets in the corporate pension fund segment of the money management industry fall below those of a market index and of mutual funds. This may signify that managers of pension funds manage their equity more conservatively than the average stock market investor. This is a testable empirical proposition. However, pension funds can modify their overall risk by changing their asset mix. Conversely, poor performance may simply mean that corporations have more complicated objectives than maximizing the funds' risk-adjusted return, or that they botch the job, or both!

Lakonishok, Shleifer & Vishny (1992) analyze the performance of 769 all-equity corporate pension funds in the United States and find that, on average, the representative (equity) fund under-performs the Standard & Poors 500 Index by 1.3 percent per year, before subtracting management fees. This is consistent with the findings of Beebower & Bergstrom (1977) for the 1966-1975 period; with those of Brinson, Hood & Beebower (1986) for the 1974-1983 period; and with the results reported in Malkiel (1990) for the 1975-1989 period. Similar results for Canada are reported by Taylor (1995) who concludes that ". . . for periods ranging from one to eight years, the annualized return of the index has outperformed the median manager by between 0.10% and 3.10%, before management fees" (p. 25).

The evidence relating to the performance of mutual funds is much less conclusive. While the classic study by Jensen (1968) and recent refinements by Grinblatt & Titman (1989) and Connor & Korajczyk (1991) cast some doubt on the capability of mutual funds to outperform the market, some recent evidence suggests that this might be the case. Ippolito (1989) finds that mutual funds outperform the market by 80 basis points, once management fees and load charges have been netted. Results similar to Ippolito's for Canada are obtained by Berkowitz & Kotowicz (1993) who conclude that the "... funds in our sample [roughly 40 mutual funds] have outperformed the market by a very significant margin" (p. 863).

The evidence thus suggests that corporate pension funds generate systematically lower returns. *Pensions and Investments* (cited in Lakonishok et al., 1992) indicates that mutual funds had a mean return 2.3 percent higher than that of pension funds over the 1971-1980 period – lower than those of mutual funds, but (more damningly) lower than the return on an index of the market. By adopting a passive investment strategy (indexing), pension funds can earn a higher return on their equity portfolio and cut costs, since typical fees for indexed funds in Canada average 43 basis points below those for actively managed funds (Taylor, 1995, p. 26).

What about the performance of public pension funds? These are the largest of all the institutional players, and they are the ones who appear to have been most active in the area of corporate governance. Public pension funds manage nearly 8 percent of all Canadian equity. Each of the two largest public pension funds, the Ontario Teachers' Pension Fund Board and the Quebec Public Employees Fund, manages as many assets as the ten largest private funds.[5]

Reviewing the evidence on the performance of public pension funds in the United States, Mitchell & Hsin (1994) conclude that "... yields on public pension fund assets have frequently been low, with public plans earning rates of return substantially below those of other pooled funds and often below leading market indices" (p. 3). Interestingly, their data (Table 3, p. 28) show that in 10 of the 17 years for which comparisons can be made, large Canadian private pension funds outperformed U.S. state and local pension plans. The authors suggest that one possible cause for this underperformance is the responsiveness of the staff managing public pension funds to political pressures. Romano (1993) also concludes her analysis of public fund activism in the United States by warning that "... public pension funds face distinctive investment conflicts that limit the benefits of their activism. Public fund managers must navigate carefully around the shoals of considerable political pressure ... ." (p. 795). Romano also finds that "[f]unds with more politicized board structures perform significantly more poorly than those with [a] more independent board" (p. 852).

THE INTERNAL ORGANIZATION OF DECISION-MAKING: MUTUAL FUNDS

WE NOW TURN OUR ATTENTION TO THE ORGANIZATION of mutual and pension funds. These institutional investors entrust money managers with the responsibility of choosing stocks. Two factors – the nature of the contract offered to money managers and the method by which pension funds select money managers – have an effect on the level of monitoring and influence exerted by institutional investors.

Generally, contracts between shareholders and money managers are regulated. In Ontario, for example, mutual funds that want to offer their money managers performance-fee contracts must obtain the approval of the Ontario Securities Commission. Performance-fee contracts link a money manager's compensation to the return on the portfolio managed. The OSC checks, among other things, that the benchmark defined in the contract is deemed "satisfactory".

Such outcome-based contracts have many advantages. For one thing, they mitigate moral hazard problems by requiring that the money manager bear a percentage of the cost of any relaxation of his/her effort. Another advantage of these contracts is the possibility of signalling. When managers have an informational advantage and are allowed to offer various contracts, good money managers can signal their superiority by selecting incentive contracts that shift more risk and profit to them.

Mutual funds might therefore be expected to rely on performance-fee contracts inasmuch as regulatory authorities permit. But this expectation is contradicted by the evidence in both Canada and the United States, where similar constraints apply. Indeed, the vast majority of mutual fund money managers are compensated on an asset-based scheme. Discussions with funds managers suggest that less than 10 percent of assets in Canada are managed under performance-fee contracts. The typical scheme provides for a fee equal to a declining percentage of the funds managed. Even in the more permissive context of the United States, Bailey (1990) mentions the lack of interest in performance-fee contracts.

This finding is somewhat puzzling. A possible explanation is offered by Berkowitz & Kotowicz (1993) for mutual funds. They suggest that asset-based contracts create an indirect link between compensation and performance. They assume that "investors believe superior management is possible and better performing funds can be identified on the basis of their past performance". It follows that the demand for better-performing funds will increase, thus endowing more capital to superior managers. Given that performance is difficult to observe because of the noisiness of the market, some inertia will characterize the evolution of market shares. In this scenario, sustained superior performance is rewarded with an expanded asset base, and higher compensation. Their empirical results support their thesis about an indirect link between performance and compensation. Hendricks, Patel & Zeckhauser (1993) also find evidence supporting the (short-run) persistence of superior performance.[6]

Given that money managers compete in a world resembling that described by Berkowitz & Kotowicz (1993), their investment behaviour will critically depend on the horizon they expect investors will use to allocate capital among them. If this horizon is quite short (a few quarters or at most a few years) money managers should be expected to focus on short-term equity returns. Holding onto stocks that offer a high potential over the long run, if it does not translate into short-term returns, is self-defeating. If, on the other hand, investors are characterized by a long-term horizon, money managers will be induced to adopt the same (long-term) horizon.

The shorter the horizon, the more liquid money managers will want to be. They will also be less inclined to spend time and energy to influence corporate managers. Coffee (1991) contends that "most mutual funds are active traders and would hesitate to make any investment the liquidation of which would require a significant block discount". (p. 1318).

To conclude on mutual funds' incentive structure, it appears that money managers are compensated mostly on the basis of the assets they manage. This contract structure can, if investors use past performance as an indicator of future performance, create a link between effort and compensation, thus alleviating the moral hazard problem. On the other hand, the uniformity of contracts in the market impedes the signalling strategy of the best money managers; and, competition for a share of investable funds depends critically on the effective horizon characterizing investors and mutual funds managers.

THE INTERNAL ORGANIZATION OF DECISION-MAKING: PENSION FUNDS

OUR DISCUSSION OF THE INTERNAL ORGANIZATION of pension funds draws heavily on the analysis of Lakonishok, Shleifer & Vishny (1992). Three important corporate decisions must be made. They concern the use of internal *versus* external management of the funds, the portion of the funds to be invested in indexed funds, and the selection of money managers. What governs these decisions, and what are the incidences on the behaviour of the agents doing the investing, the monitoring and, at times, the influencing of corporate managers?

Table 5 shows that in 1993 close to 60 percent of the top 100 pension funds in Canada were managed in-house. Of the 40 percent that were managed externally, 14 percent were by balanced funds managers and 26 percent by specialized money managers. We can also see that public pension funds rely more heavily on internal management and specialized money managers. This appears to be consistent with the perception that public pension funds have been more active.

TABLE 5

ASSET MANAGEMENT BY TOP 100 CANADIAN PENSION FUNDS (%)

| | 1990[a] | 1993 | | |
	PRIVATE & PUBLIC	PUBLIC	PRIVATE	PRIVATE & PUBLIC
In-house Management	50.1	73.3	31.1	59.7
Balanced Fund Managers	27.4	7.7	28.7	14.5
Specialized Managers	22.5	19.0	40.2	25.8
Total	100.0	100.0	100.0	100.0

Note: [a] Top 80 funds only.
Source: Benefits Canada Survey 1991, 1994.

Lakonishok *et al.* (1991) claim that treasurers can be expected to be biased against both internal management and indexing. The rationale is that treasurers are torn between two goals: they want to increase the resources under their control but at the same time want to bear as little risk as possible. They want to take charge but do not want to be held responsible for the bad returns on the assets with which they are entrusted. The solution, according to Lakonishok *et al.*, is to allocate as many funds as possible externally, but to adopt an active management policy, which calls for constant review, evaluation and selection of the money managers they hire. Choosing money managers and allocating the available funds between them becomes the treasurer's most important job.

As is the case for mutual funds, pension funds compensate money managers on an asset basis. An increase in a money manager's wealth is directly related to the extent of the increase in the size of his asset base. To make his case and convince treasurers to allocate a greater share of the funds to him, he will claim that he can outperform other money managers as well as the market. (However, the claim that money managers, on average, can beat the market is very debatable.) Now the money manager's track record plays a determinant role. How will treasurers evaluate that track record? What horizon will they favour?

Much evidence, both anecdotal and empirical, points in the direction of a very short-term bias. Coffee (1991, p. 1,325) reports on a recent survey indicating that at least 90 percent of pension funds reviewed the performance of the outside money managers they employed at least quarterly, with a mere 3 percent doing annual reviews! The problem with a short-term horizon is that performance is very elusive. Although Lakonishok *et al.* (1992) find some long-term consistency, they see very little short-term (annual or quarterly) consistency. Bauman & Miller (1994) mention several recent analyses that demonstrate the instability of performance rankings over time.

Failure to recognize the elusiveness of performance has three pernicious effects. Consider first the adverse selection bias it insinuates in the market for money managers. Many funds that use recent performance to select the "best" money managers are led to "hire high, fire low". They drop money managers who are about to recover and hire those who are bound to fall from their pedestal. The results of Lakonishok *et al.* (1992) indicate that this might well be the case, at least in the United States . The authors even speculate that the "strategy of switching to the good past performers may not be a bad one" (p. 372). Hence, a treasurer using the wrong time horizon will systematically pick money managers who will underperform.

Second, money managers know that performance is elusive, and so they develop strategies to differentiate their products and justify their short-term performance. That way, they can always come up with a good story to explain any short-term disappointing performance. This leads to window-dressing by money managers. Lakonishok, Shleifer, Thaler & Vishny (1991) and Benartzi & Thaler (1992) find evidence that money managers get rid of badly performing stocks at the end of the year and buy into trendy stocks, even if it means sacrificing performance, in order to be in a better position to impress sponsors. Mitchell & Hsin (1994, p. 5) also report that money managers who are subject to frequent performance reviews may sacrifice long-term goals for short-term objectives.

The third consequence of a failure to look ahead is a high(er) turnover rate of funds. The elusiveness of performance induces sponsors to reallocate funds among money managers too often and encourages money managers to trade too much. Regarding the last point, Lakonishok *et al.* (1992) conduct an interesting experiment: they freeze the holdings of money managers for six or twelve months and compare the returns earned by the frozen portfolios to the actual returns. This leads them to conclude that "trades made by the funds were counterproductive, costing an average forty-two basis points relative to a portfolio frozen for six months and seventy-eight basis points relative to a portfolio frozen for twelve months" (p. 354).

As a result of the selection and evaluation process developed by pension fund managers, money managers are pressured to distort their investment strategies, to trade too actively, and to trade stocks that they should not trade in order to provide their sponsors with "schmoozing" – good stories that help explain poor performance. This means either that sponsors are behaving myopically and do not know that quarterly returns are very noisy or that they know but prefer to accept lower returns and schmoozing to straight high(er) returns.

Lakonishok *et al.* (1992) claim that the second argument is true. They point out that if pension fund managers wanted straight performance they would invest heavily in indexed funds, which have outperformed the equity component of pension funds for many years. Instead, claim the authors, corporate treasurers prefer to diversify across money managers, thus achieving some averaging effect. From the vantage point of the treasurer, the problem with an indexing strategy is that it considerably reduces the work of the treasurer.

As with mutual funds, pension funds delegate investment decisions to money managers. Like mutual funds, they split investable funds between active management and passive management, in the form of indexed funds. Although pension funds involve much lower liquidity constraints than mutual funds (recent work by Berkowitz & Logue, 1987, finds the average annual turnover rates of equity for pension funds to be 61 percent compared to 76 percent for mutual funds), we find reason to doubt that money managers are chosen on the basis of long-term performance. As Lakonishok *et al.* (1992) put it, "... sponsors clearly reallocate funds in response to past performance, and because consistent performance is fairly elusive there is tremendous turnover at the top in terms of industry leadership and market share" (p. 364). Finally, since workers can only "vote with their feet", and even then only to a limited extent, the relatively poor performance of pension funds can continue (despite poor equity management) without fear that exiting capital will trigger a reaction.

Having argued that institutional investors themselves suffer from internal agency problems, we now move on to discuss how these problems interact with corporate governance activism.

The Role of Institutional Investors in Resolving Market Imperfections

ALL MONEY MANAGERS HAVE AN INCENTIVE to monitor the stocks they manage and the companies that issue them. Monitoring results in one of three possible courses of action: more monitoring, dumping the stock (exit), or an attempt to influence corporate management (voice). The first two options are clear-cut. The third, that of exerting influence, covers a wide range of possible action including: informal discussions with managers; seeking the support of other institutional investors or of a large shareholder; sponsoring a shareholder resolution; or engaging in a proxy fight (Pozen, 1994; Rock, 1991, p. 453); or becoming a relational investor (one who holds a large stake in the company, has representation on the board, and commits for the long term) (Ayres & Cramton, 1994).

The Cost-Benefit Analysis for the Sponsor

ASSUME THAT INSTITUTIONAL INVESTORS MAXIMIZE risk-adjusted returns. Under this maintained hypothesis, they will decide what action to take based on the highest net present benefit-to-cost ratio. For instance, even if some forms of activism appear to be profitable, the benefit-to-cost ratio of, say, tendering shares in a takeover may be even greater. Since the costs and benefits of each course of action vary considerably and are contingent on the business context, we can make only fairly general and speculative comments here.

It is well recognized that, by influencing managerial policy, a shareholder produces a public good: all other shareholders benefit from the disciplining action, regardless of their participation in the provision of the activity. This is the source of a fundamental free-rider problem: apathy may be rational for a shareholder who does not expect his contribution to be pivotal.

Both the likelihood that a shareholder's contribution is pivotal and the share of the public good one shareholder can appropriate are proportional to his stake in the equity of the corporation. Thus, increasing the concentration of share ownership by encouraging or allowing institutional shareholders to hold larger stakes should induce them to adopt a more active strategy. Concentration also increases the cost of exit since the sale of large blocks of shares is bound to have a depressive effect on the stock price.

Alternatively, free-riding is a rational strategy for a small institutional shareholder and in circumstances where one shareholder or a small group of shareholders is in a position of control. This is typical in Canada.

For institutional shareholders who are not rationally apathetic, the decision to influence management and the situations which provoke them to do so depend on the cost of organizing a disciplinary move as well as on the cost of possible retaliation. These costs, in turn, depend on both the nature and the subject of the intervention.

Process and procedural reforms – such as regulating the size and composition of boards (by having a majority of outside directors on the board, ensuring that compensation and other key committees are staffed by outside directors, etc.), limiting the tenure of directors and the number of boards that a director can serve on, and separating the functions of chairman and chief executive officer, etc. – imply lower search and monitoring costs than most other interventions, such as replacing the management team or influencing corporate strategy. Furthermore, large institutional investors with stakes in many widely held corporations can reap economies of scale by using the information they produce to influence the incentive structure of many enterprises. Finally, an important institutional investor can reasonably share its expertise with other large institutional investors to obtain their support. The organization of the pension fund industry in Canada (which is concentrated around the top 20 public and private investors) is conducive to the building of such coalitions. Much the same reasoning applies to informal initiatives, such as writing explanatory letters to the company's CEO or directors, or holding discussions with the firm's management.

There are four reasons why this mode of intervention is less likely to be fruitful when firm-specific issues are at issue. First, micro-management requires a level of effort and a depth of analysis that are lacking in most pension funds or mutual funds. Without such detailed knowledge, an institutional investor cannot determine what action it should take. Before endowing pension funds with the mission to straighten out the governance of Canadian firms, we must ensure that these institutions have the experience and the necessary know-how to get the job done. In our opinion, very few pension funds are properly equipped. The fact that public pension funds have often lead the corporate governance movement is consistent with that opinion: public pension funds have more resources than other institutional investors because they are much larger and because they manage a larger proportion of their assets in-house. And even then, few have ventured into micro-management.

Second, micro-managing does not confer the same economies of scale on the investor. The knowledge required to appraise a particular restructuring, for instance, may have little utility for another firm in another sector. Third, such moves are likely to be perceived negatively by corporate managers, and this increases the likelihood of retaliation. A pension fund manager may fear that the enterprise it is trying to micro-manage will retaliate by depriving the pension fund's sponsor of future business, or by cutting out the sponsor from informal information flows. The same rationale applies to banks, insurers, and so on. This retaliatory threat is a private cost that is likely to be borne by the institutional entrepreneur and is particularly credible in the Canadian context, which is characterized by a high level of ownership concentration and by the existence of a dense network of firms and directors.

Finally, while having a representative on the board is a key factor in the ability to micro-manage or monitor business policy, few institutional investors will accept the private costs of sending a representative to the board. Having a representative on the board is costly and increases the liability of the institution – important private costs that cannot be shared with other shareholders. First, there is the opportunity cost of delegating an officer or a representative of the institution to the board. Then consider the increased liability that the institution must face. Since board members cannot fully insure themselves against all risks (Daniels & Waitzer, 1994), the decision to have a representative on the board increases the risk of the institution. This delegation also limits the ability of the institutional owner to trade because of insider trading provisions. The same provisions force the institution to comply with extra disclosure rules. In addition, the institutional investor may find itself in a position of conflict of interest if holding a large equity stake, for instance, can be deemed a breach of fiduciary duty. Further analysis of this issue would take us into legal territory,[7] but we believe a case can be made that these costs and additional liabilities will tend to tip the balance toward other modes of intervention.

The incentives of institutional investors to invest in generic research to ameliorate the governance of specific firms or industries are further reduced by the public-good aspect of the information they might produce. Once it is known that a particular public pension fund or a large mutual fund devotes resources to these ends, their decisions and the actions they undertake will signal to other investors the opportunity they have identified.

Agency Problems: Monitoring by Plan Administrators and Money Managers

Assuming that it is in the interest of a given institutional investor to influence the management or the policies of some companies it invests in, will the administrators of the funds, the employees and the money managers behave in ways that foster that interest? One response could be that, were it in the interest of mutual funds or pension funds actively to engage in influence activities, they would adopt an appropriate incentive structure. Alternatively, one may study the present organization and ask: within that context, will agents behave in the principal's interest?

We argue that institutional investors do not necessarily maximize risk-adjusted returns. First, the drive to maximize profits and to undertake the influence activities can be muted because of governance defects. Second, the delegation of management to administrators and money managers may also be plagued by moral hazard and adverse selection problems.

Consequences of Moral Hazard

When a money manager is hired by a mutual fund, the typical fee-contract states that there is a duty to perform the normal proxy activity, to vote in the best interest of the fund, and to submit regular reports to an advisor. A money manager receives less than 1 percent per year on the assets he/she manages. Such fees do not cover the costs of most actions aimed at effecting a change in corporate governance (Pozen, 1994, p. 144). As a result, if money managers in this segment expend resources to monitor firms, they will generally refrain from taking steps that imply heavy costs, such as filing and preparing proxy materials, writing to all shareholders and hiring consultants and lawyers. In addition, the advisor has little information to evaluate the governance input of the managers, which is the root of the moral hazard problem.

Since the actions of the money manager are hidden, and since monitoring and influencing imply costs but generate returns that are not easily observable by the advisor, the money manager will be tempted to cut costs and to minimize the effort to influence management. This problem is compounded if the horizon of the money manager is short, since he/she will then discount any future benefits heavily. Finally, there are good reasons to believe that mutual fund money managers will favour exit over voice. This is evidenced by the higher turnover rate of equity in mutual funds. This preference for liquidity is linked to the redeemable nature of the claims on mutual funds and reinforced by the dominant exit strategy of individual investors in pension funds.

Although pension funds value liquidity much less and claim to focus on the long-term (Bauman & Miller, 1994, p. 32), we have seen that fund administrators may have problems inducing their money managers to adopt a long-term horizon. Management fees paid in Canada are also somewhat lower than those paid in the United States and the United Kingdom (30 basis points compared to 35 and 39)[8] and this means that managers have few resources to commit to monitoring (although we do not understand why the circumstances are different in the United States and the United Kingdom). In addition, pension fund money managers appear to be rewarded not only for their stock market performance, but also for their capability to produce other goods, such as schmoozing.

CONSEQUENCES OF ADVERSE SELECTION

SPONSORS APPEAR TO LACK A VALID SCREENING STRATEGY. Although this issue deserves much more research, there is evidence of a very high turnover of money managers and of some "hire high, fire low" patterns. It is possible that treasurers are satisfied with the process because it provides them with the scapegoats they seek.[9]

Activists like Black (1992), who claims that "... if monitoring is profitable, financial institutions ... will find ways to pursue that profit" (p. 876), call for the selection of managers on the basis of their level of monitoring effort. We consider this option to be interesting but it raises other questions.

First, sponsors would have to be convinced that this is a good thing, and that it should be taken into account when evaluating money managers (which does not now appear to be the case). Second, money managers will react to such contractual changes by signalling their concern and demonstrating the diligence and seriousness with which they take their fiduciary duties. Unless good signals can be devised, the outcome may just be an increase in schmoozing. The desirability of including formal measures of monitoring in the process of evaluating managers depends on the noisiness of the signals. Another possible drawback might be increased pressure on money managers by corporate managers to support the sponsor's business, thus exacerbating conflicts of interest.

The apparent high value that sponsors place on the recent track record of the managers they hire is yet another indication that the market for outside money managers is, perhaps, subject to adverse selection problems. Since performance is elusive and inconsistent, and since the benefits of sound corporate governance are long-term in nature, money managers will find it difficult to extract a higher compensation in exchange for a promise of higher quality. Lakonishok et al. (1992) confirm that conjecture (p. 372). They also state that "perceptions of the qualities of individual firms vary widely over time and across customers" (p. 364). In other words, reputations are difficult to develop and maintain and this limits the role of such reputations as bonding devices. Reputational effects are therefore not very likely to help sponsors choose good managers.

POLICY ANALYSIS AND CONCLUSIONS

EXIT AND VOICE INNOVATIONS

THIS SECTION PRESENTS A CRITICAL REVIEW of many of the propositions found in the literature aimed at enhancing the role of institutional investors in the governance of firms. The propositions intended to improve exit and voice mechanisms can be regrouped into two classes. First, those that limit the investment strategy of funds managers; second, those that address directly the monitoring problem facing investors.

RESTRICTIONS ON INVESTMENT STRATEGY

HIRSCHMAN (1970) HAS SUGGESTED THAT ONE WAY to enhance the effectiveness of voice is to restrict exit. This raises the question of whether authorities should encourage the adoption of restrictions to institutional investors' strategy in order to force money managers into a more active role. Exit could be precluded by the rules governing the fund (as the limit on foreign ownership already does), or its cost could be increased through some form of regulation (such as a "flip-tax" on capital gains) or, quite simply, by imposing some form of indexing on a percentage of the funds, thus blocking to some extent the exit option.

Underlying these reform proposals is the idea that institutional investors can be "forced" to allocate more resources to monitoring and influencing activities. These reform proposals regard institutional investors as "black boxes" and, it is argued, by constraining their choice sets, they can be induced to invest more in corporate governance. We have argued to the contrary, *i.e.*, that the governance and internal organization of investors also matter.

We disagree with such reform proposals and suggest that they are unwarranted for financial reasons. First, it is not clear that investors exit too often or that exit is ineffective when compared to voice. Those advocating such restrictions have yet to demonstrate the relative ineffectiveness of exit in the Canadian context since Canada has sophisticated and well-functioning capital markets, similar to those in the United States and the United Kingdom.

Second, it must be stressed that the effectiveness of voice also depends on the existence of a credible exit threat. The voice of CalPERS was amplified by the risk of not only the shareholder resolutions, but also massive exit – with its damaging consequence on stock price. By further constraining the exit strategy of Canadian institutions, we could also lower the efficiency of their voice mechanism.

Third, the narrowness of the Canadian equity market, its relative lack of liquidity, and the closet indexing that results from sponsors' diversification across money-manager types and through the indexing of active money managers who want to lock in their superior performance, all lead us to believe that unless radical regulations were adopted, little change in behaviour would result from increased indexing *per se*. In fact, large Canadian institutional shareholders are already locked into the relatively narrow Canadian equity market with the result that the Ontario Teachers Pension Fund, the Caisse de Dépôt et placement, the Ontario Municipal Employees Retirement Board (OMERS), and other similar large institutional investors already hold relatively large stakes in the top Canadian firms. Ownership concentration in Canada is higher than in the United States and liquidity is lower, but Canadian institutional investors' behaviour has paralleled that of their American counterparts. Again, we take this as evidence that unless very radical changes are contemplated, institutional investors are not likely to become more active.

Deliberately restraining the liquidity of Canadian institutional investors has costs of its own. For example, the overall efficiency of Canadian financial markets would decline, and the informational content of share prices would be adversely affected. In efficient financial markets, movement in share prices transmits some (noisy) information from informed investors to uninformed ones. This transfer of information improves the functioning of financial markets and contributes indirectly to the effectiveness of corporate governance. The monitoring of informed investors conveys information through prices to financial markets. The market then disciplines those firms that are not performing satisfactorily by increasing their financial costs.

The informational content of share prices provides a delicate balance between the provision of incentives for firms to perform and the provision of incentives for investors to monitor. Formally, as Grossman & Stiglitz (1976) show, in equilibrium, the proportion of monitoring financiers is such that they receive a fair financial compensation for their monitoring costs. Potential monitors, therefore, take into account the noisy leakage of the information they may acquire; they also take into account the fact that if they do not monitor, share prices will still transmit some information. We believe that these considerations are crucial and should be addressed when evaluating any restriction on the investment policy of institutional investors.

One such restriction which already generates serious by-products is the regulation on foreign ownership. In Canada, the *Income Tax Act* imposes a 20 percent ceiling on the amount of the equity (at book value) that a corporate pension fund can hold in foreign securities. By concentrating the investments of Canadian pension funds, it can be argued that fund managers are induced to improve the corporate governance of Canadian firms.

We believe, however, that this effect is likely to be small. For as we have seen, despite the relatively higher concentration of ownership in Canada, the behaviour of Canadian institutional investors does not differ markedly from that of their U.S. counterparts. On the other hand, this restriction imposes two significant costs on the Canadian economy.

First, whatever corporate governance gains are generated by the restriction should be carefully weighted against the cost to Canadian workers of limiting the diversification of their pension funds. This cost is likely to be important for two reasons: Canadian market capitalization is only a small percentage of world equity, and Canadian equity is biased towards natural resources industries.

Second, consider the implicit cost induced by the conflicts of interest spawned by this regulation. Large Canadian institutional investors are major shareholders of almost all corporate Canada and their compliance with insider trading laws and conflict-of-interest rules poses serious questions. When an important institutional investor, such as the Ontario Teachers Pension Fund, also assumes the role of dealmaker in assisting takeovers, the ethical, legal, and governance issues become even more complicated.[10] Relaxation of the foreign ownership regulation would immediately alleviate both these costs, while at the same time reinforcing the effectiveness of the exit strategy by giving it more credibility.

To reiterate, the removal of the foreign equity ownership regulation would, in our opinion, have little detrimental effect on the governance of Canadian firms. In fact, it might add power to the disciplinary role of exit.

IMPROVEMENTS IN MONITORING INCENTIVES

REFORMERS CLAIM THAT NEW INSTITUTIONS could provide stronger monitoring incentives. Two such proposals encourage the creation of a class of professional monitors and relational investing. Both suggestions contain interesting ideas, but we point out some deficiencies that are bound to impair their functioning.

Gilson & Kraakman (1991) recently proposed that a (new) class of professional monitors who would act on five or six boards and whose task would be to monitor management might be an appropriate solution to many corporate governance problems. These monitors would be remunerated by the firms themselves but, more importantly, would have the incentive to monitor by reputation effects on a newly created market for these monitors. Remember, however, that corporate governance imperfections are caused primarily by informational problems. By viewing corporate governance against this back-drop, it becomes apparent that the addition of a class of professional monitors does not address the problems at the heart of the corporate governance debate.

First, all the problems of the market for managers would be replicated in the market for monitors. How would the market evaluate these monitors? It would have to use the same performance measures as those used for managers. In our opinion, this market would have no advantage in generating reputation effects strong enough to improve monitoring and, consequently, strong enough to improve managerial effort. Second, we believe that the problem of board capture by management – although attenuated – would likely resurface with this class of professional monitors because they would join the network of managers and insiders. In the absence of clear signals on their efficiency, problems of moral hazard will plague the outside monitors. Clubability would also be a factor, particularly in the small Canadian market. Third, since the quality of monitoring is hardly observed, we should expect professional monitors to be engaged in a certain amount of schmoozing in order to convince their sponsors that they diligently accomplish their function. Finally, we note that there are at present no legal or institutional barriers to prevent the emergence of such a class of outside directors. This may be an indication that the innovation is not profitable.

Relational investing has also received some attention recently. Relational investing consists of having long-term minded investors who commit to buy and hold significant blocks of a firm's shares. Relational investors participate actively in the strategic decision-making of the firm. Ayres & Cramton (1993) discuss the advantages of relational investing in detail.

First, they claim it provides strong incentives to monitor and influence since the investor can appropriate a large share of the gains from such activities. Repeated play between the investor and management is assumed to enforce the reputation effects necessary to induce monitoring by the investor. Second, relational investing is said to alleviate moral hazard problems more effectively than takeovers, to the extent that it insulates management from inefficient takeover attempts (see our earlier discussion). Finally, they argue that a relational investor can put adequate pressure on managers while internal or external markets may apply too much, especially when there is a short-term bias in these markets. As evidenced by the weak market for corporate control in Europe and Japan, a long-term investor is certainly less likely to respond to short-term movements in profitability or share prices if those movements are transitory or not agency related.

Nonetheless, relational investing has problems of its own. First, it is important that the investor commit to hold a large percentage of the firm's shares. How can any investor, particularly an institutional investor, commit to such a strategy? Even pension funds, which assign a relatively low weight on liquidity, would be hard pressed to resist a takeover bid above current market value. Premiums paid to target shareholders in North America normally average over 30 percent and have at times been very large. Second, relational investing tilts the incentive-diversification tradeoff in favour of more incentives for monitoring and less portfolio diversification. Most institutional investors, and pension funds in particular, will shrink from such a commitment. Once again, nothing prevents institutional investors from pursuing that strategy now. It therefore appears that this tradeoff is well understood by investors and that they find micromanaging too costly in terms of reduced risk diversification and liquidity.

DISCLOSURE RULES INNOVATIONS

THIS STUDY FOCUSES ON ASYMMETRIC INFORMATION and agency problems to explain the inefficiencies found in the design of financial contracts and in the corporate governance process. The first step in alleviating informational problems is to monitor a firm's activities. Any improvement in the output of monitoring is likely to improve corporate governance. We suggest some innovations with respect to disclosure rules that would contribute to this improvement.

Recently, Quebec and Ontario proposed regulations requiring firms to disclose the compensation package of their five most highly paid managers. Such information is useful in analyzing the incentives afforded to managers, and is therefore a valid input in monitoring activities that assess moral hazard and adverse selection problems. We firmly support this innovation. In fact, we believe this regulation should be extended to include managers of mutual funds and pension funds.

These funds have their own corporate governance problems that spill over onto the governance of the firms in which they invest. Disclosing the compensation packages of fund managers can only help the corporate governance process. Investors will learn how to utilize such information and this is likely to trigger exit and/or voice reactions. This should help "monitor the monitor".

At present, money managers' contracts are based almost exclusively on the size of the assets they manage. In a static context, such compensation is likely to provide low-powered incentives. In a dynamic context, as we have seen, money managers may have an incentive to increase their asset base to increase their next period remuneration. Therefore, it is plausible that appropriate incentives are provided by these compensation packages.

We believe that better disclosure rules may attract investors' attention to the problem of designing a compensation scheme that motivates fund managers. For example, we have argued that, in a number of cases, money managers will try to maximize the expected return for a chosen level of risk. However, expected return is not the only characteristic that interests small investors. They are also interested by the level of risk. Since risk is unobservable to investors, managerial compensation could be made contingent on indices of a fund's "riskiness", using a measure such as the historical variance of the fund's returns. Finely tuned compensation packages could induce money managers to provide investors with their desired risk-return profile. Another possible innovation would consist, for investment funds, to disclose the ß value of their portfolio.

Another disclosure rule innovation that could reduce monitoring cost would be to modify accounting standards in order to include more economically relevant data in financial statements. Several areas might be considered: mandatory reporting by firms of market shares, product quality, productivity levels, labour and customer satisfaction, quality control indices, etc. These performance indices, if reported for the firm and the industry as a whole, and for, say, a five-year period, would constitute a useful yardstick in the assessment of the performance of a management team.

Economic information would complement traditional accounting and financial data. One disadvantage of such indices may be a weakening of the strategic position of some firms that compete in a global environment with other firms that are not subject to such disclosure rules. The scope of these measures must therefore be assessed carefully before being implemented.

CONCLUSIONS

CLEARLY, THE POTENTIAL FOR INSTITUTIONAL ACTIVISM is much lower in Canada than in the United States. Fewer companies are widely held in Canada, which makes for fewer pivotal institutional investors. For most investors, most of the time, a passive attitude is rational. We also believe that common sense points towards public and private pension funds as the most promising would-be activists, monitors and influence seekers.

We argue that the weaknesses in the governance of pension funds must be dealt with before any significant improvement will be seen in the internal organization of those funds and, consequently, before any dividend that might accrue from the improved governance of Canadian firms can be reaped.

Given that pension funds may play a more prominent role in the governance of Canadian firms in the near future, we believe that generic issues, of the process and procedural types, are most likely to emerge. We also conjecture that pension funds will prefer informal modes of intervention to formal modes, and conciliatory approaches to corporate governance issues to adversarial approaches. Progress could be made quickly if the largest funds developed ways and means to coordinate their behaviour. A detailed analysis of the equity portfolios of the 20 largest pension funds, for example, could shed light on this question.

We also offer some tentative comments on the desirability of a few regulatory innovations against a rather bleak portrait of proposed changes to corporate governance in Canada. It is our contention that fine-tuning financial regulation cannot bring significant changes to governance behaviour. In many ways, the Canadian context is significantly different from the American context; despite this, the behaviour of Canadian and American institutional investors is strikingly similar.

One may point to the Japanese and German regimes, which are markedly different, but there is no conclusive evidence that either the Japanese or the German system of governance is superior. Claims of superiority are generally based on the belief that Japanese and German regimes favour long-term relationships and relational investing, and avoid "short-termism". For example, there is evidence that "liquidity constraints" are more important for North American firms.[11] This suggests that internal financing is cheaper than external financing for these firms, which may mean that capital markets are plagued by informational problems.

But the liquidity constraints facing North American firms can be interpreted as optimal constraints imposed on management teams to prevent them from making non-profitable investment. Jensen's (1986) theory of free cash flows makes this point clear. Cash-constrained firms may be more efficient since they cannot invest in negative-value ventures. Whether this argument can then be extended to Japan and Germany, thereby claiming that managerial capture of investors allows them to invest too much (namely in non-profitable projects) is an empirical question. These ideas have not been proven formally in the literature nor have they been verified empirically. They are, at present, only speculation. However, they certainly deserve more attention before making radical policy changes to the Canadian system.

Moreover, there is recent evidence of moral hazard and adverse selection problems in the Japanese and German regimes. For example, the deregulation of Japanese financial markets, which has facilitated the issue of corporate bonds, has induced many Japanese firms to move away from *keiretsu* financing toward North American-type financial contracting. This is certainly at odds with the belief that Japanese financial contracting is superior. Also, recent evidence of the capture of banks by management in Germany shows that the German system is not collusion-proof nor, indeed, as efficient as it was thought to be.[12]

Our knowledge at present does not allow us to draw any firm conclusions regarding the relative efficiency of the Japanese and German models *vis-à-vis* the North American model. Without such evidence, we suggest that major or radical changes to our present system of corporate governance would be totally unwarranted. Furthermore, assuming the superiority of the corporate governance regimes of Japan and Germany, we doubt that they could be easily cloned or imitated; institutions are imbedded in history.

Conversely, we have also argued that many regulations aimed at reducing the information asymmetry between investors and money managers should improve the efficiency of the corporate governance regime in Canada.

On the one hand, we contend that some reforms could produce social benefits, but we also suggest that they would likely be marginal. On the other hand, major changes should be scrutinized for their important ramifications on the efficiency of Canadian financial markets. Those markets are embedded in a complex web of beliefs, attitudes and values and have served us very well. We should therefore ensure that important regulatory changes do not unwittingly reduce their efficiency or alter their fundamental value.

ENDNOTES

1 See Black (1992) for an ardent plea in favour of expanding the role of institutional investors in the United States.

2 *Fortune* and *Canadian Business*, 1993.

3 In Canada, as of January 31, 1995, 1077 mutual funds are listed in the Bell Charts of the *Financial Times of Canada*. In addition, entry is rather easy and has occurred, particularly by banks, following deregulation of the financial sector. Foreign competition is increasing. Information on the performance of each fund is widely available, with newspapers, specialized newsletters, and other sources regularly reviewing the performance of all funds.

4 Statistics Canada, *Trusteed Pension Funds*, 1992.

5 The Financial Post, *Canada's Largest Corporations*, 1994.

6 "A strategy of selecting, every quarter, the top performers based on the last four quarters . . . can significantly outperform the average mutual fund, albeit doing only marginally better than some benchmark market indices" (Hendricks, Patel & Zeckhauser, 1993, p. 122).

7 See Black (1990) and Daniels & Waitzer (1994) for a discussion of these questions.

8 Greenwich Associates, *Survey of Canadian Pension Funds*, 1994.

9 Why do firms allow their treasurers to entrench themselves like that?

10 "Pension Fund Power." *The Globe and Mail*, Saturday, June 17, p. B1 and B3.

11 Bascunan, Poitevin & Garcia (forthcoming), for instance, verify if there is any connection between the investment level of firms and their cash flow. They find that Canadian and American firms are liquidity constrained, while Japanese and German firms are not.

12 *The Economist* (January 29, 1994) notes that some German firms, like Siemens, Daimler-Benz, and Metallgesellschaft have been slower than American firms to spot problems. In the same article, a German analyst and lawyer blames the bad investments of many large German enterprises on the weak supervision of the banks.

BIBLIOGRAPHY

Ayres, I. and P. Cramton. "An Agency Perspective on Relational Investing", Working Paper No. 105, John Olin Program in Law and Economics, Stanford Law School, 1993.

Bailey, J. V. "Some Thoughts on Performance-Based Fees." *Financial Analysis Journal*, (July-August 1990):31-40.

Bascunan, M., M. Poitevin and R. Garcia. "Information asymétrique, centrainte de liquidité et investissement : une comparaison internationale." *L'Actualité économique.* (Forthcoming).

Bauman, W. S. and R. E. Miller. (1994) "Can Managed Portfolio Performance Be Predicted?" *The Journal of Portfolio Management*. (Summer 1994):31-40.

Baumol, W. J. *The Economics of Mutual Fund Market: Competition versus Regulation*. 1990.

Beaudry, P. and M. Poitevin. "Competitive Screening in Financial Markets when Borrowers can Recontract." *Review of Economic Studies*, 62 (1995):401-23.

Beebower, G. and G. Bergstrom. "A Performance Analysis of Pension and Profit-Sharing Portfolios: 1966-1975." *Financial Analysts Journal*, 33 (1977):31-42.

Berkowitz, S. A and D. Logue. "The Portfolio Turnover Explosion Explained." *Journal of Portfolio Management*. (Spring 1987).

Berkowitz, M. K. and Y. Kotowitz. "Incentives and Efficiency in the Market for Management Services: A Study of Canadian Mutual Funds." *Canadian Journal of Economics*, XXVI, 4 (1993).

Berkowitz, M. K., Y. Kotowitz and L. Waverman. "Enterprise Structure and Corporate Concentration: A Technical Report", Ottawa, Ministry of Supply and Services, Canada, 1977.

Berle, A. A. Jr. and G. Means. *The Modern Corporation and Private Property*. New York: Harcourt, Brace and World Inc., 1932.

Bhagat, S., A. Shleifer, and A. Vishny. "Hostile Takeovers in the 1980s: The Return to Corporate Specialization." Brookings Paper on Economic Activity, 1990.

Black, B. S. "Shareholder Passivity Reexamined." *Michigan Law Review*, 89 (1991):520-607.
_____. "Agents Watching Agents: The Promise of Institutional Investor Voice." *UCLA Law Review*, 39 (1992):811-93.

Black, F. and M. Scholes. "The Pricing of Options and Corporate Liabilities." *Journal of Political Economy*, 81 (1973):637-54.

Brinson, G., L. R. Hood, and G. Beebower . "Determinants of Portfolio Performance." *Financial Analysts Journal*, 43 (1986):39-44.

Coffee, J. C. "Liquidity versus Control: The Institutional Investor As Corporate Monitor." *Columbia Law Review*, 91, 6 (1991).

Connor, G. and R. Korajczyk. "The Attributes, Behavior, and Performance of U.S. Mutual Funds." *Review of Quantitative Finance and Accounting*, 1 (1991):5-26.

Daniels, R. and J. MacIntosh. "Toward a Distinctive Canadian Corporate Law Regime." *Osgoode Hall Law Review*, 29 (1991).

Daniels, R. and E.J. Waitzer. "Challenges to the Citadel: A Brief Overview of Recent Trends in Canadian Corporate Governance." *Canadian Business Law Journal*, 23 (1994):23-44.

Demsetz, H. "Financial Regulation and the Competitiveness of the Large U.S. Corporation." *Federal Reserve Bank of St. Louis Bulletin*, March 1993.

Demsetz, H. and K. Lehn (1985) "The Structure of Corporate Ownership: Causes and Consequences." *Journal of Political Economy*, December 1985:1155-77.

Fowler, D. J. and C. H. Rorke. "Insider Trading Profit on the Toronto Stock Exchange." *Canadian Journal of Administrative Science* (1988).

Gilson, R. J. and R. Kraakman. "Reinventing the Outside Director: An Agenda for Institutional Investors." *Stanford Law Review*, 43 (1991):863-906.

Grinblatt, M. and S. Titman. "Mutual Funds Performance : An Analysis of Quarterly Portfolio Holdings." *Journal of Business*, 62 (1989):393-416.

Grossman, S. and O. Hart. "Takeover Bids, The Free Rider Problem and the Theory of the Corporation." *Bell Journal of Economics*, 11 (1980):42-64.

Hendricks, D., J. Patel, and R. Zeckhauser. "Hot Hands in Mutual Funds: Short-Run Persistence of Relative Performance, 1974-1988." *Journal of Finance*. (March 1993):93-130.

Hirschman, A. O. *Exit, Voice and Loyalty, Responses to Decline in Firms, Organizations, and States.* Cambridge, MA: Harvard University Press, 1970.

Ippolito, R. "Efficiency with Costly Information: A Study of Mutual Fund Performance, 1965-1984." *Quarterly Journal of Economics*, 104 (1989):1-23.

Jensen, M. C. "The Performance of Mutual Funds in the Period 1945-1964." *Journal of Finance*, 23 (1968):389-416.

_____. "Agency Costs of Free Cash Flow, Corporate Finance, and Takeovers", *American Economic Review*, 76 (1986):323-29.

_____. "Takeovers : Their Causes and Consequences." *Journal of Economic Perspectives*, 2, 1 (1988):21-48.

_____. "Eclipse of the Public Corporation." *Harvard Business Review*, 67 (September-October 1989):61-74.

Lakonishok, J., A. Shleifer, and R. Vishny. "The Structure and Performance of the Money Management Industry." Brookings Papers on Economic Activity: Microeconomics 1992, (1992):339-91.

Lakonishok, J., A. Shleifer, R. Thaler, and R. Vishny. "Window Dressing By Pension Fund Managers." *American Economic Review*. (May 1991):227-31.

Mitchell, O. S. and P. L. Hsin. "Public Pension Governance and Performance," Working paper No. 4632. NBER, January, 1994.

Patry, M. and M. Poitevin. "Hostile Takeovers: The Canadian Evidence," in *Corporate Globalization through Mergers and Acquisitions*. Edited by L. Waverman. Calgary: University of Calgary Press, 1991.

Pozen, R. C. "Institutional Investors: The Reluctant Activists." *Harvard Business Review*, (January-February 1994):140-49.

Rock, E. B. "The Logic and (Uncertain) Significance of Institutional Shareholder Activism." *The Georgetown Law Journal*, 79 (1991):445-506.

Romano, R. "Public Pension Fund Activism in Corporate Governance Reconsidered." *Columbia Law Review*, 93, 4 (1993).

Sappington, D .E. "Incentives in Principal-Agent Relationships." *Journal of Economic Perspectives*, 5, 2 (1991):45-66.

Shleifer, A. and L. Summers. "Breach of Trust in Hostile Takeovers." in *Corporate Takeovers: Causes and Consequences*. Edited by A. J. Auerbach. Chicago: University of Chicago Press, 1988.

Shleifer, A. and R. Vishny. "Large Shareholders and Corporate Control." *Journal of Political Economy*. (1986):461-88.

Taylor, K. "Return on the Index Fund." *Benefits Canada*. (February, 1995):25-26.

Wang, W. Y. "Corporate versus Contractual Mutual Funds: An Evaluation of Structure and Governance." *Washington Law Review*, 69 (1994).

Stephen Foerster
Western School of Business
University of Western Ontario

10

Institutional Activism by Public Pension Funds: The CalPERS Model in Canada?

INTRODUCTION

INSTITUTIONAL INVESTORS INCLUDE PUBLIC PENSION FUNDS, private (corporate) pension funds, mutual funds and insurance companies. According to Paré's (1990) survey of chief executive officers of major U.S. companies, public pension fund managers were perceived to be the most activist group of shareholders. Given the many similarities and close proximity to Canada, public pension funds in the United States are a natural focal point for an investigation of investor activism (although, on a worldwide basis, the United Kingdom is also viewed as a world leader with respect to addressing corporate governance issues).

The California Public Employees' Retirement System (CalPERS) is the largest public pension fund in the United States, with assets of around $US 80 billion (approximately $C 112 billion) and is also regarded as the most active institutional investor in the United States. CalPERS has been involved in proxy fights since 1985. It also has a policy of targeting poorly performing companies and attempting to improve them by meeting with management, issuing shareholder resolutions, or voting against their boards of directors. Every year since 1991 the fund has issued private early warnings to targeted companies and has subsequently gone public with a revised (and usually shorter) list of companies which have not addressed its concerns raised in private meetings. A recent study by Nesbitt (1994) of 42 campaigns conducted by CalPERS between 1987 and 1992 found that targeted companies *underperformed* the S&P 500 Index by 60 percent prior to CalPERS' involvement, then *outperformed* the index by 40 percent subsequent to CalPERS' involvement.

Currently in Canada (and other countries outside the United States), there appear to be few (if any) public pension funds that approach the level of activism displayed by CalPERS. An important question for Canadian managers and regulators is why public funds in Canada have not been as visibly active as CalPERS. There are at least four different hypotheses that may explain this phenomenon.

One possible explanation has to do with regulatory differences between the two countries. A second possible explanation is that, in Canada, third-party or intermediary groups such as Fairvest Securities Corporation or the Pension Investment Association of Canada (PIAC) might be playing the activism role. A third possible explanation is the often-observed lead-lag relationship between U.S. and Canadian innovations or the sheer size differences between the largest U.S. and Canadian funds. A fourth possible explanation is the matter of style: Canadian fund managers may be more reluctant to engage in overt "American-style" confrontations.

If the first explanation is valid, then regulatory changes may accelerate the movement to CalPERS-style activism in Canada. If the second explanation is valid, then these third-party groups will continue to grow in stature. If the third explanation is valid, then examining the CalPERS model may serve as a useful benchmark for the direction of institutional investor activism in Canada as Canadian pension funds continue to grow and as Canadian fund managers become more aware of the potential rewards of institutional activism. If the fourth explanation is valid, then we should not expect to detect any *visible* change in the way public pension fund managers approach activism issues. Of course, a combination of these and/or other explanations is also possible.

The purpose of this study is to examine these four hypotheses in the context of corporate governance and institutional activism, primarily based on interviews with major Canadian public pension fund managers. Specifically, the study has the following objectives.

- Provide a detailed framework of the CalPERS model of investor activism.

- Assess the "evolution" of activism in Canadian public pension funds (relative to the CalPERS model) and determine what corporate governance issues are important to public pension fund managers.

- Provide regulators with a sense of how current regulations are viewed by institutional investors.

- Provide corporate directors with a sense of what to expect in the future in terms of institutional investor activism.

The study is organized as follows. The next section reviews public pension fund activism in North America and examines the role of public pension funds as activists. This is followed by a description of the CalPERS model and an examination of some potential future trends related to the involvement of CalPERS in corporate governance issues. The next section describes the survey methodology used in the study and this is followed by the results of interviews with Canadian public pension fund managers. The final section provides a summary and conclusions.

BACKGROUND

THE CANADIAN EXPERIENCE

ONE OF THE FIRST MAJOR PUBLIC INSTANCES of institutional activism in Canada occurred in 1986 when members of the Billes family (founders of Canadian Tire) struck a deal – later overturned by the Ontario Securities Commission – to sell 49 percent of the company's voting shares to a group of Canadian Tire dealers for a large premium over the market price, excluding from the deal many large institutional holders of Canadian Tire non-voting shares (see Stoffman, 1990 for a discussion).

Another major example of institutional activism was Inco's successful introduction of Canada's first poison pill in 1988, an action vehemently opposed by the Caisse de dépôt et placement du Québec (which held 3 percent of the stock) and other institutions. While poison pills or shareholder rights plans come in a variety of forms, most provide special rights to a company's shareholders in the event of an *unwanted* takeover attempt by another company. For example, existing shareholders may be entitled to purchase shares in their own company at a deep discount, thus diluting the value of a potential acquirer's stake. In practice, poison pills are not triggered but instead force potential acquirers to negotiate with the board. Critics claim this gives the board – not the shareholders – veto power over any offers, while proponents argue that poison pills allow the board to negotiate a higher price. In Canada, unlike the United States, companies are required by provincial law to have their poison pills ratified by shareholders. Canadian poison pills generally provide for "permitted bids" to be put to shareholders for approval and if approved the pill is not triggered. Inco's success was partially attributable to the linking of the pill to a special $10 dividend. As of 1995, poison pill proposals remained an important issue, with over 20 new proposals planned (see Mackenzie, 1994).

During the 1990s, numerous large pension funds have become more actively involved in corporate governance issues, largely because of their growing size and presence in equity markets – which makes it more difficult for them simply to sell their shares if they are dissatisfied with management. In addition to the Caisse, funds such as the Ontario Municipal Employees Retirement System (OMERS), the Ontario Teachers' Pension Plan Board (Ontario Teachers), CN Investments and other large funds have gained reputations in the investment community for their involvement in corporate governance issues, although this involvement is not always visible. A survey of Canadian institutional shareholders by Montgomery (1992) indicated perceptions among a vast majority (over 80 percent) of respondents that not only has Canadian institutional shareholder activism increased in the past, it is likely to continue increasing in the future.

Many of the issues that institutions have become involved in are structural (rather than related to day-to-day management), such as dual-class shares, various takeover defenses, executive compensation, and the size and composition of the board of directors (see MacIntosh, 1993, for a detailed examination of the role of Canadian institutional investors). In addition to institutional investors themselves, intermediaries such as Fairvest, PIAC, as well as the fund manager Jarislowsky, Fraser have acted on behalf of a larger number of institutional investors.

Fairvest Securities Corporation is a securities firm which acts exclusively as an agency trader for institutional investors. Formerly known as Allenvest (named after its founder, Bill Allen), it has played an active role in corporate governance issues. It is viewed by some institutions as providing a "conscience" for shareholders. For some institutions which do not wish to play a visible role, Fairvest provides a veil and yet allows them involvement in governance issues. Fairvest keeps institutions informed through its publication, *Corporate Governance Review*. Fairvest recently provided a submission to the Committee on Corporate Governance of the Toronto Stock Exchange.

The Pension Investment Association of Canada (PIAC) is another inter-mediary. It represents over 100 Canadian pension funds with combined assets of over $250 billion. Its purpose is to provide a forum for debate and resolution of issues facing pension funds. The role of PIAC is viewed as largely educational. PIAC has also distributed corporate governance standards to its members.

There are many aspects of the Canadian market which restrict the potential involvement of institutional investors (Montgomery & Leighton, 1993) such as the prevalence of dual-class share structure (over 200 TSE firms) and the dominance of controlling shareholders (*i.e.*, defined as those with at least 20 percent of the voting power), estimated at 70 percent of the 100 largest public companies in the early 1990s, but thought to have declined somewhat. Nonetheless, corporate governance remains a dominant issue, particularly surrounding the release of the TSE's Dey Report on Corporate Governance (see an overview by Star, 1994, and critiques by Thain, 1994, and MacIntosh, 1995).

THE U.S. EXPERIENCE

INVOLVEMENT OF CANADIAN INSTITUTIONAL INVESTORS in corporate governance issues parallels many recent developments in the United States. During the 1990s, a new form of activism has replaced takeovers in the market for corporate control (see Pound, 1992, and Pozen, 1994, for some recent examples). Institutionally-led initiatives through proxy votes have gained increasingly larger support over the years (Silverstein, 1994). Not surprisingly, public pension funds are leading the way in terms of activism (see a survey of U.S. institutional investors by Useem *et al.*, 1993) partly because of their size, but also because of their longer investment horizon and few cases of potential conflicts of interest (*e.g.*, if Company XYZ, which sells widgets, has a large private pension fund owning shares in Company ABC, XYZ will be hesitant to vote against ABC's management if ABC is a current or potential purchaser of widgets). The growth and concentration of institutional ownership in the United States has been incredible. Between 1985 and 1990, institutional holdings in the top 25 U.S. stocks grew from 36 percent to 46 percent (Chernoff, 1993). While institutional shareholders as a group now own over 50 percent of the stock in U.S. companies, it is estimated that pension funds alone will own one-third of all stock by the year 2000 (Cordtz, 1993). Institutional shareholders have recently used their power to assist in removing CEOs at such large, well-known (and often under-performing) U.S. companies as American Express, General Motors, and Digital Equipment (Stewart, 1993). CalPERS has played a leadership role in many of these initiatives.

PUBLIC PENSION FUNDS AS ACTIVISTS

WHILE THERE ARE MANY REASONS WHY PUBLIC PENSION FUNDS may be natural leaders in institutional activism – their size, their long-term horizon, and fewer potential conflicts of interest – public pension funds also face potential problems. As noted by Murphy & Nuys (1994), incentives and governance structures of some public pension funds may provide only weak incentives to increase the value of the funds. For example, they argue that with defined benefit plans, pre-specified future retirement benefits are promised to public employees with guarantees (ultimately) by state taxpayers who are the true residual claimants, yet most boards of trustees of these plans have a fiduciary responsibility to the beneficiaries (the retired public employees) and not to the residual claimants (the taxpayers). They hypothesize that boards are less interested in generating high returns and are more interested in avoiding paying high management fees and avoiding taking large risks. They note that public pension fund managers often receive low salaries and few financial incentives, and face constraints on their ability to be effective monitors of the companies whose shares they own. Fund managers often have limited expertise about specific companies and also face ownership restrictions. However, the study noted that CalPERS and some other funds have been able to circumvent some restrictions by hiring certain key employees such as the Chief Investment Officer as outside consultants.

A recent study by Wahal (1995) noted that some public funds such as CalPERS have been fairly successful in gaining acceptance for shareholder proposals and persuading firms to adopt changes. However, Wahal questions the long-term effect on stock prices of targeted companies. For the complete sample of stocks, mean "excess" performance is generally positive in the three post-target years (particularly for pre-target underperformers) but not significantly different from the market-adjusted returns. However, some results in the same study (described below) suggest CalPERS may be one public pension fund that has had some effect.

THE CALPERS MODEL

I T IS WORTHWHILE NOT ONLY TO DESCRIBE the CalPERS model of activism, but also to trace its evolution and project likely trends. This overview will allow Canadian fund managers to benefit from the CalPERS learning experience.

BACKGROUND

AS OF 1993, CALPERS WAS THE THIRD LARGEST PENSION FUND in the world (behind the New York fund TIAA-CREF and the Netherlands fund Algemeen Burgerlijk), and was the largest public pension fund in the United States. It served more than one million members: retirees from various local, county, and state governments. The fund was expected to continue to grow in the near future, since although it paid out more than $US 8 million each day in benefits, it also had over $US 15 million left each day for investment (see Ybarra, 1995, for a recent description of CalPERS and a history of its involvement with corporate governance issues).

As of 1993, CalPERS owned $US 22.4 billion in U.S. equities – over 1,000 U.S. companies with an average stake of approximately 0.6 percent of each company. Forty-one percent of assets were in fixed income, 40 percent were in equities (roughly two-thirds domestic and one-third or $US 8 billion in international equities), and the remainder in real estate, private equity, mortgages and cash. Approximately 80 percent of the equities were passively managed internally, while the remainder were managed by approximately 20 outside managers.

THE HISTORY OF CALPERS ACTIVISM

THE ROOTS OF CALPERS' INVOLVEMENT IN ACTIVISM can be traced to the corporate merger and acquisition activities of the early 1980s. In order to maintain control, management of several companies resorted to anti-takeover devices such as *greenmail, scorched earth policies,* and *poison pills.* Numerous studies have shown that these techniques often lead to a decrease in the company's stock price. Many of these stocks were held by pension funds such as CalPERS. Consequently, as early as 1985, CalPERS found itself involved in corporate governance issues, primarily through proxy battles at annual meetings. According to CalPERS representatives, one of the major reasons for CalPERS involvement was the unwillingness of corporate executives to communicate in any manner, even by simply returning phone calls.

In 1986, Jesse Unruh, a member of the CalPERS investment committee, helped form the shareholder rights organization known as the Council of Institutional Investors (CII). In the same year, Richard Koppes was hired as general counsel. In 1987, Dale Hanson was hired as Chief Executive Officer. In that year, CalPERS began issuing shareholder resolutions at annual meetings. The main focus of these resolutions was an attempt to eliminate poison pills recently instituted by various companies. According to CalPERS representatives, shareholder resolutions were used because, at the time, this was the only tool CalPERS had at its disposal.

These early CalPERS campaigns met with considerable resistance from management and were largely unsuccessful (although in 1988, CalPERS achieved its first shareholder victory over management opposition – an anti-greenmail proposal). At the time, there were also Securities and Exchange Commission (SEC) regulations (subsequently changed in 1992) which restricted communication among investors, making it difficult for large institutional investors to organize a joint effort on corporate governance issues. In addition, the only communication with management was at annual meetings. However, a major difficulty for CalPERS occurred in cases where it tried to chastise a company (about to introduce a poison pill) which had also achieved record profits and displayed a rising stock price.

In late 1989, with the assistance of outside consultants, CalPERS changed strategies. In a document titled "Why Corporate Governance?" CalPERS articulated its corporate governance philosophy. The focus was no longer on specific management actions, such as the enactment of poison pills, but rather on promoting structural changes aimed at improving performance. For example, the fund proposed to advocate stronger boards with independent directors and more qualified members. In addition, CalPERS emphasized the importance of attempting to maximize its investment return and taking a long-term investment outlook.

CalPERS continued to meet with considerable resistance during the early phase of this new approach. Companies accused it of not understanding the companies or their industries. CalPERS further inflamed corporations when, in 1990, it sent out a questionnaire to directors of S&P 500 companies asking their views of the fund's new corporate governance emphasis.

In 1990 and 1991, CalPERS met with other members of the CII and developed a list of ten principles of corporate governance, which was published in the *Harvard Business Review* (The Working Group on Corporate Governance, 1991). These principles included improving the board of directors by having outside directors evaluate the performance of the CEO, screening board candidates in a more effective manner, and having institutional shareholders acting more as owners rather than investors (for a critique of these principles, see Wharton, Lorsch & Hanson, 1991).

CalPERS attempted to emphasize the importance of dialogue between management and institutional investors. According to Dale Hanson, former CEO of CalPERS, it was important for management to know its top 20 shareholders when a company was doing well so that those same shareholders would be more understanding in bad times (*Chief Executive*, 1994). Although CalPERS attempted a "kinder, gentler" approach in 1992 by scheduling informal meetings without the threat of shareholder resolutions, this was largely unsuccessful and CalPERS decided once again to submit shareholder resolutions.

In October 1992, largely due to CalPERS involvement, the SEC changed the rule which restricted the ability of large institutions to communicate with one another. Disinterested persons not seeking proxy authority were exempted from proxy requirements and thus were permitted to communicate freely with other persons or through the media. This rule change made it easier for large institutions to plan voting strategies on key issues.

In 1992, and again in 1994, CalPERS commissioned studies by Wilshire Associates to assess the effectiveness of their corporate governance program (see Nesbitt, 1992, 1994, and a summary in *The Economist*, 1994). As noted above, the first study of 42 CalPERS' campaigns between 1987 and 1992 found that targeted companies *underperformed* the S&P 500 Index by 60 percent prior to CalPERS' involvement, then *outperformed* the index by 40 percent subsequent to CalPERS' involvement. Furthermore, the second study indicated that since 1990 CalPERS campaigns produced even more dramatic results than the earlier campaigns aimed at specific management actions. This study provided an important cost-benefit analysis of activism. According to both studies, based on the average CalPERS' holding per stock of approximately $US 35 million, the cumulative outperformance amounted to an average gain in excess of the market of about $US 2.9 million per company or $US 137 million for all such targeted companies, well in excess of the *total* annual administrative costs estimated at $US 500,000. A recent paper by CalPERS general counsel and senior staff counsel, Koppes & Reilly (1994), referred to this evidence as the "missing link" connecting the corporate governance approach of CalPERS with the improvement of a firm's stock price. Further evidence of the connection between corporate governance and performance was found in an important study by the Gordon Group for CalPERS, which highlighted the beneficial results from active investment strategies (Gordon & Pound, 1993).

A recent study by Wahal (1995) examined a number of active U.S. pension funds and found that only firms targeted by CalPERS experienced a significantly positive stock price reaction around the target date. Furthermore, Wahal's results highlight the importance (in terms of effect on shareholder wealth) of performance-based targeting, which appears to be the key contributor to any "excess" stock price reaction.

The most recent public action by CalPERS involved the promotion of the "GM Guidelines" – 28 principles related to corporate governance issues developed by General Motors in March 1993. The principles examined selection of the board chair and CEO, use of board committees, size of the board, mix of inside and outside directors, criteria for selecting new directors, evaluation of performance, succession planning, and other corporate governance issues. In the fall of 1994, CalPERS circulated copies of the guidelines to 200 of the largest U.S. companies, asking them to adopt similar principles. Follow-up letters were issued to non-respondents warning of public grading of responses (or non-responses). The grading scheme developed by CalPERS was as follows:

A+ for an excellent response, A for a good response, B for a good response but requiring more information, C for needing more information, D for missing the point, F+ for a brush off, and F for no response. In October 1994, *Business Week* published the results (Dobrzynski, 1994b). Subsequently, numerous companies which had received a failing grade of F (for non-responses) were re-graded after sending CalPERS their responses. In December 1994, CalPERS expanded the survey to the next 100 largest companies. By that time, 83 percent of the 100 largest companies had responded and almost half of these had either completed, or were in the process of completing a governance self-evaluation (*i.e.*, received grades of either A or B).

THE CALPERS MODEL AS OF 1995

IN OCTOBER 1994, CALPERS TRUSTEES HIRED as CEO former assistant executive officer for investment operations, James Burton, to replace Dale Hansen (who had resigned from CalPERS in order to join an investment firm). Burton had been involved in corporate governance issues for two years prior to the arrival of Hanson. Subsequently, Burton designated general counsel Koppes with the additional title of deputy chief executive and turned over corporate governance responsibility to him. Although less visible than Hanson, Koppes was already heavily involved in corporate governance.

The current version of the CalPERS model is a carefully timed, finely tuned approach (see Hanson, 1993, for a recent overview of the process). Around June of each year, an outside consulting firm receives a list of the approximately 1,000 U.S. companies that form CalPERS internally managed portfolio. The consulting firm assists with the initial screening by ranking the companies based on their return to shareholders over the most recent complete five-year period (it also reports the most recent six-month results). Performance relative to each firm's industry is also examined (based on 2-digit and 3-digit SIC codes), as are year-by-year results.

CalPERS then focuses on the bottom quartile – approximately 250 companies – based on each firm's five-year absolute performance. These companies are examined by CalPERS in greater detail. Other performance measures are calculated, such as return on assets, return on equity, return on sales, profitability, and payout ratios. In addition, any recently announced restructuring plans or special circumstances (such as change in management) are noted, along with the number of shares held by CalPERS.

CalPERS' own industry analysts examine these companies and also rely on other independent reports such as *Value Line*. A brief assessment of each company accompanies the report. This process usually takes place during July and August.

Several screens are put in place to reduce the bottom quartile list to the "Failing 50" list. Companies such as utilities in heavily regulated industries are eliminated. If an entire industry is doing poorly, most firms within this industry might be eliminated. Firms owned by foreign parents are not targeted;

nor are firms with either a high level of insider ownership (generally above 30 percent) or a low level of institutional ownership (generally less than 20 percent). These last screens are aimed at increasing the odds of realizing improved performance. Companies that have undergone recent restructuring are sometimes eliminated, if the restructuring is judged to be a serious effort and in the best interest of the company.

Around September, the investment committee meets to finalize the "Failing 50" list. In addition, based partly on recommendations from CalPERS' Investment Office, the committee chooses ten of the 50 companies to target for improved performance.

The worst ten companies, as well as the next-worst 20 to 25 companies are sent letters – to the Board Chairs – indicating the amount of stock held by CalPERS and a note of dismay concerning the company's performance. Firms are asked to respond to specific problems and are asked what actions are being taken to improve performance. In addition, meetings (especially with the independent board members) are requested with all of the ten worst performer companies.

During the subsequent months, if the stock performance of the next-worst firms improves dramatically, they may be removed from the watch list. If the ten worst companies are not responsive to CalPERS suggestions, they are then targeted for shareholder resolutions in the upcoming annual meeting (typically around February or March). In late January or early February, CalPERS makes public its list of the ten worst targeted companies. For example, the 1995 list included First Mississippi, U.S. Shoe, Jostens, Boisie Cascade, Melville, K Mart, Navistar International, Zurn Industry, and Oryx Energy. CalPERS attempts to meet with these companies and resolve issues before each company's annual meeting. In some cases, companies remain on the CalPERS list for several years, while other companies are removed from the list after agreeing to CalPERS' requests. For example, the list of ten worst in 1994 was reduced to just two companies (Dobrzynski, 1994a; and Anand, 1994).

FUTURE TRENDS AND ISSUES

CALPERS IS PART OF A WAVE OF INCREASING INSTITUTIONAL ACTIVISM which shows no sign of abating. There appear to be several reasons for increased investor activism by U.S. public pension funds (such as CalPERS). Given the sheer size of many public pension funds, simply voting with their feet if they are not satisfied with a particular equity investment is not always a viable option for the fund managers since the cost of selling is quite high. Part of the increase in investor activism can also be attributed to a 1988 U.S. Labor Department ruling which stated that pension funds must vote the shares in their portfolio for the exclusive benefit of plan members (rather than abstaining or automatically voting with management). Numerous issues and trends will continue to shape the evolution of the CalPERS model.

The Media

Some of CalPERS' success in corporate governance issues is attributable to the power and influence of the U.S. media. Recall that the average holding by CalPERS is only around 0.6 percent of outstanding shares. However, its influence is magnified by the media's attention to such actions as its annual "hit list" and its recent letter regarding the GM principles. As long as CalPERS is able to garner this public attention, it will continue to have influence.

New Screens

The key to CalPERS recent success appears to have been its ability to link corporate governance issues directly with poor long-term performance by companies. However, a recent additional criteria to the investment "screen" is more controversial. A study for CalPERS by the Gordon group uncovered a positive correlation between financial performance and workplace practices such as job rotation, job training, and self-management teams (see a discussion by Birchard, 1994). Time will tell whether this new screen is a natural extension, attempting to link governance issues with performance, or whether it represents a venture into social issues which may not relate to the "bottom line".

Indexing

Indexing – buying portfolios of stocks which replicate well-known indexes such as the S&P 500 – is still (relatively) far more prevalent in the United States than in Canada. For pension funds, indexing raises an interesting issue concerning the "prudence" responsibility of pension funds. Koppes & Reilly (1994) argue that indexing simply for the purpose of diversification may not be an adequate test of prudence, and pension funds may have a duty to monitor actively such "passive" funds. They suggest that to screen the index based on some form of corporate governance model may be more appropriate. This relates to the previous issue of developing an appropriate screening technique – one which is linked to the performance of the firm.

Global Diversification

As it increasingly diversifies internationally, CalPERS is taking a more active role in governance issues in foreign countries. As of 1993, CalPERS had investments of over $US 500 million in each of France, Germany, Italy, Japan, Spain and the United Kingdom, and over $US 300 million in Australia, Canada and the Netherlands. Mainly in the "study phase" now, CalPERS has an international consultant and is examining the possibility of more participation in international proxies.

Relationship Investing

The most interesting prospect for CalPERS is an increased emphasis on relationship investing which is not necessarily linked to corporate governance, but is aligned in philosophy. Relationship investing is defined by CalPERS representatives as "the conscious decision to own a large block of common or preferred stock in a single corporation, coupled with a commitment to active management over a long-term holding period" (Koppes & Reilly, 1994, pp.7-8). How the notion of "active management" evolves will ultimately be the key to the success or failure of this approach.

SURVEY METHODOLOGY

GIVEN AN UNDERSTANDING OF THE CALPERS MODEL, we are now in a position to examine the administration of public pension funds in Canada. First, a brief description of the survey methodology: between January and March 1995, in-person interviews were conducted with two groups – executives and managers (hereafter collectively referred to as fund managers) of a small number of major Canadian public pension funds, including the Caisse de dépôt et placement du Québec, Ontario Teachers, OMERS and another large fund (which wished to remain anonymous); and a representative of Fairvest Securities.

Fund managers were asked to respond to a series of questions dealing with four general areas: their portfolio composition and equity investment philosophy; their views on institutional activism in Canada; the CalPERS model of institutional activism; and their advice to CEOs, directors, and managers of Canadian companies. Many of the questions were intentionally open-ended, allowing fund managers to express their views on a range of issues.

Given the concentrated nature of Canada's public pension funds, the sample size is understandably quite small. Nonetheless, the fund managers who participated in the survey were among the largest fund managers in Canada and represented, collectively, over $90 billion in assets. According to a recent survey of pension funds (Williams, 1994), these assets represent approximately one-third of the total assets of Canada's 100 largest pension funds.

CANADIAN PUBLIC PENSION FUNDS

THE TEN LARGEST PUBLIC CANADIAN PENSION FUNDS, according to *Benefits Canada* (Williams, 1994), were (in order): Ontario Teachers, Quebec Public Employees (managed by Caisse de dépôt et placement du Québec), OMERS, Ontario Public Service, Alberta Public Sector, CN Railways, Ontario Hospitals, Ontario Hydro, BC Municipal, and BC Public Service. Numerous fund managers among this top-ten group were interviewed in order to compare and contrast the degree of institutional activism in Canada relative to the CalPERS model and to provide a basis for accepting or rejecting the four hypotheses (mentioned earlier) concerning why Canadian funds tend not to be as visibly active as CalPERS.

PHILOSOPHY AND STYLE

PHILOSOPHY AND STYLE WERE EXAMINED in order to determine whether certain styles tended to be associated with a more active stance by fund managers. Managers were presented with the following definitions of styles, as derived from MacIntosh (1993): "passive investment management" was defined as selling an investment when dissatisfied with management of the company, while "active investment management" was defined as attempting to alter management's plan of action by voting against management, participating in a proxy contest, or attempting to influence management by other means. Managers were asked to rank their funds' *philosophy* on a scale of 1 to 5, with 1 representing "totally passive" and 5 representing "totally active". In addition, managers were asked to describe their fund's equity investment style and philosophy in general terms.

"Active" public pension funds displayed a wide variety of management styles.

Some funds were very definite in describing their own style in a particular manner, for example, as being very much "bottom-up" or "value" oriented, attempting to identify good companies in attractive industries. In contrast, other funds employed a variety of styles, including indexing, growth-oriented, value-oriented, small-cap, etc. Some funds viewed these multiple styles as a form of diversification. In some cases, this variety of styles was achieved through the use of external managers. There was no apparent relationship between a fund's self-assessment of activism and the focus of its style. Interestingly, some funds distinguished between their current approach to activism (in the middle of the range) and their target (near 5), suggesting a trend toward increased activism.

One fund raised an important distinction between *reactive* and *proactive* activism. An example of reactive activism was voting against a poison pill proposal – reacting to an issue raised by the management and/or board of a corporation. In contrast, proactive activism involved approaching a corporation and trying to enact change before an issue reached the point of a vote at an annual meeting. One fund manager viewed most Canadian public funds – with the exception of the Caisse – as engaging predominately in reactive activism.

Fund managers claimed to be long-term investors, yet were also very cognizant of shorter-term performance.

Most funds claimed to be long-term investors – some even likened their style to that of U.S. investor Warren Buffet, focusing on *ownership* rather than *trading*.

Target holding periods often exceeded two years, and some cases were cited where stocks were held for more than 20 years. Funds cited the high cost of selling stocks, particularly those in the bottom 200 of the TSE 300 Index. This reluctance to sell without creating a large price impact was also a reason cited for the increased activism by the funds.

Paradoxically, most funds admitted to tracking their portfolio's performance on a quarterly, monthly, and even daily basis. In addition, many fund managers admitted to being compensated for beating the index (usually the TSE 300) over much shorter periods than their investment horizons. One fund manager emphasized this dilemma between short-term and long-term horizons.

VIEWS ON REGULATION

MANAGERS WERE ASKED TO COMMENT ON THEIR VIEWS regarding any regulatory restrictions, such as the *Foreign Property Rule* and the *Pension Benefits Act*. Prior to 1990, funds were restricted in terms of the amount of foreign assets – ten percent (of book value) – in which the fund could be invested without incurring penalties. This amount was gradually increased to 20 percent in 1994. In contrast, there are no such restrictions in the United States. There was even talk leading up to the February 1995 federal budget that foreign property restrictions might be tightened again (to less than 20 percent).

In addition, prior to the early 1990s, funds covered under the *Canada Pension Benefits Standards Act* (as well as many similar provincial Acts), were restricted in terms of the types of eligible Canadian companies in which they could invest. For example, funds were required to restrict investments to companies which had paid dividends in four of the last five years, including the most recent year. Recent changes in Canadian and most provincial Acts now focus on the "prudence" test: for example, establishing and adhering to investment policies, standards and procedures that a reasonable and prudent person would apply in respect of a *portfolio* of investments to avoid undue risk of loss and obtain a reasonable return. However, numerous Acts still restrict the amount (percentage) of stock a fund can own.

While funds preferred less regulation to more, they did not envision a complete removal of restrictions, e.g., related to foreign assets.

Fund managers viewed any constraints as restrictions on potential investment returns and welcomed the move to the prudence test. Not surprisingly, funds did not wish to see any additional restrictions, and some funds cited the strong performance (generally) of Canadian pension funds as a reason for no additional regulations.

The issue of the foreign property rule brought a wide range of responses and often the strongest (*i.e.*, most emotional) response of any topic discussed. While most managers expressed a desire for an increased foreign asset level, there was also an opinion expressed by one fund that Canada has a right to limit foreign investment of pension funds. However, another fund manager called it an "absolutely foolish rule that flies in the face of what capital markets are all about" and argued that placing walls around Canada will only serve to impoverish our nation. This manager challenged the government to present a solid economic rationale for the rule. One fund manager argued for the removal of the rule by noting that the use of derivative securities makes the rule a false barrier. Another fund manager referred to restrictions as ludicrous and a form of foreign exchange controls that will only continue to result in lost opportunities for Canadian pension stakeholders.

Some fund managers cautioned that legislators (and bureaucrats) are always looking for perceived problems and solutions, while these policy solutions were often worse than the symptoms. Other managers commented that current restrictions were simply some bureaucrat's dream. One manager lamented the fact that Canada did not have a single regulatory agency as in the United States; and another manager praised the form of regulation that requires firms to disclose more information to shareholders.

CORPORATE GOVERNANCE ISSUES

MANAGERS WERE PRESENTED WITH A LIST OF corporate governance issues and asked to comment on their perceived importance, with 1 representing "not important" and 5 representing "very important." Issues listed included poison pills, executive compensation, independence of directors, staggered boards, number of board members, and minority shareholder rights. As well, managers were asked to comment on any additional corporate governance issues which they felt were important. Results are summarized in Table 1.

TABLE 1

PERCEIVED IMPORTANCE OF CORPORATE GOVERNANCE ISSUES
BASED ON A SURVEY OF CANADIAN PUBLIC PENSION FUND MANAGERS

Independence of Directors	4.5
Poison Pill Plans	4.3
Executive Compensation	3.8
Minority Rights	3.7
Number of Board Members	3.3
Staggered Boards	3.0

Notes: 1 = not important.
5 = extremely important.

The most important corporate governance issue was the perceived lack of independence of many directors, followed by poison pill plans.

Coinciding with the draft of the TSE report on corporate governance, the independence – or more specifically, the perceived lack of independence – of directors of Canadian corporations was viewed as the major corporate governance issue. One fund manager singled out the major Canadian banks as an example of the lack of truly independent outside directors.

The second most important issue dealt with poison pill plans. Interestingly, some pension fund managers professed an evolution in thinking since Inco implemented the first such pill in Canada in 1988. Many funds routinely voted against poison pills as a matter of principle, but some have recently sought improvements in pill plans in exchange for supporting such plans. Others claimed that almost without exception they continued to vote "no". One fund manager was surprised at the large number of planned poison pills during 1995 after the recent first defeat of a poison pill (Labatt's).

Some fund mangers commented on a key difference in Canada *versus* the United States: the relative prevalence of closely held firms. CalPERS screens out most companies with at least 30 percent inside ownership, although according to CalPERS representatives, in some cases companies with up to 40 percent inside ownership would be considered. The primary reason given for this screen was to increase the chances of success for any shareholder resolutions. In Canada, since many firms are closely held, an investigation was conducted to determine the effect of this CalPERS screen on Canadian firms. The TSE has recognized the prevalence of control blocks and has incorporated it into the calculation of the benchmark TSE 300 index. The *TSE Review* provides a list of these 300 stocks, including the "available float" on which the relative weights on the TSE 300 composite index are calculated. As of January 1995, among the TSE 300 companies, 48.0 percent had 100 percent available float (*i.e.*, non-control block shares), 58.7 percent had at least 80 percent available float, 65.4 percent had at least 70 percent available float, 73.7 percent had at least 60 percent available float, and 82.0 percent had at least 50 percent available float. Thus, according to the CalPERS screen, between two-thirds and three-quarters of TSE 300 companies would be eligible for targeting or, conversely, one-quarter to one-third would not. Canadian public pension fund managers recognized this reality, but many simply viewed it as something they were required to live with. A related control issue deals with unequal or subordinate voting rights shares. As a rule, most fund managers recommended voting against any proposals that would authorize issues of new common stock that had unequal or subordinate voting rights. Thus fund managers appeared to be more concerned with ensuring that ownership concentration did not increase beyond existing levels.

Fund managers also described other corporate governance issues which they viewed as important. These included the perceived lack of planning in many companies facing Chief Executive Officer succession.

Several fund managers indicated they maintained proxy voting guidelines which they viewed as public documents and sent to most large Canadian corporations. Many of these guidelines were based strictly on the economic impact of voting for or against a particular proposal.

COMPARISONS WITH CALPERS

REACTION WAS MIXED IN TERMS OF EVALUATING the CalPERS model of activism. Some applauded the emphasis on long-term performance and its proactive stance. The CalPERS approach was generally viewed as constructive, but not the only viable approach.

Some suggested that targeting only a dozen firms and exerting pressure for change would not have a major effect on the North American economy, although perhaps it would have a small effect on CalPERS' performance. There was concern that companies' fear of antagonism might cause them to perceive shareholders as a nuisance or might create an "us *versus* them" mentality – similar to management/union struggles – rather than both parties working together to improve share value. Cases were cited of Canadian firms which underperformed both the TSE and their industry, yet managers of these companies were considered to be dedicated individuals.

Another manager suggested that up to half of the public pension funds in Canada were reluctant to get involved in corporate governance issues. Fund executives, rather than fund analysts, were most concerned about corporate governance issues. Analysts were viewed as being more concerned with keeping their contacts at various firms and did not wish to "rock the boat".

Several fund managers suggested that the best way to influence management was through private conversations rather than through proxy statement battles. Fund managers indicated they were usually just a phone call away from CEOs – usually having calls returned within fifteen minutes – and this was often an effective route. One fund manager cited a case of attempting to approach management, but being rebuffed. After creating an alliance with another group, the fund was able to attract the attention of the board and positive changes were put in place. The fund manager noted that management took full credit for the changes. Unlike many CalPERS cases, the confrontation between institutional investors and management was not reported in the media, and the fund manager was happy to let management take the credit so long as it had a positive effect on the bottom line of the fund.

Nonetheless, fund managers also supported vigorous action on the part of public funds in the (rare) case of real management abuses, provided the "quiet persuasion" route has been exhausted. Examples were cited of public advertisements which were placed in *The Globe and Mail* when fund managers wanted to make public a particularly important point. However, these last resort measures were in contrast to the annual public lists of their targeted companies supplied by CalPERS. We can now re-examine the four hypotheses with respect to why Canadian public pension funds are less visibly active than CalPERS.

Canadian pension funds tend to engage in corporate governance activism in a less visible fashion than major American counterparts such as CalPERS primarily because of style differences.

The first possible explanation was regulatory differences between the two countries. Fund managers generally did not view regulatory differences as that great and not in areas that might impact on activism. The second possible explanation was that, in Canada, third-party groups such as Fairvest or the Pension Investment Association of Canada (PIAC) might be playing the activism role. PIAC was viewed primarily as an educational vehicle, and while Fairvest was viewed as providing a voice for funds, it was not seen as precluding funds from taking an activist role. While the third explanation – the lead-lag between the United States and Canada cannot be eliminated, the fourth explanation appears to be most likely. Fund managers often differed in their views concerning corporate governance issues, yet presented a consistent picture of the "Canadian way" of dealing with management of companies – non-confrontational, except in unique circumstances.

One fund manager used the analogy of owners (shareholders), directors, and managers all in a boat together trying to navigate through difficult waters. There were enough external factors trying to sink the boat and it would be easier to survive if the three parties got along rather than screaming and shouting at one another. Another fund manager stressed the importance of keeping low visibility by referring to a fundamental law of physics: for every action, there is an equal and opposite reaction. The more a fund visibly pressed for change, the more resistant management would become, in order not to lose face in public. A third fund manager simply described Canadian fund managers as being more conservative and cautious than American counterparts.

ADVICE FOR CEOs

FINALLY, MANAGERS WERE ASKED TO COMMENT on what advice they would offer to CEOs, directors, and managers of publicly-traded Canadian companies in order to prepare them for possible increases in institutional activism. Many fund managers viewed corporate managers in Canada as generally doing a good job managing their companies. Some fund managers felt that institutions were erroneously cast in the media as always being the "saints" while managers were always the "sinners". Nonetheless, there were a few notable cases (particularly in the United States) where management was clearly incompetent and solidly entrenched.

Improve investor relations.

Fund managers felt corporate managers should be responsive to their shareholders and listen to their ideas, particularly if shareholders have knowledge or experience to offer. An example cited was a firm which held an annual dinner with representatives of its five largest shareholders. While the intent was certainly not to obtain insider information, the exchange of ideas was viewed as a positive experience.

One fund manager described the key as accountability of management and boards and better communication among all three parties: shareholders, managers and boards.

Improve the composition of boards.

The main issue appeared to be the lack of independence of board members. Fund managers sought the removal of management-appointed members with little company or industry knowledge or experience. In rare cases, fund managers indicated they sought board representation themselves.

One fund manager stressed the importance of separating the CEO from the board chair (a model more common in the United Kingdom than in most other countries). The primary argument was that a bit of "tension" (*i.e.*, the CEO having to report to someone else) is a "good thing".

Balance the short-term and long-term prospects of the firm.

Fund managers recognized the dilemma faced by CEOs who were being pushed by analysts to improve short-term performance, while at the same time trying to build a long-term strategy. Some fund managers felt the pension funds themselves should be more vocal in stating they are prepared to take a longer-term outlook for a firm's prospects, giving boards the freedom to select good managers and providing them with the time to succeed. Nonetheless, over the longer term, this flexibility should be related to performance, or fund managers will demand the removal of under-performing management. Fund managers recognized that performance relative to a peer group (such as an industry) was an appropriate way to judge a firm's performance.

SUMMARY AND CONCLUSIONS

THIS STUDY INVESTIGATED WHY PUBLIC PENSION FUNDS in Canada have not been as *visibly* active as the California Public Employees' Retirement System (CalPERS) in the United States. Primarily based on interviews with major Canadian public pension fund managers as well as with CalPERS representatives, this study provided a detailed framework of the CalPERS model of investor activism, described how Canadian public pension fund managers viewed this model, examined what corporate governance issues were important to Canadian public pension fund managers, and provided corporate directors with a sense of what to expect in the future in terms of investor activism. There are several lessons to be learned from this study: lessons for pension fund managers, regulators and corporate managers.

The results of this study are not to suggest that all Canadian public pension funds should try to be just like CalPERS, but rather that they should benefit from many of the CalPERS' experiences, particularly the relatively recent focus on company performance. Pension fund managers must do their homework: know what questions they wish to ask managers and articulate what it is they are looking for. They must do research on companies, especially examining performance (total shareholder return) and any factors related to performance. They must recognize that they are partners with managers and boards.

Regulators should resist any temptation to install additional regulations which might restrict public pension fund ownership, and should, in fact, consider removing regulations. Specifically, funds should be allowed to maximize returns to their stakeholders based on desired risk levels and utilize an *unconstrained* global opportunity set of securities. In addition, any regulations that restrict public fund mangers from being effective monitors of corporations should be removed. For example, public pension funds should be allowed to own a larger stake in any company in which they invest.

Corporate managers should be concerned with improving shareholder return, and should recognize emerging evidence linking performance with corporate governance issues. In particular, corporate managers should consider recommendations – made by public pension funds as well as others – for making boards more effective. Communication with shareholders should also be strengthened.

While governance issues will continue to dominate the concerns of public pension funds (and other institutional investors), and while these funds will become increasingly active and continue to search for ways to improve the long-term performance of Canadian firms, they will do so in a less visible fashion than major American counterparts such as CalPERS. Nonetheless, Canadian pension funds have much to learn from the U.S. experience, as do Canadian managers and regulators.

ACKNOWLEDGEMENTS

THE FINANCIAL SUPPORT PROVIDED by the Financial Research Foundation of Canada is gratefully acknowledged. I also wish to acknowledge with thanks the research assistance of Rod Graham and Dave Thomas. My thanks to Carl Bang for useful comments and to the discussants and seminar participants at Industry Canada's Conference on Corporate Decision-Making in Canada. I also wish to thank Karin Estes and Maureen Reilly from the California Public Employees' Retirement System and representatives of the Canadian public pension fund industry (some of whom wished to remain anonymous) for agreeing to be interviewed for this project. Any errors are solely attributable to the author.

BIBLIOGRAPHY

Anand, V. "CalPERS Gunning for Poor Performers." *Pensions & Investments*. (January 24, 1994):4, 80.

Birchard, B. "The Call for Full Disclosure." *CFO*. (December 1994):31-42.

The California Public Employees' Retirement System. "Why Corporate Governance?" (November 7, 1989):1-21.

Cordtz, D. "Corporate Hangmen." *Financial World*. 162, 7 (March 30, 1993):24-8.

Chernoff, J. "Institutions Strengthen Grip on Companies." *Pensions & Investments*. (March 8, 1993):1, 34.

Chief Executive. "The New Governance Paradigm." (April 1994):40-54.

Dobrzynski, J. H. "Cool it! It's the CalPERS Cops." *Business Week*. (January 31, 1994a):6.

_____. "An Inside Look at Calpers' Boardroom Report Card." *Business Week*. (October 17, 1994b):186-88.

The Economist. "Reluctant Owners." (January 29, 1994):16-7.

Gordon L. A. and J. Pound. "Active Investing in the U.S. Equity Market: Past Performance and Future Prospects." The California Public Employees' Retirement System. (January 11, 1993):1-43.

Hanson, D. M. "Much, Much More than Investors." *Financial Executive*. (March/April 1993):49-51.

Koppes, R. H. and M. L. Reilly. "An Ounce of Prevention: Meeting the Fiduciary Duty to Monitor an Index Fund through Relationship Investing." Working Paper, The California Public Employees' Retirement System. (March 25, 1994):1-56.

MacIntosh, J. "If it Ain't Broke... ." *Canadian Investment Review*. (Winter 1994/95):37-9.

MacIntosh, J. G. "The Role of Institutional and Retail Investors in Canadian Capital Markets." *Osgoode Hall Law Journal*, 31, 2 (1993):371-472.

Mackenzie, W. "Corporate Governance News." *Corporate Governance Review*, 9, 1 (December 1994/January 1995):10-12.

Montgomery, K. E. "Shareholder Activism in Canada: A Survey of Institutional Shareholders." National Centre for Management Research and Development Working Paper NC 92-014-B. Western Business School, University of Western Ontario, 1992.

Montgomery, K. E. and D. S. R. Leighton. "The Unseen Revolution is Here." *Business Quarterly*. (Autumn 1993):39-46, 48.

Murphy, K. J. and K. V. Nuys. "State Pension Funds and Shareholder Inactivism." Working Paper. Harvard Business School, 1994.

Nesbitt, S. L. "Rewards from Corporate Governance." California Public Employees' Retirement System. (February 12, 1992):1-5.

_____. "Long-term Rewards from Shareholder Activism: A Study of the CalPERS Effect." *Journal of Applied Corporate Finance*, 6 (1994):75-80.

Paré, T. P. "Two Cheers for Pushy Investors." *Fortune*. (July 30, 1990):95, 98.

Pound, J. "Beyond Takeovers: Politics Comes to Corporate Control." *Harvard Business Review*. (March-April 1992):83-93.

Pozen, R. C. "Institutional Investors: The Reluctant Activists." *Harvard Business Review*. (January-February 1994):140-49.

Silverstein, K. "Pension Funds Increase Presence in Corporate Boardrooms." *Pension World*. (May 1994):4-5.

Star, M. G. "Measuring up in Canada." *Pensions & Investments*. (April 18, 1994):22.

Stewart, T. A. "The King is Dead." *Fortune*. (January 11, 1993):34-7,40.

Stoffman, D. "Look who's Calling the Shots." *Canadian Business*. (July 1990):45-7.

Thain, D. "The TSE Corporate Governance Report: Disappointing." *Business Quarterly*. (Autumn 1994):77-86.

Useem, M., Bowman, E. H., Myatt, J. and C. W. Irvine. "US Institutional Investors look at Corporate Governance in the 1990s." *European Management Journal*, 11, 2 (1993):175-89.

Wahal, S. "Pension Fund Activism and Firm Performance." Working Paper, The Kenan-Flagler Business School. The University of North Carolina, 1995.

Wharton, C., J. Lorsch and L. Hanson. "Advice and Dissent: Rating the Corporate Governance Compact." *Harvard Business Review*. (November-December 1991):136-43.

Williams, P. "Benefits Canada Top 100 Pension Funds." *Benefits Canada*. (April 1994):41-61.

The Working Group on Corporate Governance. "A New Compact for Owners and Directors." *Harvard Business Review*. (July-August 1991):141-43.

Ybarra, M. "Money Talks." *California Lawyer*. (February 1995):50-5, 90.

Ben Amoako-Adu & Brian F. Smith
School of Business and Economics
Wilfrid Laurier University

11

Outside Financial Directors and Corporate Governance

INTRODUCTION

A S CORPORATE LONG-TERM STRATEGISTS FOCUS THEIR ATTENTION on global competition, environmental concerns and corporate restructuring, the role and effectiveness of the board of directors in positioning the company to meet these challenges is being re-examined. Weitzer (1991) states that the goal of corporate governance is to realign the interests of shareholders, managers and other stakeholders of the corporation so as to enhance the long-term growth of the company. Directors should, therefore, represent stakeholders' interests, monitor the actions of management and provide advice, which should enhance corporate value (Gillies, 1992).[1] Mace (1972) argues that the role of corporate boards is not well understood and that there appears to be a gap between what boards are expected to do and what they actually do. Although he states that boards provide advice, exercise discipline on executives and act in crisis periods, his interviews with board members reveal that CEOs exert significant influence on their boards.

In order to offset any undue influence of management and to represent the interests of shareholders, it is argued that a minimum number of outside directors[2] should be on the board. Outside directors are generally considered to be more independent of management than inside directors who are usually senior officers of the firm. This argument is reflected in both federal and provincial corporate legislation that requires a minimum number of outside directors on the boards of public corporations.[3] Furthermore, a major recommendation of the draft report of the Toronto Stock Exchange Committee on Corporate Governance in Canada (1994) was that a majority of directors on the boards of listed companies should be unrelated.[4]

Another benefit to the firm of outside directors is the expertise they can bring to the board which may not be present among officers of the firm. For example, directors from the financial sector may bring special knowledge with respect to underwriting of securities, bank financing, takeovers and/or corporate restructuring; they are also expected to have extensive knowledge of other industries and the national economy.

The degree of independence and net benefit to the firm of outside directors has been disputed. First, it is argued that outside directors tend to act in management's interests because the selection of directors is influenced by senior executives and these outside directors generally hold few shares. Second, outside directors are often investment dealers, pension fund managers, bankers and insurers who may face a potential conflict of interest given an existing or prospective business relationship between the financial institution and the firm. Even if they have no current business dealings with the firm, outside financial directors may not wish to challenge senior management for fear of losing future business. In addition, since their companies take invest-ment positions in stocks as well as provide financial advice to clients, there is a potential conflict of interest that inside information from the corporate boardroom may be used for the financial institution's direct gain or to counsel their investment clients. Mace (1986) argues that financial directors do not have a monopoly on financial expertise and, hence, their presence on a board should not necessarily be value-enhancing.

Shleifer & Vishny (1986) contend that large shareholders may be more effective at monitoring management and, if necessary, they can initiate takeovers. Such large shareholders may be family trusts, institutional or corporate investors who are represented on the board. The implication of this argument is that insofar as the marginal benefit of concentrated ownership outweighs the marginal cost of entrenchment, there should be an economic incentive for large shareholders to increase their ownership. This would, therefore, lead to a concentrated corporate ownership structure as found in Canada. However, whether concentrated ownership is beneficial or injurious to the Canadian economy is an unresolved empirical question.

The primary objective of this study is to evaluate empirically the effectiveness of outside financial directors of a large sample of non-financial Canadian public corporations.[5] After controlling for other determinants, three different measures of corporate performance are related to the proportion of outside financial directors to ascertain whether the presence of such directors on the board enhances corporate value. Outside financial directors have been classified in previous research as "grey area" directors.[6] As discussed in Byrd & Hickman (1992a), grey area directors have some type of affiliation with the firm that may limit their ability to challenge management. In addition to out-side financial directors, lawyers, consultants, customers, suppliers and those having transactional or familial ties to management have also been labelled grey area directors.

A secondary goal of this study is to examine the effect of directors in the same line of business. We expect such directors to add value because of their special knowledge of the industry in which they work. As in the case of out-side financial directors, there are factors that offset the benefits related to directors in the same line of business. For example, they may face a conflict of interest where the firms for which they act as managers and directors are competing for the same customers. In addition, the expertise that directors from the same line of business can offer may be available from within the firm or from industry consultants.

INDEPENDENT AND AFFILIATED OUTSIDE DIRECTORS

THE NEED FOR REQUIRING CORPORATE BOARD composition to include outside directors is based on the assumption that outside directors will be independent of management or the corporation and, hence, will bring independent thinking and objectivity into corporate boardroom discussions or debates. In line with this thinking, the *Canada Business Corporations Act* requires that public corporations appoint at least two directors who are not employees of the corporation or its affiliates. On the other hand, the *Ontario Business Corporations Act* requires that a minimum of one-third of the directors of a public corporation be outside directors.

For outside directors to be effective in monitoring and advising management and (at times) voting against management on issues deemed not to be in the interest of stakeholders, they must be independent of management or the company. This means affiliated or related directors appointed from outside the corporation may be ineffective in monitoring management performance because of their links with management or the corporation. Such affiliated or captive directors, also referred to as grey area directors, include individuals who are linked to the corporation or management through either transactional or familial ties. Thus, the corporation's consultants, creditors, underwriters and directors related to management through blood or marriage are considered affiliated directors. Any outside director who faces a potential conflict of interest may be categorized as an affiliated or grey area director. Such potential conflict of interest will impair the effectiveness of such outside directors. Mace (1986) goes to the extent of suggesting that securities underwriters should not be allowed to serve as outside directors because of the potential conflict of interest. The importance of this issue underscores the recent TSE Committee on Corporate Governance in Canada's (1994) guideline that a majority of the board members should be unrelated or independent directors and also that the board's nominating committee should be comprised exclusively of unrelated outside directors. At present, however, corporate disclosure of the background of outside directors is not sufficient to provide us with the data needed for any analysis of the effectiveness of affiliated or related directors.

METHODOLOGY

IF OUTSIDE FINANCIAL DIRECTORS AND DIRECTORS in the same line of business are effective in their role as representatives of stakeholders and provide unique advice and monitor the performance of management, then their presence on corporate boards should be value-enhancing. On the other hand, if these outside directors do not hold a monopoly on the information they provide to the board or if they face a conflict of interest in their role as bankers, underwriters and competitors, then corporate performance may not be enhanced with more of these outsiders on the board.

Two methodological research approaches are used in assessing the effectiveness of outside directors in adding value to the corporation. One approach is to make indirect inference from stock market reaction to events surrounding board of directors' decisions, such as the appointment of outside directors (Rosenstein & Wyatt, 1990; and Byrd & Hickman, 1992). The second method is to use a multiple regression to relate directors' attributes to corporate performance measures after controlling for other relevant variables which may affect performance (Baysinger & Butler, 1985; Morck, Shleifer & Vishny, 1988 and Hermalin & Weisbach, 1991). Because of an inadequate number of common board-related events we chose the regression methodology for this study.

The null hypothesis being tested is that the presence of outside financial directors and directors in the same line of business on a board should not be associated with incremental corporate value different from that of other outside directors. Since Morck et al. (1988) show that there is an empirical relationship between ownership and corporate performance, the test will also control for ownership.

The directors of the firms in the sample were classified into four groups: i) inside directors, ii) outside directors from financial institutions, iii) directors in the same line of business, and iv) other outside directors. Inside directors are employees and officers of the firm or related companies or shareholders who control at least 10 percent of the votes of the firm. Financial institutions include banks, trust companies, investment dealers, pension funds and insurance companies. Personal investment companies are not classified as financial institutions because these firms are usually a tax-incentive alternative to owning shares directly. Identification of such firms was somewhat subjective because of a lack of detailed disclosure.

The financial institution directors are subclassified into a narrow definition (N) which includes only employees of financial institutions and a broad definition (B) which includes both employees and directors of financial institutions. Directors in the same line of business are those who are either directors or officers of firms in the same industry. Other outside directors are all directors who are not insider, financial institution or same-line-of-business directors.

Cross-sectional regressions are used to examine the relationship between corporate value and outside financial directors and directors from the same line of business, respectively.[7] The data for the regression are averaged over a ten-year period, from 1984 to 1993. In order to capture the expected long-term effects of many board decisions, a ten-year period of analysis is required.

Three different performance measures are used in this study. The first is the ratio of the year-end market value of common equity to the book value of common equity. This performance measure serves as a proxy for Tobin's Q measure of performance which has been used in U.S. studies. The denominator of Tobin's Q is the replacement cost of assets, but in Canada data are not available on replacement cost of corporate assets. The market value of common equity equals the number of common shares outstanding multiplied by the market price at year end.

The other performance measures – return on assets and asset turnover – rely exclusively on accounting figures. The return on assets is calculated as earnings before interest and taxes divided by total assets. Asset turnover, defined as total sales divided by total assets, is considered to be devoid of accounting deductions, such as depreciation, and research and development expenses, which tend to distort net profit positions of corporations.

The annual variables are averaged over the number of years for which data are available. The cross-sectional regression used for the subsequent tests follows this general functional form.[8]

$$Performance \quad = \quad f \; (Control \; Variables, \; Outside \; Financial \\ Directors, \; Same \; Line \; of \; Business, \\ Other \; Outside \; Directors) \qquad (1)$$

The control variables include a measure of size (log of market value of equity), systematic risk (beta) and ownership measured as percentage of stock holdings of all directors.[9] In the financial literature, insider ownership of shares is suggested as one solution to the principal-agent problem. Executive ownership in the company is expected to enhance the alignment of the interest of the executives and shareholders and hence reduce agency costs. Morck, Shleifer & Vishny (1988) show that the relationship between corporate value and ownership is non-monotonic so ownership is delineated into three parts: zero to 5 percent, 5 percent to 20 percent, and more than 20 percent holdings. We used 20 percent as the threshold because the Ontario Securities Commission allows cumulative share acquisition up to 20 percent of votes (bright line) before a takeover offer must be extended to all shareholders. It should be noted that for the U.S. study, Morck et al. (1988) used 5 percent and 25 percent as the thresholds, after using a piecewise regression to determine the slopes. Following the argument put forward by Morck et al., we expect ownership of zero to 5 percent (Own 5) to be positively related to stock value, ownership between 5 percent and 20 percent (Own 20) to be negatively related to value, and ownership in excess of 20 percent (Own 20+) to be positively related to value.[10] The regression specification for the first performance measure is

$$MVB \; = \; \alpha_0 + \alpha_1 \, Log \, (Equity) + \alpha_2 \, (Beta) = \alpha_3 \, (Regulated) + \alpha_4 \, (Own \; 5)$$

$$+ \, \alpha_5 \, (Own \; 20) + \alpha_6 \, (Own \; 20+) + \alpha_7 \, (Fin \, (N)) + \alpha_8 \, (Same)$$

$$+ \, \alpha_9 \, (Other \; Outside) + e_{jt} \qquad\qquad (2)$$

MVB	=	ratio of market-to-book value of equity
Equity	=	market value of common equity (a measure of size)
Beta	=	Dimson (1979) adjusted systematic risk coefficient with a lead and a lag[11]
Regulated	=	Dummy variable is 1 if regulated and zero otherwise
Own 5	=	ownership by directors between zero and 5%, and 5% if ownership is > 5%
Own 20	=	zero if ownership is ≤ 5%, ownership −5% if ownership is > 5% and ≤ 20%, and 15% if ownership is > 20%
Own 20+	=	zero if ownership is ≤ 20%, and ownership −20% if ownership is > 20%
Fin (N)	=	Narrow definition of financial directors. This is the percentage of directors who are current employees of financial institutions.
Fin (B)	=	Broader definition of financial directors. These include Fin (N) and percentage of other directors who are just directors of financial institutions.
Same	=	Percentage of outside directors who are directors or officers of firms operating in the same industry.
Other Outside	=	Percentage of outside directors, other than those from the financial industry defined in Fin (B), and those defined as same-line-of-business (Same). This includes politicians, academics, public sector employees, consultants and lawyers.

The cross-sectional regression uses market value of equity to book value of equity, a proxy for Tobin's Q, as a performance measure.

Tobin's Q was the performance measure used by Morck et al. (1988) and Hermalin & Weisbach (1991). However, we modify this approach to control for both size, regulation and risk. While the sign of the size and regulated variable cannot be determined *a priori*, the relationship between value and risk is expected to be negative. In order to control for risk, we include beta in the cross-sectional regression and expect $n_2 < 0$ because higher risk should be inversely related to value. From Morck et al. (1988), we expect $n_4 > 0$, $n_5 < 0$ and $n_6 > 0$. If financial and same-line-of-business directors are effective in increasing the value of the corporation, then $n_7 > 0$ and $n_8 > 0$. If the other outside directors also add significant value to the corporation then $n_9 > 0$.

DATA

THE MONTHLY STOCK PRICES AND SHARES outstanding were obtained from the Canadian Financial Markets Research Centre stock database. Corporate financial data, such as book value of common equity, were taken

FIGURE 1

AVERAGE COMPOSITION OF BOARD OF DIRECTORS OF 150 TSE LISTED COMPANIES (1984 - 1993)

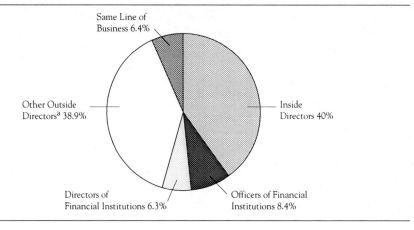

Note: a Other outside directors include consultants, lawyers, former politicians, academics, and employees from the public sector or non-profit organizations.

from the Compact Disclosure Canada CD-Rom Database as well as Microfiche copies of the annual reports. The names, positions and professional background of the directors of 200 of the *Financial Post 500* public corporations each year were compiled and coded into a workable database from the shareholder proxy circulars and the Compact Disclosure Canada CD-Rom database. The names of all shareholders holding more than 10 percent of the votes were also taken from these two sources. From an initial sample of 200 public companies, the final sample reduced to 150 because of either missing financial, ownership or director information, or insufficient monthly stock returns for the estimation of the beta. Five years of monthly stock returns were used to estimate the betas but in cases where there were not enough monthly returns, at least 24 months of stock returns were required.

BOARD COMPOSITION AND SAMPLE CHARACTERISTICS

FIGURE 1 SHOWS THE COMPOSITION OF CORPORATE BOARDS in the sample for the full period from 1984 to 1993. For the sample of 150 Canadian public corporations listed on the Toronto Stock Exchange over the period from 1984 to 1993, inside directors constitute 40 percent of the board and all outside directors comprised 60 percent. These proportions compare with 34.4 percent and 65.6 percent of insiders and outsiders, respectively, reported in Rosenstein & Wyatt (1990) for the United States. Thus, in Canada, about 60 percent of board directors are outsiders while in the United States about 66 percent are outside directors.

TABLE 1

SAMPLE CHARACTERISTICS OF 150 CANADIAN COMPANIES, 1984 TO 1993

VARIABLE	MEAN	STANDARD DEVIATION	MINIMUM	MAXIMUM
Equity Beta	0.937	0.379	0.066	2.132
Market-to-Book Value of Equity	1.416	1.042	0.240	6.184
Proportion of Inside Directors	0.400	0.175	0.068	1.00
Proportion of Outside Directors	0.600	0.175	1.00	0.932
Proportion of Financial Directors (N)[a]	0.084	0.083	0.00	0.350
Proportion of Financial Directors (B)[b]	0.147	0.128	0.00	0.627
Proportion of Directors from the Same Line of Business[c]	0.064	0.091	0.00	0.500
Market Value of Equity ($ millions)	710	1,380	2.7	11,200
Total Assets ($ millions)	1,700	3,889	33.6	38,998
Operating Profit Margin[d] (%)	10.08	12.54	–1.59	80.70
Return on Assets[e] (%)	7.81	4.75	–4.21	24.55
Asset Turnover[f]	1.30	0.90	0.08	5.80

Notes:
[a] Financial Directors (N) are narrowly defined as outside financial directors who are employees of financial institutions.
[b] Financial Directors (B) are broadly defined to include both outside financial directors who are either employees or directors of financial institutions.
[c] Directors from the same line of business is defined as outside directors who are current CEOs or employees, retired employees or directors of the same line of business.
[d] Earnings before interest and taxes divided by sales.
[e] Earnings before interest and taxes divided by total assets.
[f] Asset turnover is defined as total sales divided by total assets.

Using the broader definition of outside financial directors, about 15 percent of the directors are either employees or directors of financial institutions. These proportions are reported in Table 1. Thus, one-seventh of all directors are associated either directly or indirectly with financial institutions. This is a significant proportion considering the limited number of financial institutions in Canada. For a sample of U.S. firms, Rosenstein & Wyatt (1990) find that financial directors represent 10.7 percent of all directors. For our study, only 8.4 percent of the directors were current employees of financial institutions. Directors from the same line of business or industry comprised 6.4 percent of the board.

Table 1 indicates that the mean equity beta for the sample of companies is 0.937. This low average equity beta corresponds to the fact that the sample

TABLE 2

CHARACTERISTICS OF BOARDS OF DIRECTORS OF 150 CANADIAN PUBLIC COMPANIES, 1984 TO 1993

VARIABLE	MEAN	STANDARD DEVIATION	MINIMUM	MAXIMUM
Number of Directors per Company	11.25	3.88	5.0	25.0
Percentage of Votes Held by Inside Directors	40.75[a]	30.84	0.01	100.00[b]
Percentage of Companies where CEO is Chair[c]	26.70	n/a	n/a	n/a
Tenure of Directors in Years	8.60	4.15	0.20	27.60

Notes: [a]   The percentage of votes held by inside directors is high for our sample of Canadian firms in relation to that reported in studies of U.S. companies. We attribute the higher percentage to the closer ownership of Canadian firms.

   [b]   The company which had directors holding 100.00 percent of votes between 1984 and 1993 had dual class equity. The voting shares were held by insiders whereas the non-voting shares were held mainly by outsiders.

   [c]   The percentage includes all companies that had a chief executive officer who also served as chair of the board of directors.

   n/a   Not applicable.

represents the largest public corporations in Canada. These firms tend to have relatively low systematic risk. The mean market value of equity and total assets are $710 million and $1.7 billion, respectively.

The three performance measures have a wide range of values for the sample of companies even though they represent an average across a number of years. The market-to-book value of equity varies from 0.240 to 6.184. Return on asset and total asset turnover range from −4.21 percent to 24.55 percent and 0.08 to 5.80, respectively. The firms with the highest operating profitability tend to be utilities which have a high level of offsetting interest expense. These utilities also have the lowest asset turnover.

As shown in Table 2, the number of directors per company ranges from five to twenty five. On average, over the period from 1984 to 1993, there were 11.25 directors per company, of which about 6.9 were outside directors. The *Ontario Business Corporations Act* (section 115), and the corresponding Federal Act (section 97) requires that at least one-third of the board or two directors, respectively, should be outside directors. Thus, large Canadian public corporations tend to have more outside board members than is legally required.

Table 2 shows the percentages of votes held by all directors. The mean total votes held by directors for each company is 40.75 percent with the minimum and maximum held being 0.01 percent and 100.0 percent, respectively. Byrd & Hickman (1992) report that the average vote ownership by directors of a sample of U.S. firms was 15 percent. The 100 percent voting control was for Xerox Canada which issued dual-class shares. The directors of Xerox Canada held all voting shares and outside investors owned the non-voting shares. A further analysis of the data in the sample suggests that most of the votes controlled by directors are owned by a few inside directors. These data indicate that although the proportion of outside directors on the board is larger, relative to insiders, only a small fraction of the company's votes is held by outside directors.

In 26.7 percent of the firms, the chief executive officer (CEO) is the chair of the board. The potential for undue influence on board decisions of this dual role has been raised as a concern in the literature on corporate governance. The mean and maximum tenures of directors in our study are 8.6 years and 27.6 years, respectively. This indicates substantial board experience among directors of Canada's largest public companies.

ANALYSIS OF REGRESSION RESULTS

THE REGRESSION RESULTS OF THE TEST using three different performance measures as the dependent variable are presented in Tables 3 through 5. In column one of each table, the results indicate that the proportion of total outside directors is not significantly related to corporate performance. The absence of a significant relationship between outside board composition and corporate performance is consistent with the findings of Hermalin & Weisbach (1991). When the composition of outside directors is analyzed, neither the proportion of directors who are employees from the financial sector nor the proportion of directors broadly defined to include financial sector employees and directors is consistently related to the performance measures at the 5 percent significance level. Only the proportion of financial directors defined broadly (B) and market-to-book value of equity are related at the 10 percent significance level. In addition, other outside directors do not have a significant relationship with any of the performance measures. With one exception, this is also the case for the same-line-of-business directors. Asset turnover has a significant negative relationship with the proportion of directors from the same line of business. This implies that companies with more directors from the same industry generate less sales per dollar of assets.

The overall results indicate that the experience of outside directors classified by involvement in the financial sector and the same line of business does not consistently add more value than that provided by other directors. This contrasts with Rosenstein & Wyatt (1990) who find that the appointment of outside directors from the financial sector increases shareholder wealth. In addition, there is no incremental value to having a higher proportion of other outside directors on the boards.

The results of the control variables indicate that the systematic risk variable, beta, is positively related to market-to-book value ratio. This implies

TABLE 3

REGRESSION RESULTS OF PERFORMANCE AND ITS DETERMINANTS

DEPENDENT VARIABLE: MARKET VALUE OF EQUITY-TO-BOOK RATIO[a]

CONSTANT	−0.403	−0.130	−0.188	0.043
	(0.36)	(0.12)	(0.17)	(0.04)
Log (Equity)	0.124	0.128	0.091	0.125
	(1.02)	(1.05)	(0.74)	(1.02)
Beta	0.467	0.444	0.467	0.453
	(1.99)**	(1.87)*	(2.00)**	(1.92)*
Regulated	0.341	0.381	0.382	0.381
	(1.21)	(1.33)	(1.35)	(1.33)
Ownership[b] 5	7.462	7.870	7.212	9.002
	(0.65)	(0.68)	(0.17)	(0.77)
Ownership 20	−3.125	−3.617	−3.031	−4.058
	(0.86)	(1.01)	(0.85)	(1.11)
Ownership 20+	0.459	0.440	0.505	0.368
	(0.95)	(0.90)	(1.05)	(0.76)
Outside Directors	0.277	—	—	—
	(0.673)			
Financial Directors (N)[c]	—	0.516	—	—
		(0.45)		
Financial Directors (B)[d]	—	—	1.324	—
			(1.66)*	
Same Business Directors	—	—	—	−0.485
				(0.45)
Other Outside Directors	—	−0.139	−0.220	−0.299
		(0.25)	(0.38)	(0.54)
Adjusted R^2	0.02	0.01	0.03	0.01
Number of Companies	138	138	138	138

Notes: Numbers in parentheses are t-statistics.
* Coefficient is statistically significant at the 10% level.
** Coefficient is statistically significant at the 5% level.
a The average annual ratio of the market capitalization of common equity to the book value of common equity.
b Ownership is defined as the percentage of corporate votes held by inside and outside directors.
c Financial Directors are narrowly defined as outside financial directors who are employees of financial institutions.
d Financial Directors are broadly defined as outside financial directors who are either employees or directors of financial institutions.

TABLE 4

REGRESSION RESULTS OF PERFORMANCE AND ITS DETERMINANTS

DEPENDENT VARIABLE: RETURN ON ASSETS[a]				
CONSTANT	0.106 (2.04)**	0.090 (1.77)*	0.094 (1.86)*	0.111 (2.11)**
Log (Equity)	−0.003 (0.49)	−0.003 (0.53)	−0.003 (0.48)	−0.003 (0.57)
Beta	−0.011 (0.93)	−0.012 (1.08)	−0.011 (0.97)	−0.010 (0.93)
Regulated	0.026 (2.08)**	0.026 (2.02)**	0.025 (1.92)*	0.026 (2.01)**
Ownership[b] 5	−0.078 (0.15)	−0.123 (0.24)	−0.065 (0.12)	0.011 (0.02)
Ownership 20	−0.017 (0.10)	−0.005 (0.033)	−0.013 (0.08)	−0.057 (0.34)
Ownership 20+	0.032 (1.41)	0.038 (1.67)*	0.034 (1.49)	0.029 (1.27)
Outside Directors	−0.000 (0.01)	—	—	—
Financial Directors (N)[c]	—	0.067 (1.25)	—	—
Financial Directors (B)[d]	—	—	0.005 (0.13)	—
Same Business Directors	—	—	—	−0.060 (1.13)
Other Outside Directors	—	0.032 (1.27)	0.024 (0.87)	0.011 (0.42)
Adjusted R^2	0.02	0.03	0.02	0.03
Number of Companies	130	130	130	130

Notes: Numbers in parentheses are t-statistics.
* Coefficient is statistically significant at the 10% level.
** Coefficient is statistically significant at the 5% level.
[a] The average annual ratio of the market capitalization of common equity to the book value of common equity.
[b] Ownership is defined as the percentage of corporate votes held by inside and outside directors.
[c] Financial Directors are narrowly defined as outside financial directors who are employees of financial institutions.
[d] Financial Directors are broadly defined as outside financial directors who are either employees or directors of financial institutions.

that growth companies tend to be more risky. Tables 4 and 5 indicate that regulated firms behave differently from non-regulated firms when considering corporate governance issues. In Table 4, the results show that regulated firms tend to perform better than non-regulated firms if return on assets is used as a performance criterion, while Table 5 indicates that regulated companies have lower asset turnover.

The size of the company, measured by the log of market value of equity, is statistically significant as a control variable in the case where the dependent variable was measured as asset turnover. Larger companies tend to have lower asset turnover. This is not surprising, given that many of the larger companies in the sample were utility companies, such as Bell Canada Enterprises.

In contrast to Morck et al. (1988), ownership up to 5 percent and ownership between 5 percent and 20 percent is not significantly related to performance. However, ownership in excess of 20 percent is found to be significantly and positively related to corporate performance, measured as asset turnover or return on assets. This provides weak support for the argument that a high concentration of ownership more closely aligns the interest of shareholders and management and, hence, concentrated ownership makes companies perform better.

Generally, the results indicate that there is no convincing evidence of significant incremental value associated with the presence on the board of outside directors from the financial industry and outside directors in the same line of business. This is consistent with the findings of Hermalin & Weisbach (1991) for outsiders in general. The results also indicate that the non-monotonic relationship between ownership and corporate value as postulated and observed by Morck et al. (1988) holds only for ownership levels above 20 percent.

CONCLUSIONS AND POLICY IMPLICATIONS

IN THIS STUDY, CANADIAN CORPORATE DATA over the period from 1984 to 1993 were used to test whether the presence on corporate boards of outside financial directors and directors from the same line of business is value-enhancing. In other words, is there a statistically positive relationship between these outside directors and corporate performance? The study also examines the significance of other determinants of corporate performance, such as systematic risk and size as well as the non-monotonic relationship between board ownership and corporate performance.

Generally, the results suggest that there is no statistical evidence of a relationship between corporate performance and proportion of outside directors on the board. The findings for this large sample of Canadian firms are consistent with those reported by Hermalin & Weisbach (1991) in the United States. In addition, when the composition of the board is analyzed, there is no convincing evidence that outside directors from the financial industry or from the same line of business enhance the value of the corporation. The results, however,

TABLE 5

REGRESSION RESULTS OF PERFORMANCE AND ITS DETERMINANTS

DEPENDENT VARIABLE: ASSET TURNOVER[a]				
CONSTANT	5.345	5.168	5.201	5.786
	(6.79)**	(6.69)**	(6.75)**	(7.39)**
Log (Equity)	−0.486	−0.492	−0.512	−0.508
	(5.56)**	(5.66)**	(5.78)**	(5.93)**
Beta	−0.128	−0.153	−0.116	−0.131
	(0.76)	(0.91)	(0.70)	(0.80)
Regulated	−0.598	−0.600	−0.605	−0.586
	(3.03)**	(3.06)**	(3.03)**	(3.01)**
Ownership[b] 5	4.340	3.374	3.737	7.049
	(0.52)	(0.41)	(0.45)	(0.87)
Ownership 20	−2.052	−1.854	−1.622	−3.455
	(0.78)	(0.73)	(0.63)	(1.35)
Ownership 20+	1.001	1.080	1.053	0.884
	(2.94)**	(3.17)**	(3.12)**	(2.65)**
Outside Directors	−0.004	—	—	—
	(0.01)			
Financial Directors (N)[c]	—	1.108	—	—
		(1.35)		
Financial Directors (B)[d]	—	—	0.818	—
			(1.45)	
Same Business Directors	—	—	—	−2.003
				(2.64)**
Other Outside Directors	—	0.385	0.486	−0.150
		(0.98)	(1.17)	(0.39)
Adjusted R^2	0.315	0.320	0.322	0.345
Number of Companies	144	144	144	144

Notes: Numbers in parentheses are t-statistics.
 * Coefficient is statistically significant at the 10% level.
 ** Coefficient is statistically significant at the 5% level.
 a The average annual ratio of the market capitalization of common equity to the book value of common equity.
 b Ownership is defined as the percentage of corporate votes held by inside and outside directors.
 c Financial Directors are narrowly defined as outside financial directors who are employees of financial institutions.
 d Financial Directors are broadly defined as outside financial directors who are either employees or directors of financial institutions.

indicate that corporate size is positively related to performance, that corporate value increases when ownership exceeds 20 percent, and that the governance structure of regulated firms has a different effect on their performance compared to that of non-regulated companies.

The two public-policy implications of this research are related to the effectiveness of outside directors and the disclosure of the background of outside directors which will enable analysts, investors and securities regulators to identify and therefore separate affiliated and independent directors. First, the effectiveness of outside directors may not be due to knowledge *per se*, but may rather be dependent on other personal attributes. This stems from the empirical finding that the presence of highly informed outside financial directors on the board has no significant causal relationship to corporate performance. Thus, legislation that sets a minimum proportion of independent outside directors is not likely to have a significant positive or negative effect on corporate performance. Second, improvements are needed regarding the disclosure of background, affiliation, interlocking directorships, and tenure of outside directors. Especially weak is the requirement to disclose whether firms with which a director is associated – either as an employee or a director – are related by common ownership. At present it is difficult to identify who is an unrelated or independent outside director. Without better disclosure, legislation based on a minimum proportion of independent outside directors will not be effectively monitored.

ENDNOTES

1 It appears that the issue as to whose interests are represented by directors is debatable. Wainberg & Wainberg (1987) state that directors, acting as a board, are agents of the corporation. They are agents in the sense that they have the responsibility of managing the assets of the corporation to make profit and they are also trustees in the sense that they have the responsibility of preserving the assets of the corporation. Hatton (1990) also argues that legally, directors are required to represent the best interests of the corporation and not the interests of shareholders and other stakeholders because the powers of directors to manage the operations of the company come from legal statutes and not the shareholders. Gillies (1992) and Mace (1986) take the broader approach and argue that directors have a fiduciary responsibility to all stakeholders including shareholders, creditors, employees, consumers and society as a whole.

2 With some exceptions, most empirical studies have found either a positive or neutral relationship between the proportion of outside directors on the board and corporate performance. Rosenstein & Wyatt (1990) in analyzing

the effectiveness of outside directors find that positive wealth effects result from the appointment of outside directors. Kaplan & Minton (1994) find that the appointment of outside directors leads to higher executive turnover and a modest improvement in performance. Brickley, Coles & Terry (1994) report that the stock market reaction to the announcement of poison pills is positive when the board has a majority of outside directors and negative when it does not. Brickley, Lease & Smith (1988) also provide evidence indicating that institutional investors and blockholders are more likely to vote against management when they think that a corporate proposal would harm shareholders. However, Murphy (1985), Hermalin & Weisbach (1988, 1991) and Kaplan & Reishus (1990) find no evidence that outside directors add value to the company. In addition, Pound (1988) provides evidence which indicates that due to conflict of interest pressures, institutional investors and outside board directors are more likely to vote in support of management but against their fiduciary responsibilities to shareholders and other stakeholders.

3   The *Canada Business Corporations Act* (CBCA) requires that public corporations have at least two directors who are not employees of the corporation or its affiliates. On the other hand, the *Ontario Business Corporations Act* (OBCA) states that a minimum of one-third of the directors of a public corporation must be outside directors. In this case, the minimum proportion of outside directors required may be at conflict. Two outside directors on a board of ten will meet the CBCA but not the OBCA requirements.

4   The draft report of the Toronto Stock Exchange Committee on Corporate Governance in Canada defines an unrelated director as "a director who is free from any interest and any business or other relationship which could, or could reasonably be perceived to materially interfere with the director's ability to act with a view to the best interests of the corporation". Unrelated directors are those outside directors who would be considered independent of management. It is unclear whether firms would classify their outside financial directors as unrelated.

5   Empirical studies from the United States and Japan on the role of directors from the financial sector do not provide consistent results. In a study of U.S. firms, Van Nuys (1993) shows that even directors from financial institutions that do not have existing business with the firm tend to support managers on anti-takeover announcements more frequently than other groups. However, Rosenstein & Wyatt (1990) find that in the United States appointments of outside directors from any particular industry have no different impact from any other industry. Kaplan & Minton (1994) report that Japanese directors who are employees of banks are appointed in companies that are financially distressed and have large bank borrowings. Directors from non-financial firms are appointed to companies that have temporary problems. In both cases, the outside directors play a monitoring role.

6 For a discussion of "grey area" directors, see Baysinger & Butler (1985), Hermalin & Weisbach (1988), and Byrd & Hickman (1992a).

7 Byrd & Hickman (1992) argue that the cross-sectional analysis relating corporate performance to board composition used in this study and in U.S. studies such as Hermalin & Weisbach (1991) are unlikely to find significant results because the presence of outside directors has an impact only at the time of extraordinary events such as takeover attempts or the adoption of poison pills.

8 The literature is unclear as to the direction of causality between corporate performance and board composition. The reverse causality where the board composition can be determined by corporate performance is analyzed in St-Pierre, Gagnon & Saint-Pierre (1992).

9 A number of Canadian companies have foreign parent companies. In almost all cases, executives from the foreign parent company were directors on the board of the Canadian subsidiary. The percentage of votes controlled by directors includes those votes controlled by the foreign parent company.

10 Morck et al. (1988) argue that the relationship between corporate value and ownership can be positive reflecting convergence-of-interests hypothesis or negative indicating that the entrenchment hypothesis outweighs the convergence-of-interests hypothesis. Their piece-wise linear regression of Tobin's Q on ownership indicated that the slope was positive to ownership between zero and 5 percent, negative for the 5 percent and 25 percent range, and positive but weaker for ownership in excess of 25 percent.

11 The systematic risk was estimated with the adjusted beta of Dimson (1979). This measure adjusts for possible thin trading. The Dimson beta is the sum of the β_is from the following regression:

$$R_{jt} = \alpha_0 + \sum_{i=-1}^{+1} \beta_i R_{mt+i} + e_{jt}$$

where R_{jt} and R_{mt} are the monthly holding period returns for the stock and the TSE 300 Composite Index. The regression was run over the five-year period prior to the cross-sectional analysis in equation (2).

12 Brickley, Lease & Smith (1988) distinguish between outside directors from "pressure-sensitive" financial institutions (banks, trust companies, investment dealers and insurance companies) and those from "pressure-resistant" financial institutions (public pension funds and mutual funds). No distinction is made in this study because insufficient information was available to separate underwriters from other institutional investors.

ACKNOWLEDGEMENT

THIS RESEARCH WAS FUNDED WITH A Social Sciences and Humanities Research Council Grant and a Wilfrid Laurier University Short-Term Research Grant. We would like to thank our research assistants, Yuxing Yan, Yuhui Liu and Raman Krishnaprasad, for the data collection and programming work. This study was presented at the Conference on Corporate Decision Making in Canada, organized by Industry Canada and the Financial Research Foundation of Canada, March 20-21, 1995.

BIBLIOGRAPHY

Ang, J. S., and J. H. Chua. "Corporate Bankruptcy and Job Losses Among Top Level Managers." *Financial Management*. (Winter 1981):70-74.

Arnold, Hugh J., and Patrick F. O'Callaghan. "The New Board of Directors: A Survey of Chief Executive Officers." *Business Quarterly*. (Summer 1988).

Barr, Joseph W. "The Role of the Professional Director." *Harvard Business Review*. (May-June 1976).

Baysinger, Barry D., and Henry N. Butler. "Corporate Governance and the Board of Directors: Performance Effects of Changes in Board Composition." *Journal of Law, Economics, and Organization*, 1, 1 (Fall 1985):101-124.

Brancato, C. K. and P. A. Gaughan. "Institutional Investors and Their Role in Capital Markets." Monograph, Columbia University Center for Law and Economics, 1988.

Brickley, J. A., J. L. Coles and R. L. Terry. "Outside Directors and the Adoption of Poison Pills." *Journal of Financial Economics*, 35 (1994):371-390.

Brickley, J. A., R. C. Lease and C. W. Smith, Jr. "Ownership Structure and Voting on Antitakeover Amendments." *Journal of Financial Economics*, 20 (1988):267-91.

Byrd, J. W. and K. A. Hickman "Do Outside Directors Monitor Managers? Evidence From Tender Offer Bids." *Journal of Financial Economics*, 32 (1992a):195-221.

_____. "The Case for Independent Outside Directors." *Journal of Applied Corporate Finance*, 5 (1992b):78-82.

Coughlan, A. T. and R. M. Schmidt. "Executive Compensation, Managerial Turnover, and Firm Performance: An Empirical Investigation." *Journal of Accounting and Economics*. (1985):43-66.

DeAngelo, L. E. "Managerial Competition, Information Costs, and Corporate Governance." *Journal of Accounting and Economics*. (January 1989):3-36.

Demsetz, H. "The Structure of Ownership and the Theory of the Firm." *Journal of Law and Economics*, 26 (1983):375-90.

Demsetz, H. and K. Lehn. "The Structure of Corporate Ownership." *Journal of Political Economy*, 93 (1985):1155-77.

Dimson, E. "Risk Measurement When Shares are Subject to Infrequent Trading." *Journal of Financial Economics*, 7 (1979):197-226.

Easterbrook, F .H. and D. R. Fischel "Voting in Corporate Law." *Journal of Law and*

Economics, 23 (1983):395-427.

Epstein, Edward M. "The Corporate Social Policy Process and the Process of Corporate Governance." *American Business Law Journal*, 25 (1987).

Fama, E. F. and M. Jensen. "Separation of Ownership and Control." *Journal of Law and Economics.* (1983):301-25.

Fredrickson, J. W., D. C. Hambrick, and S. Baumrin. "A Model of CEO Dismissal." *Academy of Management Review.* (April 1988):255-70.

Furtado, E. P. H. and V. Karan. "Causes, Consequences, and Shareholder Wealth Effects of Management Turnover: A Review of the Empirical Evidence." *Financial Management.* (1990):60-75.

Gaughan, P. A. *Mergers and Acquisitions.* New York: Harper Collins Publishers Inc., 1991.

Gillies, James. *Boardroom Renaissance: Power, Morality and Performance in the Modern Corporation.* Toronto: McGraw-Hill Ryerson Limited, 1992.

Hatton, Michael J. *Corporations and Directors: Comparing the Profit and Not-for-Profit Sectors.* Toronto: Thompson Educational Publishing, Inc., 1990.

Hermalin, Benjamin E. and Michael S. Weisbach. "The Effects of Board Composition and Direct Incentives on Firm Performance." *Financial Management*, 20, 4 (Winter 1991):101-12.

_____. "The Determinants of Board Composition." *Rand Journal of Economics*, 19, 4 (Winter 1988), 589-606.

Holderness, C. G. and D. P. Sheenan "The Role of Majority Shareholders in Publicly Held Corporations: An Exploratory Analysis." *Journal of Financial Economics*, 20 (1988):317-46.

Jensen, M. C. "Eclipse of the Public Corporation." *Harvard Business Review.* (1989):61-74.

Jensen, M. C. and W. H. Meckling. "Theory of the Firm: Managerial Behaviour, Agency Costs and Ownership Structure." *Journal of Financial Economics.* (1976):305-60.

Jensen, M. C. and J. B. Warner. *The Modern Corporation and Private Property.* New York: Macmillan Inc., 1988.

Kaplan, S. N., and B. A. Minton. "Appointments of Outsiders to Japanese Boards: Determinants and Implications for Managers." *Journal of Financial Economics*, 36 (1994):225-58.

Kaplan, Steven N., and David Reishus. "Outside Directorships and Corporate Performance." *Journal of Financial Economics*, 27 (1990):389-410.

Kovacheff, J. D. "Managing the Board: A Survey of Chairmen of Canadian Corporations." London, ON: National Centre for Management Research and Development, University of Western Ontario, 1991.

Leighton, David S. R. and Donald H. Thain. "The Role of the Corporate Director." *Business Quarterly.* (Autumn 1990).

Mace, Myles L. *Directors: Myth and Reality.* Boston, Harvard Business School Press, Division of Research, 1986.

_____. "The Board and the New CEO." *Harvard Business Review.* (March-April 1977).

_____. "The President and the Board of Directors." *Harvard Business Review.* (March-April 1972):37-49.

Morck, R., A. Shleifer, and R. W. Vishny. "Management Ownership and Market Valuation: An Empirical Analysis." *Journal of Financial Economics.* (March 1988):842-52.

_____."Alternative Mechanisms for Corporate Control." *American Economic Review.* (September 1989):293-315.

Murphy, K. J. "Corporate Performance and Managerial Remuneration." *Journal of Accounting and Economics.* 7 (1985).

Osler, Hoskin and Harcourt. "Directors' Duties: A Guide to the Responsibilities of Corporate Directors in Canada", Toronto, 1993.

Patton, Arch and John C. Baker. "From The Boardroom." *Harvard Business Review.* (November-December 1987):10-18.

Pawling, John D. "The Crisis of Corporate Boards: Accountability *vs.* Misplaced Loyalty." *Business Quarterly.* (Spring 1988):26-8.

Pound, J. "Proxy Contests and the Efficiency of Shareholder Oversight." *Journal of Financial Economics,* 20 (1988):237-65.

Rosenstein, S. and Jeffrey G. Wyatt. "Outside Directors, Board Independence and Shareholder Wealth." *Journal of Financial Economics,* 26 (1990):175-91.

St-Pierre, Josée, Jean-Marie Gagnon and Jacques Saint-Pierre. "Takeover Bids, Structure of Ownership and Board Composition." Working Paper, Laval University, 1992.

Shleifer, A. and R. Vishny. "Large Shareholders and Corporate Control." *Journal of Political Economy,* 94 (1986):461-88.

Thain, D. H. and D. R. S. Leighton. "Ownership Structure and the Board." *Canadian Investment Review,* IV (Fall 1991):61-5.

Toronto Stock Exchange Committee on Corporate Governance in Canada. "'Where Were the Directors?': Guidelines for Improved Corporate Governance in Canada." Toronto: Toronto Stock Exchange, 1994.

Vance, Stanley C. *Corporate Leadership: Boards, Directors and Strategy.* New York: McGraw-Hill Book Company, 1983.

Vancil, R. F. *Passing the Baton: Managing the Process of CEO Succession.* Boston, MA: Harvard Business School Press, 1987.

Van Nuys, K. "Corporate Governance Through the Proxy Process: Evidence from the 1989 Honeywell Proxy Solicitation." *Journal of Financial Economics,* 34 (1993):101-32.

Wainberg, J. M. and Mark I. Wainberg. *Duties and Responsibilities of Directors in Canada.* Toronto: CCH Canadian Limited, 6th Ed., 1987.

Waitzer, E. J. "Are Institutional Investors Really Impacting Corporate Governance?" *Canadian Investment Review,* IV (1991):9-14.

Warner, J. B., R. L. Watts and K. H. Wruck. "Stock Prices and Top Management Changes." *Journal of Financial Economics.* (March 1988):461-92.

Weisbach, M. S. "Outside Directors and CEO Turnover." *Journal of Financial Economics,* 20 (1988):431-60.

Mark R. Huson
Faculty of Business
University of Alberta

Commentary on Part IV

MUCH OF THE EXISTING LITERATURE on the agency problems in firms is devoted to understanding the conflict of conflicting interests between shareholders and bondholders, and between shareholders and managers. Solutions to these conflicts include debt covenants, incentive compensation schemes and monitoring by shareholders. Increasingly, institutional shareholders are playing an important role in the process of monitoring managers in the United States. The studies presented in this session investigate the extent to which Canadian institutional investors are active in creating firm value.

Because of the unique ownership structure that exists in Canada, the extent to which Canadian institutional investors are active in corporate governance and the effect of their presence on firm value should not be compared too directly to the activities of U.S. institutional investors. The presence of controlling shareholders provides an additional agency conflict: the shareholder/shareholder conflict. The ability of the controlling shareholder to affect corporate direction reduces incentives for institutional investors to engage in governance activities.

In the realm of governance, institutions are faced with a number of decisions. First, they have to decide whether or not to monitor. Then, based on the information set they choose, they must decide whether to exit, exercise voice, or remain loyal. Patry and Poitevin consider the institutional incentives to monitor as well as incentives to exit, exercise voice or remain loyal. Foerster looks at a potential model for monitoring and discusses the types of governance activism that are currently being used in Canada. The effectiveness of these activities are examined by MacIntosh and Schwartz and Amoako-Adu and Smith. MacIntosh and Schwartz examine the effect of the presence of institutional investors on firm value. Amoako-Adu and Smith investigate the effect of the presence of outside financial directors on firm performance. It should be noted that failure to reject the null hypotheses of these empirical studies means that one cannot distinguish between two alternatives – i.e., that institutions do not try to influence corporate performance, or, that they try, but are ineffective.

Patry and Poitevin look specifically at the governance and organizational structures of institutional investors to determine if these have any effect on their incentives to monitor. In order to do so, they first discuss the nature of the agency problem in firms, the exit/voice mechanisms, and then they highlight the increasing importance of institutions in financial markets. They go on to discuss the governance structure of institutional investors and how it affects monitoring incentives. They consider two types of institutions: mutual funds and pension funds.

Their analysis leads them to conclude that the nature of mutual funds leads fund managers to behave in a manner that results in maximizing return to investors. However, the liquidity concerns of mutual fund managers do not allow for long-term investments. Pension fund managers, on the other hand, do not have the same liquidity constraints and therefore can accommodate a longer-term investment horizon. The problem is that since most pension funds have captive investors, there is no incentive to maximize investor return and, therefore, there is low incentive to monitor.

The analysis assumes that mutual fund managers act to maximize shareholder return. Failure to maximize returns will result in a removal of funds from a manager's discretion. If returns can be augmented through monitoring, then mutual fund managers who monitor should outperform other funds. In outperforming other funds, a fund manager will draw more funds to his management, and liquidity concerns will be less pronounced. This suggests that if monitoring is a value additive, mutual fund managers will engage in monitoring. The lesson to be learned from the lack of monitoring by mutual funds is not altogether clear. Is it that the very structure of mutual funds makes it inconceivable, or is it that monitoring is not a value additive?

I would like to raise three additional points with regard to this analysis. The first and second have to do with the assumption that mutual fund managers act to maximize shareholder return. In motivating this assumption, the authors claim that mutual fund shareholders do not have a comparative advantage in selecting stocks and should therefore leave the management of the portfolio in the hands of the manager. They go on to suggest that because there is sufficient information to enable investors to judge the manager's performance and also enough suitable alternatives available to investors, fund managers are forced to maximize return.

My first point deals with the idea that mutual fund shareholders should leave the management of the fund to the fund managers. This should be kept in mind since it deals directly with the concept of "relational investing" (discussed elsewhere) as a means of corporate governance. The second point has to do with the presence of readily available substitutes for specific mutual funds as a way of inducing individual fund managers to maximize value. This is related to the foreign investment constraints placed on Canadian institutional investors.

My third point is aimed at the notion that pension fund managers lack the incentive to monitor. I suggest this could be handled *via* incentive compensation contracts. In addition, the high level of activism shown by CalPERS and other pension funds in the United States demonstrates that pension funds do indeed have an incentive to monitor.

The CalPERS monitoring and activism model is analyzed by Foerster, who also looks at monitoring and intervention techniques of Canadian public pension funds. Foerster asks why Canadian institutional investors have not been as "visibly" active as their American counterparts. He offers four possible reasons. The first is that there are regulatory differences that limit the activity of Canadian institutions. The second is that Fairvest and PIAC assume the activist role on the part of institutions. The third is that Canadian institutions have only recently become large enough to act effectively, but more activity should be expected now that they are large. The final possibility is that the "Canadian style" of activism is not as visible as the American style.

Foerster writes:

> During the 1990s, numerous large pension funds have become more actively involved in corporate governance issues, largely because of their growing size and presence in equity markets – which makes it more difficult for them simply to sell their shares if they are dissatisfied with management. In addition to the Caisse, funds such as the Ontario Municipal Employee's Retirement System (OMERS), the Ontario Teachers' Pension Plan Board (Ontario Teachers), CN Investments and other large funds have gained reputations for their involvement in corporate governance issues.... [1]

If these statements are accurate, then Canadian institutional investors do indeed engage in activist pursuits. This statement also lends credence to the third explanation offered by Foerster. It would be interesting to know what were the issues involved in these institutional interventions, as well as something about their effects.

Foerster describes the screening method used by CalPERS to identify problem companies and the methods employed to induce change. He goes through an example of the screening process, using a sample of Canadian firms, to show that it can be done with Canadian data. The question Foerster does not answer, however, is what percentage of the firms identified as requiring intervention have controlling shareholders. He states that CalPERS systematically avoids firms with high levels of insider ownership. Considering that approximately 80 percent of the TSE 300 have insider ownership over 20 percent, it would be interesting to see the correlation between relative performance and the presence of a controlling shareholder. This is necessary since the presence of a controlling shareholder influences the effectiveness of CalPERS' intervention style. In fact, CalPERS' style of intervention may not even be relevant, given the ownership structure of Canadian firms.

Additionally, Foerster's use of return series that exclude dividends makes it likely that high-dividend-paying stocks will under-perform relative to the index and low-dividend-paying stocks will over-perform relative to the index. To illustrate, however, consider two stocks that have the same total return to an investor; one pays a dividend and one does not. Calculate the return excluding dividends and the performance of these firms relative to a *sans* dividend index. Even though both stocks provide the same total return, the dividend-paying stock will appear to under-perform the index. This should not be used as an example of how to rank companies.

In describing the "Canadian style", Foerster reports a reactive style that emphasizes non-public communication with management to air grievances about performance. He makes an effort to contrast this with the confrontational CalPERS style. I think the difference in style is more perceived than real. CalPERS' system is also reactive. It targets firms that have performed poorly. It then tries to alleviate the problems through private discourse with management. Only if it is rebuffed does CalPERS launch a public campaign to change managerial practices. I consider this to be very similar to the "Canadian style".

Whereas Foerster's analysis suggests that Canadian institutional investors are involved in governance issues, MacIntosh and Schwartz examine the effect of the presence of institutional shareholders on the performance of the firm. They discuss the nature of the shareholder/shareholder conflict that exists in firms with controlling shareholders. Specifically, the controlling shareholder has an incentive to monitor managers in order to maximize firm value. He also has the further incentive to redirect the flow of value to himself and away from minority shareholders. With this in mind, the presence of controlling shareholders should be positively related to accounting measures of performance, but inversely related to market measures of performance.

Their evidence is consistent with the theory that controlling shareholders help to control the manager/shareholder conflict of interest but exacerbate the shareholder/shareholder conflict of interest. The evidence on whether institutional investors affect firm value is a little more difficult to interpret. They find that institutions tend to have more ownership in firms with high accounting numbers (earnings, ROA) but an inverse relation between institutional holdings and a market measure of performance. While this is consistent with institutions monitoring managers (since institutions cannot redirect resources to themselves), both measures of performance should be positively related to the presence of institutions. Given the timing mismatch of the measures, I think the evidence is more supportive of the theory that institutions follow value-based strategies of buying stocks with high earnings-price ratios and selling stocks with low earnings-price ratios. They do, however, provide some evidence that institutions tend to control the shareholder/shareholder conflict. Nonetheless, the results of this study, as it stands, do not allow for conclusions to be drawn or for policy statements to be made.

Amoako-Adu and Smith look at the effect of the presence of outside financial directors on firm value. This research is important because it bears directly on the question of the efficacy of putting representatives of institutional investors on the board. However, in its current state the research does not separate captive from non-captive financial directors. Also, by including any holder of a block greater than 10 percent in the insider group, the authors potentially include representatives of institutional investors as insiders.[2] They conclude that their results indicate no value associated with the presence of outside financial directors or outside directors in the same line of business. These results are interesting in light of the recommendations of the Dey Committee and those contained in other studies presented in this session – that more outsiders be placed on boards. However, I cannot overemphasize the need for more compelling evidence about the effects of board composition than that presented in Amoako-Adu and Smith before policy recommendations are made.

One interesting result in the Amoako-Adu and Smith study that the authors do not make much of is the differential effect that a large control block has on ROA and Asset Turnover. Define the following.

$$ROA_i = \frac{EBIT_i}{Assets_i}$$

$$Asset\ Turnover_i = \frac{Sales_i}{Assets_i}$$

$$Costs_i = \frac{Sales_i - EBIT_i}{Assets_i} = \frac{Sales_i \, \alpha_i}{Assets_i}$$

If there were no correlation between ownership structure and cost structure, the coefficient in the ROA regression would be 0.10 multiplied by the coefficient in the asset turnover regression, since that is the average profit margin. The fact that the coefficient in the ROA regression is less than 10 percent of the coefficient in the asset turnover regression indicates a positive correlation between ownership structure and cost structures. This is consistent with controlling shareholders removing value that other shareholders cannot share.

The discussion in MacIntosh and Schwartz as well as the information contained in Foerster indicate that, despite the problems enumerated in Patry and Poitevin, institutions do become involved in corporate governance. Additionally, this involvement appears to be beneficial. The results in Amoako-Adu and Smith suggest that the reform advocated by the Dey Committee is, at best, ineffective. This begs the question, what other reforms, if any, are needed to improve corporate governance in Canada?

Given the evidence of increased activism by public pension funds, it is not clear that reform is needed. Additionally, reforms that reduce the ability of controlling shareholders to siphon off the gains from their monitoring of managers may not benefit minority shareholders. It is true that minority shareholders would now get a bigger slice of the pie; however, the pie itself may well get smaller and, if the pie does not get smaller (or larger), then the most reform(s) will do is legislate a wealth transfer. Nevertheless, since institutional investors can potentially monitor the manager/shareholder conflict, it may be beneficial to reduce the inter-shareholder conflicts. One way to achieve this is to reduce the costs of institutional involvement along with the insulation from punitive measures currently enjoyed by controlling shareholders. I will now discuss some of the reforms mentioned in the papers as well as offer some of my own thoughts on how to improve corporate governance in Canada.

Patry and Poitevin suggest mandatory fund indexation and flip taxes on capital gains. Both of these reforms would increase the cost of funds exiting, thereby increasing their incentives to use voice. Exit *is* using voice; it tells management in no uncertain terms that their practices are not acceptable. Exit strategies are already costly for Canadian institutions, given the size of their holdings and the thinness of Canadian equity markets. Besides, increasing exit costs would prove beneficial to controlling shareholders because it would force the institutions to stand still longer while their wealth is being expropriated.

Another suggestion that runs through the papers is the use of relational investing. The general idea behind relationship investing seems to be that institutions should take large stakes and then participate in "active management". However, the meaning of the term "active management" is not clear. Does it mean direct involvement in strategic decisions? Does it mean involvement in day-to-day business decisions? Recall from an earlier reference here that Patry and Poitevin indicated that investors in mutual funds would not think of telling the managers which stocks to buy. Why then should we expect a fund manager to have the ability to tell an operating manager the best way to make widgets?

In my opinion the way to achieve increased institutional activism is to reduce the costs of using voice and exit. To this end I suggest the following.

- Change the proxy solicitation rules as they apply to institutional investors to allow communication on governance issues without the cost of formal solicitation.

- Change the definition of "control person" as it now applies to institutional investors. Doing so would allow such investors to act in concert against controlling shareholders. It would also remove the need to have secondary distributions to exit, and free them from concerns of insider trading violations if they do exit.[3]

- Change the valuation technique when shareholder appraisal rights are used. There are certain actions taken by firms that are known to reduce value. Poison pills and greenmail come to mind. In cases like these, the change in value attributable to managerial action is fairly clear. In these cases, an investor should be able to put the stock back to the issuer at the pre-event price level.

- Link the pay of outside board members to the value of the non-voting shares of stock.

- Remove the foreign investment limits from the portfolios of institutional investors.

I would like to elaborate more on the last point. The size of the Canadian equity market and the inter-relatedness of the ownership of Canadian firms makes exit a questionable strategy if an investor is dissatisfied with management. The dissatisfied investor utilizing an exit strategy merely goes from Bronfman I to Bronfman II.

Additionally, one of the costs borne by a controlling shareholder for expropriating wealth from minority shareholders is a higher cost of capital. The higher cost of capital is a result of funds being diverted to uses where investors are not held up. By limiting the ability of investors to take their money out of Canada, a captive investor pool is maintained. This keeps the supply of investment capital high and prevents the cost of capital from rising to a level that reflects the amount of self-dealing engaged in by controlling shareholders. Relaxing the foreign investment criteria is similar to providing a vast pool of mutual funds to retail investors. It provides a larger market where entrepreneurs compete for funds. This, in turn, gives entrepreneurs incentives to maximize shareholder value if they want a low cost of capital.

ENDNOTES

1 Similar claims are made by MacIntosh and Schwartz. They state that Canadian institutional investors have voted against management proposals (sometimes in conjunction with other institutional investors), and have also threatened to use dissent rights and sue managements. This is also evidence that Canadian institutions are actively and visibly involved in governance issues.

2 I would also like to add that they should consider utilities separately. For one thing, utilities have an additional layer of regulatory oversight that should control agency problems. Additionally, utilities have low asset turnover and large asset bases. The authors document an association between board composition and asset turnover. Are they just picking up utilities?

3 The last point should take effect only if the institutional investor sunshine trades.

Michael S. Weisbach
College of Business and Public Administration
University of Arizona

Commentary on Part IV

Institutional Investors and the Governance of Canadian Corporations: An American Perspective

IT WAS A PLEASURE TO READ AND TO THINK ABOUT the four interesting studies on the topic of the influence of institutional investors on Canadian corporate governance, by Macintosh and Schwartz, Patry and Poitevin, Foerster, and Amoako-Adu and Smith. In doing so, I feel that I have learned a great deal about the way corporate finance is practiced here in Canada. Since it has been a long day I will try to keep my remarks brief.

My first reaction to the studies is that their tone is overly deferential to the United States. The general theme tends to be: "Such and such is done this way in the United States and we do it differently here in Canada, so what can we change?" I find this kind of amusing, because it seems that every time I go to a conference in the United States, the theme is that we are doing everything wrong and we should be copying the Japanese or the Germans.[1] When you think about what we do south of the border, you should be careful to remember that we are not quite sure if American corporate governance practices and the associated regulations make sense for us, let alone whether they should be copied by other countries.

A question that summarizes the agenda of the studies presented in this session is: "How can Canadian institutional investors be encouraged to monitor Canadian Companies better?" One important issue here is the extent to which Canadian institutions utilize the blocks of Canadian stock they currently hold. Canadian institutional investors should probably be encouraged to hold onto those blocks and to gain as much influence as they can on the governance of the corporations affected – including the possibility of obtaining a seat on the board. I would also caution against underestimating the amount of influence being exerted by institutions at this time. At least in the United States, most influence activity goes on quietly behind the scenes so it is easy to underestimate the extent to which this type of activity already occurs by concentrating on what one reads in the press.

When we think about the issue of institutional ownership, one issue that has come up repeatedly throughout this conference is the restrictions that are placed on Canadian financial institutions with respect to ownership of foreign equity. In finance theory, it is quite clear that the benefits of diversification are maximized when the set of risky assets held is the value-weighted portfolio of all the risky assets in the world. This means that since the Canadian equity market is probably (at most) one or two percent of the world's equity market, Canadian institutions should have at most one or two percent of their investments in Canadian equities. In addition, one ought to consider the human capital of the beneficiaries. Since the beneficiaries are Canadians, the value of their human capital will vary according to how well the Canadian economy is doing. Because of the positive correlation between Canadian human capital and the Canadian stock market, the optimal fraction of pension wealth that ought to be held in Canadian securities is actually lower than this one or two percent. In fact, if one were to be persistent about having some sort of foreign equity restrictions, perhaps the most sensible rule would be to *prohibit Canadian institutions* from owning any Canadian securities at all, rather than the current rule which forces them to own Canadian securities. Such a restriction would encourage financial institutions to act in the interest of their beneficiaries, providing them with the diversification they desire.

Let me briefly discuss the studies individually. The one that I found to be the most inflammatory was the paper by Foerster on CalPERS. He puts the question: "Why haven't pension funds in Canada been as visibly active as CalPERS?" I would phrase the question somewhat differently: "Why haven't pension funds anywhere been as visibly active as CalPERS?" I think the answer has something to do with the fact that highly visible activism as practiced by CalPERS is costly and does not help the beneficiaries of the fund. Foerster relies on studies by Nesbitt, which claim a 40 percent stock price improvement following CalPERS involvement. I have not seen these studies, nor have they been published in an academic journal, so it is difficult to know what to make of them. One issue that seems relevant is a growing literature documenting that stock prices tend to exhibit mean reversion over certain horizons. Therefore, if one picks *any random* group of stocks that has done extremely poorly and follows them over time, it is likely that they will have positive abnormal performance. Since CalPERS targets stocks based on their poor performance, this may be one alternative explanation for Nesbitt's findings of high subsequent performance.

A recent study by Wahal is relevant here.[2] He finds that there are small (about 1 percent) increases in the prices of a stock on the announcement of CalPERS' involvement in a company, and no long-term effects on either stock prices or accounting measures of performance. Especially with Wahal's results in mind, it seems to me that Foerster drastically overstates the effectiveness of CalPERS' monitoring on American corporations.

The Patry and Poitevin study surveys a large literature and raises a number of different issues. One of their proposals that intrigues me calls for mandatory indexing of pension fund assets. Pension fund investment policies are a puzzle to many economists for the following reason: Indexing appears to be the best way to maximize risk-adjusted returns net of expenses, yet few funds are indexed. The market apparently has not found the optimal solution. The reason why the market has not found the optimal solution is not clear, but Patry and Poitevin's explanation of moral hazard on the part of fund managers is as plausible as any I have heard.

I tend to think that this sort of regulation isn't such a bad idea. However, a potential cost associated with regulating portfolio strategies is that such regulation reduces flexibility on the part of the pension funds. Perhaps a better solution would be to allow Canadian funds to follow the example of TIAA-CREF, whose trustees and managers voluntarily decided to index a large portion of their stock portfolio.

The two remaining studies, by Macintosh and Schwartz, and Amoako-Adu and Smith, both use the methods developed by Morck, Shleifer & Vishny (1988) to measure the effect of corporate governance on firm performance. The technique is to regress an estimate of Q, the ratio of the market value of the firm's assets to the replacement cost, on variables representing the firm's governance structure. Presumably, higher Qs are representative of better operating performance, so that the empirical relations uncovered would capture the effect of alternative ownership structures on firm performance. In the case of the Macintosh and Schwartz study, the governance variables represent institutional ownership of the firm, and in the Amoako-Adu and Smith study they represent the composition of the firm's board of directors.

I think an important issue for the authors of these studies is to consider what economists call endogeneity problems. These problems arise if corporate governance structures are themselves determined by the firm's performance and not *vice versa*, as the authors (of both studies) claim. For example, institutional investors could be attracted to firms that have performed well historically and could purchase shares in these firms after a run-up in the firm's stock price. If this were true, it would imply that there would be a relation between firms with high Qs and institutional ownership, but for reasons different from those put forward by Macintosh and Schwartz. Similarly, if firms adjust their board composition in response to their performance, we would find a relation between composition and performance, but the causality would be different from that discussed by Amoako-Adu and Smith.

ENDNOTES

1 This practice did slow a bit with the collapse of the Japanese stock market several years ago.

2 This study came to my attention following the conference in Toronto at which these remarks were made; so it was not mentioned in the comments I made there. See Wahal, S., "Pension Fund Activism and Firm Performance," Unpublished Ph.D. Dissertation, Kenan-Flagler Business School, University of North Carolina, Chapel Hill, NC,1995.

Part V   *International Aspects of*
         Corporate Governance

Randall Morck   *&*   Bernard Yeung
Faculty of Business   School of Business Administration
University of Alberta   University of Michigan

12

The Corporate Governance of Multinationals

INTRODUCTION

G LOBALIZATION IS A RESULT OF AN INCREASING NEED for companies to gain access to larger markets in order to recoup the costs associated with the increased pace of innovation in many industries. This study argues that globalization and multinational firms are likely to be even more important to Canada's competitive position in coming years than they have been in the past. This global competitive pressure may render moot many of the contemporary public policy concerns about corporate governance. In a global economy, customers, investment capital and highly skilled employees need not tolerate poor management; they can simply do business with better-run rivals. Canadian firms must deal with their governance problems not because they are legally required to do so, but because their survival will depend on it. In this context, government's best option for improving Canadian corporate governance may well be to foster competition and openness while providing good legal and educational infrastructure. This entails weaning firms from subsidies and captive markets, and providing sound basic public services like education, health care and law. Some specific issues as to the governance of multinational subsidiaries in Canada do arise, especially with regard to minority Canadian shareholders. We advocate tighter disclosure requirements to increase transparency, and also argue that the boards of foreign subsidiaries with Canadian minority public shareholders should have *conduct committees* charged with approving non-arm's-length transactions with the parent or other related companies. Indeed, requiring this of all firms with controlling blockholders and publicly traded minority shares might solve many of Canada's corporate governance problems in one stroke. Before we can formulate suggestions about corporate governance in multinationals, we must make clear why multinational firms are important and how they are different from purely domestic firms.

Multinationals have always been an important source of capital for Canada. As of 1990, there was $108 billion worth of foreign direct investment in Canada, or 6.6 percent of the world's total stock.[1] In 1987, foreign owned subsidiaries accounted for 64.8 percent of total manufacturing sales, 75.4 percent of manufacturing exports and, in 1985-88, 88.3 percent of manufacturing imports (Corvari et al., 1993). The flow of new foreign direct investment into Canada has averaged about $10 billion per year in recent years, mostly from the United States. (Knubley et al., 1994).

Canada's public policy toward inward foreign direct investment has thus been central to its relations with the United States. In the 1960s and early 1970s cool relations with Washington and popular fears of U.S. domination led to the establishment of the Foreign Investment Review Agency (FIRA) in 1974. FIRA was allegedly designed to ensure that inward foreign direct investment brought significant benefits to Canada. Similar emotions brought about the National Energy Program (NEP), a system of partial expropriation of foreign investments in the energy sector.

In 1985 the conservative election victory brought about a sharp change in policy. The NEP was eliminated. FIRA was recast into Investment Canada and given the mandate of *attracting* new foreign direct investment to Canada. The 1989 Canada-U.S. Free Trade Agreement (FTA) and the subsequent North American Free Trade Agreement (NAFTA) further opened the Canadian economy, although both provided special status for specific industries, most notably the so-called "cultural" industries. Investment Canada was made part of the Department of Industry in 1993, and ceased to exist as an independent agency in 1994.

Economic policies in the twentieth century have been products of political ideology, popular opinion and economic realism. Political ideology seems a spent force, and popular opinion seems increasingly aligned with economic realism. The growing realization that governments are not monopolies, but are in competition for footloose investment by global businesses reflects this. One effect is the on-going development of free trade and regional investment blocs which is resulting in the multilateral trade and investment liberalization envisioned in the Uruguay Round of the General Agreement on Tariffs and Trade (GATT) and the new World Trade Organization (WTO). Given this so-called "GATTization" of our economy, what policy should Canada adopt toward foreign-owned subsidiaries in the remaining years of this century and beyond?

It is difficult to over-emphasize the importance to Canada of the globalization of business. Rapid advances in information and communications technology and the economic liberalization of entire regions of the globe like China, Eastern Europe, and (it is hoped) Latin America have been accompanied by an explosive growth in foreign direct investment. Business success often depends on globally integrated marketing, production, research and development, and human resources management. The increased competition due to globalization has brought about substantial improvements in management skills and in the way business is conducted in many countries. This free flow of ideas means that firms now strive to learn from the best of their rivals all over the world. Constant innovation is a requirement for survival. Multinational enterprises are a conduit of this globalization phenomenon. They are vital for prosperity and yet they are ruthless enforcers of the "survival of the fittest".

Canada's policy toward foreign-owned subsidiaries in the new economic order must be informed by an understanding of the economics of multi-national firms. In the next section of this study, we explore the following issues: Why do multinationals come to attain a competitive advantage over uninational firms? How has the behaviour of subsidiaries changed over time? What effect does foreign direct investment have on a host economy? We then explore how the international environment for foreign direct investment is changing. Finally, we present our views on the policy challenge and make some suggestions.

OUR THEORETICAL AND EMPIRICAL UNDERSTANDING OF MULTINATIONAL FIRMS

WHY FIRMS ESTABLISH FOREIGN SUBSIDIARIES

INTERNATIONAL OPERATIONS ARE NOT SIMPLE TO RUN. when a company enters a new environment, it must start from scratch to build up an understanding of the local culture, legal system, regulatory environment, and the business environment in general. Moreover, doing business is more than just building a factory or a marketing outlet, it involves making local contacts, hiring correctly in the local labour and management markets, building up a good working relationship with suppliers, distributors, and transportation service companies, as well as with the local government. These considerations suggest that foreign entrants have an information disadvantage relative to indigenous firms. In the business literature, the assumption is often referred to as the "home-court" advantage of local firms. For example, foreign entrants may often have to pay a premium in hiring local workers. They may make costly mistakes in building up working relationships with local suppliers and distributors. The question is: Why, given all these difficulties, would foreign entrants be interested in establishing overseas operations in the first place, and what allows them to overcome their local rivals' home-court advantage?

Practitioners offer several answers: access to inexpensive raw materials and/or labour; access to markets, for example by jumping trade barriers; strategic response to a competitors' presence; improved flexibility in production or marketing; access to business intelligence, like the development of the latest products, production techniques, marketing ideas, etc.; and reducing taxes by shifting income to subsidiaries in countries with low tax rates.

Since all these ideas seem *prima facia* legitimate, researchers have sought to understand more precisely what creates the synergies in a multinational network of affiliates. Does a multinational structure, in itself, create enough value to overcome local firms' home-court advantage, or is there a deeper economic reason for the survival of multinationals?

Recent research suggests that the intrinsic value of a multinational structure stems from the *internalization* of markets for a company's intangible assets; and that the above reasons are all tactics to achieve this. Intangible assets are *information-based*. They include innovative production techniques, new marketing skills, brand names, company images, company-based management skills, and new organization routines. In short, they are innovations that bestow a competitive advantage or "edge" to the firm.

Because such intangible assets are information-based, expanding the scale or scope of their application adds few costs and does not deplete the intangible assets, but greatly increases the return on their up-front development costs. The firm should thus try to take advantage of its edge to as great an extent as possible in order to gain the most from its innovation.

It is difficult to sell another firm the rights to use an information-based asset. For example, a buyer might reasonably demand information about a new marketing technique before paying for it; but once the buyer has the information, there is no further need to pay for it, since the buyer already has everything he needs. Patents and copyrights mitigate these problems to some extent, but not completely. Licensing a new technology to a foreign firm may create a vigorous future competitor.

To employ its innovative edge to the greatest extent possible while preserving exclusive control requires that the firm itself expand. In the international context, this means foreign direct investment. This is what is meant by internalizing the market for these information-based intangible assets.

Morck & Yeung (1991) examine the relationship between firm value and multinational structure. Their purpose is to discover whether a multinational structure indeed enhances firm value, and to uncover the source of any changes in firm value.[2] They find that a multinational structure is correlated with enhanced firm value to the extent of about 8¢ per dollar of total physical assets. Without intangible assets, a multinational structure either has no effect on firm value, or decreases it. More importantly, Morck & Yeung find that this increase in firm value is strongly correlated with a firm's past R&D or advertising spending. Without intangible assets, a multinational structure either has no effect at all or a decreased effect on firm value. This implies that information-based intangible assets are required for a multinational structure to add value, and that without them a multinational structure is a potential liability. Morck & Yeung (1992) find that announcing the acquisition of a foreign firm adds an average of 2 percent to the total value of a U.S. firm. This positive stock price reaction is also restricted to firms with probable intangible assets.[3] The announcement of a foreign acquisition by a U.S. firm without intangible assets either does not change or decreases its value. This indicates that expanded multinational structure causes the increased firm value in the presence of intangibles, but without intangibles expanded multinational structure destroys firm value. It also shows that, in firms with intangibles, foreign acquisitions cause the value increase and not the converse. Additional studies show that, on average, multinational firms have a much higher propensity to invest in intangibles than purely domestic firms.

Upon reflection, it is apparent that the reasons cited by practitioners derive from increasing the scale of a firm's edge. A firm with such an innovative edge can afford to enter difficult markets and source raw materials in ways that would be unprofitable for other firms. Flexibility, strategic moves, and obtaining intelligence are all long-term investments that a competitive edge makes possible. Income shifting is most useful when a firm has extra income to shift, and because the increasing sophistication of the tax authorities is making transfer pricing more difficult, intra-firm transactions involving intangibles are becoming the income shifting method of choice (Harris et al., 1993).

In short, from a firm's point of view, international expansion is fundamentally a way to expand the scale and scope of application of its intangible competitive edge. International expansion is not an end in itself; rather, it is a means to combine firm-specific assets with local assets and thereby enhance profits.

Furthermore, both for Canadian firms going abroad and for foreign parents establishing subsidiaries in Canada, a multinational structure demands continuous investment in new intangibles. Intangibles are not everlasting. Like physical assets, they depreciate and become obsolete. They need continuous replacement and replenishment by on-going R&D, new marketing initiatives, new organizational structures, etc. If a firm allows its intangibles to become obsolete, it loses the edge that helped it overcome local firms' home-court advantage. Its multinational structure then becomes a liability.

Innovation is thus both more profitable and more essential for a multinational than for a uninational firm. It is more profitable because a multinational structure lets a firm use its innovations on a larger scale and scope, and thereby more readily recover its up-front costs. It is more essential because a multinational structure becomes a liability when a firm lacks intangible information-based assets. Constant innovation is required for a multinational to maintain an edge.[4]

From a policy point of view, foreign direct investment enhances the productivity of the local economy because of the intangibles it brings along. Furthermore, from an efficiency point of view, an economy with an open competition policy should have little fear of foreign multinationals exploiting its local factor inputs. A foreign subsidiary can overcome the home-court advantage of indigenous firms only because its intangibles make local inputs more productive in its hands, and thus allow it to outbid competing potential employers.

THE BEHAVIOUR OF SUBSIDIARIES OVER TIME

ALTHOUGH AN EDGE DUE TO INTANGIBLE ASSETS can overcome the home-court advantage of domestic firms, international expansion is risky (Mitchell et al.,

1992) and many subsidiaries fail early (Newbould *et al.*, 1978; Evans *et al.* 1991). Unfortunately, the literature does not compare the exit or failure rates of foreign-owned subsidiaries with those of domestic firms. It is therefore not clear how to interpret the reported considerable failure and exit rates of foreign-owned subsidiaries. Specific case studies reveal reasons such as inability to adapt to the local business environment, insufficient expertise in running foreign operations, and insufficient benefits to the parent firm from the subsidiary.[5] It is comforting to know that parents do fold up failed operations. Overall, these reasons are consistent with multinationals (whose intangibles are insufficient to offset the home-court advantage of domestic firms) being forced to retreat.

Surviving foreign operations appear to increase their involvement in the host country's economy over time. Aharoni (1966) documents a gradual increased in local involvement from exporting to licensing to the establishment of a fully fledged subsidiary. Teece (1985) argues that American and British firms' offshore operations develop from sales branches into contractual production and ultimately into foreign direct investment as the firms gradually accumulate more information about the offshore market. Shaver (1994) finds that, of the 354 foreign acquisitions or greenfield construction of new production plants by foreign firms in the U.S. manufacturing sector in 1987 recorded by the U.S. Department of Commerce (International Trade Administration), 205 (or fully 58 percent) were by foreign firms that already had a presence in the United States. Moreover, 107 (or 30 percent) were by foreign firms already present in the United States in the same industry. In short, a substantial portion of foreign direct investment is by multinationals that are already committed to the host country.

Such a sequential approach makes sense. With so many disadvantages on domestic firms' home turf, the foreign entrant moves cautiously; perhaps it begins by exporting into the market. This allows management to accumulate information about the host economy and about whether the firm's competitive advantages can outweigh the home-court advantage of local firms. If the host economy looks promising enough, the foreign entrant commits more resources. If the host country's home-court advantage is too formidable – for example, if strong political connections are needed for business success – the foreign entrant retreats.

A result of this sequential approach is that multinationals gradually increase their involvement in a host country that provides a favourable investment climate. A hospitable environment entices the multinational to expand and deepens the synergies between its intangibles and local economic resources. In doing this, multinationals serve the local economy as a conduit to global markets, a source of information and innovations, a stimulant of new business opportunities, and a source of competitive pressure.

THE IMPORTANCE OF MULTINATIONALS FOR CANADA

BECAUSE OF THE POLITICAL CONTROVERSY SURROUNDING IT, the economic effects of multinationals on the economies of their host countries deserves special attention. The traditional approach to understanding the effect of foreign direct investment on an economy is to model it in terms of capital migration and analyze it using the traditional tools of international trade theory. This may not be the most useful approach. Canada is a small open economy; changes in its factor endowments due to capital migration are unlikely to change the prices of its products and thus its terms of trade. With no change in prices, classical static trade theory, which links factor returns to product prices, predicts no change in factor return.[6]

Public debate about foreign direct investment often turns to the issue of job creation. If there is genuine involuntary unemployment, an injection of investment can indeed create jobs in the short run, and that is important. However, such market disequilibrium is usually temporary, and therefore should not be the paramount consideration in determining a long-term public policy strategy. Distortions in national or regional labour markets that cause sustained unemployment often reflect poor macroeconomic or regional economic policies. These problems should be dealt with directly. Various federal and provincial policies have decreased the cost to a worker of being unemployed and have therefore raised Canada's *natural unemployment rate*: the level of unemployment in a healthy economy due to workers taking their time searching for the best job.

Under these circumstances, the criterion for "desirable" foreign direct investment is not more jobs, but better jobs. The creation of better-paying jobs can only be based on a potential employer's ability to make Canadian workers more productive. In general terms, "desirable" foreign direct investment must make Canadian capital, labour, and material inputs more productive.

Does foreign direct investment make Canadian inputs more productive? Empirical research generally produces an affirmative answer.[7] Globerman (1979) shows that labour productivity in Canadian production plants is positively related to the degree of foreign ownership in an industry. Corvari *et al.* (1993) conclude that foreign-controlled plants are usually more productive than domestically owned plants and that the former have, in particular, a higher level of labour productivity.[8]

Why is foreign direct investment positively correlated with productivity? We can point to several reasons. First, successful multinationals possess intangible assets. Their more innovative production, marketing and managerial skills let them use other inputs, such as labour, more productively.

Second, multinational firms are a conduit through which local labour, capital and raw materials become a part of the world economy. For example, multinational software firms employ Indian programmers to develop products that will eventually be marketed in the West. In the absence of multinationals, these skilled Indian workers would probably not be able to find comparably attractive employment in India. Also, local firms that establish business relationships with multinationals become indirectly linked to global markets. Doing business with a multinational may allow a local firm to supply overseas markets that would otherwise be too costly to access. This indirect access to broader markets greatly expands the scope of opportunities available in the local economy.

Third, multinationals serve as information gathering and processing machines. Through their presence in multiple markets they collect and, where possible, exploit information from all over the world about new production techniques, new market opportunities, or changed business conditions. They are uniquely able to create global synergies, that is, they gain edges in one market by applying information they gather elsewhere. For local firms, this aspect of multinationals is a two-edged sword. The spillover of new techniques and information, as well as the indirect access to global markets a multinational provides, benefit local firms and workers by helping them increase their productivity beyond what might otherwise be possible. But at the same time, because the multinational is constantly searching for newer, better ways to do business, local firms are under constant competitive pressure. Doing business with a multinational forces local firms to invest more in innovation and productivity enhancement than they might otherwise do.

Indeed, because of their information-based intangible assets and global connections multinational enterprises stimulate improved local production, marketing, and management. Clark et al. (1987) argue that Japanese transplants in the United States served both as stimulants of and conduits for the transfer of skills to the lagging U.S. auto-industry's productivity. Eden (1994) argues that multinationals serve as agents of change in the Canadian economy.

Fourth, multinationals stimulate competition. In a small closed economy, optimal economies of scale may lead to a small number of local firms in each industry, and a consequent tendency toward oligopolistic pricing. Foreign entrants can increase the number of competitors and thus make collusion more difficult. The dynamic implications of this are especially important. Collusion reduces the need for firms to maintain a level of innovation and may result in an industry sliding into a cosy stagnation. By breaking entry barriers and competing for business, foreign entrants force entrenched firms to be more innovative and productive, or to lose business. Poor corporate governance of local firms becomes more obvious and more dangerous in the presence of multinational competitors.

Also, because their market power is weakened by this increased competition, entrenched local firms are less able to exploit their suppliers, investors, workers or customers. They must pay workers, investors and suppliers factor prices that are closer to marginal values. They must also charge their buyers reduced prices that are closer to marginal costs. Generally, there should be an improvement in overall economic efficiency.[9]

This increase in competition certainly displaces some workers, especially in old and marginal firms. While not painless, however, this displacement is valuable. Improving economic efficiency usually involves replacing low-productivity jobs with high-productivity jobs, and replacing stagnant firms with innovative ones.

In summary, foreign direct investment increases host-country productivity *via* an immediate transfer of information-based intangible assets. However, this is a one-shot static improvement. More important, foreign direct investment provides continuous conduits to global markets for the local economy, ongoing transfers of information and innovations to the local economy, and sustained pressures on local firms to innovate and increase their productivity. These dynamic pressures lead to an increased level of Schumpeterian creative destruction, and therefore a higher long-run growth rate for the economy.

THE CHANGING ENVIRONMENT FOR MULTINATIONALS

THE ENVIRONMENT IN WHICH FOREIGN DIRECT INVESTMENT takes place is changing rapidly. The most visible changes are the development of NAFTA, the European Community (EC), the Asia Pacific Economic Cooperation organization (APEC), and the new World Trade Organization (WTO), established in the Uruguay Round of GATT. Less visible, but perhaps more important, is a rapid evolution in the way business is done – popularly described as "globalization".

DECLINING TRADE AND INVESTMENT BARRIERS

REDUCED TRADE BARRIERS SHOULD LEAD TO AN INCREASE in foreign direct investment that achieves synergies between multinationals' information-based intangible assets and the assets of host countries. They should also reduce foreign direct investment aimed at jumping trade barriers.

The Uruguay Round of GATT produced the World Trade Organization along with promises of general tariff cuts, reductions in subsidies on agricultural products, the "tariffication" of non-tariff barriers, the elimination of voluntary export restraints, and the phasing out of the Multifiber Agreement. The rules on safeguards, anti-dumping actions and subsidies are to be reviewed. The effectiveness of these changes is in question because the long phase-in periods will greatly delay most of the changes, especially for developing countries.

The Trade Related Investment Measures component of the WTO directly affects foreign direct investment. It prohibits WTO member-countries from imposing local content requirements, trade balance requirements, or foreign exchange balance requirements. In the past, these measures have constrained trade in motor vehicles, chemicals, pharmaceuticals and high-tech products. Unacceptable requirements must be eliminated within two years by developed countries, within five years for most developing countries and within seven years for the least developed countries. The Uruguay Round Agreements also strengthen intellectual property rights and include a General Agreement on Trade in Services. Major features in the latter are national treatment and a most-favoured-nation clause, as well as a framework for further negotiation on the liberalization of trade in services.

The full effect of this shift is not yet clear. What is clear, however, is that despite the success of the Uruguay Round, significantly freer international trade and investment are neither imminent nor assured. Indeed, the ingenuity of protectionists in devising new trade and investment barriers should not be underestimated; they have repeatedly undermined the liberalization efforts of previous GATT rounds. One major insight in the trade literature is the equivalent of domestic tax and subsidy policies to trade barriers. For example, a tariff is equivalent to a consumption tax plus a production subsidy. In the WTO agreement, research subsidies and regional development subsidies are permitted. Complex and "progressive" tax codes can be rigged to affect different firms or industries in different ways. For example, a progressive corporate income tax is essentially a tax on highly productive firms. Tax codes can discriminate against foreign ownership and can punish the import of foreign inputs (Slemrod, 1995). The opportunity for hidden trade barriers clearly remains.

Therefore, despite the Uruguay Round, economic regionalism will certainly continue to affect trade and investment. This means that direct and secure access to regional free trade and investment blocs *via* wholly owned subsidiaries will remain attractive to many businesses. Many companies have established European subsidiaries to gain access to the European Community's market. Similarly, foreign firms have come to understand that secure access to North American markets is best assured by direct investment in North America.

NAFTA creates a rigorously non-discriminatory investment environment within North America. It requires all signing countries to treat investors from other NAFTA countries no worse than domestic investors or any other foreign investors from NAFTA countries or elsewhere. Performance requirements for investments are either eliminated or phased out. Restrictions on capital movement, like payments and profit remittances, are banned except for balance of payments reasons. Expropriation is outlawed unless enacted under ordinary domestic law. Broadly speaking, NAFTA has put competition for investment between the United States, Canada and Mexico on purely economic terms.

THE GLOBALIZATION OF BUSINESS

ADVANCES IN COMMUNICATIONS TECHNOLOGY and improved transportation efficiency allow companies to scatter their production and other value-chain activities throughout the world. Some companies, General Electric for example, actually pull intercontinental teams together to design and engineer products without ever needing to put them under the same roof. Some companies are able to manufacture a product by shipping components from Hong Kong to Panama. Better inventory control techniques, systems management and the like allow companies to work with affiliates and other supporting companies around the world.

Improvements in organization and related management techniques have been made possible by these developments and made necessary by intensified global competition. For example, companies now farm out activities to specialists, thus improving overall efficiency and productivity. The North American auto-assembly industry has gone through a well-publicized slimming down to "lean" production techniques. These firms now produce a much smaller number of parts than previously, and internal and external units have learned how to collaborate and cooperate. Ford and Chrysler are now able to form new-car design teams that include people who are not employees and even people who are not in North America. Many previously hierarchical companies, such as Xerox and AT&T, are now engaged in so-called "lateral blending".

These developments have several implications. First, companies are now more focused in their development of core competencies (Prahalad & Hamel, 1990). During the 1980s, overtly integrated conglomerates were shown to be inefficient organizations. Unrelated integration and expansion were viewed unfavourably by financial markets (Morck et al., 1990) and were seen by many observers as signs of managerial agency problems. Less cross-industry diversification means that companies are now more agile and alert for changes in the markets upon which they are focused. Second, the scale of plants and companies is substantially reduced.[10] Large massive and integrated plants are rarer than in the past. Smaller physical facilities with more flexible product design and mix possibilities are seen as preferable. Changes in product design need not await the development of mass consumption, nor do they require the high adjustment costs typical in large plants. At the same time, because smaller facilities are easier to establish and dispose of, exit and entry are becoming more prevalent. Third, companies are now competing in groups rather than alone. For example, Nike and Addidas each have an associated group of suppliers and shippers, and it is these two networks of firms that compete.[11]

Multinationals must excel at developing information-based intangible assets, the innovative edges upon which their survival and success depend. For example, multinational pharmaceuticals companies compete to amass and blend their R&D capabilities globally, and take advantage of whatever tax, regulation, and labour-cost advantages various host countries offer. Retailers, like Benetton and Toys' R Us, apply much of their competitive effort to being cost effective and consumer conscious, developing improved inventory systems, better marketing flexibility, and more efficient co-ordination among their suppliers. Motorola is an example of a high-tech multinational that relies on its technological capability and its ability to manage its work force to produce new high-quality products faster and better than anyone else.

In this environment, multinationals become extremely sensitive to all of the factors that affect productivity. Besides managing internal operations and strategy, foreign subsidiaries also serve as team leaders, creating productivity and synergies between themselves and local support firms. In this context, they demand a pool of qualified local managers, a highly efficient local workforce, and very competitive local support firms. It is in the provision of these that the United States and Canada are really competing for foreign investment.

Multinationals and Canadian Corporate Governance

THIS SECTION CONSIDERS CANADA'S PUBLIC POLICY OPTIONS for dealing with foreign multinationals. We first examine some specific issues that arise in the governance of foreign-controlled subsidiaries. We then turn to public policy on corporate governance in general and examine how it should reflect what we know about globalization and the increasing importance of multinational business.

Unique Corporate Governance Problems in Multinationals' Subsidiaries

REVENUE CANADA AND OTHER TAX AUTHORITIES around the world have long been concerned about a practice of many multinationals that economists call *income shifting* or *transfer pricing*. Harris *et al.* (1991), Grubert & Mutti (1991), and Hines & Rice (1994) all present evidence that U.S. multinationals shift taxable income from subsidiaries in high-tax countries to low-tax countries. They do this by setting artificial prices for patents, copyrights, insurance, assets being transferred to or from subsidiaries, and services provided to or by the subsidiary; and by having highly taxed subsidiaries issue a disproportionate amount of the firm's debt.

While tax authorities have succeeded in limiting blatant income shifting, they are unlikely to eliminate many of the more subtle practices. These often involve the transfer of intangibles such as patents, copyrights, insurance services, etc. for which no clear benchmark prices exist. Aggressive taxation of multinationals is likely to drive profits to other subsidiaries and may thus actually reduce tax revenues.

Income shifting is a manifestation of a deeper issue that also affects many domestic firms in Canada: non-arm's-length transactions among affiliated corporations. If multinationals shift income out of their Canadian subsidiaries, the value of the subsidiary's Canadian minority shares is depressed. This is essentially the same problem as a purely domestic Canadian conglomerate shifting income from a subsidiary with public shares to one that is entirely owned by insiders, thus depressing the value of the first subsidiary's public shares. When Canadian shareholders buy into greenfield expansions or existing controlled subsidiaries of multinationals or other conglomerates, they arguably know what they are getting into. However, where a multinational or conglomerate acquires control of a previously independent Canadian company, there is a serious likelihood that remaining public shareholders may be harmed by subsequent non-arm's-length transactions. This is a fundamental problem in an economy characterized by closely held conglomerates and multinational subsidiaries, but it is also a general issue that Canadian corporate governance rules must address.

Moreover, there is a conflict of interest for corporate directors, especially those appointed by the controlling shareholder, who must decide which comes first, their duty to the firm as a whole to help it avoid unnecessary taxes, or their duty to Canadian shareholders of the subsidiary to maximize the value of their shares. In foreign-controlled subsidiaries, most directors are appointed by the parent company's top management. Frequently, these directors hold jobs in the parent firm. Their careers are not likely to be helped by challenging head-office decisions.

Requiring multinationals to appoint Canadian citizens to serve on the board of their Canadian subsidiaries is unlikely to solve this problem. In general, multinationals appoint top executives of the subsidiary to its board to fulfill this requirement. These Canadian executives are therefore unlikely to criticize overtly head-office decisions for fear of damaging their careers in the firm.

One option is to require that these Canadian directors also be outsiders. But they must then be totally free of any commercial links with the firm. Replacing Canadian executives with partners of the Canadian law firm that handles the multinational's Canadian business is not likely to lead to a more independent board. Still, unless independent directors form a majority on the board, they may well be unable to block non-arm's-length transactions with the parent or other subsidiaries that may harm Canadian minority shareholders. Moreover, foreign multinationals are likely to see a requirement for a majority of independent Canadian directors as overly onerous.

A reasonable compromise might be to require the boards of subsidiaries with minority public shares to have *conduct committees*. Such committees could have a majority of independent Canadian directors, and could be required to approve all transactions with related companies. Directors on the conduct committee would be specifically charged to protect the subsidiary's minority shareholders. At the same time, these directors would be helping Revenue Canada enforce its transfer-pricing tax rules.

However, conduct committees would be objectionable if they were required only of foreign-controlled subsidiaries, especially under the NAFTA agreement which requires equal treatment of both domestic and foreign-owned firms. As we have argued, the problem of minority public shareholders being harmed by non-arm's-length transactions is a general issue in Canadian corporate governance. It is a concern in conglomerates and closely held firms in general, not just in foreign-controlled subsidiaries. Perhaps there might be a general requirement that all firms with a controlling or dominant shareholder have a conduct committee charged with protecting public shareholders from non-arm's-length transactions. Foreign subsidiaries would, of course, be included.

An alternative policy might take a two-pronged approach: improve disclosure about non-arm's-length transactions by subsidiaries and other controlled firms, and make it easier for shareholders to sue controlling shareholders who engage in such transactions. Improved disclosure could take the form of federal rules similar to Ontario's section 9.1 rules which require that publicly traded firms must disclose details of all non-arm's-length transactions. Small shareholders might then be allowed the option of class action suits against controlling shareholders who abuse their positions. A policy combining these requirements could be as effective as the conduct committee.

The general problem is non-arm's-length transactions, and the solution as we see it is some combination of greater empowerment for shareholders and greater transparency for complex corporations. The introduction of conduct committees is a solution that leans toward empowerment; disclosure rules like those in Ontario's section 9.1 lean toward greater transparency. In our opinion, it would not be unreasonable to require large, complex controlled firms with public shareholders to have both conduct committees and disclosure of non-arm's-length transactions.

An alternative policy might be to require multinationals to buy all the shares of Canadian corporations they acquire, so there are no minority shareholders to protect. While this neatly solves the corporate governance problem, it does nothing to help Revenue Canada. Moreover, it restricts access to Canadian equity markets by foreign firms. Unless similar rules were put in place for domestic conglomerates, the legal status under NAFTA of such a requirement is dubious. Furthermore, multinationals with Canadian minority shareholders must produce separate annual reports, proxies, etc. for their Canadian subsidiaries. This makes multinationals' Canadian operations considerably more transparent than they would otherwise be. These broader legal and public-policy issues tip the balance toward conduct committees or greater transparency as solutions to corporate governance concerns about foreign-controlled subsidiaries.

GLOBALIZATION, MULTINATIONALS, AND CANADIAN PUBLIC POLICY ON CORPORATE GOVERNANCE

IN HIS 1942 BOOK *Capitalism, Socialism and Democracy*, Joseph Schumpeter first described the process of continuous productivity growth we have outlined above, calling it "creative destruction" – if firms do not constantly create new ideas, they are destroyed. There is increasing agreement among mainstream economists that this process underlies the success of the capitalist democracies. In our view, the ultimate effect of the worldwide reductions in trade barriers and the globalization of business described above is to make the world more Schumpeterian: more than ever before, firms must innovate in order to survive.

This has direct implications for the corporate governance debate. Indeed it may render most concerns about poor corporate governance moot within a few years. When the economy is changing rapidly, when competitors from previously remote parts of the world are entering Canadian markets, and when Canadian firms must sell to foreign markets to pay for their own increased costs of innovation, poor corporate governance is untenable. Canadian firms must quickly find real solutions to their corporate governance problems or they will fail.

The government has a critical role to play in the new economy, a role that is quite different from its traditional part. The central theme that underlies this new role for the government is that, to help Canadian firms compete abroad, the Canadian economy must be as efficient as possible at home. An efficient economy both attracts foreign investment that brings with it new ideas, and encourages local firms to innovate and grow, which makes our economy even more efficient – a positive spiral of growth. In contrast, an inefficient economy fails to attract foreign investment and thus misses out on new developments that could increase its efficiency – a negative spiral of stagnation described by Murphy et al. (1991, 1993).

The fundamental long-term goal, from which improved corporate governance will result and which it will promote, is an efficient, innovative, and internationally competitive economy. In the new global economy, multinational subsidiaries will come here if Canada has an efficient economy, but they are neither a means nor an end in the master game plan.

In our opinion there are three broad philosophical principles that Canadian policy makers should bear in mind as they consider different options for improving Canadian corporate governance.

First, (as we argue above) if the world is becoming more Schumpeterian, Canada probably needs foreign multinationals more than they need Canada, especially in the NAFTA era. Rules about the governance of multinational subsidiaries should not be so onerous as to compromise the attractiveness of the Canadian economy to foreign investors and thereby limit Canada's long-term prospects for productivity growth.

Second, public policy must aim at providing a stable environment with as few economic pitfalls as possible. Transparency and predictability are important. Uncertainties and frequent sharp changes in regulations and laws drive out existing investment and discourage future investment. They make corporate governance more difficult than necessary.

Third, the role of government outlined in the 1995 federal budget is to provide public goods that the people want and that private industry cannot provide as efficiently. In the new economy, government must be especially resistant to lobbying by special interest groups for government subsidies or other favours. If firms find that investing in lobbying government is more profitable than investing in new technology, corporate governance becomes perverted. The best lobbyists may serve their shareholders well, but they are hardly advancing the national interest.

Given these three overarching philosophical considerations, we can formulate some specific actions that government ought to take and others that it ought not to take in regard to corporate governance and multinational firms. We turn first to the list of actions *not* to take.

First, domestic firms should not be given preferential access to natural resources, subsidies, special preference in submitting bids for government contracts or other advantages over multinationals. Protectionism and favouritism of domestic firms hurt a country's competitiveness and frustrate innovation (Lenway *et al.*, 1995). Such policies shelter Canadian companies from the full force of international competition and thereby allow them greater leeway to survive despite poor corporate governance.

Second, foreign firms should not be restricted on the grounds that such restriction would give Canadian firms more freedom to become competitive and innovative. Substantial empirical evidence backs the contrary view, that the presence of foreign firms increases competitive pressures and fosters innovation (Caves, 1974; Globerman 1979; Blomström, 1989; and Chung *et al.* 1994). Creative destruction means that poorly governed firms fail, and some of them are going to be domestic firms.

Third, the government should not try to pick winning firms or industries. New research indicates that the often-repeated stories about the success of Japanese industrial policy are probably fables inspired by the political interests of the Liberal Democratic Party. Beason & Weinstein (1994) show that the Japanese government directed subsidies mainly at losers, not winners, and that Japanese government assistance either had no effect or a negative effect on industry productivity. An industrial policy of subsidizing "expected winners" encourages managers concerned about maximizing share value to invest in lobbying government for subsidies. If investing in lobbying is more lucrative than investing in R&D, the social value of good corporate governance is subverted.

Fourth, requirements that multinationals place more Canadians on the boards of their subsidiaries in Canada are not advisable. From time to time popular writers and commentators allege that multinationals do not promote foreign host-country managers to senior positions, underpay locals, do not invest enough in increasing productivity in their foreign subsidiaries, etc. While this sort of behaviour may have occurred in the past, in our opinion it is less likely to occur in the future. Multinationals cannot afford to tolerate less than optimal productivity. Underinvestment, passing over qualified candidates for senior positions, and underpaying workers are simply not viable options in the highly competitive global economy that is now emerging. Stiff competition makes discrimination very expensive.

In general terms, government policy should not be based on the assumption that multinationals view their Canadian subsidiaries as second-class affiliates.

Under adversity, multinationals do retreat from foreign markets and strive to retain their home-country operations. But this is more a reflection of open global competition (multinationals go where productivity is high and costs of production are low) and the fact that the home-court advantage held by domestic firms makes overseas subsidiaries vulnerable. Pullouts by multinationals are likely to reflect higher costs, deteriorating economic conditions, etc. in the host country and they should be viewed as the economic equivalent of the canary falling silent in the mine shaft. They are a signal that something is wrong. Accusations about the fickle nature of multinationals mask the real issue.

Fifth, corporate governance rules should not be used as social policy tools. Trying to shift social policy costs through, for example, director liability for back wages, simply decreases the attractiveness of doing business in Canada and thereby adds to our long-term problems. Globalization has exposed fundamental weaknesses in Canada's social programs, but it did not cause them. Canada is in a fiscal crisis because government revenues have consistently fallen short of spending commitments. The long-run solution is higher overall productivity so that our social programs are sustainable as a smaller fraction of a larger economy. Exposing the Canadian economy to international competitive pressures to innovate is critical to raising productivity.

Sixth, legislation forcing multinationals to locate head-office activities like corporate finance, strategic planning, R&D, marketing strategy, and organization planning in Canada would be unwarranted interference in corporate governance.

Multinationals are likely to keep activities that are vital to their competitiveness in the safest economic environment – usually the home country. For example, Honda is famous for its engine and power train and the company keeps production of these elements in Japan as much as possible. In short, companies are keeping jobs most directly related to the establishment and possession rights of their intangible edges at home. These jobs probably do involve the highest return from both private and societal standpoints – that is, the so-called "spillovers" these activities generate – in that innovative activity attracts more innovative activity. For example, new computer companies are most likely to be able to recruit the professionals they need if they locate near established computer companies. Keeping the "goodies at home" is a sensible economic decision. Maintaining possession of the innovative edges that make their multinational structures profitable is vital to these firms' prosperity and survival. There is no reason to think these companies are the slightest bit concerned with scheming to oppress foreigners.

However, globalization means that multinationals are fast losing allegiance to their home countries. The economies of scale in centralizing head-office activities can be achieved elsewhere too. Why, then, do multinationals keep the most critical of their activities in their historical home countries? We believe there are three key reasons. First, their home countries provide a pool of professionals that is at least as good as the alternatives available in other countries, and who are more familiar with the managerial and social culture of the headquarters environment. Second, their home countries have legal and economic systems that protect and foster the sorts of innovative intangible assets multinationals need. Third, there is the intangible that economists refer to as "path dependence" and others call "history".

These points require some clarification. The continual development of new information-based intangible assets gives a firm the edge it needs to prosper abroad. These activities are carried out in the home country head office before the company goes abroad. Once the firm is international, it already has routines, physical assets and organizational structures centred around that (head) office. Moving these activities abroad would require costly new investments. Thus, even if another country provides a pool of well-trained professionals and an attractive legal and economic system, multinationals will not normally move their core activities there.

Yet, such transfers of high value-added activities do occur. For example, in Sweden, the transfer of head-office activities out of the country by its domestic multinationals is becoming a major public issue. Over time, the tangible and intangible assets in a multinationals' home country will depreciate. In a more globalized economy, new assets may well be located wherever the best economic opportunities for the firm are to be found.[12]

How can Canada attract these high value-added head-office activities? Specifically, how do we attract spillover-generating activities that initiate a positive feedback loop of innovation stimulating more innovation? The fundamental issue is to *make the Canadian economy more amenable to Schumpeterian creative destruction*. That is what public policy OUGHT to do!

We now turn to our second list – positive policy options for government. First, under increased global competition Canadian firms with poor governance practices are likely to decline rapidly and eventually fail. This is a socially costly way of eliminating corporate governance problems. Many of the suggestions for improving corporate governance in other studies in this volume are really ways to decrease the cost of correcting poor corporate governance. They would make Canadian capital markets less forgiving to managers.

Elsewhere in this volume, the point is made that most Canadian firms are closely held. The main corporate governance concern here, therefore, is entrenched insiders extracting private benefits. Shleifer & Vishny (1991) raise the possibility that entrenched managers might divert corporate resources into avenues that preserve their control even though this subtracts from the value of their firms. Magee *et al.* (1985) and Morck *et al.* (1988) present empirical evidence supporting the proposition that entrenched managers can become liabilities to their firms. Morck & Stangeland (1995) study the relationship between different categories of dominant shareholders and firm performance, and find that closely held firms controlled by their founders' heirs perform significantly worse than all other firms in several dimensions. The apparent long-run viability of these firms is a tribute either to the forgiving nature of

Canadian capital markets and institutions, or to their inability to discipline errant managers.

Second, better disclosure rules would help Canadian shareholders improve corporate governance. For example, Canadian companies need not disclose how much R&D they are doing. The Giammarino study in this volume shows that U.S. financial markets penalize firms with low R&D spending by depressing their share prices. Investors are attracted to innovative firms, and the current Canadian rules protect stagnant firms from their shareholders.

Third, stiff competition leads to good corporate governance. Broad access to markets allows innovations to yield the highest returns by enabling innovators to reach more potential customers. To foster Schumpeterian creative destruction, remaining international and interprovincial trade barriers should be dismantled. This will cause some protected "fat cats" to lose business or even fail, but it will also give innovative Canadian firms access to markets large enough to make a higher level of continuous innovation profitable. Foreign entrants into Canada provide local firms with indirect access to international markets, elicit more innovative effort from domestic firms by increasing competition, and act as a conduit for innovations from abroad.

Fourth, a firm, credible commitment to eliminate subsidies to corporations is critical. Lobbying for government assistance is an attractive substitute for investing in innovation, as Lenway *et al.* (1995) show using U.S. data. Canadian firms must see "mining" the government as a less profitable investment than R&D. Otherwise managers, acting in their shareholders' interests, will quite rationally invest in lobbying rather than R&D, to the long-run detriment of the economy.

This is emphatically not a call for government to subsidize R&D spending by corporations. The risk is too high that some firms will take advantage of such subsidization and become innovative only at extracting public money. Consumers will reward results; the government need not reward apparent effort.

Fifth, poorly governed firms must be allowed to fail, and workers must be allowed to be unemployed if creative firms are to displace stagnant ones. Social programs and labour laws have important roles to play in Canada, but they must not interfere too much with the process of creative destruction or they will destroy the economic activity that supports them. In our opinion, much of the government's current difficulty in maintaining its program spending ultimately stems from this interference.

Sixth, fostering good corporate governance means letting firms pass on the fruits of successful innovation to their shareholders. Corporate income taxes and personal taxes on investment income must be low. Shareholders will not be concerned about poor corporate governance if confiscatory taxes prevent them from benefitting from good corporate governance.

Politically, general reductions in the level of corporate taxation are probably impossible at this juncture, but certainly no increases should be contemplated.

Also, general tax-rate reductions would be preferable to faster accelerated depreciation, tax write-offs, etc. as the former would reward success while the latter reward effort.

Seventh, in coming years, good corporate governance will increasingly come to be synonymous with innovation. Canada must have legal and economic systems that protect the property rights that innovators hold on their innovations. Canada ranks far ahead of many other countries in this regard, and might therefore attract R&D and other high-value-added operations from foreign multinationals. Certainly a lack of protection for intangible property rights is becoming widely seen as a serious barrier to development in some Asian countries.

Eighth, education – from kindergarten through graduate school – should be a top public policy priority. Sound education at the grade-school level, and in community colleges, producing workers and technicians capable of learning, will make Canada competitive. Good universities are needed to train scientists, professionals and managers. Whether education should be public or private, especially at the high-skill level, is a complex issue. However, in Canada the political consensus appears still to favour public education. We must therefore take care that our public investment in Canada's general human capital is protected.

It appears that Canada is doing a rather good job at education, at least relative to the United States. Doubtless, there is fat in the Canadian educational system and this should be eliminated, but care should be taken not to lower the quality of Canada's stock of human capital. Clearly, if we are to concentrate on higher value-added activities in Canada, we need highly skilled scientists, managers, professionals, technicians and workers. As global competition speeds up innovation, Canadians must be equipped to embrace continuous learning of new ideas and technologies. This is the ultimate purpose of education today, and is thought by many to be the secret to the success of countries like Japan, Korea and Singapore. The public good inherent in education makes it an obvious choice as one of the government's core businesses.

Finally, research and development at universities should be supported. Basic research, the investigation of new ideas and theories that have no immediate commercial application, is essential to fostering more overall innovation in our economy in the future. Because of their lack of immediate applicability, it is almost impossible to place a value on these ideas or to say whether one university is producing more or better basic research than another. Because of these ambiguities, artificial, pointless research aimed only at generating publications and more grant dollars is often confused with genuine contributions. Although improving the governance structure of Canadian universities and granting agencies is beyond the scope of this study, we believe there are several options. The fundamental problem is that Canadian universities and granting agencies must, like Canadian businesses, reward success and not effort. Given the problems inherent in measuring research productivity, this is much easier said than done. However, we believe there are analogies in business, and we hope there will be opportunities in the future for further exploration of governance problems in universities and granting agencies.

CONCLUSIONS

TO REITERATE THE POINTS MADE IN THE INTRODUCTION, globalization stems from an increasing need for companies to have larger markets that let them quickly recover the costs of the rapid innovation that is overtaking many industries. This study argues that globalization and multinational firms are likely to be even more important to Canada's competitive position in coming years than they have been in the past.

In the long run, this global competitive pressure may render moot many of the contemporary public policy concerns about corporate governance. In a global economy, customers, investment capital and highly skilled employees need not tolerate poor management. They can simply take their business and skills to better-run rivals. Canadian firms will have to deal with their governance problems not because they are legally required to do so, but because their survival will depend on it. In this context, government's best option for improving Canadian corporate governance may well be simply to foster competition and openness while providing good legal and educational infrastructure. This entails weaning firms from subsidies and captive markets, and providing sound basic public services like education, health care and law.

In the short run, some specific issues as to the corporate governance of foreign-controlled subsidiaries in Canada do arise, especially with regard to the value of public minority shares. These are related to multinationals' practice of shifting income among subsidiaries for tax and other reasons. If profits are systematically shifted out of Canada, some Canadian public shareholders may be harmed. We argue that the boards of all closely held Canadian companies with public shareholders, including foreign-controlled subsidiaries, should have conduct committees that monitor non-arm's-length transactions with the parent and other related companies. Subsidiaries should be required to disclose publically all non-arm's-length transactions with their parent firms, and this should make it easier for subsidiaries' minority shareholders to take action in cases of oppressive non-arm's-length transactions.

ENDNOTES

1 U.S. Department of Commerce 1990 data.

2 Morck & Yeung (1991) report results obtained by regressing Tobin's Q on various representations of a multinational structure: a firm's number of foreign subsidiaries, the number of host countries in which a firm has subsidiaries, or dummies based on these two variables. They find positive and significant regression coefficients. They find that these positive coefficients are due to the presence of intangibles, proxied for by past R&D and advertising spending. For firms with little past spending on R&D and advertising, the multinational structure variables attract negative and sometimes significant regression coefficients. Morck & Yeung (1992) report that the stock price reactions of U.S. firms' stock to news of its foreign acquisitions are, on average, positive. They use multiple regression analyses to show that the stock price reactions are most positive for U.S. firms with large past investment in R&D or advertising, or with an optimal level of management ownership. Their regression analyses also reveal that, net of these variables, the stock price reactions to foreign expansions are on average negative.

3 Other studies yield similar results, *e.g.*, Harris & Ravenscraft (1991) and Eun *et al.* (1995).

4 We infer the need for multinationals constantly to innovate from the cross sectional results in Morck & Yeung (1991, 1992) described in this subsection. In on-going research, we find preliminary evidence in a time series analysis that high R&D spending increases firms' chances of survival. Also, increased R&D increases profit rates, but international expansion alone does not. Finally, using Granger causality tests, we find that international expansion causes an increase in R&D spending, but not the converse.

5 It is rather difficult to study the systematic determinant of the survival of foreign-owned subsidiaries because segmented data are hard to come by or may not even exist. Of course, results based on parent firm survival is not good enough because the survival of parents does not imply the survival of subsidiaries.

6 The classical theory predicts that in a world of constant returns to scale and competitive markets for input factors and outputs, there is a one-to-one correspondence between factor returns and output prices. The exception is the case of complete product specialization, which is very unrealistic for Canada.

7 See *e.g.*, Blomström (1989).

8 The same study concludes that foreign-owned subsidiaries do not seem to offer higher wages than domestically owned plants. This indicates that foreign-owned subsidiaries are able to extract most of the rents related to their intangible assets that lead to higher labour productivity. The concern that multinationals pay substandard wages because their multi-location

production facilities gives them more bargaining power is not borne out.

9 Chung et al. (1994) show increased competition to be the main short run mechanism by which multinationals increase host-country productivity. This increased competition leads to better allocation of resources within as well as among firms. Mitchell et al. (1993) find higher exit rates in industries where multinationals have greater market share.

10 Carroll (1994) presents descriptive statistics on firm downsizing.

11 Some suppliers may be shipping both Nike and Addidas.

12 Hines (1994) suggests that localized R&D is a response to high royalties. In the NAFTA context, this is not viable even if Hines is right.

ACKNOWLEDGEMENTS

WE ARE GRATEFUL TO Stephen Jarislowsky, Brad Kilaly, Will Mitchell, Paul McCracken, Marina Whitman and the conference discussants Roberta Romano and Adrian Tschoegl for insightful suggestions. Rachelle Sampson provided excellent research assistance.

BIBLIOGRAPHY

Aharoni, Yair. "The Foreign Investment Decision Process." Boston: Harvard Business School, Division of Research, 1966.

Beason, Richard and David Weinstein. "Growth, Economies of Scale, and Targeting in Japan (1955-1990)." Review of Economics and Statistics, 1994.

Blomström, Magnus. Foreign Investment and Spillovers. London: Routledge, 1989.

Carroll, Glenn R. "Organizations ..., The Smaller They Get." California Management Review, 37, 1 (Fall 1994):28-41.

Caves, Richard E. Multinational Enterprise and Economic Analysis. Cambridge: Cambridge University Press, 1982.

_____. "Multinational Firms, Competition, and the Productivity in Host-Country Markets." Economica, 41 (May 1974):176-93.

Chung, Wilbur, Will Mitchell and Bernard Yeung. "Foreign Direct Investment and Host Country Productivity: The Case of the American Automotive Components Industry (Discussion Paper No. 367)." University of Michigan, Institute of Public Policy Studies and Department of Economics. 1994.

Clark, Kim B., Bruce W. Chew and Takahiro Fujimoto. "Product Development in the World Auto Industry." Brookings Papers on Economic Activity, 3 (1987):729-71.

Corvari, Ronald and Robert Wisner. "Foreign Multinationals and Canada's International Competitiveness (Working Paper No. 16)." Investment Canada, June 1993.

Eden, Lorraine. "Multinationals as Agents of Change: Setting a New Canadian Policy of Foreign Direct Investment (Discussion Paper No. 1)." Industry Canada, November 1994.

Evans, Wendy, Henry Lane and Shawna O'grady. *Border Crossings: Doing Business in the U.S.* Scarborough, ON: Prentice Hall Canada Inc., 1991.

Globerman, Steven. "Foreign Direct Investment and Spillover Efficiency Benefits in Canadian Manufacturing Industries." *Canadian Journal of Economics*, 12, 1 (February 1979):42-56.

Harris, David, Randall Morck, Joel Slemrod and Bernard Yeung. "Income Shifting in U.S. Multinational Corporations," in *Studies in International Taxation*. Edited by A. Giovannini, G. Hubbard and J. Slemrod. Chicago: University of Chicago Press, 1993, pp. 277-302.

Hines, James R. "Taxes, Technology Transfer and the R&D Activities of Multinational Firms." NBER Working Paper. October 1994.

Knubley, John, Marc Legault and Someshwar Rao. "Economic Integration in North America: Trends in Foreign Direct Investment and the Top 1,000 Firms." Industry Canada Working Paper No. 1. January 1994.

Lenway, Stefanie, Randall Morck and Bernard Yeung. "Rent-Seeking and Protectionism in the American Steel Industry: An Empirical Analysis (Discussion Paper No. 349)." University of Michigan, Institute of Public Policy Studies and Department of Economics, 1993.

Morck, Randall and Bernard Yeung. "Why Investors Value Multinationality." *Journal of Business*, 46, 2 (1991):165-87.

_____. "Internalization: An Event Study Test." *Journal of International Economics*, 33 (August 1992):41-56.

Mitchell, Will, Myles Shaver and Bernard Yeung. "Performance Following Changes of International Presence in Domestic and Transition Industries." *Journal of International Business Studies*, 24, 4 (1993):647-69.

Newbould, G. D., Peter Buckley and J. C. Thurwell. *Going International – The Experiences of Smaller Companies Overseas.* New York: John Wiley & Sons, 1978.

Shaver, James Myles. "The Influence of Intangible Assets, Spillovers, and Competition on Foreign Direct Investment Survival and Entry Time." Doctoral dissertation, School of Business Administration, University of Michigan, 1994.

Slemrod, Joel. "Emerging Issues in the Interface Between Trade, Investment and Taxation Working Paper." OECD, Fiscal Affairs Division, January 1995.

Teece, David. "Multinational Enterprise, Internal Governance, and Industrial Organization." *American Economic Review*, 75, 2 (May 1985): 233-38.

Lewis D. Johnson & Edwin H. Neave
School of Business
Queen's University

Corporate Governance and Supervision of the Financial System

INTRODUCTION

CANADA'S FINANCIAL SERVICES INDUSTRY has changed dramatically since the mid-1970s. Technological change, increasing trade and the increasing volatility of exchange rates have stimulated an explosion of global financial innovation. The changes have attenuated the former distinctiveness of the banking, insurance, trust and brokerage industries, and have also stimulated several rounds of financial deregulation. There is now inter-industry competition, both domestically and internationally, for the same clientele. Structural and regulatory changes continue, and their pace may even be increasing.

Since past change seems to have led to a spate of failures, and since dealing with those failures has been costly for many parties, it is useful to ask whether current and proposed changes in regulation might enhance future system supervision. Improved regulation cannot (and should not try to) prevent failure. It can, however, aim to ensure first that bad management receives full publicity as early as possible and, second, that the consequences of unwise decisions are borne by the decision-makers and investors who are responsible for them.

CANADA'S FINANCIAL SYSTEM TODAY

SUPERVISORY POWERS IN A NUMBER OF JURISDICTIONS have been revised several times since the mid 1970s, usually to accommodate new realities retroactively. The removal of minimum commissions in the United States in 1975 was principally in response to pressures for change, as was the United Kingdom's "Big Bang" in 1986. While Quebec's 1984 deregulation had a greater proactive element, Canada's national reforms have been largely reactive. The latter include the 1987 deregulation of the securities industry, establishing the Office of the Superintendent of Financial Institutions, and the 1992 revisions to financial legislation. The latter encompassed changes to the *Bank Act*, the *Trust and Loan Companies Act*, the *Insurance Companies Act* and the *Cooperative Credit Associations Act*.

Canadian banks have long dominated the domestic financial system, accounting for just over half of Canada's total institutional assets at the 1992 year end. Although it is less well-known, financial conglomerates also hold a healthy proportion of institutional assets.[1] Indeed, some conglomerates are as large as some banks, and are also more diversified. At present, different financial institutions have different powers. The large Schedule I banks are constrained to have diffuse ownership, but smaller banks and trusts can still have controlling shareholders. As a result, the latter can have closer connections to the activities they finance than is the case in the larger institutions.

PROBLEMS AND RESPONSES

WITH A VIEW TO LEARNING FROM OUR EXPERIENCE, it is worthwhile to reflect on the difficulties experienced by Canadian financial institutions in the recent past, and also to consider in detail the regulatory responses to them that are currently being proposed. Four banks, 36 trust companies, ten insurance companies and seven brokerage houses have failed in Canada since 1980. In addition to investor losses, the cumulative costs of managing bank and trust failures led to a $1.65 billion deficit at the Canada Deposit Insurance Corporation (CDIC) and, following the demise of Confederation Life, to a multi-million dollar deficit at Compcorp.

The principal reasons for these failures were poor investment decisions, poor management, and self-dealing. Many regional firms failed because of poor investment decisions. In particular, the smaller regional banks failed as a result of over-investment in energy and real-estate loans. The failed trusts either invested too aggressively in real estate or were victims of self-dealing and other similar activities. The insurance company failures were largely attributable to poor real-estate investments. In the case of the failed brokerage houses, inadequate capital and poor management seem to have been common.

These difficulties have stimulated several calls for regulatory reform. Michael Mackenzie (former Federal Superintendent of Financial Institutions), Douglas Peters (Secretary of State for Financial Institutions), and the Senate Banking Committee have all called for tighter regulation in the insurance industry. Suzanne Labarge (Deputy Federal Superintendent of Financial Institutions) has suggested that mutual funds require more regulation. The federal government is again trying to set up a national securities commission, and the Vancouver Stock Exchange is the object of renewed scrutiny and criticism. The 1995 Finance Department White Paper recommends refinements to the current regulatory regime, including increased power for earlier intervention by the Office of the Superintendent of Financial Institutions (OSFI), increased transparency of the supervisory process, and the provision of more public financial data about federally regulated companies.

RESPONSIBILITIES FOR SUPERVISION

HOWEVER MUCH IT IS IMPROVED, regulation alone cannot address all industry problems; other parties also bear responsibilities. First, while the role of directors is theoretically limited (Neave, 1995) the board is nonetheless charged with controlling and directing management. Some boards fail to discharge this responsibility even to the limited extent of their practical capabilities. Such boards are sometimes dominated by controlling shareholders, or sometimes overwhelmed by the vastness of large institutions with diffuse ownership. In Canada, unlike the United States, boards are seldom assisted by other outside stakeholders, as few financial institutions vote their shares.[2]

Two examples illustrate how boards have not fully discharged their duties. According to *The Report on Business* of July 19, 1993, Royal Trustco failed because the board did not constrain management's over-ambitious strategy of expanding its commercial real-estate investments in Canada, the United States and the United Kingdom. Jack Hickman noted that: "Managements don't fail. Boards fail. The failure of Royal Trustco is a board problem, pure and simple". Donald Thain said: "The function of any board is to stop management from taking survival-threatening risks". Examination of events suggests that management convinced the board that a risky loan package was secure, in spite of evidence to the contrary. The board apparently asked appropriate questions, but failed to evaluate the answers.

Confederation Life Insurance Company ventured into areas in which it had little experience and no expertise, setting up a trust company, buying part of Midland Walwyn (brokerage), and starting a leasing business. The company foundered in part because of its own risky real-estate investments, which amounted to 71 percent of its assets by 1989. However, the trust company also contributed to the failure. Its management was weak, but despite this the parent (insurance) company allowed it to pursue an aggressive, largely uncontrolled growth strategy, which led to further losses from risky real-estate investments.[3]

The boards of both Confederation Life and the trust company exercised only weak supervision. Confederation Life board member André Monast stated: "...the directors received the reports and advice of management in good faith. Confederation Life was so big, directors couldn't be expected to have detailed knowledge of the operating subsidiaries and so relied on management's advice".[4] Since no insurance company board members sat on the trust company board, an important channel of information remained unused by the parent board.

External rating agencies and analysts also influence the financial services industry by public reporting of their analyses. Bond rating agencies provide relevant information, but usually with a time lag that impairs its usefulness. Brokerage house analysts provide more timely information, but their reports tend to be biased by an unwillingness to produce negative information about current or prospective clients. TRAC Insurance Services provides quantitative assessments of the financial health of insurance companies, but the validity of their reports is criticized (mostly by insurance company executives) because of the small number of factors used in the analysis.

DEALS AND GOVERNANCE

COPING WITH THE CHANGING ENVIRONMENT JUST OUTLINED, and with the difficulties it creates, presents challenges for regulators and management alike. The remainder of this study develops a theory that both explains the developments outlined, and establishes principles for guiding future regulatory reform. In contrast to the functional analyses of Diamond (1984) and Merton (1992), this study builds a theory of the financial system based on the individual financial deal.[5] This theory permits finer analyses of institutional incentives and the supervisory approaches likely to prove most successful in governing them.[6]

Any financial system facilitates and governs the making of a variety of individual financial deals, some intended mainly to provide new funds, others mainly to manage risks. The deals made within a financial system and the funding it provides can have a profound effect on an economy's rate and type of capital formation. (In some respects, the deals *not* made have an equally profound effect in terms of the funding *not* provided.) Availability of funding cannot stimulate capital formation, but a lack of funding can restrict it. Capital formation, especially if it involves technologically innovative projects, can also be inhibited by a dearth of risk-management capabilities. The risks associated with a technologically innovative project will not attract financing unless those risks can be structured to appeal to financiers' interests.

Thus, if financiers are not sufficiently creative certain types of capital formation, particularly the technologically innovative forms, can be inhibited. There is no single recipe for creative structuring, since different types of deals demand different kinds of financial and risk management structures. However, encouraging diversity within a financial system is one of the best ways to ensure that new deals receive creative, constructive financing.

TYPE S AND TYPE N DEALS

THERE ARE MANY TYPES OF FINANCIAL DEALS, and each has its own key attributes. For present purposes, the many possible combinations of attributes can be summarized using two categories – standard and non-standard.[7] Standard deals (Type S) are those that require screening before they are agreed, but relatively little monitoring and control afterward. Non-standard deals (Type N) also require screening before they are agreed, but it may be more intensive than for standard deals. More importantly, Type N deals subsequently require continued monitoring, as well as possible control over operations and adjustment of contract terms. Type S deals have all (or nearly all) relevant information available at the outset, while information regarding

Type N deals is typically revealed with the passage of time after the financing has been agreed. Type N deals are unfamiliar, non-standard, and are characterized by greater uncertainty regarding their payoffs.

With regard to funding, Type S deals finance relatively liquid assets; Type N deals finance illiquid assets.[8] Financiers find it easiest to fund acquisitions of assets with readily determined market values;[9] asset illiquidity usually implies payoff uncertainty. For example, projects whose success rests on the talent and commitment of particular individuals offer an extreme example in which financiers look to earnings rather than to the capital value of assets to secure their funds. With regard to risk management, Type S deals use standardized instruments. Since the same instruments are employed in numerous transactions, agreeing the individual deal does not typically involve high fixed costs relative to potential profits.

Financiers secure their positions in Type N deals through enhanced governance capabilities, such as by using discretionary and incomplete agreements rather than rule-based financing contracts covering all possible contingencies. The ability conveyed by a discretionary agreement (to exercise continuing supervision and control unfavourable outcomes), can be crucial to the success of a project where financiers' returns depend on earnings rather than on easily realized asset value.

The Attributes of Deals

Increasing Information Differences
Perceived Greater Risk
Uncertainty rather than Risk
Decreasing Liquidity of Assets Financed
Greater Need for Continued Monitoring
Greater Need for *ex post* Adjustment
Increasing Cost of Default

S   N

TYPE M AND TYPE H GOVERNANCE CAPABILITIES

FINANCIERS THEMSELVES CAN ALSO BE CHARACTERIZED as having differing capabilities which, for the sake of simplicity, are here referred to as Type M (market) and Type H (hierarchy), respectively. Type M financiers have considerable research and information-processing capabilities regarding readily observable short-term changes in the market values of the instruments they normally trade. Type H financiers have relatively greater capabilities for estimating the potential of illiquid assets to generate cash flows and to monitor and control the management of those assets. Those financiers who specialize in trading liquid instruments have Type M capabilities, those who supervise portfolios of illiquid instruments have Type H capabilities.

The Governance Capabilities of a Financier

------➤   Greater Monitoring Capabilities   ------➤
(particularly on a continuing basis)

Greater Control Capabilities
(auditing, replacement of key personnel)

Greater Adjustment Capabilities
(ability to alter contracts as circumstances change)

Increasing Governance Cost

M   H

Financiers acting as principals for very short periods of time usually specialize in market instruments and have less well-developed Type H capabilities than financiers holding instruments in their portfolios for relatively long periods of time. The trader in government treasury bills and the real-estate developer both act as principals. However, the assets they hold differ greatly in terms of both their liquidity and their time frames.

PROFIT MAXIMIZATION

AGENTS WILL ONLY MAKE THE DEALS THEY PERCEIVE TO BE PROFITABLE. In a competitive environment, agents can only make deals profitably if they possess the requisite governance capabilities and use them cost-effectively.

Type M governance is generally cheaper than Type H (Williamson, 1987; Garvey, 1993). Thus, the cost of using market governance for standard deals is less than the cost of using hierarchical governance. Symbolically, the costs are related by $C(SM) < C(SH)$, where $C(SM)$ is the cost of governing a standard deal with Type M capabilities, and $C(SH)$ the cost of governing the same standard deal with Type H capabilities. With Type S there is little to be gained, in terms of risk reduction or increased revenue, by acquiring the extra capabilities (and incurring the extra costs) of hierarchical governance. It follows that $V(SM) > V(SH)$, where V is the value to the financier of doing the deal. Value is defined as earnings discounted at a rate adjusted to reflect the risk involved.

Despite its greater cost, Type H governance offers a profitable alternative to Type M if the marginal benefits of its command, monitoring and control capabilities exceed the marginal information and coordination costs involved. This is usually the case when the financing environment is uncertain rather than risky. For Type N deals, $V(NH) > V(NM)$ because even though $C(NH) > C(NM)$ the reduced risk or increased return to the extra resources expended on hierarchical governance more than compensate for their increased cost. In part, the extra return results from the fact that financiers can earn super-normal profits on appropriately governed Type N deals until the deal becomes familiar enough to attract competition. In summary, the profit-maximizing combinations of deal and governance types are SM and NH.

FINANCIAL FIRMS

FINANCIAL FIRMS SPECIALIZE IN DEALS they can govern cost-effectively. The decisions on which types of deals to support, in which types to specialize, and whether to make the deals as principals or as agents are the main determinants of both financial system organization and change. These decisions are, of course, affected by the economics of individual deals when they are first made. We first discuss static organization, then consider organizational change.[10]

Financial firms find it profitable to assemble specialized portfolios for several reasons. Both screening and monitoring are characterized by fixed costs, and therefore offer increasing returns as the number of deals using the same kind of screening and monitoring increases. If many deals use the same fixed inputs (such as the same computer system, for example), savings called scope economies can also be realized. Financial firms rarely find possibilities to realize both scale and scope economies (e.g., Benston, 1986; Nathan & Neave, 1992). There appear to be few limits to enjoying scale economies; there also appear to be more clearly defined limits to enjoying scope economies. Financial firms tend to encounter difficulties, and attendant costs, in coordinating relatively different types of activity. Thus, financial firms have incentives to be large and to emphasize closely related kinds of activities.

TRANSACTION AND OPERATING COSTS

TRANSACTION COSTS ARE THE COSTS BORNE BY A CLIENT – both those paid directly to the financier and any search costs incurred in identifying an accommodating financier. From the financier's point of view, the governance cost of a deal is determined by the deal's share of total costs. These costs include the resource costs of setting up and operating the governance mechanism, the additional costs associated with setting the contract terms of an individual deal, plus any provisions for losses on deals of the type in question.

On average, financiers must recover their costs from the deals they conclude. Indeed, if they could perform the necessary computations, financiers would accept only those deals on which they can earn an appropriately risk-adjusted marginal rate of return, after allowing for the marginal funding and governance costs implied by the acceptance.[11] If two agents had the same cost structures but the second had higher capability, the second would be able to consummate deals for lower transaction costs than the first. The first would not be able to consummate the same deal profitably unless he could somehow overcome his competitive disadvantage.

CHOOSING SPECIALIZED PORTFOLIOS

THE SPECIALIZED CAPABILITIES OF DIFFERENT FIRMS lead them to assemble different portfolios. For simplicity of discussion, we suppose a given firm's assets are either Type S or Type N, and that its liabilities are also of one type.[12] Thus we define four polar types of firm: SS, SN, NS, and NN, where the first letter refers to asset type, and the second to liability type. Similarly, there are four types of governance used with the four portfolios: MM, MH, HM and HH. Since Type S deals are governed cost-effectively using Type M capabilities, and Type N deals using Type H capabilities, portfolios can be classified either by asset-liability or by governance type. Cost-effectiveness identifies deal type and governance method on a one-for-one basis.

Our discussion focuses on polar types, but our analysis extends beyond these extremes. For example, a diversified portfolio of (say) Type N credit card advances might be able to support an issue of Type S securities, and can thus be securitized. A firm assembling such a portfolio uses Type HM capabilities. Note the classification shows immediately that more than Type M governance is needed even when securitization is possible because the original assets supporting the instruments used for securitization cannot themselves be governed using Type M capabilities. Even in a high-technology environment, individual credit card advances typically require Type H capabilities for continued monitoring, but most purchasers of Type S securities have only Type M capabilities.

Managing a portfolio effectively also demands capabilities to govern aggregate effects. For example, a portfolio's risk-return tradeoff can be altered either by changing deal terms (e.g., substituting floating for fixed-rate loans) or by hedging some risks (e.g., with interest-sensitive derivatives). Typically, the differing choices will utilize differing specialized capabilities; experts in setting Type N deal terms will not normally be expert in trading Type S derivatives.

GOVERNING SPECIALIZED PORTFOLIOS

THE FOUR TYPES OF SPECIALIZED PORTFOLIOS DEFINED ABOVE pose different governance challenges. Understanding the differences is critical to effective supervision of the different types of firms.

MM GOVERNANCE[13]

IN PRACTICE, MARKET AGENTS ADD VALUE BY ASSEMBLING PORTFOLIOS of Type S deals because they can spread the costs of trading and research over relatively large numbers of deals. For example, they can enjoy scale economies both by spreading the fixed components of transactions costs across several large purchases, and by spreading the fixed costs of information production over large amounts of invested funds.

The principal challenge in managing portfolios of Type S assets and Type S liabilities is achieving trading profitability. Profits flow from acquiring capabilities to trade quickly and to value market instruments speedily and accurately; *i.e.*, from acquiring Type M capabilities for managing both assets and liabilities. Securities firms offer examples of firms with MM governance. Whether market agents act as principals (dealers) or as agents (brokers), they enjoy scale economies in both trading and research activity. The essential economic difference between a broker and a dealer is the trading return on an average deal relative to its inventory risk – if return is high relative to risk, the firm acts as principal; if return is low, it acts as agent.

Since portfolio theory has been largely developed with reference to Type S instruments, it is not surprising that, generally, firms with SS portfolios have better developed capabilities for determining and governing portfolio risk-return tradeoffs than do firms with NS, SN or NN portfolios.

MH GOVERNANCE

A COST-EFFECTIVELY GOVERNED FIRM WITH A TYPE SN PORTFOLIO will utilize Type M asset governance capabilities and Type H liability governance capabilities. Such firms add value through intermediation; *i.e.*, transforming a particular kind of asset, through internal diversification, into a liability with different characteristics. For example, a typical insurance company or pension fund creates value by entering into many individual liability contracts (with clients purchasing insurance or pension benefits) and combining them into a portfolio of predictable risks. Managers of SN firms try to avoid undefined liabilities, chiefly through continued monitoring. Thus, fire and casualty companies usually acquire capabilities to investigate claims and to supervise payout procedures.

Typically, firms with Type MH management have assets, the market values of which are relatively easy to ascertain; and liabilities the market and indeed actuarial values of which are both relatively difficult to ascertain (transparent asset values, opaque liability values; see Ross, 1989). Apart from their cash management capabilities, most firms with Type MH governance have only weakly developed capabilities for determining and governing portfolio effects.

HM GOVERNANCE

BANKS AND OTHER LENDING INTERMEDIARIES ARE EXAMPLES of firms with Type N assets and Type S liabilities. Deposits are marketable instruments (or instruments whose values are close to marketable values); loans are illiquid and many require continued monitoring. Thus banks acquire Type H capabilities for governing assets, and Type M capabilities for governing liabilities. The emphasis on governance is to avoid assets likely to default and to sell liabilities aggressively in order to fund lending. The values of liabilities of Type NS companies are relatively transparent, but the values of their assets can be opaque (difficult to establish).

Type NS firms can face important cash management problems because they hold illiquid assets funded by liabilities whose levels can fluctuate rapidly and over relatively wide ranges. By changing the terms of loans from fixed to floating, and by using negotiated swaps, firms with Type NS portfolios have been able to reduce the interest-rate risk on their portfolios. However, in part because earnings patterns on Type N assets are relatively more difficult to quantify than patterns on Type S assets, Type NS firms usually have only weakly developed capabilities for determining portfolio risk-return tradeoffs.

HH Governance

Type NN firms, that is, firms with both illiquid assets and infrequently traded or non-tradeable liabilities, find Type HH governance to be cost-effective. In part because NN firms create the most difficult governance challenges, there are very few of them within the financial system to use as examples. However, some real estate development companies and some financial conglomerates (especially closely held ones) offer examples. From a valuation point of view, both asset and liability values are difficult to establish. If asset values are perceived to be uncertain the firms can face relatively important liquidity management problems. Investors in such firms may seek short-term rates of return, but the firms' investments can make it difficult to post steady earnings on a quarterly or even an annual basis.

Agency Activities

Stock brokers have always acted as agents for their clients. Increasingly, financial firms are acting as agents on behalf of clients, particularly in the field of risk management which is growing at almost explosive rates. When a firm trades marketable assets in the capacity of an agent, its risks and/or contingent liabilities are limited, but when it begins to negotiate individual contracts in the capacity of a principal, the risks expand accordingly. Since these activities are new, the firms may not have well-developed assessment procedures in place, and may also be peculiarly vulnerable to portfolio effects. This vulnerability often stems from the difficulties financial firms have in identifying and assessing potential losses from new kinds of business.

Present financial practice is relatively weak in determining and in governing the portfolio effects resulting from combining a new form of agency business with other activities. For example, banks facing credit risk in their lending activity, and market risk in their derivatives trading, have considerable difficulty in devising overall measures of risk-return tradeoffs.

INCENTIVES AND GOVERNANCE

WHILE GOVERNANCE STRUCTURES MAINLY REFLECT the nature of the portfolios assembled, they are modified in individual firms by management incentives.

MANAGEMENT WITH LITTLE OWNERSHIP INTEREST

CEOS WITH LITTLE OWNERSHIP INTEREST act as agents on behalf of shareholders. If they direct Type MM firms, CEOs are likely to emphasize trading profitability and want to be paid by bonuses. The ease with which asset and liability values of Type MM firms can be established in the marketplace means the actions taken by their CEOs are usually well-scrutinized by at least the firm's major shareholders.

If they manage Type MH firms, CEOs will try to avoid large, undefined liabilities, and will focus some of their attention on the management of particularly troublesome individual liabilities. However, the market values of those liabilities are relatively difficult to estimate and shareholders are unlikely to be critical of individual management decisions.

CEOs of Type HM firms will emphasize acquiring relatively safe assets, and will focus some of their attention on managing assets identified as potentially troublesome. The values of those assets are relatively difficult to estimate and shareholders are (again) unlikely to be critical of individual management errors.

CEOs of Type HH firms will seek to design profitable projects, and to manage both assets and liabilities. However, because their expertise is usually limited, they are likely to focus on either asset management or liability management. Individual decisions regarding both are difficult for shareholders to scrutinize.

FINANCIERS WITH LARGE OWNERSHIP INTERESTS

A FINANCIER WITH A SUBSTANTIAL OWNERSHIP STAKE IN A FIRM has an incentive to use the firm's resources to improve his/her own fortunes, particularly if firm portfolios are relatively difficult to value. Financiers managing Type MM firms emphasize trading profitability, and account for large market shares of trading activity. Since the market values of Type M assets and Type M liabilities are readily established, these managers have little incentive to manipulate the quality of the instruments in their portfolios.

A financier with a large stake in a Type MH firm has an incentive to underestimate the risks, and overestimate the profitability of liabilities associated with other closely held investment interests. These incentives are strengthened by the difficulty of valuing the financial firm's liabilities.

Owner-managers of Type HM firms face incentives to invest the firm's funds in closely held activities. These financiers face incentives to underestimate the risks and to overestimate the profitability of such closely held assets, and the incentives are strengthened by the difficulty of valuing the financial firm's assets.

In the case of Type HH firms, owner-managers may both underestimate liquidity risks and overestimate the profitability potential of favoured projects. The opacity of both assets and liabilities encourages these owner-managers to become highly independent individuals. They have little incentive to recognize and deal with the concerns of outside stakeholders.

OUTSIDE STAKEHOLDERS WITH LITTLE OWNERSHIP INTEREST

OUTSIDE STAKEHOLDERS WITH LITTLE OWNERSHIP INTEREST have concerns similar to those of managers with little ownership interest. Outside stakeholders are not usually concerned with monitoring individual assets or liabilities. Rather, their principal interest in the case of Type MM firms is to assess the market value of the firm's equity or other instruments it uses to raise funds. They have the same concern in the case of Type MH firms, but tend to overestimate liability risks in difficult times because they have little information about the value of the liabilities. For the same reasons, stakeholders of Type HM firms overestimate asset risks in difficult times. Stakeholders in Type HH firms tend to place their faith in existing management, principally because they have little other information on which to base assessments.

CHANGE

THE MAJOR FORCES OF CHANGE IN THE FINANCIAL SYSTEM are new computing and communications technologies that alter the economics of deals and affect the nature of competition. The effects of change include more rapid rates of new product development, more rapid adoption of new technologies, increasing internationalization of financial systems, and dissolution of traditional boundaries (e.g., domestic/international, banking/insurance, and increasing worldwide homogenization of financial regulation). Regulatory changes can also stimulate adaptation, chiefly by affecting management incentives. For example, flat rate deposit insurance stimulates banks to take on greater risks than they would willingly assume if they were subjected to risk-based premiums (Benston, 1986; Kane, 1984, 1989; Kaufman & Litan, 1993).

CAUSES OF CHANGE

CHANGE IN THE FINANCIAL SYSTEM IS INFLUENCED both by existing capabilities and by accidents of history. Successful innovation is a trial-and-error response to changing economics. It takes place as clients present new types of deals and as financiers become aware of new technologies which they can profitably implement.

An emerging opportunity will be seized only as and when financiers perceive it to be profitable. When new opportunities are perceived, financiers attempt to exploit them, learning as they enter the new form of business. The focus of learning changes in the direction of doing deals more efficiently as firms become more familiar with the methods of dealing in the new business area.

Learning is incremental, but action taken in a learning environment does not always reflect smooth adjustment. Financiers may overreact to perceived new profit opportunities for at least two reasons. First, change occurs in an atmosphere of uncertainty, and it is not always easy to find an appropriate method to exploit change. Second, the most profitable way to enter a new line of business is often through establishing a dominant market position as early as possible. Thus financiers are sometimes inclined to offer new products before their profitability is clearly established, and to expand the line of business before its sources of loss are fully understood. Nevertheless, their responses indicate attempts to identify and to govern the key profitability attributes of their deals.

For the same reasons that financiers sometimes enter a new business too quickly, both the financiers and their clients may overreact to emerging losses. For example, at the first sign of trouble a Type S share ownership position or a Type S bondholding may immediately be reclassified as Type N, and a former overvaluation may, in a very short time, swing to an undervaluation. There is usually a return to near-market valuation eventually, but it can be quite protracted.

Processes of Change

Over time, a financial firm will adjust its portfolio to its governance capabilities, and *vice versa*. If at a given point in time governance capabilities and portfolio types are not fully aligned, adaptive alterations in either the portfolio or the firm's capabilities will be initiated, and will continue until a closer match is achieved. A firm with Type H capabilities will sell off assets whose attributes have evolved to demand only routine governance, and will also seek new Type N products to replace the original investments.

Merton (1992) observes that institutions change their product lines in the manner just described. However, the functions performed by institutions adapt much more slowly, if at all. Thus an institution with established Type HM capabilities usually substitutes new forms of Type N assets to replace investments in what were formerly Type N assets, but which have now become Type S. Based on this analysis, the future demise of banks is unlikely. For example, as corporate borrowers have increasingly learned to use market instruments rather than bank loans, some banks have compensated by taking on other Type N functions such as risk management. Today, some banks inter-mediate clients' risk instruments just as they formerly intermediated debt instruments. Securitization means the kinds of deals they do are different from those done formerly, but their function of providing Type H governance remains largely unchanged.

PRINCIPLES OF SUPERVISION

SUPERVISORY CHALLENGES DIFFER with respect to the type of firm involved and with respect to whether or not the firms are changing their traditional activities. The discussion first considers differences related to firm type, then examines the challenges associated with changing activity.

DIFFERING CHALLENGES

THIS SECTION IS DEVOTED TO FIRMS WITH DIFFUSE OWNERSHIP, since closely held firms are considered separately in the subsequent analysis of the (February 1995) White Paper recommendations. For deals with familiar attributes, governance routines and methods for producing information about the deals are equally familiar. In such a setting, supervisors strive mainly to encourage probity of conduct and to ensure the safety of certain stakeholders' claims.

If the firms are Type MM, the principal regulatory concerns are liquidity management, capitalization, transparency of trading activity, and prevention of market cornering. With Type MH firms, regulators aim to reduce solvency risk, but seldom attempt to develop more public information regarding the firms' liabilities. For example, the question of whether a Type MH firm is prone to take on too many liabilities of a type it does not have the capability to govern is seldom raised publicly by regulators. But raising such an issue in private with the firm concerned is even less likely to result in corrective action being taken, since private discussion utilizes only the incentives provided by the supervisors themselves.

In the case of Type HM firms, supervisors aim to reduce solvency risk. Sometimes, but with insufficient frequency and rigour, supervisors attempt to promote information about asset valuations. Supervisors seldom investigate whether the firm is prone to take on too many assets of the type(s) it does not have the capability to govern. With regard to Type HH firms, one of the principal regulatory tasks is to assess the capability and honesty of management. Questions of competence also arise: for example, do management capabilities extend beyond liquidity management to portfolio management? Since both assets and liabilities are difficult to value, it is often equally difficult for supervisors to assess management responses.

New Forms of Business

As a financial firm changes, supervisors face the additional challenge of having to assess whether management has systems that will enable it to learn quickly from whatever mistakes it may make. Supervisory concerns vary according to the type of change, as shown by the following examples.

MM to MH

Does the firm have experience in writing the new forms of liabilities? Does management know how to avoid pitfalls such as the long tails to claims often associated with new kinds of insurance policies? Does management understand and have a plan for dealing with the underwriting cycle? Does management have the incentive(s) to take action of the sort(s) just mentioned?

MM to HM

Does management have experience with lending as opposed to trading market instruments; *i.e.*, does management understand the difference between market and credit risk? Does management know about the write-off patterns typical of entry into the lending or investment business? Does management face incentives that encourage prudent fund administration, or perverse incentives to take on additional risks without incurring penalties?

MH to HH

Does management understand the forms of technological change being financed? Does it understand the portfolio effects of the new business? Does management understand how to weather the liquidity crises to which NN portfolios are periodically subject?

HM to HH

Does management understand the differences between negotiated deals on the asset side and negotiated deals on the liability side? Other questions are similar to those for MM to MH.

White Paper Recommendations

This section examines the recommendations of the federal government's White Paper on Canadian Financial Regulation (February 1995) in light of the paper's theory, along with some additional possibilities for reform not addressed by the White Paper. Since the desirability of changing the deposit insurance framework and of enhancing information production have been analyzed earlier (*e.g.*, Neave, 1989), this section considers each of the following proposals in turn, offering commentary in addition to that already published.

The February 1995 White Paper recommendations include the following proposals.

- Enhanced Disclosure of Financial Information
- An Early Intervention Framework
- Changes to Deposit Insurance
- Protection for Policyholders of Life and Health Insurance Companies
- A Stronger Prudential Framework for Federal Financial Institutions
- Changes to Reduce Systemic Risk in Clearance and Settlement Systems

ENHANCED DISCLOSURE

THE MOST IMPORTANT FINANCIAL INFORMATION A FIRM can disclose is its economic value – determined as the difference between the value of its assets and its liabilities. Enhanced disclosure of asset and liability attributes can also help determine a firm's value, but only up to a point. For example, if the deals are Type N they generally have no readily established market values, for the theoretical reasons discussed above. In such cases supervisors should consider providing incentives for management to report their assessments of the economic values of Type N assets, and Type N liabilities truthfully.[14] Where management fails to discharge its responsibility for reporting truthful and timely information, it should be subject to penalties.

The principle of enhanced disclosure promises improvement, but it is not a panacea. Since any financial system will always have Type N deals, and since the valuation of Type N deals is necessarily difficult, full disclosure of all the economic value of all deals is simply unattainable. But supervisors need not let the best be the enemy of the good; improvements in information, even if imperfect, can help investors make better decisions.

To obtain improvements, the benefits to additional information release must exceed the costs of gathering the information. In most cases it is necessary to make qualitative judgments about the costs and benefits involved; more nearly precise calculations are not likely to be possible. The difficulty of comparing value to cost is compounded by a problem of incidence: the costs of producing information are not always borne by the parties who benefit from it. There may also be legal and institutional obstacles to greater information release. Analyzing cost-benefit questions, incidence questions, and remaining obstacles is beyond the scope of this study. But, if the principle of greater information release is accepted, it will be possible to begin addressing the problems involved.[15]

EARLY INTERVENTION

THE POWER OF EARLY INTERVENTION IS A VALUABLE ADDITION to the present supervisory framework. Whether intervention is early enough depends, however, on the abilities of supervisors to detect emerging difficulties. The White Paper contains much on the steps to be followed when intervening, but little on how to detect possible difficulties; i.e., the signals which might trigger intervention.

The questions to be asked before deciding on early intervention go beyond assessing a firm's value. They include: Do management capabilities cover the kind(s) of business the firm is currently conducting? Has the firm recently entered a new area without acquiring the capabilities to conduct the new activities without undue loss? What percentage of its capital is at stake in these ventures? An institution entering a new line of business without appropriate forms of risk control might merit extra supervision, but a decision to intervene should also depend on whether an appreciable amount of capital is likely to be placed at risk by the new business activity.

An early warning system will not work well if supervisors wait for signs of trouble rather than implement extra supervision when management enters an important (new) area of business without acquiring the appropriate governance capabilities. Increases in deposit insurance premiums, reductions in the institution's safety rating, or both, could be appropriate if a large amount of capital is at risk and if management risk control systems are inadequate. It would also be well for Canada if the proposed legislated mandate for OSFI could be extended to include provincial supervisors.

Whether early intervention is best pursued by OSFI or by CDIC is a difficult matter to resolve. OSFI usually tries to save a troubled institution by improving its operations rather than by closing it down. CDIC usually tries to limit payouts by closing down a troubled institution quickly, especially one whose operations appear likely to continue declining. OSFI can afford optimism because it has little to lose from continuing the operations; CDIC faces higher losses if it (over) optimistically permits an ultimately doomed firm to continue in operation. Theoretically, this conflict between optimism and pessimism could be governed internally, possibly under better informational conditions, if the two institutions were merged. Conversely, keeping OSFI and CDIC separate encourages debate over whether a troubled institution is capable of continuing. Such debate could be in the public interest, since markets work better if they are as fully informed as possible. Since we consider the benefits of public information to be greater than the costs of the attendant disruption that information release sometimes brings, we favour the continuance of separate organizations.

DEPOSIT INSURANCE

RISK-BASED PREMIUMS ARE A HIGHLY DESIRABLE INNOVATION because they provide financial institutions with the incentive to balance the promise of extra return against the extra risks involved.[16] With risk-based premiums, the financial institutions that are willing to accept higher risks will pay more for funds than their more conservative counterparts, thus reducing some of the present subsidization of risky institutions by safer ones. For example, a bank with a high proportion of relatively risky real-estate loans would normally pay a higher deposit insurance premium than another with a lower proportion. However, if the first bank securitized the real-estate loans in such a way that it did not bear any of the remaining default risk, its portfolio would be less risky than it was initially and, other things being unchanged, its deposit insurance premium would then be lower.[17] It is clear from the theory, and substantiated by the present example, that risk-based deposit insurance premiums carry with them a need for substantially closer involvement in the governance of individual firms. Selling deposit insurance is a Type N transaction which cannot be conducted on an informed basis without adequate assessment of the risks involved.

While depositors should also face incentives to balance risk against return, co-insurance is both unnecessary and too complex for this purpose. Co-insurance is unnecessary because the elimination of stacking helps bring home the idea of risk to a depositor without requiring the depositor to attempt valuation of assets. The incentive provided by eliminating stacking can be strengthened by informing depositors that deposit insurance payouts resulting from the difficulties of a given group of firms will be based on a maximum of $60,000 per social insurance number. Co-insurance is probably too complex for the small depositor because it requires a level of knowledge close to that of a professional. Yet even professionals can find valuation of Type N deals difficult, as the foregoing analysis has shown.

POLICYHOLDER PROTECTION

INCREASED PROTECTION OF INSURANCE POLICYHOLDERS is a highly desirable move. While Canadian policyholders have not suffered substantial losses from insurance company failures to date, that experience does not mean that strengthened protection is unnecessary. The question for supervisors is whether the probability of potential difficulties in the future can be reduced by increasing policyholder protection. Potential future difficulties will certainly be reduced if premium assessments are risk-based, as it is with deposit insurance. Possible future difficulties could be reduced even further if provincially organized insurance companies were required to contribute to the fund. Even more important, the amounts of individual savings held by pension funds are very substantial and all pension funds should contribute to a similar insurance scheme. Such a scheme should also use risk-adjusted premiums.

PRUDENTIAL FRAMEWORK

A STRONGER PRUDENTIAL FRAMEWORK IS NEEDED at both the federal and provincial levels. Supervisory authorities, both federal and provincial, should carry a legislated responsibility to disclose material information to the public in a timely manner, and should be subject to penalties in law if they fail to do so. In the past, the public has sustained losses because provincial authorities have been slow to identify troubled institutions.

SYSTEMIC RISK

CHANGES TO REDUCE SYSTEMIC RISK IN CLEARINGS are a useful way to reduce potential for future losses. Netting clearings reduces the settlement risk now borne by institutions. On the other hand, possible domino effects resulting from the insolvency of a given financial firm remain to be addressed. The recent failure of Barings Bank indicates the kinds of difficulties that can arise even after clearings risks are reduced.

Reducing the remaining systemic risks begins with ensuring that individual firms have good risk control systems in place, and that supervisors report their ratings of how these systems are working. Supervisors should ask such questions as: How quickly is management moving to establish good internal risk control? How do the risk control activities in Canadian financial institutions measure up against the best systems in other parts of the world? How vulnerable is a given institution to the failure of another?

Supervisors can also help reduce systemic risk by producing aggregate data that individual firms do not assemble. For example, had it been known in early 1995 that very large amounts would be at risk if the Nikkei index were to move substantially, institutions doing business with Barings might have identified the positions Barings was taking, and might then have moved earlier to limit their risks of dealing with the firm. As a second example, supervisors might discuss the quality of other supervisors' governance with the firms in their own jurisdiction, thus improving the subject firms' assessment of the kinds of international risks they might be facing.

CLOSELY HELD FIRMS

CLOSELY HELD FIRMS PRESENT SUPERVISORY CHALLENGES that the White Paper does not fully address. On the positive side, closely held firms can bring a greater degree of benefits of Type H governance to the Type N deals with which they are involved. The closely held firm's intimate connection between financier and project conveys substantial capability to control its uncertainties, largely because of the kind of information and control the financier has. Widely held banks have a lesser degree of Type H capabilities for governing such deals.

The potential difficulties presented by closely held firms stem largely from the incentives that large proportional ownership creates. Closely held Type MH firms are vulnerable to the excess issue of closely held liabilities; *i.e.*, to underwriting the risks of other businesses owned by the financial firm's

CEOs. Closely held Type HM firms are vulnerable to excess investment in other projects of owner-managers. Closely held Type HH firms are peculiarly vulnerable to being operated in the interests of owner-managers rather than of other stakeholders. The incentives to overemphasize owners' interests, and the difficulty of valuing firm operations, argue for particularly careful supervision of their activities.

Closely held firms thus present supervisors with a finely balanced governance challenge. If they impose stringent conflict-of-interest restrictions, they could inhibit deals that would otherwise contribute to economic growth. However, if they supervise only closely held firms in the same way as widely held firms, they may encourage losses stemming from the incentive problem just discussed. For example, widely held banks may create few conflicts of interest, but they can also be highly conservative in financing innovative deals in which they have no ownership interest. In contrast, closely held trust companies have sometimes identified their interests with those of the principal shareholders, at the cost of failing to safeguard depositors' funds. The key to managing the tradeoff is to seek a balance between the two types of costs. This balance, moreover, is probably best found on a firm-by-firm basis using the exercise of supervisory judgment.

SUMMARY

SUPERVISION SHOULD BE DESIGNED FIRST OF ALL TO ENCOURAGE economic activity. Such encouragement is best achieved by favouring the development of a varied spectrum of financial arrangements. There is no single best regulatory posture for every financial firm. Different firms have different capabilities and different vulnerabilities; the task of regulation is to be sensitive to the mix of regulatory problems each firm is likely to present.

Supervision should seek to ensure that portfolio quality is known to the public and that management is prudent. The two goals may conflict, and regulation has therefore to balance them. Public ratings can help make the values of illiquid portfolios more transparent, but both the virtues of public information and the difficulties of obtaining it (particularly when valuing Type N assets is involved) are not yet widely understood. Conflict-of-interest regulation may safeguard the public but at the cost of inhibiting deals that contribute to economic growth.

Supervisory reform should try both to recognize the change(s) in past financial systems and to anticipate future change. Encouraging change can conflict with protecting the public but the tradeoffs can be clarified using the economics of change and of learning. It is important for regulators to inform the public about changes in the financial system so that, whenever possible, perceptions can be allowed to adjust gradually rather than suddenly. Supervisory discipline is especially important with new, illiquid deals, but it is difficult for supervisors to assess these deals better than financiers.

ENDNOTES

1 Laurentian Group, Trilon, E-L Financial, Crownx, Power Financial, Eaton Bay Financial Services, and Caisses Populaires Desjardins are the principal Canadian examples.

2 However, the picture is beginning to change: see the *Journal of Canadian Business Law*, September 1995.

3 *Report on Business*, August 13, 1994, p. B3.

4 *Toronto Star*, August 21, 1994, p. D1.

5 For further discussion of how the theory relates to the financial literature, see Williamson (1988).

6 The relations between transaction economics and agency theory are discussed in Williamson (1988); the application of transaction economics to financial system analysis in Neave (1991). See also the comments by Romano (this volume) concerning the payoff to transactions economics analyses.

7 In practice, deals usually present differing mixes of the two polar types, but discussion is still furthered by examining the extreme types.

8 A deal involving illiquid assets can be a Type S deal if it is secured by other (liquid) assets.

9 Williamson (1988) demonstrates the importance of asset specificity as a deal attribute; in the present context it is useful to refer to asset specificity as asset liquidity.

10 Incomplete contracting arises from bounded rationality (Williamson, 1988); *i.e.*, from uncertainties that cannot be specified quantitatively when a deal is arranged.

11 Johnson & Neave (1994) demonstrate this cost-benefit relationship in a CAPM environment.

12 A real life firm might have, say, both types of assets. For practical purposes, we would analyze this firm as exhibiting a combination of two of our polar types.

13 Merton (1992) argues that transactions economics has not stressed the kinds of improvements achieved by completing markets. While transactions economics has not previously emphasized this aspect of financial development, our study attempts to show that the transactions economics framework can incorporate explanations of these activities.

14 Financial theory offers many suggestions for designing incentives that induce unbiased reporting.

15 The principles of early information release and risk-based deposit insurance premiums, advocated in Neave (1989) were strongly opposed at the conference where this study was first presented. Both principles have since gained greater acceptability, but the work of implementing them is a long-term task.

16 The problems of level premium insurance schemes are examined in, for example, Kane (1989).

17 This is not to advocate continuously varying deposit insurance premiums; for practical purposes it seems likely that changes would be made no more frequently than annually.

APPENDIX

RECOMMENDATIONS

1. Supervision must strike a balance between encouraging innovative activity and protecting stakeholders through rigidity-inducing rules.

2. The tradeoffs can be mitigated by encouraging information production where asset valuations, liability valuations, or contingent risks are now difficult to establish.

3. Supervision should take account of financial firms' differing capabilities and vulnerabilities as defined by their portfolio types and governance capabilities.

4. In times of change, regulatory supervision should principally assess management capabilities to enter the new lines of business and the adequacy of management procedures to assess the risks.

5. Encouraging continued release of information rather than sudden announcements of change helps stakeholders to revise their portfolio positions at minimal adjustment cost.

6. Supervision should be especially cognizant of the incentives affecting closely held firms, and the consequent dangers these firms face. These dangers must be traded off against the benefits of using highly capable forms of Type H governance for the most difficult forms of Type N deals.

7. Only regulators can govern the domino effects that individual firms have no incentive to recognize (*e.g.*, systemic effects of failure in an active derivatives market).

ACKNOWLEDGEMENTS

WE GRATEFULLY ACKNOWLEDGE THE FINANCIAL ASSISTANCE of Industry Canada and the Financial Research Foundation of Canada. Our study has benefitted from comments by Ron Daniels, Randall Morck, Roberta Romano and Adrian Tschoegl.

BIBLIOGRAPHY

Benston, George J., et al. Perspectives on Safe and Sound Banking: Past, Present, and Future. Cambridge: MIT Press, 1986.

Canada: Department of Finance. "Enhancing the Safety and Soundness of the Canadian Financial System." A White Paper on Canadian financial regulation, February 1995.

Diamond, Douglas W. "Financial Intermediaries and Delegated Monitoring." Review of Economic Studies, 51 (1984):393-414.

Garvey, Gerald,"Does Hierarchical Governance Facilitate Adaptation to Changed Circumstances?" Journal of Economic Behavior and Organization, 20 (1993):187-92.

Johnson, Lewis D. and Edwin H. Neave. "Governance and Comparative Advantage." Managerial Finance, 20 (1994):54-68.

Kane, Edward J. "Technological and Regulatory Forces in the Developing Fusion of Financial Service Competition." National Bureau of Economic Research Working Paper 1320, 1984.

_____. "How Incentive-Incompatible Deposit Insurance Funds Fail." National Bureau of Economic Research Working Paper 2836. 1989.

Kaufman, George G. and Robert E. Litan, (eds.). Assessing Bank Reform: FDICIA One Year Later. Washington: Brookings Institution, 1993.

Merton, Robert C. "Operation and Regulation in Financial Intermediation: A Functional Perspective." Harvard University Graduate School of Business Administration Working Paper. September 1992.

Nathan, Alli and Neave, Edwin H. "Operating Efficiency of Canadian Banks." Journal of Financial Services Research, 6 (1992):265-76.

Neave, Edwin H. "Canada's Approach to Financial Regulation." Canadian Public Policy, XV (1989):1-11.

_____. "Directors and Corporate Control." Canadian Business Law Journal. (September 1995).

Ross, Stephen A. "Institutional Markets, Financial Marketing, and Financial Innovation." Journal of Finance, 44 (1989):541-56.

Williamson, Oliver E. "Transaction Cost Economics: The Comparative Contracting Perspective." Journal of Economic Behavior and Organization, 8 (1987):617-25.

Williamson, Oliver E. "Corporate Finance and Corporate Governance." Journal of Finance, 43 (1988):567-91.

Randall Morck   &   Masao Nakamura   14
Faculty of Business   Faculty of Commerce
University of Alberta   University of British Columbia

Banks and Corporate Governance in Canada

INTRODUCTION

IN GERMANY AND JAPAN, AND ALSO IN OTHER COUNTRIES such as Switzerland
and Korea, banks play a pivotal role in corporate governance. Typically, in
these countries banks own, both directly and indirectly, large blocks of stock
in non-financial firms. Banks can be represented on boards and can have
strong influence on management decisions. The term "universal bank" is used
to describe financial institutions that engage in some or all of deposit-taking,
lending, trust services, underwriting, merchant banking, insurance, or equity
investment activities.

It is equity investment by banks that concerns us here. Criticism of the
corporate governance of U.S. firms by economists like Mace (1986) and
Jensen & Meckling (1976), and subsequent analogous criticism of Canadian
corporate governance, e.g., Leighton & Thain (1990), has been severe.
These and other critics view boards of directors as cosy reunions of old boys
that are generally powerless to prevent, or even recognize, potentially disastrous
corporate policies. Managers, the critics argue, are self-interested and,
unhindered by effective board oversight, run corporations to suit themselves.
Empirical evidence such as Morck et al. (1988, 1989, 1990) and Jensen &
Murphy (1988) provide econometric support for the existence of corporate
governance problems in many large U.S. firms. Given all of this, reformers
have begun to speculate about alternative institutional frameworks that
might work better.

Shleifer & Vishny (1986) argue that even one large, sophisticated shareholder might provide a valuable counterweight to management, and
McConnell & Servaes (1990) report that the existence of such a shareholder
does enhance firm value. In Canada, financial deregulation has opened the
way for large chartered banks to become equity investors in non-financial
firms. Should public policy encourage banks to become large shareholders in
Canadian firms as a means to improve overall corporate governance?

To answer this question, we begin with an examination of the development of the financial systems of countries that allow bank ownership of non-financial firms. We then consider the nature of corporate governance problems in large Canadian firms, and argue that bank ownership of equity is unlikely to provide the sort of benefits its supporters envision.

THE HISTORY OF UNIVERSAL BANKING

THE STRUCTURE OF FINANCIAL INSTITUTIONS is increasingly seen by economists as "path dependent" – that is, history matters! We therefore examine the origins of bank ownership of equity in European industrialization, and then turn to the two banking systems that are often held up as examples of the constructive role of equity ownership – the German and the Japanese.

ORIGINS

THE FIRST UNIVERSAL BANK WAS THE Société Générale du Crédit Mobilier, established in November 1852 by Emile and Isaac Péreire, who were followers of the utopian socialist Claude-Henri, Comte de Saint-Simon.[1] The Saint-Simonians saw banks as an irrigation system for flooding parched areas of the economy with capital. To achieve this, the Péreire brothers employed what we would now call "securitization" – they repackaged their bank's loans to industries as short-term bonds called *valeurs omnium*, which they sold to the public. The reputation of the bank was to enable it to raise funds more cheaply than the uncertain credit of individual industrialists would permit. Unfortunately, securitization was not very successful for the Crédit Mobilier, and it ultimately relied more on deposits and its own capital as well as straightforward underwriting. To retain the confidence of depositors and investors, the Crédit Mobilier considered it essential to maintain the value of its shares, and so engaged in heavy purchases of its own stock whenever the price waned. Companies for which the Crédit Mobilier underwrote securities had to maintain current accounts with the bank. Unprofitable investments in the North of Spain railway, a real estate firm, and reverses on the stock market caused the collapse of Crédit Mobilier in 1867.

Numerous financial institutions modelled on the Crédit Mobilier were set up throughout German-speaking Europe. The Bank für Handel und Industrie was established in Darmstadt in 1853. The Rothschilds founded the Kaiserlich-Königliche Privilegirte Österreichische Credit-Anstalt für Handel und Gewerbe in 1855. Others include the Schweizerische Credit-Anstalt in Zurich (now one of the three main Swiss banks), the Allgemeine Deutsche Credit-Anstalt in Leipzig, the Vereinsbank in Hamburg, the Norddeutsche Bank in Hamburg, the Mitteldeutsche Credit-Bank in Meiningen, the Schlesischer Bank-Verein in Breslau, the Dessauer Credit-Anstalt, the Coburg-Gothaische Credit-Anstalt, and the Preussiche Handelsgesellschaft in Königsberg and the Magdeburger Handelscompagnie.

Branches of the Crédit Mobilier were also established by the Crédit Mobilier itself in Amsterdam, Turin, and London. Rivals were also established in London (the General Credit and Finance Company) and in Paris (the Société Générale pour Favoriser le développement du Commerce et de l'Industrie en France and the Crédit Lyonnais). Heavy losses in equity investments by these banks (including Société Générale's "guano affair" debacle in Peruvian bonds) along with the spectacular collapse of the Crédit Mobilier convinced French bankers of the wisdom of separating commercial banking from equity investment, and gave rise to the present division between banques de dépôts such as the Crédit Lyonnais, and banques d'affaires. In England, the General Credit and Finance Company was liquidated after 90 percent of its capital was wiped out in the panic of 1866. Its managers renounced all "financing" and transferred its commercial banking activities to the General Credit and Discount Company of London, which was merged into the Union Discount Company. The meteoric fate of General Credit confirmed the informal separation of commercial banking from equity investment that still characterizes British banking. In Italy, universal banking existed until the banking crisis of April 1931, when the government intervened, imposing a legal separation of commercial and investment banking, and took over banks' holdings of non-financial firms' shares. These were placed in a state-owned holding company, the Istituto per la Ricostruzione Italiana or I.R.I., one of the largest conglomerates in Europe. Similar legislation was imposed in Belgium.

The late 19th century was a turbulent period in Germany's financial history. Kleeberg (1995) counts 20 bank collapses, 15 bank liquidations, one forced merger, and 10 narrowly averted bank collapses in Germany between 1850 and 1910. Germany also had a severe banking crisis in 1931. In the 1920s German banks had made large loans to highly leveraged industrial firms, especially those controlled by the industrialist heir Hugo Stinnes. As these companies failed, German banks accumulated their equity, which had been pledged as collateral. In the later part of the decade, German banks also spent large amounts of their depositors' money buying their own shares to maintain their stock prices. The fact that the share prices were being maintained at an artificially high level no doubt contributed to the banks' later insolvency. By 1931, when all the major German banks were recognized as clearly insolvent, the Deutsche Bank und Disconto-Gesellchaft owned 27 percent of its own shares, the Dresdner Bank owned 34 percent, the Commerz und Privatbank 50 percent, and the Darmstädter-Nationalbank owned 60 percent. To bail them out, the Weimar government took over these blocks, effectively partially nationalizing the banks.

Several proposals were put forward to reconstruct the German banks along the lines of those in other European countries . However, in 1933, a committee established to consider banking reform quickly recommended against any changes when the National Socialist Party came to power. Hitler toyed with the idea of fully nationalizing the banks, but never implemented such plans. In 1946, following the war, banks in the Soviet occupation zone were "temporarily" closed (Kleeberg, 1987), by 1957 those in West Germany had rebuilt their prewar structures.

Banking reform was also a low priority in the smaller European countries like Switzerland, Holland and the Scandinavian countries. The trade war that followed the Smoot-Hawley tariff, which was passed by the U.S. congress in 1930, virtually shut these small nations out of international trade.[2] Given the resulting economic devastation in these countries, public policy attention was centred on trade initiatives like the Oslo Agreement; banking reform was of negligible importance so a number of aspects of the universal banking system survived in these countries. In Switzerland especially, cosy cartels were established to protect the stability of the system. When barriers to entry were relaxed in 1990, 130 of the then existing 625 banks either lost their independence or disappeared.

In summary, universal banks were established throughout Europe, but did not survive in France, England or Italy. The Canadian banking system followed the French and English models. Reform of the banking system in the early 1930s was pre-empted in Germany by the rise of National Socialism (Kleeberg, 1986).

THE GERMAN BANKING SYSTEM

HEAVY BANK INVOLVEMENT IN INDUSTRIAL FIRMS in Germany is thought by economic historians (Calomiris, 1992) to have played a key role in that country's rapid industrialization between 1870 and 1914. Citing the German electrical industry as an example, Calomiris (1992) argues that universal banks helped "coordinate decision-making among firms", but that banks "did not encourage the development of cartels to impede entry or stunt technological innovativeness at the crucial early stage of industrial development", although he does not deny that cartels may have arisen later. Calomiris (1992) also argues that Germany's cost of capital during industrialization was both lower and more geographically equalized than was America's, at least in part because bank financing was more difficult in the United States. Typical underwriting spreads in the United States were about 20 percent, as compared to about 4 percent in Germany. This, he continues, led to a more capital-intensive industrialization in Germany. Benston (1995) argues that the traditional arguments used in the United States to justify separating commercial from investment banking are bogus creations of populist politicians. He points out that banks with securities operations had lower failure rates and did not push stocks they were underwriting.

Even if Germany's banking system did provide cheaper capital than was available in the United States, it is not clear how this should be interpreted. The U.S. banking system is unlike the others in almost every dimension. Was Germany's cost of capital lower because of greater economies of scale implicit in nationwide multi-branch banking, or was bank involvement in corporate governance through equity ownership the critical factor? Kleeberg (1987) presents substantial evidence that it was not the latter, arguing that German universal banks were remarkably poor at "picking winners" during the country's industrialization, that they invested in a depressing series of financial debacles, and that they may actually have impeded Germany's development by sustaining poorly run firms.

Germany industrialized rapidly because it was a latecomer and the path it had to follow was clear, not because of its universal banks. Of course, other factors were also important, but these were often specific to individual industries. The good fortune of having mineral deposits led to coal, zinc and potash industries. It is arguable that the social benefits provided by collieries meant that, unlike British miners, Ruhr miners rarely went on strike. However, Germany's latecomer advantage may have helped here too – the problems in Britain were clearly to be avoided. A good system of education was an undeniable advantage for Germany. Well-educated workers helped the Saxon and Franconian printing industries grow to become world leaders in colour printing before 1914. It became fashionable for German aristocrats to endow universities, and a dense network of institutions of higher learning provided personnel for the chemicals industry. Germany's latecomer advantage and these other factors were clearly much more important than universal banks, which Kleeberg argues were more a hinderance than a help.

Figure 1 illustrates the structure of a German bank's equity holdings under the present rules.[3] The universal bank may own a direct controlling stake in some firms, but more often its shareholdings are held through an investment company. These investment company subsidiaries are analogous to mutual funds in that they pool small investors' funds together to form large portfolios. A critical difference between a German investment company and a North American mutual fund is that investors in the German variant are not shareholders and have no voting rights. Investors sign a contract with the bank's investment company that specifies management fees, etc. German law allows the investment company to alter these contracts provided the Federal Banking Supervisory Authority approves the changes. The bank is the controlling shareholder of the investment company and it exercises voting rights in the stocks the investment company owns.

This results in banks controlling majority stakes in most large German companies, as illustrated in Table 1. Clearly, corporate governance power in Germany is effectively concentrated in the hands of the top managers of the major banks. Other shareholders are essentially irrelevant. There are no pension funds in Germany, as pensions are organized on a "pay-as-you-go" basis and are guaranteed by the federal government. Insurance companies are generally affiliated with banks. Thus, institutional investors other than banks and their subsidiaries are not a force. Finally, German law allows management to disenfranchise dissident shareholders at annual meetings, so criticism of

TYPICAL STRUCTURE OF A GERMAN UNIVERSAL BANK

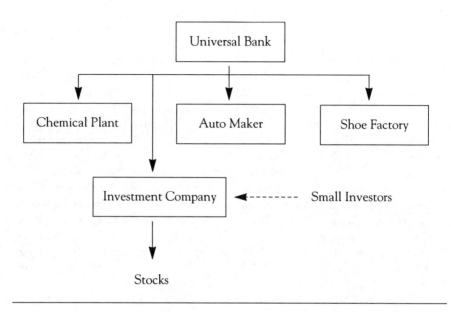

Note: The intercorporate ownership structure typical of German universal banks involves an "investment
        company" subsidiary that pools small investors' funds together to hold a large equity portfolio. The
        Universal bank usually exercises all voting rights on stock held by its investment company. The direction
        of arrows indicates ownership.

corporate policy is somewhat muted. Such criticism is, in any case, usually about "politically correct" issues like racism or the environment, not the competence or track record of management.

It is arguable that Germany has also both actively and passively suppressed financial markets, banks' main competitors in other countries. The active suppression is in the form of punitively high capital gains taxes that both lock banks into their equity positions and discourage the development of active securities markets. The passive suppression takes the form of lax disclosure standards and a tolerant attitude toward insider trading. Thus, relatively primitive financial markets in Germany leave banks with immense power, almost by default.

The scope for banks to abuse their positions is immense. Product market competition among banks and their investment company subsidiaries is not intense. No reliable comparison of the performance of German investment companies is made available to the public. The reputation of the bank is considered a guarantee against incompetence or fraud. However, there are surely

TABLE 1

VOTING RIGHTS EXERCISED BY BANKS IN GENERAL MEETINGS OF THE LARGEST
NON-BANK WIDELY HELD GERMAN CORPORATIONS IN 1992 (%)

FIRM	BANKS' DIRECT STAKE	SUBSIDIARY INVESTMENT FUNDS' STAKE	PROXY VOTES CONTROLLED BY BANKS	TOTAL BANK CONTROL
Siemens	–	9.87	85.81	95.48
Volkswagen	–	8.89	35.16	44.05
Hoechst	–	10.74	87.72	98.46
BASF	0.09	13.81	81.01	94.71
Bayer	–	11.23	80.09	91.32
Thyssen	6.77	3.82	34.98	45.37
VEBA	–	12.82	78.23	90.85
Mannesmann	–	7.78	90.35	98.11
MAN	8.67	12.69	28.84	48.20
Preussag	40.65	4.51	54.30	99.48
VIAG	10.92	7.43	30.75	49.10
Degussa	13.65	8.65	38.35	60.65
AGIV	61.19	15.80	22.10	99.09
Linde	33.29	14.68	51.10	99.07
Deutsche Babcock	3.22	11.27	76.09	90.58
Schering	–	19.71	74.79	94.50
KHD	59.56	3.37	35.03	97.96
Bremer Vulkan	–	4.43	57.10	61.53
Strabag	74.45	3.62	21.21	99.28
Average	13.02	10.11	60.95	84.09

Note: Includes shares on own account, depositary voting rights as proxies and shares held by subsidiary investment
funds expressed as a percentage of all shares represented at the meeting.
Source: Baums (1995).

instances where a bank's interests as a creditor conflict with the interests of its
investors. Since banks' dividends from their investment companies can be
enhanced by churning, etc. there appears to be another potential conflict of
interest here.[4] In addition, banks and their investment companies can sell
blocks of equity to each other in private transactions, and investment companies'
fees paid to their banks for miscellaneous services are only loosely regulated
and are thus another possibility for non-arm's-length transactions harming
small investors. Baums (1995) points out that German banks' investment
companies frequently buy blocks of shares their parents are underwriting, and he
raises the possibility that German banks may be "dumping the trash" on small
investors. He argues that German law is not effective at preventing such dumping.

German corporate governance, then, is entirely overseen by the country's
large banks. How well does this system work? Kaplan (1993) finds that
German directors have much more job security than their American peers;

TABLE 2

VOTING RIGHTS OF THE FIVE LARGEST STOCK CORPORATION BANKS AT THEIR OWN
SHAREHOLDERS' MEETINGS IN 1992 (%)

BANK	DEUTSCHE BANK	DRESDNER BANK	COMMERZ-BANK	BAYR. VEREINSB	BAYR. HYPO	ALL BANKS
Deutsche Bank	32.07	14.14	3.03	2.75	2.83	54.82
Dresdner Bank	4.72	44.19	4.75	5.45	5.04	64.15
Commerzbank	13.43	16.35	18.49	3.78	3.65	55.70
Bayr. Vereinsb.	8.80	10.28	3.42	32.19	3.42	58.11
Bayr. Hypo	5.90	10.19	5.72	23.87	10.74	56.42

Note: Includes depositary voting rights and shares held by subsidiary investment funds. Figures are percent of
all shares represented at the meeting.
Source: Baums (1995).

Aufsichtsrat or supervisory board turnover is uncorrelated with firm performance; but turnover on the *Vorstand* or management board is related somewhat to sliding stock prices, but more to very poor earnings. This suggests that if banks do play a role in disciplining managers of non-financial firms, they do so mainly from the perspective of creditors – not shareholders.

Even assuming no conflict of interest exists between banks and investors, this system depends on the quality of the top management at Germany's banks. Incompetence at the helm of a great bank could lead to a domino effect of mismanagement. Unfortunately, bank managers themselves are totally protected from oversight. Together, the largest German banks control majorities of their own shares, as shown in Table 2.

Overall, the German banking system appears singularly unsuited to provide corporate governance. While Germany's large firms have prospered under the system in the post-war period, signs of strain are beginning to show. In 1982 the Schröder Münchmeyer Hengst bank collapsed because of its heavy exposure to the machinery firm IBH-Holdings, which was heavily leveraged and failed when the market for construction and farming machinery dried up. The recent financial debacles involving the gigantic German property development firm Jürgen Schneider and the metals giant Metallgesellschaft AG, which threatened the Deutsche Bank itself, have raised concerns in Germany that German banks are not able to keep up with the doings of corporate management. Reflecting this, financial journalist Günther Ogger wrote about the incompetence of German bankers in his best-seller *Nieten in Nudelstreifen*. In 1994, responding to public concern, the Social Democrats proposed Bundestagsdrucksache 13/367, which calls for a 5 percent limit on the shares banks could hold in non-financial companies, and a requirement that shares above 3 percent be disclosed (down from the current 20 percent).

The Japanese Banking System

Following the 1868 *Meiji* restoration in Japan, that country imitated what it saw to be the best features of several Western countries. Japan chose Germany's banking system as its model, despite the collapse the previous year of the Crédit Mobilier (the template on which the German system had been modelled). The feature of the German system that made it attractive to the Japanese was the same feature that appealed to Bismarck: bank control of capital allocation kept economic power out of the hands of political enemies. Both Germany and Japan were modernizing in the face of concerted opposition from previously entrenched aristocratic classes. Of course, the banks were not always ideological allies. The Deutsche Bank was also known as *die rote Bank*, and in 1848 David Hausemann, founder of the Diskonto-Gesellschaft, was a left-wing leader. Bismarck certainly cared more about controlling the army than the banks; *Gegen Demokraten helfen nur Soldaten!* (against democrats, only soldiers help).

Prior to 1945, the Japanese economy was characterized by groups of industrial companies called "zaibatsu", often organized around a bank, and controlled by a powerful *Meiji* family.[5]

When the family corporate group was highly profitable, their bank invested excess cash flow elsewhere in the economy. These banks, which we shall call *zaibatsu* banks, include the Mitsubishi, Mitsui, and Sumitomo Banks, lent only 10 percent to 20 percent of their loans to related firms. They were well diversified and survived the financially troubled 1920s and 1930s.

Other Japanese corporate groups had greater need for outside capital, and so used their banks to raise money for themselves. These captive banks, called "organ" banks, were poorly diversified. For example, 94 percent of the Nakazawa Bank's loans were to insiders, as were 75 percent of the Watanabe Bank's loans. Prior to their collapse in 1927, 72 percent of the loans of Suzuki's captive bank, the Taiwan Bank, were to Suzuki companies and 75 percent of the loans of Matsukata's Jugo Bank were to Matsukata family firms. In the crisis of 1927, triggered by the financial frauds of Mme. Ione Suzki and the closure of the Tokyo Watanabe Bank, 37 banks failed. All were organ banks. It is notable that organ banks typically held less equity (about 15 percent of the value of their loans) than did the highly diversified *zaibatsu* banks (about 21 percent).

Another wave of bank failures occurred as the great depression took hold in Japan. In 1930, 19 banks failed; 33 closed their doors in 1931; and 13 more failed in 1932. Again, large diversified *zaibatsu* banks survived, and organ banks failed; again, equity ownership was lower in banks that failed.

Following World War II, the U.S. occupation force in Japan oversaw a full-scale revamping of Japan's financial system. Banks were forbidden from underwriting securities issues. Although the U.S. government exerted considerable pressure for a complete ban on bank ownership of the stock of non-financial firms, (as was the U.S. practice) the Allied Forces ultimately decided against this. Banks' share ownership in other companies was limited to a 10 percent stake, and *zaibatsu* firms were ordered to disgorge their share holdings in each other. (A further reduction to 5 percent was implemented between 1977 and 1987.) As a result, in the immediate postwar period large Japanese companies were, to a great extent, widely held. Reconstruction following the war also entailed high interest rates and low equity prices. Sheard (1991) documents a series of hostile takeover bids during this period. Immediately before the end of the U.S. occupation in 1952, Japanese firms began buying up each others' shares again with the explicit purpose of preventing hostile takeovers (Sheard, 1991). This resulted in a considerable increase in intercorporate share ownership between the former Mitsubishi, Mitsui and Sumitomo *zaibatsu* firms between 1949 and 1951. In the late 1960s a renewed spate of takeover bids and greenmail payments accelerated Japanese firms' intercorporate stock purchases, particularly between firms in the newly emerging Sanwa, Fuji, Daiichi, and Kangyo bank groups. The result is the present grouping of Japanese firms into *keiretsu*, groups of firms that, together, own controlling blocks of each others' shares. Corporate groups that contain a large bank as a key member are called *financial keiretsu*. Morck & Nakamura (1994) argue that *keiretsu* arose primarily as anti-takeover barriers. Figure 2 illustrates a typical financial *keiretsu*.

The potency of *keiretsu* as anti-takeover defences is illustrated by the bid of American financier T. Boone Pickens for the Japanese firm *Koito* in 1990. Pickens accumulated stock on the open market until he was by far the largest single shareholder, yet he was unable even to gain a seat on the board. Together, other firms in the *keiretsu* owned a majority of *Koito* stock and, acting in concert, they blocked Pickens' every move.

Banks do serve a corporate governance role in contemporary Japan. Morck & Nakamura (1994) show that new bank representatives are appointed to the boards of Japanese companies when their financial performance lags. Kaplan & Minton (1994) confirm this, and also show that these banker appointments are accompanied by increased turnover of top managers. This is confirmed by Kang & Shrivdasani (1995) and is consistent with banks exercising a greater governance role in troubled firms. However, both Morck & Nakamura (1994) and Kaplan & Minton (1994) find that indicators of possible loan repayment problems, rather than more general indicators of financial health, are the strongest predictors of increased bank attention. Under most circumstances, Japanese banks appear relatively unconcerned with the welfare of small shareholders or the decisions of management.

Moreover, the globalization and deregulation of the securities markets appears to be undermining what governance roles Japanese banks do play. Hoshi *et al.* (1993) argue that, in recent years, the most profitable of Japan's large firms seem to be reducing their dependence on banks and turning to financial markets to raise capital. This is consistent with the view that

FIGURE 2

TYPICAL STRUCTURE OF A JAPANESE FINANCIAL KEIRETSU

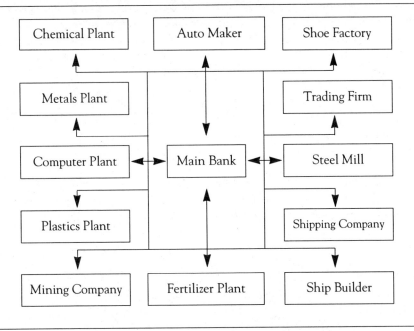

Note: In a Japanese financial *keiretsu*, group firms hold blocks of each others' stock, with banks being forbidden by law from owning more than 5 percent of any non-financial company's stock. Together, the stakes of *keiretsu* firms usually add up to a control block.

Japanese financial regulations simultaneously protect banks and constrain the capital market activities of other firms.

Like German banks, Japanese banks themselves cannot be taken over. They are protected by the same web of intercorporate ownership that shields industrial companies. Also, the largest shareholders of major Japanese banks are affiliated life insurance firms. Since these firms have "mutual" ownership structure (*i.e.*, the policyholders are owners) they are unlisted and essentially management-controlled.

BANKS AND CORPORATE GOVERNANCE IN CANADA

CANADIAN BANKS ARE AMONG the largest corporations in the world.[6] Because of their vast systems of branches, they have attained a degree of economic importance that far surpasses that of U.S. commercial banks. According to Breckenridge (1910), the Canadian nationwide branch banking system was a deliberate adoption of Alexander Hamilton's vision of a banking system for the United States. However, the American free banking philosophy did not take root here. (A brief experiment with free banking in Ontario was not seen as a great success.) The parliamentary charters granted to form Canada's first banks in the early 1800s limited the activities of banks to issuing notes and lending for commercial purposes at multiple branches, and required periodic reports to the government. After Confederation, their activity was governed by the *Bank Act* of 1871 and its subsequent revisions every ten years. The general trend of these revisions has been to broaden steadily the scope of banks' businesses.

In 1907, a financial crisis which threatened the stability of the banks was precipitated when many indebted farmers experienced crop failures. This brought an injection of credit by the federal government and a new government concern with the stability of the system. The early 1920s were a period of recession in Canada and the failure of the Home Bank in 1923 led to increased government oversight. Many banks became unprofitable and were merged into other banks. The number of chartered banks was reduced by two-thirds to only ten during the 1920s. Well-known names like the Bank of Hamilton, the Bank of Ottawa and Molson's Bank vanished.

Although 27 banks failed in Canada between 1867 and 1940 (Kryzanowski & Roberts, 1994), none failed during the Great Depression. This latter fact has perhaps given Canada's banking system an exaggerated reputation for stability. Kryzanowski & Roberts (1994) describe archival evidence that the Canadian government gave a 100 percent implicit guarantee to all banks following the 1923 Home Bank failure. They further show that all but one bank were technically insolvent in the 1930s and survived only because of forbearance by government regulators. Thus, Canadian banks are a poor example for supporters of multibranch banking to cite when they list greater stability as a virtue of such systems.

Canadian banks were very conservative about expanding the definition of "banking" in the immediate postwar period. In 1944, they were offered the mortgage business, but collectively turned it down. Only in 1954 did they begin handling N.H.A. mortgages. General mortgages were not part of banking until 1967.

In the 1960s and 1970s the Canadian financial system was compartmentalized by function into five groups (known as the "four pillars" of the financial system): chartered banks, trust and mortgage companies, cooperative credit movements, life insurance companies, and securities firms (Freedman, 1986). This division was underscored by federal regulation of chartered banks and provincial regulation of securities firms. However, the distinctions became steadily blurred over time as innovations by the various institutions encroached on each others' territory. For example, chartered banks increased their mortgage lending while trust companies and credit unions moved into commercial banking and life insurance policies came increasingly to resemble fixed-term deposits.

Nonetheless, the introduction of deposit insurance in 1967 created a fundamental difference between banking and other financial businesses that is now politically impossible to undo. That same year, a 10 percent limit was imposed on bank ownership of voting stock in non-financial firms, except for very small companies and for equity obtained as collateral. Prior to this, there had apparently been no rule explicitly barring banks from being equity block-holders, although banks seem not to have taken advantage of this. Even now, the 10 percent limit in Canada is generous compared to that of 5 percent in Japan. Yet Canadian banks collectively hold very little equity, only about $10.4 billion out of total assets of $800 billion.[7] The reason given by practitioners and by the Bank of Canada is that "equity ownership is not part of banking".

In the 1980s it became apparent that changing demographics might soon begin to erode banks' lending opportunities as baby boomers aged and became net savers. Bankers began to fear (legitimately) that mortgage lending and other traditional bank activities were likely to be low-growth industries. Also, the admission of subsidiaries of foreign banks (Schedule II banks) into Canada allowed in the 1981 revision of the *Bank Act* increased competition in commercial banking as the number of chartered banks rose to 66 by 1991. Finally, both the Canada/U.S. Free Trade Treaty (FTA) and the North American Free Trade Agreement (NAFTA) require that new federal regulations must give "national treatment" to financial institutions.

In addition, inflation and interest rate volatility made the banks' traditional business of taking deposits and making loans more risky. New financial products were developed to manage this risk, but these sorts of innovations were part of the traditional business of securities firms, not banks. Indeed, the global trend towards securitization is undermining banks' traditional financial intermediation business (*i.e.*, taking deposits and making loans). Mortgages and student loans, (and perhaps, soon, small business loans), are being repackaged into securities and sold to investors. This trend is likely to accelerate following the 1995 introduction of a tax on bank capital in Canada. Overall, these movements point to a long-term decline in conventional banking. Thus, strong pressures for financial deregulation arose in the 1980s, mainly from the chartered banks. Fearing bank dominance, other financial institutions, especially insurance companies, opposed deregulation.

In the late 1980s various interim measures were introduced that allowed banks to buy securities firms and trust companies, and enter real estate development. These measures were consolidated in the 1991 *Bank Act* revisions, along with an elimination of reserve requirements. All financial institutions are now free to enter all financial businesses, with the sole exception of insurance which, because of intense lobbying, is protected by rules that bar banks from selling insurance in branches and from using information about their customers to target insurance sales. Banks were also kept out of the automobile leasing business. All of Canada's major securities firms are now subsidiaries of chartered banks, as are many large trust companies.

493

TABLE 3

FINANCIAL PERFORMANCE AND FIRM CHARACTERISTICS OF CANADIAN FIRMS WITH AND WITHOUT BANK EXECUTIVES ON THEIR BOARDS OF DIRECTORS

CHARACTERISTIC	FULL SAMPLE		NO BANKER ON BOARD		BANKER ON BOARD		T-TEST PROBABILITY LEVEL
Sales Growth (%)	11.4	(492)	11.7	(455)	7.07	(37)	.19
Assets Growth (%)	10.4	(460)	11.0	(423)	3.41	(37)	.01*
Income Growth (%)	141.00	(256)	131.00	(247)	275.00	(18)	.52
Five-year Income Growth (%)	180.00	(254)	197.00	(234)	−17.6	(20)	.01*
Return on Investments (%)	13.7	(334)	14.0	(306)	10.7	(28)	.05**
Return on Equity (%)	11.4	(293)	11.7	(269)	9.04	(24)	.04**
Income/Assets (%)	3.06	(399)	3.11	(365)	0.55	(34)	.37
Income/Sales (%)	2.97	(404)	2.99	(370)	2.78	(34)	.80
Income/Worker ($)	39.4	(391)	41.62	(357)	15.6	(34)	.23
Sales/Worker ($)	2,158	(485)	2,305	(448)	389	(37)	.03**
Assets/Worker ($)	2,709	(454)	2,895	(417)	601	(37)	.07***
Sales ($)	1,079	(500)	922	(463)	3,042	(37)	.01*
Employment ($)	4,710	(485)	3,981	(448)	13,543	(37)	.01*
Assets ($)	1,547	(466)	1,393	(429)	3,343	(37)	.01*
Foreign Ownership (%)	34.6	(500)	34.2	(500)	38.9	(37)	.53
Insider Ownership (%)	67.7	(499)	69.3	(462)	48.8	(37)	.01*

Notes: * Statistically significant at 99% probability.
** Statistically significant at 95% probability.
*** Statistically significant at 90 % probability.
Data are for fiscal years ending in 1994. Growth rates are from 1993 to 1994.
Five-year income growth in 1989 to 1994.

Canadian chartered banks are currently well represented on the boards of the country's largest non-financial firms.[8] Of the 1994 *Financial Post* 500 firms, 37 have executives from the major chartered banks on their boards. Table 3 shows some rough measures of growth, profitability, labour force utilization, size, and ownership for Canadian firms without and with bankers on their boards. Firms with bankers are growing more slowly and are less profitable, their workers generate lower sales *per capita* and they are less capital-intensive, they are much larger in terms of sales, employees and assets, and they are less closely held.[9] From this, it is not clear whether bankers are appointed to boards in response to declines in firm performance, as in Japan, or whether they are simply more likely to accept honorific board positions from large, slow growing, less profitable firms. In any case, bankers on boards are not *prima facie* correlated with superior overall performance. More technical research in this area is in progress.

All Canada's chartered banks have long been widely held. This status is preserved by legislated voting caps that prevent any shareholder from acquiring more than a 10 percent stake. Thus, like their German and Japanese counterparts, Canadian chartered banks cannot be taken over. Other financial institutions in Canada can be closely held, so in establishing equal treatment of all financial institutions, financial deregulation might perhaps call for the elimination of these voting caps. It does not. Instead, all federal financial institutions with capital greater than C$ 750 million are required to have at least 35 percent of their stock widely held by 1996 and to be fully widely held by 2001. Only banks that are controlled by widely held financial companies can be closely held. Smaller institutions and provincially incorporated institutions can come under Schedule II, and thus be exempt from being widely held.

These ownership rules are reasonable in that they prevent the formation of the sorts of "organ" bank subsidiaries of non-financial firms that proved so disastrous in prewar Japan. However, by insulating the top managers of Schedule I banks from both the market for corporate control and from oversight by a large shareholder, the current *Bank Act* almost guarantees that these Canadian banks will suffer from the sorts of governance problems that plague large widely held U.S. firms. While improved audits and outsiders on bank boards might provide some check on managers, the overall ability of the system to discipline under-performing bank managers is questionable.

Indeed, the current rush by the chartered banks to diversify into insurance, leasing, securities, etc. is itself disturbing. In other industries, diversification is now almost a dirty word. Morck, Shleifer & Vishny (1990) show that when industrial firms launch diversifying takeovers, their share prices promptly fall. Elsewhere in the economy, firms are returning to their core businesses and shedding unrelated operations. Diversified companies are now viewed as expensive failures in corporate governance, and are being broken up. Much of the takeover activity in North America in recent years has actually been the transfers of assets from these diversified firms to firms that specialize in particular industries. Why, then, are banks setting up conglomerates when every other industry is getting back to basics?

A likely answer is that traditional banking produces substantial cash flows (barring Latin American debt disasters, etc.), but offers few growth prospects. Banks are thus following tobacco and steel companies by trying to diversify into growth. When firms in a declining industry try to buy growth by acquiring firms with better prospects than their own, their share prices fall (Morck, Shleifer & Vishny, 1990). Indeed, this sort of behaviour in other industries would doubtless lead to calls for better corporate governance to force firms to disgorge their cash as dividends to shareholders.

Colossal losses from investments in Latin American debt, London real estate, or New York office buildings have not led to the termination of senior bankers. Indeed, Canadian banks seem to have adopted a herd mentality. As long as all the banks make the same investments at the same time, no individual banker can be blamed if money is lost. This sort of logic would do little to convince angry shareholders not to tender in a takeover bid. Canadian pension fund manager Stephen Jarislowsky (1994) reports the following exchange: "After the annual meeting of Canada's largest bank, The Royal Bank of Canada, I quipped to the CEO Rowland Frazee, 'What does it take to get fired as CEO of a Canadian bank?' He responded, 'What do you mean, Stephen?' I said, 'Rolly, you lost $1.5 billion this year.' His answer: 'I see what you mean!'"

SHOULD PUBLIC POLICY PUSH CANADIAN BANKS TOWARD A CORPORATE GOVERNANCE ROLE?

CANADA'S FINANCIAL SYSTEM IS AT A UNIQUE POINT in its history. Recent financial deregulation has removed most constraints on banks, and a spate of takeovers of other financial firms has greatly broadened the economic role of the banks. At the same time, corporate governance is becoming a major public policy issue. Pension fund managers are increasingly critical of poor corporate performance, and shareholder advocates such as Fairvest are becoming increasingly vocal. Is there a solution to our corporate governance problems that involves a further expansion of the functions of the banks in the Canadian economy, similar to the experience of Germany or Japan?

We contend that the answer to this is "no" for three reasons. First, as we showed earlier, the German and Japanese systems have serious problems of their own. Even if we could switch to their models immediately and without cost, it is far from clear that this would be an improvement. Second, as we also discussed earlier, Canadian banks are required by law to be widely held. Thus, almost alone among major Canadian firms, they are likely to be subject to the same serious corporate governance problems that plague large widely held U.S. firms. Putting banks in charge of corporate governance is uncomfortably like putting the fox in charge of the hen-house. Third, there are several facts of political and economic life in Canada that make German- or Japanese-style bank oversight less attractive here. We now turn to these.

First, the political fact of deposit insurance must be taken into consideration in any expanded role for Canadian banks. In recent years some economists have deplored the apparent political impossibility of downgrading or eliminating deposit insurance. In our view, this popularity should be taken as revealing a strong public preference for the existence of a readily accessible, minimally risky asset. Certainly, standard portfolio theory is consistent with such an asset being welfare enhancing. If, to create such an asset, the government is guaranteeing large amounts of the banks' debts (i.e., their deposits), then a case can be made that banks' assets (i.e., their mortgages, loans and other investments) ought to be limited to investments that can be monitored effectively by government supervisors. One straightforward demarcation line might be that investments where tangible assets are put up as collateral are acceptable, but others are not. This clearly excludes equity investments by banks.

A second fact that distinguishes corporate governance issues in Canada from those in the United States is that most Canadian firms are closely held, not widely held. Morck & Stangeland (1994) show that the poorest performers among Canadian firms are not those with diffuse ownership, but those with entrenched family control. Shleifer & Vishny (1986) demonstrate that a stake by a large outside investor (such as a bank) might improve the performance of a widely held firm. However, large U.S. institutional investors such as CalPERS avoid closely held firms. Presumably this is because institutional investors are less able to mitigate problems associated with entrenched management than those associated with diffuse ownership.

Related to this, a third fact that distinguishes the Canadian case from Germany and Japan is the existence of large institutional investors here. Because of legal limits on the foreign investments they can make, institutional investors like the ($35 billion) Ontario Teachers' Pension Plan are forced to take large stakes in Canadian firms' equity. Increasingly, Canadian pension funds are working to improve the governance of firms in which they invest, since the alternative of selling their large blocks of equity onto the open market pushes the price down before the sale is complete. Both private-sector and public-sector pension funds are exerting steadily increasing pressure on corporate managers to improve performance. In both Germany and Japan, pension plans are managed on a pay-as-you-go basis, so there are no pension funds as such. Other financial institutions in Canada, like venture capital funds, also play governance roles in other sections of the economy. Kroszner (1995) argues that in the United States, given the existence of these substitutes, letting banks hold equity stakes would add little. The same argument applies here. Indeed, given the potential problems in the governance of Canadian banks themselves, other institutional investors might be preferable as checks on management in the 16 percent of large Canadian firms that are widely held.[10]

A fourth fact is that Canada does have active financial markets and a market for corporate control. While hostile takeovers are rare, they do happen. Nova's takeover of Polysar *via* a hostile proxy fight is a good example. The recent $1.2 billion leveraged buyout of Maple Leaf Foods Inc. by the ousted McCain Foods CEO Wallace McCain (backed by the Ontario Teachers' Pension Plan) is an example of the market for corporate control in action. Hees International Bankcorp's equity workouts in the 1980s are another. Most Canadian takeovers are friendly since they are aimed at closely held firms, but these are still ways of replacing top management.

A fifth fact of contemporary Canada is the existence of active and sophisticated financial markets and investors. Organizations like Fairvest Securities Corp. and the Canadian Shareholders' Association both lobby for shareholders' rights and against the poison pills that widely held Canadian companies are increasingly adopting. In contrast, especially in Germany, financial markets are relatively primitive.

Sixth, Canada's banks do not seem especially interested in being equity blockholders. They seem more intent on diversifying out of their low-growth core business and into possibly higher growth lines of business like securitization – in imitation of the financial conglomerates that exist in Britain.

A final political fact is the already considerable public anxiety about concentration of economic power in too few hands in Canada. In Germany, because of their intercorporate ownership stakes and trusteeship role, the large banks indirectly control a majority of their own voting stock. In Japan, bankers are protected by networks of intercorporate equity holdings that exclude outsiders from exerting any control. In Canada, banks are insulated from corporate governance challenges by government mandated voting caps. The banks may watch other firms, but who watches the watchers? Encouraging bank ownership of blocks of equity might very well only further entrench Canadian managers and exacerbate the political problems that flow from overly concentrated economic power.

CONCLUSIONS AND PUBLIC POLICY OPTIONS

HISTORICAL STUDIES AND ECONOMETRIC ANALYSES of banking in both Germany and Japan suggest that the concept of banks as guarantors of good corporate governance owes more to wishful thinking by economic theoreticians than to hard evidence. Both the German and Japanese systems have serious shortcomings of their own.

The Canadian banking system evolved in a different direction, and Canadian banks are now poorly equipped to perform a monitoring role over the managers of other firms. Indeed, it can be argued that Canadian banks are showing signs of serious corporate governance problems themselves. Any role for banks in improving the corporate governance of other firms must be predicated on first improving corporate governance in the banks themselves.

One easy way to do this would be to relax banks' voting caps for investments by *independent* pension funds to, say, 20 percent while keeping the caps at 10 percent, or perhaps even lowering them to 5 percent, for all other investors. Pension funds managed by corporations, or even provincial governments, might also be bound by the lower limit. This would allow hardnosed institutional investors to oversee bank managers, but would prevent the formation of "organ" banks.

Another way to improve corporate governance in the banks would be to open up the Canadian banking system to further (possibly foreign) competition. Scholnick (1994) reports that the average spread between mortgage rates and G.I.C. rates in Canada has risen from between 1 percent and 2 percent in the 1980s to between 2 percent and 3 percent in the 1990s, while the overall costs of commercial banking have declined slightly. This should not be possible in a competitive industry. If banks can use their market power to pass on the costs of mistakes in corporate governance to depositors, pressure from shareholders can be deflected. Heightened competition for depositors' dollars in commercial banking would make shifting costs to depositors less viable and would force banks to confront their own corporate governance issues.

If bank ownership of equity in non-financial firms does come into effect in Canada, regulators should be on the alert to protect both depositors and taxpayers. The "liabilities" on a bank's balance sheet that correspond to the debt of an industrial company are largely its deposits. Financial economists theorize that the bondholders of the industrial firms perform a sophisticated monitoring function. It is unrealistic to ascribe a similar role to the depositors of the banks, who are the quintessential unsophisticated investors. Through their political support for deposit insurance, Canadian depositors have made it clear that they want a maximally safe asset in bank accounts. While it is certainly true that many stocks are much less risky than Brazilian bonds or New York real estate, equity is an investment without collateral. In light of this, a policy option that deserves consideration is to amend bankruptcy laws to give depositors absolute priority in all the companies a bank controls. Even if this is unlikely to improve corporate governance, it would at least protect the taxpayers from footing the bill *via* the Canadian Deposit Insurance Corporation for any of the banks' equity misadventures.

ENDNOTES

1 Much of the historical discussion here closely follows Kleeberg (1987), who gives a fascinating description of the history of universal banking in Europe, focusing on Germany. His work is not well-known to economists, but should be.

2 The "beggar thy neighbour" devaluations following the September 1931 collapse of Sterling, and the adoption of Imperial preferences at the Ottawa conference, were also key events.

3 The next paragraphs draw heavily on Baums (1995).

4 "Churning" is a legal term for unnecessary transactions generating commissions for financial managers.

5 The discussion of the prewar Japanese banking system follows Hoshi (1995).

6 The historical description of the Canadian financial and banking systems draws from Siklos (1994) and Freedman (1986).

7 *Bank of Canada Gazette*, Fall 1994.

8 Romano (1993) reports that bankers are also well represented on the boards of top U.S. companies.

9 Nakatani (1984) finds that Japanese firms in financial *keiretsu* also grow

more slowly and are less profitable than firms with weaker link to these banks.

10 Morck & Stangeland (1995) report that only 16 percent of the largest 550 firms in Canada in 1989 had no single shareholder controlling more than 20 percent of their votes.

ACKNOWLEDGEMENTS

WE ARE GRATEFUL FOR ASSISTANCE FROM Clyde Goodless of the Bank of Canada and John Kleeberg of the American Numismatic Society. Comments by Roberta Romano were especially useful. Trevor Katz and Jane Jiang provided outstanding research assistance.

BIBLIOGRAPHY

Baums, T. "Universal Banks and Investment Companies in Germany," Unpublished Manuscript, New York University Salomon Centre Conference on Universal Banking, 1995.

_____. "Corporate Governance in Germany, The Role of the Banks," Unpublished Manuscript, 1994.

Benston, G. "The Banking and the Securities Industries in Historical Perspective," Unpublished Manuscript, New York University Salomon Centre Conference on Universal Banking, 1995.

Breckenridge, R. *The History of Banking in Canada*. Washington, DC, U.S. Government Printing Office, 1910.

Calomiris, C. "The Costs of Rejecting Universal Banking: American Finance in the German Mirror, 1870-1914." National Bureau of Economic Research Working Paper, Cambridge, MA. 1992.

Freedman, C. "Universal Banking: The Canadian View," in *Financial Regulations Changing the Rules of the Game*. Edited by Dimitri Vittas. Washington, D.C.: World Bank, 1992, pp. 369-90.

Hoshi, T. "Back to the Future: Universal Banking in Japan," Unpublished Manuscript, New York University Salomon Centre Conference on Universal Banking, 1995.

Hoshi, T., A. Kashyap and D. Scharfstein. "The Choice Between Public and Private Debt: An Analysis of Post-Deregulation Corporate Financing in Japan," Unpublished Manuscript, 1993.

Jamieson, A. *Chartered Banking in Canada*. Toronto: The Ryerson Press, 1957.

Jarislowsky, S. "Corporate Performance: A Canadian Point of View." *The Edge*, Faculty of Business, University of Alberta, 1994.

Jensen, M. and W. Meckling. "Theory of the Firm: Managerial Behavior, Agency Costs and

Ownership Structure." *Journal of Financial Economics*. 3 (1976):305-60.

Jensen, M. and K. J. Murphy. "Performance Pay and Top Management Incentives." *Journal of Political Economy*. 98 (April 1990):225-64.

Kang, J. and A. Shrivdasani. "Firm Performance, Corporate Governance and Top Executive Turnover in Japan." *Journal of Financial Economics*. (Forthcoming 1995).

Kaplan, S. "Top Executive Turnover and Firm Performance in Germany (Working Paper No. 374)," C.R.S.P. University of Chicago, 1993.

Kaplan, S. and B. Minton. "Appointments of Outsiders to Japanese Boards." *Journal of Financial Economics*, 36 (1995):225-58.

Kleeberg, J. "Some Notable German Bank Collapses, and Why They Happened," Unpublished Manuscript, The American Numismatic Society, New York, 1995.

_____. "The Disconto-Gesellschaft and German Industrialization," Ph.D. Thesis, Oxford University, 1987.

_____. "Universal Banks: The Sonderweg of German Finance," Unpublished Manuscript, The American Numismatic Society, New York, 1986.

Kroszner, R. "The Evolution of Universal Banking and its Regulations in Twentieth Century America," Unpublished Manuscript, New York University Salomon Centre Conference on Universal Banking, 1995.

Kryzanowski, L. and G. Roberts. "Canadian Banking Solvency." *Journal of Money, Credit and Banking*. (Fall 1994).

Leighton D. and D. Thain. "The Role of the Corporate Director." *Business Quarterly*. (Autumn 1990).

Mace, M. *Directors: Myth and Reality*. Cambridge, MA: Harvard Business School Press, 1986.

McConell, J. and H. Servaes. "Additional Evidence on Equity Ownership and Corporate Value." *Journal of Financial Economics*, 27, 2 (1990):595-610.

Morck, R. and M. Nakamura. "Banks and Corporate Control in Canada (Working Paper No. 6-92)," Institute for Financial Research, University of Alberta, 1994.

Morck, R., A. Shleifer and R. Vishny. "Management Ownership and Market Valuation: An Empirical Analysis." *Journal of Financial Economics*, 20 (1988):293-315.

Morck, R., A. Shleifer and R. Vishny. "Alternative Mechanisms for Corporate Control." *American Economic Review*. (September 1989):842-52.

_____. "Do Managerial Objectives Drive Bad Acquisitions?" *Journal of Finance*. (March 1990):31-48.

Morck, R. and D. Stangeland. "Corporate Performance and Large Shareholders in Canada (Working Paper No. 4-94)," Institute for Financial Research, University of Alberta, 1995.

Nakatani, I. "The Economic Role of Financial Corporate Groupings," in *The Economic Analysis of the Japanese Firm*. Edited by M. Aoki. Amsterdam: Elsevier North Holland, 1984, pp. 227-58.

Romano, R. "A Cautionary Note on Drawing Lessons from Comparative Corporate Governance." *Yale Law Journal*, 102. (1993):2021-29.

Sheard, P. "The Economics of Interlocking Shareholdings in Japan." *Richerche Economiche*, 45, 2-3 (1991):421-48.

Shleifer, A. and R. Vishny. "Large Shareholders and Corporate Control." *Journal of Political Economy*, 95 (1986):461-88.

Scholnick, B. "Commercial Bank Spreads: Evidence from Canada," Working Paper, University of Alberta, Faculty of Business.

Siklos, P. *Money, Banking and Financial Institutions: Canada in the Global Environment*. Toronto: McGraw-Hill Ryerson, 1994.

Roberta Romano
Professor of Law
Yale Law School

Commentary on Part V

THERE IS A COMMON THEME DIRECTED AT POLICY MAKERS in the three studies in this section. It is that protectionist regulations are not welfare-maximizing for the society undertaking them, and (therefore) that in today's world of global markets, less regulation is, in general, better than more regulation. This is the thesis of Morck and Yeung's study on the appropriate public policy toward foreign-owned subsidiaries (encouragement of foreign investment),[1] of Johnson and Neave's study on policy toward financial institutions (encouragement of disclosure rules, supervisory flexibility and discretion over more restrictive regulation),[2] and, albeit indirectly, of Morck and Nakamura's study on the bank-centered system of corporate governance in Germany and Japan. (Morck and Nakamura do not argue against the deregulatory trend concerning the ability of banks to undertake equity investments, but rather, against requiring or encouraging such investments.)[3]

I believe there is a second important lesson to be drawn from these studies – a lesson directly connected to the comparative corporate governance issues raised by Morck and Nakamura, which, I think, is also related to the other two studies: the ingenuity of humans to shape their private institutions, and behaviour to mitigate, if not stymie, regulatory efforts. My impression is that such regulatory efforts have occurred throughout time; the comparative corporate governance debate is an example. The studies by Morck and Yeung, and Johnson and Neave drive this point home forcefully, albeit indirectly: with the increasingly global economy populated by multinational manufacturing and financial firms, less effort may be necessary to devise institutional innovations to avoid a nation's regulatory regime because firms can more easily select an alternative regulator by reallocating their business across operating divisions.

Morck and Yeung's analysis of what drives foreign investment (the desire to protect and capitalize on investments in certain [information-based] intangible assets), and the competitiveness of multinationals (successful innovation amid competition), and their conclusion that Canada should foster such investments, are reasonable and, I believe, would not be seen as controversial among economists. I have little to add to their lucid analysis but to urge its reading by policy makers in Canada and elsewhere who are concerned about foreign investment and tempted to restrict such activity.

I do have a few questions about some points in their argument and policy proposals. The first question has to do with the implications they draw from their thesis that multinationals must perpetually innovate. Morck and Yeung suggest that if a multinational's innovation ends, its foreign subsidiaries will become disadvantaged *vis-à-vis* domestic rivals. It seems to me, however, that after a time the foreign subsidiary becomes an established enterprise and develops the local contacts and personnel, and consequent knowledge of local conditions, which are equal to the "edge" that local firms initially possess. We need more evidence about comparative costs to determine whether perpetual innovation is required for a multinational to retain established subsidiaries profitably or whether the benefits or uses of the organizational form change over time. It may be that multinationals must constantly innovate to compete successfully in global markets, but the connection between innovation (perpetual or not) and organizational form over the long term is less clear. More data on items such as operating costs and revenues than Morck and Yeung provide is necessary in order to determine what the effects of a slow-down in new product or process innovation are on the organizational forms of multinational firms. Does a multinational whose innovation has come to an end shut down established subsidiaries and replace them with contracting arrangements to compete in international markets, or does it withdraw from those markets entirely? In this context, I cannot help thinking of General Motors, whose European subsidiary has been doing extremely well, while the parent firm is doing poorly at home and has not been a perpetual innovator.

My second question concerns the gist of the policy recommendation that appears to suggests the need for increased government subsidization of education through graduate school. I question whether education is as pure a public good as Morck and Yeung maintain to support this recommendation. A substantial proportion of education, particularly the higher technical skills the authors emphasize, is best characterized as a private good that increases the individual's human capital and labour market power. It is far from obvious, however, that this should be subsidized by the state, without more evidence than Morck and Yeung provide – such as evidence that there is a capital market failure that makes it extremely difficult for individuals to borrow in order to train themselves adequately for the relevant professions. In other words, public good arguments make more sense to me in connection with the acquisition of basic literacy skills as provided at the elementary school level rather than at the level of higher learning, or in connection with funding basic research (a separate policy recommendation of the authors), where individuals cannot capture the returns to their investment.

There is also a troubling distributional aspect to such a policy, at least insofar as how such policies have been manifested in the United States. My impression is that U.S. state subsidies to higher education have largely benefitted middle and upper income individuals and not the poor. (The poor are less likely to attend the state-subsidized institutions of higher learning, or to complete their studies if they do attend.) I expect the pattern is not much different in Canada. In fact, the United States is considered to be the world leader in higher education, but the subsidies provided by government are far less than those provided by other nations, including Canada.

But these minor questions sidetrack us unnecessarily from the overall contribution of their study to the Canadian policy debate on foreign investment and from its connection to what I have already identified as the common theme of this session. As I alluded to earlier, and the authors have made clear, their explanation of the process of international competition and innovation serves as a warning against over-regulation. (They conclude with suggestions to move in the other direction, such as to loosen restrictive labour laws, reduce taxes on investment, etc.)

Their study is also relevant to my second theme – the resourcefulness or adaptability of private institutions when confronted by restrictive regulation. For instance, what would happen if Canada decided to forego the benefits identified by Morck and Yeung and banned foreign direct investment? It is not obvious that the market presence of U.S. multinationals in Canada would decrease significantly. To the extent that these firms have found that doing business in Canada is profitable, rather than exit they would be more likely to alter the form of their presence, such as by using extensive relational contracts (or some other mechanism) rather than direct investment to conduct their Canadian business. Of course, the new institutional arrangements would probably be less efficient organizational forms than those previously established without such a ban, because the choice set has been reduced. Some firms may even completely disinvest. There is, however, no reason to believe that Canadians will benefit from imposing higher costs on multinationals and some reason to believe that they will be harmed. By imposing higher costs on multinationals there will be losses from the spillovers that direct foreign investment provides (identified by Morck and Yeung) unless a Canadian firm is thrust into the position of a monopoly supplier of services to the multi-national by the elimination of direct investment competitors, and so must engage in bilateral bargaining rather than market competition. In addition, given its higher operating costs, the multinational will reduce the share of the profits going to its contractual partners that was provided to the subsidiary's Canadian inputs under the previous system. Moreover, the multinational's ability to relocate its business undercuts the bargaining power of even a monopolist contractor.

Johnson and Neave offer a useful classification of financial institutions by associating the liquidity of an institution's assets and liabilities with its organizational structure – an interesting application of the transaction-cost economics approach. Their presentation would gain from the addition of more concrete examples to illustrate the categories, as it may be difficult for policy makers to appreciate the relevance of the approach. It would, for example, be helpful to illuminate more specifically how the framework can be used for a broad set of policy issues, paralleling the discussion relating to the choice of deposit insurance premium levels, and which would depend on whether banks have securitized their loan portfolios or whether they hold risky non-liquid real estate loans. But this is not a pressing objection and I have little to add to their classification structure.

Putting this expositional concern aside, Johnson and Neave share Yeung and Morck's approach – cautioning regulators that inappropriate regulation can cause substantial damage to the private sector, particularly in global markets. In keeping with this theme, the authors recommend adopting a flexible regulatory policy that varies with the characteristics of the institutions' balance sheets – the direct payoff of the classification analysis. Moreover, by identifying risk management and information disclosure as the key issues for regulation of financial institutions, the authors helpfully direct the attention of regulators to market-oriented solutions that should enhance, rather than reduce, firm value by increasing firm competitiveness.

The variation in financing deals described by the authors not only provides the basis for their policy recommendations but also points to the resilient inventiveness of private institutions to find the cheapest mechanism for "getting things done"; this is my second theme. If a nation's regulation bears more heavily on one form of capital than another, financial institutions will first alter what kinds of deals are used where, thereby putting domestic firms in need of financing at a disadvantage. Second, as domestic firms seek cheaper means of financing to remain competitive, they will either come up with new forms of financing that avoid the regulation, or do the deals in foreign markets to avoid the tax, thus creating powerful incentives to repeal the offending regulations in order to regain domestic business. A good case in point is the use of the Eurobond market by U.S. corporations, which led eventually to a reduction in the disclosure and registration requirements of public-debt financing in the shelf registration regime.

Morck and Nakamura examine the German and Japanese systems of corporate governance which depend principally on bank control of non-financial corporations – either by direct investment or by control over votes. This contrasts with both the Canadian and the U.S. systems, where banks play no such role. Other types of investors – individuals, families and the government – play a key role with respect to Canadian firms, whereas for the vast majority of U.S. corporations there is no controlling shareholder, and the market for control is the crucial monitor for the dispersed shareholders. The purpose of Morck and Nakamura's inquiry is to consider whether the differences merit a regulatory response: should Canadian regulators encourage, if not require, banks to buy shares and to assume a central monitoring function of corporate management? They conclude that there would be little benefit in transplanting the German and Japanese approach. I share their skepticism. In my own work in the debate over the merits of adopting German and Japanese corporate governance institutions for U.S. firms, I have reached a similar negative conclusion. I offer some additional data on the issue, which have influenced my conclusion.

In the corporate governance debate in the United States, it is often argued that the Japanese and German bank-centered systems of corporate governance are preferable to U.S. institutions because Japan and Germany are more competitive in world markets. Typically, competitiveness is measured in terms of productivity, and both countries have surpassed the United States in productivity growth for some time. It should be noted that these arguments are based on relative growth rates because, in terms of absolute productivity, the United States has retained the lead and, for the last decade, U.S. productivity growth has exceeded Germany's, and Japan's has not been much better than that in the United States.[4] The best explanation of the difference in productivity growth rates over the post-war period is not, in my judgement, attributable to superior governance mechanisms. Rather, it is, as Baumol, Blackman & Wolff contend, a result of the phenomenon of international convergence: when one nation's productivity is superior to that of other nations, the nations that are not too far behind can catch up as they learn from the leader, through the transfer of technology, and eventually performance levels converge.[5] The laggard countries have more to learn from the leader than the leader has to learn from those behind and, consequently, "those who were initially behind must advance more rapidly than those who were ahead".[6] In addition, the key factors that economists believe affect absolute productivity are the national savings rate (investment), the level of education of the labour force, and the magnitude of the effort devoted to basic and applied research.[7] There is no theory or evidence relating any of these factors to corporate governance arrangements. Furthermore, the different corporate governance institutions in these countries were in place well before the postwar years when the productivity growth rate in the United States began its steep relative decline. Comparative productivity data, and changes in the rate of growth of productivity in particular, cannot therefore be readily attributable to differences in corporate governance. Since improved productivity is the focus of any comparative corporate governance debate, the debate over which system is superior misses the mark.

My reason for reviewing the comparative productivity growth rate findings is not to endorse the restrictions on banks' equity ownership in the United States, or to reverse Canada's deregulatory move permitting such ownership. There would probably be little harm to the financial system by allowing banks to own corporate stock. But, like Morck and Nakamura, I question whether such a reform would radically alter U.S. corporate governance patterns to resemble the German and Japanese systems, just as I observe that it has not yet appreciably altered the Canadian corporate landscape. I also question whether greater bank ownership of U.S. and Canadian firms will improve performance. I offer two anecdotal examples, one historical and one contemporary, in support of the predicted lack of impact. First, long before the United States passed the *Glass-Steagall Act* prohibiting bank ownership of corporate equity in the late 19th century, some American banks (notably in New England) voluntarily abandoned their relationships with firms in favour of intermediation, for reasons of efficient risk-reduction.[8] There is some evidence of similar developments operating in Germany and Japan today.

Second, although British banks can own equity, we see the same sort of dispersed stock ownership of U.K. firms as we see in the United States.[9] The difference may be due to historical accident: the thesis associated with the economic historian Alexander Gerschenkron, that variation in industrialization is related to a country's economic backwardness at the time of its industrialization, offers one plausible explanation.[10] Industrialization occurred considerably later in Germany than in England, at a time when the optimal plant size was much larger and technology was more complex, required greater capital and more informed entrepreneurial guidance. Given this temporal difference, the fledgling German manufacturing firms, in contrast to the comparable industrializing U.K. manufacturers, were unable to grow by reinvesting earnings or by relying on small private banks. This necessitated new financial institutions, such as innovative alliances between Rhenish firms and private bankers, and joint-stock issue banks. As a consequence, German banking developed along different lines from British banking, and that difference also resulted in different systems of corporate governance (as equity-investing universal banks required greater involvement in management). Whatever the significance of fortuity in historical development in explaining contemporary differences between England and Germany, their presence makes it clear that regulatory barriers to bank ownership are not sufficient to explain the differences between U.S., Canadian, German and Japanese governance institutions.

There is a further institutional difference between German, American and Canadian firms that makes piecemeal comparisons of their arrangements difficult and bolsters the theme that corporate governance mechanisms are part and parcel of an entire economic system. German workers are formally represented in corporate decision-making by their statutory representation in the two-tier corporate board system; this is referred to as "codetermination", and ensures that workers constitute half of the supervisory board. In this context, dispersed shareholders could be at a disadvantage, compared to the better-organized workers, in terms of maintaining decisional control; concentrated voting powers in banks, as well as bank block ownership, could be beneficial by providing equity with a countervailing organized force on the board. Such a need is not present in the United States, the United Kingdom or Canada, where firms do not operate under the codetermination board system, and correspondingly, there is less need for a bank-centered monitoring system.

As I have already noted, I agree with Morck and Nakamura that it is not patently obvious that the German and Japanese systems are better for shareholders. They provide suggestive evidence that those systems apparently offer greater protection for, and interest in, creditor rather than shareholder concerns. In addition to the data Morck and Nakamura furnish, I offer another anecdote, this time from the work of the business historian, Alfred Chandler who chronicled U.S. Steel's loss of its early leading position due to poor management decisions.[12] David Teece, in a review of Chandler's work noted that,

"U.S. Steel provides one of the very few examples of banker control in American industry".[13] As Teece concludes, "Chandler leaves little doubt that he believes that the financiers and lawyers running U.S. Steel made serious mistakes".[14] But anecdotes from U.S. business history are muddy on the performance issue. Contrary to the experience of U.S. Steel, one study found that adding a J.P. Morgan banker to a corporate board increased equity value by 30 percent.[15] We do not know whether that increase in value was due to the expectation that there would be more effective corporate governance with a banker on the board, or that there would be increased monopoly rents from business interconnections established with other Morgan firms. In addition, the study does not indicate whether Morgan had equity or debt positions in the firms on whose boards its partners served.

The conclusion I draw from the comparative corporate governance research is that different systems develop in response to the needs of private parties – and one of those needs includes the desire to minimize the effect of regulation. The new German banking institutions created by Rhenish financiers and entrepreneurs to finance industrialization were, in fact, a mechanism to circumvent the Prussian government's restrictions on economic development.[16] In Japan, restrictions on capital market development forced firms to rely on bank financing, and, as Morck and Nakamura indicate, when the regulations were removed, there was a dramatic shift away from bank financing to public debt financing. Moreover, the separation between banker and management in the United States is not as stark as is sometimes maintained. Some large U.S. corporations have important relationships with banks, even though banks cannot own corporate stock. For example, one study found that the impending insolvency of a major U.S. bank had a significant negative effect on the stock prices of corporations whose primary lending relationships were with that bank.[17] In addition, seven of the top ten *Fortune* industrial firms have bankers on their boards, and two of these have financial relations with the directors' banks that are material enough to report in their proxy statements.[18] Undoubtedly, the relation-specific investments between U.S. firms and banks are far more attenuated than those in Germany and Japan. My point is simply that banks enter into long-standing relationships with corporations even in the United States under a regime that restricts banks' equity ownership, so ownership is not a prerequisite to such relationships (and the managerial monitoring that is a byproduct). Banks are motivated to monitor debtors to ensure loan repayment whether or not they are also stockholders in the debtor. As in the cases of Germany and Japan, we do not know the extent to which such relationships produce benefits for shareholders.

In short, there is no reason to assume that one set of corporate governance institutions is superior to or worse than another. We should, instead, understand the differences as evincing the resourcefulness of private parties to organize their affairs so as to produce maximum financial benefits in disparate regulatory contexts. These are all solutions to constrained optimization problems.

Perhaps the most useful thought to keep in mind when considering the relation between regulation and economic organization is that private parties will persist in devising institutions that minimize the effect of political constraints on economic activity. This is the lesson I draw from comparative corporate governance. Moreover, when we consider the implications of this lesson in the context of global markets, confiscatory protectionist regulation will spur not only institutional innovation to circumvent the regulator, but it will also surely drive firms to relocate their business in more favourable regulatory regimes, wherever they may be.

ENDNOTES

1 Morck, Randall and Bernard Yeung, "The Corporate Governance of Multinationals," this volume.

2 Johnson, Lewis and Ted Neave, "Corporate Governance and Supervision of the Financial System," this volume.

3 Morck, Randall and Masao Nakamura, "Banks and Corporate Governance in Canada," this volume.

4 The literature is reviewed in Roberta Romano, *The Genius of American Corporate Law*, American Enterprise Institute, Washington, DC, The AEI Press, 1993, pp. 140-43.

5 Baumol, William J., Sue Anne Batey Blackman and Edward Wolff, *Productivity and American Leadership: The Long View*, Cambridge, MA, The MIT Press, 1989.

6 *Ibid.*, p. 90.

7 *Ibid.*, pp. 258-60.

8 Lamoreaux, Naomi R., "Information Problems and Banks' Specialization in Short-Term Commercial Lending: New England in the Nineteenth Century," in *Inside the Business Enterprise: Historical Perspectives on the Use of Information*, edited by Peter Temin, Chicago, University of Chicago Press, 1991, p. 161.

9 Coffee, John C., "Liquidity versus Control: The Institutional Investor as Corporate Monitor," *Columbia Law Review* , 91, 1991, p. 1277 .

10 Gerschenkron, Alexander, *Economic Backwardness in Historical Perspective: A Book of Essays*, Cambridge, MA, Belknap Press of Harvard University Press, 1962.

11 Tilly, Richard, *Financial Institutions and Industrialization in the Rhineland, 1815-1870*, Madison, WI, University of Wisconsin Press, 1966, pp.134-35; Francke, Hans-Hermann and Michael Hudson, *Banking and Finance in West Germany*, New York, St. Martin's Press, 1984, p. 4.

12 Chandler, Alfred D. Jr., *Scale and Scope: The Dynamics of Industrial Capitalism*, Cambridge, MA, Belknap Press of Harvard University Press, 1990, p.131-40.

13 Teece, David, "The Dynamics of Industrial Capitalism: Perspectives on Alfred Chandler's Scale and Scope," *Journal of Economic Literature*, 31, 12 (1993):199-205.

14 *Ibid.*, p. 205 n.12.

15 De Long, J. Bradford, "Did J.P. Morgan's Men Add Value? An Economist's Perspective on Financial Capitalism," in *Inside the Business Enterprise: Historical Perspectives on the Use of Information*, edited by Peter Temin, Chicago, University of Chicago Press, 1991, p. 205.

16 Tilly, Richard, *Financial Institutions and Industrialization in the Rhineland, 1815-1870*, Madison, WI, University of Wisconsin Press, 1966, pp. 134-38.

17 Slovin, Myron, Marie Sushka and John Polonchek, "The Value of Bank Durability: Borrowers as Bank Stakeholders," *Journal of Finance*, 48, 1993, p. 247.

18 Romano, Roberta, "A Cautionary Note on Drawing Lessons from Comparative Corporate Law," *Yale Law Review*, 102, 27, 1993, pp. 2021, 2029.

Adrian E. Tschoegl
The Wharton School
University of Pennsylvania

Commentary on Part V

SINCE THE EARLY PART OF THIS CENTURY when Joseph Schumpeter published his *Theory of Economic Development*, economists have argued that financial intermediaries make possible technological innovation and economic development. "The banker ... authorizes people, in the name of society as it were, to ... [innovate]" (Schumpeter, 1911, p. 74). Recent work by Ross & Levine (1993) presents evidence that supports Schumpeter's view and shows that financial development correlates positively with economic growth. Still, intermediaries are only part of the structure of the financial system, and allocation of credit, time deferral and risk-bearing are only some of the functions of the financial system. The financial system is part of a governance structure that works to reduce or eliminate the harmful effects of opportunism and error on economic growth.

I have commented both at this conference and privately on the three studies presented in this session. My comments, however, included only minor suggestions for strengthening these interesting and knowledgeable studies. What follows here is an attempt on my part to organize some general thoughts on the issue of corporate governance. The section below considers the question of function and addresses the nature of the problems that bedevil the corporate governance system. The function of the governance system is to reduce or eliminate these problems. The next section looks at the structures that comprise corporate governance as a system. In that context, I briefly review some of the literature on the Japanese, German and U.S. systems. The final section, the conclusion, raises some issues in relating structure to function. That is, I address a number of caveats that one should keep in mind when trying to relate a particular structure to a particular function. Last, I express some cautionary concerns as to the risks involved in copying models from other countries.

FUNCTION: GOVERNANCE PROBLEMS THE SYSTEM MUST ADDRESS

THE CORPORATE GOVERNANCE SYSTEM must deal with two separate problems – opportunism and error. By opportunism I mean circumstances in which individuals expend resources to carve out a larger chunk of the pie (usually for themselves) rather than to add to the pie. By error I mean mistakes made by executives in exercising business judgement.

Opportunism frequently involves malfeasance of some sort, but opportunism encompasses more than malfeasance. Theft and fraud are clearly wrong. But negligence is a form of theft; negligence represents an agent's failure to carry out his or her professional obligations. Still, there are several forms of opportunistic behaviour that are socially sub-optimal without being criminal. These forms include both failing to perform desirable actions and undertaking actions that exploit others.

Shirking, for instance, is a failure to perform up to the level of one's ability. In this sense, a person may shirk even though he or she may be performing as required. The shirker contributes only exactly what he or she has contracted to provide – no more, no less – rather than contributing to the full extent to which he or she is capable. In such circumstances, both the venture (or firm) and society are the losers.

Exploitative actions include circumstances where parties to a contractual relationship seek out *lacunae* in the contracts so they can take advantage of these flaws in order to transfer resources from their partners to themselves. Examples include cases where owners enrich themselves at the expense of their creditors, and controlling shareholders enrich themselves at the expense of non-controlling shareholders.

Criminal law attempts to deal with theft; contract law is intended to deal with forms of opportunism that are not criminal. However, preventing error is less amenable to law.

In Common law, there is a presumption against judges ruling on issues of business judgement. Law can help with errors due to negligence, particularly when the negligence contributes to decisions being made with inadequate information. Thus we have laws requiring due diligence and disclosure. Still, the law is uncomfortable with second guessing what use people make of the information they have available to them.

From time to time, the law does attempt to limit the possibility of error. One example is the "prudent man" rule. This is the legal requirement that parties in a fiduciary situation behave as would a "prudent man". The fiduciaries may not assume unnecessary and excessive risks. Obviously, the question of when a risk is unnecessary or excessive is a matter of judgement as to degree rather than a determination of kind.

This is an example of a larger problem that I can easily express by means of the metaphor of escaping the Sirens' song. Homer's *Odyssey* offers one of the earliest examples of the problem of management becoming enraptured by a course of action and being blind to the course's (potentially) disastrous consequences. Odysseus' solution was to have his crew bind him to the mast and to put wax in their ears. These measures freed him to hear and enjoy the Sirens' song, but also ensured that he would be unable to steer his vessel toward the Sirens and the rocks they sat upon.

In the context of corporate governance, the equivalent of the binding materials that tie one to the mast is the body of law, corporate charters, and other devices that impose blanket rules and limitations on management's discretion. Examples from the United States include limitations on how much of its capital a bank may lend to one borrower or who may own banks. These rigid and crude rules often involve the imposition of arbitrary limits – such as percentage limits (of 5 percent, 8 percent and 20 percent).

If these rules are to improve on discretion, *i.e.*, if they are to make sense, we must believe that managers do, occasionally, make avoidable mistakes. Normally, we do not think that imposing crude, rigid constraints enhances a situation. In linear programming, the imposition of new constraints cannot improve the previously optimal solution. New constraints, if they are not binding, do not worsen the situation but they cannot improve it. Apparently in the case of human judgement, we believe that circumstances exist in which constraints can help.

The economics literature has long dealt with the issue of rules *versus* discretion. The usual argument rests on cognitive limitations. Rules are better than judgement when, for example, we cannot know enough in time to fine-tune the rate of growth of the money supply. The problem of the Sirens' song is more subtle. It is not that we cannot know enough for discretion to be better than rules; it is rather that we may find ourselves in circumstances like those facing the unfortunate mariners in Homer's Greece. We can become enraptured, ignore what we would otherwise know, and so destroy ourselves. Like Odysseus, therefore, we must bind ourselves to the mast.

THE GOVERNANCE SYSTEM

THE GOVERNANCE SYSTEM IS A RING WITH THREE SEGMENTS: the governed, the governors and the regulators. Each segment has a structure (interaction of firms and individuals) that performs a governance function over the segment before it. What completes the ring is that the governed must themselves govern the regulators.

THE GOVERNED

THE DISCUSSION OF A RING MUST, BY DEFINITION, begin somewhat arbitrarily. Here I begin with firms and individuals, and concentrate on individuals.

The motto of the University of Pennsylvania, where I currently teach, is: *Leges sine moribus vanae* – Laws without morals are futile. This motto implies that if people are to obey the laws, the laws must embody society's values. The motto also implies that laws cannot make up for the absence of self-restraint based on individual morality.

The corporate governance system begins with the selection and training of managers. In a recent article on culture and economic growth, Casson (1993) points out that culture is an enforcement mechanism. Through the values a culture imparts to its members, internal supervision replaces external supervision and internal emotional sanctions (such as guilt and shame) replace external legal sanctions. For our purposes, the relevant cultures include not only the general societal culture but also its subsets, including the business culture and each firm's own culture.

Similarly, Huang & Wu (1994) model the control of corruption in principal-supervisor-agent relationships. They argue that the presence or absence of social norms and organizational cultures determines the equilibria that result. Expectations concerning the likelihood of corrupt behaviour can influence decisions to engage in such behaviour. The key regulating factor is the magnitude of the remorse the individual feels as a consequence of his decisions. Thus, expectations can be self-reinforcing, for good or ill.

The Governors

HIRSCHMANN (1979) IN HIS INSIGHTFUL AND SEMINAL BOOK, distinguishes between two governance mechanisms – exit and voice. By exit, he means the market itself, or the freedom of parties to associate, deal or contract with those they trust and to disassociate themselves from those they do not trust. By voice, he means the action large owners or creditors take to impose sanctions on firms or managers who perform badly.

In the context of "exit", firms are subject to the discipline of their reputation and other investments that have the force of a bond for good behaviour (Klein & Leffler, 1981). Individuals and other firms can ostracize a firm that behaves opportunistically so that the firm that misbehaves loses the value of its investment in the bond. Sometimes firms and individuals will continue to deal with firms with a poor reputation but may take other measures to protect themselves. For instance, consumers will not pay as much for a car from a firm with an uncertain reputation as for a car from a firm with a good reputation. These measures impose costs on the firm with the poor reputation.

Telser (1980), in his paper on self-enforcing agreements, examines the conditions under which the pay-off from continuing to co-operate will exceed the pay-off from behaving opportunistically. When the necessary conditions are in place, firms (or individuals) behave as if they were parties to an implicit contract whose terms they honour.

Nonetheless, much of the literature on corporate governance has focused on the role of "voice", (that is, as mentioned above, on the role of large owners or creditors who impose sanctions on firms or managements that are performing poorly). In this context, I shall deal briefly not with the market for corporate control, but rather with the issue of governance by firms that combine the roles of large owner and large creditor.

The literature on comparative financial systems distinguishes two major types, with some sub-variants. The two major types are the bank-orientated and the market-orientated. Rybczynski (1984) adds a third category, the strongly bank-orientated. Walter (1992) distinguishes between outsider (market-oriented), insider (bank-orientated) and ultra-insider (bank-orientated with cross-holdings) systems. These classifications parallel some others. We could just as well divide systems into the Anglo-Saxon and the European-Japanese, or into Common-law-based and Code-law-based.

Japan

The Japanese post-World War II experience and the development of the "main bank" system have given rise to an extensive literature on the subject of banks holding company shares. Much of the literature on the Japanese case has focused on the implications of bank ownership (Aoki, 1993; Aoki, Patrick & Sheard, 1994; Hoshi, Kashyap & Scharfstein, 1990; Morck & Nakamura, 1992; Sheard, 1989 and 1994; Weinstein & Yafeh, 1994a).

Firms holding each others' shares also receive some attention. Explanations for firms owning large blocks of each others' shares include the desire of managments to retain control in friendly hands and as a mechanism for collusion (Flath, 1993; Hodder & Tschoegl, 1985 and 1993; Miyajima, 1994; Weinstein & Yafeh, 1994b; Wallich & Wallich, 1976).

What makes the Japanese *keiretsu* unique among groups is the mutuality of their cross-holding. Unlike other group structures, such as bank-controlled or family-owned groups, in a *keiretsu* no one party dominates; unlike widely held conglomerates, all related parties collectively control any one participant. The group's control rests on a firm legal foundation, especially when a member is in financial distress. As the holder of the collateral, the "main bank" has strong legal powers over borrowers. However, the controllers are themselves controlled. The Ministry of Finance regulates the bank and the members of the group together own the bank. It is this last point that the literature on the "main bank" relationship ignores.

Because groups are independent (Mitsubishi does not own Mitsui or *vice versa*), and because there are several of them, competition between the groups disciplines each group. However, no group can acquire any other group and there is only a small number of groups. Therefore, oligopoly, in the sense of each participant having to take the other participants' actions into account, is a concern. In this oligopolistic setting firms do not compete on price. Rather, firms compete on quality (including service) and all work together to create an environment, (which extends to regulation) that is hostile toward new entrants (Schaede, 1994).

Germany

The English-language literature on the German banking system is less extensive. The empirical literature, in particular, is not as extensive as that on the Japanese system. However, Cable (1985) provides an interesting examination of alternative views of the German situation.

Cable's main hypothesis is that bank participation in ownership could confer advantages that relate to internal capital markets. By being both debtor and creditor, and by having representation on company boards, the bank can remove informational asymmetries and incentives to transfer assets from debt to equity. Bank ownership then reduces any tendency on the part of lenders to impose credit-rationing or onerous lending terms.

Two other hypotheses also link bank ownership to profitability. First, bank ownership across related firms could facilitate cartel arrangements and raise their effectiveness. Second, banks could raise companies' profitability through providing financial expertise. Cable makes logical arguments that call these two hypotheses into question. More important, he argues that his empirical results are consistent with the internal capital markets hypothesis. Last, Kleeberg's (1986) historical study of German universal banks undermines the notion that these banks are particularly adept financiers of long-term investments.

Japan, Germany and the United States

Much of the attention that the Japanese and German systems have attracted stems from a simple (perhaps even simplistic) comparison and argument. Observers contrast bank-orientated systems (Germany and Japan) with market-orientated systems (the United States) and associate the systems with rapid economic growth in Germany and Japan and slow economic growth in the United States.

Porter (1992) argues that the U.S. market-orientated system fosters a focus on short-term performance. Porter does stress that the U.S. system has advantages too, but on balance argues for reforms to ensure that managers maximize long-run value.

Allen (1993) challenges Porter's view. He argues that the predominance of institutional investors and transitory ownership in the U.S. financial system are not necessarily the cause of the lack of competitiveness of U.S. firms. Instead, he suggests that the competitiveness of German and Japanese corporations may be due to the managerial incentives that high growth rates make possible.

Interestingly, Wintrobe & Breton (1986) earlier made a related, formal argument in which rapid economy-wide economic growth leads to productivity growth within firms through the incentives that managers can then offer workers. Together, the articles by Allen and Wintrobe & Breton suggest that the Japanese and German governance systems accompanied rapid growth but did not cause it. Dufey (1983) suggests that regulation in Japan might even have impeded growth had it not been for the existence of offshore markets that acted as a relief valve.

THE REGULATORS

REGULATORS OVERSEE THE GOVERNORS. Any discussion of corporate governance must include the regulatory system, for two reasons. First, as Winston Churchill said, "We shape our buildings and then our buildings shape us." That is, we create laws and then contract under those laws. Walter (1992) notes that the U.S. and U.K. (outsider) market-oriented systems owe much to the limited role of the state in their development. In contrast, the French and Japanese (insider and ultra-insider) bank-orientated systems are, in part, the outcome of a government propensity to direct the economy.

Second, corporate governance involves the financial system and, when dealing with financial systems, regulation is typically an important part of the system. The effectiveness of a governance system depends, in part, on the fit (or the lack of fit) between the governance system and the economy that it serves, as each evolves over time.

Highly developed securities (debt or equity) markets are slow to develop and represent a later stage of the evolution of financial systems. Securities markets require an infrastructure of disclosure, sophisticated accounting information backed up by arm's-length observers such as accounting firms, securities regulators, and financial economists employed by securities firms. Well-operating securities markets also require a capable and determined government to bring about effective regulatory institutions over a considerable period of time.

As part of the governance system, a well-designed regulatory system is not only appropriate at present, it can evolve as the economy changes to be appropriate in the future. However, we must note the warning raised around the world by the long life of regulatory measures taken in the 1930s in response to the problems of that era (Cassese, 1984).

An unchanging regulatory system is not only a potential impediment to an effective corporate governance system; it may also impede further evolution. Kanda (1993) has an illuminating article on the role of regulation in code-law-based legal systems, especially in Japan. He argues that regulation has stifled innovation in financial markets and has slowed the evolution of the financial system toward a greater use of markets.

To close the circle that began this discussion, I must return to the question Juvenal raised 2,000 years ago: *Sed quis custodiet ipsos custodes?* (But who guards the guardians?). Regulators are not saints. To keep them from becoming demons, a well-functioning system of corporate governance ultimately requires that the governed govern the regulators. At the very least, there is the problem of collusion between the governors and the regulators, a collusion that may or may not be in the general interest. Breton & Wintrobe (1978) have an interesting theory of "moral suasion" in which they suggest that moral suasion is a mutually advantageous exchange between the central bank and the commercial banks. The commercial banks co-operate with the central bank not simply because the banks fear administrative or legal sanctions. Rather, the central bank offers a *quid pro quo* of information, rules and other services that facilitate collusion among the banks.

At its extreme, a system in which the regulators are themselves free from oversight will degenerate into corruption. Klitgaard (1988) developed an insightful formulation: corruption = monopoly + discretion – accountability. Similarly, and in a more formal vein, Schleifer & Vishny (1993) argued that the structure of government institutions and of the political process are very important determinants of the level of corruption in a society.

CONCLUSION

IN MODIFYING THE SYSTEM OF CORPORATE GOVERNANCE we are faced with the task of modifying structures so they will better perform their functions of limiting the exercise of opportunism and of reducing the likelihood of errors of judgement. Riggs (1970) suggests three axioms of Structural-Functionalism that provide a good starting point for thinking about some of the problems involved in trying to improve the corporate governance system.

- Structures tend to survive despite changes in their functions.

- Although a given structure normally performs a given function, there is no assurance that it always will do so.

- Under the constraints of existing social technology, some functions can only be performed by a given structure or set of structures.

These axioms raise cautionary notes to our attempts to identify structures in terms of functions: historic roles may not be a good guide to current roles: similar structures across countries may not perform the same functions; and we are not free to design any system we like.

Finally, this discussion of the Japanese, German and U.S. systems suggests that we are not free to pick and choose, nor are we free to mix and match, drawing on this model from here and on that model from there. Systems constitute a coherent whole. The different financial systems around the world are the result of differences in historical evolution and political values. The different systems also reflect different economic circumstances. Any well-developed system of corporate governance is a complex entity within which the relationships (of the parts to each other and the structures to the functions) are not entirely clear or well-understood. We must, therefore, beware of unanticipated consequences of attempts at reform.

ACKNOWLEDGEMENTS

A GAIN, I WOULD LIKE TO THANK Randall Morck, Industry Canada and the Financial Research Foundation for inviting me to participate in this session and in this conference on so important an issue.

SELECTED REFERENCES

Allen, Franklin. "Strategic Management and Financial Markets." *Strategic Management Journal*, 14 (1993):11-22.

Aoki, M. "Monitoring Characteristics of the Main Bank System: An Analytical and Historical View," Center for Economic Policy Research. Publication No. 352, Stanford University, 1993.

Aoki, M, Hugh Patrick and Paul Sheard. "The Main Bank System: An Introductory Overview," in *The Japanese Main Bank System: Its Relevancy for Developing and Transforming Economies*. Edited by M. Aoki and Hugh Patrick, New York: Oxford University Press, 1995.

Breton, Albert and Ronald Wintrobe. "A Theory of 'Moral Suasion'." *Canadian Journal of Economics*. 11 (1978):210-19.

Cable, John. "Capital Market Information and Industrial Performance: The Role of West German Banks." *The Economic Journal*, 95, 1 (1985):118-32.

Cassese, Sabino. "The Long Life of the Financial Institutions Set up in the Thirties." *Journal of European Economic History*, 13, 2 (1984):273-94.

Casson, Mark. "Cultural Determinants of Economic Performance." *Journal of Comparative Economics*, 17 (1993):418-42.

Dufey, Gunter. "Banks in the Asia-Pacific Area," in *Asia Pacific Dynamics*. Edited by R. Moxon, J. F. Truit and T. Roehl. Greenwich, CT: JAI Press, 1983.

Flath, David. "Shareholding in the Keiretsu, Japan's Financial Groups." *Review of Economics and Statistics*, 75 (1993):249-57.

Hirschmann, A. O. *Exit, Voice and Loyalty: Responses to Decline in Firms, Organizations and States*. Cambridge, MA: Harvard University Press, 1979.

Hodder, James E. and Adrian E. Tschoegl. "Some Aspects of Japanese Corporate Finance." *Journal of Financial and Quantitative Analysis*, 20 (1985):173-91.

Hodder, James E. and Adrian E. Tschoegl. "Corporate Financing in Japan," in *Japanese Capital Markets*. Edited by Shinji Takagi. Cambridge, MA: Basil Blackwell, 1993.

Hoshi, Takeo, Anil Kashyap and David Scharfstein. "Bank Monitoring and Investment: Evidence from the Changing Structure of Japanese Corporate Banking Relationships," in *Asymmetric Information, Corporate Finance, and Investment*. Edited by R. Glenn Hubbard. Chicago: University of Chicago Press, 1990, pp. 105-26.

Huang, Peter H. and Ho-Mou Wu. "More Order without More Law: A Theory of Social Norms and Organizational Culture." *Journal of Law, Economics and Organization*, 10, 2 (1994):390-406.

Kanda, Hideki. "The Regulatory Environment for Japanese Capital Markets," in *Japanese Capital Markets*. Edited by Shinji Takagi. Oxford: Basil Blackwell, 1993, pp. 196-211.

King, Robert G. and Ross Levine. "Finance and Growth: Schumpeter Might Be Right." *Quarterly Journal of Economics*, 108, 3 (1993):717-37.

Kleeberg, John M. "Universal Banks: The Sonderweg of German Finance", St. Catherine's College, Oxford. Unpublished paper, 1986.

Klein, Benjamin and Keith B. Leffler. "The Role of Market Forces in Assuring Contractual Performance." *Journal of Political Economy*, 89, 41 (1981):615-41.

Klitgaard, Robert. *Controlling Corruption*. Berkeley, CA: University of California Press, 1988.

McKinnon, Ronald I. *The Order of Economic Liberalization*. Baltimore: Johns Hopkins University Press, 1991, 1993.

Miyajima, Hideaki. "The Transformation of Zaibatsu to Postwar Corporate Groups – From Hierarchically Integrated Groups to Horizontally Integrated Groups." *Journal of the Japanese and International Economies*, 8 (1994):293-328.

Morck, Randall and Masao Nakamura. "Banks and Corporate Control in Japan," Institute for Financial Research, University of Alberta, WP 6-92, September 1992.

Porter, Michael. "Capital Disadvantage: America's Failing Capital Investment System." *Harvard Business Review*. (September-October 1992):65-82.

Riggs, Fred W. "Systems Theory: Structural Analysis," in *Approaches to the Study of Political Science*. Edited by Michael Haas and Henry S. Kariel. Scranton, PA: Chandler, 1970.

Rybczynski, Tad M. "Industrial Finance System in Europe, U.S. and Japan." *Journal of Economic Behavior and Organization*. 5 (1984):275-86.

Schaede, Virike. "Change and Continuity in Japanese Regulation." Roundtable on the International Economy, Working Paper 66, University of California, Berkley, March 1994.

Schleifer, Andrei and Robert W. Vishny. "Corruption." *Quarterly Journal of Economics*. 108, 3 (1993):599-617.

Sheard, Paul. "The Main Bank System and Corporate Monitoring and Control in Japan." *Journal of Economic Behavior and Organizations*. 11 (1989):399-422.

_____. "Reciprocal Delegated Monitoring in the Japanese Main Bank System." *Journal of the Japanese and International Economies*. 8 (1994):1-21.

Schumpeter, Joseph A. *The Theory of Economic Development*. Cambridge, MA: Harvard University Press, 1911.

Telser, Lester G. "A Theory of Self-Enforcing Agreements." *Journal of Business*, 53, 1 (1980):27-44.

Wallich, Henry C. and Mabel I. Wallich. "Banking and Finance," in *Asia's New Giant: How the Japanese Economy Works*. Edited by Hugh Patrick and Henry Rosovsky. Washington, D.C.: The Brookings Institution, 1976.

Walter, Ingo. "The Battle of the Systems: Control of Enterprises and the Global Economy." *Journal of International Securities Markets*, 6 (Winter 1992):309-17.

Weinstein, David E. and Yishay Yafeh. "On the Costs of a Bank Centered Financial System: Evidence from the Changing Main Bank Relations in Japan." Harvard University, Dept. of Economics, unpublished, June 1994a.

_____. "Japan's Corporate Groups: Collusive or Competitive? An Empirical Investigation of Keiretsu Behavior," Harvard University, Dept. of Economics, unpublished, May 1994b.

Wintrobe, Ronald and Andre Breton. "Organizational Structure and Productivity." *American Economic Review*, 76, 3 (1986):530-38.

Part VI   Corporate Governance
           and Social Responsibility

Robert Howse & Ronald J. Daniels
Faculty of Law
University of Toronto

15

Rewarding Whistleblowers: The Costs and Benefits of an Incentive-Based Compliance Strategy

INTRODUCTION

CANADIANS TODAY ARE VERY MUCH CONCERNED about corporate crime and about corporations that do not comply with regulatory requirements, especially those related to the environment, securities law and occupational health and safety regulations. This increased concern has led to proposals to extend liability for illegal corporate conduct[1] (by making directors *personally* liable for the actions of their companies, for example); it has also led to arguments in favour of greatly increasing the sanctions on corporations (and individual wrongdoers within those corporations) for wrongful conduct. The recent academic literature reflects a lively debate as to the effectiveness of such proposals in reducing illegal behaviour in corporations and their consequences for the functioning of the corporation as an economic institution.[2]

With some notable exceptions,[3] the focus of the debate on sanctions and liability rules has resulted in the relative neglect of an essential ingredient in effective deterrence; the capacity to monitor and detect wrongdoing within the corporation. The lack of attention to the potential for increased compliance through improved monitoring and detection is surprising for several reasons. First, as Jennifer Arlen notes, "[m]any corporate crimes – such as securities fraud, government procurement fraud, and some environmental crimes – cannot be readily detected by government".[4] Second, there is a significant body of literature on regulatory reform that relates the ineffectiveness of many traditional "command and control" forms of regulation to the costs and difficulties which are inherent in government monitoring and detection of wrongdoing.[5] Third, one of the most generally held tenets of contemporary criminology is that increasing the likelihood of detection and prosecution tends to be a more effective means of strengthening deterrence than making sanctions more severe. In other words, it is better to put another cop on the beat than to build more jail cells.[6]

This study is intended to help redress the inadequate emphasis on monitoring and detection in the current debate on corporate criminal and regulatory responsibility. Accepting the proposition that direct monitoring of corporate conduct by government as a means of detection is unlikely to be cost-effective, our concern is to identify agents *within* the corporation who can be enlisted in the cause of monitoring and detection,[7] and to consider how public policies can provide stronger incentives, and make it easier, for these agents to identify and disclose wrongdoing within the corporation. In conducting this analysis, we begin by considering one such policy that has generated sustained public attention and controversy over the last decade: so-called "whistleblower protection."

Recognizing that agents within corporations (and government institutions) risk retaliation in the form of dismissal if they disclose corporate wrongdoing, many jurisdictions in North America have adopted legislation to protect employee whistleblowers, either by providing them with a private right of action when dismissed in retaliation for whistleblowing or through outright prohibition of dismissal or other disciplinary measures motivated by retaliation.[8] It is not, however, these modest protective provisions that have captivated the public imagination, nor have these provisions contributed significantly to the disclosure of spectacular corporate frauds. Rather, it is the offer (or prospect) of substantial rewards or bounties to whistleblowers, most notably under the *False Claims Act*, a federal U.S. statute (as amended in 1986), that has produced this result.[9] Under the provisions of this statute,[10] an individual[11] who discovers wrongdoing that has injured the U.S. federal government (fraud in defence procurement, for example) may launch a private lawsuit against the corporate wrongdoer. The government has the option to join the action or not, but the individual may nevertheless proceed even if the government declines to do so. If successful, the whistleblower may recover a bounty calculated to be between 25 percent and 30 percent of the total penalties or other damages assessed against the wrongdoer. In cases where the Justice Department joins the action, the *minimum* recovery is reduced to 15 percent. If unsuccessful, the whistle-blower is responsible for her own legal costs but is not responsible for the legal costs of the defendant *except* where the court is convinced that the action is vexatious. The most spectacular whistleblower suits have centred on multi-million dollar frauds, particularly in the areas of defense and health-care procurement and have usually resulted in convictions. In these instances, whistleblowers have often received what appear to be very large payoffs, which, in effect, reflect the size of the scam uncovered and the enormous savings to government.

Despite the arguable savings to the public from this type of action, under the *False Claims Act* the practice of providing bounties to whistleblowers has been controversial. First, there is the argument that much of the information divulged through actions under the *False Claims Act* would have been divulged even if much smaller bounties had been offered. Second, corporations are vulnerable to false claims made by opportunistic whistleblowers who may be motivated to force corporations into financial settlements in order to avoid the adverse reputational and related effects caused by highly public, albeit ill-founded, accusations. Third, it is sometimes argued that rewards for external whistleblowing frustrate efforts at internal compliance, or act as disincentives to "internal" whistleblowing. For instance, an employee may be dissuaded from reporting a misconduct in a timely fashion within the corporation because of the prospect of receiving a large reward by disclosing corporate wrongdoing through litigation, thereby undermining internal efforts at corporate compliance (the importance of which is often stressed in a wide range of the relevant policy and legal literature).[12] Fourth, it is often suggested that the calibration of the amount of the reward from whistleblowing directly to the amount of the penalty (and thereby to the degree of seriousness and extent of the wrongdoing) provides whistleblowers with an incentive to report wrong-doing later rather than earlier, and to do so only after the corruption has produced much more serious consequences, rather than disclosing evidence of corruption in the corporation immediately.

Finally, some analysts worry that the practice of rewarding whistleblowing may have deleterious effects on trust and team spirit within corporations, ingredients seen by many as critical to the success of corporations as economic institutions. As is evident from the variety of pejorative colloquial expressions for whistleblowing (ratting, squealing, tattling, etc.), reporting co-workers, associates or superiors to the authorities often has negative moral connotations. These connotations have been powerfully reinforced in our time by the frequent use of "informers" by totalitarian regimes, both left and right, a practice often closely identified with the repellent nature of those regimes.

This study draws primarily on analytical techniques and empirical studies from the literature of the law, economics and organizational behaviour. Since understanding the effects of rewarding whistleblowers depends on an under-standing of their motivations and the effects of their actions on the essential ethical life of the corporation (as a human association), it is our hope that this study will also contribute to the more subtle and informed debate over the morality of whistleblowing.

DO WE NEED MORE INCENTIVES?

THE OBVIOUS QUESTION IN THE DEBATE over whistleblowing is: Is there any need for new instruments that may be used to increase the probability of detecting criminal or quasi-criminal conduct by corporations? If, as the economics literature suggests,[13] penalties set for corporate wrongdoing are based on the social consequences of the impugned behaviour divided by the probability of detection, the total social costs of corporate regulation and wrongdoing should be minimized – which consequently maximizes social welfare.[14] According to this theory, any weakness in detection and prosecution can be offset by increasing the weight of the penalty that is imposed. However, in practice there are several impediments to this theory. As mentioned earlier, there is a growing awareness in the criminology literature that increasing the magnitude of sanctions cannot easily compensate for low probabilities of detection. Another factor that weighs against relying on added penalties as a way of constraining corporate wrongdoing relates to the marginal deterrence problem; that is, there is a tendency for optimal fines to become level across different types of crimes, which reduces the incentive for wrongdoers to refrain from engaging in more socially damaging forms of conduct. Further, to the extent that financial penalties are relied on principally to enforce desired forms of conduct, the efficacy of those penalties is contingent upon the financial solvency of wrongdoers. Where fines exceed the assets of wrongdoers, then the magnitude of the expected penalty is effectively capped, possibly at levels far below what is socially optimal.

This problem is particularly acute in the case of corporations, where shareholders, the nominal principals of the corporation, enjoy limited liability (i.e., the amount of their financial exposure from corporate wrongdoing is limited to the amount of funds that they have actually invested or committed to have invested in the corporation). For shareholders, therefore, increasing the magnitude of financial penalties above their existing wealth levels will have only a limited effect on their behaviour, and therefore on the behaviour of the corporation.[15] However, there is some evidence to suggest that shareholders are not generally the driving force behind corporate wrongdoing, at least within widely held public corporations.[16] As Jennifer Arlen notes, "[c]orporate crimes are not committed by corporations; they are committed by agents of the corporation".[17] Nevertheless, the limited liability of shareholders *does* inhibit the deterrent effect of fines and penalties in that it reduces shareholders' incentive to engage in active monitoring of the corporation's agents. Moreover, while other investors (namely creditors) may suffer financial losses in the event that the shareholders' equity is less than the magnitude of the fine levied on the corporation for wrongdoing, contractual and legal restrictions limit the scope for creditor voice.[18] In this vein, Polinsky & Shavell (1993) have argued that the difficulties in raising fines to the levels necessary to create optimal penalties provide a rationale for relying on state sanctions for wrong-doing, particularly imprisonment of individual corporate actors.[19] Nevertheless, while imprisonment may be effective for some types of corporate wrongdoing, its utility is impaired by endemic information problems which make it difficult for the state to identify the corporate agents responsible for wrongful corporate conduct.[20]

If increasing the magnitude of the penalty is not an effective way to constrain corporate wrongdoing, then why not rely on state monitoring to increase the probability of detection, thereby securing optimal levels of corporate compliance? An overriding consideration militating against reliance on external monitoring is, of course, the strained fiscal resources of the public sector.[21] Since the beginning of the post-war period, as the breadth and intensity of public demands upon governments in industrialized democracies have increased, so too has their inability to generate the revenues necessary to fund new programs, even where it is clear that the new programs can yield greater social benefits than those generated by existing programmes. In the case of marginal investments in monitoring-related activities, the lack of demonstrable showcase effects emanating from such expenditures, combined with the existence of stable and powerful coalitions in favour of existing programmes, undercuts the ease with which public officials can re-direct scarce public resources to allegedly more valuable activities, such as increased monitoring to ensure corporate compliance with public goals.

The inability of the public sector to muster or re-direct resources to monitoring, however, is only part of the reason why additional expenditures are not made. The comparative inefficiency of public *versus* private monitoring mechanisms is also implicated. First, in contrast to external public monitors, private actors within the corporation can gain access to real-time, on-the-spot information with fewer additional resources. To coordinate internal corporate activity, shareholders (or their managerial representatives) make fixed investments in internal information and control systems which can also be used to acquire, transmit and analyze information respecting corporate compliance decisions, thereby exploiting economies of scope. In contrast, external government monitors may have difficulty accessing firm information systems, and may therefore have to invest in duplicative (and perhaps more costly) information systems.

Second, while duplicative investments in monitoring can be avoided to some extent by having government concentrate its efforts on auditing rather than on continuous monitoring, the reliability of information gleaned from such activity is very low. Firms can easily manipulate the data culled by government authorities, thereby conveying a more favourable impression of their compliance effort than is accurate. Alternatively, even in the absence of a deliberate attempt to "cook the books", the information obtained by government auditors may be unreliable due to stochastic variances in the way a corporation's production functions. For instance, government environmental monitors could inadvertently sample the emissions discharged by a corporate polluter during periods when the level of regulated emissions was unusually low.

Even if government did have the technological capability to gather raw information regarding the incidence of wrongful corporate conduct, it often encounters significant barriers in being able to interpret and analyze these data against firm and industry practices. In part, this impediment is a function of public-sector compensation constraints, which weaken the attraction of government service to highly qualified industry specialists. In part, it is also a function of the difficulties that any industry outsider confronts in understanding and assessing the effects of novel corporate practices in a setting of rapid and profound organizational and technological change. Regulation of financial markets is a case in point; the ingenuity and contrivances of unscrupulous market actors typically outstrip the analytical expertise of government inspectors and compliance officers, with the result that wrongdoing is often effectively hidden from public regulatory authorities.[22]

Even if public authorities were able to generate optimal levels of enterprise liability for corporations without having to rely on excessive financial penalties, a great many daunting compliance problems would be raised by internal agency conflicts. Commencing with Berle & Means (1932), numerous scholars of corporate behaviour have focused on the issue of accountability in the modern corporation, particularly with respect to the responsibilities of managers to shareholders.[23] The concern is that management will exploit the delegation of power it receives from shareholders to advance its own interests. Subsequently, law and economics scholars have formalized and generalized these account-ability problems through the use of agency analysis. The analysis focuses on the accountability problems that arise in the modern corporation when principals delegate power to agents in the absence of perfect information.[24] In the context of corporate wrongdoing, the concern is that managers will ignore the share-holders' direction to comply with legislated responsibilities because of the private benefits they realize from engaging in sanctioned behaviour, namely increases in compensation or other perquisites. For instance, by chiselling or scrimping on the expenditures required to be made pursuant to various types of regulatory compliance programs (e.g., environmental or occupational health and safety), managers may be able to increase the level of reported earnings, which, assuming the existence of incentive-based compensation arrangements, will result in their receiving increased compensation. Although there is the risk that the misconduct will be detected and punished by the state (with losses imposed on shareholders), the existence of substantial lags between misconduct and detection, difficulties in determining levels of personal responsibility for culpable conduct within the organization, and problems of collective action that undermine the ability of shareholders to discipline managerial misconduct, all combine to reduce the likelihood that wrongdoing will result in sanctions (including job losses) for senior managers. Of course, to the extent that managers are risk-averse because of their high levels of firm-specific human capital investment, this propensity may undercut the willingness of managers to engage in wrongdoing that entails the threat of job loss.

So far, we have focused on the agency problems that exist between shareholders and senior managers. However, as the organizational behaviour literature demonstrates, issues of accountability are not confined to senior levels of the corporation; these problems are also inherent in the relationships that exist among senior-, mid- and lower-level employees. For instance, lower-level management may pursue goals that conflict with those set out by senior managers because the private gains from deviation more than offset the accompanying costs. These internal agency problems (often referred to as "sub-goal pursuits") are also manifested in distorted information flows from lower-level managers to senior managers (often expressed as "information impactedness"). The net effect is to hobble the capacity of senior management to implement and operate an effective compliance regime.[25] These problems are undoubtedly exacerbated by "collective folly", the documented tendency of groups to engage in excessive forms of risk-taking (compared to the levels of risk that individuals would be willing to assume). Thus, to the extent that middle- and lower-level management coalesce as a group, they may be willing to run greater risks, even of job loss, in failing to adhere to firm-mandated compliance strategies.

In combination, the factors enumerated suggest the need for additional instruments to align corporate and social interests in ensuring responsible corporate conduct. In the next section, we consider the role for one such instrument – whistleblowing – in fostering this alignment.

THE CASE FOR WHISTLEBLOWING

THE CASE FOR WHISTLEBLOWING AS AN INSTRUMENT of corporate control rests on its ability to induce corporate actors with local knowledge of corporate misconduct to report that information in real time to internal and external monitors. Essentially, rewards for whistleblowing seek to destabilize coalitions within the firm that are committed to conspiring against the public weal by enhancing the attraction of personal defection strategies. Whistleblowing inducements are also attractive for their ability to exploit existing internal information systems. As mentioned earlier, in contrast to external monitoring mechanisms, whistleblowing draws on the benefits of sunk investment costs in existing internal management and information systems. Against these benefits, however, there are certain costs.

First, the existence of whistleblowing inducements may distort optimal information flows and decision-making structures within the corporation. To the extent that senior managers are committed to wrongdoing and lack the confidence that lower-level employees will support their activities by keeping quiet, they can be expected to recast organizational routines and decision-making systems in order to limit the access of potential "employee-defectors" to information that indicates or suggests any wrongdoing. Obviously, if decision-making and information systems for compliance are also used to coordinate firm production, the distortion of these systems to support managerial misconduct can be expected to inflict significant costs on the productive efficiency of the firm. This concern is especially relevant given the growing premium that the organizational literature places on the benefits derived from decentralized decision-making in securing firm-competitive advantage.

A second and related point is that whistleblowing may cause senior managers to make lower-level employees over-invest in firm- or industry-specific human capital in order to magnify the downside costs of whistleblowing. High levels of firm- or industry-specific human capital, particularly when the costs of such investment are borne principally by employees in return for future compensation, increase the vulnerability of employees to retaliation by the firm for whistleblowing, particularly through job displacement.

A third concern has to do with the effect of whistleblowing on firm culture and teamwork. Some analysts claim that by creating strong individual incentives for defection from perverse corporate policies, whistleblowing subverts the ability of managers to create durable commitments to firm culture and teamwork. However, it is important to avoid overstating the importance of this concern. Whistleblowing incentives will not undermine a corporate culture that is based on honesty and fair play; rather, it will jeopardize only those cultures that are based on a perverse commitment to conspire against the public weal.

Whistleblower awards of the magnitude frequently seen over the last decade in the United States are unquestionably costly. Like other government payments intended to influence conduct (such as subsidies to businesses), an obvious question is whether the cost of these payments is justified in terms of its ability to procure benefits by altering the conduct of the recipient. There is the possibility that much of the action taken by the whistleblower might occur even without a payment or with a lesser inducement. Perhaps an appropriate starting point for investigating the costs and benefits of whistleblower awards is to examine the "base-line" of human conduct upon which the awards operate. That is to say, apart from whistleblowing awards, what are the incentives that operate upon individuals, particularly upon actors within the corporation, to report wrongdoing? What are the disincentives?

One major factor that probably influences reporting of corporate misconduct is a sense of public duty or responsibility, and the satisfaction that comes from performing that duty.[26] There are cases, as well, where the corporation's wrongdoing exposes whistleblowers, their friends and/or their families to risks that may constitute genuine hazards (for example, hazards created by non-compliance with regulations relating to occupational health and safety, nuclear and aviation safety, etc.). Such risks provide employees with a powerful incentive to engage in whistleblowing. Third, continual serious wrongdoing may have disastrous reputational effects on the corporation and its management. This can lead to the corporation's economic decline, which in turn can result in greater risk of employee job loss or, in the case of senior management, a decline in the value of their stock in the corporation or other performance-related compensation. Fourth, in some corporations, senior management may actually reward employees who report wrongdoing where this leads to avoidance of liability, or reduced liability for the corporation itself.[27] Finally, in some instances, the opportunity to neutralize one's rivals or punish one's enemies within the corporation may provide a motivation for whistleblowing.

The most powerful disincentives to whistleblowing derive from the prospect of retaliation by fellow employees or by the corporation itself, including dismissal of the whistleblower.[28] Other disincentives include the fear that detection of wrongful conduct will harm the corporation, thereby increasing the risk that the employee will lose her job or that her own reputation will be tarnished by association with the corporation when the wrongdoing is exposed.

Given the range of incentives to whistleblowing identified above, one might expect a high rate of whistleblowing to be achieved merely by removing the principal disincentive – the fear of retaliation. However, existing statutory protection for whistleblowers (statutes that allow whistleblowers to sue for wrongful dismissal or which otherwise deter retaliatory conduct) has serious limitations. In the first place, most whistleblower-protection statutes do not provide remedies for retaliatory actions that fall short of dismissal – such as demotions, unwanted geographical transfers, failure to consider an employee for promotion, freezing an employee out of a decision-making role consonant with level of seniority, inordinate scrutiny and surveillance in and outside the workplace, and psychological pressures.[29]

Of course, individually and/or cumulatively, some of these acts might be regarded as "constructive dismissal". However, even assuming a creative application of the constructive dismissal doctrine, and allowing for statutory protections that extend to forms of discipline or revenge that stop short of dismissal, serious evidentiary and interpretative obstacles exist in judicial or regulatory surveillance of employer treatment of an employee *ex post* an act of whistleblowing. In some instances, action taken by the employer that an employee attributes to revenge may have legitimate corporate purposes, or it may be cloaked under legitimate corporate purposes. A presumption that any *ex post* treatment of an employee that is sub-optimal from the perspective of that employee's interests constitutes retaliation would risk constraining other-wise efficient business decisions. Conversely, placing too great a burden of proof on the employee to show a retaliatory intent could easily lead to under-sanctioning retaliatory acts that can be more-or-less masked as normal personnel policies. Even assuming that the right balance could be struck, in most instances, deterring the more subtle forms of retaliation would involve on-going judicial scrutiny of micro-decisions within corporations – at a considerable cost to the whistleblower, the corporation, and the public purse.

Even where a whistleblower can ultimately exit the firm with a wrongful dismissal settlement, the reputational effects of having blown the whistle may harm the whistleblower's prospects of re-employment elsewhere in the same industry or community. (However, depending on how other employers view the wrongful conduct disclosed, they *might* welcome a whistleblower; but this is not a prospect a potential whistleblower can count on.) Glazer & Migdal studied the fates of some 41 whistleblowers whom they characterized as ethical resisters. Of the 41, 28 (68.3 percent) had difficulty finding employment after blowing the whistle and, of the 28, 18 had to settle for employment in "fields unrelated to their previous work".[30]

Common law and statutory protection against retaliation insulates whistleblowers and their families even less effectively from the severe psychological pressures that come from standing up to the corporation. Whistleblowers must be prepared to have their personal backgrounds investigated, to have their charges challenged as lies, to lose the support of fellow-employees, and to be accused of threatening jobs and prosperity in the firm and perhaps in the broader community. In some circumstances, whistleblowers may even risk physical harm. Of course, where whistleblowers are able to survive (psychologically and physically) until the corporation or the wrongdoers within the corporation are brought to justice, they may become heroes – compensating for their earlier vilification. However, whistleblowers must also face the risk that the information they divulge, however persuasive, may not be sufficient to sustain a criminal conviction, in which case the corporation may well be vindicated in the eyes of colleagues and the community. Thus, if it is unlikely that the legal protection of whistleblowers against retaliation is sufficient to redress the imbalance between the disincentives and incentives for whistleblowing, there is a plausible *prima facie* case that additional incentives are needed to achieve a socially optimal level of whistleblowing. This appears to be supported by anecdotal evidence that the 1986 changes in the *False Claims Act* elicited responses and brought forth information about fraudulent practices that might have been, but was not, reported before the legislation offered substantial rewards to whistleblowers.[31]

ISSUES IN CALCULATING INCENTIVES TO WHISTLEBLOWERS

UNDER THE *FALSE CLAIMS ACT*, THE WHISTLEBLOWER'S REWARD is calculated as a percentage of the total penalties and other damages assessed against the corporation. It has been argued that this method of determining the amount of the reward creates perverse incentives for whistleblowers to withhold information or to come forward significantly later than when they first suspect wrongdoing (on the assumption that the longer the wrongdoing continues, the more serious it will become and the larger the ultimate reward will be). In the well-known case of *United States et al.* v. *General Electric*,[32] the U.S. Justice Department sought to have the Court reduce the award to the whistleblower, Chester Walsh, from $14.9 million to $4.5 million, on the grounds that Walsh and his lawyers could have avoided loss to the United States by reporting the wrongdoing in question immediately after it first came to Walsh's attention. The Court, however, accepted Walsh's claim that much of the delay was justified by the difficulty of obtaining sufficient evidence of wrongdoing without undue risk to his own security. It therefore reduced Walsh's reward only by a small amount, from 25 percent to 22.5 percent. The Justice Department initially sought to appeal the decision but eventually settled with Walsh for $11.5 million, a reduction from the $13.4 million ordered by the Court.

The ability of a whistleblower under the *False Claims Act* to increase the amount of a reward through delay in the reporting of wrongdoing seems like an obvious moral hazard problem. However, there are good reasons to favour the Court's cautious approach in addressing this problem in the *General Electric* case. Encouraging immediate or precipitous reporting of wrongdoing may have undesirable effects, given the characteristics of whistleblowers and of the situations they face. First, whistleblowers are likely to be persons who have a strong sense of loyalty to the corporation as a whole.[33] Confronted with the initial evidence of wrongdoing, their immediate reaction may well be disbelief. If whistleblower awards are tied to immediate reporting, such individuals may well not come forward at all since they will be disinclined to jump quickly to a conclusion that an organization for which they have a long-standing respect is guilty of major wrongdoing. Second, the empirical evidence suggests that employees are more likely to consider whistleblowing as justified in instances of clearly illegal, serious misconduct than where it appears that the conduct in question in merely unethical.[34] This suggests that if, in order to obtain an award that provides sufficient compensation for the risk of retaliation, it is necessary to act before one has been able to determine unambiguously that serious wrongful conduct is occurring, some individuals will simply not feel prepared to come forward.

This leads to a related point. In order to recover an award, the whistleblower must obtain a conviction of the wrongdoer in court. The whistleblower bears the risk that a court will find insufficient evidence of wrongdoing, thereby saddling the whistleblower with legal costs in addition to all of the harmful reputational effects that may result from having blown the whistle (apparently) unjustifiably. For this reason, whistleblowers may be unlikely to come forward before they have assembled a body of evidence that makes a conviction all but certain. This will often occur considerably later than the first suspicions of wrongdoing given that the whistleblower may be required to assemble evidence surreptitiously, often at considerable personal risk. This is reinforced by the fact that the whistleblower will not know *ex ante* of blowing the whistle whether the Justice Department will join the action with its investigatory resources or whether the whistleblower herself will have to bear all of the responsibility for assembling the evidentiary record. Furthermore, while earlier whistleblowing may in some instances avert further wrongdoing, in other circumstances it may provide the opportunity for wrongdoers to conceal or destroy evidence of more serious wrongdoing.

In addition to these legitimate reasons for delayed reporting, it is also important to recall that a purely opportunistic strategy of delaying the reporting of wrongdoing in order to obtain a larger reward is not without serious risks to the interests of the whistleblower. The longer the whistleblower delays taking any action, the higher the risk that another whistleblower will come forward to relate information of the wrongdoing and capture all or part of the reward. Moreover, delay may result in evidence being destroyed or rendered unavailable or unuseable, either intentionally or inadvertently. Computer tapes may be erased, potential witnesses may die or be assigned overseas, and so forth. The existence of these risks inherent in delay impose an intrinsic curb on whistleblower opportunism.

The implications of this analysis are that, while it may be appropriate to allow courts some discretion to reduce a reward where purely opportunistic or inexplicable delay in relating information has occurred, the requirement to report wrongdoing immediately should not be a condition for recovering a substantial reward.

Another important implication has to do with the nature of the financial bounty provided to whistleblowers and the clash between compensation and deterrence objectives entailed thereby. Given that the rewards to whistleblowers offered under the *False Claims Act* are based on a percentage of the penalties ultimately assessed against the corporation, the bounty is generally understood as giving expression to deterrence goals; the corporation is not expected to compensate whistleblowers in excess of the fines prescribed by optimal penalties. Nevertheless, it is clear that using a percentage of the fines ultimately levied against the corporation as a basis for bounties paid to whistleblowers may cause payments to diverge systematically from the levels necessary to compensate whistleblowers for the risk of loss to their human capital from corporate retaliation. In some cases, the specified percentage of the fine levied against the corporation will undercompensate whistleblowers, while in other cases, it will have the opposite effect. From an economic perspective, under-compensation is more vexing because a prospective whistleblower who determines *ex ante* that the bounty will not be sufficiently large to compensate for the risk to her human capital will refrain from whistleblowing. Over-compensation is less of a problem as it merely constitutes a windfall transfer from the corporation to the whistleblower, which should not affect actual behaviour.[35] For these reasons, it may make more sense to consider the adoption of a minimum floor for whistleblowing bounties. This would ensure that a whistleblower always obtains sufficient compensation to cover the risks to her human capital.

INTERNAL AND EXTERNAL WHISTLEBLOWING: CONFLICTS OR COMPLEMENTS?

A MAJOR STRAND IN THE FABRIC of contemporary scholarship about regulation and corporate responsibility suggests the desirability of encouraging internal mechanisms of self-regulation and self-monitoring within the corporation.[36] It is sometimes claimed by corporations that providing substantial rewards to external whistleblowers frustrates efforts to create such internal mechanisms. If an employee can collect millions of dollars by reporting wrongdoing externally, why would she wish to report internally in the first instance?[37] Based on this logic, a plausible case can be made that an employee should have to attempt to deal with the problem internally before she can bring an (external) lawsuit for the reason that it does involve a potential reward for whistleblowing.[38]

A closer examination of the relationship between external and internal whistleblowing, however, puts in doubt whether such a requirement would produce desirable results. First, recent studies of employee attitudes toward whistleblowing suggest that, generally, employees *are* inclined to report wrong-doing internally before reporting such information to authorities outside the firm *as long as they do not fear retaliation from internal whistleblowing*.[39] Second, employees may justifiably be afraid that internal whistleblowing mechanisms (such as supposedly anonymous "hotlines") will be abused to identify trouble-makers, and may allow wrongdoers the opportunity to destroy, conceal or tamper with evidence or intimidate potential witnesses by tipping them off that wrongdoing has been discovered.[40] Even where shareholders, directors, or senior management are strongly committed to positive internal disclosure policies, employees may still fear retaliation from immediate supervisors or middle managers. As Near & Miceli conclude, an organizational strategy to "encourage valid [internal] whistle blowing may be difficult to implement even if accepted by top managers. The weak link in such a strategy appears to be the immediate supervisors and managers who retaliate against the whistle blower, seemingly at will".[41] These findings are consistent with the application of the theory of agency costs to corporate wrongdoing, which suggests that the interests of shareholders, senior managers, and other stakeholders within the corporation may diverge significantly with respect to corporate wrongdoing.[42]

If, as argued, a requirement of prior internal disclosure acts as a disincentive to external whistleblowing, then it may, in turn, actually operate as a disin-centive to corporations that adopt internal disclosure policies to protect workers against retaliation for – and thereby encourage – *internal* whistleblowing. The fear of being exposed to prosecution as a consequence of external whistleblowing may be an important incentive for some corporations to adopt *credible* internal disclosure policies and procedures. Such policies might very well gain employee trust and increase the number of internal disclosures.[43]

While we do not believe that weakening incentives for external whistle-blowing is likely to increase incentives for internal whistleblowing (in fact, we would expect the contrary to be true), it is also important that an external whistleblower not be disadvantaged in recovering a reward by virtue of having pursued internal channels before engaging in external whistleblowing. The fact that delay in relating information may be due to the employee's efforts to seek a solution to the problem within the corporation is an additional reason for *not* requiring that the whistleblower disclose immediately after learning of the wrongdoing.

A rather different concern about the relationship between internal and external whistleblowing is that internal whistleblowing (even where it does not result in retaliation, destruction of evidence etc.) may produce an outcome that is not favourable to the public interest. First, internal whistleblowing may afford the corporation or specific corporate actors an opportunity to pay hush money to an internal whistleblower. Second, even where the corporation takes steps to avoid future wrongdoing, it may be disinclined to inform the authorities of past wrongdoing because of the prospect of having to pay sub-stantial penalties. This problem is particularly acute in the case of corporate fraud, where keeping the matter within the corporation may well lead to the government foregoing recovery of substantial past losses. Again, since whistle-blowers tend to be conservative individuals with strong loyalty to the corporation, they may well be satisfied by an outcome that prevents future wrongdoing and entails internal discipline of past wrongdoers.

WHISTLEBLOWER COMPLICITY IN CORPORATE WRONGDOING

A SPECIAL DIFFICULTY IS APPARENT when a whistleblower is involved in the wrongdoing she has reported, either through complicity or through active initiative. At the crudest level, the prospect of obtaining a large reward for reporting wrongdoing in which one is involved may actually encourage mis-conduct. Moreover, since obtaining a reward obviously depends upon other employees also being involved in the wrongdoing, there may be an incentive to corrupt other employees. Finally, since the reward is determined as a percentage of the total penalties assessed against the corporation, a wrongdoer-whistleblower has an incentive to increase the amount of wrongdoing by other employees as much as possible. (Increasing her own wrongdoing may, of course, lead to a larger award but it could also lead to larger criminal sanctions against the whistleblower, thereby mitigating the effect of the former).

While these considerations appear to militate in favour of a hard-and-fast rule that a whistleblower should not be entitled to a reward for reporting wrongdoing to which she is a party, other factors may weigh against such a rule. For example, in some cases insiders are likely to be the only plausible whistleblowers or the only individuals with access to the kind of evidence likely to secure a conviction. It is well-known that, in the context of organized crime, successful prosecutions have often depended on inducing members of a conspiracy, criminal organization or ring to "turn state's evidence".

Similarly, under a rule that largely eliminates the incentive to whistleblow where the erstwhile whistleblower is herself implicated in wrongdoing, the "leaders" of crime within the corporation have a strong incentive to induce other employees to engage in wrongdoing so as to immunize them against becoming whistleblowers – an incentive which, of course, is mitigated by the risk that the employees will refuse and, now alerted to the wrongdoing, will blow the whistle *before* becoming implicated.

A related concern is that some employees who become involved in wrongdoing may do so under pressure from managers or co-workers, or under threat of retaliation. These employees are excellent candidates for whistle-blowing. Too weak to do the right thing on principle but not inherently corrupt, they may well be induced to whistleblow by the prospect of a reward that mitigates the risks of doing so. It would seem perverse, then, to exclude this class of individuals from eligibility for a whistleblowing reward. Nonetheless, it can be argued that the prospect of such a reward in the first instance should have been sufficient to induce such persons to whistleblow when pressure was first put on them to engage in wrongful activity. However, when they first succumb to such pressure these individuals may not yet be aware of the seriousness or extent of wrongdoing. They may, for instance, think that they are only being asked to cheat a little "around the edges", to help out a colleague or the corporation or, alternatively, they may not (yet) have access to the kind of evidence required to be confident of securing a conviction and therefore obtaining a reward.

These considerations suggest that it would be undesirable to have a hard-and-fast rule preventing an individual who is implicated in wrongdoing from recovering a whistleblowing reward. Arguably, the best approach is to provide the court with discretion to examine, on a case-by-case basis, whether the nature of the individual's wrongdoing in the circumstances justifies a reduction or elimination of the award. Here, relevant factors will include whether the individual has been a "leader" or a "follower" in the wrongdoing, whether she became involved under pressure from co-workers or supervisors, at what point she could have been expected to identify a clear pattern of serious wrongful activity, and the extent to which she profited from wrongful activity before blowing the whistle.

This suggests that the existing approach of the *False Claims Act* is not off the mark. The Act allows the court to reduce an award where the action is brought by an individual who herself has been involved in wrongdoing, but only where the whistleblower has "planned and initiated" the wrongful conduct. Furthermore, even in the case of an action by a whistleblower who planned or initiated the wrongdoing, recovery is not barred altogether and the reduction is not required by the statute, but rather is a matter for the discretion of the judge, depending on the circumstances. This is somewhat offset, however, by the proviso that a whistleblower who receives a criminal conviction for the wrongful conduct that is the basis for the action shall be barred altogether from recovery. This means that for the incentive of a reward to operate on a whistleblower who herself is implicated in the wrongdoing, the whistleblower might have to be assured of immunity from criminal prosecution.

THE RISK OF FABRICATED CLAIMS

As CALLAHAN & DWORKIN (1992) NOTE,[44] it is often claimed that the prospect of large awards to whistleblowers provides an incentive for employees to fabricate claims of wrongdoing for personal profit. If this were true, one would anticipate that serious costs would follow, including harm to the corporation's reputation and that of individual employees, wasted time and money in defending against false claims, and a deterioration of morale within the corporation. However, as Callahan & Dworkin further note,[45] there are several features of the *False Claims Act* that make fabricating claims of wrongdoing a very high-risk strategy. First, the whistleblower must either convince the Justice Department to pursue an action against the corporation or bear the costs of the action herself. In the latter case, this involves either significant out-of-pocket legal and investigatory expenses or persuading a lawyer that the chances of success are sufficient to merit investing time on a contingency-fee basis. Second, if the court determines that the action "was clearly frivolous, clearly vexatious, or brought primarily for purposes of harassment",[46] the whistleblower may be required to pay the corporation's costs. A more serious risk is that a fabricated or exaggerated claim may be used by a whistleblower to obtain a settlement from the corporation. This risk is probably greatest in the case of a disgruntled employee who already doubts her future within the corporation, or where the potential settlement is sufficiently large to outweigh possible dismissal and other retaliation for such conduct. (This is also the risk that the reputational effects attached to such behaviour may lead to "blacklisting" by other potential employers).

At one level, one might ask why a corporation (usually a "deep-pocket" litigant) would be prepared to settle a meritless claim for a substantial amount of money. It is possible to imagine a scenario where even unfounded allegations of corruption could effect a decline in the value of a corporation's shares. Unproven allegations could, perhaps, also dissuade governments from entering into new contracts with a corporation until the matter is "cleared up". A fraudulent whistleblower could time her demand for a settlement strategically; for example, at a time when the corporation is on the verge of winning a major contract, is about to float a new equity issue, is about to be acquired, or is about to undertake a merger.

The main difficulty facing the fraudulent whistleblower in these circumstances is that a large settlement of the whistleblower's claim is unlikely to save the corporation's reputation. Shareholders and others may well infer from such a settlement that wrongdoing has in fact occurred. It is true that the corporation might be able to keep a settlement secret for a time, but eventually a large disbursement must be reflected in the corporation's books and somehow accounted for in its regular reporting to shareholders. Nevertheless, a settlement might have the short-term value of pulling the corporation through a critical period. In some circumstances, it might also be possible to disguise a settlement as a generous "golden handshake". Furthermore, if agency theory is introduced into the analysis, even where it is not in the corporation's best interests to settle with the whistleblower, individual employees or managers may be quite happy to spend the corporation's money to silence a troublemaker, particularly where the whistleblower's allegations impugn their personal reputations.

These considerations qualify the claim of Callahan & Dworkin that "settlement leverage to be gained from a meritless claim is minimal".[47] However, it is important to recognize that this leverage has little to do with the availability of an award if the whistleblower has the option of being able to succeed with the claim in court. Rather, it has everything to do with the ability to do reputational harm to the corporation and/or its managers and employees *before* the claim can be judicially scrutinized. The likelihood that a corporation would settle, not because of this immediate threat but because of the risk that a court might actually accept a truly fraudulent or fabricated claim *is* probably minimal.

A related concern is that of vigilantism. In the hope of gaining a large reward if they actually uncover wrongdoing, employees may invest inefficient amounts of time and resources in attempting to detect wrongdoing. This would likely occur where at least some of the time and resources expended are corporate, for which the individual employee does not bear the full opportunity cost. Moreover, vigilantism may have subtle negative effects on corporate interests where, for example, potential whistleblowers break into confidential files or spy on other employees in the hope of uncovering wrongdoing. It is important to note that it is not a requirement of the *False Claims Act* that a whistleblower obtain information about wrongdoing either inadvertently or in the normal course of her duties. Conversely, vigilante-like conduct, particularly where no wrongdoing exists, can be legitimately and effectively disciplined within the workplace – ultimately by dismissal if necessary. Intuitively, it is unlikely that a potential whistleblower would run such risks unless she already had plausible evidence of misconduct. Nevertheless, in some circumstances, a disgruntled employee facing termination for other reasons might decide there is little to lose in such behaviour.

While it might prevent some inefficient employee investments of company time and resources in detecting wrongdoing, a rule preventing recovery where the informer has not obtained information in the course of her normal duties might also deter some efficient investments. Moreover, even if she discovers some hint of wrongdoing in the normal course of her duties, it will often be unlikely that she can gather decisive evidence of wrongdoing except through active efforts. In fact, in many circumstances, using company time and resources to gather evidence may be inevitable. Finally, given that whistle-blowers typically consider themselves to be acting out of loyalty to the *corporation*, they will be most inclined to make investments of corporate time and resources in uncovering wrongdoing where they believe that doing so is in the best interests of the *corporation*.

Guarding the Guardians: The Case for a Private Right of Action

A DISTINCTIVE ASPECT OF THE WHISTLEBLOWER provisions of the *False Claims Act* is that they allow the whistleblower to pursue a private right of action where the Justice Department refuses to take up the claim. A much higher *minimum* level of award is provided to the whistleblower, where she pursues an action on her own (25 percent as compared to 15 percent). This seems reasonable, given the greater costs and risks of a whistleblower bearing the carriage of the action. However, it is sometimes argued that allowing a private right of action invites frivolous claims, which would otherwise be screened out by public prosecutors.

In fact, as noted by Callahan & Dworkin, of the nearly 300 claims filed between 1986 and 1992, only 42 were joined by the Justice Department.[48] At first glance it may seem odd that it could be socially efficient for a private individual to pursue a whistleblower action but it is not socially efficient for the Justice Department to do so. Callahan & Dworkin suggest that the government may actually be saving money by allowing private individuals to bring actions. However, any such savings are likely outweighed by the higher payment generally owed to a whistleblower in compensation for having brought the action (unless we assume that whistleblowers are able to use legal resources more efficiently than the government, which may very well be the case). This may also be partly explained by the departmental budgets which put ceilings on internal resources for investigation and prosecution and which cannot easily be raised in the short term. Under these circumstances, it can be predicted that Justice Department lawyers will decline to prosecute even where it is socially efficient to do so if the anticipated benefit is outweighed by the opportunity cost of foregoing prosecution of a more promising claim. If there were no fixed limits on prosecutorial resources, the Justice Department would pursue every action where the marginal social benefit[49] of doing so is equal to the marginal cost in prosecutorial resources and where the marginal cost of prosecutorial resources that are *equal in effectiveness to those that would be marshalled by the whistleblower herself* is less than the cost to the government of the whistleblower pursuing her own action (i.e., where a higher percentage of the total recovery goes to the whistleblower to reflect her carriage of the action, with a corresponding smaller recovery for the public purse).

If we introduce assumptions related to public choice, the government's decision whether to prosecute or not may not be determined solely by considerations of maximizing social welfare or the public interest. The government's decision will also be influenced by agency theory assumptions that the decisions of bureaucrats regarding individual prosecutions will be affected by their own interests and not only the government's (whether the latter is defined in terms of public interest or public choice). Moreover, the availability of a private right of action may have much broader consequences than the above account suggests. From a public choice standpoint, the government may be reluctant to prosecute a corporation that wields influence on government generally and to which it is indebted for, or from which it expects to receive, political contributions. A government may also be reluctant to prosecute where an investigation and trial could reveal government complicity in corporate wrongdoing.

The possibility of the government failing to prosecute wrongdoing for such reasons reinforces the value of a private right of action as a means of "guarding the guardians". The potential for using whistleblower legislation in this way is important to bear in mind when considering some of the specific issues in design and interpretation of whistleblower provisions in the *False Claims Act*. First, the possibility that a government may not prosecute in order to conceal its own complicity with wrongdoing suggests that governmental complicity should not act as a bar or a kind of estoppel defence against an action whose carriage is born by the whistleblower herself. This supports the result in the case of *Hagood* v. *Sonoma County Water Agency*, where the United States Court of Appeals, Ninth Circuit, held that awareness by government officials of the falsity of a contractual claim did not provide a valid defence to a whistleblower suit against the contractor.[50]

A more subtle issue in the design of an optimal whistleblower statute is also raised by the facts of this case. The legislative history of the *False Claims Act*, reviewed by the Court in *Hagood*, suggests a preoccupation with designing statutory provisions which do not require that the government forego significant revenue to compensate a whistleblower for information already available to the government. The assumption is that it is inefficient to pay for something that one already owns. However, it is precisely when the government is in complicity with the wrongdoing that the information, by definition, will already have been available to it. The latest version of the *False Claims Act*, as amended in 1986, allows a whistleblower to recover even where she was not the primary source of the information, although it does provide for a reduction in the amount of the award to a maximum of 10 percent when the whistle-blower has not been the primary source, provided the information had not previously been made public.[51] However, where the Justice Department does not intervene, there is no requirement that an award be discounted even where the information provided by the whistleblower would already have been available to government. This has precisely the salutary effect of not deterring whistleblower actions where the government has deliberately decided not to act on information independently available to it.

From an agency theory perspective, even where the government itself is acting in the public interest, delegated decision-makers within government, such as prosecuting attorneys or investigators, may have interests that are not fully aligned with those of government. For example, where prosecutors are not fully compensated for overtime, they may shirk from undertaking a case that involves significant extra work unless they believe it offers them strong career advantages. Bureaucrats who want to leave open the possibility of a private sector career upon leaving government may be disinclined to offend major corporate interests. In the case of the defense sector, defense contractors are a major source of employment for former government employees, as are major government contractors generally. This consideration may weigh less on Justice Department lawyers themselves and more on officials in the line department that signed the government contract who would likely be consulted on whether prosecution is warranted.[52] A third factor is that there appears to be some institutional bias against whistleblowers in the Justice Department, which may explain why the Department frequently declines not only to recommend that the Department join an action but often seeks to frustrate a whistleblower's own recovery, arguing on various grounds that the whistleblower's reward should be reduced. As the Court pointedly noted in one whistleblower's suit,

> [n]o one likes snitches but they can be valuable. In view of their widespread use, it is worthy of note that the Department of Justice has considered such individuals as adversaries rather than allies. This is not the first case where this Court has noted the antagonism of the Justice Department to a whistleblower. The reason continues to be unknown, but the attitude is clear.[53]

On the basis of common explanations of bureaucratic conduct, a number of reasons come to mind why Justice officials might have a bias against whistleblowers despite the apparent social utility of their role. First, Justice officials are themselves "team players" in a large organization and may be distrustful of dissenters or apparent traitors within other large organizations. Lennane (1993) suggests in a study of Australian whistleblowers that: "It is disappointing that statutory authorities so often fail to help, seeming, like most workmates, to side with employers as part of the authority system."[54] Second, where whistleblowers pursue an action that the Justice Department fails to join, they may in effect second-guess the judgement of Justice Department officials in deciding not to prosecute. Finally, officials may react out of jealousy or envy at the large awards that whistleblowers and/or their lawyers may receive if successful.

CONCLUSIONS

THIS STUDY HAS EXPLORED THE SCOPE for whistleblowing to serve as an important instrument in the arsenal of public policy designed to ensure corporate compliance with broad social responsibilities. We believe that attention to whistleblowing serves as a welcome addition to the debate over corporate social responsibility. Traditionally, this debate has focused on issues of discretionary directorial duties at the expense of dealing with more mundane but significantly more important issues of corporate compliance. Whistleblowing holds considerable promise as an instrument capable of increasing the probability of detection of perverse corporate behaviour, but at a relatively low resource cost. In this respect, whistleblowing bounties are similar in nature to other types of insturments that permit valuable corporate information to be disseminated in a timely and accurate way to public authorities, and which in turn enhance the quality of the regulatory system governing corporations. While there are certainly vexing and subtle design issues involved in the creation of workable whistleblowing schemes, we view these concerns as not so formidable as to militate against the adoption of such schemes, and we recommend them strongly to Canadian policy makers.

ENDNOTES

1 Illegal corporate conduct means illegal actions undertaken by the corporation's agents for personal gain.
2 See, *e.g.*, B. Fisse and J. Braithwaite, *Corporations, Crime and Accountability*, Cambridge: Cambridge University Press, 1993; J. Arlen, "The Potentially Perverse Effects of Corporate Criminal Liability", *Journal of Legal Studies*, 23, 1994, p. 833; J. C. Coffee Jr., "'No Soul to Damn: No Body to Kick': An Unscandalized Inquiry into the Problem of Corporate Punishment", *Michigan Law Review*, 79, 1981, p. 386; R. H. Kraakman, "Corporate Liability Strategies and the Costs of Legal Controls", *Yale Law Journal*, 93, 1984, p. 857; various articles in symposium issue on corporate criminal liability, *Boston University Law Review*, 71 (2), 1991, pp. 189-453.
3 See, *e.g.*, Arlen, *ibid.*
4 Arlen, *ibid.* at 835.
5 See, *e.g.*, W. K. Viscusi and R. J. Zeckhauser, "Optimal Standards with Incomplete Enforcement", *Public Policy*, 27, 1979, p. 437; R. B. Stewart, "Regulation, Innovation, and Administrative Law: A Conceptual Framework", *California Law Review*, 69, 1981, p. 1259; C. R. Sunstein, *After the Rights Revolution: Reconceiving the Regulatory State*, Cambridge, MA: Harvard University Press, 1990; R. Howse, J. R. S. Prichard and M. J. Trebilcock, "Smaller or Smarter Government?", *University of Toronto Law Journal*, 40, 1990, p. 498.; I. Ayres and J. Braithwaite, *Responsive Regulation: Transcending the Deregulation Debate*, Oxford: Oxford University Press, 1995.
6 See particularly, R. J. Herrnstein and J. Q. Wilson, *Crime and Human Nature*, New York: Simon & Schuster, 1985.
7 See R. Howse, "Retrenchment, Reform or Revolution? The Shift to Incentives and the Future of the Regulatory State", *Alberta Law Review*, 31, 1993, pp. 455 at 476-477; Arlen, *supra* n. 2 at 835.

8 For overviews of such protection in the United States, see M. H. Malin, "Protecting the Whistleblower From Retaliatory Discharge", *University of Michigan Journal of Legal Reference*, 16, 1983, Ref. p. 277; S. M. Kohn and M. D. Kohn, "An Overview of Federal and State Whistleblower Protections", *Antioch Law Journal*, 4, 1986, p. 99; and more recently, T. Barnett, "Overview of State Whistleblower Protection Statutes", *Labor Law Journal*, 43, 1992, p. 440. For Canada, see L. J. Brooks, "Whistleblowers ... Learn to Love Them", *Canadian Business Review*, 20, 1993, pp. 19-21.

9 *False Claims Act*, 31 U.S.C. § 3730.

10 For a much more detailed analysis of the development and wording of the statute, see E. S. Callahan and T. M. Dworkin, "Do Good and Get Rich: Financial Incentives For Whistleblowing and the False Claims Act", *Villanova Law Review*, 37, 1992, 273 at pp. 302-18.

11 The individual need not be an employee or officer of the corporation in order to recover under the statute, which extends its incentive effect to clients, customers, competitors and others who have the opportunity to discover corporate wrongdoing.

12 See Fisse & Braithwaite, *supra* n. 2; Arlen, *supra* n. 2.

13 See, *e.g.*, G. Becker, "Make the Punishment Fit the Corporate Crime", *Business Week*, 13 March, 1989, 22, col. 2; M. K. Block, "Optimal Penalties, Criminal Law and the Control of Corporate Behaviour", *Boston University Law Review*, 71(2), 1991, p. 395; J. S. Parker, "Criminal Sentencing Policy for Organizations: The Unifying Approach of Optimal Penalties", *American Criminal Law Review*, 26, 1989, p. 513; W. M. Landes, "Optimal Sanctions for Antitrust Violations", *University of Chicago Law Review*, 50, 1983, p. 652; and R. A. Posner, *Economic Analysis of Law*, Boston: Little Brown and Company, 1986, 2nd ed., c. 7.

14 However, as J. Arlen, *supra* n. 2 at 842, has stressed, the standard analysis of corporate crime should be broadened to incorporate sensitivity to "the relationship between corporate enforcement expenditures, the probability of detection, and the corporation's expected liability".

15 See discussion Kraakman, *supra* n. 2; R. H. Kraakman, "Gatekeepers: The Anatomy of a Third-Party Enforcement Strategy", *Journal of Law, Economics and Organization*, 2, 1986, p. 53.

16 C. R. Alexander and M. A. Cohen, "Why Do Corporations become Criminals?" (unpublished manuscript, Dec. 1994).

17 Arlen, *supra* n. 2 at 834.

18 For a more extensive discussion of this issue in the setting of bank debt interests, see R. Daniels and G. Triantis, "The Role of Debt in American Corporate Governance", *California Law Review*, (forthcoming, 1995).

19 A. M. Polinsky and S. Shavell, "Should Employees Be Subject to Fines and Imprisonment Given the Existence of Corporate Liability?", *International Review of Law and Economics*, 13, 1993, p. 239.

20 As A. Etzioni has noted in "Going Soft on Corporate Crime", *Washington Post*, 1 April, 1990, C3, col. 1, "[b]ecause the crimes may involve complex financial transactions over long time periods, it may not be possible to determine exactly which individuals are responsible for what actions".

21 See M. Trebilcock, *The Prospects for Reinventing Government*, Toronto: C. D. Howe Institute, 1994.

22 The recent debacles over the misuse of financial derivative instruments by financial institutions and public issuers underscores this point. Normally, these instruments are a device for limiting or at least controlling corporate risk exposure, but with only modest changes in contractual arrangements, the riskiness of these instruments for the sponsoring institution can be increased dramatically. The difficulty for public authorities is, first, in being able to determine when derivative instruments are being used and, second, in being able to distinguish those cases of benign risk management from perverse risk-taking.

23 A. Berle and G. Means, *The Modern Corporation and Private Property*, New York: Harcourt, Brace & World, 1932.

24 These accountability problems are observed in a number of different relationships within the corporation: between shareholder and manager, between shareholder and creditor, and between majority and minority shareholders. For an introduction to agency theory in the corporate context, see: A. Barnea, R. A. Haugen, and L.W. Senbet, *Agency Problems and Financial Contracting*, Englewood Cliffs, New Jersey: Prentice-Hall, 1985, or W. A. Klein and J. C. Coffee, *Business Organizations and Finance: Legal and Economic Principles*, Mineola, New York: Foundation Press, 1990, 4th ed.

25 Recent trends toward organizational de-layering and increased focus reduce, although do not obliterate, the scope for sub-goal pursuit.

26 J. B. Dozier and M. P. Miceli, "Potential Predictors of Whistle-Blowing: A Prosocial Behaviour Perspective", *Academic Management Review*, 10, 1985, p. 823; M. P. Miceli, B. L. Roach, and J. P. Near, "The Motivations of Anonymous Whistle-Blowers: the Case of Federal Employees", *Public Personnel Management*, 17, 1988, p. 281; M. P. Glazer and P. Migdal, *The Whistleblowers: Exposing Corruption in Government and Industry*, New York: Basic Books, 1989, c. 4, "The Power of Belief Systems for Ethical Resisters".

27 See Arlen, *supra* n. 2.

28 See J. P. Near and M. P. Miceli, "Retaliation Against Whistle Blowers: Predictors and Effects", *Journal of Applied Psychology*, 71, 1986, p. 137; E. S. Callahan and J. W. Collins, "Employee Attitudes Toward Whistleblowing: Management and Public Policy Implications", *Journal of Business Ethics*, 11, 1992, p. 939.

29 Glazer and Migdal, *supra* n. 26; a catalogue of the "Ways of Punishing Whistleblowers" can be found in B. D. Fisher, "The Whistleblower

Protection Act of 1989: A False Hope for Whistleblowers", *Rutgers Law Review*, 43, 1991, p. 355 at 363-68.

30 Glazer and Migdal, *supra* n. 26 at 210.

31 F. Strasser, "When the Big Whistle Blows ...", *National Law Journal*, 8 May, 1989, p. 1; R. B. Schmitt, "Honesty Pays Off", *Wall Street Journal*, 11 January, 1995, A1-2, col. 6.

32 808 F. Supp. 580 (S.D. Ohio 1992).

33 Dozier and Miceli, *supra* n. 26; F. Elliston *et al.*, *Whistleblowing Research: Methodological and Moral Issues*, New York: Praeger, 1984, p. 26.

34 Callahan and Collins, *supra* n. 28 at 944-55; Miceli, Roach & Near, *supra* n. 26.

35 A further difficulty is the inherent uncertainty of the value of the whistle-blower award; not only must the prospective whistleblower worry about the likelihood and costs of corporate retaliation, but she can only speculate on the expected value of the bounty in the event that her claim succeeds. Here, as mentioned earlier, the prospective whistleblower must consider the actual social damages inflicted by the corporation, the extent of corporate culpability (if this is an element of the offence), the level and quality of resources expended by the state on prosecution, and the ultimate disposition of the claim. The uncertainty inherent in these calculations creates risks for the whistleblower which must be offset with additional compensation. The design of incentive-based contracts is discussed in P. R. Milgrom and J. Roberts, *Economics, Organization and Management*, Englewood Cliffs, New Jersey: Prentice-Hall, 1992, at c. 7.

36 Ayres and Braithwaite, *supra* n. 5.

37 A. K. Naj, "Internal Suspicions; GE's Drive to Purge Fraud is Hampered by Workers' Mistrust", *Wall Street Journal*, 22 July, 1992, A1-2,6, col. 1.

38 See T. M. Dworkin and E. S. Callahan, "Internal Whistleblowing: Protecting the Interests of the Employee, the Organization, and Society", *American Business Law Journal*, 29, 1991, p. 267 at 273.

39 Callahan and Collins, *supra* n. 28; T. Barnett, D. S. Cochran and G. S. Taylor, "The Internal Disclosure Policies of Private-Sector Employers: An Initial Look at Their Relationship to Employee Whistleblowing", *Journal of Business Ethics*, 12, 1993, p. 127.

40 For anecdotal evidence of such abuse, see M. Mason, "The Curse of Whistle-Blowing", *Wall Street Journal*, 14 March, 1994, A14, col. 3.

41 Near and Miceli, *supra* n. 28 at 142.

42 See generally, J. R. Macey, "Agency Theory and the Criminal Liability of Organizations", *Boston University Law Review*, 71(2), 1991, p. 315.

43 Barnett, Cochran and Taylor, *supra* n. 39 at 129, 134.

44 Callahan and Dworkin, *supra* n. 10 at 325.

45 *Ibid.* at 326-27.

46 31 U.S.C. § 3730 (d) (4) (1988). However, as W. Kovacic notes, "Whistleblower Bounty Lawsuits as Monitoring Devices in Government

Contracting" (unpublished manuscript, October 1994), there has not yet been a reported case where a court has ordered a *qui tam* plaintiff to pay the defendant's costs under this provision of the *False Claims Act*. This fact may mitigate, at least to some degree, the extent to which this cost-rule actually creates a disincentive to fabricated claims in practice.

47 Callahan and Dworkin, *supra* n. 10 at 326.

48 *Ibid.* at 325.

49 Here, the social benefit includes not only recovery of public moneys lost due to fraud but also the specific and general deterrence effects that result from sanctioning wrongful conduct.

50 929 F.2d. 1416 (9th Cir. 1991), foll'd *Heckler, Secretary of Health and Human Services v. Community Health Services of Crawford County, Inc., et al.*, 467 U.S. 51 (3rd Cir. 1984).

51 31 U.S.C. § 3730(d)(1) (1988).

52 A related issue is the extent to which government employees or former employees should be entitled to bring whistle-blower law suits based on information about corporate wrongdoing learned while fulfilling their duties as agents of the government. For a thorough consideration of this issue, see Kovacic, *supra* note 46.

53 *U. S. v. General Electric, supra* n. 32 at 584.

54 K. J. Lennane, "'Whistleblowing: A Health Issue", *British Medical Journal*, 307, 1993, p. 667 at 669.

ACKNOWLEDGEMENTS

WE ARE INDEBTED TO Jennifer Arlen for extensive comments on an earlier draft of this study. We are also grateful to Jody Langhan and Wayne Bigby, LL.B. students at the Faculty of Law, University of Toronto for research assistance.

Alice Nakamura
Faculty of Business
University of Alberta

John Cragg
Faculty of Arts
University of British Columbia

&

Kathleen Sayers
International Wordsmiths
Vancouver

16

Corporate Governance and Worker Education: An Alternative View

CANADIAN EMPLOYERS, WORKERS, GOVERNMENTS AT VARIOUS LEVELS, and the voting public all have stakes in the amount, the quality, and the allocation and payment mechanisms for education and training available to the Canadian labour force. We contend, however, that there are important differences in the nature of the stakes of these different interested groups, and that these differences are at the root of shifts in prevailing views on *what aspects* of worker education should be expanded or improved, *which workers* should have more invested in them, and *what are the preferred policy options* for accomplishing the desired increases and improvements in worker learning investments. In addition, we argue for policy initiatives that reaffirm the vital importance of the Canadian tradition of public education while improving the efficiency, effectiveness and fairness of education and training programs for the Canadian labour force. Our conclusions are summarized in a final section.

EMPLOYER, WORKER, GOVERNMENT AND PUBLIC STAKES

EMPLOYERS, WORKERS, GOVERNMENTS AND THE PUBLIC all have stakes in worker education and training, but for different reasons.

Employers buy and use labour as an input in the production of goods and services. Worker education alters the ways in which workers can be used in production processes and improves worker productivity. However, employers in Canada have no way of obtaining long-term rights to, or ownership of, the labour services of particular workers.

Workers own their labour services and can count on benefitting in the future from investments that they or others make in their job-related expertise – provided, of course, that they can find employment where the expertise they have acquired is needed and will command a return.

The public includes Canadian labour force participants, employers, government officials, and the taxpayers who must pay the cost of subsidized government programs. Furthermore, the *parents* of the next generation of labour force participants, of employers and of government officials are part of the public. Thus, the public has a broad stake in the amount, the quality, and the allocation and payment mechanisms for job-related education and training.

The divergent interests of the various stakeholder groups within the voting public result in differences of opinion as to what changes are needed in our education and training systems and how those changes should be funded. Government policies cannot accommodate all the differences in voter opinion at any one point in time. As a consequence, the political choices made can shift dramatically over time.

BUSINESS INTERESTS

HYPOTHETICALLY, BUSINESSES COULD PROVIDE all the education and training for their own workforces, with workers paying some share of the cost directly, or in the form of lower wages. The reasons why this is not done are also the reasons why Canadian businesses want public education and training opportunities to be available.

Labour Cost Considerations

Modern businesses need workers who have a wide array of learning skills as well as more specialized expertise. In turn, providing this needed education and training requires a wide range of teaching expertise as well as instructional materials and facilities. There are economies of scale and scope to be had by centralizing the delivery of much of this education and training in established institutions of learning. Most businesses would not find it practical to maintain teaching resources for everything from reading to computer basics to chemistry.

A second labour cost consideration is that in the earlier stages of the education and training process the talents and interests of the students are usually unclear. If businesses were responsible for earlier levels of education and training, they would have to invest in some individuals who would subsequently turn out to be poorly suited for the available employment opportunities in those businesses. In fact, some of those in whom learning investments were made could turn out to be poorly suited for employment of any sort. Businesses can avoid many of these potential worker suitability risks when most worker education and training is provided by public institutions. Also, there are shifts over time with respect to the types of education and training that individual businesses need their workers to have. These shifts are caused both by changes in the product and service lines of the businesses themselves, and by more general developments in business processes, such as the increase in the use of computer technology. To the extent that worker education and training is provided by public institutions, Canadian businesses can avoid some of the adjustment costs that result from ongoing needs to alter and update worker education and training offerings.

Public education and training that helps to lower business labour costs provides a subsidy to Canadian businesses. One advantage of the subsidy in this form – rather than, say, as a direct cash transfer – is that possible charges of unfair competition from trading partners are avoided. Investment in education and training for the populace is an internationally accepted means by which governments provide aid to their country's industries and businesses.

Avoiding Underinvestment by Businesses

Employee training, like R&D, represents a long-term investment that can yield high returns to employers for many years in the future, but only from those employees who in fact continue to work for an employer. Any returns to the employer cease at the point when a worker in whom the employer has invested is no longer needed and is permanently laid off or takes a job else-where. The future returns to employers from the investments they make in employee education and training are fundamentally contingent on the outlook concerning the employers' future needs for, and the likelihood of holding onto, the workers in whom those investments are made.

Employers require both general and specific expertise. For example, employees must have general reading, writing, and numeracy skills, as well as highly specific knowledge about where and how to do their day-to-day jobs. The more general the education and training investments that businesses make in their workers, the more likely it is that other businesses can capture the returns on those investments. But even so-called "firm-specific" knowledge can, in fact, enhance an employee's employment and earnings prospects with other employers. A worker who has acquired specific knowledge in one employment situation has already demonstrated his or her capability to acquire details of this sort. Also, other businesses may want to learn about the operational specifics of a competitor's business. Thus, when employers make investments of even firm-specific learning in their workers, the effect may be to make those workers more attractive to other businesses. When trained workers are hired away, the businesses that invested in the workers cease to collect any further return on their investments. This can result in collective under-investment in worker learning by businesses. Public education and training is one way to deal with this potential under-investment problem.

Escalating Business Expectations of Public Education and Training

Certain skills and work procedures constitute proprietary business property (to be carefully guarded in much the same way as businesses seek to protect impor-tant physical inventions with patents or through secrecy). Also, businesses recognize that public education and training institutions cannot always give students access to expensive, highly specialized machines, particularly in areas where such machines are constantly changing. Businesses recognize that they must provide some worker training themselves. Nevertheless, businesses will be better off if a high percentage of the share of needed worker education and training is provided, and paid for, by others.

There is an additional consideration that encourages businesses to favour giving public educational institutions the responsibility for providing general worker education. As already noted, businesses that provide education and training risk losing their trained employees to other firms that are willing to pay somewhat more for experienced workers, with this risk increasing as the training becomes more general. But the knowledge that is general in an economy-wide or industry-wide sense continues to increase, making it inevitable that businesses will always want more from education and training institutions than is being delivered.

The ongoing upward adjustments with respect to what the business sector wants from public educational institutions is evident not only in commentary by business leaders, but also in the writings of scholars who study and try to foresee the evolving needs of successful businesses. Examples include the writings of Drucker, who coined and popularized many of the terms that have become part of the everyday vocabulary of the effects of technology on our economy and on future business prospects and the implications of technology for education and training requirements in the years ahead. Drucker (1993) writes:

> The basic economic resource – "the means of production," to use the economist's term – is no longer capital, nor natural resources (the economist's "land"), nor "labor." It is and will be knowledge. ...

> The leading social groups of the knowledge society will be "knowledge workers" – knowledge executives who know how to allocate knowledge to productive use, just as capitalists knew how to allocate capital to productive use; knowledge professionals; knowledge employees. ... The economic challenge of the post-capitalist society will therefore be the productivity of knowledge work and the knowledge worker (p. 8).

The Business Wish List for Public Education and Training

Employers want public educational institutions to provide more of the education and training their workers need, at no additional cost, or at someone else's expense — in the form of higher tuitions, for example. This will improve their own unit costs, competitiveness and profitability, all of which are natural and appropriate business interests in a free-market, capitalist economy.

The message for all who will listen is that Canadian business wants and needs better-trained workers at all levels. But Canadian business particularly wants adequate numbers of personnel who have the sort of education and training that is expensive for employers to provide in-house, or to have to pay for by subsidizing selected employees to take this training at schools outside Canada. Of course, this latter sort of education and training can also be very expensive when it is provided through formal educational institutions. This causes conflicting pressures on those responsible for the direction of education and training in Canada, since most of our formal educational institutions are publicly subsidized, and since the business community is also concerned about rising taxes and public-sector deficits and debt.

WORKER INTERESTS IN WORKER EDUCATION

EMPLOYED WORKERS RISK LOSING THEIR JOBS if the enterprises they work for lose competitive ground and are therefore forced to downsize, or are taken over or go bankrupt. Because of these considerations, there are overlaps in the employee's stake in worker education versus the stake of business owners and managers. Both workers and business owners stand to lose from education and training deficiencies that put Canadian companies at risk. Workers also recognize that they will have lower education and training costs if their learning opportunities are publicly subsidized; and workers, like businesses, usually benefit from being able to seek out the sorts of jobs that suit them *after* they have completed a substantial amount of their education and training rather than having to join (and stay with) a business in order to be trained and before acquiring sufficient knowledge about their own talents and work preferences.

Beyond these areas where worker and business interests overlap, the interests of both parties in worker education diverge sharply.

Points of Divergence

In Canada, education and training courses for adults at formal learning institutions are typically subsidized. The degree of subsidization has been greater for universities and colleges and for full-time degree programs than for programs at technical and vocational institutions and for short course, part-time and certificate programs. Even with the public subsidies, however, there are tuition fees for almost all adult learning programs. Workers have an obvious financial interest in keeping tuition fees low, and in having employers provide directly, or pay the fees for, the instructional programs they need to do their jobs.

In tight job markets where employers are competing for the workers they need, promises of subsidized education and training or other instruction to be provided by the employer become important inducements to attract good quality workers. For example, in the late 1970s, better-qualified Bachelor of Commerce graduates were sometimes given job offers that included the possibility of having their expenses paid to attend graduate programs in areas of specialization that were in short supply. Employers will rarely make offers of this sort unless they feel they must in order to find the workers they need.

Workers, on the other hand, always like to have opportunities for employer-supplied or employer-financed education and training, since otherwise they must pay the costs of such training themselves, and often without any assurance that they will have a job once they finish their training programs. Workers lose in terms of direct financial outlay, and often with respect to increased job risk as well, when they rather than the employers are the ones who must take responsibility for their educational expenses beyond the elementary and secondary school levels.

A second point of divergence is that workers often like to have more general, as well as job-specific, education and training. This tends to be the case particularly for workers who are afraid that they may eventually be laid off by their present employers and who therefore anticipate having to find new jobs; and for workers who dislike, or would like to improve upon, their present jobs and want to acquire marketable qualifications through education.

A third potential point of divergence has to do with the allocation among workers of the employer's investment in worker education. Presumably, employers want to concentrate these investments, to the extent practical, on the core of employees who are expected to stay with the firm over the long run, and who can not be readily replaced. Yet, it is the workers who know they are expendable and vulnerable to being laid off who, in many respects, have the most pressing personal need to gain access to employer-provided or subsidized instructional opportunities.

A fourth point of divergence arises when Canadian educational institutions do not produce sufficient numbers of certain types of highly skilled workers who are readily available in other countries. This point becomes even more contentious when those foreign workers can be hired by employers in Canada for wages that are relatively modest by Canadian standards. When this is the case, Canadian firms typically request permission to hire foreign workers and to bring them into Canada as immigrants. Canadian workers, on the other hand, typically favour restricting this sort of immigration, so that firms must train Canadian workers in these skills.

Finally, there are large numbers of *unemployed* workers – that is, persons in the workforce who have no employers – who want access to on-the-job or other forms of subsidized instruction or training in order to improve their chances of finding jobs that provide a living wage. These unemployed workers would like employers to be encouraged, or even forced, to offer training not only to their current employees but also to others (including the unemployed) who want to acquire more marketable job skills.

Why Workers may Underinvest

Unlike employers, workers own their own expertise. Wherever they go, their knowledge goes with them. Thus, the reasons why businesses may underinvest in worker education and training do not apply for workers. In the case of workers, underinvestment is a potential threat because of the risks associated with job opportunities and problems of finding the funds to pay for education and for living expenses while in educational programs.

While workers do own their expertise, they do not usually own the other necessary factors of production. To be able to make use of their expertise, most workers must sell their labour to employers. Furthermore, it is the businesses (employers) who do most of the forward planning about what will be produced and how, and in what quantities. Because of this, it is primarily businesses that have the advance information about job prospects. Workers must guess about this based on what they can observe and on recent trends in job openings, employment and earnings. Also, even if there are many job openings for workers with specific skills, there is no guarantee that a newly qualified person will be hired, especially if there are also many other more qualified and experienced applicants competing for those jobs.

Because individuals have no control over labour demand, and are not usually in a position to foresee shifts in either labour demand or supply, it is inevitable that some will make some job-related education and training investments that pay off poorly relative to their original hopes and expectations. In some cases an individual may not even recover the out-of-pocket and opportunity costs of the education and training programs he or she has chosen to take. This risk factor tends to discourage individual and family investments in more education and training – particularly for those individuals of lesser means who cannot afford to lose on their investments. For similar reasons, financial institutions are reluctant to make loans to individuals for most sorts of education and training unless those loans can be secured by something other than the hoped-for future return on the education and training.

These are thought to be the main reasons why individuals and families will tend to under-invest in work-related education and training.

PUBLIC AND GOVERNMENT INTERESTS

PUBLIC INTEREST IN WORKER EDUCATION AND TRAINING is rooted in the fact that Canadian employers and workers, and their parents and families, are all members of the public. Also, the public is the source of the revenues – through taxes – that support public education and training programs.

Governments are the official representatives of the voting public. Because governments cannot satisfy all of the public at any one point in time, governments make ongoing choices about *which* public groups to listen to. Governments also produce and shape much of the information on which public perceptions and choices are based.

Governments have a stake in worker education and training for several reasons. First, the voting public is concerned with the subject. Second, large numbers of public-sector jobs are involved. Third, public education and training programs are believed to affect other areas of government responsibility such as unemployment insurance and welfare caseloads. Workers with low levels of education are believed to be more likely to rely on public income support. Finally, all levels of government in Canada must now cope with tight budgets, and funds that are spent on public education and training cannot be used for other purposes.

THE SHIFTING ALLIANCES OF GOVERNMENTS

GOVERNMENT POLICY POSITIONS ON WORKER EDUCATION and training are inherently unstable because of the divergent interests of those who make up the voting public, public sector employee interests, and budgetary problems. The difficulty is that government policy positions related to education and training represent shifting alliances with business *versus* worker *versus* taxpayer interests.

Attributing our Economic Problems to a Learning Deficit

Many members of the business community have been eager to attribute Canada's recent employment woes to deficiencies in publicly provided education and training – not in their own training efforts. The message from the business sector is not that more should be spent on education and training, but that the money already allocated should be better spent. Consider the following summary conclusions based on an extensive survey of B.C. businesses commissioned by the British Columbia Chamber of Commerce (1994).

> The issue is not "more money from government". The issue is effective use of resources. Our public spending as a percent of Gross Domestic Product ranks at about the median in comparison to other economies in the developed world.
>
> However, our human resources are not being developed to achieve success in the new economy. In spite of high education spending, unemployment remains stubbornly high (1,618,000 in Canada, 182,000 in B.C.), yet over 400,000 Canadian job openings are vacant because employers cannot find people with the skills they need at a competitive price. In the opinion of senior executives, Canada ranks behind almost all other developed countries in this respect (p. 61).

What the business community is saying, effectively, is that businesses *would* hire more Canadians if only it were more cost effective to do so.

Cost effectiveness depends in part on the education and skills workers have at the time they are hired. Workers with good reading and other learning skills, who are prepared to master the instructional materials on machine operation or other company processes on their own, will be far cheaper (for employers) to train than those who must be taught virtually everything they need to know by more-experienced staff in an on-the-job, hands-on mode. Those who have already had direct experience with the machines or processes related to their new jobs will require even less training from their new employers to achieve a given level of on-the-job productivity. This side of the determination of worker cost effectiveness is clear from the following remarks in the B.C. Chamber of Commerce (1994, p. 52) survey.

> Clearly increased training results in less unit cost by assuring more efficient production – whether this is provided by the public sector or the private sector. If public education and training is improved, then productivity of individual firms can increase since they are required to invest less overhead cost for in-house training.

In its recent review of Canada's social security programs, the federal government joined with large segments of the business community in arguing that our national employment problems are a consequence of inadequately educated and trained workers. A discussion paper titled *Improving Social Security in Canada*, prepared by Human Resources Development Canada (1994), makes the following points.

> To make the most of our future, we need more jobs. And that means pulling in more investment from inside Canada and abroad to create jobs. We need to be an investment magnet. Key to this is to overcome Canada's "skills deficit" – to offer the best-educated, best trained workforce in the world and that must be our common goal in the coming years (p. 10).

Two main explanations are offered for how our apparent "skills deficit" has developed. The discussion paper suggests that globalization of markets and production activities is one reason.

> ... in the long haul unskilled and labour-intensive manufacturing is declining here as Third World producers expand. Services and knowledge-based industries are the major areas of economic growth (p. 15).

The discussion paper then points to technological change as a second explanation.

> If Canadians are to regain a measure of security in the tumultuous, uncertain new world of work, their world of learning will have to catch up. Adapting to technological and economic change is the biggest challenge facing the world of learning (p. 18).

Job openings today require higher levels of education as well as more advanced and specialized skills. Even many lower-skill jobs that once required only basic schooling now call for high school graduates at a minimum (p. 19).

There are at least three separate themes bound up in these explanations in the discussion paper of how globalization and technological change are changing the schooling and training needs of Canadians.

The first theme is that these changes are eliminating many jobs, with the most severe losses occurring in those areas where jobs have traditionally been performed by less educated workers. This is indisputably the case, so far at least. The second theme is that disproportionate numbers of the new (and more desirable) jobs being created are going to more educated workers. This is also indisputably so. As a consequence of these patterns of job loss and hiring for newly created jobs, we learn in the discussion paper quoted above that

"... in the past three years jobs held by university graduates expanded 17 per cent, while the number of jobs held by people not completing high school fell 19 per cent" (p. 19).

The third theme is that disproportionate numbers of those with more education are being hired for the newly created jobs *because these are higher-skill jobs incorporating new technologies.*

Unemployment rates are, in fact, far lower for those with more education. Earnings also rise dramatically with higher levels of schooling. One inference often drawn from these facts is that we would have much less unemployment and poverty if we could decrease the numbers of those with low levels of schooling.

Expectations that reducing the numbers of those with low levels of schooling would help alleviate the problems of joblessness and low earnings are bolstered by the human-capital and wage-determination concepts of economists. Investments in education and training are viewed by economists as having long-run public as well as private returns. Applied research in the growth accounting area of economics has attempted to quantify the effects of public investment in education on national economic growth. The basic conclusion drawn from growth accounting is evident in the following quotation from the report by Newton and his associates (1992).

The growth-accounting method has been used by many researchers to estimate the contribution of education to economic growth over a variety of time periods. The conclusion has always been that education contributes positively to growth. On average, research shows that on an annual basis education con- tributes approximately one-half a percentage point to economic growth (p. 3).

This assessment draws on a comprehensive examination of estimates of the contribution of education and training to Canadian economic growth carried out by the Canadian Labour Market and Productivity Centre (1989-90).

The judgement that Canada's employment deficit problem is primarily attributable to a "skills deficit" serves to deflect worker and public concerns away from business practices and other aspects of government policy that affect employment levels. Instead, attention is focused on our education and training systems: inappropriately, so we believe, despite the growth accounting estimates and the fact that unemployment rates are much higher for those with less schooling.

More Public Money for Education is Not the Answer

In addition to echoing business leaders in claiming that our national skills deficit is an important cause of Canada's widespread unemployment and underemployment problems, the federal government has joined those in the business community and certain taxpayer advocates who argue that more public money for education and training is not the answer. Consider, for example, the following passage from the discussion paper in which the theme that improving the education and training of our workforce will help preserve and restore Canadian prosperity is coupled with assertions that Canada is already a high spender on learning. The implication is that we must spend smarter – not more – on worker education.

> Clearly the enormous investment in education over the years by provincial governments, buttressed by federal financial support, has paid big dividends. As a nation we spend the equivalent of 2.6 per cent of the value of our entire economy each year on post-secondary education alone. That's a greater share of GDP than any other nation. Fully 60 per cent of Canadian high school graduates go straight on to some form of higher learning at a post-secondary institution. ...

> [A]s a new century beckons, we again must push our nation's learning yardsticks further out – much further. In the balance is our ability to preserve our position as one of the world's most prosperous societies. If our standard of living is to be secure, one of our urgent tasks must be to strengthen our learning and training systems (pp. 57-8).

Siding with Workers on Access

In other respects, however, the federal and several of the provincial governments have tended to side with workers rather than employers as to the nature of the needed reform of our education system. Governments have chosen to stress greater access to education and training opportunities, particularly for those who are able-bodied and classified as employable but who have been dependent on unemployment insurance or welfare.

Evidence of the nature of the federal position on how our educational systems should be reshaped is provided by the following rhetorical remarks from the discussion paper.

> Yet don't we as a society have a stake in doing more, in helping people who suddenly find their job skills inadequate and out-of-date to retool themselves for the good jobs in today's economy? (p. 8)

> Long-term unemployment, and the growing number of people who repeatedly fall back on Unemployment Insurance, show that people aren't getting the help they need to help themselves. Too many young people leave school unprepared for the world of work. Too many people on social assistance or in low wage jobs can't afford – or are not allowed by the system – to upgrade their skills. Too many people with careers derailed by change are not receiving the appropriate training (p. 22).

At the same time, governments have begun cutting back funding for more advanced education and research. Governments are not admitting that advanced graduate training and research are being severely pruned as a deficit reduction measure, but this is the inevitable consequence of the nature of some of the cuts that are being made and how they are being implemented.

Students and Businesses Must Pay More

In relation to funding, federal government policy statements run contrary (in some respects) to the stated concerns of business, workers, and taxpayers. Reflecting budgetary imperatives, the government position seems to be that tuitions must rise for publicly subsidized adult learning programs. There are also suggestions that businesses must do more to help train not only their own workers but also others with serious employability problems. The discussion paper states the following.

> One fundamental obstacle to successful skills development faced by many Canadians is their lack of basic learning skills. ... These skills are not only required for most jobs; they are the foundation for development of more advanced skills. People lacking such skills are disadvantaged in today's world and will be more so in the future, unless they get help. ... In designing enhanced employment development services, Canadians will have to decide how basic skills training can best be improved. ... Enhanced employment development services could give employers a greater role in training (pp. 34-5).

Businesses always seem to want more say in the types of education and training provided at public expense. But do businesses also want to become part of the public education and training establishment? Do businesses wish to have more direct control as well as a larger share of the direct costs and the public accountability responsibilities that are an essential part of providing a service that affects the public? Would these sorts of changes make Canadian businesses more competitive and increase their labour demands? Would these sorts of changes even be desirable from the perspective of a worker or the general public?

Looming Pressure on Businesses

Regardless of the responses to the above questions, in the coming years businesses probably will face increasing pressure to contribute more financially as well as in other ways to the education and training of workers, including those who are out of work. There are at least three reasons why this is so.

- Governments are out of money.

- Individuals seem prepared to fight to avoid paying more them- selves for learning programs.

- Canadian firms are regarded as spending too little on worker education and training.

It is unlikely that more public money will be added to existing alloca- tions for education and training in the immediate future. The discussion paper is filled with statements acclaiming the importance of learning to Canada's prosperity and anecdotes about how many Canadians are not receiving the education and training they need. Yet the same federal government that is responsible for this document just brought down a three-year budget plan that effectively reduces federal transfers to the provinces for higher education, and reduces federal support for the provincial welfare programs that help subsidize and provide vocational training for many of those with serious employability problems. None of the provinces is promising to replace fully the lost federal dollars for education and training, and all of the provinces are struggling with their own severe fiscal deficits and debt problems.

Betcherman (1993) provides summary information from 14 different surveys that have attempted to measure training in Canadian firms. In an earlier study, Betcherman (1992) also attempted comparisons of the training investments of Canadian firms with those of other countries. Betcherman (1993) concludes:

Given the difficulties involved in measuring training in industry, it should not be surprising that any international comparisons need to be made with great caution. In addition to the definitional and sampling problems that have already been noted, the structural and institutional differences across countries add a further serious complication. Nevertheless, available data offer a strong sense that Canadian firms do train less than their counterparts in other major industrialized countries. This conclusion is based on a range of indicators (standardized across countries to the extent possible) including the percentage of employees receiving employer-based training, the percentage of enterprises providing training, private-sector expenditures on training, and the incidence of apprenticeship (p. 23).

Some Canadian business leaders agree that firms in this country should probably spend more on worker education. In fact, last year the B.C. Chamber of Commerce (1994, p. 37) reported that 91 percent of the businesses they surveyed agreed with the statement: "To become more competitive, B.C. businesses themselves must expand worker skill training". There are grounds for the argument that public policy measures that encourage businesses to invest more in developing their workers would benefit these businesses. But, if so, why are these businesses failing to make these expenditures now? Shortsightedness is sometimes suggested as an explanation.

In any case, much of the public would probably be sympathetic to forcing businesses to spend more on worker education, whether or not those businesses derive a direct benefit from a profit-maximization perspective. In a democracy like ours, the implicit social contract between the public and the businesses community is that businesses and their capitalist owners should be allowed to earn profits, but that they, in turn, should provide decent employment for the public – "decent" meaning employment that is plentiful enough and that pays well enough and is stable enough to allow workers and their families to enjoy decent standards of living. Increasingly, businesses are perceived as shirking on their end of this social contract, using the threats of capital flight and lost market shares in a global economy as excuses. One likely result is an erosion of public respect for business well-being, even though this may further harm employment prospects for Canadians.

MECHANISMS FOR INDUCING EMPLOYERS TO INVEST MORE IN WORKER EDUCATION

ALTERNATIVE MECHANISMS FOR INDUCING EMPLOYERS to invest more in worker education are already under consideration by various government departments. The mechanisms being considered most seriously fall into two categories: taxes or subsidies that would make it financially more attractive to businesses to invest more in worker education and training programs; and changes in corporate governance that would motivate businesses to become more concerned about the employment and earnings prospects of their employees. In this section we examine some of the differences, advantages and disadvantages of these two approaches.

EDUCATION INVESTMENT TAXES OR SUBSIDIES FOR EMPLOYERS

THE DISCUSSION PAPER NOTES THE RANGE of financial incentives to employers investing in worker education that are being considered, and some of the perspectives influencing the degree of interest in the various options:

> While there are payoffs for the employer from work-based training, these may be indirect or longer-term. Such training has important benefits for society because well-trained workers are more employable, and can adapt more easily if they are forced to change jobs. It may therefore be appropriate for governments to consider incentives for employers to undertake these activities. This would apply especially to small- and medium-sized businesses which often lack the resources to do much formal training on their own.

> Commentators have suggested various ways to promote employer-led training, such as employer tax credits, levies for training, wage subsidies and direct government assistance, paid educational leave, individual training accounts and work-sharing arrangements. These possibilities will need to be explored fully, bearing in mind that it makes good business sense for employers to invest in developing their employees (pp. 35-6).

A key aspect of the financial incentives approach to trying to increase employer investment in worker education is that no attempt is being made to alter the basic decision-making mechanisms of businesses. Rather, these are attempts to use the existing business decision-making mechanisms to achieve socially desired human-capital-investment goals. These are relatively non-invasive options that would be relatively non-threatening to established business interests, although levies for training could increase business costs.

Some other countries, France, for example, do have training taxes that are rebated to businesses that meet clearly defined training-expenditure standards. A training tax program with rebates for firms providing education and training has the advantage that it would help redress the problem that firms that do invest in their workers often suffer ongoing losses of trained employees to other firms that pay more but invest far less in training and education. For smaller firms that lack the economics of scale for worker-training programs enjoyed by large firms, a training tax and rebate program would provide a mechanism for them to pool their resources to achieve worker learning levels more in line with large firms. Learning tax payments from those smaller firms that do not provide or subsidize worker learning programs themselves would flow into a revenue pool to be used to provide publicly run worker education and training programs for which workers in firms not offering learning opportunities would be eligible. For other smaller firms, a training tax and rebate program would probably serve as an inducement to band together or to work through industry or worker associations to find ways of offering shared education and training programs for their workers.

A key challenge for implementing any program of financial incentives for employer training is to find practical ways to decide which education and training activities will qualify (or be rewarded), and to monitor these activities effectively on an ongoing basis. This problem is akin to that of collecting meaningful survey information on workplace education and training. Betcherman (1993) offers the following observations on surveys of education and training provided or subsidized by employers.

> Looking first at the firm-based studies, the most recent survey with broad coverage and a formal definition of training was the 1987 Human Resource Training and Development Survey where 30.7 per cent of the respondents reported training programs.

> It should be noted that this figure has been disputed. ... In fact, this concern led to the most recent data collection effort – the National Training Survey, sponsored by the Canadian Labour Market and Productivity Centre (CLMPC) – where the definition of "training" and other methodological issues were jointly worked out by business and labour representatives. ...

> Estimates are considerably higher when informal training is recognized. The CFIB Small Business Panel Survey (1988) and the Human Resources Survey (1979) gathered firm-based training data that included informal activities; ... the incidence rates for both were between 60 and 70 per cent. ... (pp. 20-1)

The point is that if it is difficult to produce meaningful and accepted measures of very simple dimensions of workplace education and training activities (such as the number of firms providing training, and the number of employees receiving training), clearly it will be difficult to develop meaningful and accepted criteria for what will count as employer-provided or subsidized worker education and training for the purpose of administering financial incentives for employer investment in worker education. The resulting disagreements and paper work are aggravations that could motivate Canadian businesses to make even more effort to downsize their workforces in favour of more computers and other technology combined with overseas production. Care must be taken to avoid this outcome since the main reason for worker and public concern about worker education is inadequate levels of employment aggravated by very limited opportunities for jobs that are attractive in terms of working conditions, job security and remuneration.

CHANGES IN CORPORATE GOVERNANCE

A DIFFERENT APPROACH TO ATTEMPTING TO INCREASE employer investment in worker education is to alter the decision-making mechanisms used by businesses in ways that might reasonably be expected to lead to a greater commitment to worker education and training. One possibility, for instance, is to require businesses to have worker representation on their (company) boards of directors. The rationale for this is that companies would be forced to pay more attention to the interests of their employees in longer-run business planning and investment decision-making. From a social point of view, it is vital that business produce employment and consumer buying power as well as competitive goods and services. From this perspective, altering business decision-making mechanisms so that businesses will choose to invest more in their employees makes sense, even if there are some costs to the organizations affected in terms of productive efficiency for the goods and service outputs. Another feature of this approach is that, in contrast to most of the options involving financial incentives, there are essentially no direct dollar costs to government beyond the government administrative or regulatory overhead expenses required to institute the program and ensure business-sector compliance with the new corporate governance provisions.

However, this approach also has obvious disadvantages. First, it is invasive in the extreme. It could surely be an inducement for companies to move out of Canada over time, unless the changes enacted were also adopted by most of Canada's trading partners. A second drawback has to do with the well-documented phenomenon of unions representing the interests of their members in ways that are occasionally contrary to the interests of workers who do not belong to those particular unions, or without regard for the interests and problems of certain types of workers who have different needs from other workers and are too few in number to influence union objectives. Workers on corporate boards of directors would have incentives to pursue policies that benefit *present* company employees at the expense of company growth over time horizons that stretch well beyond the working lifespans of existing employees. Also, under present conditions they would have virtually no incentive to make sacrifices to improve the job qualifications or to create job opportunities for those who are trying to enter or re-enter the workforce.

At best, this approach would help remedy only a narrow range of employment and earnings problems that have stimulated worker, public and business interest in worker education and training.

OTHER AVENUES

WE BELIEVE THAT THERE ARE INDEED PROBLEMS related to worker education and training in Canada that should be addressed. On this point it is important to understand, however, that solving the problems of worker education and training will not solve Canada's larger national problem of high levels of unemployment.

BEING HONEST ABOUT THE NATURE OF OUR EMPLOYMENT PROBLEMS

AT PRESENT, MOST DEVELOPED COUNTRIES ARE EXPERIENCING high levels of unemployment and underemployment. The discussion paper notes the following.

> An apparent decoupling of economic growth from job growth now seems to afflict most advanced industrial countries. Total unemployment was fairly stable between the 1950s and the early 1970s in the 24 countries then belonging to the Organization for Economic Cooperation and Development (OECD). Since then, the unemployment total has more than tripled, with steep increases in the early 1980s and 1990s. Canada, with a current unemployment rate of just over 10 per cent, is comparable to the European Union, where unemployment averages 10-11 per cent (pp. 16-17).

Many Canadians consider the economic management of the country and job creation to be the shared responsibility of the federal government and business. The claims of the federal government and business that the present unacceptably high levels of unemployment are due primarily, or even substantially, to an education and training deficit may help to deflect public criticism for awhile. However, as argued in Nakamura, Cragg & Sayers (1994), these diversionary arguments may also delay efforts to deal with the real causes of job loss and the growing strains on Canada's labour-based system of income distribution. In addition, it may push reform of our education and training systems in inappropriate directions.

ENCOURAGING LONGER EMPLOYMENT RELATIONSHIPS

THERE IS A RESIGNED ACCEPTANCE of increasingly ephemeral employment relationships in the materials emanating from governments these days. The following passage from the discussion paper provides an example.

> For too many of those who find jobs, the jobs do not last long. Almost 40 per cent of the people on Unemployment Insurance in 1993 had claimed UI benefits at least three times in the previous five years – and the number is rising. ...

> Even for those who have managed to escape the unemployment rolls, the world of paid work is not the stable place it was just 20 years ago. No one is sheltered from the changes sweeping through the economy. Gone for many is the idea of "lifetime employment" with a single employer, once the automatic reward for hard work and loyal service. Reflecting the high degree of fluidity

that now characterizes the world of work, in any given year, up to one-quarter of all employees have been in their job for a year or less (p. 18).

We believe it is vital for all levels of government to work together with the business sector to try to restore job security for a large share of the workforce. Measures to encourage the spread of employee compensation systems and industrial relations practices that allow earnings adjustment without layoffs during economic downturns might help improve job security in industries that are subject to frequent fluctuations in consumer demand. The Japanese-style bonus compensation mechanism is one of many ways in which this objective might be achieved. Correcting features of the Unemployment Insurance system that penalize firms for using full-time workers, as argued in Nakamura (1995) and Nakamura & Diewert (forthcoming) should also help. Yet another approach to this problem that could help is the committed employment UI proposal (Nakamura, 1995).

The essence of the committed employment proposal is that both employers and workers would pay lower UI tax rates for hours of work committed to substantially in advance by employers and voluntarily designated by the employers as "committed hours". Workers laid off from committed hours would be automatically eligible to collect UI for those hours, and the employers making committed hours layoffs would be assessed penalty charges. This UI option would allow employers to make credible employment security commitments that are more flexible, limited, and worker- and situation-specific than the usual contractual and collective bargaining job-security arrangements. As a consequence of the credible job-security commitment and the lower UI tax rates for both workers and employers for committed hours, employers would presumably be able to hire better-quality workers for less money in cases where they can plan far enough ahead to be able to hire on the basis of committed hours.

If a greater sense of long-term commitment could be rekindled on both the employer and the employee sides of ordinary work relationships, it would help restore the economic incentives and reduce the risks for investments in worker education and training by both employers and workers.

MOVING TOWARD ZERO TOLERANCE FOR ILLITERACY

THERE IS AN UNDERSTANDABLE TENDENCY FOR GOVERNMENT to emphasize measures that might help people move off public income support rolls. In this connection, governments can become overly focused on the education and training needs of adults with serious employability problems. However, measures designed to help prevent employability problems would also help, over time, to reduce reliance on Unemployment Insurance and welfare. Improving the delivery of basic learning skills in our elementary and secondary schools is important in this regard.

Just as businesses have moved toward policies of zero tolerance for defects, Canadians need public policies to help move us toward zero tolerance for children being passed on from grade to grade in public school without mastering such essential learning skills as reading. As a start toward this objective, we need nation-wide testing of basic learning skills at multiple points in the elementary and secondary learning processes, with summary results made available in a timely manner to all interested parties. Each student, and the student's teachers and parents or guardians, should receive the student's personal results. Such a testing program would allow children who are falling behind in basic learning skills to be identified so help can be directed to them. It would also allow teachers, programs and schools that are not succeeding in their educational missions to be identified, making it more likely that future failures will be avoided. The public pronouncements of support for lifelong learning that have become fashionable seem out of place as long as substantial numbers of Canadian children are passing through elementary and secondary programs without properly mastering the basic skills needed to qualify for even those jobs classified as low-skill! The discussion paper reports, for instance, that "Almost 3 million Canadians have very limited literacy skills. Another 4 million have some difficulty with everyday reading tasks" (p. 19). Some of these illiterate and semi-literate Canadians completed several levels in elementary school and often attended secondary school as well. Undoubtedly also, many of those who drop out of school do so because, without the skills to keep up in school, they become frustrated and bored. Better monitoring of learning performance in elementary and secondary education programs would reduce the burden on both post-secondary and employer-supplied learning programs of having to deal with students who do not have basic learning skills.

HELPING CANADIANS TO AFFORD POST-SECONDARY EDUCATION AND TRAINING

THERE ARE TWO DISTINCT GROUPS IN NEED of post-secondary education and training. The first group is new high school graduates. Typically, members of this group are not married and have few or no children or other dependents. Many still live with their parents. Full-time education and training programs make sense and are affordable for much of this group because their living costs are still relatively modest. Also, the young people in this group typically need more from education and training programs than simply to master the subject matter. Most are still maturing as individuals and learning how to interact effectively with others – objectives that are difficult for teachers to promote without substantial ongoing, face-to-face contact between teachers and students, and among the students themselves.

The second group is mature labour force participants, many of whom are highly motivated to improve their job qualifications in order to do better in their present jobs, or to qualify for better paying or more interesting jobs, or because they have been (or fear they may be) laid off. This group needs education and training programs designed to be compatible with full-time work. Such an arrangement would eliminate the major cost of education and training programs for adults: the opportunity cost of not working. Also, this would mean that mature students with jobs would not have to sever their job connections in order to pursue post-secondary education and training programs, leaving them vulnerable to spells of unemployment while they search for new jobs after they complete their training programs.

Many students in both categories would benefit from a revision of financial arrangements designed to help individuals finance investments in their own job-related human capital. As Michael Trebilcock suggested in his comments on an earlier version of this study, revisions of financial arrangements could include tax sheltered savings plans, tax credits, learning vouchers, and income-contingent and other loan programs backed by government guarantees to lending institutions, and repayment arrangements implemented through the tax system to minimize abuse and financial losses. As Trebilcock & Daniels (1994) have pointed out, these financial measures could also help to improve the functioning of the Canadian education and training systems by encouraging more supply-side competition.

PROVIDING PUBLIC INFORMATION ON THE EMPLOYMENT AND EARNINGS OF GRADUATES

THE EFFECTIVENESS OF PUBLIC ELEMENTARY AND SECONDARY school programs could be monitored by regular, mandatory testing of student achievement. At the post-secondary level, however, the content of education and training programs varies so widely that standardized tests are less practical and less suitable for monitoring program effectiveness. At this level, what might be more helpful is public information on the employment and earnings outcomes of the graduates of all publicly subsidized post-secondary learning programs. In this regard, all that is available now on a nation-wide basis are the results of national surveys, such as the national census conducted periodically by Statistics Canada, which provides information on the amount of schooling individual respondents have, but not the details of the institutions and programs attended. Composite educational records should be compiled for properly chosen samples of students enrolled in publicly subsidized educational programs. The annual earned incomes and other employment information from their Records of Employment and from their tax returns should be added to their composite educational records. This data would permit factual *ex post* examinations of employment and earnings outcomes of various sorts of post-secondary educational and training investments.

Public information on the employment and earnings outcomes of publicly subsidized education and training programs would help adults to become better-informed consumers of education and training programs. This, in turn, should help to introduce more market discipline into the provision of post-secondary learning programs.

CONCLUSIONS

DESPITE THE FACT THAT THE BUSINESS COMMUNITY, workers, and government officials all seem to want more and better worker education and training in Canada, the interests of the different groups are divergent in many respects.

Rather than changing corporate governance mechanisms in an attempt to induce businesses to invest more in worker education and training, we propose a number of alternative reform measures. First, we recommend the use of standardized student testing as a means of monitoring and encouraging the effectiveness of elementary and secondary school programs. Next, for post-secondary programs, we recommend that data on the employment and earnings outcomes of all publicly subsidized programs be collected and that appropriate summary information be made available to the public. This would help to introduce a measure of market discipline into the provision of post-secondary learning programs. We also recommend that special learning programs that are compatible with full-time work be developed for mature labour force participants, and that financial instruments be revised to help adults afford the job-related learning programs they need.

We note a number of advantages with respect to tax and subsidy incentives that could be adopted to encourage businesses to invest more in worker education and training. However, the most powerful inducement in this regard would be a reversal of the trend toward more ephemeral employment relationships. Changes in government policy that could help in this regard are briefly discussed. All Canadians have high stakes in the outcomes of government policies that affect worker education and training in this country.

ACKNOWLEDGEMENTS

THIS STUDY WAS PREPARED FOR THE CONFERENCE on Corporate Decision-Making in Canada, March 20-21, 1995 in Toronto. The research was partially funded by a grant from the Social Sciences and Humanities Research Council. We are grateful to Ron Daniels, Michael Trebilcock, and Erwin Diewert who provided helpful comments on an earlier version. We also thank the other conference participants for their comments. All errors and misinterpretations are the sole responsibility of the authors.

BIBLIOGRAPHY

Betcherman, G. "Are Canadian Firms Underinvesting in Training?" *Canadian Business Economics*, 1, 1 (1992):25-33.

_____. "Research Gaps Facing Training Policy-Makers." *Canadian Public Policy*, 19, 1 (1993):18-28.

British Columbia Chamber of Commerce. "Moving Forward: The Vision of B.C. Business." Vancouver, BC, 1994.

Canadian Labour Market and Productivity Centre. "The Linkages Between Education and Training and Canada's Economic Performance." *Quarterly Labour Market and Productivity Review*. (Winter 1989-90).

Drucker, Peter F. *Post-Capitalist Society*. New York: Harper Business Publishers, 1993.

Human Resources Development Canada. *Improving Social Security in Canada: A Discussion Paper*. Ottawa: Minister of Supply and Services, 1994.

Nakamura, A. "New Directions for UI, Social Assistance, and Vocational Education and Training." *Canadian Journal of Economics*. (Forthcoming, 1995).

Nakamura, A., J. Cragg and K. Sayers. "The Employment-Social Security Reform Connection," in *A New Social Vision for Canada?* Edited by K. Banting and K. Battle. Kingston, ON: School of Policy Studies, Queen's University, 1994, pp. 47-56.

Nakamura, A. and W. E. Diewert. "The Canadian UI Program: Problems and Suggested Reforms." (Forthcoming, 1996).

Nakamura, A. and P. Lawrence. "Education, Training and Prosperity," in *Stabilization, Growth and Distribution: Linkages in the Knowledge Era*. Edited by T. J. Courchene. Kingston, ON: The John Deutsch Institute for the Study of Economic Policy, Queen's University, 1994, pp. 235-79.

Newton, K., P. DeBroucker, G. McDougall, K. McMullen, T. T. Schweitzer and T. Siedule. *Education and Training in Canada*. A Report prepared for the Economic Council of Canada, Minister of Supply and Services Canada, Ottawa, 1992.

Trebilcock, M. and R. Daniels. "Choice of Policy Instruments in the Provision of Public Infrastructure," in *Infrastructure and Competitiveness*. Edited by J. Mintz and R. Preston, Ottawa and Kingston, ON: Industry Canada and the John Deutsch Institute, 1994, pp. 416-28.

Ronald M. Giammarino
Faculty of Commerce and Business Administration
University of British Columbia

Patient Capital?
R&D Investment in Canada

INTRODUCTION

R&D SPENDING IS ONE OF THE MOST WIDELY USED indicators of a country's future competitiveness. More R&D spending is considered good; less is considered bad. The Conference Board of Canada clearly reflects this view in its most recent survey of R&D spending intentions.[1]

> Canada's preparedness for the "new economy" is often called into question due to, among other issues, the level of resources allocated to performing R&D. Compared with other industrialized nations ... the level of business enterprise expenditure on R&D in Canada in 1991 as a percentage of GDP at 0.8 per cent ... [is] far behind the allocation of leading economies such as Japan (2.2 percent), the United States (1.9 per cent), Germany (1.8 percent) and Sweden (1.6 percent).

While the debate on Canada's industrial policy clearly benefits from this focus on aggregate numbers, it is important to remember that the objective of R&D policy, ultimately, is to enhance economic output. Increasing aggregate spending levels is consistent with this objective if the spending is economically efficient.

An alternative focus, and the one taken in this study, is to consider the quality of the R&D expenditures. That is, are R&D opportunities appropriately evaluated and implemented? When firms are efficient in responding to R&D investment opportunities they create wealth and, under these circumstances, larger levels of aggregate R&D investment are better than smaller levels. The next main section of this study provides a brief overview of the conceptual issues involved.

In principle, specific R&D investment decisions are like any other investment decision: resources are taken out of current consumption to provide for future consumption. R&D expenditures are distinguished by great uncertainty, and the considerable length of time required to develop the fruits of an investment. To some, the nature of R&D investment opportunities implies that they will not be correctly evaluated by managers who behave myopically. In this view, there are two potential causes of this myopia. The first is the concern that managers who are trained to "maximize the value of the firm's shares" and who are rewarded on the basis of the performance of a company's common stock, will fail to internalize the long-run benefits of R&D expenditure. In the next section of this study I review the literature that relates to this issue – which examines the extent to which market value reflects capital investment in general and R&D investment in particular.

A second concern is that myopia on the part of managers derives from corporate restructuring and the extent to which such restructuring drives managers to maximize short-term cash flows. In the section of this study dealing with "Corporate Control, Restructuring, and R&D Spending" I review the studies that deal explicitly with this issue.

Ultimately, the decision to invest in R&D is based on the valuation placed on a project by the managers of a firm. Various well-established principles of capital budgeting can be used to value firms. Some recently developed tools are particularly well-suited to the evaluation of R&D projects. In the section on "The Management of R&D Spending: A Capital Budgeting Approach" I review some of these principles and discuss evidence on the way that Canadian managers evaluate investment opportunities. The study concludes with a summary, some suggestions for future research and some overall conclusions.

An Overview of the Problem

There is a dramatic conflict between the popularly held explanation for the decline in R&D spending in North America and the conventional view found in corporate finance theory. Under perfect financial markets, corporate finance theory does not in general consider R&D expenditure to be different from any other long-term capital investment. Finance theory argues that the merits of all capital investments are evaluated on the basis of capital market forces that determine discount rates, impounding an economy's collective impatience and risk adjustments. These forces are brought together through standard capital budgeting techniques that implement a simple rule for decision-making: undertake investment if it increases the market value of the firm. R&D investments can be distinguished by a higher degree of uncertainty and a longer development period, but both of these features are accommodated by essentially the same mechanism that applies to other investments. Moreover, the form of financing used to exploit the opportunity is irrelevant.[2] If a project is viable, money will be available from the capital market.

While we do not expect to find many perfect market implications (such as the irrelevance of financing) supported by data, they do provide valuable reference points. If we find that the perfect market implications are not descriptive of practice (if, for instance, the form of financing seems to be relevant to R&D) the responsible market imperfection must be identified.

The market imperfection that has attracted much of the blame for low levels of R&D investment is an inefficient capital market, specifically a "myopic" capital market that does not recognize the long-run value of R&D investment. The basic argument is that, because markets are believed to be efficient, managers are trained to rely on market signals when making investment decisions. But markets are both inefficient and myopic. As a result, managers behave myopically as well.

Hayes & Abernathy (1980) make a typical contribution to this debate with their argument that managers are short-sighted and that they ignore the importance of long-term competitiveness. Woolridge (1988) notes that managers often defend themselves against these charges by arguing that market inefficiencies force them to behave myopically. He cites a *Business Week* interview with Andrew Sigler, CEO of Champion International, as providing a typical response: "There is intense pressure for current earnings, so the message is: don't get caught with long-term investments. And leverage the hell out of yourself. Do all the things we used to consider bad management".[3] A survey of major corporations is also used to further this view: 89 percent of the CEO respondents felt that American companies had lost some of their competitive edge by failing to recognize the importance of long-term investment in their capital budgets. In turn, this myopia was largely felt to be due to the importance placed on quarterly earnings reports by investors.[4]

Furthermore, it is commonly argued that the myopia induced by a market that does not value long-term investment is exacerbated by corporate restructuring. In this case the prime suspects are leveraged buyouts. Here, it is argued, any firm that does not maximize its short-term cash flows will be subject to a debt-financed takeover by a raider who will reorganize corporate activity to satisfy the newly acquired debt repayments. According to this view, debt payments preclude patient investment.

Again, the conflict between popularly held views and finance theory is striking. In contrast to this popular view, corporate finance theory predicts that any manager who fails to exploit valuable long-term investment opportunities will be replaced by a manager who will invest where value is greatest. Moreover, as Haugen & Senbet (1979) pointed out, capital structure and capital budgeting are inherently separate decisions. If a debt payment cannot be made because of the cash requirements of a long-term investment, debt and equity holders will refinance and reschedule. If they fail to do so, other agents will first purchase the debt and equity at prices that reflect sub-optimal decisions, then make optimal corporate investment and capital structure decisions, and derive benefit from the attendant value increase.

POLICY ISSUES

A NUMBER OF POLICY QUESTIONS in the area of R&D investment derive from these considerations. To the extent that some of the benefits from R&D investment are social and/or cannot be expropriated by the investor, private investment decisions will not be efficient. If the externality can be assessed, the policy issue is how best to subsidize production so as to restore efficiency. This implies that, since each case presents its own externality, the policy decisions are idiosyncratic and there is little that can be said in general about what government should or should not do.

The more difficult case, and the one that is the focus of this study, arises if, as suggested above, the market failure is due to myopia. In this case and depending on the source of the problem, the government might take one of the following courses of action. First, it can provide direct incentives for R&D investment to offset the undervaluation that myopia brings. Indeed, according to the Conference Board survey of R&D investment intentions, Canadian-owned firms rely more heavily on government funds for R&D investments than their foreign-owned counterparts. Second, action might be taken to induce investors (particularly institutions) to take a longer-term position in a company's shares. This, it has been argued, can be accomplished by taxing short-term trading gains or by taxing trading activity in general. Third, the market for corporate control could be restrained so that managers will be relieved of the pressure to provide short-term cash flows in order to avoid a takeover. Finally, if leverage-increasing reorganizations are the problem, a solution might be to restrict the use of debt financing.

The essence of the general-policy choice in this case rests on two empirical questions: Is the capital market myopic in its valuation of corporate securities? and Do corporate restructurings induce myopic behavior in management? A brief review of the evidence on these issues follows.

HOW PATIENT IS THE CAPITAL MARKET?

MANY INVESTORS IN TODAY'S CAPITAL MARKETS are interested primarily in short-run gain. Investment dealers and fund managers whose livelihood depends on regular performance evaluations must often be more concerned about short-term trading profits than long-term capital gain and dividend income. It is argued that such investors are unwilling to hold the shares of companies that make R&D investments with long-term payoffs.

Such an argument flies in the face of conventional finance theory. This body of knowledge holds that investors, whether they plan to hold shares for the long run or the short run, rationally anticipate having to sell their shares to other investors at the end of their investment horizon. Hence, they are interested in the price at which they will sell, which depends on the future holding period of some unknown investor. Even if it is assumed that shares will be sold to a succession of short-term investors, the price at any point in time will anticipate the chain of prices at which the shares will be sold and this chain, taken as a whole, reflects the long-run value of the firm.[5]

There is a significant body of evidence supporting the notion that share prices reflect the long run value of the firm. For instance, the shares of numerous companies have positive prices even though the companies themselves fail to report positive earnings or pay a dividend. A more systematic examination of this issue is provided by McConnell & Muscarella (1985) who evaluate the joint hypothesis that managers maximize the value of the firm, and that the value of the firm reflects long-term capital investments. To evaluate this joint hypothesis, the stock market reaction to corporate announcements of unexpected increases and decreases in capital expenditures was examined. The joint hypothesis predicts that an increase in capital spending will lead to an increase in market value and that a decrease in capital spending will lead to a reduction in market value.

The study by McConnell & Muscarella focuses on the firms that made announcements regarding company-wide capital spending plans and covers the period from 1975 to 1981. The authors were able to construct a sample of 547 announcements made by 285 different industrial companies. The empirical results support the joint hypothesis inasmuch as the market reaction was of the predicted sign and was statistically significant. Unfortunately, although some information was available as to the specific type of capital spending, only eight of the 547 announcements specifically mentioned an increase in R&D expenditure and none indicated a reduction. Moreover, the results reported for this sub-sample indicated that R&D spending was different from other capital budgeting, and so the small sample size precludes any firm conclusions.

Hirschey (1982) is an early study that focused on R&D specifically. Rather than deal with the announcement effects of corporate action, Hirschey examines the relationship between the ratio of the market-to-book value of assets at a point in time and a weighted sum of current and previous expenditures on R&D. Hirschey argues that the market-to-book ratio can be viewed as approximately equal to Tobin's Q, an indicator of investment value.

Tobin (1978) proposed that the ratio of the market value of a firm to the replacement value of the assets held by the firm, Q, is a measure of the attractiveness of new investment. When Q >1 firms should find new investment attractive since they are worth more than they cost. When Q<1 firms should be inclined to contract their operations. Hence, Hirschey evaluates the importance of intangible investment to market value and, through the reference to Tobin's Q, implicitly links R&D investment to future tangible and intangible investment.

Hirschey examined the end-of-year value of the market-to-book ratio for 390 firms taken from the 1977 *Fortune 500*. In a cross-sectional regression of the market-to-book value ratios for these firms on a number of factors, a positive and statistically significant influence was found for both R&D and advertising expenditures.

The Canadian capital market does not appear to differ noticeably from the U.S. market in this respect. In a recent study of Canadian firms, Johnson & Pazderka (1993) test the hypothesis that the market places a positive value on R&D expenditure. Using data from the period from 1985 to 1988, they estimate the relationship between the market value of equity on the one hand, and book value of equity, a measure of market power, R&D expenditures and other investment expenditures on the other hand. The analysis is conducted for a number of sub-periods and in all cases supports the hypothesis that the market value of the firm is significantly and positively related to R&D expenditure.

Pakes (1985) also examines the relationship between stock market valuation and R&D investment, but in a dynamic model. In this model R&D investment is a productive input and patent applications are the output of the firm. The stock-market value of the firm is then taken as a reflection of the market's assessment of the process. Managers are assumed to maximize the stock-market value of the firm in selecting input levels, which implies a relationship between the dynamic behavior of R&D expenditure, patents, and market value.

The empirical relationship between these variables is estimated from annual data for 120 firms during the period from 1968 to 1975. It should be noted that annual data does not allow a very refined measure of the dynamic relationships since leads and lags of less-than-annual frequency will appear to be contemporaneous.

Based on the model estimation, Pakes concludes that

> ... it is clear that the events that lead the market to reevaluate the firm are indeed significantly correlated with unpredictable changes in both R&D and the patents of the firm. Moreover, the estimates imply that, on average, unexpected changes in patents and in R&D are associated with quite large changes in the market value of the firm.

Thus, managers seem to select R&D levels that lead to large changes in market value.

These studies indicate that the market value of a firm is related to R&D activity and that managerial actions are apparently consistent with market-value maximization. Woolridge (1985) provides a more refined view of the relationship between what he refers to as strategic investments and stock market valuation. Strategic investments are those investments which Woolridge considers to have a long run and highly uncertain return. The announcements studied were taken from the "What's News" column of the *Wall Street Journal* over the period from 1972 to 1984. This provided a sample of 634 strategic announcements made by 347 firms. The announcements were further classified according to Joint Venture Formation (161 announcements), Research and Development (45), Product Strategies (168), and Capital Expenditures (260). For the announcements overall and for each category separately, the market reaction was positive and statistically significant.

Hence, this study provides further evidence to support the view that financial markets do take a long-run view of the firm. Unfortunately for our purposes, the conclusions are somewhat limited by the small number of R&D announcements in the sample.

The studies discussed to this point have focused on R&D and strategic investment decisions without considering the role played by current earnings in the market's reaction. It is possible, however, that the firms studied invested in R&D only in good times, when reported earnings were positive and pressure to improve short-run performance was negligible. In a more recent study Chan, Martin & Kensinger (1990) (hereafter CMK) address this concern directly and, in the process, provide additional support for the view that stock markets are generally not myopic.

CMK considered R&D announcements over the six-year period from 1979 to 1985. They restricted their search to firms that had available stock price data and further restricted their sample in a number of ways[6] so that their final sample consisted of 95 announcements. The announcements lead to a market reaction only if the information provided is not previously known to the market. The authors rather conservatively classify an announcement as providing new information if it indicated a change in R&D spending from the previous year. As the market is likely to expect some increase in R&D in general, this classification will, if anything, bias the estimated market reaction to R&D information downward.

The empirical results are striking. The announcement-day abnormal return of 0.85 percent is statistically significant and economically quite large. Moreover this is followed by a post-announcement-day return of 0.53 percent which is again statistically significant.

To address directly the question of how current earnings affect the market's reaction, CMK split the sample into those firms that announced an earnings increase in the quarter in which the R&D announcement was made (62 firms) and those that announced an earnings decrease (33 firms). The estimated two-day abnormal return for both groups was positive and statistically significant. Moreover, although the estimate is 1.54 percent for the earnings increase group and 1.01 percent for the earnings decrease group, the authors were unable statistically to reject the hypothesis that the announcement effect was the same for the two samples.

While, on average, R&D announcements are greeted positively by investors, there are cases where the market reaction is negative. CMK attempt to shed light on why R&D investment by some firms is viewed negatively by the market, while for others the reaction is positive. They find that announcements by firms considered to be in low-tech industries generated negative and weakly significant abnormal returns, while announcements by firms in the high-tech sector reported significantly positive returns. While there is no reason to suggest that R&D cannot be valuable in low-tech industries, the chances of it being so are less likely and the market may react accordingly.

To understand further the market's reaction to announcements, CMK also estimate the cross-sectional relationship between the announcement effect and: i) the intensity of the firm's R&D relative to an industry norm, ii) the level of technology in the industry, iii) the increase in R&D relative to the company's sales, iv) industry concentration, and v) a measure of the firm's market power. The only significant explanatory variable is the ratio of the firm's R&D intensity relative to an industry norm, and here only when the firm is in the high-tech sector.

IS THE MARKET PATIENT?

THE EMPIRICAL EVIDENCE DISCUSSED ABOVE suggests that the market is generally patient in its valuation of a firm, in that value does reflect long-run decisions. We have seen that long-term investments are linked to market value both statically and dynamically. The market responds to announcements of long-term strategic decisions generally and R&D decisions specifically. Moreover, the response is generally positive and significant, although the market does seem to differentiate R&D investment according to industry type. The positive response may be restricted to those firms in high-tech industries. Interestingly, this response is also found among firms that report operating losses in the period in which the R&D announcement is made. Hence, these results do not generally support the notion that capital market myopia has forced managers to abandon long-term investment in R&D in favour of enhancing short-run earnings.

HOW PATIENT ARE MANAGERS?

IT APPEARS, THEN, THAT THE CAPITAL MARKET IS NOT MYOPIC. Nonetheless, investment decisions made by managers may be myopic. In fact, Stein (1988) has pointed out that myopic management may be consistent with the market reactions noted above. If managers prefer investments with short-term payoffs, they may only accept long-term strategic investments when the returns on these investments are exceptionally high. If this is so, then the market treats R&D announcements positively despite the fact that R&D management overall is inefficient.

There are two possible sources of managerial myopia. The first is the risk of, or implementation of, corporate restructuring. The second is the possibility that the capital budgeting techniques currently in use in North America are inherently conservative and biased against long-term, high-risk investments. Unfortunately, it is difficult to observe directly the extent to which managerial decisions are myopic since it would be necessary to observe the characteristics of the investment opportunities along with the investment decisions actually made. As a result, the discussion in the following section deals with indirect evidence.

Corporate Control, Restructuring, and R&D Spending

MANAGERIAL MYOPIA MAY BE DEFENSIBLE on the grounds that it is necessary to avoid costly disruptions brought on by a myopic market for corporate control. Stein (1988) formally develops a model that delivers this prediction. Managers are assumed to know more about the value of the firm and the firm's investment options than does the market as a whole. In particular, the informational asymmetry is greater for long-term projects than for short-term projects. Consequently, when managers with valuable long-term prospects are threatened by a takeover, they will respond by shifting to short-term projects that the market can better value. The social and private cost is the loss of valuable long-term investment opportunities. In this setting is it possible to increase the value of the firm by sheltering managers from takeover threats.

The evidence on the reaction of the stock market to the adoption of such protection in the form of an anti-takeover charter amendment is mixed. Linn & McConnell (1983) find positive abnormal returns, while DeAngelo & Rice (1983) and Jarrell & Poulsen (1987) find insignificant returns. While these results are interesting, they are not conclusive because they do not distinguish between Stein's theory and others (such as Giammarino & Heinkel, 1986) that show how value can be increased by giving managers increased bargaining power during a takeover. Hence, we are not sure that firm value does increase if managerial protection increases and, if it does, we are not sure if this is due to more efficient R&D investment or to the greater bargaining power given to corporate managers.

To address the issue more directly, Meulbroek et al. (1990) consider the level of R&D investment undertaken by firms before and after they adopt anti-takeover provisions. Meulbroek et al. base their study on a sample of 554 anti-takeover amendments proposed between 1979 and 1985. The authors exclude firms that did not report any R&D expenditure during the sample period, leaving a total of 203 proposals (of which 179 were passed during the last three years of the sample period).

The authors compute the ratio of R&D to sales and examine the change in this ratio for three periods (windows) surrounding the date of adoption of the amendment. The windows considered are (−1, 1), indicating the period beginning the year prior to the amendment through to the year after the amendment, (−1, 2) and (−1, 3). They find that none of the estimated changes are statistically different from zero. The authors go on to adjust the figures to reflect general changes in R&D expenditure during this period by subtracting the rate of growth of R&D/sales for all firms covered by the Compustat data base. Here, significantly negative changes in R&D are reported for all windows: relative to the market, R&D fell by 15 percent in the (−1, 1) window, 25 percent in the (−1, 2) window and 36 percent in the (−1, 3) window.

The authors consider the possibility that the reduction in R&D spending results from the fact that there was substantial takeover pressure despite the

GIAMMARINO

anti-takeover amendments. In fact, 52 of the 203 firms were subsequently subject to a successful or unsuccessful merger or tender offer. The authors report that the results are similar for the subsample of firms that were not subsequently subject to a takeover attempt. Hence, it appears that reducing the threat of a takeover does not lead to an increase in R&D activity.

The other (related) potential cause of myopic behavior is a takeover or restructuring itself. Here, the concern is that a firm that is highly leveraged, either because of a leveraged takeover or for other reasons, cannot afford to invest in valuable R&D because this will diminish its ability to service the debt in the short run. In an extensive study of this issue Hall (1988) examines a panel of annual data for 2,500 manufacturing firms. The data covers the period from 1959 to 1987 and contains information on R&D spending and other corporate characteristics. The objective of Hall's study is to determine the effect on R&D spending of: leveraged buyouts, mergers and acquisitions, and increases in debt not accompanied by ownership changes.

Although, as Hall points out, leveraged buyouts (LBOs) have received a great deal of attention, they are a relatively small portion of total activity. Of the 780 acquisitions that were identified from among the firms studied, only 76 could be classified as LBOs. In a LBO the firm is taken private by a group that uses extensive debt financing to facilitate the acquisition. As already noted, the resulting debt load is believed to result in a reduction in R&D spending.

However, Hall reverses this argument by suggesting that for this very reason, companies for which R&D spending is considered to be important will not be subject to an LBO. In fact, of the 76 LBOs in the Hall study, only six were in industries that had invested a significant amount (*i.e.*, more than 3.5 percent of sales) in R&D. The unimportance of LBOs to R&D activity is further illustrated by the fact that firms subject to LBOs accounted for only 1 percent of the total R&D activity in 1982. The post-LBO investment in R&D is difficult to determine since firms that go private are not required to provide the same reports as others. Hence it is difficult to draw conclusions about how LBOs change R&D behaviour, but it is not difficult to conclude that, whatever the effect, it is unlikely to be important to overall R&D performance.

Hall also examines the R&D intensity (R&D/sales) of the 336 firms involved in acquisitions during the period. She performs a regression analysis to determine whether firms that have acquired other firms change their R&D intensity relative to other firms in the same industry. The analysis is performed for all acquisitions and then separately for the group of firms that did not report any R&D activity during the period. The result is that R&D intensity does, in fact, decline and while the estimated effect is statistically insignificant for the entire sample, it is significant for those firms that reported R&D activity. That is, firms that engage in R&D activity and acquire other firms reduce their R&D intensity relative to the mean level of R&D intensity in their industry. This undoubtedly reflects economies of scale in R&D activity through elimination

584

of duplication and better co-ordination of activities and support services. In fact, these economies of scale may provide the synergy that motivates the takeover in the first place. It is important to note, however, that such a reduction does not reflect an inefficiency.

Finally, Hall considers the effect of leverage on R&D intensity. A total of 177 firms were classified as having engaged in a leveraged restructuring – by virtue of the fact that they had increased their long-term debt by more than 75 percent of the firm's total market value at the beginning of the year. The analysis here was similar to the analysis for acquisitions. The results indicate that leveraged restructurings are associated with significant reductions in R&D intensity relative to the industry. In addition, Hall ran separate regressions to control for acquisitions and found that the effect of acquisitions on R&D is essentially the result of the increase in leverage that accompanies the acquisition.

The overall result of these studies is that acquisitions and leverage increases are both correlated with reductions in R&D intensity. However, the threat of a takeover does not appear to have a significant effect on R&D intensity. What does this imply about the R&D decision? Unfortunately, these studies report correlation and do not allow us to determine cause and effect. It may be that higher levels of leverage force managers to reduce valuable R&D spending. However, if the capital market is not myopic, why would managers voluntarily take action that increases leverage if this forces value-reducing decisions to be made? An alternative explanation for this correlation is that, because of asymmetric information, managers of firms with R&D opportunities do not engage in leverage, financing instead with internally generated funds. Conversely, managers of firms that have exhausted valuable R&D opportunities are able to issue debt and do so to take advantage of the tax benefits of debt.

THE MANAGEMENT OF R&D SPENDING: A CAPITAL BUDGETING APPROACH

SEVERAL METHODS ARE USED IN PRACTICE to evaluate capital investments. The most widely accepted approach is to compute the net present value (NPV) of an investment and accept all projects that have a positive NPV. Other widely used approaches include the internal rate of return (IRR), the payback method, and the accounting rate of return. NPV requires that the analyst estimate the incremental cash flows generated by an investment, estimate the appropriate required return on investment, and use the estimated rate to discount the cash flows. The valuation consequences of leverage (due, for instance, to the tax deductibility of interest payments) can be estimated separately and then added to the base case net present value to calculate a total value of the project. If the project is valuable, actual financing is assumed to be available in a perfect capital market. Table 1 summarizes the features of each of these techniques.

TABLE 1

A COMPARISON OF CAPITAL BUDGETING TECHNIQUES

ACCOUNTING	PAYBACK	RETURN	IRR	NPV
Recognizes All Cash Flows	No	Yes	Yes	Yes
Recognizes the Time Value of Money	No	Yes	Yes	Yes
Uses a Market-Determined Discount Rate	No	No	No	Yes

A recent survey by Jog & Srivastava (1994) indicates that the practice of capital budgeting in Canada takes several different approaches. Conducted in 1991, the survey was sent to 582 firms, including those who form the TSE 300 as well as other large, foreign-owned and private corporations. Responses were received from 133 firms indicating their use of a number of different capital budgeting techniques. In many cases, several techniques were applied simultaneously. Specifically, the survey, found that either the NPV or the IRR is widely used by corporations in evaluating expansion plans. In addition, however, about 50 percent of the firms reported using the payback period and a number of firms continue to use the accounting rate of return. The use of the latter two techniques is surprising given that these techniques are conceptually flawed and, especially in the case of accounting rate of return, may lead to resource misallocations.

With respect to the estimation of the opportunity cost of funds, Jog & Srivistava find that over 50 percent of their respondents use the weighted average cost of capital. Surprisingly, however, about 25 percent of the respondents use the cost of debt as the firm's cost of capital, despite the fact that there is little justification for using the debt rate. In contrast, a much earlier study of American firms by Schall et al. (1978) found that only 17 percent of the respondents in the United States used the cost of debt at that time.

While it is encouraging to see the increased adoption of discounted cash flow methods, there is no indication that refinements of these methods are being used. Specifically, there are two aspects of applying standard capital budgeting techniques to R&D investments which, if not correctly handled, can make investment decisions appear myopic.

The first problem is with the fact that standard applications of discounted cash flow methods may not recognize all of the changes that can take place with respect to the risk of an investment over the life of a project. Instead, it is typically the case that a single discount rate is estimated and applied to each cash flow over what can be a lengthy investment horizon. Given the uncertainty involved in the investment, it is often the case that the discount rate is quite high. This approach is not usually correct for an R&D investment. For instance, often an initial investment is made in some sort of pilot project. The result of the pilot project will determine the viability of subsequent development stages and at each stage information is provided that can refine the risk. That is, the risk of the new project may be great initially but then, conditional on success in early stages, diminish substantially. By applying the large initial discount rate to long-term cash flows, the analyst overstates the risk and the risk adjustment and consequently underestimates the value of the project.

The second and related concern is the failure to recognize the real options inherent in any long-term and high-risk project. When a firm enters a new market or attempts to develop a new technology, it is investing in the option to exploit the opportunities that may result from the initial investment. The important point here is that the firm need not invest additional future funds in new capacity and, in addition, has the option of abandoning any productive capacity it has put in place if information becomes available to suggest that the investment is not worth advancing. Recently, real option applications to R&D expenditures have been developed by Schwartz & Moon (1994). Although evaluating real options is a complex problem, especially in terms of R&D investment, the important general point is that the value of an option increases with underlying risk and with the amount of time that the firm can wait before having to make a final decision on exercising the option. Both of these factors suggest that real options generated by R&D initiatives are likely to be particularly valuable and that managers who ignore those options run the risk of seriously undervaluing investment opportunities.

CONCLUSIONS AND AN AGENDA FOR FUTURE RESEARCH

THIS STUDY HAS EXAMINED THE WIDELY HELD CONCERN that Canada is losing a competitive advantage due to the relatively low levels of R&D expenditure by Canadian industry. The approach taken here has been to determine whether the low levels of R&D expenditure are caused by myopia or by impatient investment decisions and to consider whether or not this problem stems from a myopic capital market or from myopic management.

The studies reviewed indicate that the capital market is not entirely myopic. Long-term, high-risk investments are viewed as valuable by capital market participants. Furthermore, the value placed on long-term investments is not simply a fair weather effect – a positive response is found even when corporations report reductions in earnings.

This study has also considered the possibility that managers may be myopic even if capital markets are not. Unfortunately, a direct test of this proposition is not possible and I have instead focused on indirect evidence, finding that there is no support for the notion that the threat of a takeover causes managers to forsake long-term R&D expenditures. On the other hand, firms that did increase leverage subsequently reduced their expenditures on R&D. This may be due to the fact that the higher leverage requires greater cash flow to service the debt, leaving less money available for long-term investment. In the absence of an inefficient market, however, this explanation implies inconsistent behaviour on the part of managers who selected the level of debt in the first place. An alternative explanation is that firms with R&D opportunities keep their leverage low until such time as the opportunities are exploited. At that point they increase leverage to take advantage of the tax subsidy.

Finally, I reviewed the basic capital budgeting techniques used in Canada. In the context of current practice, I conclude that myopic decisions can result from either overstating the risk of a project (a result of failing to recognize how risk might decline through time), or from ignoring expansion and abandonment options that are particularly valuable for R&D investment.

In the Introduction I raised several policy issues which can be discussed in light of the research reviewed. First, as there is no evidence that the market is myopic, it seems inappropriate to base government grants and incentives on this market failure. It also seems inappropriate to try to induce longer term holdings of securities through capital gains taxes and/or transaction taxes. A market populated by investors who worry about short-term trading profits should (and apparently does) recognize value in long-term R&D investment. Second, while less clear, the evidence suggests that there is no need to restrict takeover activity. The threat of a takeover does not appear to drive myopic decisions. Moreover, the decrease in R&D activity following a takeover, to the extent that it exists, appears to reflect an increase in leverage. Finally, the link between leverage and a decline in R&D, while empirically well-established, does not imply causality. As a result, it would be premature to restrict the use of high levels of debt.

The review of this literature suggests several areas for additional research. In my view, perhaps the most important is work that attempts to link R&D investment to managerial incentive contracts. For example, any firm that rewards managers on the basis of earnings-per-share will induce a preference for short-term cash flows, perhaps at the expense of long-term R&D. A systematic review of the incentive contracts actually used by Canadian companies and of the corresponding R&D investment decisions, would shed light on an aspect of the problem that has not received much attention. A second area for research is an examination of the capital budgeting techniques used to evaluate R&D investments. While we have a broad view of how capital investment decisions are made, we need to know more about how R&D is handled. It would be particularly useful to know how long-term risk and the options generated by R&D expenditures are evaluated by management.

ENDNOTES

1 Robert J. Squires, "R&D Outlook 1995", The Conference Board of Canada, 1994.
2 This ignores the role of taxes and bankruptcy costs. The point, however, is that even when these forces are included, capital structure has the same affect on R&D spending as it does on any investment decision, whether it be long-term and high-risk or short-term and safe.
3 Judith H. Dobrznyski, "More than Ever, It's Management for the Short Term", *Business Week*, (November 24, 1986), pp. 92-93, as cited in Woolridge (1988).
4 Business Bulletin, *Wall Street Journal*, (June 12, 1986) p. 1, as quoted in Woolridge (1988).
5 This argument appears in most finance textbooks. See, for example, chapter 4 of Brealey *et al.*, (1992).
6 There were six additional restrictions covering such factors as duplicate announcements and R&D projects that were funded by customers and/or the government.

BIBLIOGRAPHY

Brealey, Richard, Stewart Myers, Gordon Sick, and Ronald Giammarino. *Principles of Corporate Finance*. Toronto: McGraw-Hill Ryerson, 1992, Second Canadian Edition.

Chan, Su Han, John D. Martin, and John W. Kensinger. "Corporate Research and Development Expenditures and Share Value." *Journal of Financial Economics*, 26 (1990):255-76.

DeAngelo, Harry, and Edward M. Rice. "Antitakeover Charter Amendments and Stockholder Wealth." *Journal of Financial Economics*. 11 (1983):329-59.

Giammarino, Ronald M. and Robert L. Heinkel. " A Model of Dynamic Takeover Behavior." *Journal of Finance*. (1986):465-80.

Hall, Bronwyn H. "The Impact of Corporate Restructuring on Industrial Research and Development." Brookings Papers on Economic Activity. (1990):85-135.

Haugen, Robert A. and Lemma W. Senbet. "The Insignificance of Bankruptcy Cost to the Theory of Optimal Capital Structure." *Journal of Finance*, 33 (1978):383-93.

Hayes, Robert A., and William J. Abernathy. "Managing Our Way to Economic Decline." *Harvard Business Review*. (July-August 1980):67-77.

Hirschey, Mark. "Intangible Capital Aspects of Advertising and R&D Expenditures." *Journal of Industrial Economics*, 30 (June 1982):375-90.

Jarrell, Gregg A. and Annette B. Poulsen. "Shark Repellents and Stock Prices: The Effects of Antitakeover Amendments Since 1980." *Journal of Financial Economics*, 19 (1987):127-68.

Jog, Vijay M. and Ashwani K . Srivastava. "Corporate Financial Decision Making in Canada." *Canadian Journal of Administrative Sciences*, 11 (1994):156-76.

Johnson, Lewis D. and Bohumir Pazderka. "FIrm Value and Investment in R&D." *Managerial and Decision Economics*, 14 (1993):15-24.

Linn, Scott C. and Mohn J. McConnell. "An Empirical Investigation of the Impact of 'Antitakeover Amendments on Common Stock Prices." *Journal of Financial Economics*, 11 (1983):361-99.

McConnell, John, J. and Chris J. Muscarella. "Corporate Capital Expenditure Decisions and the Market Value of the Firm." *Journal of Financial Economics*, 14 (1985):399-422.

Meulbroek, Lisa K. , Mark L. Mitchell, J. Harold Mulherin, Jeffrey M. Netter, and Annette Poulsen. "Shark Repellents and Managerial Myopia: An Empirical Test." *Journal of Political Economy*, 98 (1990):1108-17.

Pakes, Ariel. "On Patents, R&D, and the Stock Market Rate of Return." *Journal of Political Economy*, 93 (1985):390-409.

Schall, L. D. K., G. L. Sundem and W. R. Geijsbeek. "Survey and Analysis of Capital Budgeting Methods." *Journal of Finance*, 33 (1978):281-87.

Squires, Robert J. *R&D Outlook 1995*. Ottawa: Conference Board of Canada, 1994.

Stein, Jeremy C. "Takeover Threats and Managerial Myopia." *Journal of Political Economy*, 96 (February 1988):61-80.

Tobin, James. "Monetary Policies and the Economy: The Transmission Mechanism." *Southern Economic Journal*, 37 (April 1987):421-31.

Woolridge, Randall. "Competitive Decline and Corporate Restructuring: Is a Myopic Stock Market to Blame." *Journal of Applied Corporate Finance*, 1 (Spring, 1988):26-36.

Ron Hirshhorn
Consulting Economist
Ottawa

The Governance of Nonprofits

A LTHOUGH LARGELY UNEXPLORED AND POORLY UNDERSTOOD, the nonprofit sector constitutes an important component of the Canadian economy. Sometimes referred to as the "third sector", its members include such notable groups as social service agencies, health service providers, religious organizations, arts groups, educational institutions, special interest organizations, and various forms of associations. From a governance perspective, nonprofit organizations – or "nonprofits", as they are more generally known – raise special concerns. Falling between the public and the private sectors, nonprofits are subject neither to the disciplinary forces that apply to private firms, nor to the public sector controls that apply to government corporations. Some of the literature suggests, however, that nonprofits represent an important institutional form precisely because they are able to resolve many of the contractual problems associated with specific economic activities more effectively than either for-profit or public-sector providers.

This study examines this argument and considers its relevance to a number of Canadian nonprofit organizations. Following a review of available data on the Canadian nonprofit sector, there is a general overview of governance issues. The comparative advantages of nonprofits, in terms (primarily) of transaction cost considerations, are then examined in more detail. The next section examines a number of areas where nonprofit provision has some potential advantages over public and for-profit provision. This is followed by a section that focuses on the internal governance problems that may erode, or eliminate, any gains from the use of the nonprofit form.

The considerations that emerge from the preceding sections are then applied to assess the use of nonprofits in two quite different areas, health services and airport operations. In the next section universities are used as an example to illustrate the problems associated with the governance of nonprofits that provide relatively complex services. This section also looks at some specific policy reforms designed to alleviate governance problems. The final section provides the conclusions of the study.

NONPROFITS IN THE CANADIAN ECONOMY

NONPROFITS ARE DISTINGUISHED FROM MOST OTHER organizations by the existence of a non-distribution constraint. The surplus that remains after all expenses have been deducted from revenue cannot be distributed to directors, managers or other influential stakeholders. Nonprofits are free to run financial surpluses and some researchers believe that decision-makers in these organizations may indeed strive to earn and accumulate surpluses.[1] The absence of a claimant with a right to appropriate such surpluses, however, distinguishes nonprofits from proprietary, co-operative, and government-owned enterprises.

A wide range of disparate organizations is subject to non-distribution constraints. A recent study by Quarter (1992) provides a useful way to categorize the diverse organizations that comprise the nonprofit sector. Quarter distinguishes between nonprofits that serve the general public and mutual nonprofits that serve a defined membership. Included among mutual nonprofits are religious organizations, labour organizations, professional associations, business organizations, consumer groups, social clubs, and various socio-political organizations.

Nonprofits serving the general public can be subdivided into three groups according to their major funding source. First, there are those organizations that are heavily (if not entirely) supported by sales revenue. These include commercial entities (such as Blue Cross, the Canadian Automobile Association and Travel CUTS); non-profit homes for the aged and daycare centres; private elementary and secondary schools; performing arts groups; and youth organizations such as the YMCA, Boy Scouts and Girl Guides.

The second group comprises organizations that are heavily dependent on volunteers and financial donations. "Donative" nonprofits include major humanitarian organizations (such as the Red Cross, CARE Canada and CUSO); domestic fund-raising and volunteer organizations (such as the Shriners, the John Howard and Elizabeth Fry Societies, service clubs such as Lions, Rotary and Kiwanis, and various family service agencies); "food and shelter" organizations (such as the Salvation Army, Meals-on-Wheels, and food banks); and health support and advocacy agencies (such as the Canadian Cancer Society and the Canadian Diabetes Association).

The third group consists of nonprofit organizations that rely largely on government funding. This group includes hospitals along with nursing homes, and alcohol and drug abuse treatment centres; and post-secondary institutions and research institutes. Although these organizations are often regarded as part of the public sector, they are generally more independent than public corporations that are accountable to a provincial legislature or the federal government through a Minister. Virtually all hospitals and universities meet some of their requirements through their own fund-raising activities and, in addition, are not subject to the accountability and control regimes that apply to most government corporations and agencies.

Quarter estimates that in 1992 there were about 175,000 mutual-interest and general nonprofits (excluding unincorporated nonprofit associations) in Canada. Information is available through Revenue Canada on the subset of approximately 70,000 nonprofits that qualify as registered charities (Table 1). In 1993 over $86 billion passed through charities; 56 percent of that amount was provided by governments. Hospitals and teaching institutions comprised only 5 percent of the number of registered charities in 1993, but they accounted for 58 percent of total revenue and 56 percent of all employees.

Charities employed 1.3 million Canadians in 1993. If output is measured on the same basis as government production (*i.e.*, using labour payments), the production of registered charities amounted to 5.6 percent of 1993 GDP – excluding the contributions of volunteers. According to Sharpe (1994), 1.6 million Canadians offered their services on a steady basis over 1993, and another 3 million Canadians volunteered over peak periods. Volunteer services can also be estimated using Statistics Canada's 1992 *General Social Survey on Time Use*. Applying data on the opportunity cost of time for males and females to survey results on the time devoted to civic and voluntary activity yields an estimate of over $40 billion (for 1992),[2] which is slightly higher than the salary and benefit payments made by charities to their employees. Both sources suggest that the contribution of volunteer services is much higher than estimated in earlier studies[3] and that the output of registered charities (measured in terms of the value of all labour services) is probably in excess of 10 percent of GDP.

GOVERNANCE ISSUES

ACCORDING TO THE PROPERTY RIGHTS THEORY of the firm, nonprofit corporations should perform less efficiently than for-profit or proprietary corporations. The lack of clearly defined residual claimants and the nontransferability of ownership in nonprofits introduce a number of governance problems. As Furubotn & Pejovich (1972) point out, managerial decisions are more costly to evaluate because the future consequences of those decisions cannot be capitalized. Managers who have limited horizons are rarely inclined to take account of all expected future costs and benefits. More troubling, there is an increased opportunity for managers to use potential profits in the pursuit of nonpecuniary sources of utility. Moreover, it is difficult for anyone to take control of the enterprise and put the assets to better use.

Property rights arguments recognize that the shareholders of for-profit corporations are also subject to attenuation problems and that the mechanisms to alleviate these problems have limitations. Capital-market and other constraints on managerial behaviour, however, put the governance problems of proprietary corporations into a very different category from those of nonprofits.

The literature on property rights has less to say about the difference between nonprofits and government corporations. In government corporations,

TABLE 1
REVENUES AND EXPENDITURES OF REGISTERED CHARITIES

CHARITY TYPE	NUMBER[a]	% OF ALL CHARITIES	REVENUES ($ MILLIONS)	% OF ALL REVENUES	EXPENDITURES ($ MILLIONS)	% OF ALL EXPENDITURES
Places of Worship	25,177	36.4	5,128	5.9	4,859	5.9
Hospitals	1,071	1.5	26,314	30.4	25,970	31.5
Teaching Institutions	2,516	3.6	23,763	27.5	22,513	27.3
Other Charitable Organizations						
Welfare	10,157	14.7	8,275	9.6	7,890	9.6
Health	4,910	7.1	5,030	5.8	4,795	5.8
Education	6,365	9.2	4,978	5.8	4,710	5.7
Religion	3,729	5.4	2,972	3.4	2,647	3.2
Benefits to the Community	8,602	12.4	4,116	4.8	3,912	4.7
Other	522	0.8	117	0.1	93	0.1
Subtotal	34,285	49.5	25,488	29.5	24,046	29.2
Public Foundations	3,148	4.5	4,731	5.5	4,366	5.3
Private Foundations	3,033	4.4	1,088	1.3	675	0.8
All Charities	69,230	100	86,512	100	82,428	100

Note: Percentages and dollar amounts may not add due to rounding.
    a Provided by Revenue Canada staff, November 1993.
Source: Sharpe (1994).

as in nonprofits, the costs of detecting, policing and enforcing desired behaviour are substantial because ownership is nontransferable. In government corporations, however, the residual claimants are at least well-defined, and political and bureaucratic mechanisms of accountability and control are in place to protect the interests of shareholders.

From a property rights perspective, the significant role of nonprofits in Canada, as well as in other industrialized economies, is puzzling. In the nonprofit literature, attempts to resolve this conundrum have focused on the need for alternative institutional arrangements to address both market and government (or political) failures. In Weisbrod's view (1975, 1988), the advantage of nonprofits has to do with their ability to provide collective goods when demand is heterogeneous. Nonprofits can be relied on to provide so-called "trust goods", which involve severe information asymmetry problems, for example, because managers are subject to a nondistribution constraint and therefore do not have the same incentive to downgrade quality as the managers of proprietary corporations. While trust goods can also be publicly provided, governments, which are majoritarian and consensual and must provide "equal access", are ill-equipped to satisfy diverse demands from minorities.[4] Therefore, nonprofits are a response to inadequacies in goods and political markets.

Douglas (1983) has elaborated persuasively on the arguments for nonprofit involvement in public functions. A service provided by the state is subject to the constraints of political feasibility and political justice. The nonprofit sector, which is not subject to these constraints, can help give expression to a wide diversity of views and social values that must be respected in a pluralist democracy. Nonprofits can also facilitate experimentation in the introduction and delivery of new services. This fills an important gap because governments have difficulty introducing services on a limited basis – especially experimental services that may subsequently have to be abandoned because they are not worth pursuing.

Hansmann (1980) explains non-profits in terms of various forms of contract failure in markets served by for-profit providers. Contract failure may be due to the usual sorts of market failures (*i.e.*, public goods, information asymmetry, imperfect loan markets) as well as to special problems associated with donative (charitable) activities. Individuals who purchase (*i.e.*, contribute to) foreign aid, for example, must rely on the trustworthiness of the intermediary (the charity) to ensure that the service paid for is provided. Because the nondistribution constraint removes the incentive to exploit informational advantages, many people prefer to provide time and money to nonprofit organizations. Fama & Jensen (1983b) regard the agency problems faced by donors generally as central to the role of nonprofits. Donors need to be assured that their contributions will not be expropriated by residual claimants. Fama & Jensen (1983b, p. 342) contend that "the absence of residual claims avoids the donor-residual claimant agency problem and explains the dominance of nonprofits in donor-financed activities".

Theories of nonprofits fit well with more general theories of institutional choice, which have been directed mainly to understanding why firms, rather than markets, are chosen to co-ordinate some activities. In the same way that firms may be preferable to markets because they economize on transaction costs, use of nonprofits as distinct from for-profits may offer savings in the costs of monitoring and enforcing contracts (where the costs include the losses incurred because full enforcement is prohibitively expensive). McManus' (1975) observation that different forms of organization have different behaviour constraints, which entail different costs of enforcement, is central to understanding the role of nonprofits. In the case of charitable nonprofits, however, there are two outside stakeholders, donors and recipients, whose interests must be addressed. Both bear a cost if nonprofits are poorly run and in that sense both can be said to have residual claimant status.[5] The appeal of the nonprofit form relates to its potential to minimize enforcement costs and maximize consumption possibilities for these two stakeholders.

When examining the normative question of whether, and under what conditions, nonprofits do, in fact, successfully resolve contracting problems,[6] there are a number of factors to be considered. In his comparison of firms and price systems, McManus (1975) notes that the methods of allocation have different biases and entail different "external effects". The latter refers to the incentive individuals have to impose damages on others through activities that are not constrained because of high enforcement costs. The shift from a price system to a centralized system of allocation reduces external effects along some margins and increases them along others. There is a gain from this shift if there is an overall reduction in the losses from such external effects. A firm would gain from contracting out certain activities, for example, if the costs of controlling the pursuit of purely monetary gains by contractors are lower than the costs of controlling non-monetary consumption on the job by its employees.

Similarly, the savings that derive from adoption of the nonprofit form depend on the balance from lower external costs in some areas and increased costs in other areas. Managers of nonprofit firms, for example, generally have less incentive than their for-profit counterparts to take advantage of information asymmetries by reducing quality. Because of the non-distribution constraint, managers of nonprofits have little to gain personally from providing less of those qualitative features that are difficult to monitor. Moreover, if, as Weisbrod (1988) suggests, there is a managerial self-selection process at work, nonprofit managers would tend to be those who are attracted by the service mission and would also be likely to value the high service standards of these organizations. But while the external effects arising from the difficulties of monitoring product attributes are likely to be less of a problem, the external effects associated with consumption on the job are more of a concern in non-profit than in for-profit organizations. For the reasons highlighted in the property rights literature, the enforcement of constraints on non-monetary consumption is costly and difficult in nonprofit organizations. The desirability of having a service provided by a nonprofit relative to a for-profit agency depends on the balance between the gains and losses from these two external effects.

Tradeoffs are also involved in determining the nature and extent of the advantages of nonprofit over public provision. While nonprofits can respond more closely than governments to the needs of specific sub-sectors of the population, unlike governments, they lack the coercive power to compel payments from those stakeholders who can afford to pay for the services they are receiving. Individuals can "purchase" services that better reflect their preferences through a nonprofit provider, but they will incur a loss to the extent that their contributions also go to support free riders.

Where it is possible to form a club that restricts its services to paying members, individuals can overcome the free-rider problem. Compared to governments, however, clubs must spread the costs of organization and administration over a few services and a few individuals. As long as the resulting diseconomies of scale and scope are not sufficient to overcome the advantages of having a club satisfy divergent consumer preferences, clubs will be an attractive alternative to having to rely on the public sector.

What all this suggests is, first, that the governance issue with respect to nonprofits is appropriately viewed as a set of contractual problems involving decision-makers within the organization, and donors and recipients, both of whom may be regarded as residual claimants. Second, the ability of nonprofits to resolve these problems, and hence their appeal relative to alternative organizational forms, is likely to depend on the balance between the gains from lower transaction costs in some areas and the losses from higher costs elsewhere. Compared to for-profit corporations, the advantage of nonprofits is likely to depend, to a great extent, on the size of the enforcement costs savings related to the elimination of monetary incentives relative to the losses from the increased costs of monitoring non-monetary consumption.

The balance between such external effects depends on a number of factors. The nature of the output produced is a major factor. Nonprofits have advantages in providing particular types of output which pose certain difficulties for for-profit and public producers. Also of importance are those factors that have a particular influence on the incentives for managerial efficiency within non-profits. These include the composition of the nonprofit's board of directors and the structure of the market for the nonprofit's outputs. Internal control problems may undermine, and perhaps even eliminate, the advantages of non-profits relative to for-profit or public provision.

The next section considers the comparative advantage of the nonprofit form in satisfying the demand for certain types of output. The section there-after looks at factors relating specifically to the internal governance of non-profits. The issues in both sections are relevant to an understanding of the performance of nonprofits and to an assessment of their role relative to for-profit and public organizations.

Nonprofits as Producers of Different Types of Output

WHILE NONPROFITS MAY BE SUBJECT TO significant governance problems, transaction costs could conceivably be much higher if the relevant activities were performed by governments or proprietary firms. An examination of the organizational alternatives for providing particular outputs, and the limitations of for-profit and public provision, helps put the governance problems of nonprofits into perspective. In this section the focus is on nonprofits producing four different types of outputs: club goods, other collective goods, trust goods and donative goods.

These categories correspond with the major contractual problems that may give rise to nonprofit provision.[7] Contractual problems derive from the collective (or "nonrival") attributes of some goods; the difficulty of assessing the quality of certain types of service (*i.e.*, trust goods); and the special monitoring difficulties associated with the purchase of goods and delivery of services to unknown beneficiaries (*i.e.*, donative goods).

In the first group, a distinction is made between those collective goods that are generally provided by clubs for their members, and other goods, such as nonprofit television telecasts, which are produced for the general public. In each case of contract failure, the impact of the contracting problem on the costs of for-profit and public provision must be balanced against the inefficiencies of nonprofit delivery.

Nonprofits as Providers of Club Goods

THE POTENTIAL ADVANTAGE OF MUTUALS (OR CLUBS) in supplying certain types of collective goods was formally outlined by Buchanan (1965). At the centre of the theory of mutuals (clubs) are goods that are excludable but only partially rivalrous. Most goods are rivalrous, which means that they can be consumed by only one person. Where a good is nonrivalrous additional users do not reduce the benefit derived from the good after it has been used by the initial consumers, and collective provision is therefore desirable. This is relevant to club goods such as a swimming pool or a golf course, although they are partially rivalrous; additional members create congestion and thereby impose some additional cost. Excludability (or exclusivity) makes it possible for groups to form and restrict access to the relevant good to members.

While governments often satisfy needs for collective services, alternative collectivities become more appealing when heterogeneous consumers are taken into account. Whereas governments must serve all individuals within the defined jurisdiction, a club can tailor its services to meet the needs of those with specific needs or tastes. As noted earlier, the advantages of flexible groupings which are not tied to physical boundaries is an important theme in Weisbrod's theory of nonprofits.

Mutuals include trade unions and professional associations, which exist to represent the collective interest of their members, as well as sporting and social clubs that offer facilities and services not unlike many of those that can be purchased from for-profit providers. In this latter case, some of the popularity of the nonprofit form has been attributed to the desire of individuals to regain some of the influence they lose when goods are provided collectively. The influence of the individual diminishes because it is more efficient to package and sell club-type services as a bundle, generally for an annual fee, rather than to impose a separate charge for each service. Douglas (1987) suggests that the influence individuals gain through their voting power as club members helps compensate for the weakening influence of "exit" when goods are provided collectively.

Hansmann (1980) provides an alternative explanation. He views non-profit provision as a response to concerns that for-profit providers of club services have considerable monopoly power. This arises because part of the appeal of clubs is the opportunity they provide to their members to associate with others who are seen to have certain desirable characteristics. Profit-maximizing producers have an incentive to charge something in excess of costs and to capture some of the value individuals place on the social benefits of belonging to an exclusive organization. By forming a nonprofit club which they, as members, can control, individuals are able to prevent such monopolistic exploitation.

In the theoretical ideal, heterogeneous individuals not only divide them-selves optimally among various clubs but also force clubs to compete for their membership. The latter creates pressures for the efficient provision of club goods.[8] The theory of clubs has more relevance to some types of mutuals than others. In many areas (i.e., professional, labour and consumer associations), individuals are not presented with a wide variety of choice, nor do they enjoy the benefits of competition. Similarly, concerns about the potential market power of proprietary club owners arise because there is limited scope for competition between exclusive social clubs. In these circumstances, members can voice their displeasure with the club's operation but they rarely "vote with their feet" by moving to another club that provides similar services with a preferable mix of price and quality.

Notwithstanding the potentially limited competition, clubs are comparatively well-suited to satisfying certain consumer needs. Members of mutuals are often better off than they would be if the only alternative is to rely on proprietary firms, which have an incentive to take advantage of the lack of competition, or on governments, which have a broad constituency to satisfy and are subject to pressures to focus attention on the needs of the median voter.

599

NONPROFITS AS PROVIDERS OF OTHER COLLECTIVE GOODS

CLUBS OR MUTUAL NONPROFITS ARE NOT APPROPRIATE for all types of collective goods. A different example of a collective good is a performing arts production (such as an opera), which is characterized by high fixed costs. The latter derive from the considerable expense of mounting a production and represent the nonrival aspect of theatre consumption.[9] With operas, and similar productions catering to a limited audience, the demand curve typically lies below the average cost curve at all output levels. As O'Hagan & Purdy (1993) point out, total benefits may still exceed total costs if benefits vary widely and there is a group of opera lovers prepared to pay well above average cost. Nonprofits are able to satisfy the unmet demand by encouraging much-needed donations from those who place a high value on its productions.

Having a for-profit organization provide a service such as an opera is an alternative when proprietary firms can tap into the high demand of opera lovers through price discrimination. However, effective price discrimination is often difficult and costly. Moreover, for-profit firms that can effectively price discriminate have an incentive to take advantage of the high demand of opera lovers and earn monopoly rents.

The nonprofit form provides donors with the assurance that their funds are not being used to benefit equity holders. It is less clear that their funds are being utilized efficiently. Performing arts theatres are under pressure to mount productions of sufficiently high quality and appeal to meet established objectives in terms of box-office revenue. They also have to pay special attention to those factors that influence donor contributions. The nature and quality of the performances is important in this respect, as are the special services and amenities the theatre offers to cultivate a sense of community among donors.[10] The ability of a theatre's management to achieve attendance goals and financial targets can be assessed relatively easily; these indicators are likely to attract much of the board's attention.

It is more difficult for the board to ensure that the costs for mounting theatre productions and carrying out related activities are adequately con-trolled. The combined revenue from donations and box-office receipts can conceivably establish a low ceiling that offers little opportunity for excessive spending and on-the-job consumption, but there is nothing to ensure that will be the case. If the theatre is publicly owned, the government can attempt to establish a level of funding support that encourages cost-cutting and more efficient management. However, one might reasonably question governments' ability to determine an appropriate level of funding and enforce budgetary discipline.

Moreover, to the extent that donations reflect individuals' valuations of the theatre's activities, donations establish a link between costs and benefits that is lost when public funds replace donations. With budgetary controls there is an incentive to shift towards productions that have wide public appeal and are therefore more likely to attract large audiences. This does not necessarily result in greater net benefits, however.

NONPROFITS AS PROVIDERS OF TRUST GOODS

MANY COMMERCIAL NONPROFITS ARE INVOLVED in activities where service performance is especially difficult to assess. The conceptual discussion in the previous section suggested that nonprofits have some advantages in the provision of trust goods, and it raised the possibility that they could be the preferred provider notwithstanding potentially significant governance problems.

While available evidence is not conclusive, some studies support the expectation that nonprofits are less likely than proprietary corporations to take advantage of information asymmetries by reducing service quality. For example, in a study of nursing homes, Weisbrod and Schlesinger (1986) find that for-profit homes perform more poorly than non-profit homes when quality is difficult for outsiders to observe. A recent study of psychiatric hospitals in the state of California (Mark, 1993) finds, similarly, that nonprofit hospitals are less likely to exploit information asymmetries. A Manitoba study (Manitoba Department of Community Services and Corrections, 1986) points to the higher quality of service provided by nonprofit, compared to for-profit, day care centres. In addition, Weisbrod (1988) identifies a number of significant differences between nonprofit and proprietary organizations in three long-term care industries: nursing homes, facilities for care of the mentally handicapped, and psychiatric care facilities. He found, in particular, that consumers are more likely to be satisfied with their surroundings and various aspects of the service provided in nonprofit facilities.

These results are consistent with theoretical models emphasizing the distinct incentives of nonprofit providers. They also correspond with anecdotal evidence highlighting the important role of stakeholders who have strong ideological perspectives on establishing and running nonprofit "trust" organizations (discussed later in this study in relation to the role of the board).

Empirical research also provides some tentative support for the argument that, compared to for-profits, nonprofit trusts are subject to weaker pressures to achieve efficient performance. Cost comparisons are complicated by the difficulty of adjusting for differences in quality of care and in the characteristics of the clientele(s) served by different organizations. Adjustments must also be made for the cost savings achieved through the use of volunteer labour. While researchers have had varying success in allowing for such differences, studies across different sectors and different countries have produced generally similar results.[11] For example, a U.S. study of nursing homes found proprietary homes had costs significantly below nonprofit homes and substantially below government homes.[12] Similarly, a study of residential child care in the United Kingdom found that for-profit homes had the lowest costs.[13] A recent study of Canadian long-term care facilities for the elderly revealed a similar pattern:

"average *per diem* costs were generally highest in the public category, followed by the private not-for-profit category and then the private for-profit category".[14]

Among other things, these findings reflect the higher costs of detecting and policing managerial decisions in nonprofit, compared to proprietary, organizations. Although "commercial" nonprofits derive much of their revenue from user fees, they nonetheless tend to operate in highly imperfect markets. Because of the support nonprofits receive through charitable donations, volunteer labour and tax exemptions, financial results are a misleading indicator of performance. Outside directors who take their monitoring function seriously must look beyond the financial statements to assess a variety of other more detailed indicators of organizational efficiency.

The relative size of the gains and losses that are clearly attributable to the organizational form of the provider – nonprofit as opposed to proprietary – depends on a number of factors. The benefits from the trustworthiness associated with nonprofits increase as monitoring becomes more difficult and the losses from a poor choice of provider become greater. Monitoring is more problematic in some situations because the ultimate consumers of the service being provided are not in a position to assess service performance. At the same time, because of the critical nature of the services being provided, *ex post* compensation may provide an inadequate remedy for poor service delivery. The comparative advantages of having a nonprofit provider also depend on how effectively for-profit firms have responded to consumer concerns through mechanisms or arrangements that reduce uncertainty. By using brand names and franchise arrangements to certify product quality, for example, for-profit firms may actually be able to offer savings in consumer enforcement costs approaching those which are achieved under nonprofit provision.

For-profit provision also becomes a more attractive option if governments can incorporate contract features into their purchasing arrangements that reduce the risk of inadequate service quality. It has been shown, for example, how a shift from a per diem payment scheme to a reimbursement scheme that adjusts for the medical condition of patients and includes a bonus for improvements in patient health can contribute to significantly higher quality care by for-profit nursing homes.[15]

NONPROFITS AS PROVIDERS OF DONATIVE GOODS

DONATIVE NONPROFITS ENGAGE IN A WIDE RANGE of activities, many of which do not, in themselves, involve any special problems of contract specification and enforcement. Issues of concern do arise, however, regarding the contractual arrangements between these organizations and their donors. While donations cannot be expropriated by residual claimants, they can be absorbed by other internal agents in the absence of adequate monitoring mechanisms.

These problems are not unique to donative nonprofits, but in organizations such as CARE Canada and the Salvation Army the question of how donors can get "more bang for their buck" is central. However, while the governance properties of donative organizations may leave much to be desired, alternative institutional options are likely to have more serious limitations. Proprietary organizations are an inappropriate alternative to nonprofits because of the donor-residual claimant-agency problem identified by Hansmann and highlighted by Fama & Jensen; donors have no incentive to contribute to an organization if their donations can be used to benefit residual claimants who share in the organization's net income. The activities of donative organizations could be assumed by governments, but this would disadvantage individual donors who, as well as losing the freedom to allocate their contributions to charitable activities of their choice, would forego the psychological rewards that derive from voluntary donations. Moreover, as the empirical findings on the performance of organizations that provide "trust goods" illustrates, public provision involves its own significant agency problems.

Individuals can, of course, forego the use of an intermediary, and contribute directly to the intended recipients. However, the high transaction costs of direct transactions tend to make this unreasonable, except in a small number of specific circumstances. Since the costs involved in identifying recipients and evaluating their claims are fixed, charitable organizations that are involved in large numbers of repeated transactions enjoy important economies of scale.[16]

Some mechanisms do help to reduce the costs associated with the monitoring of nonprofits. Corporate legislation which applies to nonprofits assures donors that the organization's resources shall be used exclusively for the stated purpose of the organization. In Canada, the relevant federal law is the *Canada Corporations Act* (CCA), Part II. An additional check is provided by the *Income Tax Act*, which requires that organizations registered as charities are actually engaged in charitable activities and that their services are not restricted to a select group of beneficiaries. Charitable purposes, as defined under Common law, include four types of activities: the relief of poverty; the advancement of religion; the advancement of education; and other activities beneficial to the community. As well, donors can reduce uncertainty through the choices they make. As Posnett & Sandler (1988) have documented, small donors who have no significant influence over nonprofit activities tend to favour organizations with clearly defined objectives and where the discretion afforded trustees is closely constrained.[17] With clearly specified objectives, donors can be reasonably certain that particular groups will benefit from their charitable contributions.

These mechanisms do not address concerns about the performance of nonprofit organizations, however. The CCA, Part II simply ensures that nonprofits adhere to certain basic requirements, by, for example, having a board of at least three directors, holding an annual meeting, filing an audited annual financial statement, and adopting by-laws that are acceptable to the Minister. Neither corporation law nor tax law does much to assuage those who are concerned that resources may be used inefficiently or to benefit internal agents.

Individuals who are sensitive to the governance problems of nonprofits are likely to pay more attention to the distribution of their charitable contributions. They may also be inclined to increase their contributions to smaller, local organizations, with whom they have some familiarity. At the same time, concerns about waste and inefficiency may lead some donors to reduce their donations to some nonprofits whose missions they value highly. It is through such choices, rather than through choices between alternative institutional arrangements, that individuals attempt to maximize the satisfaction they derive from their charitable donations.

OTHER FACTORS AFFECTING THE GOVERNANCE OF NONPROFITS

AMONG NONPROFITS THAT PROVIDE SPECIFIC TYPES of output, performance depends on internal governance arrangements and the nature of the resulting incentives for managerial efficiency. Two of the most important factors that affect the motivation of nonprofit mangers are discussed below.

THE ROLE OF THE BOARD OF DIRECTORS

IN THE ABSENCE OF THE DISCIPLINE exercised by the takeover market, there is a greater onus on the board to monitor managerial behaviour and to ensure that inadequate managers are replaced. Fama & Jensen (1983a) emphasize the role of outside directors as proxies for shareholders in monitoring management activities. They observe that board members are often large donors whose commitment(s) of time and wealth assures other donors that the organization is being adequately monitored. Nonetheless, inside (as distinct from outside) directors do play an important role in some nonprofits. Moreover, outside directors may also be motivated by a number of factors, which include (but are not limited to) altruism. While it is not in the interest of directors to be associated with a wasteful organization, the monitoring of charities is both complicated and time consuming – and most board members have limited time to commit to voluntary activities. Seibel (1992), for example, emphasizes the role of nonprofit boards as sociopolitical institutions offering important networking benefits:

> The boards of trustees or boards of directors ... do more than just control organizational performance. It is even questionable whether performance control is a board's primary function. Boards act as knots within networks of reputational, financial and power elites. Mutual interests are balanced through this arrangement. From the organization's point of view, rich, influential, and reputable persons on the board of trustees are a prerequisite for successful fund raising; at the same time, being a member of a board brings one an increase in

reputation and reinforces old networks and knits new networks of interpersonal relationships.

In one of the few attempts to test the influence of nonprofit boards empirically, Callen & Falk (1993) examine whether an increase in the proportion of outside directors has any significant impact on the efficiency of charitable activities.[18] Indices of technical efficiency were derived by using data envelope analysis (DEA) on a sample of Canadian charities with a specific focus on health. The results led the authors to conclude that neither technical nor allocative efficiency is affected by the composition of the board of directors. This could reflect a lack of motivation and commitment on the part of outside directors. It could also indicate that managers who sit as inside directors are themselves committed to efficiency goals, or they are at least as committed as outside directors.

While high monitoring costs attributable to the absence of tradeable equity, combined with the limited commitment of board members who derive a strictly non-monetary return from their contributions, is a concern for all nonprofits, there are a few special situations. First, in mutual organizations, the lines of accountability are clearer and stronger than in other nonprofits. The members are the only important outside stakeholder in mutuals, and elections provide a means for members to hold the board accountable. In large organizations, however, transaction costs and free-rider problems may reduce the ability of the members to exercise effective control over the organization's management. Alternatively, control may be exercised by a small subset of members with especially strong preferences.[19]

Second, in certain nonprofits, the board is dominated by stakeholders who want to use the organization to give expression to their particular ideologies or philosophies. Organized religious groups, for example, have been behind the establishment of nonprofits delivering a variety of social services.[20] Secular groups with specific beliefs, such as those promoting particular theories of child development, have also been influential in the founding and operation of nonprofits.[21] It is not apparent that such corporations are more successful than other nonprofits in eliminating waste and inefficiency. But the boards of these corporations are motivated to hire managers who support the organization's objectives. They are also motivated to ensure that rules and operating procedures are in place to achieve the types and standards of service envisioned by the founders of the organization.

MARKET CHARACTERISTICS

WHILE THE USUAL INDICATORS OF MARKET PERFORMANCE are often of limited use in monitoring nonprofits, in some circumstances market information can significantly reduce monitoring and enforcement costs. Monitoring is less of a problem where nonprofits are subject to market competition or to a demanding contractual agreement that imposes significant discipline on nonprofit providers.

Generally, mutual nonprofits face limited competition in their particular areas of activity. One mutual that comes close to satisfying the conditions of efficient club performance, however, is the local religious organization (*i.e.*, the church congregation) in major urban centres. While it is difficult to measure the production of religious institutions, individuals know whether and to what degree their congregation is providing the services they value. In urban centres, members of the major religious denominations have a reasonable degree of choice, and congregations are under pressure to offer a price-service package that compares favourably with available alternatives.

The benefits of competition and choice are not available when churches are part of the public sector, as is the situation in some countries and was the case at one time in North America. The privatization of religion is seen as a factor underlying the growth of the church in the United States, and as the main reason why the religious services sector in the United States is so much larger than in Europe.[22]

Similarly, markets for services provided by so-called "commercial" non-profits are less imperfect in some situations than others. Market performance is a more revealing indicator where information asymmetry is not a major problem, and where nonprofits derive the bulk of their revenue from user fees. While the playing field may not be entirely level, measures of market performance can still provide a useful indication of an organization's success in sustaining quality and controlling costs relative to competing nonprofit and for-profit providers. However, these conditions are likely to apply in only a few circumstances; if they do apply, and markets are reasonably competitive, there is probably little justification for nonprofits, rather than for-profits to provide commercial services. Perhaps for this reason, the nonprofit literature is not very helpful in assessing the influence of market structure on performance. Still, evidence pointing to the positive impact of competition on the performance of governments, and of state-owned enterprises is instructive.[23] This literature suggests that, under competitive conditions, the monitoring problems associated with nontransferable ownership claims are much more tractable.

One of the most significant attempts to inject competitive incentives into nonprofit activities is occurring in the U.K. hospital sector.[24] As part of the wide-ranging reforms introduced in the National Health Service (NHS) and the *Community Care Act* of 1991, hospitals are being transformed into independent self-governing trusts that must compete for business. District Health Authorities and general practitioners with large practices receive government payments based on the number and the characteristics of their client population. They are free to use these funds to purchase hospital services on the most favourable terms possible. Although all of the effects of this reform are not yet known, a recent OECD study (1993, p. 81) observes that "internal markets" of this sort "have considerable potential for allocating available resources more efficiently between establishments, for generating productivity gains and for improving capacity utilization".

Where the consumer is a government, rather than groups or individuals, the nature of the contractual arrangement determines the incentives for efficient performance. There may be less reason for concern about the relatively high costs of nonprofit provision, for example, if the government can devise a system of compensation based on the performance of a reasonably efficient provider whose costs can be used as a benchmark. Alternatively, the government may be able to introduce some of the beneficial incentives of competitive markets by establishing a system of competitive tendering. Here again, results may be distorted if the activities of the nonprofits are subsidized heavily through donations of funds and voluntary labour and there is no appropriate allowance for these cost advantages.

SOME CONCLUSIONS

BASED ON THE FACTORS IDENTIFIED IN THIS SECTION, some types of nonprofits offer a greater potential for transaction cost savings than others. Despite concerns about the internal governance of donative nonprofits, these organizations have a strong comparative advantage simply because of the inability of alternative types of organizations to satisfy the requirements of donors. Mutual nonprofits also tend to have a significant comparative advantage over alternative arrangements with respect to the provision of certain types of collective services. The internal governance arrangements of mutuals have some desirable features. While members of some large organizations may not effectively exercise their authority, it is less likely in mutuals than in other types of nonprofits that internal agency problems will undermine the advantages of nonprofit provision. In the case of the other types of nonprofits, "commercial" nonprofits and government-funded nonprofits, the factors influencing the optimal organizational arrangement are more balanced. It is not surprising, therefore, that both for-profit and nonprofit entities can be found providing post-secondary education, health care, and various other social services.

TRANSACTION COSTS AND THE PROBLEM OF ORGANIZATIONAL CHOICE: AN EXAMINATION OF COMMUNITY HEALTH CENTRES AND AIRPORTS

IN THIS SECTION WE LOOK AT TWO VERY DIFFERENT nonprofit organizations – community health centres and airport authorities – with a view to shedding some further light on the problem of organizational choice. It has already been argued here that, for nonprofit provision to be preferable to for-profit provision, a necessary (although not sufficient) condition is the potential for improvements in monitoring and enforcement along some dimension. There must be an area where the potential for lower external costs can be identified. It will be argued that the application of this test leads to quite different results in the cases of health centres and airport authorities.

COMMUNITY HEALTH CENTRES

NONPROFIT COMMUNITY HEALTH CENTRES serve a small fraction of the Canadian health-care market, but represent a potentially significant alternative to traditional fee-for-service medical care. The community health concept is most fully developed in Quebec, where a network of primary care clinics known as centres locaux des services communautaires (CLSCs) were established as part of the government's reform of the province's health and social services in 1972. There are now about 170 CLSCs in the province providing primary healthcare, along with homecare and a range of other social services. In other provinces, nonprofit health centres have evolved through the efforts of community activists. There are approximately 50 community health centres (CHCs) in Ontario, and a dozen or so in each of Manitoba and Saskatchewan.[26]

Both CHCs and CLSCs are independent nonprofit organizations headed by boards comprised of users and other stakeholders.[27] As well as providing users with a voice, CHCs and CLSCs allow non-medical staff, such as nurses and social workers, to exert influence and play a major role in the delivery of health care. As distinct from private for-profit clinics, nonprofit health centres emphasize a multi-disciplinary approach to health care. They also devote more time and attention to preventative and health-promotion services.

From a governance perspective, what is most significant about nonprofit health care is that physicians, along with other staff, are paid salaries, rather than fees for services rendered. This change in compensation arrangements addresses a significant agency problem in the contractual arrangements between government providers of health insurance and physicians. In a system with fee-for-service compensation and comprehensive public health insurance, neither physicians nor patients have an incentive to economize on the use of medical services. Indeed, at a time when improving technology is increasing the scope for medical intervention significantly, and a declining population-to-physician ratio poses a threat to the earning capacity of individual physicians, there are strong incentives to increase the use of physician services. Accordingly, between 1977 and 1988, the number of medical services provided to each Canadian increased by over 30 percent. Recently, provincial governments have attempted to deal with this problem by, among other things, imposing "utilization controls" that require doctors to bear part of the costs of increases in service beyond some specified base.

With a salary form of compensation, the bias in the system shifts toward the provision of less care. Physicians and other providers have no financial incentive to provide more than minimal levels of care. However, as with most other nonprofit providers of "trust" goods, CHCs and CLSCs tend to be managed and staffed by individuals who are committed to the organization's mission. This means that physicians and other health care workers tend to have a significant personal stake in the provision of a high standard of community health care.[28] Moreover, community health centres that are attempting to carve out a niche in a market dominated by fee-for-service health care cannot survive unless they provide a high quality of service. These factors reduce the risk that a change in the nature of contractual arrangements between government providers of health insurance and physicians will be accompanied by a significant deterioration in the quality of health care.

Available evidence lends support to the argument that the overall losses from external effects are lower with nonprofit community health care than with traditional fee-for-service medical care. A study of matched groups of patients served by community centres and private clinics in Saskatchewan, for example, found that per capita health service costs were 17 percent lower for community clinic patients.[29] Part of the cost difference was due to the lower hospital utilization rate of community centre patients. This is consistent with other studies that show that fee-for-service compensation tends to be associated with significantly higher rates of hospital utilization than other compensation systems.[30] In an examination of the quality of care provided for six "tracer" conditions, a St. Catherines nonprofit centre performed better than the fee-for-service alternatives.[31] A number of studies have documented the comparatively high-quality medical care provided by Quebec CLSCs.[32] After assembling the evidence on the cost-effectiveness of nonprofit community health care relative to fee-for-service care, Angus & Manga (1990) observe that they "have not encountered a single study that demonstrates the contrary".

Community health centres highlight the inefficiency of conventional contractual arrangements between government insurers and fee-for-service physicians. The nonprofit model gives rise to its own decision-making biases, but these tend to result in lower enforcement costs and significantly smaller losses. While it is not clear that it could be replicated on a national scale, the community health centre model represents a promising application of the nonprofit organizational alternative.

CANADIAN AIRPORT AUTHORITIES

As part of a massive restructuring of the airport system, the operation of Canada's major airports is being transferred to independent, not-for-profit corporations, designated Canadian Airport Authorities (CAAs). Authorities have been operating airports in Vancouver, Calgary, Edmonton and Montreal since 1992. According to current plans, CAAs will be established at all the country's 26 largest airports, which account for approximately 94 percent of the country's scheduled airline passenger traffic.

As with other nonprofits, CAAs have no shareholders. Accumulated surpluses must be reinvested in the airport. The airports are headed by boards comprised of directors nominated mainly, but not exclusively, by governments and intended to be representative of the community.[33] Aside from its continuing responsibilities for the regulation of air safety, the federal government's relationship to each CAA is that of a landlord. Sixty-year leases are being negotiated, with a rental formula designed to allow the federal government to share in any increase in gross revenue above some base-case forecast.

Through the creation of CAAs, the federal government hopes to: allow airports to better serve community interests; enhance regional economic development potential; and permit the nation's airport system to operate in a more cost efficient and commercial manner.[34] Another important underlying objective is to eliminate the financial burden associated with federal assistance now being provided to the major airports. It is expected that operating subsidies and most federal capital assistance can be phased out within five years.

CAAs represent a unique approach to the operation of airports. The application of the nonprofit form of organization is appealing because there are problems with both public and for-profit provision of airport services. The current restructuring is largely a response to the difficulties experienced by the federal government in operating Canada's major airports, although these inefficiencies may reflect less on public provision *per se* than on some particular features of federal airport policy.[35] For-profit provision would be problematic because of the market power that would be in the hands of private operators – although this would vary between both services and airports. In terms of the services provided to airlines, airports will have greater market power in relation to direct origin and destination traffic,[36] as distinct from connecting traffic. In its dealings with other commercial firms, airports will have their greatest market power where those granted an exclusive concession face limited competition from off-airport facilities. Airports possess a high degree of market power *vis-à-vis* passengers; in setting terminal access or facility charges airports are in the favourable position of selling a service subject to relatively inelastic demand.

Nonprofit provision, however, is accompanied by its own very significant problems. First, there are the usual governance problems arising from the absence of transferable ownership claims in nonprofit organizations. The federal government has attempted to strengthen the accountability of CAAs by imposing various requirements. Perhaps most significant, is the requirement that an independent review of the CAA's management, operation and financial performance be undertaken every five years. Reporting and public disclosure requirements may help check some more significant forms of waste and inefficiency, but they are not a substitute for the disciplinary mechanisms that exist in organizations with transferable ownership claims. Second, under CAA operation, the market power of the major airports remains as a significant concern. While there are no residual claimants to benefit from the exercise of market power, neither are there disciplinary mechanisms to ensure that the resulting revenues are invested efficiently. One might reasonably expect that the availability of significant revenue sources coupled with the interests of local firms in promoting airport development will generate pressures for new investment, including the initiation of projects with relatively low expected rates of return.

A third concern relates to what might be regarded as the social, or non-commercial, role of the CAAs. Investments and other activities that do not satisfy commercial criteria, might be seen to be justified to the extent they help the airport better serve local community interests or enhance the potential for regional economic development. But, to accept this justification we must be prepared to accept a significant delegation of what is essentially public decision-making power to non-elected individuals. Managers and unelected board members are being empowered to tax the users of airports and to decide how the proceeds of those taxes can best be used to serve the interest of the local population.

As with community health centres, the nonprofit form of organization introduces its own decision-making biases. In the case of CAAs, however, these biases give rise to concerns that are at least as significant as those under alternative organizational arrangements. The CAA model is unlikely to lead to behavioural changes that result in clear savings in monitoring and enforcement costs, compared to alternative options. CAAs give rise to concerns about monopolistic pricing similar to those that exist under for-profit operation, but this cost is incurred without the benefits of for-profit governance. CAAs retain a capacity for non-commercial decision-making, but without the procedural controls and accountability structures that exist in the public sector.

UNIVERSITIES AND THE PROBLEMS OF NONPROFIT GOVERNANCE

UNIVERSITIES HIGHLIGHT THE PROBLEMS inherent in establishing an effective governance structure within nonprofits – particularly "complex nonprofits". The difficulties in assessing university performance, and the role and effectiveness of university boards have been a focus of much concern and debate.

Universities are relatively autonomous non-profit organizations, incorporated under provincial jurisdiction, either through a general university act or by an individual charter. A number of theories have been offered to explain the use of the nonprofit form. Both Hansmann (1980) and Fama & Jensen (1983b) emphasize the advantages of nonprofits in securing donations. Hansmann (p. 860) regards alumni donations as an inter-generational transfer that is required because of the inability of students to borrow against their future earnings: They are "... in large part, simply a means by which past generations of students help to finance the education of the present generation of students". McCormick & Meiners (1988) focus on the difficulty of monitoring academic output, and the need for a system in which faculty members can be relied upon to assess their colleagues' research and teaching fairly. This is most likely to be achieved where faculty members are themselves residual claimants who stand to lose personally from a monitoring system that results in a low-quality department.

Different nonprofit models have been employed in an attempt to explain the behaviour of universities. Some depict universities as being akin to public enterprises that pursue managerial goals subject to market and regulatory constraints.[37] From this perspective, performance problems arise because regulators do not possess the information they need to establish a system of direction and control that will achieve their objectives, and university managers are able to use the resulting gaps in the regulatory framework to their own advantage.[38] Public enterprise models do not help us understand how government regulators establish objectives for some activities, such as research and teaching, which are difficult to measure, nor do they shed light on the internal control problems within a university.

Internal control problems are a central focus for Fama & Jensen (1983a), who are interested in understanding the disciplinary mechanisms within a university that compensate for the absence of an outside takeover market. They find the answer in a strong board of trustees, comprised primarily of donors and supported by diffuse decision-making systems within universities. Trustees, who do not have specialized knowledge themselves, can rely on the information produced by the complicated decision hierarchies and mutual monitoring systems within universities.

In a third approach, models of labour-managed co-operatives are used to help explain the behaviour of universities. In a labour-managed firm selling a tradeable output, the emphasis is on maximizing net revenue per employee. Barriers to entry allow the realization of net incomes above the competitive level. In their analysis of universities, James & Neuberger (1981) and James (1990) assume initially that all faculty members have the same objective function. The possibility for faculty to earn rents arises from the lack of market competition and the difficulty of monitoring academic activities, which limits the influence of other stakeholders, including administrators, donors, students and legislators. Rents are seen primarily to take the form of distortions in the output mix of the university. Those activities which academics prefer, such as research and graduate education, are therefore overproduced, relative to what would occur in a competitive, profit-maximizing organization. The university is seen to engage in profitable activities that society is willing to pay for in order that it be able to perform utility-maximizing activities that society will not fully finance directly. Since the utility function of staff may differ between departments, so, too, the mix of outputs (as for example, between teaching and research) may vary from department to department.

While all three models are highly stylized, the concepts derived from the literature on labour co-operatives appear to be most relevant to Canadian universities. Despite their heavy dependence on government financial support, Canadian universities enjoy a high degree of autonomy. They have not had to provide governments with detailed information to support their funding requirements nor have they had to provide an *ex post* justification for their expenditures. Even now, when publicly funded universities in most countries are being confronted with new reporting requirements and controls, Canadian institutions continue to enjoy considerable autonomy.[39] Moreover, as West (1993) points out, this decision-making freedom has not been substantially constrained by competitive pressures.[40]

While the theory of an influential government regulator does not apply very well to Canadian universities, neither does the concept of a strong, independent board. Cameron (1992) has described how the original concept of a bicameral governing structure, which was intended to balance academic independence with external decision control broke down during the sixties. The growth in academic influence at Canadian universities and the erosion of the power of the president and the board of governors continued through the subsequent period of intense collective bargaining. While Canadian academics have been subject to the scrutiny of their colleagues, these mutual monitoring systems have not been subject to the effective independent oversight envisioned by Fama & Jensen and others.

The expectation that faculty governance affects university quality is supported by evidence from the United States gathered by McCormick & Meiners. There have been no comparable Canadian studies, but there are some indications that the output mix at Canadian universities differs from what would be produced if there were strong pressures to satisfy student or societal preferences. The Commission of Inquiry on Canadian University Education (1991, hereafter the Smith Commission), for example, observed that research publications are more important than teaching excellence at Canadian universities. Research and teaching are, to some extent mutually reinforcing, but as the Association of Universities and Colleges of Canada (AUCC) has itself noted in a Task Force report (1992, p. 2), the reward system at Canadian universities is "inappropriately skewed in some instances in favour of research output". At the same time, universities have coped with increased enrolments mainly by expanding class sizes and hiring part-time faculty, including teaching assistants. There has been a reluctance to increase the number of scheduled teaching hours of full-time faculty, although, as the Smith Commission points out (p. 55), "... by letting active researchers teach so little, and putting sessional lecturers in their places, universities are putting at risk ... the quality of university education". The Smith Commission also noted that the practice of assigning the most senior and distinguished members of a department to the teaching of introductory courses, a practice supported by the literature emphasizing the importance of students' first exposure to a subject, had become less prevalent. The Commission attributes this change to the preference of senior professors to teach graduate and higher-level undergraduate courses.

While such findings should be treated cautiously, and with a sensitivity to the significant differences among, as well as within, universities, they are indicative of the general sense of discomfort with the governance of Canadian universities. The latter, in turn, underlies the current search for new mechanisms that will increase the accountability of these important nonprofit institutions.

IMPROVING THE ACCOUNTABILITY OF NONPROFITS

PROPOSALS FOR IMPROVING ACCOUNTABILITY have focused on strengthening competition in markets for nonprofit services, increasing the independence and role of the board of directors, requiring independent management reviews, and imposing more stringent reporting requirements. While there is no obvious solution to the problems of nonprofit governance, some recent initiatives hold promise. Government's role both as a major nonprofit funder and as a major purchaser of nonprofit services, coupled with its responsibility for the legal framework governing the provision of nonprofit services, offers opportunities for promoting better nonprofit governance.

For government-funded services where consumer-information problems are not so serious as to jeopardize the operation of markets, new funding arrangements that strengthen competitive forces may be an attractive option. The efforts being made in the United Kingdom to inject competition into the provision of hospital services bear watching. In Canada, the desire to strengthen competition among universities partly underlies recent proposals for new funding arrangements that would result in students having to bear a larger portion of their schooling costs. The intention is to make students more discriminating "purchasers" and to create a stronger financial incentive for universities to tailor their services to student needs. Expanded public loan programs, and income-contingent loan programs, could help ensure that higher tuition fees do not limit access to higher education. At the same time, separate funding arrangements, which also incorporate competitive incentives, could be introduced to support the universities' research activities.[41]

When using their influence as funders to improve accountability, governments must respect the independence of nonprofits. For universities, as for most other nonprofits, substantial autonomy is necessary for the effective fulfilment of their responsibilities. Governments must also respect the interests of other contributors who donate a significant share of the revenue and are important stakeholders in many types of nonprofits. Other stakeholders may be discouraged from contributing and participating if they perceive that there are efforts under way to transform the nonprofit organization with which they are involved into an instrument of public policy.

While respecting these constraints, governments can use their influence to ensure that nonprofits have an adequate internal system of accountability and control and an adequate reporting system. Like other major contributors, governments must satisfy themselves that the objectives of the nonprofits they are assisting deserve support and that these objectives are being pursued efficiently. Accordingly, each nonprofit should be encouraged to establish a reporting system that clearly identifies objectives and assesses the organization's progress in achieving those objectives.

Admittedly, for some of the services provided by nonprofits, the development of adequate performance measures poses a major challenge. Measures that capture only part of the relevant attributes of a service can be very misleading. They can also send the wrong signals and lead providers to concentrate on the measurable at the expense of the unmeasurable. Nonetheless, progress is being made in developing meaningful performance measures, even for such complex services as post-secondary teaching.[42] Realistically, the construction of performance measures is a long-term process, which will involve ongoing reassessment and refinement.

Along with reforming government's approach to funding nonprofit activities, there is a need to consider how framework policies can be used to encourage an improved system of nonprofit governance. The relevant federal legislation, the *Canada Corporations Act*, Part II (CCA) has not been changed fundamentally since its enactment in 1934. The CCA establishes a less detailed framework of rules than the *Canada Business Corporations Act* (CBCA), which applies to for-profit corporations, and accords greater discretionary power to the Minister of Industry Canada, who must approve all by-laws filed by nonprofit corporations.

From a governance perspective, the lack of any provision in the CCA to identify those to whom the organization is accountable is of particular concern. There is nothing comparable to the provisions in the CBCA, which support owners of for-profit corporations in the exercise of their rights. While the matter of identifying ultimate principles in nonprofit organizations can be complex, reasonable rules can be established to determine who qualifies as a significant stakeholder based on his/her contributions to the organization. A legal regime analogous to that which applies to for-profit corporations, would specify a process for conferring membership status on qualified stakeholders and clarify the rights of members. The legislative changes necessary to implement such reforms deserve consideration. More effective framework law for nonprofit organizations could make a significant contribution to alleviating current governance problems.

CONCLUSIONS

THE GOVERNANCE OF NONPROFITS IS IMPORTANT because nonprofits constitute an important component of the Canadian economy. A large and diverse group of organizations are subject to a nondistribution constraint. By some estimates, the output of charitable organizations (a subset of all nonprofits) in itself accounts for over 10 percent of GDP.

Nonprofits can be an efficient organizational arrangement in certain circumstances – notably where there are significant failures in the operations of private and political markets. In the provision of collective goods, nonprofits may be preferable to governments, because they are better able to respond to the particular needs of various subgroups of the population. At the same time, because they reduce the risk of certain forms of opportunistic behaviour, nonprofits offer advantages over for-profit provision of some market services. In some situations (most notably donative activities) nonprofit provision may be the only reasonable alternative. In most circumstances, however, the desirability of nonprofits depends on the careful balancing of transaction-cost savings in some areas against the increases in enforcement costs in other areas. This examination is somewhat analogous to the assessment firms must make in determining whether they can economize on transaction costs by internalizing certain market activities.

The incentive to improve managerial efficiency is generally weaker in nonprofits than in for-profit organizations. To some extent, these internal governance problems undermine the ability of nonprofits to carry out those activities efficiently that are ill-suited to other types of organizations. These problems tend to be less severe where oversight is provided by an elected board and where a competitive market structure reduces the costs and difficulty of assessing nonprofit performance. Internal governance is less of a concern in mutual nonprofits. It is, however, very much of a concern in commercial and government-funded nonprofits, where the tradeoffs between gains and losses from the use of nonprofits as opposed to other organizational alternatives require careful assessment.

These concepts have been applied to an examination of the roles of nonprofits in two very different areas – health centres and airports. Available evidence suggests that, although community health centres account for a small portion of health services, they have been relatively successful as an organizational innovation. As with most other successful applications of the nonprofit model, gains were achieved because the new arrangement (and the associated change in the nature of physician compensation) resulted in a fundamental change in provider incentives. There has not been sufficient time to evaluate the overall performance of Canadian Airport Authorities, but it is nonetheless difficult to identify the contribution that the nonprofit form can make to the delivery of airport services. There is a need to reconsider whether nonprofit provision can help establish an incentive structure superior to that which could be achieved under for-profit or public operation.

While community health centres and airport authorities offer some lessons on the use of the nonprofit form, universities shed some light on the governance problems in nonprofits, and especially "complex nonprofits". Models comparing universities to labour-managed co-operatives appear to have some relevance to Canadian experience. In universities, as in other nonprofits, there is a need for mechanisms that will improve accountability without jeopardizing the autonomy these organizations need to fulfil their roles. In some circumstances, there may be scope for strengthening competitive forces to make nonprofits more accountable to their clients. Through the reform of corporation law, nonprofits can be made more accountable to important stakeholders. As well, nonprofits should be encouraged to develop a reporting system that demonstrates to stakeholders that they are indeed efficient vehicles for satisfying legitimate societal objectives.

Endnotes

1 Tuckman and Chang (1992) hypothesize that administrators of nonprofits have an incentive to accumulate surpluses because this enhances their operating freedom and it is often, in itself, regarded as a measure of performance. Data tested by the authors lends support to their hypothesis.

2 Estimates of the opportunity cost of time for males and females were taken from Chandler (1993). Gross rather than net hourly earnings were used, since the focus was on the opportunity cost to society, not on the opportunity cost to the individual.

3 For example, Ross (1990) estimates the value of volunteer time at only $13.2 billion in 1990. This was derived by applying an average service-sector wage to volunteer time estimates provided by a 1986/87 Statistics Canada survey.

4 There is less need for nonprofit provision to the extent responsibilities for service provision can be assigned to local governments and individuals can sort themselves into relatively homogeneous communities. In reality, however, most differences in individual values and preferences cut across geographic boundaries.

5 This point is made by Williamson (1983).

6 I distinguish between a "normative" approach, which involves an assessment of the activities undertaken by nonprofits, and a "positive" approach, which is directed at understanding why nonprofits exist. Theories of regulation fall into the latter category, although their findings have normative implications.

7 It differs from the classification criteria in the first section of the study, where nonprofits serving the general public were subdivided according to their major funding source. Nonprofits categorized as "commercial" on the basis of funding are largely involved in the provision of "trust" goods. Nonprofits that rely largely on government funding produce both "trust" goods and "donative" goods. The latter reflects the fact that, in some cases, the government faces contracting problems similar to those of individual donors.

8 Efficient provision requires that clubs be of optimal size. For "impure public goods" that are subject to crowding effects, optimal size occurs where the cost of admitting an additional member equals the average cost of providing the public good. Buchanan (1965) shows that an optimal division of clubs is possible as long as the total number of consumers in the economy is a multiple of the optimal club size.

9 Opera also has rival consumption aspects – notably the seat at a performance. Because opera is excludable (unlike some public goods) and it has both rivalrous (unlike other public goods) and non-rivalrous components, it might be regarded as a "mixed good". The potential role for nonprofits in the provision of mixed goods was initially recognized by Hansmann (1980).

10 The latter is discussed in James & Rose-Ackerman (1986). The objective is to create psychic benefits for donors from which free riders are excluded.

11 The hospital sector is an exception. While the evidence, obtained largely from the United States, does not indicate that privately-owned, for-profit hospitals operate more efficiently than nonprofit hospitals, this can be attributed to the unique incentives in this sector – in particular, to payment systems that have allowed high-cost, for-profit hospitals in the United States to earn healthy profits. See, for example, Stoddart & Labelle (1985).

12 Caswell & Cleverly (1983).

13 Knapp (1989).

14 Greb et al. (1994).

15 Norton (1992).

16 This point is made in Posnett & Sandler (1988).

17 By contrast, nonprofit organizations that serve to facilitate the transfers of a single donor, or a small number of large donors, tend to have broader mandates and allow for a high degree of trustee discretion.

18 Although the importance of outside directors was suggested by Fama & Jensen (1983a), the empirical test was proposed by Williamson (1983).

19 Ben-Ner (1986) develops a model in which high-demand members dominate the organization leading to prices and outputs that do not reflect the interests of the majority of members.

20 This is discussed by Estelle James in her "Comments" in Rose-Ackerman (1986), Chapter 8.

21 The application to day care is discussed in Rose-Ackerman (1983).

22 Olds (1994).

23 For example, Donahue (1989), Vickers & Yarrow (1991), and Borins & Boothman (1985).

24 While hospitals are mainly commercial nonprofits in the United States, Hansmann contends that the usual justification for adopting the nonprofit form for commercial activities does not apply to hospitals. The services hospitals provide are mainly routine (i.e., room and board, laboratory tests, nursing care) and are sold to physicians, not to patients. Hence, the nonprofit form is not needed to provide protection to vulnerable consumers.

The use of the nonprofit form in this area is attributed to historical factors, and to the influence of physicians who have been well-served by the organization of hospital services.

25 Innovative contractual features, however, can have different effects. As we noted in the discussion of "trust goods", one result might be to allay concerns about the risks of contracting with for-profit providers. The development of new contractual features and mechanisms may not necessarily result in a greater reliance on nonprofit provision.

26 Data comes from Rachlis & Kushner (1994).

27 The composition of CLSC boards is prescribed. Each board consists of: five representatives elected by the public in the region served by the CLSC; two public representatives with specialized skills chosen by other public representatives; an elected representative of each of the three staff groups (medical, clinical and clerical); a member of a sponsoring foundation (if one exists); a representative of a related nursing home; and the director, who is a non-voting member.

28 Studies of Quebec physicians confirm that there are significant differences in attitudes and practice styles between CLSC doctors and fee-for-service practitioners. See Pineault et al. (1991).

29 Saskatchewan Department of Health (1983).

30 For example, Evans (1984).

31 Birch et al. (1990)

32 Studies indicate that CLSCs provide better quality care for patients with headaches, more complete childhood immunization, more appropriate cancer screening, and better cancer prevention services. The evidence is reviewed in Angus & Manga (1990) and Rachlis & Kushner (1994).

33 The boards must include at least one representative from the business community, one representative from organized labour, and one representative of consumer interests. To reinforce the CAAs' independence from government, elected officials and government employees are explicitly prohibited from serving as directors.

34 From Government of Canada, "A Future Framework for the Management of Airports in Canada," April 1987.

35 This is discussed in Hirshhorn (1992).

36 Origin and destination traffic is much more important than connecting traffic at major Canadian airports. Data compiled for 1989 showed that even at Pearson, Canada's major hub airport, origin-destination traffic accounted for almost 70 percent of total emplaned-deplaned traffic. By contrast, at Hartsfield Atlanta International Airport, a major American hub, origin-destination traffic was estimated to account for only 30 percent of total traffic. From Hirshhorn (1992)

37 Cave, Dodsworth & Thompson (1992) maintain that the conduct of universities in the United Kingdom is best understood through the application of public enterprise models.

38 Such models are explored in Bos (1988).

39 The autonomy of Canadian universities relative to publicly funded universities in other countries is discussed in Watts (1992).

40 Uniform pricing is cited by West as one symptom of the lack of competitiveness. He observes that a competitive system would be characterized by both fee reductions in response to increased efficiency, and tuition increases where new and expensive courses were introduced to satisfy demands.

41 As noted previously, there are complementarities between research and teaching. This does not preclude the introduction of separate financing arrangements, but it does complicate the problem of distinguishing between research and teaching costs.

42 Efforts to monitor the performance of U.K. universities are described in Davies (1992). Attempts to develop value added measures of educational output, which assess the difference between a student's knowledge and ability on entering and on leaving an institution, are discussed in Cave & Weale (1992).

ACKNOWLEDGEMENTS

THE AUTHOR IS GRATEFUL FOR the helpful comments received from Bruce Chapman, Ron Daniels, Randall Morck and Robert Weist.

BIBLIOGRAPHY

Angus, D.E. and P. Manga. "Co-op/Consumer Sponsored Health Care Delivery Effectiveness." Research study prepared for the Canadian Co-operative Association (August 1990).

Association of Universities and Colleges of Canada Task Force. "Report of the Commission of Inquiry on Canadian University Education." Ottawa (1992).

Ben-Ner, A. "Non-Profit Organizations: Why Do They Exist in Market Economies?" in The Economics of Nonprofit Institutions. Edited by S. Rose-Ackerman. New York: Oxford University Press, 1986.

Bos, D. "Recent Theories in Public Enterprise Economics." European Economic Review, 32 (1988).

Birch, S., J Lomas, M. Rachlis, and J. Abelson. "HSO Performance: A Critical Appraisal of

Current Performance," CHEPA Working Paper 90-1, Centre for Health Economics and Policy Analysis, McMaster University, 1990.

Borins, S.F. and B.E. Boothman. "Crown Corporations and Economic Efficiency," in *Canadian Industrial Policy in Action*. Edited by D. G. McFetridge. Toronto: University of Toronto Press, 1985.

Buchanan, J.M. "An Economic Theory of Clubs," *Economica*, 33 (February 1965).

Cameron, D. M. "Institutional Management: How Should the Governance and Management of Universities In Canada Accommodate Changing Circumstances?" in *Public Purse, Public Purpose: Autonomy and Accountability in the Groves of Academe*. Edited by J. Cutt and R. Dobell. Halifax: Institute for Research on Public Policy, 1992.

Caswell, R. and W. Cleverly. "Cost Analysis of the Ohio Nursing Home Industry." *Health Services Research*, 18 (Fall 1983).

Cave, M., R. Dodsworth and D. Thompson. "Regulatory Reform in Higher Education in the U.K.: Incentives for Efficiency and Product Quality." *Oxford Review of Economic Policy*, 8, 2 (1992).

Cave M. and M. Weale. "The Assessment: Higher Education :The State of Play." *Oxford Review of Economic Policy*, 8 (1992).

Commission of Inquiry on Canadian University Education. *Report*. (Ottawa 1991).

Chandler, W. "The Value of Household Work in Canada." Statistics Canada Cat. No. 13-001, Fourth Quarter 1993.

Davies, K. "Monitoring Performance in U.K. Universities," in *Public Purse, Public Purpose*. Edited by Cutt & Dobell, *op. cit.* 1992.

Donahue, J. D. *The Privatization Decision: Public Ends, Private Means*. New York: Basic Books, 1989.

Douglas, J. *Why Charity?* Beverly Hills, CA.: Sage Publications, 1983.

_____. "Political Theories of Nonprofit Organization," in *The Nonprofit Sector*. Edited by W. W. Powell. New Haven: Yale University Press, 1987.

Evans, R. G. *Strained Mercy: The Economics of Canadian Health Care*. Toronto: Butterworths, 1984.

Fama, E. F. and M. C. Jensen. "Separation of Ownership and Control." *The Journal of Law and Economics*, V. XXVI (June 1983a).

_____. "Agency Problems and Residual Claims." *Journal of Law and Economics*, V. XXVI (June 1983b).

Furubotn, G. F. and S. Pejovich. "Property Rights and Economic Theory: A Survey of Recent Literature." *Journal of Economic Literature*. (December 1972).

Greb, J., L. W. Chambers, A. Gafni, R Goeree and R. Labelle. "Interprovincial Comparisons of Public and Private Sector Long-Term Care Facilities for the Elderly in Canada." *Canadian Public Policy*, XX (1994).

Hansmann, H. "The Role of Nonprofit Enterprise." *Yale Law Journal*, 89 (1980).

Hirshhorn, R. "The Ownership and Organization of Transportation Infrastructure – Roads and Airports," *Research Report 13*, Royal Commission on National Passenger Transportation, 1992.

James, E. "Decision Processes and Priorities in Higher Education," in *The Economics of American Universities*. Edited by S. A. Hoenack and E. L. Collins. Albany, N.Y.: State University of New York Press, 1990.

James, E. and E. Neuberger. "The University Department as a Non-Profit Labour Co-operative." *Public Choice*, 36 (1981).

James, E. and S. Rose-Ackerman. *The Nonprofit Enterprise in Market Economics*. New York: Harwood, 1986.

Knapp, M. "Intersectoral Differences in Cost Effectiveness: Residential Child Care in England and Wales," in *The Nonprofit Sector in International Perspective*. Edited by E. James. New York: Oxford University Press, 1989.

Manitoba Department of Community Services and Corrections. "A Brief Submitted to the Special Committee on Child Care by the Government of Manitoba." Winnipeg, June 1986.

Mark, T. L. "Nonprofit Ownership as a Response to Market Failure in the Provision of Psychiatric Care." Working Paper. Washington: Office of Technology Assessment, 1993.

McCormick R. E. and R. E. Meiner. "University Governance: A Property Rights Perspective." *Journal of Law and Economics*, XXXI (October 1988).

McManus, J. C. "The Costs of Alternative Economic Organizations." *Canadian Journal of Economics*, VIII (August 1975).

Norton, E.C. "Incentive Regulation of Nursing Homes." *Journal of Health Economics*, 11 (1992).

OECD. Managing with Market-Type Mechanisms. Paris: OECD, 1993.

O'Hagan, J. and M. Purdy. "The Theory of Non-Profit Organisations: An Application to a Performing Arts Enterprise." *The Economic and Social Review*, 24 (January 1993).

Olds, K. "Privatizing the Church: Disestablishment in Connecticut and Massachusetts." *Journal of Political Economy*, 102 (1994).

Pineault, R. *et al.* "Characteristics of Physicians Practicing in Alternate Primary Care Settings: A Quebec Study of Local Community Center Physicians." *International Journal of Health*, 21 (1991).

Posnett, J. and T. Sandler. "Transfers, Transaction Costs and Charitable Intermediaries." *International Review of Law and Economics*, 8 (December 1988).

Quarter, J. *Canada's Social Economy*. Toronto: James Lorimer & Company, 1992.

Rachlis, M. and C. Kushner. *Strong Medicine*. Toronto: Harper Collins Publishers Ltd., 1994.

Rose-Ackerman, S. "Unintended Consequences: Regulating the Quality of Subsidized Day Care." *Journal of Policy Analysis and Management*, 3 (Fall 1983).

_____ (ed.). *The Economics of Nonprofit Institutions*. New York: Oxford University Press, 1986.

Ross, D. P. *Economic Dimensions of Volunteer Work in Canada*. Ottawa: Department of Secretary of State, 1990.

Saskatchewan Department of Health. *Community Clinic Study*. Regina: Policy Research and Management Services Branch, 1983.

Seibel, W. "Government-Nonprofit Relationships in a Comparative Perspective: The Cases of France and Germany," in *The Nonprofit Sector in the Global Community*. Edited by K. D. McCarthy, V. A. Hodgkinson, R. D. Sumariwalla and Assoc. San Francisco: Jossey-Bass Publishers, 1992.

Sharpe D. *A Portrait of Canada's Charities*. Toronto: Canadian Centre for Philanthropy, 1994.

Stoddart, G. L. and R. J. Labelle." Privatization in the Canadian Health Care System," prepared for the Minister of National Health and Welfare. Ottawa: Minister of Supply and Services, 1985.

Tuckman H.P. and C.F. Chang. "Nonprofit Equity: A Behavioral Model and Its Policy Implications." *Journal of Policy Analysis and Management*, 11, 1 (1992).

Vickers J. and G. Yarrow. "Economic Perspectives on Privatization." *Journal of Economic Perspectives*, 5, 2 (1991).

Watts, R. "Universities and Public Policy," in *Public Purse, Public Purpose*. Edited by Cutt & Dobell, *op. cit.*, 1992.

Weisbrod, B.A. "Toward A Theory of the Voluntary Nonprofit Sector in a Three-Sector Economy," in *Altruism, Morality and Economic Theory*. Edited by E. Phelps. New York: Russell Sage Foundation, 1975.

_____. *The Nonprofit Economy*. Cambridge, MA: Harvard University Press, 1988.

Weisbrod, B. A. and M. Schlesinger. "Public, Private, Nonprofit Ownership and the Response to Asymmetric Information: The Case of Nursing Homes," in *The Economics of Nonprofit Institutions*. Edited by S. Rose-Ackerman. New York: Oxford University Press, 1986.

West, E. G. "Higher Education and Competitiveness," Government and Competitiveness Discussion Paper 93-26, School of Policy Studies, Queen's University, 1993.

Williamson, O. E. "Organizational Form, Residual Claimants, and Corporate Control." *Journal of Law and Economics*, XXVI (June 1983).

Michael J. Trebilcock
Faculty of Law
University of Toronto

Commentary on Part VI

Corporate Governance and Worker Education: An Alternative View

IN THIS STUDY, ALICE NAKAMURA, JOHN CRAGG AND KATHLEEN SAYERS usefully review the divergent perspectives of employers, workers, and the public at large on issues such as: what aspects of worker learning should be expanded or improved; which workers should have more invested in them; and what are the preferred policy options for encompassing the desired increases and improvements in investments in worker education. Not surprisingly, they conclude that while employers would prefer to have better trained workers available to them, they would also prefer not to be required to absorb the costs of providing the training themselves or to fund training externally through means such as payroll taxes. Conversely, workers in many industries, facing a higher degree of employment insecurity than in the past, would wish to have enhanced job training opportunities provided at the expense of someone other than themselves. As taxpayers, the general public clearly has an interest in ensuring that any publicly financed job-training programs are provided as efficiently as possible. Nakamura *et al.* also accurately identify, at least in the case of more general forms of human capital, a particular form of market failure in the educational and/or training market. Employers as a group face incentives to under-invest in the training of their existing workforces, given the incentives of other employers to hire away workers that they have trained and thereby free-ride on the investment in training made by the initial employers.

I also believe that Nakamura *et al.* are correct in expressing some skepticism about two public policy measures that are commonly advocated for redressing this problem.

The first measure is learning taxes on, or subsidies for, employers. Here, their concern is that it is almost impossible to define what an employer must do either to qualify for exemption from a learning tax or to attract a subsidy, thus engendering significant risks of opportunism on the part of employers and/or significant monitoring costs on the part of public agencies that administer such programs.

The second measure is changes in corporate governance that require worker representation on corporate boards of directors on the premise that this will ensure heightened sensitivity on the part of corporate management to the need to provide existing workers with on-the-job training. The authors' concern here is that representatives of the existing workforce are likely to promote policies that benefit existing company employees at the expense of company growth over time horizons that stretch beyond the working lifetimes of existing employees, and that those policies may indeed reduce future employment levels. Moreover, worker representation on corporate boards has much broader and more controversial implications for corporate performance than on-the-job training and should be evaluated in this broader perspective.[1]

While recognizing the force of her reservations, I am less impressed with the alternative prescriptions offered by Nakamura, Cragg and Sayers. They propose that we get better value for our public education dollars by adopting nation-wide testing of basic learning skills at multiple points in the elementary and secondary learning process, and by extending the information base that this would provide to subsequent employment outcomes associated with alternative learning processes. The authors also propose reducing hiring and other non-wage labour costs of employers, for example, by: instituting an electronic bulletin board or hiring hall for job listings; reducing the scale of payroll taxes such as unemployment insurance contributions which make domestic labour relatively more costly compared with foreign labour or other substitutes such as machines; and encouraging longer employment relationships through arrangements such as short-time employment in industries subject to economic down-turns.

While there may be merit in these proposals in and of themselves, none of them directly addresses the need for adult job training or retraining. In this sense, they largely avoid the issue. In order to confront public policy options more squarely, I believe it is important to develop a sharper focus on the following issues.

First, which groups of workers or prospective workers are most likely to be in need of job training or retraining services? Here it seems to me crucial to disaggregate the potential demanders for job training or retraining services, in part because the appropriate policy responses may well vary substantially from one constituency to the next. There may be employed workers who need skills upgrading either to advance in their present occupation or to avoid redundancy by qualifying for other occupations where the firm or industry in which they are currently employed is contracting. There are also displaced workers who may need skills upgrading in their former occupation; retraining to enter a new occupation; mobility assistance; and/or job search assistance. Finally, there are persons who may be entering the workforce for the first time or re-entering it after a long absence, such as youth, the long-term unemployed, and some women.[2]

Second, as we think about what policy options may be appropriate with respect to each of these constituencies, key issues arise as to the relative emphasis to be placed on: passive income-support programs such as unemployment insurance, which may, incidentally, facilitate job search; programmes that reduce the information costs of job search (such as electronic billboards); subsidized forms of classroom training or retraining; and subsidized forms of on-the-job training. The empirical evidence on the efficacy of these various policy options provides limited grounds for optimism. At least with respect to displaced workers, the comparative empirical evidence appears to suggest that job-search assistance programmes, if properly structured and efficiently administered, have a significant positive impact, while evidence on both classroom training and on-the-job training programmes suggests very limited efficacy.[3] However, the evidence also tentatively suggests that the efficacy of classroom training could be enhanced by matching it to the needs of identified employers and that contracts with training providers should be performance-based. In addition, I would argue for more supply-side competition, in contrast to the existing Canadian practice where the federal government under various job training programmes purchases "seats" in community colleges. At present, this entails a heavily centralized and fallible role in forecasting future labour market needs, and tightly restricted competition in the provision of classroom-training programmes (specifically through the exclusion of private for-profit and other non-profit institutions).[4] In my view, public policy should encourage much more competition in the supply of classroom training, more mixed class-room and on-the-job training programmes (based on the co-op model) and more employers offering mixed formal and on-the-job training programmes to both employees and non-employees. The question then becomes, how is this competitive process to be driven?

I believe that we need to place much more weight on the demand side, and allow workers or potential workers in each of the categories identified above a high degree of freedom of institutional choice, on the premise that different training programmes are likely to emerge, which are specialized to different training needs. It is true, of course, that private markets in many of these training services have already evolved, but we need to know whether they are being optimally demanded. This does not implicate the free-rider/externality problem associated with employer-provided on-the-job training to existing employees, but rather the question of whether workers or potential workers will under-invest in their own on-going training. One argument in support of subsidization has a purely distributional basis and is put forward for much the same reasons that we underwrite or subsidize all or some of the costs of elementary, secondary, and post-secondary education. Another rationale may be that the social costs of subsidizing training are likely to be lower than the social costs of having unemployed workers making claims on other social programmes.

I am at least tentatively persuaded that there is a case for subsidization but, unlike some of the proposals reviewed critically in this study (such as a learning tax on employers or subsidies to employers for on-the-job training), I would strongly prefer to provide the subsidies on the demand side, much like the arguments in support of school voucher programs, on the grounds that demanders will have much stronger incentives to spend these subsidies wisely than governments (or opportunistic employers). I am not clear at this juncture whether demand-side subsidies for job training or retraining might most appropriately take the form of tax deductions, tax credits, vouchers, or income contingent loan programmes. Nevertheless, it seems to me there is considerable promise in exploring the possibilities of a combination of a much more competitive and decentralized supply of job-training and retraining services and subsidized demand, complemented by enhanced access by workers and potential workers to electronic information banks on both the relative efficacy of alternative job training and retraining programmes, and job opportunities (through job search and placement programmes).

While the empirical evidence suggests there is a need for caution both in designing job training policies and in committing large financial resources to them, as well as for moderating excessive optimism in their potential, none of these reservations seems to warrant taking job training and retraining programs off the public policy agenda altogether. Both politically and socially, this is one policy option that we do not have.

ENDNOTES

1 See Robert Howse and Michael Trebilcock, "Protecting the Employment Bargain," *University of Toronto Law Journal*, 43, 1993, p. 751.
2 See Michael Trebilcock and Ronald Daniels, "Choice of Policy Instruments in the Provision of Public Infrastructure," in *Infrastructure and Competitiveness*, edited by Mintz and Preston, Industry Canada and John Deutsch Institute, 1994, pp 416-28.
3 Duane Leigh, *Does Training Work for Displaced Workers?*, Kalamazoo Michigan: W. E. Upjohn Institute, 1990.
4 Trebilcock and Daniels, *op.cit.*

Bruce Chapman
Faculty of Law
University of Toronto

Commentary on Part VI
The Governance of Nonprofits

IN MY COMMENTS, I WANT TO EMPHASIZE Ronald Hirshhorn's characterization
of the non-profit sector as "the third sector" of our economy. It is distinguished from both the pure market, private goods, or "for profit" sector, on the
one hand and from the political, public goods, or "governmental" sector on
the other. To focus my remarks, I concentrate my analysis on the charitable
nonprofits, which comprise 40 percent of the non-profit sector according to
Hirshhorn's own estimates.

Specifically, I want to make two arguments: first, charitable nonprofits
can do some things that would be destabilizing if done in the public sector
and, second, charitable nonprofits can effectively supply some things that
would be subject to an agency cost problem if supplied by for profit firms. For
both arguments, I emphasize supply-side analysis, which is quite different from
the essentially demand-side analysis provided by Hirshhorn, and by the two
theorists on which Hirshhorn's argument most relies – Burton Weisbrod and
Henry Hansmann. I also show that this supply-side analysis has some quite
different and unique policy implications.

POLITICS AND CHARITABLE NONPROFITS

DIFFERENT PEOPLE HAVE QUITE DIFFERENT DEMANDS for different goods. In
competitive markets for private goods, this range of demands is
accommodated when individuals buy different quantities of goods at the
same competitive prices. Indeed, the fact that they buy *different* quantities at
the *same* prices is what allows them to bring their marginal rates of substitution
for the different goods into equality with one another, so that efficient
consumption across individuals is achieved.

In the public sector, where public goods are supplied, and where everyone must consume the same quantity of the public good, variable demand at
equal prices shows itself as a range of political disagreement that must, somehow, be resolved collectively – by majority voting, for example. One method
of reducing the range of political disagreement or conflict, at least in principle,
is to have various individuals pay different prices for the same quantity of public
good. Ideally, it should be possible to accommodate this disagreement perfectly
well, and to achieve efficient consumption of the public goods by employing a
system of price discrimination across individuals with different demands for

the public good. Thus, where in the private-goods market, variable demand is accommodated at the same competitive prices with variable quantities purchased by each individual, in the public goods or political market, this same variable demand is accommodated (and political conflict avoided) when different individuals buy the same quantity of the good at variable prices.

However, in practice, such a scheme of price discrimination for public goods is very difficult to achieve. Individuals would seem to have every incentive to misrepresent their true evaluations of these public goods if they recognize that their high demands will be priced accordingly – that is, those with the highest demands pay the highest prices. Nevertheless, I suggest that, to some extent, this is exactly what nonprofits, and certainly charitable nonprofits, seek to do. The same quantity of public charitable good is provided at variable prices. The high demanders for the public goods in question make higher voluntary contributions to the relevant charitable non-profit, and low demanders make lower such contributions. But each such contribution attracts a tax subsidy because of the favourable tax treatment attached to such contributions, and it is a tax break that tracks the willingness to pay. Thus, there is more of a tax break and, therefore, more of a tax subsidy, the more one is willing to pay. This has the effect of making the scheme of price discrimination more voluntary and, for reasons which turn on the significance of reciprocity for charitable giving, also has the effect of inducing more charitable contributions towards the public good.[1]

Now this may seem to be undramatic and even obvious. Some might even say that the real concern is still whether this scheme of voluntary price discrimination brings us any closer to the optimal supply of the public goods at issue. Thus, the question for most theorists is whether we are closer to that optimum if we begin with voluntary contributions encouraged by a tax subsidy, or whether the optimum is more closely approached by requiring tax contributions sufficient to fund some collectively determined amount of public good.

Nevertheless, I suggest that there is some benefit to charitable nonprofits (however optimal or non-optimal the level of public goods so achieved) just in having political disagreement and conflict (together with all the associated costs of rent-seeking, cycling, and instability) removed from the political arena. Moreover, I also argue that some quite specific policy implications follow from viewing charitable nonprofits in this manner. These implications for the governance of charitable non-profit activities do not follow from the more conventional economic analysis, cited and used by Hirshhorn, which treats nonprofits only as a necessary add-on to the inadequate supply of public goods demanded by the median voter.

While, in the name of greater political stability, a tax subsidy might usefully be provided for individually variable voluntary contributions to some public good (a tax subsidy that will be greater for high demanders than low demanders because of their greater contribution, for example), no such subsidy ought to be provided to such demanders if others in the political jurisdiction viewed the public good in question not as a good at all, but as a "bad". A bad might be defined as something for which demanders would naturally seek compensation (a negative price), not just want to pay a low or zero price, to have it. To do so would be to subsidize and, therefore, to exacerbate political disagreement, not reduce it as intended. Moreover, if compensation were not forthcoming, demanders of such a good (those who actually considered it a bad) would be tempted to organize themselves politically to control this (publicly subsidized) bad. It would be better, therefore, to avoid this problem altogether, or at least its worst manifestations, by restricting charitable status (and the tax advantages that go with it) to those activities or organizations with less politically controversial goals. This is exactly what we observe the law seeking to do.[2]

Furthermore, since the point of these arrangements is to reduce – at least to some degree – the sorts of political disagreement that might be destabilizing in the public sector, it would not be acceptable to have taxed subsidized charitable nonprofits organizing themselves to make policy proposals and to lobby for those proposals in the political arena. If they were to do so, then this too would be grounds for taking away their special charitable status, and the accompanying tax advantage. The law now forbids charities from engaging in political activity. However, policy prescriptions need not always call for reform; there are cases where the policy makers may already have "got it right"!

Generally, I am suggesting that the charitable non-profit sector operates as more than merely an add-on to politics (as for Weisbrod and Hirshhorn, where government *inactivity* is thought to need supplementing by private non-profits). Rather, the charitable non-profit sector can be seen as an important substitute for what, in this alternative view, is an unstable excess of political activity. Hence, this sector should be kept apart from politics in the way that I suggest and that is reflected in the current regulation of charities.

DONOR CONTROL AND PRIVATE MARKET TRANSFERS-IN-KIND

HENRY HANSMANN IS THE SECOND KEY THEORIST on whom Hirshhorn relies for his argument. Both Hansmann and Hirshhorn describe cases of "contract failure" to explain the need for the non-profit sector. The example of sending aid to some distant country illustrates the problem. A for-profit firm could be contracted to deliver some given amount of aid to a distant place, but there would be obvious difficulties in monitoring that the delivery had actually taken place. (This is unlike the case of sending flowers to a friend or relative, for example, where monitoring is achieved when the call of thanks is received.) This problem of contract failure can be controlled to some extent through the use of a non-profit. Because the non-profit has no residual claim above the costs of performance, there is less incentive to chisel on the performance which the purchaser desires. For this reason, those who wish to send foreign aid are more inclined to use a nonprofit firm.

This is essentially demand-side analysis. Donors are said to purchase the relief of other individuals from poverty through a charitable intermediary. The possibility of contract failure arises because of the geographical separation between the donor/purchaser and delivery. Other examples, beyond foreign aid, include nursing homes and day care. In these cases, delivery of the services contracted for are also difficult to monitor because the actual recipients of the services are often too old or too young to make the appropriate assessments.

However, it is difficult to look at the usual list of nonprofits, a list which includes, for example, social service agencies, health service providers, religious organizations, arts and cultural groups, and educational institutions, without thinking that there must be some sort of charitable altruism operating on the supply side as well. These are all public services or, to use an old fashioned term, public "callings", where for-profit motivation seems somehow out of place.

Why "out of place"? Certainly not because "profit" is a nasty word, but rather because the nonprofits, as suppliers of the service, (even commercial nonprofits supported by sales revenues earned in the market) are making transfers of very specific goods to (often) equally specific targeted individuals; that is, they are making so-called "transfers-in-kind". They will therefore want to control both the price at which the good is sold, choosing perhaps something less than the profit-maximizing price, and the quality of the good that is delivered. These concerns, rather than the notion of profit maximizing, provide the motivation for the supply-side decisions of nonprofits.

This interpretation of nonprofits is slightly different from that of Hansmann and Hirshhorn, and provides in turn a slightly different explanation of the non-distribution constraint that characterizes nonprofits, as well as certain restrictions nonprofits require on the transfer of ownership. Now the idea is not so much to reduce risk of "contract failure" for donor/purchasers who are distanced from the delivery of the service, but rather to remove the temptation *amongst supply-side investors*, who might well be on the site, to defect from the "mission" because higher profits might be achieved by doing so. Ideologically motivated supply-side investors do not want their organization to be captured by investors who are more interested in profits than in specific forms of transfers-in-kind. Furthermore, they do not want their ideologically motivated fellow investors to sell out to these profit-oriented investors. Such profit-oriented investors would be likely to appoint managers of the charity who would be interested only in profit. Thus, such investors would remove supply-side temptations by organizing themselves as a non-profit and, further, by restricting the transfer of ownership in their non-profit firm.

The same sort of worries about what might be termed "ideological drift", or drift away from the mission perceived by the original investors, applies even to how the organization, once formed as a non-profit and subject to transfer of ownership restrictions, might be managed thereafter. In this last respect, some specific policy implications, which can only be listed here, follow from the analysis.

First, to control managers' "free cash flow", and the managerial discretion that goes with it,[3] there is good reason to have a regular disbursements obligation of the sort imposed on charities by the *Income Tax Act*.[4] This keeps managers honest by forcing them to come back regularly to their ideologically motivated investors and donors. Second, and this is also related to free cash flow, there should be limits on the investments which charities can make and on the sorts of "unrelated business activities" in which they can engage. Moreover, this last restriction should continue to hold even if management requires that the money so obtained be used for charitable purposes. The idea is not to subsidize just any charitable purpose, but rather to subsidize the one that the original investors chose to promote through their specifically chosen transfers-in-kind.

Even if charities were permitted to earn unrelated business income,[5] it does not follow, because of their charitable status, that they should receive any kind of special tax relief on the earning of this income. Such tax relief may be appropriate for donated income, since donors would not be much encouraged by a tax subsidy on donations if they perceived that the donation was only to be taxed later in the hands of the charity. But it would not be appropriate on income from unrelated business activity since, again, the idea is not to aid all charitable activity (even that chosen by managers of charities), but only those selected by donors and investors. Thus, a tax break on donated income only is needed; anything more is in danger of subsidizing the managers of charities in their "altruistic" use of other people's money.

Finally, nothing in the argument so far requires that income from related business activity be non-taxable. This last recommendation is different from some prevailing views and from current legal practice.[6] Nevertheless, it is a common criticism that the current tax subsidy on related business income operates as an unfair government subsidy favouring nonprofits in their competition with for-profit firms.[7] The analysis presented here would allow this subsidy to be removed although it would not require its removal. The point here is that there can be a charitable transfer-in-kind in selling a good (or providing a certain quality in the good) in a commercial market at *less* than market price. But if that is so, there is no donation in the price that is charged and, therefore, no charity in the income that is received commercially. Therefore, at least on the basis of the argument presented here, there is no need to exempt a charity's related business income from corporate income taxation.

CONCLUSION

THIS COMMENT ADVANCES AN ALTERNATIVE ACCOUNT of the role that is played by the third sector of our economy from that put forward in

Hirshhorn's study. Charitable nonprofits, it is argued, can be used to supply public goods in a way that avoids problematic and destabilizing political conflict that might occur were the goods provided in the public sector. My comments also advance a slightly different analysis of the choice of the non-profit form of organization from that argued by Ron Hirshhorn. The argument presented here is that the non-profit form is an effective device not only for preventing contract failure, but also for donors and investors on the supply side to control the specific nature of the transfers-in-kind that frequently characterize charitable nonprofits. Both of these general arguments are also shown to have a number of specific policy implications for the governance of charitable nonprofits.

ENDNOTES

1 The significance of knowing that by giving, one can require matching contributions from others, say, through a tax subsidy, and that one might give more as a consequence, is highlighted in the literature on reciprocity and in the literature on the "assurance game". On these, see, respectively, Robert Sugden, "Reciprocity: The Supply of Public Goods Through Voluntary Contributions," *Economic Journal*, 94 (1984):772, and Amartya Sen, "Goals, Commitment, and Identity," *Journal of Law, Economics, and Organization*, 1 (1985):341, 350.

2 For example, if an animal rights group were to organize for a complete ban on animal experimentation to the point where certain advances in medicine are jeopardized, we should expect such activity to become very controversial and so attract countervailing attempts at political regulation. On the other hand, a position limited to banning gratuitous cruelty to animals, while not something everyone would want to pay much for, is unlikely to attract the same negative political response and could, there-fore, be deemed charitable, attracting the usual tax subsidies. On these sorts of issues, see *National Anti-Vivisection Society v. Inland Revenue Commissioners* [1948] A.C. 31 (H.L.).

3 See Michael Jensen, "The Agency Costs of Free Cash Flow: Corporate Finance and Takeovers," *American Economic Review*, 76 (1986).

4 *Income Tax Act*, S.C. 1990, c.35, s.149.1(2).

5 Charities can earn unrelated business income through their passive investments in other organizations, which are not themselves charities. It is difficult to see how it could be otherwise; charities are not expected to keep donated income tucked away in mattresses. Needless to say, it is often difficult to distinguish between passive business investments (which are permitted to charities) and an active investment programme in an unrelated

activity (which is not). For litigation on this issue, see *Church of Christ Development Co. Ltd. v. MNR*, [1982] C.T.C. 2467.

6 See *Income Tax Act*, S.C. 1990, c. 35, s.149.

7 For a good discussion of this criticism, which has the effect of sharply limiting its scope, see Susan Rose-Ackerman, "Unfair Competition and Corporate Income Taxation" in *The Frontiers of Non-Profit Institutions*, edited by Susan Rose-Ackerman, Oxford: Oxford University Press, 1986.

Jennifer Arlen
Professor of Law
University of Southern California Law Center

Commentary on Part VI

Rewarding Whistleblowers: The Costs and Benefits of an Incentive-Based Compliance Strategy

THE DANIELS AND HOWSE STUDY, "Rewarding Whistleblowers: The Costs and Benefits of an Incentive-Based Compliance Strategy", is an important contribution to the literature on controlling corporate crime. It is one of the few studies to analyze thoroughly the deterrent effect of offering bounties to employees who provide information of wrongdoing to the government.[1] The authors provide a thoughtful and thorough analysis of the benefits of, and problems associated with, awarding bounties to whistleblowers. They conclude that policy makers should consider making greater use of bounty provisions.

Although the authors' ultimate conclusion that the government should make greater use of bounties is undoubtedly correct, bounty provisions generally should not be enacted unless they are accompanied by a thorough reform of corporate criminal law. Bounty provisions are one of several mechanisms that governments can use to deter corporate crime. Another is to hold corporations criminally liable for crimes committed by managers or employees (agents). This comment shows that the type of corporate liability rule employed has a direct influence on the effectiveness of bounty provisions. Bounty provisions, in turn, alter the effect of the prevailing corporate liability rule. Specifically, if corporations are held absolutely criminally liable, offering bounties to whistleblowers will not necessarily reduce crime. Indeed, introducing bounty awards may actually increase the amount of corporate crime by causing corporations to reduce their own efforts to deter crime. In this situation, bounties should not be employed unless the law governing corporate criminal liability is also reformed.

The effect of absolute corporate criminal liability on bounties is of particular concern because, in both Canada and the United States, corporations generally are held absolutely liable for crimes committed by their managers. In the United States, corporations are held directly or vicariously liable for crimes committed by both managers and other employees within the scope of employment, with some intent to benefit the corporation.[2] In Canada, in cases of crimes requiring *mens rea*, corporations are criminally liable for crimes committed by managers who are a "directing mind" of either the corporation or the area in which the criminal act occurred, provided that the manager was acting within the scope of his authority and to benefit the corporation. In the case of absolute liability regulatory crimes, Canadian corporations also are liable for crimes committed by lower-level employees. This liability generally is subject to a due diligence defense, however, based on corporate monitoring and investigation. This due diligence defense generally does not apply when a manager who is a "directing mind" commits a regulatory crime, however, because the manager's act will be treated as an act of the corporation. The corporation, thus, generally will be unable to show that it exercised due diligence to avoid the crime.[3] Thus, crimes involving "directing mind" managers generally are governed by absolute liability. This legal regime must be changed if bounties are to be applied to such crimes.

A central reason why Canada and the United States hold firms liable is to deter crime. Often corporations can most effectively deter crime by monitoring agents, investigating wrongdoing, and reporting to the government.[4] Certain forms of corporate liability can be used to induce optimal monitoring and reporting. Absolute corporate criminal liability, however, cannot necessarily be used to induce optimal corporate monitoring, investigation and whistle-blowing. Indeed, in some cases, absolute corporate liability may deter firms from engaging in such activities for fear that evidence obtained will be used against them.[5] Introducing bounty provisions in these circumstances may only reduce firms' willingness to monitor by increasing the risk that the information will be used against them. Under an absolute liability regime, therefore, bounties may have the opposite of the desired effect.

This comment has four parts. The first summarizes the argument in favour of bounties: bounties deter crime by increasing the government's access to monitoring information. The second part evaluates whether bounties will indeed increase the amount of monitoring information in a cost-effective manner, focusing on those crimes which expose the firm to absolute criminal liability.[6] The third part argues that the problems with bounties can be reduced (perhaps even eliminated altogether) by changing the corporate liability rules. Alternative corporate liability rules – such as mitigation rules, negligence-based corporate liability or an evidentiary privilege – may be superior to holding corporations absolutely liable for their managers' and employees' crimes, and would greatly increase the effectiveness of bounty provisions.

WHEN SHOULD BOUNTIES BE CONSIDERED?

THE GOVERNMENT SHOULD CONSIDER OFFERING bounties to whistleblowers when the standard mechanisms for deterring corporate wrongdoing – individual liability and corporate liability – are unable to optimally deter crime.[7] To determine when bounties might be justified, we must examine the causes and cures of corporate wrongdoing, taking explicit account of agency costs.

Corporate crimes and torts are not actually committed by corporations themselves. Corporate crimes are committed by the firm's managers and employees acting in their own self interest.[8] In a perfect world, corporate wrongdoing could be optimally deterred by sanctioning the individual wrongdoer, imposing a fine equal to the social cost of the wrong divided by the probability of detection. In this case, neither corporate liability nor bounties would be necessary.[9]

Generally, the government cannot rely solely on agent liability to optimally deter corporate wrongdoing, however, because agents[10] will often be insolvent with respect to the optimal sanction. Agent insolvency is particularly likely to be a problem where the probability of detection is low, since in this case the sanction necessary to deter wrongdoing efficiently is very high.[11] When agents are insolvent, the state cannot rely only on individual criminal liability. To deter wrongdoing, the state must employ other methods to increase the agents' cost of crime or to prevent the agent from committing the crime.[12]

One way to increase an insolvent agent's expected cost of crime is to increase the likelihood that agents will be sanctioned for their crimes (hereafter referred to as the probability of detection). In many cases, the agent's corporate employer is better able than the state to increase the probability of detection. The corporation often is better able to monitor agents and/or investigate wrongdoing to identify the agents responsible for the crime. Both monitoring and investigation expenditures are here referred to as "enforcement expenditures".

The government attempts to induce firms to make enforcement expenditures by holding them liable for agents' wrongdoing.[13] If corporate liability achieves its goal, corporations will monitor their agents in an attempt to reduce expected liability by deterring crime. Corporations will also investigate crimes that do occur in order to sanction the employee privately; if the liability regime is properly designed, corporations will pass on information about criminal wrongdoing to the state which can then sanction agents. When corporate liability regimes succeed in inducing firms to engage in optimal enforcement activities, bounties are unnecessary.[14]

Corporate liability will not necessarily induce firms either to monitor agents optimally or to disclose this information to the state, however. As Howse and Daniels recognize, agency costs may reduce the effectiveness of corporate liability regimes generally. Bounties are one possible solution to this problem. When corporate liability is absolute, however, an additional problem arises which the authors do not address. Bounty provisions not only will not solve this problem, they may exacerbate it.

Two different levels of agency costs may undermine corporate liability regimes. Shareholders (who bear the burden of corporate liability) cannot always induce non-owner managers to monitor optimally and to disclose evidence of wrongdoing. This is a problem both for manager-controlled firms (common in the United States), and for owner-controlled firms, which hire non-owner managers (common in Canada). In addition, agency costs plague managers' efforts to monitor. Information about employee wrongdoing is often held by lower level employees who may have reasons not to disclose it to managers. Bounties may solve these agency cost problems by giving managers and employees a direct financial incentive to collect information about wrongdoing and to disclose it to the state.[15]

Absolute corporate liability suffers from an additional problem, however. Absolute corporate liability may be unable to induce optimal enforcement even in the absence of agency costs. Under a regime of absolute corporate liability, enforcement expenditures have two effects on the firm's expected liability: one is beneficial, the other is not. On the one hand, enforcement expenditures reduce the expected number of crimes by increasing the agents' expected liability. This benefits the firm by reducing its expected liability. On the other hand, any information a corporation obtains about wrongdoing committed by its agents may be used against it if the crime is detected. This increases the firm's expected liability. Under plausible conditions, the expected liability cost of enforcement may exceed the benefits. Specifically, if firm enforcement expenditures increase the firm's expected liability for the crimes that will be committed by more than it reduces its expected liability by deterring crimes, incurring additional enforcement expenditures will reduce profits. The firm will respond to absolute liability by not engaging in additional enforcement. Indeed, introducing absolute corporate liability may actually cause firms to reduce enforcement expenditures below the levels which would prevail if firms were never held liable for agents' crimes. In this situation, corporate liability is said to have "perverse effects."[16] The issue is whether bounties reduce or exacerbate the potentially perverse effects of absolute corporate criminal liability.

PROBLEMS WITH BOUNTIES

BOUNTIES, IT IS ARGUED, CAN IMPROVE on the current regime of corporate liability by increasing the government's access to information about wrongdoing, thereby increasing the probability that wrongdoers will be sanctioned. The question is, will bounties in fact increase the government's access to information about crime, and will they do so at an acceptable social cost? This section argues that under a regime of absolute corporate liability, bounties may not increase the government's access to information; firms may respond to bounties by decreasing enforcement. Moreover, even if bounties do increase information flows, they may do so at excessive cost.

BOUNTIES MAY NOT INCREASE ENFORCEMENT INFORMATION

BOUNTIES WILL INCREASE THE FLOW OF INFORMATION to the government in some, but not all, circumstances. Bounties operate to redress the agency cost problem when owners (or managers) want to deter wrongdoing but are unable to provide their agents with adequate incentives to inform them about wrongdoing. Bounties may not be effective, however, when owners (or managers) do not want such information disclosed because disclosure is, on net, costly to the firm. Disclosure is costly if the benefit of the expected resulting reduction in crimes is less than the cost of the expected resulting increase in the firm's expected liability.[17] Indeed, in this case bounties will reduce the firm's enforcement expenditures only in some circumstances.

To see this, consider the case where, before bounties are imposed, the firm is engaging in an amount of enforcement at which the marginal cost of enforcement equals the marginal benefit (the standard equilibrium condition). Assume that much, but not all, of the information the firm obtains about crimes is disclosed to the state; the firm keeps some information private, sanctioning wrongdoers privately. Assume, as well, that the expected sanctions (government and corporate) are not optimal (i.e., that they are insufficient to deter employees).

In this scenario the state wants to be informed about crimes in order to increase the probability of detection, thereby increasing the expected cost of crimes.[18] Bounties would appear to serve the state's goal of increasing the probability of detection. This is not necessarily the case, however. Bounties will not increase the probability of detection because, in some circumstances, firms will respond to bounties by reducing enforcement expenditures. This reduces the amount of information available to the state. Firms recognize that bounties increase the likelihood that the state will obtain firm enforcement information, thereby increasing the firm's expected liability for any wrongdoing it uncovers. The firm's cost of monitoring its employees thus is higher under bounties than without bounties (which follows because the firm would otherwise have disclosed all the information it obtained to the state). The increase in the cost of enforcement will cause the firm to reduce enforcement expenditures. The firm may even reduce enforcement expenditures so much as to reduce the probability of detection below the pre-bounty level. Bounties thus may reduce the number of crimes which are detected, thereby increasing the amount of crime by reducing the expected cost to agents of wrongdoing.

The potentially perverse effects of bounties can also be demonstrated by a numerical example.[19] Consider a firm that has 15 agents, each of whom has an opportunity to commit a crime. The firm is absolutely liable for its employees' crimes. The fine (F) is $300 per crime. The firm can attempt to reduce crime by monitoring its employees. This increases the cost of crime to the agent by increasing the probability of detection. Assume that the firm will spend either $10 or $20 on monitoring.[20] Without bounties, if the firm spends $10 on monitoring, the probability of detection is 1/30 and 14 employees commit a crime. If the firm spends $20 on monitoring, the probability of detection is 1/15 and only six employees commit a crime. In this case, if the firm spends $10 on monitoring; the firm's expected costs are[21]

$$10 + (14/30) F = 150$$

If it spends \$20 on monitoring, its expected costs fall to

$$20 + (6/15) F = 140$$

Corporate liability thus will induce this firm to spend \$20 on monitoring.

Assume, however, that the socially optimal level of monitoring exceeds \$20, but that the firm will only spend \$20, given existing liability rules.[22] Now assume that the state attempts to increase the amount of monitoring by offering a bounty. Bounties increase the probability of detection: with bounties, the probability of detection is 1/20 if the firm spends \$10 on monitoring and 1/10 if the firm spends \$20. Assume that seven agents commit a crime when the probability of detection is 1/20; four commit a crime when the probability of detection is 1/10. Now, if the firm spends \$10 on monitoring, the its expected costs are

$$10 + (7/20) F = 115$$

Spending \$20 on monitoring increases the firm's expected costs to

$$20 + (4/10)F = 140$$

In this case, regardless of the level of the fine (F), the firm's expected costs are lower if it spends \$10 on monitoring than if it spends \$20 because, when the bounty regime is in place, increasing enforcement increases the firm's expected liability.[23] By increasing the probability of detection, bounties increase the cost of monitoring sufficiently to deter it altogether. Thus, introducing bounties causes the firm to reduce monitoring from \$20 (in the pre-bounty scenario) to \$10. This reduces the overall probability of detection from 1/15 (without bounties) to 1/20 (with bounties), thereby increasing the number of crimes from six to seven. Therefore, in those cases where bounties increase the net cost of monitoring to the firm, introducing bounties may cause firms to reduce enforcement expenditures resulting in increased crime.

In addition, under absolute liability bounty provisions may adversely affect the firm's production methods. In response to bounties, a firm may attempt to reduce information flows within the firm by adversely altering methods of production. For example, a government contractor who is having trouble meeting the government's specifications may respond to bounties by involving fewer workers in manufacturing and production problems. The firm may avoid involving many workers for fear of increasing the likelihood that someone will whistleblow if the firm is unable to fix the problem. The firm may feel compelled to do this even though involving additional expert workers would likely improve the product (and the firm's chances of meeting the specifications).[24]

Finally, absolute liability may increase the cost of using bounties in addition to reducing their effectiveness. Bounties will not induce employees to disclose information to the government if the cost to them of doing so exceeds the benefit. The higher the bounty required to induce disclosure, the higher the cost of bounties to the government. The cost to agents (employees and managers) of revealing information depends on whether the firm is likely to punish them for whistleblowing. This, in turn, depends on whether the firm is injured when information about a crime is disclosed. Under absolute liability, disclosing information about wrongdoing may injure the firm. If the firm is likely to be injured, it will attempt to deter agents from whistleblowing by threatening to sanction them if they do so. Since the firm can affect the agent's life-time earning stream, it can increase significantly the cost of whistleblowing to the agent. This dramatically increases the size of the bounty government must pay.[25] Legal limitations on a firm's ability to fire whistleblowers can reduce, but not eliminate, this problem since the firm can severely sanction its employees without actually firing them. Reducing the cost of bounties, therefore, will require that the government also reduce the cost to firms of informing the government about crimes.

A COSTLY WAY TO PRODUCE INFORMATION

EVEN WHEN BOUNTIES DO INCREASE INFORMATION FLOWS, they may be an expensive way to do so. As suggested above, bounties are likely to be particularly expensive if the firm does not want the information to be produced for fear of the consequences of its release to the government. In this case, bounties may cause the firm to alter its production practices in order to reduce its employees' ability to obtain information about wrongdoing. Also, firms will sanction the agents who do blow the whistle (thereby increasing the amount of the bounty necessary to induce whistleblowing).

Bounties also create other costs, however. Bounties may reduce the amount of internal whistleblowing if the agent's reward for external whistleblowing is higher than the award for internal whistleblowing. This may be inefficient if the corporation can respond more quickly and accurately than the government to allegations of potential wrongdoing. Reducing internal whistleblowing may prolong the duration of corporate wrongdoing and reduce the accuracy of the investigation.[26] In addition, whistleblowers may delay reporting because whistleblowers are not generally entitled to a reward unless the wrongdoer is convicted in court.[27] Thus, external whistleblowers will report wrongdoing later than internal whistleblowers since the evidence necessary to obtain a conviction usually exceeds the evidence sufficient for a firm to determine if wrongdoing has occurred (given the greater information the firm has about the employee). Reporting delays, which also delay private reporting to the firm, are rarely in society's best interests. These delays will increase the social costs of wrongdoing if the firm would have acted to prevent or terminate the wrong had it been notified earlier.[28]

Whether bounties will dissuade agents from reporting crimes depends on several factors. One of them is whether the firm will adequately reward agents for reporting internally. Corporate liability rules affect firms' attitudes towards internal reporting. If firms are absolutely liable for the crimes of their employees, and internally reported information is likely to reach the government (for example, because bounty provisions allow an agent to collect a bounty for reporting to the government), then firms may not reward internal reporting because it increases the probability of detection. Indeed, if subject to absolute liability, profit-maximizing firms may find their best strategy is to deter internal reporting by threatening to sanction whistleblowers. In this case, the combined effect of absolute corporate liability and bounties may be to delay reporting.

Bounties may also increase social costs by inducing excessive monitoring by employees of each other. Under bounty regimes, employees benefit personally from reporting wrongdoing. Yet much of the cost of obtaining this information is borne by the firm. Thus, bounties may result in excessive enforcement because the agents in control of firm enforcement decisions will receive the full benefit of the bounty although they do not bear the full cost of the monitoring.[29]

A PARTIAL SOLUTION: CHANGE THE CORPORATE LIABILITY RULE

THE PREVIOUS SECTION SHOWS THAT BOUNTY PROVISIONS will not be as effective as they might be – and in any event will be more costly – if bounty provisions are simply added to a regime of absolute corporate liability for managers' (or employees') wrongdoing. If bounties are to serve their purpose, substantial reform is necessary. The rules governing corporate liability must be changed so that corporate liability does not deter firms from monitoring their employees and disclosing evidence of wrongdoing to the government. There are several ways to do this. Among the more promising alternatives are mitigation rules (under which the firm's liability is reduced if it engages in efficient enforcement);[30] a negligence-based corporate liability rule (under which the firm is not liable if it engaged in efficient enforcement);[31] and an evidentiary privilege for information the corporation obtains about crimes committed by its agents (under which the information provided by the firm cannot be used against the firm, but can be used against the employee). In theory, each of these alternatives could be designed to eliminate any disincentive to detect or report wrongdoing and to induce efficient enforcement.[32]

Reforming corporate liability so that the firm necessarily benefits from detecting and reporting wrongdoing would dramatically improve the effectiveness of bounties. Such reform would also reduce the need for bounties by increasing firms' incentives to detect and report wrongdoing.

Under an optimal corporate liability rule, firms would not respond to bounty provisions by reducing monitoring because any wrongdoing they detect would not injure them. Similarly, firms would not alter their production processes to reduce the risk of whistleblowing. In addition, firms would have less incentive to punish agents for whistleblowing and, indeed, might even reward them. This, in turn, should increase agents' willingness to report corporate crime (internally and externally), thus increasing the speed of reporting, and reducing the size of the bounty needed to induce optimal whistleblowing.

In addition, certain changes in the rules of corporate liability might reduce the risk of excessive monitoring. For example, both mitigation provisions and negligence-based corporate liability would establish a standard of optimal monitoring. Firms could use that standard to judge the behaviour of their employees: employees who engaged in excessive monitoring could be sanctioned. Such alternative rules would not entirely eliminate excessive monitoring, however. Court standards could well be inaccurate and certain types of excessive monitoring might also be difficult to detect. Nonetheless, changing the corporate liability regime could reduce the problem.

CONCLUSION

HOWSE AND DANIELS' SUGGESTION THAT POLICY MAKERS should make greater use of bounty awards deserves serious attention. In many circumstances, bounties may well be an excellent mechanism by which the government can obtain information about corporate wrongdoing. This analysis suggests, however, that to be successful, bounty provisions cannot simply be added to existing regimes of absolute corporate criminal liability. For bounties to be successful, policy makers in both Canada and the United States must reform the laws governing corporate criminal liability and sanctions. Special consideration should be given to eliminating absolute corporate liability for crimes committed by corporate agents and replacing it with a rule that encourages corporate enforcement expenditures. If corporate liability rules can be thus reformed, a stronger case can probably be made for using bounties to reduce corporate crime. The precise nature of optimal bounty rules, and the precise circumstances under which bounties should be used, however, require further study.[33]

ENDNOTES

1 For an additional discussion of whistleblowing bounties that focuses primarily on government contracting, see William Kovacic, "Whistleblower Bounty Lawsuits As Monitoring Devices in Government Contracting", unpublished manuscript, October 1994.

2 See Jennifer Arlen, "The Potentially Perverse Effects of Corporate Criminal Liability," *Journal of Legal Studies*, 23, 1994, pp. 833, 838-40

(summarizing U.S. law). The statement that corporations are absolutely liable for crimes committed by its managers slightly over-simplifies both U.S. and Canadian law. In the United States, corporations are liable for crimes against others committed by their employees within the scope of their employment. Corporations are liable even if the crime was contrary to express company policy. This liability is very broad and includes crimes committed by nonsupervisory employees. Nevertheless, the legal liability regime is not entirely absolute. The sentencing provisions governing federal crimes provides for fine reduction (mitigation) if the firm has an effective monitoring program. These provisions do not appear to operate effectively in the case of crimes committed by supervisors, however. Under the U.S. Sentencing Guidelines, corporations are presumed *not* to be entitled to mitigation, based on having monitoring programs, if the crime was committed by a manager. Most major corporate crimes, such as securities fraud or antitrust violations, are generally committed by managers. In addition, there is no reason to believe that the amount of mitigation is sufficient to overcome the effects discussed in this commentary. If the mitigation is not optimal, corporate criminal liability can still have the perverse effects discussed below. See Id. at 838-40, 862-65.

3 *Canadian Dredge & Dock Co. Ltd. et. al. v. The Queen*, 19 C.C.C.3d 1 (Canadian Supreme Court 1985); see generally Eric Colvin, *Principles of Criminal Law*, 2nd edition, 1991, pp. 67-68 and 362-63; Bruce Welling, *Corporate Law in Canada: The Governing Principles*, 2nd edition 1991, pp. 152-173. Canada differs from the United States in rejecting corporate vicarious liability for crimes involving a *mens rea* requirement. The firm is liable only if it can be identified with the person with the guilty mind: thus, only if the guilty party was a "directing mind" of the corporation (or of the area in which the guilty act occurred). *Canadian Dredge and Dock Co. Ltd. v. R.*; see generally Colvin, *supra*, at 67; Welling, *supra*, at 152-73. In Canada, this rule results in corporations being held liable for criminal acts of a wide variety of employees. There is no due diligence defense. Welling, *supra*, at 158-60. Moreover, in Canada, as in the United States, a firm is liable for the acts of managers (agents) even if the agent acted contrary to specific or general instructions prohibiting the conduct in question. *Canadian Dredge & Dock Co. Ltd. et. al. v. The Queen.*

4 See, *e.g.*, Arlen, *supra* note 2; Jennifer Arlen & Reinier Kraakman, "Controlling Corporate Misconduct" (unpublished manuscript, 1995); Lewis Kornhauser, "An Economic Analysis of the Choice Between Enterprise and Personal Liability for Accidents", *California Law Review*, 70, 1982, p. 1345; Reinier Kraakman, "Corporate Liability Strategies and the Costs of Legal Controls," *Yale Law Journal*, 93, 1984, p. 857; Alan Sykes, "The Economics of Vicarious Liability," *Yale Law Journal*, 93, 1984, 857.

5 This claim is discussed in detail in Arlen, *supra* note 2.

6 See *supra* note 3 and accompanying text; see also *supra* text accompanying

note 2. This commentary does not consider other possible problems with bounty provisions. Other problems are discussed, however, in Daniels & Howse, this volume, and Kovacic, *supra* note 1.

7 For a more thorough analysis of the relative merits of bounties and other mechanisms for controlling corporate crime, see Arlen & Kraakman, *supra* note 4.

8 A recent empirical analysis of corporate crime confirms the claim that corporate crime is a product of agency costs, not the result of shareholder pressure to commit crime. Cindy R. Alexander & Mark A. Cohen, "Why Do Corporations Become Criminals?" (unpublished manuscript, Dec. 1994).

9 Accordingly, contrary to the Howse and Daniels analysis, optimal deterrence is possible provided that agents are not "judgement-proof"; in this ideal world, the fact that shareholders enjoy limited liability would not impede efforts to optimally deter corporate crime. Shareholder limited liability thus in and of itself does not justify bounties. Corporate, and thus shareholder liability, is relevant only when the state cannot rely on pure agent liability to deter corporate wrongdoing. See, *e.g.*, Arlen, *supra* note 2; Kornhauser, *supra* note 4; Sykes, *supra* note 4.

10 The term "agents" refers to people who work for the firm, including directors, managers and regular employees.

11 The optimal sanction for individual wrongdoers equals H/p, where H is the social cost of harm and p is the probability of detection. This sanction is optimal because it forces the individual wrongdoer to internalize fully the social costs of his crime: the expected fine (pF) equals H. For any given H, the lower the probability of detection, the higher is H/p, and thus the higher the optimal sanction. See Gary Becker, "Crime and Punishment: An Economic Approach", *Journal of Political Economy*, 76, 169, (1968).

12 In some cases, the state can also increase an agent's expected sanction by employing non-monetary sanctions. However, this solution is not always available, nor is it invariably desirable. Concerns about marginal deterrence and "justice" may limit the amount of jail time that can be awarded to less than the amount required to deter the crime; deterring crime by imprisoning criminals also may be more expensive than deterring crime by increasing the probability of detection. See Arlen, *supra* note 2, at 853-84; John C. Coffee, "'No Soul to Damn, No Body to Kick': An Unscandalized Inquiry into the Problem of Corporate Punishment," *Michigan Law Review*, 79, 1981, p. 386, 401; Reinier Kraakman, "The Economic Functions of Corporate Liability," in *Corporate Governance and Directors' Liabilities*, edited by Klaus Hopt and Gunther Teuber, 1985, pp. 178 and 195; see also Daniels & Howse, this volume (noting that the empirical literature suggests that increasing the probability of detection is a better deterrent than it increasing the magnitude of the sanction).

13 See Arlen, *supra* note 2.

14 The effect of vicarious liability on firm enforcement expenditures is analyzed more thoroughly in Arlen, *supra* note 2.

15 In Canada, there is a third possible argument in favour of bounties. In Canada firms are not liable for *mens rea* crimes committed by nonsupervisory employees. See *supra* note 3. Generally, therefore, firms have insufficient incentive to spend resources on enforcement measures designed to deter employees from committing such crimes. Bounties may increase the amount of monitoring for those crimes by inducing employees to monitor each other. Further analysis is required, however, to determine whether bounties would be superior to (or should be introduced in addition to) some form of corporate liability for crimes committed by those employees.

16 Arlen, *supra* note 2. Moreover, even where corporate liability induces firms to monitor employees, it may not induce firms to optimally reveal the information to the state. Arlen & Kraakman, *supra* note 4.

17 For a more detailed discussion of where corporate liability has this effect see Arlen, *supra* note 2.

18 Indeed, if the firm is not doing this, bounties might not be necessary.

19 For a more detailed analysis of this perverse effect of corporate liability see Arlen, *supra* note 2.

20 This example implicitly assumes that the state cannot increase corporate enforcement by increasing the corporate fine. This may be the case either if increasing the fine reduces enforcement, see Arlen *supra* note 2, or if marginal deterrence concerns limit the size of the corporate fine. See *supra* note 12.

21 To simplify the discussion, this analysis assumes that the crime neither benefits nor harms the firm. For a more complete analysis, which recognizes that firms benefit from some crimes and are harmed by others, see Arlen, *supra* note 2.

22 For an example of this see Arlen, *supra* note 2.

23 The firm's liability is 7/20 F if it spends $10 on enforcement and 8/20 F if it spends $20 on enforcement.

24 See Kovacic, *supra* note 1.

25 See Howse and Daniels, this volume.

26 As Howse and Daniels recognize, laws that base the size of the bounty on the magnitude of the harm encourage whistleblowers to delay reporting because greater harms produce larger bounties. Howse and Daniels, this volume; Kovacic, *supra* note 1, at 24-25.

27 Howse and Daniels, this volume.

28 Howse and Daniels recognize this problem but appear to conclude it is not serious. The present analysis suggests that they are correct in some circumstances but probably not in others. The issue is to define the circumstances under which they are correct.

29 See Arlen & Kraakman, *supra* note 4. There are, in addition, other potential problems with bounties. See Howse and Daniels, this volume; Kovacic, *supra* note 1.

30 The mitigation rule discussed in this comment differs from the mitigation provisions governing corporate criminal sanctions currently employed in the United States. Arlen, *supra* note 2, at 840, 862-865.
31 Canada already has a form of negligence-based corporate liability in cases involving corporate liability for regulatory offenses by lower level employees. See *supra* note 3.
32 The precise circumstances where these rules are efficient is discussed in Arlen, *supra* note 2, at 861-866.
33 For additional analysis, see Arlen & Kraakman, *supra* note 4.

BIBLIOGRAPHY

Alexander, Cindy R. & Mark A. Cohen. "Why Do Corporations Become Criminals?" (Unpublished Manuscript, December 1994).
Arlen, Jennifer. "The Potentially Perverse Effects of Corporate Criminal Liability." *Journal of Legal Studies*, 23 (1994):833.
Arlen, Jennifer & Reinier Kraakman. "Controlling Corporate Misconduct." (Unpublished Draft, 1995).
Coffee, John C. "'No Soul to Damn, No Body to Kick': An Unscandalized Inquiry into the Problem of Corporate Punishment." *Michigan Law Review*, 79 (1981):386, 401.
Colvin, Eric. *Principles of Criminal Law.* 2nd Ed. 1991, pp. 67-8, 362-63.
Karpoff, John & John Lott, Jr. "The Reputational Penalties Firms Bear From Committing Criminal Fraud." *Journal of Law and Economics*, 36 (1993):757.
Kraakman, Reinier. "Corporate Liability Strategies and the Costs of Legal Controls." *Yale Law Journal*, 93 (1984):857.
Kornhauser, Lewis. "An Economic Analysis of the Choice Between Enterprise and Personal Liability for Accidents." *California Law Review*, 70 (1982):1345.
Kovacic, William. "Whistleblower Bounty Lawsuits as Monitoring Devices in Government Contracting." (Unpublished Manuscript, October 1994).
Sykes, Alan. "The Economics of Vicarious Liability." *Yale Law Journal*, 93 (1984):857.
Welling, Bruce. *Corporate Law in Canada: The Governing Principles.* Toronto: Butterworths, 2nd ed. 1991.

Roger Heath
Industrial Innovation Division, Industry and Science Policy Branch
Industry Canada

Commentary on Part VI

Patient Capital? R&D Investment in Canada: An Interim Report

GIAMMARINO MAKES SEVERAL IMPORTANT POINTS that are not sufficiently acknowledged by those of us who study innovation financing. To demonstrate this, my comments on "Patient Capital" are grounded in my knowledge of innovation policy. They attempt to show how this paper, coming from a different stream of the literature, is important to innovation study.

One must first address the distinction between research and development (R&D) and innovation. Giammarino's strict use of "R&D" is right in that most quantitative work centres on R&D investment only because the statistics on innovation investment are inadequate. I think in terms of innovation, because R&D is only a (small) part of the process whereby firms move innovation into the market – the process that drives long-run growth. While there are efforts to address the gap in innovation data, at present, innovation analysis tends to treat R&D as a marker for innovation activity because the presence of R&D always indicates some innovation. This is unsatisfactory in many ways: R&D is not always part of innovation and, when present, the proportions may vary, haphazardly or systematically by size of firm, sector, or other factors. Despite its immeasurability, it is nevertheless fruitful to use the term innovation whenever possible, since it is more central to the larger issues than R&D.

Innovation financing presents a number of difficulties. The literature identifies at least five special characteristics:

- Asymmetric information – the borrower invariably has a more detailed technical knowledge than potential funders. Thus, funders tend to impose uncertainty premiums that may only be acceptable to high-risk (as assessed by borrowers) ventures. In true Akerlof fashion, this winnowing process may generate instability because different lending pools will be crowded out by the poorest risks.[1]

- Uncertainty – innovation commonly has uninsurable, Knight-type uncertainty because, by its very nature, the new cannot be known.[2]

- Deferred pay-off – initial investments occur long before there is any possibility of reaping the rewards of an innovation. In fact, as the investment proceeds there are multiple decision points when a project may be realigned or even eliminated with no further cost incurred. As a result, innovation investments require an unusual degree of monitoring throughout their long life.[3]

- Innovation is largely intangible – this makes it difficult for potential funders to review the "numbers" or take comfort from residual ownership in the case of bankruptcy.

- Innovation investment commonly surges – cash requirements for innovation are generally not even (uneven) over the life of a project. Costs may, for instance, be particularly high when going to market and a sales/service system must be built up. Surges complicate relations with funders.[4]

These characteristics have direct effects on innovation funding. Consider two kinds of potential funders: a patient and involved funder, who is prepared to follow developments and wishes to share in the profits, *versus* a contract funder who will make little effort to monitor an investment or loan after an initial selection. Loan contracts are largely irrelevant to innovation funding – uncertainty, the lack of detailed knowledge, the lack of collateral, and the deferred pay-off. All drive lenders to impose such a heavy risk premium on their loan that borrowers go elsewhere. Similarly, normal stock market investors who manage their portfolios based on a standard set of financial ratios cannot address the twists and turns of innovation investment, particularly the surge in financial need as the innovation approaches the market. Consequently, a patient and involved investor minimizes information asymmetries by following developments and offsets the inherent risk through ownership of the windfall gains that successful innovation investment engenders.

Partly as a result of this pattern, much of the literature on innovation funding, and most policy discussion in this area, focus on developing patient involved funders. This idea underlies discussion of *keiretsus*, merchant banks, venture capital firms, angels, etc. Giammarino's paper is not in this tradition. The unstated assumption behind his study is that the bulk of R&D (note my switch) takes place in medium-to-large firms and is financed internally. For instance, in 1991 about 70 percent of the R&D tax claims, by value, were from large firms. The top 50 performers account for more than half of business-funded R&D. Even medium-sized companies finance most of their R&D out of retained earnings. Thus, Giammarino's paper focuses on where most of the action is taking place.

Giammarino's conclusions are important to innovation funding in Canada. First, he finds that the stock market does pay an innovation premium for innovative industries – individual firms in innovative industries are valued in a way that reflects their competitive need to invest in R&D. However, the market may not reward higher-than-average innovation, because innovative firms in traditional industries receive little or no premium. This conclusion is "partial good news". It challenges policy makers to improve the ability of the market to identify the merit of individual innovating firms. This is particularly important since so many of Canada's most important sectors are not commonly considered to be innovation-led. Second, he finds that takeovers do not significantly diminish R&D investment – not because the associated increase in debt does not reduce R&D somewhat, but because firms in R&D-intensive industries are seldom subject to takeover. Finally, he finds that the internal valuation methods for R&D in Canadian companies are considerably weaker than methods commonly employed in the United States. They particularly do not recognize the repetitive and tentative nature of R&D investment costs, so that costs are invariably overemphasized. Canadian financial-planning techniques are therefore strongly biased against R&D and innovation.

Giammarino takes innovation policy in an important, but relatively neglected direction. Instead of focusing on the tantalizing search for a patient and involved funder, his paper raises two important policy issues where the bulk of the action is now taking place. First, since most innovation investment is self-financed, can the country's extensive innovation advice networks, or other policy levers, promote better internal valuation techniques for innovative expenditures within Canadian companies? This is critical since so much innovation is self-funded. Second, is there any way to heighten the market's inadequate valuation of better-than-average innovators? Considerable research indicates that innovative firms are unusually profitable. If the market does not reflect this additional value, then it suggests some kind of information failure that ought to be corrected. If these two issues were effectively addressed to any significant degree, the effects on growth and competitiveness would be significant.

ENDNOTES

1 Schaller, Huntley, Asymetric Information, Liquidity Constraints, and Canadian Investment," *Canadian Journal of Economics*, August 1993, pp. 552-74.

2 Lipsey, Richard G. & Cliff Bekar, "A Structuralist View of Technical Change and Economic Growth," CIAR Program in Economic Growth and Policy, Working Paper No. 45, March 1995.

3 *Ibid.*

4 OECD, "National Systems for Financing Innovation," Working Group on Innovation and Technology, 1994.

Jean-Claude Delorme
Chairman of the Board and CEO¹
Caisse de dépôt et placement du Québec

19

Corporate Governance in the Year 2000

A Speech given at the Industry Canada Conference on
Corporate Decision-Making in Canada

T HE THEME OF YOUR CONFERENCE IS CORPORATE DECISION-MAKING. It is my
intention to approach it from the standpoint of corporate governance.
Indeed, in my view, corporate governance and corporate decision-making are
very much inter-related.

Corporate governance has been uppermost in the minds of business
executives, investors and academics in recent years. The issue has been debated
at length and significant progress has been made. More progress will no doubt
be realized in the foreseeable future. It is in that perspective that I invite you
to join me in attempting an exercise in futuristic projection regarding the
principles of corporate governance in, say, the year 2000. Will the questions
we are asking today still be at the top of the agenda then? Will experience
validate the expected effectiveness of the principles we now consider relevant?
Will the 14 principles put forward by the Toronto Stock Exchange in the
report it has just adopted, and which will take effect on July 1, 1995, still be
part of corporate culture? We should remember that Peter Dey, the Chairman
of the TSE Committee, has already said that more than half of all Canadian
companies do not abide by any of the 14 rules adopted by the Task Force.

THE GROWING POWER OF INSTITUTIONAL INVESTORS

M Y FIRST POINT IS TO HIGHLIGHT the fact that one factor we will need to
take into account in the future evolution of corporate governance is the
growing power of institutional investors. By institutional investors, I mean
pension funds, mutual funds and insurance companies. The most recent
statistical analyses show that the presence of institutional investors is growing
strongly in almost every industrialized country.

In the United States, assets under management by institutional investors
represented $6,500 billion in 1990, or more than 20 percent of all U.S. financial
assets. Today, these investors are very active in the stock market and they control

about 50 percent of the price/earnings ratio of the top 1,000 American corporations. Fifteen years ago, that figure was barely 30 percent. For example, institutional investors recently held over 50 percent of the shares of companies like IBM, General Electric, Philip Morris, Bristol Myers, Coca Cola and many others.

In Canada, there has also been a very sharp rise in the activities of institutional investors. Pension funds have grown by 16 percent annually over the past 13 years and now account for $290 billion in total assets. The growth of mutual funds has been even stronger: a 30 percent annual increase over the past 12 years. Assets held by mutual funds now total $115 billion, while insurance companies hold about $125 billion in assets. Overall, it is therefore possible to speak of an industry that manages $530 billion in total assets, almost the equivalent of the Canadian federal public debt, or over $18,000 per capita! In Canada, institutional investors trade over two-thirds of the shares listed on the Toronto Stock Exchange.

With its $47 billion in assets, including $12 billion invested in Canadian equities, the Caisse de dépôt et placement du Québec is the number one stock market investor and the leading manager of public funds in Canada. We hold shares in over 250 Canadian companies and our equity portfolio accounts for approximately 4 percent of the securities traded on the Toronto Stock Exchange.

In short, institutional investors represent a growing force. They can and, in my view, will have a significant impact on corporate governance and the development of investment practices.

What Principles of Corporate Governance will Apply in the Year 2000?

LET US NOW RETURN TO MY EXERCISE IN ECONOMIC FICTION or futurology. In that perspective, let us see how and to what extent models of corporate governance can be expected to evolve by the year 2000. Will the independence of the majority of board members still be considered an essential factor? Will we still consider it necessary to separate the role of Chairman of the Board from that of Chief Executive Officer? What size of corporate boards will be considered appropriate? How will relations evolve between corporate boards and corporate management?

I think you will agree that the first factor to consider when discussing corporate governance is its capacity to increase shareholder value and corporate profitability. I submit that this factor, currently of paramount interest, will be just as important in the year 2000 as it is now. It remains to be seen, however, whether all the principles that we apparently recognize now as helping to increase the value of corporate equity will still be perceived in the same way in the year 2000.

The Toronto Stock Exchange Committee report proposed guidelines for efficient corporate governance. That report specifies that the main responsibility of the Board of Directors is to supervise and control the company's activities. More precisely, the report goes on, the Board should ensure the adoption of a strategic planning process and communications policy. It should also ensure the integrity of the company's internal information and management system. It should also seek to ensure an orderly succession of senior executives by selecting, training and supervising senior executives. Finally, it should identify the risks related to the company's activities, as well as new types of financial risks, including those arising from the use of derivatives, to cite only one example, which has generated a lot of noise in recent years.

The fundamental responsibilities of board members should not be expected to change in the years ahead. With global markets, increased competition and economic interdependence, the duties and workload of board members will not diminish. Quite the contrary.

A Brief Analysis of Experience with Corporate Governance

THE QUESTION CAN BE ASKED AS TO WHETHER corporate governance principles will succeed in maintaining and fostering a harmonious balance between executive management power and board authority. American specialists, including Michael Useem in his book, *Executive Defense*, published in 1993, have studied how models of corporate governance have evolved over time. They have also observed that top executives have almost always succeeded in retaining effective control over the companies they headed. This analysis probably reflects the prevailing situation in the United States where three out of four companies are widely held. In Canada, the proportions are reversed and only one out of four companies falls into the category of widely held companies.

Nevertheless, we must also acknowledge that active and effective participation by boards is not necessarily part of the traditional corporate culture. Not so long ago, and still today, (although less often) boards were expected to be no more than supportive of management rather than proactive. Quite often, they were satisfied to ratify the recommendations of upper management without asking challenging questions or criticizing the way things were done. Fortunately, things are evolving and as the saying goes: "Every cloud has a silver lining".

Indeed, over the past ten or 15 years, gigantic financial disasters have thrown companies into turmoil. Corporations once considered invincible have seen their market share and profitability shrink dramatically. There has been an unprecedented wave of takeover bids and these events, in turn, have triggered a process of evolution. They have made shareholders more vigilant and corporate executives more receptive to corporate governance matters.

These events caused shareholders to react, including a number of institutional investors like CalPERS of California, which certainly can still be regarded as a pioneer in corporate democracy. Such institutional investors did not shrink from administering shock treatment to certain companies, getting things moving to obtain adoption of the increasingly recognized and accepted principles of corporate governance. One may wonder why all institutional investors have not been as active as CalPERS. This theme, I believe, was discussed today or will be discussed tomorrow.

Overall, therefore, shareholders (particularly institutional shareholders) have become much more attentive to the quality of management without, however, closing their eyes to quantitative results. In specific cases, institutional investor activism has generated concrete spinoffs. For example, a study by the Boston firm New Generation Research, cited in a recent issue of *Pension and Investment*, revealed that, in seven out of nine cases analyzed, the changes resulting from pressure applied by institutional investors to correct faulty management led to an increase in price per share, and thus in the company's value. Among the cases studies, we should mention those of Allied Signal, American Express, GM, IBM and Kodak.

In Canada, everything happened rather more gradually because the circumstances and the corporate ownership structure were different. In fact, everything happened in a typically Canadian way. We were able to draw some valuable lessons from the American experience, which was developing before our very eyes, and institutional investors did not hurl thunderbolts at our companies. Adjustments were made and actions were taken in a more serene climate, especially at a time when corporate management was much more receptive to the idea of complying with the principles of corporate governance.

THE ADAPTABILITY OF COMPANIES AND THEIR OFFICERS

ON THE WHOLE, AS I MENTIONED EARLIER, clear progress has been made. Furthermore, and I think this is an important point, management's capacity to adapt to the requirements of the firm's environment – regardless of whether those requirements are imposed by lawmakers or institutional investors – remains notable. Likewise, in my view, principles of corporate governance should be capable of adaptation with time and with the benefit of experience.

One question that we are likely to address in this context is whether the principles of corporate governance should apply uniformly to all companies. I personally believe they should not. In my view, they should display flexibility and adapt to the corporate ownership structure. In general, these principles have been defined with companies of a certain size in mind. For smaller companies listed on stock exchanges, particularly those in which the founding entrepreneur is still a significant shareholder, there is genuine risk that corporate governance will remain a matter of theoretical importance. This pitfall must be avoided – and it can be avoided – provided there is a way to introduce a reasonable measure of flexibility into the corporate governance rules for the purpose of recognizing the positive characteristics of such companies. In the case of an entrepreneurial company, management often devotes major effort and capital to the business, and its growth is often linked to the leadership qualities of the founder. Such effort, investment and growth are very much influenced by his or her interest, as a significant shareholder, in the success of the company. Corporate governance should take this into account, as it is likely that there will be many more entrepreneurial companies in the new economy.

In the case of a holding company, the minority shareholders' interests must somehow be taken into account so that the interests of all shareholders are adequately balanced. It is with that in mind we at the Caisse thought it absolutely essential to establish the principle that the make-up of the board of directors should reflect the equity capital structure.

Finally, in a widely held company, executives may tend to take up a lot of space, as you know. To keep this from leading to abuses, the Board of Directors must see its role as that of a counterweight to management, again in the interests of all shareholders.

Another issue, which may need to be revisited, is that of the size of boards. A recent survey of 100 major American corporations by the firm Spencer Stuart has revealed that the size of corporate boards is shrinking (to an average size of 13 members, compared to 15 a few years ago) and that these now include more independent directors (a four-to-one ratio). However, the same study concludes that boards meet less often than before and that their committees are gaining importance. Therefore, is real power likely to become concentrated in the hands of a few individuals or a few key committees, of which only a select group of board members will be a part? Without being able to give a categorical answer to this question, it seems to be important enough to merit considerable vigilance on our part, otherwise the objective of corporate governance, which is to enhance corporate democracy, could somehow be undermined.

Another subject of interest is the anticipated growth in mutual funds as individuals choose to be more self-reliant in planning for their own retirement. How active can mutual funds be expected to be in corporate governance matters? Let us not forget that according to forecasts, one out of four workers will be self-employed in the year 2000. Should we expect, therefore, that mutual funds and, by the same token, insurance companies will have a higher profile and display more interest in corporate governance? If they have expressed their views up to now, this probably happened in the corridors of power more often than in public forums. Will things change in the future? It is no doubt conceivable that they will, but this will depend effectively not only on the mutual funds managers and insurance company managers but also on the support they will get from their own clientele, which in turn will depend on the perceived capability of corporate governance principles and practices to enhance corporate profitability and shareholder value over time. Hence, it is necessary to protect the credibility of corporate governance and its relevance in terms of corporate performance.

INFORMATION: WHAT PEOPLE DEMAND AND WHAT THEY USE

MOVING ON TO ANOTHER ASPECT OF THE ISSUE, I believe it will be necessary to focus more attention, not only on the role of boards, but also on the tools they require to perform their duties. Indeed, a great deal of attention has so far been paid to the characteristics of the boards of directors such as their independence, the nomination process, their size, etc. These are no doubt essential characteristics. However, if the boards are to provide effective oversight of management, it will become increasingly important for firms to have clearly defined corporate objectives, supported by an effective management information system.

In the year 2000 we will indeed be living in an information-based economy, in which knowledge will no doubt provide access to a great deal of power. If we took a survey of board members now, I think we would learn that they want more of both factual and strategic information, that they require ever more up-to-date management monitoring tools, and that they will be demanding more participation in the preparation of corporate strategic decisions. In my view, this would be the response from most board members and it would be in line with corporate governance theory.

In practice, however, the questions to be asked are: how are boards using management information, to what extent are boards effective in specifying the information they need, and how do they manage to perform their role in the development of corporate strategic directions? Quite often, interventions by board members are still timid and focus more naturally on daily operational questions rather than on major strategic orientations. Is this due to a lack of interest or preparation? Is it out of fear of committing an error? Should one blame corporate management or the Chairman of the Board for failing to motivate the troops or manage the board dynamics? Is it due to a lack of training on the part of less experienced board members? Regardless of the reasons, there is here a malaise that hampers the development of sound corporate governance or the application in practice of the corporate governance theory. If this malaise is not dispelled, corporate governance will not result in better management information and will never have the desired concrete effect of surrounding corporate management with directors capable of feeding the decision-making process, especially the strategic direction-setting process. In short, it is the very credibility of corporate governance which, in my opinion, is at stake in the sense that it runs the risk of becoming obsolete unless it is seen as a positive factor in enhancing shareholders' interests.

I think that an efficient management information system must be articulated around strategic objectives and key corporate success factors. This requires major inputs from management, significant time, effort and dedication on the part of directors and a constructive ongoing dialogue between the two. Being at the core of corporate governance, it is essential. This system should also allow board members to be aware of and to measure in a timely manner the real risks to which the company is exposed. This appears essential if we want the board members to be true participants in the company's strategic orientations. It means, therefore, that corporations must move forward from corporate governance theory to corporate governance practice.

By performing its duties correctly, a board can hope to initiate a constructive dialogue with corporate management and bring it, in a timely manner, to correct certain situations or make the necessary changes in direction to ensure long-term growth. It is, therefore, not enough for a board to be independent, of the right size, to be chosen by an external committee and to have a chairman who is not also its CEO. It must also play its role and carry out the supervisory and control tasks I discussed earlier. I therefore suggest that greater attention be paid to the role of the boards and to the tools they require, including, to the extent necessary of course, training programs for those directors who may not be as familiar as they should be with the corporate decision-making process or with the complexities of the business of the company of which they are directors.

INTEREST GROUPS AND CORPORATE GOVERNANCE

ONE CANNOT SPEAK OF THE YEAR 2000 IN THE CONTEXT of corporate governance without also evoking the emergence of a new force, which will influence the models of corporate governance we have developed so far. By this I mean increasingly powerful and well-organized interest groups. The progress and spread of technology – there is now a computer in one out of every three houses – as well as the increase in the education of the general public will, in my view, foster a more active role for interest groups, from youth organizations to golden-age groups, including pacifists, ecologists and supporters of a plethora of socio-economic issues. All of these groups will try to make their voices heard. Better equipped than ever before, the advocates of these various positions can be expected to use corporate channels to advance the causes they defend. This will call for corporations (and, specifically, corporate management) to be particularly sensitive to these trends. We should expect a resurgence of interventions on a wider range of themes at general meetings. Officers will have to learn how to deal with these dynamics, regardless of whether they feel at ease with this kind of debate. Institutional investors – and their depositors and beneficiaries to whom they are accountable – will also be influenced by the opinions of these groups. Investment projects could be delayed or simply abandoned because of pressures by interest groups.

Companies therefore will have to consider not only the interests of their shareholders, but also those of such very heterogeneous groups and attempt to balance them with legitimate corporate interests. The success of business corporations will depend increasingly on their ability to arbitrate among this wide variety of sometimes divergent interests. The search for a long-term balance between the expectations of shareholders, workers and interest groups appears to be a priority.

Until now, to my knowledge, relatively little attention has been paid to interest groups. The Dey Report, otherwise a very valuable document, barely scratches the surface of this subject. If this trend solidifies, and it is my opinion that it will, it certainly deserves more immediate attention.

CONCLUSIONS

IN SHORT, I BELIEVE THAT CORPORATE GOVERNANCE, as currently perceived, will have to go through not only evolutionary changes over the next few years, but also through significant refinements in order to remain relevant. While contributions to the issue of corporate governance have so far been worthwhile, we must acknowledge that some principles, which we consider to be absolutely unchallengeable at this time, could prove to be less relevant in the future and, more importantly, may not survive analyses once more experience has been accumulated by companies, investors, academics and any other individuals interested in the question. Conversely, principles as yet unknown may well arise as new priorities and models of corporate governance evolve.

Of all the corporate governance questions that might be raised in the next five years, the most fundamental appears to be the following: will it be possible, in the year 2000, to demonstrate that a corporate governance policy is effectively contributing to a company's performance and to shareholder value? Furthermore, can we expect investors to be more willing to take a longer-term view of corporate profitability so that issues coming under the wider umbrella of corporate governance can be accommodated? For the time being, we cannot establish a cause-and-effect relationship between corporate governance and corporate performance. As long as we do not show that a relationship exists between the two, the principles of corporate governance, in the best of cases, will be the object of polite attention or, perhaps more often, the object of generalized skepticism.

Indeed, getting a company to adopt and apply a corporate governance policy is a good thing. Ensuring that the company improves its performance through such policies is even better. Indeed, the key ingredient of a corporate governance policy should be its ability to sustain and enhance corporate performance. Therefore, if corporate performance is the objective, and given that the corporate world will continue to evolve rapidly in the foreseeable future, I want to underscore the need for systematic research in the coming years to determine the real effectiveness of corporate governance principles with regard to corporate dynamism and growth. More specifically, I wish to address a special invitation to the academic community to initiate research projects along those lines and to work with the business and institutional investor communities so that each can benefit from the views and experience of the other. This, in my view, will be the most productive way to ensure that corporate governance remains relevant and focused on its fundamental objective while at the same time allowing it to evolve with time and with the benefit of experience.

To conclude and, in a way, to highlight what I believe should characterize corporate governance practices when we look at them again in the year 2000, allow me to add two final points. First, if enhanced corporate performance is to remain the object of corporate governance, as it must, it is essential that corporate performance be seen in the broader perspective of the corporation's longer-term interests. Shareholders and directors, as well as corporate executives, must look beyond the next quarter or next year's financial results; otherwise, corporate governance will have generated nothing but a wide misunderstanding. Secondly, corporate governance must no doubt be focused on the role of the boards of directors. Nonetheless, corporate performance also requires executive leadership and management efficiency. Therefore, corporate governance cannot be seen as a substitute for qualified, efficient and enlightened management executives. Sound corporate governance must generate a co-operative partnership spirit between executives, boards and investors.

ENDNOTE

1 Jean-Claude Delorme joined the Caisse de dépôt et placement du Québec as Chairman and Chief Executive Officer in July 1990. He resigned from this position on March 30, 1995.

Ronald J. Daniels   &   Randall Morck
Dean of Law   Faculty of Business
University of Toronto   University of Alberta

20

Canadian Corporate Governance: Policy Options

INTRODUCTION

PEOPLE WITH MONEY OFTEN LACK GOOD BUSINESS IDEAS, and people with good business ideas often lack money. Financial markets and institutions bring these people together; they allow the people with money to invest in companies whose managers need funds to expand or to finance new projects. The purpose of corporate governance law is to keep the people who are running the companies from wasting or stealing investors' money.

It is difficult to overstate the importance of sound corporate governance rules. They are the basis of investor trust. When investors trust corporate managers, capital is readily available; when investor trust breaks down, the resulting spillover of anxiety affects everyone, and even well-run companies may have difficulty raising external funds. Pagano, Panetta & Zingales (1994) describe the extraordinary difficulties Italian firms have raising external capital, and attribute these difficulties to governance problems. Shleifer & Vishny (1995) point to even more extreme problems in post-socialist economies.

Canada's corporate governance problems are benign compared to those of Italy and Russia, but Canadian investors, too, need assurance that their money will not be stolen or wasted. Investors who fear such things demand high returns on whatever stock they do buy; markets provide those returns by allowing investors to buy at low prices. This is evident in Italy and other countries where average investors have learned to expect poor or dishonest corporate governance. It is also evident in the United States, where the share prices of those firms perceived to have governance problems are discounted (Morck et al., 1988).

It would be naïve to assume no such problems exist in Canada. Indeed, many of the studies in this volume make it clear that corporate governance in this country could be improved. The principle effect of such improvement would be to give Canadian firms better access to investors' money without penalizing investors. This lowering in financing costs would, in turn, improve the competitive positions of Canadian firms relative to their foreign rivals.

Despite the long list of potential corporate governance problems considered in this volume, many Canadian firms are very well run. Typically, this is a reflection of the ethical principles of those in charge. However, there are exceptions – cases of questionable conduct and decision-making by top managers ranging from self-interested transactions to outright theft. In an imperfect world where such behaviour is always a threat, investors cannot rely solely on the lofty principles of managers. There is a clear role for law. Standards of behaviour and accountability must be upheld, and must be seen by investors to be upheld. Consequently, many of the policy options recommended below are intended to improve disclosure and transparency as well as the conduct and accountability of managers.

Corporations, and the laws that guide them, have evolved powerful checks on managerial excesses. In this chapter, we examine some of those checks and we propose a number of specific policy options to strengthen them. These policy options are based on the studies contained in this volume, and on the extensive and rapidly growing body of empirical research literature on corporate governance. In addressing economic issues of the sorts raised in this volume, individual studies are seldom definitive. The mainstream position of the economics profession tends to shift only in response to very persuasive findings. Not surprisingly, public policy formulation follows a similar pattern. We therefore adopt a hands-off approach where we feel the evidence is inadequate, and we advance concrete proposals only where we are convinced there is sufficient evidence to justify them. At the end of this chapter, we reflect on this philosophy of corporate governance regulation, and discuss why we consider it appropriate for Canada in the coming years.

OPTIONS FOR IMPROVING CANADIAN CORPORATE GOVERNANCE

MANAGERIAL EQUITY OWNERSHIP

IF MANAGERS OWN SHARES IN THEIR OWN CORPORATION(S), they should be less willing to make decisions that are likely to reduce share prices. Thus, share values should generally be higher when managers own more stock. At some point, however, increasing ownership begins to entrench management. Consequently, when that point is reached, share values should begin to fall as management ownership rises. This pattern is found in data for large U.S. firms by Morck et al. (1988), and is illustrated in Figure 1. Share value rises with stock ownership by management, except in the range between 5 percent and 20 percent, suggesting that this is the range within which entrenchment occurs.

Other studies confirm this general pattern, although there is disagreement as to exactly which ownership levels correspond to entrenchment. For example, McConnell & Servaes (1990) place the entrenchment range around

FIGURE 1

THE RELATION BETWEEN MANAGEMENT EQUITY OWNERSHIP AND FIRMS' Q
(OR MARKET-TO-BOOK) RATIOS FOR LARGE U.S. FIRMS

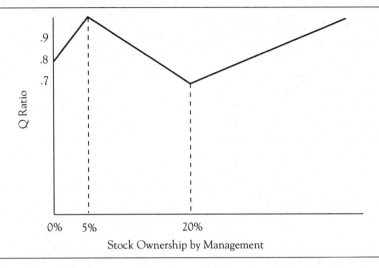

Source: Morck et al., 1988.

40 percent, but they use smaller firms for most of their analysis. Also, their findings do not include an upward sloping segment beyond 20 percent. Both their result in this range, and that of Morck et al. (1988) are tenuous because of the scarcity of data on publicly traded, closely held firms in the United States.

Amoako-Adu and Smith provide a similar analysis for Canadian firms. They find no statistically significant pattern in the data for firms with insider ownership below 20 percent. This could be due to the small number of Canadian firms in that range, or to the fact that in Canada stakes below 20 percent are not generally disclosed, or both. However, among firms with more than 20 percent managerial ownership, they find a positive relationship with share value, similar to that found by Morck et al. (1988). Rao and Lee-Sing find no linear relationship between insider ownership and firm performance, but do not search for a nonlinear relationship of the sort shown in Figure 1. Jog and Tulpule divide firms into four groups ranging from very low to very high levels of insider ownership and find no difference in their long-term returns to shareholders or their accounting performance. As they recognize, an important limitation of their stock market analysis is that it looks only at returns. Consequently, if the stock prices of some of their firms (say, the widely held firms) were depressed due to their ownership structures by roughly the same amount throughout the period studied, they would find exactly the same result. Their study does show, however, that between 1977 and 1981 there was no statistically significant change in the relative pricing of stocks in widely held *versus* closely held firms. Also, their accounting-based results are not strictly comparable to Rao and Lee-Sing or to other studies in the research literature because they are not compared with industry and firm-size benchmarks.

On the whole, we share Barone-Adesi's lack of surprise that results obtained for U.S. firms do not hold up in Canada. There are many institutional differences between the two countries (Daniels & MacIntosh, 1991 and MacIntosh, 1993). Canadian managers are relatively free of class-action suits by shareholders and can use dual-class shares to retain control despite issuing large amounts of equity. Also, friendly sales of control are more difficult in Canada because of legislated equal-opportunity rules, and Canadian institutions may be more passive on corporate performance issues. All of these differences make management entrenchment easier in Canada. The studies by Amoako-Adu and Smith, and by Rao and Lee-Sing are both consistent with the view that most Canadian firms already have entrenched management, so increasing insider ownership further is more likely to increase than depress share prices. In this context, Canadian firms are located along the farthest right segment of Figure 1. Share values are already depressed by full entrenchment, so further increasing insider holdings can do little, if any, harm. Therefore, if managers are equally entrenched by holding 50 percent or 60 percent, it is preferable that they own 60 percent; then their personal interests are at least marginally closer to the firm's.

If this view were confirmed by overwhelming evidence, it would support a policy of actively encouraging greater insider ownership among firms that already have dominant shareholders. However, the evidence is not yet overwhelming. Jog and Tulpule, for instance, are not supportive of this, although their methodology is aimed at addressing other issues and is ill-suited to answer this question. Because we consider the evidence to be too equivocal to support a robust policy recommendation, we make the following, more modest, suggestion.

Policy Implication 1

- Government should neither encourage nor discourage any level of insider ownership.

OUTSIDERS ON BOARDS OF DIRECTORS

THE CANADA BUSINESS CORPORATIONS ACT CURRENTLY REQUIRES at least two unrelated directors on the board of a public firm. In theory, these outsiders monitor management and publicize, if not prevent, decisions that might depress share values. Weisbach (1988) shows that U.S. firms whose boards have outsider majorities are more likely to sack their CEOs following unusually poor financial performance than are firms with boards dominated by insiders. Also, Rosenstein & Wyatt (1990) find that the share prices of U.S. firms tend to rise with the news that outsiders are coming onto their boards. However, Hermalin & Weisbach (1991) find no statistically meaningful relation between outsiders on the board and share values. These findings can be reconciled if outside directors have little effect under normal circumstances, but force action when performance is very bad. Despite this decidedly mixed evidence, the Toronto Stock Exchange Committee on Corporate Governance in Canada (the Dey Committee) recommended that a majority of all directors of listed companies be unrelated.

It is important to note that Weisbach's (1988) result is for the United States where most firms are widely held. In Canada, most firms are closely held and their top managers are arguably entrenched. Also, the clout of outside directors may be decidedly limited when the CEO controls a majority of shareholder votes. In a closely held economy, does having outsiders on the board really matter?

The evidence presented in this volume is that it does not seem to matter. Neither Amoako-Adu and Smith nor Gagnon and St-Pierre finds any statistically discernible relation between the percentage of outsiders on the board and firm performance. Rao and Lee-Sing actually find a positive relation between several performance measures and the percentage of *insiders* on the board. These findings are consistent with recent work by Hermalin & Weisbach (1995), who argue that rules requiring a certain percentage of the board to be outsiders are likely to be ineffective because dominant shareholders and managers can always find compliant and passive outsiders. They argue that outside directors must be given both more power and stronger incentives if they are to improve economy-wide corporate governance.

It may, however, be too early to give up on outside directors. Amoako-Adu and Smith make the valid point that Canadian disclosure rules often fail to establish whether outside directors are truly independent. For example, unrelated directors who are also the lawyers or accountants for the firm, or for its controlling shareholder, cannot be considered to be truly independent. The same is true for executives of companies that are suppliers or customers of the firm, or of other firms controlled by its dominant shareholder. Such directors are less likely than truly independent directors to challenge the CEO for fear of jeopardizing their other business interests.

The Dey Committee recommended that the board be charged with the task of determining who among its members is unrelated, and then be required to disclose publicly the basis upon which that decision is made (subsequently adopted in TSE Bylaw No. 636). While this recommendation confers considerable latitude on shareholders and directors to craft governance arrangements tailored to specific circumstances, it comes at the cost of engendering some confusion among investors as to what exactly "unrelated" means. Therefore, in response to the issue raised by Amoako-Adu and Smith, we suggest the following.

Policy Implication 2

- The current requirement in the *Canada Business Corporation Act* – that there be a minimum of two public directors on the boards of public companies – should be retained. However, the definition of an outside director should be tightened considerably. For a firm to characterize a director as an outside director (in accordance with the *Canada Business Corporations Act*), that director should have no commercial link of any kind with the firm or its controlling shareholder(s). In other words, an outside director should be truly independent of management and owners. The controlling shareholder, the firm's lawyers, its advertising account managers, the executives of firms dependent on it for business, etc. should not be considered as outside directors. We further recommend that firms be required to disclose *all* their directors' commercial links, direct or indirect, with the firm and with *all* entities controlled by the firm's controlling shareholder.

Hermalin & Weisbach (1995) point out that requiring a specific *number* of outside directors is, by itself, unlikely to improve corporate governance. They argue that outside directors must also be given sufficient power to influence management and sufficient incentives to use that power. We return to the issue of increasing the power of directors later in the chapter, but turn now to directors' incentives.

One such incentive comes from director-liability rules, which, in our opinion, should be reasonable, focused and well-balanced. The present regime weighs on the side of severity. We suggest that the ultimate effect of overly-severe director-liability rules is to discourage good outside directors from serving on boards. Director liability should therefore be invoked only in carefully limited, sharply focused circumstances, or it will be counter-productive. Another more balanced, less severe – rational – incentive scheme is needed. We believe changes in the form of director compensation might accomplish this.

Paying outside directors solely in publicly traded shares, or call options on them, would make directors more attentive to shareholders' interests. This would address the incentive issue raised by Hermalin & Weisbach (1995), and lead outside directors to exert a stronger influence on firm performance. Although compensation paid to outside directors is usually quite modest, linking it to the price of publicly traded shares would be an important symbolic reminder to directors of where their discretionary duty lies. We therefore suggest that governments adopt the following recommendation.

Policy Implication 3

- Outside directors should be paid solely in publicly traded stock or stock options. If options are used, their exercise prices should *not* be adjusted *ex-post* when the share price falls. (This practice, regrettably common in CEO compensation schemes, defeats the entire purpose of option-based compensation schemes, which is to link pay to performance.) A better way to maintain proper incentives as the market fluctuates is to define explicitly the exercise price as the value of a portfolio of the stocks of other firms in the industry. A director's compensation would then rise when the shares of the company outperform the benchmark portfolio of shares of industry rival firms. Director compensation, and how it is determined, should be fully disclosed.

The effect of this requirement would be to empower shareholders by giving directors stronger incentives to safeguard shareholders' interests.

An issue raised repeatedly in this context is the alleged myopia of shareholders. Directors, the argument goes, should not be paid in options or stock because the perspective of shareholders is too short-term, and the rosy long-term prospects of the board's plans are thus beyond markets' collective ken. Giammarino documents the large and increasingly conclusive empirical literature on this issue and thoroughly debunks the folk wisdom that shareholders are more myopic than managers. He shows convincingly that share prices respond sensibly to changes in firms' long-term prospects. Accounts to the contrary simply do not stand up to close scrutiny.[1]

If director compensation is linked to firm performance, a related issue is whether good directors will serve in a firm where there is likely to be continued poor performance while a turnaround is engineered. A basic compensation could be built into options by setting their exercise prices below the current stock price. (We consider the Toronto Stock Exchange rule that now prevents this to be inadvisable, and we recommend that it be changed.) If the directors oversee a continued price decline (relative to the shares of other firms in the same industry) that renders their options worthless, investors are presumably collectively unimpressed by the board's long-term turnaround strategy. In such circumstances, shareholders would probably be relieved if the directors responsible for the decline resigned or were replaced. Presumably, not paying them would hasten the former and render the latter unnecessary. If, initially, a firm is unable to persuade an outside director to come onto its board, the interests of the shareholders would be better served by offering such a director more options or stock, rather than by offering cash. In our view, *there is no economic justification for a guaranteed component in directors' compensation.* After all, the people in whose interests the directors are supposed to act – the shareholders – have no guaranteed compensation either. We believe most directors would welcome a switch to stock or options as compensation if it were accompanied by the rationalization of director liability we suggest.

There are two dangers with respect to paying potentially unscrupulous directors in stock or options: insider trading, and stock price manipulation. Such directors might exercise their stock options when they know the stock is overvalued, and thus harm public shareholders; or they might actively orchestrate information releases or discretionary accruals in earnings to inflate the share price around exercise dates. There is considerable evidence in the accounting research literature that firms *do* manipulate information releases and accounting data in this way for other purposes. Nonetheless, one straightforward way to address this problem is to require that directors' stock or options be unuseable until some time after they have left the board. If directors must wait, say, two years after leaving the board, until they can trade or exercise the stocks or options they receive as compensation, their information advantage over ordinary shareholders should be largely dissipated.

Under the proposals we advance here, the job of an outside director is likely to become more difficult. Public companies should therefore review their directorial compensation arrangements regularly to ensure that the level of compensation received by directors corresponds to the time, energy, and commitment required of them in a rapidly changing, highly complex business environment.

BOARD SIZE

IS SMALL BETTER? RAO AND LEE-SING FIND A NEGATIVE CORRELATION between board size and performance. There is also a strong conviction held by many practicing directors that the boards of some large Canadian corporations are already too large to allow effective decision-making. Nonetheless, in our opinion it would be inadvisable to legislate the number of directors on boards. We contend that large boards are a symptom of deeper governance problems rather than a fundamental cause of poor corporate governance. Rather than encumber firms with an array of laws aimed at such symptoms, public policy should address root causes. We believe the positive recommendations we set out here focus on those root causes and thus would empower shareholders to demand smaller boards where they might improve performance.

Policy Implication 4

• Governments should not attempt to control board size.

SEPARATION OF POWERS

RAO AND LEE-SING FIND THAT IN ALMOST 66 PERCENT of the Canadian firms comprising the sample for their study, the CEO *does not* chair the board. In contrast, in roughly 60 percent of the firms in their U.S. sample, the CEO *does* chair the board.

Among students of constitutional law, the separation of powers is widely considered to be an essential component of good government. Power in the public sector must not be concentrated in too few hands, or some day an error in judgement by the electorate might confer on a rascal unchecked scope for villainy. Does this recipe for good government also apply to good corporate governance? There is some evidence that it does.

Morck *et al.* (1989) find that boards are more likely to replace CEOs following unusually bad corporate performance if the CEO is not also serving as both president and chairperson of the board. Moreover, where the three positions are held by one person, poor firm performance tends to increase the odds of a hostile takeover rather than the dismissal of the CEO. Perhaps too much power in the hands of the CEO paralyses the board and leaves the firm vulnerable to more drastic remedies like takeovers for poor governance.

Rao and Lee-Sing find no discernable relationship between firms' general performance and a separation of powers in either U.S. or Canadian data. (They actually find a positive relation between *concentration* of power and firm growth.) They do not explore whether or not Canadian boards might be more willing to dismiss CEOs subsequent to very poor performance, however.

Allowing one talented executive to assume greater power by acting as CEO and chairperson of the board may benefit shareholders by reducing, if not eliminating, "needless" discussion and by speeding up the decision-making process. However, the same can be said of a dictatorship. Arguably, the purpose of political democracy is to restrain great men: that is also the purpose of shareholder democracy. Yet despite this, we believe a legislative requirement that these roles be separated is unnecessary and might well be ineffective. A dominant CEO is as likely to find a compliant and passive chairperson of the board as to find compliant and passive outside directors.

The purpose of separating the roles of chairperson and CEO is to foster a climate in which dissident directors can confront a CEO or a controlling shareholder. Elsewhere in this commentary, we propose both better disclosure and conduct committees as ways to accomplish this. In our opinion, this represents a better general strategy to ensure that shareholders are empowered and informed; they can then elect whom they please to chair the board.

Policy Implication 5

- Governments should not legislate a separation of the roles of CEO and chairperson of the board.

CEO COMPENSATION

IN CANADA AND THE UNITED STATES, CEO compensation is a hot topic. As Elitzur and Halpern point out, in the United States CEO compensation is thought by many to be too high and, more importantly, too unrelated to corporate performance. Presumably, most shareholders would not mind high CEO pay if it were related to superb performance. However, if CEOs can continue to earn the same compensation no matter how well (or badly) they run their companies, this is clearly a problem.

It is important to emphasize that this problem is mainly confined to widely held firms. In closely held firms, especially where the dominant shareholder is also the CEO, the firm's fortunes are intertwined with those of the CEO. In such cases, tying compensation to firm performance through salaries, bonuses or option plans is redundant.

In Canada there are some widely held firms, and sometimes the managers of closely held firms are not their dominant shareholders. In such cases, tying executive compensation to firm performance makes sense. Elitzur and Halpern argue in this volume that in these firms CEO compensation is not tied closely enough to performance. We do not believe requiring a closer tie is wise. A better policy would be to empower shareholders in more basic ways and then allow them to determine appropriate compensation packages for CEOs.

Stock options are one alternative shareholders should reconsider. These have deservedly earned a bad name in recent years because of the willingness of boards to rewrite their terms at the CEO's request. For example, if a CEO were given options to buy his company's stock at $50 and the share price fell to $25, the board too often happily rewrites the options to let the CEO buy at $20. CEOs and boards rightly understand that a CEO cannot be held responsible for every movement in her firm's stock price. However, allowing options to be adjusted freely in this way can protect the CEO from stock price declines that are her responsibility.

To sidestep this, we suggest that firms pay their CEOs in options with adjustable exercise prices tied to the stock price performance of rival firms. The CEO's stock option could let her buy a share of her company's stock at a price that moves up and down with the share prices of other firms in the industry. This would adjust the terms of the option when industry-wide or economy-wide factors affect the share price, yet would still hold the CEO accountable when her own firm's share price alone rises or falls.

Policy Implication 6

- CEOs should be paid in stock options. These should partially or completely replace salaries, not supplement them. Boards should not be allowed to revise the terms of such options after they are issued. To protect CEOs from price fluctuations beyond their control, the exercise prices of their options should move auto-matically with industry or market indexes. A CEO compensated in this way should not be subject to excess compensation suits if she achieves superior performance relative to her industry rivals. In addition, CEO compensation and the way it is determined should be disclosed.

It is important that CEOs share some of their shareholders' downside risk. Therefore CEOs should originally be compensated with in-the-money options[2] in order to produce expected compensation sufficient to attract and retain highly qualified CEOs. Although we understand the sentiments that led to it, we believe the current TSE rule forbidding in-the-money options should be changed. As it is now, the rule prevents options from replacing salary and bonuses, yet leaves open the possibility of huge amounts of compensation.

We recommend against tying CEO compensation to accounting perfor-mance measures such as earnings. These are too subject to manipulation. By timing accruals, for example, managers can manipulate current earnings to almost any extent desired. Elitzur and Halpern provide a quick overview of the extensive empirical evidence that this does occur. Of course, stock prices can also be manipulated by orchestrating information releases. To prevent this, CEOs' options, like those of directors', should not be exercisable until after retirement.

If a CEO's pay is to be geared to her firm's stock market performance, that CEO must also be permitted to reap the rewards – in the form of very high pay – when the firm's performance is superior. There has recently been much grumbling in Canada about the magnitude of CEO pay. In the United States many lawsuits by shareholders against managers are "excess compensation" suits. Jensen (1990) argues that the real scandal is not the size of the CEO's pay, but its failure to reflect firm performance. He contends that the fear of excess compen-sation lawsuits partly explains why CEO pay in the United States is not closely tied to performance. CEOs there are unwilling to accept low pay when firm performance is poor because they doubt that they will be able to keep high pay when firm performance is good. Because of this, some argue that CEO pay should not be disclosed in order to allow it to be tied more closely to firm per-formance without raising shareholders' ire. We believe this would be unwise.

It is in the public interest that shareholders know how much money top insiders are taking from the firm. We therefore endorse strongly the recent changes to the Regulations under the *Ontario Securities Act*, which require more extensive and detailed disclosure of executive compensation practices. However, while there is value in disclosure, it is also in the public interest that good management be rewarded. Thus, when a manager receives very high compensation from an option-based incentive scheme that seemed reasonable at the time it was instituted and that shareholders accepted at the time, law-suits alleging excess compensation should not be allowed.[3]

We do not believe government should legislate how CEOs are paid. Our suggestion with respect to the use of options with moving exercise prices is directed mainly to shareholders and boards of directors. It is important, however, that governments continue to require disclosure of CEO and top executive compensation, and that the courts are not required to hear excess compensation suits where high compensation derives from superior performance.

DIRECTOR LIABILITY

THERE HAS BEEN A GROWING TREND IN CANADA toward increased directors' liability. In contrast to the United States, Canadian legislatures are inclined to support explicitly legislated corporate duties and obligations with explicit liability for directors. One researcher recently identified no less than 106 different federal and provincial statutes that impose personal liability on directors and officers in Ontario. There has also been an increase in non-statutory, typically tort-based, liabilities. It is noteworthy that this expansion in liability has occurred without any substantial change in the corporate law relating to duty of care, which governs the liability of directors and officers for negligence.

The rationale alleged for legislating these duties is straightforward: directors must have strong incentives to monitor corporate activities and prevent corporate wrongdoing. However, while there may be a need for increased control of corporate wrongdoing in Canada, it is not at all clear that the imposition of personal liability on directors is an effective way to achieve this goal. Imposing liability on directors not only fails to provide consistent and compassionate levels of recovery to injured stakeholders (owing to vagaries in the personal resources of directors), it may also bias directorial decision-making in the direction of low-risk, unimaginative projects (Daniels, 1994). In a setting of intense competitive pressures, a board gripped by fear because of its liability is an uninspired instrument for vigorous and creative leadership. Even worse, fear of liability may cause the board to resign when its leadership and expertise are most needed (when, for example, a firm is near insolvency) and the threat to stakeholder interests is greatest – the so-called "board overboard" phenomenon (Daniels, 1993). Indeed, fear because of personal liability under provincial employment standards legislation has resulted in en masse resignations of board members from troubled public companies in Canada (e.g., PWA and Westar).

These problems are accentuated by various weaknesses in Canadian corporate director and officer insurance policies. Daniels & Hutton (1993) find that, as a specialty or fringe line of insurance, the supply of director and officer (D&O) coverage is subject to abrupt and quite dramatic fluctuations, as measured by several variables: price and deductible increases, growth in coverage exclusions, and compression of coverage periods. The use of these restrictions means that, at some points in the insurance-cycle, coverage for certain D&O liability risks is literally unavailable at any price. For example, in 1987, 91 percent of the insurance policies written in Canada excluded liability for pollution and environmental damage and 17 percent excluded liability for actions taken by various regulatory agencies. Furthermore, most insurance policies were written on a claims-made basis and allowed for only relatively short discovery periods after termination. The net effect of these restrictions has been to make trusting D&O insurance an extremely speculative strategy for most directors.

To address these problems, we recommend the following.

Policy Implication 7

- Directors should be liable to class action suits by shareholders for explicitly legislated corporate responsibilities *provided that the directors' act or omission is the reasonably proximate cause* of the harm in question. This liability should never be absolute – it should always be subject to a *due diligence defence*. Directors and officers who exert a reasonable effort to uncover and prevent potential harm to shareholders should be protected from lawsuits. Directors who go on the record as opposing decisions later found to have harmed shareholders or stakeholders should also be protected from lawsuits arising out of those decisions. We endorse the recommendation of the Dey Committee that the government departments responsible for the administration of corporate law in their jurisdictions undertake systematic and comprehensive reviews of all legislation that imposes personal liability on directors and officers to ensure that the provision is cost-effective as measured against the policy goals sought.

It is our expectation that much of this legislation will not justify its cost. In cases where social responsibility, the environment and other broad public objectives are being backed up with director liability, such liability should be capped, at least for outside directors. It might also be reasonable to cap outside directors' liability for breach of duty of care, as this duty can be somewhat open ended. We would not, however, limit the exposure of directors for either oppressive conduct or breach of the duty of loyalty, both of which involve aspects of self-dealing.

Generally, there has not been any expansion in the scope of liability under the corporate law duty of care. This is desirable since, by and large, courts are ill-equipped to second guess directorial business decisions. The danger is that, in order to be able to point the finger at someone when corporations lose money, shareholders will attempt to hold directors and officers responsible for actions that were perfectly responsible at the time they were made. Corporate decision-making is inherently about risk-taking, and it is undesirable for directors to be held liable for legitimate risks that later turn sour. This is why courts have traditionally strained against the imposition of liability for business decisions and judgements that are well-informed and not tainted by any hint of self-interest; it is also why we believe director liability should be precisely defined and subject to a due diligence defence.

Another reason is the serious risk of deterring competent outsiders from accepting positions on boards if liability rules are too strict. The responsibilities of directors and officers should be limited to what they can reasonably be expected to control. There are better tools for improving corporate governance than broad and open-ended liability for officers and directors. This is especially true for outside directors who benefit little from firms' exploitation of their shareholders yet who may bear huge liabilities. Imposing excessive liability undoubtedly deters highly qualified people from serving as directors, especially in troubled firms where there is a high likelihood of legal action. Yet these are the firms where competent outsiders are most needed.

We believe directors' responsibility should be simple and clear: maximize share value. The substantial body of empirical literature discussed by Giammarino in this volume suggests that the allegations of shareholder myopia and related criticisms of financial markets are largely unjustified. Although financial markets may be subject to occasional irrational fluctuations, for the most part share prices move in response to investors' rational perceptions of a firm's performance and long-term future prospects. Share prices are valuable, though admittedly imperfect, measures of how well shareholders think the firm is doing. Except for annual shareholder meetings, no other such gauge of shareholders' views is available. Therefore, we feel the law should recognize financial markets as delivering a democratic, albeit imperfect, expression of shareholders' opinions.

Policy Implication 8

- The shareholders' interests in a derivative suit should be defined as the *maximal current share value*.

Although earlier studies came to conflicting conclusions, there is now fairly widespread acceptance that management entrenchment devices like poison pills lower share prices. We concur with Huson's suggestion that these sorts of effects be factored into valuation calculations in such suits.[4]

CONTROLLING SHAREHOLDERS

CANADA'S IS A CLOSELY HELD ECONOMY, and *dealing with controlling shareholders is consequently the central issue in Canadian corporate governance*. In our judgement, the policy implications in this section are the most important in this volume. Although the studies here do not point to pervasive problems related to controlling shareholders, the same methodological difficulties we discussed when interpreting them as to the desirability of fostering more or less concentrated ownership apply here too. Moreover, there is considerable evidence in the corporate finance research literature that concentrated ownership can be a problem. Holderness & Sheehan (1988) show that different types of dominant shareholders have different effects on U.S. firms' performance. Along these lines, Morck & Stangeland (1995) find that the performance of Canadian firms is depressed when the controlling shareholder is an heir, but not other-wise. The studies of large blockholders in the United States cited by Holderness also provide ample reason for concern. Finally, there is a large body of empirical evidence from other countries, reviewed at length in Shleifer & Vishny (1995), which concludes that dominant shareholders do extract significant value from firms they control. The preponderance of evidence, we believe, supports an active public policy in this area. However, we believe the primary goal of public policy here should be the empowerment of shareholders and outside directors.

The high level of share ownership concentration in Canada makes problems between controlling and minority shareholders the crucial axis of agency conflict. The problem is not one of managerial fidelity to shareholders, but rather one of fidelity to some shareholders – controllers – at the expense of others, minorities (Daniels & MacIntosh, 1991). As MacIntosh and Schwartz argue in this volume, controlling shareholders usually make the corporation's managers work harder, but the rub is that the fruits of such effort may not go equally to all shareholders – the controlling shareholder can siphon off a disproportionate share.

In this setting, it is indeed ironic that Canadian courts (in contrast to their American counterparts) were loathe to develop a clear fiduciary duty from majority to minority shareholders (see MacIntosh, 1993, for a thorough discussion of this issue). Indeed, in a closely held economy such as ours, a clear fiduciary duty of dominant shareholders to minority shareholders along the lines of French law, described by Barone-Adesi, would seem appropriate.

This omission has been redressed through the adoption of the statutory oppression remedy in federal and provincial corporate law, and through the development of a range of minority shareholder protections in provincial securities law, such as Ontario Securities Commission Policy 9.1, which sets out disclosure, valuation, disinterested director review, and shareholder approval requirements for insider bids, issuer bids, going private transactions, and related party transactions.

Although it may appear that having multiple and overlapping instruments available to redress abuses by a controlling shareholder strengthens the protections available to minority shareholders, there are several infirmities within the current system that hobble its general effectiveness. First, there are simply too many different instruments in the minority shareholders' arsenal. This engenders overlap and confusion. Depending on whether a minority shareholder's action against a controlling shareholder is framed as an alleged breach of securities law, the corporate fiduciary duty, or the oppression remedy, quite different consequences ensue. This is due to the different substantive rights and remedies in each, the different modes of prosecution (public for securities law, private for corporate law), and the different forums for resolution (administrative review and possibly a hearing for securities law, the courts for corporate law). Second, the multiplicity of instruments hobbles the creation of an extensive body of precedent under any single instrument. Consequently, it is difficult for both controlling and minority shareholders to know how the law will balance their respective interests in particular circumstances. Third, we are concerned that OSC Policy 9.1 has subverted the incentive (indeed, the capability) of shareholders and directors of Canadian corporations to negotiate directly the resolution of disputes over related-party transactions. The excessively detailed code of conduct elaborated in OSC Policy 9.1 insinuates OSC staff into the heart of disputes over self-dealing transactions, attenuating the need for those parties with the economic stakes to argue with controlling shareholders and management over related-party transactions (Daniels & Waitzer, 1994). The code has further undercut the incentive for board members to take the responsibility for crafting review processes for self-interested transactions tailored to specific circumstances. In this respect, in some circumstances the policy is far too stringent (in prescribing directorial review and disinterested shareholder voting, for example), whereas in others it is too lax (such as for significant transactions that are less than the 25 percent market capitalization tripwire for its non-disclosure obligations).

We regard the rationalization of the system of minority shareholder protection to be an urgent priority for the federal government, given the need to protect the integrity of the federal corporate law regime and to reduce costs for Canadian shareholders. At present, the substantive rights and remedies set out in OSC Policy 9.1 encroach on the corporate governance regime contemplated by the *Canada Business Corporation Act*. That is not to say, however, that the existing corporate law regime alone affords adequate protection to minority shareholders. There is a need for the federal government to review its own legislative scheme to determine which modifications are appropriate in light of the experience of the corporate and investor communities with both the oppression remedy and OSC Policy 9.1.

Policy Implication 9

- The federal government should commence a review of the various federal and provincial regulatory initiatives affecting minority share-holder rights to ensure that minority shareholders enjoy effective and rational protection against abuse by controlling shareholders.

As part of its review of the existing regime of minority shareholder protections, the federal government should also consider the desirability of expanding the disclosure and directorial voting provisions respecting interested material contracts or transactions to include those contracts or transactions involving the corporation and controlling shareholders. We suggest that class-action suits by minority shareholders against controlling shareholders be allowed when there is evidence of serious abuse.

We have argued (above) that mandating a certain number of outside directors on boards is unlikely to be effective unless three conditions are met. First, as suggested in Policy Implication 2, outside directors must be completely independent of the firm, *i.e.*, they must have no commercial relationship whatsoever with the firm, nor with any other firm controlled by the firm's controlling shareholder. Second, outside directors must have strong incentives to protect public shareholders. We believe this can be accomplished by giving outside directors performance-related compensation, and by rationalizing director liability, as proposed in our Policy Implications 3, 7 and 8. The third condition required for outside directors to be effective is that they must be empowered. We now turn to this.

There are sensible economic reasons for having insiders on boards of directors; they bring expertise and experience that outsiders seldom have. Nevertheless, external oversight and the vetting of self-interested transactions is a fundamental underpinning of effective corporate governance in a closely held economy such as Canada's. We believe that the board of directors of a closely held company is unlikely ever to be an effective forum for monitoring such transactions. The power and influence of the dominant shareholder are simply too pervasive. Therefore, we recommend that a new forum be established.

We suggest that a special committee of the board monitor and review the corporation's activities with controlling shareholders, other entities controlled by the controlling shareholders, and other insiders (non-shareholder officers and directors) to ensure fairness to minority shareholders. This would permit some institutional experience and memory to be accumulated with respect to non-arm's-length transactions and contracts.

Policy Implication 10

- The board of directors of any public Canadian company with a dominant shareholder should be required to establish a *conduct review committee* to approve significant non-arm's-length transactions and contracts. This committee should be composed *entirely* of outside directors (as defined in Policy Implication 2). Members of the conduct review committee and other members of the board should be liable to class-action lawsuits by minority shareholders when they deliberately, or negligently, allow improper non-arm's-length transactions or contracts to occur, but should be protected by a due diligence defense. To avoid frivolous suits, the courts should not hear cases unless there is evidence of grievous harm.

Conduct review committee approval could substitute for minority shareholder votes in many, perhaps most, cases. This would address a key criticism of Ontario's rule 9.1; that its requirements for shareholder consultation are too onerous and costly.

If the duties of controlling shareholders toward minority shareholders are to have any real content, minority shareholders must know when and how their interests might be threatened. Therefore we believe another critical issue is the timely disclosure of related party transactions.

Policy Implication 11

- Timely and full disclosure to all shareholders of all material contracts and transactions proposed between controlling shareholders, or the entities they control, and the corporation should be required.

INSTITUTIONAL INVESTORS

A RECURRING THEME IN SEVERAL OF THE STUDIES in this volume has to do with the recent growth in power and importance of institutional investors. Rao and Lee-Sing show that institutional investors now control 38 percent of the dollar value of the Canadian firms in their study. While this is less than the comparable figure for the United States, 53 percent, it is nonetheless large – and it is increasing rapidly.

Public pension funds, such as the Ontario Teachers fund, and private pension fund managers, like Jarislowsky and Fraser, now control multibillion-dollar stock portfolios. By threatening to use their substantial equity blocks to back takeovers or proxy challenges by dissident shareholders, these large institutional investors can displace managers whom they believe are not serving the shareholders. In the United States, institutional investors have caused a revolution in corporate governance, much to the dismay of many top corporate managers. Foerster examines pension funds in Canada, and argues that the same is likely to happen here. MacIntosh and Schwartz find a correlation between institutional ownership and corporate performance. This leads them to be relatively optimistic about the contribution institutional ownership can make to the Canadian system of corporate governance. However, Rao and Lee-Sing find no relationship between institutional ownership of Canadian firms and indicators of corporate strategy (like R&D spending and foreign market penetration), or general performance indicators (like return on assets or firm growth). In contrast, among U.S. firms they do find a link between high institutional ownership and good general performance. This is consistent with McConnell & Servaes (1990) who also document a relationship between institutional investors' stakes and high market-to-book ratios in U.S. firms. Many other studies argue for similar links.

However, as Patry and Poitevin explain, an increasing number of studies suggest institutional investors are overrated. A key issue in this connection is skepticism about pension fund managers learning enough about diverse business operations to make reliable business decisions. In the 1960s, conglomerates were touted as a way for a single team of superb managers to run numerous disparate businesses. The conglomerates of that era were largely failures. *Post mortem* examinations show problems in managing diverse divisions and subsidiaries to be the prime cause. Perhaps all the best conglomerate managers moved on to pension funds?

Expecting pension funds to be the holy grail of good corporate governance is unrealistic. However, even if pension fund managers take only measured and focused action to prod recalcitrant directors to do their jobs, substantial improvements in corporate governance might result. Some studies that are critical of pension funds and other investors seem to doubt that even this is likely, however. They point to serious governance problems within pension funds that may undermine their effectiveness.

Who are the people who run pension funds? How well do they do their jobs? What incentives do they face? To what extent do they promote their own interests, or interests other than those of their beneficiaries? These are critical questions that have largely gone unasked in Canada, despite the fact that pension fund managers regularly make multibillion-dollar decisions that constrain the decisions of large corporations and affect the retirement security of millions of people.

In public-sector funds, there is a nagging fear that those in control of pension funds might be there more for their political connections than for their financial expertise. Romano (1994) finds that public-sector pension funds earn statistically significantly lower returns than private sector funds, and attributes this to politically motivated "local initiative" investments.

In corporate pension funds, Lakonishok et al. (1991, 1992a, 1992b) present disturbing evidence that pension fund managers choose portfolio managers less for the performance of their investments than for their ability to generate good excuses when their portfolios do poorly. Lakonishok et al. document surprisingly poor portfolio returns on corporate pension funds. In general, most corporate pension funds would do better on a risk-adjusted basis simply to buy and hold broad market indices. Lakonishok et al. argue that conflicts of interest between plan beneficiaries, plan sponsors, and portfolio managers are largely responsible for this poor showing. Corporate treasurers in sponsoring firms may be more interested in expanding the influence of their office than in earning optimal returns. Also, portfolio managers may be more interested in pleasing the corporate treasurer (and thus getting their investment contracts renewed) than in producing optimal financial returns.

In Canada, the sheer size of institutional investors, particularly public pension funds, may itself be a double-edged sword. Fearing the public scrutiny that often accompanies vigorous action, even in circumstances where it is appropriate, public-fund managers may shun activism that is not in response to a discreet management-initiated transaction, like a poison pill plan or a change in corporate capital structure.

If pension funds themselves have serious governance problems, assigning them an important watchdog role over corporate governance may be akin to setting the fox to guard the henhouse. Before they can adequately play such a role, public- and private-sector pension fund managers' incentives must be properly aligned. This suggests a need to clarify the underlying economic purpose of both public and private pension funds – which is to provide retirees with financial security. Pension fund portfolios should be managed to benefit the beneficiaries – not politicians, not political insiders, not corporate treasurers, and certainly not fund managers.

Ultimately, the most powerful way to ensure that pension funds are managed in the interests of their beneficiaries would be to introduce direct competition for beneficiaries' pension dollars. This could be accomplished by allowing employees themselves to allocate their pension money among several portfolios, each with stated investment strategies and performance records. Pension fund management could even be completely divorced from corporate management. For example, employees of Bell Canada could choose to put their money in any certified pension fund, not just those assigned contracts by Bell Canada. This would amount to moving toward defined contribution pension plans and away from classical defined benefit plans.

Defined contribution or money purchase plans are akin to Registered Retirement Savings Plans (RRSPs), but in this case either the employer alone or both the employer and employee make regular contributions. The beneficiary receives the accumulated amount of these contributions when she retires. Also, the employee can allocate her share of the asset pool as she chooses among several investment funds associated with the pension plan.

In defined benefit plans, the employer promises a specific level of benefits related to the retirees' years of service, top five years' wages, etc. Either the employer alone or both the employer and the employee make regular contributions. Theoretically, both the investment strategy and the responsibility for shortfalls rest with the employer only. In practice, when a defined benefit plan becomes seriously underfunded, the employees are usually asked for higher contributions or given lower defined benefits – or both – as occurred recently for public-sector employees in Alberta. Even when the contributions come solely from the employer, those contributions (and the benefits they pay for) are a part of labour contract negotiations and are subject to change. It is arguable that there is really no such thing as a "pure" defined benefit plan, in that in all pension plans employees potentially pay some costs for poor investment performance.

Hybrid plans, part defined benefit and part defined contribution, are also common. Most corporate plans are *de facto* defined contribution plans with defined benefit floors. Employers make "voluntary inflation adjustments" in the defined benefit when the fund's assets do well, but guarantee a basic floor level of payments, and sometimes even a basic partial inflation adjustment, when they do poorly. In such plans, the employees gain the benefits of good pension fund management and so should worry about the funds' investment strategies.

From a detached economic standpoint, defined contribution plans are preferable because the beneficiaries' property rights are clearly defined: they own the fund's assets. In defined benefit plans, although the employer is the *de jure* owner of the fund's assets, real property rights are vague. Since it is not clear who bears the costs of poor performance and who gains the benefits of good performance, no one has a clear incentive to press for good governance of these pension funds.

Given the advantage of defined contribution plans, why are most large pension plans defined benefit plans? First, the sponsors retain day-to-day control of the assets in defined benefit plans. Pension funds' investment strategies can be altered in the interests of the firm or government that sponsors them, often to the detriment of the beneficiaries. Second, defined benefit plans provide corporations with tax-free savings accounts. Bodie *et al.* (1985) show that U.S. companies with extra cash overfund their defined benefit pension plans so that in times of cash shortfalls they can adjust their contributions downward. This is accomplished by strategically altering the actuarial assumptions used to calculate the firm's contribution. Third, defined benefit plans are more forgiving of poor portfolio management because the ownership of the assets being managed is muddier. (Do they belong to the beneficiaries or to the employer?) Finally, defined benefit plans offer employees a false sense of security by promising a fixed annual dollar amount during their retirements. In fact, new securities like Government of Canada inflation-indexed bonds, allow defined contribution schemes to offer even more security than defined benefit plans.

We believe none of these reasons justifies the current reliance on defined benefit plans, and that a shift to defined contribution plans would be in the broad public interest.

Policy Implication 12

- Corporate and public-sector pension plans should be shifted away from a defined benefit system toward a defined contribution system. This could be accomplished by requiring that all pension plans offer beneficiaries a *defined contribution option*. Beneficiaries should then be given as much choice as possible as to how their pension dollars are to be invested.

In defined contribution plans, the ownership of the pension assets is clear: *they are the sole property of the beneficiaries*. Pension fund managers should therefore be acting solely for and in the interests of the beneficiaries. Thus, we make the following recommendation.

Policy Implication 13

- The fiduciary duty of pension fund managers to the beneficiaries of pension funds should be clarified and strengthened. This fiduciary duty should be to maximize the value of the portfolio while exercising prudent risk management. Pension fund managers who deliberately or negligently fail to do this should be liable to *class-action lawsuits* by the beneficiaries. A reasonable effort to fulfill these duties should constitute a defense against such lawsuits.

To ensure further that senior pension fund managers represent beneficiaries, we would like to see more democracy within pension funds. Pension fund managers should not be appointed by corporate management or by politicians. If shareholders elect the directors charged with safeguarding their interests, should not pension plan beneficiaries have analogous power? If CEOs must disclose their compensation, ought not the same apply to pension fund managers?

Policy Implication 14

- The senior managers of corporate and public sector pension funds should be elected by the beneficiaries. In addition, the compensation of top pension fund managers should be disclosed to beneficiaries.

A system that allowed proxy challenges would also make it possible for outsiders to challenge the fund's management strategy. In short, we are proposing the *corporatization* of public and corporate pension funds. Pension funds should be run like firms and, as in firms, their top decision-makers should have responsibilities and liabilities similar to those of a board of directors.

If beneficiaries are to challenge the decisions of pension fund managers, information about the performance and composition of the funds' assets must be available to them.

Policy Implication 15

- Pension funds should disclose information as to the contents and performance of their portfolios to beneficiaries on a quarterly basis. The average length of time the fund has held each asset should also be disclosed. The individual components of market index portfolios need not be specified. These reports should be subject to uniform accounting standards and be audited regularly.

One cost of such a disclosure rule is that it might possibly deter innovative forms of fund management because of the risk that expensive investment strategies adopted by some fund managers would be appropriated by others – the public good problem. However, particularly in the time-sensitive environment of capital markets, we are skeptical that historical reporting of investments would unduly compromise innovating firms.

An important issue that arises here is so-called "window dressing" by fund managers. This occurs when fund managers sell their "dogs" to buy stocks that have done well just prior to reporting the contents of their portfolios. The result of window dressing is that funds sell low and buy high – not exactly a formula for financial success. Lakonishok *et al.* (1991, 1992b) report that this practice is common among pension funds in the United States, because having high performers in the portfolio shows that fund managers chose at least some good investments, even though others were less profitable. (Some suggest that window dressing also explains the positive correlation between institutional ownership and firm performance identified in some studies.) Apparently this increases the portfolio manager's chances of retaining the investment contract with the fund sponsor. To stop this practice, we propose that pension funds also disclose the length of time they have held the assets in their portfolios.

It is our hope that these reporting requirements will encourage more pension funds to hold more indexed portfolios. We agree with Patry and Poitevin's conclusion, supported by Weisbach, that pension funds ought to be indexed more than they are. However, we also consider this to be a symptom of deeper governance problems. We believe our suggestions in this section address the cause of this symptom, in that they would improve pension fund governance so that pension funds would move independently to index more of their portfolios. There are valid reasons for pursuing more complex investing strategies, and pension funds should have some flexibility in this regard. Preventing pension funds from following such strategies by requiring a certain level of indexing would, in our view, be a mistake.

Despite overblown claims and legitimate questions, pension funds and other institutional investors can probably become a strong force for better corporate governance in Canada. At present, however, the effect of institutional investors may be undermined by a number of legal impediments that limit their voice in corporate governance matters. For instance, there is concern that the shareholder proposal process, which is intended to make it easier and less costly for dissident shareholders to communicate with all shareholders by allowing them to piggyback on management's information circulars, may be of limited value in disputes over corporate governance. This stems from the argument that such matters as information circulars are for the purpose of "promoting general economic, political, racial, religious, social or similar causes". The corporation can thus refuse to circulate a dissident proposal. There is also concern with the 200-word limitation on the size of the statement that can be made in support of a proposal. Finally, there is concern with the breadth of the definition of "solicitation" set out in the proxy rules of Canadian corporate legislation. The issue is that this definition could require large dissident shareholders who are talking with each other in contemplation of activism to file a dissident proxy circular, which is extremely costly.[5]

While the precise effect of these legislative restrictions on institutional voice is a matter of dispute, we believe that little would be lost by relaxing these rules, especially given our earlier recommendation calling for heightened disclosure of institutional ownership in Canada. As is clear from our earlier discussion, we regard informed, measured, and responsible institutional shareholder activism to be one of the linchpins of a modern system of corporate governance. We are also of the opinion that, given the right legal framework, Canadian institutional investors can play a constructive and responsible role in corporate governance. This accounts for our reluctance to codify rigid governance structures in corporate legislation that are inappropriate in a range of settings. By empowering large institutional shareholders to play a role in Canadian corporate governance, corporate and securities regulators will be free to play a more passive, enabling role. Such a regime is much more likely to result in optimal governance arrangements than one driven by governmental or quasi-governmental action. Therefore, we make the following recommendation.

Policy Implication 16

- The federal government, in association with the provincial securities commissions, should establish a joint task force to carry out a systematic review of corporate and securities legislation in order to remove any unnecessary impediments to institutional shareholder voice.

Key issues to consider in this review should be the status of institutional investors as insiders or controlling shareholders, and institutional investors' freedom to communicate with each other to address corporate governance problems. When institutional investors take large stakes in companies but do not become involved in detailed management decisions, there should be a way for them to avoid being designated as controlling shareholders, and still be free to communicate with each other about certain general corporate governance problems.[6] One can envision cases where pension funds truly become controlling shareholders and might oppress minority investors. However, the circumstances under which a founding family is designated as a controlling shareholder and those under which a pension fund should be so designated should perhaps be different.

One important factor that lessens the positive effect of mutual and pension funds on corporate governance in this country is the rule(s) restricting foreign securities in their portfolios (Daniels & MacIntosh, 1991; MacIntosh, 1993; Daniels & Halpern, 1995). Although the use of derivatives allows pension funds to reproduce the risk characteristics of foreign portfolios, the fact remains that they are restricted to the basic return they can earn in Canada.

The rule confining mutual and pension funds to Canadian investments has two effects on corporate governance. The positive effect is that, since mutual and pension funds have few other places to put their money, they cannot simply sell out when a firm has management problems. They have little choice but to intervene to try to improve the governance of their investments. The negative effect is that if the funds cannot improve the governance of firms whose stock they own, they are nevertheless stuck with it and have only a limited pool of other Canadian companies as possible alternative investments. If there are intractable governance problems in a preponderance of the companies, the funds may be forced to hold stocks they would otherwise shun. This allows poorly governed firms to raise capital by issuing securities on artificially favourable terms, which, in turn, enables corporations to make investment and operating decisions that are economically perverse. Indeed, we suspect that such mercantilist policies have had a devastating effect on the growth and development of the Canadian economy.

On balance, we believe the foreign investment restrictions on Canadian mutual and pension funds to be detrimental. The additional fact that these restrictions prevent mutual and pension funds from diversifying as much as they otherwise would (although derivatives help here), tips the verdict firmly on the side of free international capital flows.

Notwithstanding, there is yet another reason for allowing Canadian mutual and pension funds to diversify freely. It would not be economically healthy for Canadian finance to become completely dominated by pension funds. Might small shareholders need protection from oppression by large funds as much as from any other large shareholder? At present, we think the answer is "no" because mutual and pension funds are generally not inside parties to the sorts of corporate decisions that raise concerns about oppressive non-arm's-length transactions – such as asset transfers, securities issues, and the like. However, if the assets of mutual and pension funds continue to increase rapidly and their portfolio choices continue to be restricted to Canadian securities, there is a danger that the funds might come to so dominate Canadian finance that small investors might be slighted. In our opinion, this is another argument for allowing Canadian mutual and pension funds to diversify internationally without restrictions.

Policy Implication 17

- Canadian mutual and pension funds should be free to invest as much or as little in Canada as they see fit.

We recognize that adopting this policy will affect the finances of both governments and corporations. Governments can finance their deficits more easily when they can draw on captive investors. It should be recognized, how-ever, that the current Canadian content rule constitutes a hidden tax on Canadians' savings. If Canadian governments obtain funds on better terms because pension money is forced to remain here, this means Canadians' retirement savings are earning less than they would if invested at globally competitive rates. Current thinking in public finance favours consumption taxes, or taxes on the part of income people spend on consumption goods. Taxes on savings are seen to be bad because they discourage capital formation. Although public-sector governance is beyond the scope of this study, we speculate that Canadian governments might have been forced to begin their current fiscal house cleaning sooner if they had had to compete for capital in global markets, and that the present task would not have become as great as it is.

COMPLEX FIRMS: CONGLOMERATES AND MULTINATIONALS WITH PUBLIC SHARES

THE MAIN FEATURE OF THESE FIRMS that raises concerns related to corporate governance is the ease with which money can be transferred between parts of the group of companies when each of the parts has a different set of share-holders. This is the same basic problem that causes concern in closely held firms in general, but here it can arise in many different ways. In our view, these problems are best addressed through the initiatives discussed earlier in respect of controlling shareholders. The most important initiatives in this context are that, if they have publicly traded shares, the subsidiaries of multi-nationals and firms in conglomerate groups should have conduct committees and should be required to disclose the details of non-arm's-length transactions.

Requirements that Canadian citizens serve on the boards of the Canadian subsidiaries of multinationals are unlikely to have any real effect. By choosing Canadian employees of the multinational, or Canadian employees of firms dependent on the multinational for business, the force of this rule can be largely dissipated. Rao and Lee-Sing find no strong correlation between the nationality of board members and firm performance. (Actually, they find weak and mixed evidence that more foreign directors might boost performance.) There appears to be no strong case for continuing this requirement unless it is strengthened to require completely unrelated Canadian directors. Even then, it is more important that the directors be unrelated than that they be Canadian.

If it is thought to be important for political reasons to require Canadian citizens in key positions in the Canadian subsidiaries of multinationals, our recommendation (Policy Implication 10) could be modified to require that the outside directors on conduct review committees be Canadian citizens. Economically, however, the citizenship of directors is unimportant. What is critical to the economic basis of Canadian corporate governance law is that directors be subject to lawsuits by Canadian shareholders.

Policy Implication 18

• Directors should be sueable.

Directors of Canadian companies resident in the United States and other developed countries are not judgement-proof. Canadians can sue in foreign courts. The important issue here is that shareholders should know what they are getting into. If a company moves to allow its directors to reside permanently outside Canada, this should require at least one-time shareholder approval and should be clearly disclosed in the prospectuses of all new securities.

We see no problem in the proposal, mentioned in the *Canada Business Corporations Act* Discussion Paper on Directors' and Other Corporate Residency Issues (August 1995), to allow shareholder meetings outside Canada. Again, the key issue is that shareholders know what they are getting into. One-time shareholder approval should be required and prospectuses for all new securities should disclose this practice. We also see no problem in the same discussion paper's suggestion that the *Canada Business Corporations Act* allow certain records to be kept outside of Canada as long as those records are readily available electronically.

However, there are some suggestions in the discussion paper that we consider inadvisable. One is that non-resident directors post a bond. We believe this to be unnecessary. If a security's prospectus states clearly that directors can reside abroad, the investors know what they are getting into. Another inadvisable proposal is that director residency requirements be replaced with a "community interest" clause requiring director attention to "stakeholders" rather than to shareholders. Since directors now have clear duties to ensure that the firm honours its contractual and other legal duties to all its stakeholders, a general discretionary duty (such as that to shareholders) would serve only corporate insiders. We argue at length in our introduction to this volume that *a duty to all stakeholders is too multidimensional and vague to be a serious constraint on the actions of directors.* Boards can always find some group whose interests are promoted by even the most foolhardy decision. Theoretical accountability to everyone boils down to real accountability to no one.

WHISTLEBLOWERS

EVEN WITH THE BEST AUDITED FINANCIAL STATEMENTS and the most principled directors possible, it is still conceivable that corporate insiders might bilk shareholders directly or expose their firm(s) to lawsuits by violating environmental rules, etc. In such cases, protecting whistleblowers is in the interest of the public as well as the shareholders. The U. S. government pays a bounty to whistleblowers who expose fraud in government contracting. (This is why so many $700 toilet seats and $400 hammers come to light there.) There is an equally strong case in Canada for laws to protect whistleblowers from

687

retribution in both the public and private sectors. However, retribution can take subtle and intangible forms, so such laws might be impossible to enforce. This supports the idea, developed in this volume by Daniels and Howse, of offering a bounty to potential whistleblowers.

Policy Implication 19

- Protect whistleblowers from reprisals. Offer them bounties where public money is involved. Permit shareholders to vote to offer bounties in private firms.

TAKEOVERS AND FRIENDLY SALES OF CONTROL

ONE OF THE DISTINCTIVE FEATURES OF CANADIAN CORPORATE LAW (compared to that of the United States) is that friendly sales of control fall within the statutory takeover regime. For instance, the *Ontario Securities Act* precludes any party who wishes to purchase control from a controlling shareholder or group of shareholders at a premium in excess of 115 percent of a baseline market price from doing so, unless such an acquisition occurs pursuant to an offer made to all shareholders in accordance with the takeover regime. This means that the bid is subject to minimum bid periods and a *pro rata* take-up, among other things. The purpose of such a rule is to promote fairness for minority shareholders by ensuring that they have an equal opportunity to share the control premium with the controlling shareholder when there is a change in control. The equal opportunity rule is also thought to deter sales of control to opportunistic acquirers who want to loot the corporation by transferring corporate assets to themselves on unfair terms. Because the rule prevents a controlling shareholder from cashing out her position completely (at a high premium), the controlling shareholder is bound to take the plight of minority shareholders into account when parting with a part of a control block. Nevertheless, against these alleged benefits, the rule imposes significant costs. A controlling shareholder might not want to hold any equity after control is relinquished. If so, she is forced either to take a more modest control premium (*i.e.*, to the 115 percent ceiling) or to encourage the acquirer to buy all of the outstanding shares. In tandem, both effects increase the cost of control transfers, thereby discouraging their frequency.

We believe that the problems generated by entrenchment of lacklustre controlling shareholders are both significant and severe. Therefore, we think that a more appropriate way to deal with the prospect of *ex post* looting by an acquiring shareholder is through the use of the various disclosure and review mechanisms identified above in our discussion of controlling shareholders. We believe that such selective, substantive review, reinforced by shareholder oversight, would provide effective and more nuanced constraints on self-dealing activities by acquiring shareholders. We are dubious, however, of the claims to equal sharing of control premiums rooted in general ethical norms or in specific shareholder expectations. In robust, efficient capital markets, the price of a company's shares generally include a discount for minority status.[7]

Policy Implication 20

- The application of the takeover rules now included in provincial securities legislation and applicable to friendly sales of control should be revoked.

DISCLOSURE

WE DO NOT BELIEVE IT IS ECONOMICALLY DEFENSIBLE to use a specific threshold of ownership (like 20 percent) to trigger a required takeover bid for 100 percent of a firm's stock. The main effect of this would be to entrench managers further by increasing the costs of takeovers. We do, however, believe that the disclosure of large shareholders' stakes is reasonable. Minority shareholders should know who the large shareholders are, and the public should know which companies are subject to influence by which institutional investors.

In the United States, section 13d of the *Williams Act* requires that the stakes of all shareholders who own more than 5 percent of a publicly traded firm be disclosed. In Canada, disclosure is required only of stakes greater than 10 percent, which means that Canadian shareholders and managers often do not know the identity of the shareholders of the corporation. In the United States, investors reaching the 5 percent threshold must declare their intentions if they are launching a takeover. This makes sense because most U.S. firms are widely held and, compared to the Canadian case, shareholders with stakes greater than 5 percent are rare. Section 13d is often criticized because the mandatory early disclosure of a takeover in the works usually causes the share price to rise, making the pursuit of the takeover more expensive for the acquirer. Requirements in other countries that trigger automatic takeover bids for 100 percent of a company's stock when an investor's stake exceeds 20 percent create the same problem. In both cases, attempts to protect the interests of small shareholders actually harm them instead – by deterring takeovers.

A very large body of empirical work, alluded to throughout this volume, supports the claim that the possibility of a takeover stimulates good corporate governance. This means takeovers must be a credible threat to poor managers. The public interest is therefore served by allowing the secret accumulation of stock in preparation for a takeover.

There is, however, an offsetting public interest in the full disclosure of significant shareholdings. In the highly concentrated Canadian economy many large public pension funds are fast gaining staggering clout. Individual pension funds now own 10 percent or more of many firms' voting stock. Inevitably, as these institutions become more activist, the sheer size of their holdings will raise important and legitimate concerns regarding their concentrated economic and political power. In this respect, we believe that the harsh glare of public scrutiny is the best way to ensure that large shareholders, like the corporations in which they invest, operate in a constructive and responsible manner. Therefore, we propose the following.

Policy Implication 21

- The identities and stakes of all shareholders holding in excess of 5 percent of the voting shares of Canadian public companies should be disclosed.

We do not recommend that a 5 percent stake trigger a bid for control. Nor do we recommend that it mandate a declaration of intentions regarding a possible future takeover.

BANKS AND CORPORATE GOVERNANCE

IN GERMANY, JAPAN, AND SOME OTHER COUNTRIES, banks own large blocks of stock and play an active role in the governance of non-financial companies. In those countries, it is common for directors to be appointed by banks and for banks to be intimately involved in the strategic and tactical decisions of the firms whose stock they own. Some argue that this bank oversight is a powerful stimulus to good corporate governance and that it might obviate the need for takeovers, pension fund activity, etc. However, Morck & Nakamura (1994) proffer a less rosy view of this system, arguing that it effectively entrenches a network of insiders and depresses share prices. In this volume Morck and Nakamura trace the somewhat tainted historical development of bank-centred financial systems in Germany and Japan, and discuss some of the potentially serious problems of such systems.

Could more equity ownership by Canadian banks improve corporate governance in Canada? Amoako-Adu and Smith find no consistent pattern in Canadian data relating firm performance to a firm having directors affiliated with financial institutions. Morck and Nakamura find a negative relation between firm performance and the presence of directors affiliated with Canadian banks. Although this could reflect banks and other financial institutions taking a more active role in the governance of troubled firms, and thereby perhaps performing a useful service, we must conclude that there is no compelling evidence to support a broader role for banks or other financial institutions in Canadian corporate governance. It is probably more socially useful to explore other options for improving corporate governance.

Policy Implication 22

- The role of banks in corporate governance should not be expanded.

PUBLIC-POLICY OBJECTIVES AND CORPORATE GOVERNANCE

THE DECISIONS OF CANADA'S LARGE CORPORATIONS can either support or undermine the ability of governments to pursue their objectives. In the past, governments have used targeted taxes and subsidies to influence corporate decisions. This has caused enormous increases in the complexity of the tax code, leading many to conclude that it is hopelessly capricious. Recently, some have advocated using director liability as an alternative tool to achieve social policy objectives.

Nakamura, Cragg and Sayers argue that this is an inefficient approach to realizing such objectives. All the arguments for precise and well-defined liability raised in the section above on director liability are overwhelmingly relevant here. Exposing directors to liability for back wages, environmental damage, or failure to achieve social policy objectives is likely only to deter competent directors from accepting seats on a board. Directors must be able to control the things for which they are liable. We believe required disclosure of firms' contributions to public-policy objectives is a much more appropriate course. It is also likely to be more effective.

It is commonly alleged, for example, that North American shareholders have short time horizons and that this results in lower R&D spending than in Japan or other countries where managers are allegedly free to have long-term outlooks. Giammarino's study in this volume presents fairly conclusive evidence that R&D spending raises share values, not just in the long term, but immediately. Thus, we have a case where both public policy and shareholders appear to want more R&D spending. The absence of a requirement that Canadian firms disclose their R&D spending serves only to protect managers of firms that do little R&D from scrutiny by shareholders. We therefore suggest the following.

Policy Implication 23

- Firms should be required to disclose their research and development spending. Those that do no R&D should be required to say so.

We believe other social policy objectives might be approached the same way. For example, if worker retraining were a national priority, companies might be required to disclose their annual spending in this area. If the social policy objective is actually important to the public, consumers can choose to support companies with their business in response to their disclosures.

GOVERNANCE IN NONPROFIT ENTERPRISES

HIRSHHORN RAISES THE ISSUE OF ACCOUNTABILITY in not-for-profit firms. Increasing fiscal pressure on all levels of government makes efficient governance at not-for-profit institutions such as hospitals and universities critical. Governments are also increasingly willing to contract out certain public goods and services to the third or not-for-profit sector. Thus, we believe Canadian governments should undertake a comprehensive review of the legislative framework for nonprofits to determine the adequacy and effectiveness of the mechanisms of accountability to taxpayers, donors and beneficiaries. This legislation should be updated regularly in light of changing practices and demands.

Policy Implication 24

- Both the federal and the provincial governments should establish special advisory committees of professional advisors to and representatives of various not-for-profit organizations, as well as independent experts, to review and suggest changes to legislation concerning the governance of nonprofit institutions such as public service organizations, hospitals and universities.

Hirschhorn's suggestions of independent reviews and stringent reporting requirements for nonprofits should serve as a starting point for such a review. A central issue the review should address is to whom should the directors of a nonprofit organization be accountable. Should hospitals be run in the interests of patients (the customers), physicians (the skilled workers), or taxpayers (the providers of capital)? To whom should the directors of nonprofit organizations have fiduciary duties? A comprehensive examination of the governance of Canada's hospitals, universities, Crown Corporations, and other nonprofit organizations is long overdue. The motivation for such an endeavour should not be any allegation of wrongdoing or waste, but rather the simple – somewhat sobering – facts that these institutions are tremendously important and that governments are running out of money.

ARBITRATION

IF THE RIGHTS OF SHAREHOLDERS AND PENSION FUND BENEFICIARIES are to have any real content, they must be enforceable at reasonable cost and within a reasonable time frame. The various proposals we have advanced here are aimed at creating new legal rights and obligations and at clarifying and sometimes modifying old ones. Canada's legal system is already cumbersome and clogged. We do not want new corporate governance rules merely to add to the logjam.

We are also skeptical that the current adversary legal system can provide fair, prompt and reasonable settlements to corporate governance disputes. Long and costly legal battles deter shareholders from challenging corporate insiders. Since managers can use shareholders' money to pay legal bills, they have greater staying power. The formal legal system tips the balance too far in favour of big players.

The United Kingdom has developed an interesting way of dealing with this problem. *The Cadbury Report*, a detailed investigation into British corporate governance, established arbitration, rather than the formal adversary legal system, as the way to resolve corporate governance disputes. We believe a system of compulsory arbitration would be sensible in Canada too.

Policy Implication 25

- Corporate governance disputes should be settled by arbitration. They should only enter the legal system if the arbitration process is not properly followed.

One approach is for government to legislate compulsory arbitration. A more *laissez faire* approach would be to allow firms to include clauses in their corporate charters binding them, their directors, and their managers, to the decisions of arbitration committees. Shareholders would then be informed *via* prospectuses, proxies and annual reports as to whether the firm has so bound itself. Shareholder pressure would probably quickly result in almost universal acceptance of arbitration.

The arbitration committees should follow the laws and regulations established by governments. In corporate governance disputes, some variant of the following process might be used: each side names one arbitrator, and the two arbitrators then name a third; arbitration committees could then hear and rule on corporate governance disputes quickly and cheaply. Analogous systems could be established to arbitrate disputes related to pension fund governance.

A PUBLIC-POLICY PHILOSOPHY ON CORPORATE GOVERNANCE

THE ACCELERATING INTEGRATION OF WORLD FINANCIAL MARKETS is fast making distinctions between the corporate governance systems of different countries irrelevant. If Canadian companies fail to provide adequate corporate governance, Canadian investors will simply move their money abroad. Canadian companies will soon be forced to compete with rivals from all over the world. All else being equal, the company with the best governance will prevail. Therefore, the best way for the government to improve corporate governance in Canada is to open up the country to international competition quickly rather than slowly, and to prevent poorly governed firms from surviving on subsidies or other government favours.

Coercive corporate governance rules should not be used to promote general societal goals such as more R&D, increased worker training, or low unemployment. Ontario's rules making directors personally liable for back wages did not achieve the goal of reducing unemployment in the province. Their only effect was to encourage directors to resign when they feared the firm might be in trouble. But that is precisely the time when it is most important to have a well-functioning board.

R&D spending has been shown fairly conclusively to increase share values, not just in the long run, but immediately. The link between a well-trained work force and high share prices is less well documented, but common sense says it must surely exist. By first "getting the legal and economic environment right" and then allowing boards, CEOs, institutional investors, and other players in corporate governance to focus on boosting share prices, government will indirectly promote these broader goals. Therefore, most of our specific recommendations are different ways of saying "Do not". Do not interfere too much in firms' internal affairs. Do not legislate the structure of the board or its size. Do not favour any particular ownership structure; etc. If government sticks to free market policies, Canadian firms will find that better corporate governance is in the cards whether they like it or not.

A free-market economy depends on visibly fair legal and economic systems. For political and historical reasons, concentration of economic power is a concern in Canada. It is therefore reasonable to require full disclosure and outside oversight where there is any possibility of unprincipled behaviour by powerful insiders. It is for this reason that whistleblowers should be protected. It is also why we advise full disclosure of compensation paid to insiders, and why we strongly recommend that conduct committees review non-arm's-length transactions and that the details of such transactions be disclosed.

In the global economy, no country can afford to make its corporate governance laws too onerous without encouraging companies to find other, friendlier, jurisdictions in which to do business. Neither can a country afford to make its rules too lax or investors will simply find other places to put their money. Establishing a balance, while a bold challenge, imposes a comforting, practical constraint on law makers.

ENDNOTES

1   Also, since we would link compensation to how well the firm's shares do relative to those of other similar firms, the directors are insulated from any overall market fluctuations due to alleged myopia.
2   Such an option is initially "in-the-money" if, at the time it is written, it permits the CEO to buy stock at a discount from the current market price.
3   Exceptions should be made if corporate waste can be demonstrated; that is, if corporate resources were paid out to corporate management without any corresponding benefit to the firm.
4   However, the debate surrounding poison pills is not yet over. If managers use them to drive up offer prices in takeover bids, poison pills may actually benefit shareholders. A recent study by Comment & Schwert (1995) takes this view.
5   For a more thorough discussion, see MacIntosh (1993).
6   See also MacIntosh (1993).
7   See also MacIntosh (1993b).

BIBLIOGRAPHY

Bodie, Z., J. Light, R. Morck and R. Taggart. "Funding and Asset Allocation in Corporate Pension Plans: An Empirical Investigation" in *Issues in Pension Economics*. Edited by Bodie, Shoven and Wise. National Bureau of Economic Research Conference Volume, University of Chicago Press, 1987.

Comment, R. and G. Schwert "Poison or Placebo? Evidence on the Deterence and Wealth Effects of Modern Antitakeover Devices." *Journal of Financial Economics*, 9, 1 (1995):3-44.

Daniels, R. and P. Halpern "The Role of the Closely Held Public Corporation in the Canadian Economy and the Implications for Public Policy." *Canadian Business Law Journal*. (Forthcoming 1995).

Daniels, R. and J. MacIntosh, "Toward a Distinctive Canadian Corporate Law Regime." *Osgoode Hall Law Journal*, 29 (1991):863.

Daniels, R. J. and E. J. Waitzer, "Challenges to the Citadel: A Brief Overview of Recent Trends in Canadian Corporate Governance." (1994) *Canadian Business Law Journal*, 23 (1994):23.

Hermalin, B. E. and M. S. Weisbach. "The Effects of Board Composition and Direct Incentives on Firm Performance." *Financial Management*, 20, 4 (1991):101.

_____. "Endogenously Chosen Boards of Directors and their Monitoring of the C.E.O." (Unpublished Manuscript, 1995).

Lakonishok, J., A. Shleifer and R.W. Vishny. "The Impact of Institutional Trading on Stock Prices." *Journal of Financial Economics*, 32 (1992):23.

_____. "The Structure and Performance of the Money Management Industry." Brookings Papers on Economic Activity - Microeconomics. (1992):339-91.

Lakonishok, J., A. Shleifer, R. Thaler and R. Vishny, "Window Dressing by Pension Fund Managers." *American Economic Review*, 81 (1991):227.

J. G. MacIntosh, "The Role of Institutional and Retail Investors in Canadian Capital Markets." *Osgoode Hall Law Journal*, 31 (1993):2371.

MacIntosh, J. "The Canadian Securities Administrators' Takeover Proposals: Old Wine in New Bottles." *Canadian Journal of Business Law*, 22 (1993b):231.

McConnell, J. and H. Servaes. "Additional Evidence on Equity Ownership and Corporate Value." *Journal of Financial Economics*, 27 (1990):595.

R. Morck and M. Nakamura. "Banks and Corporate Control in Japan." (Unpublished Manuscript, 1994).

R. Morck, A. Shleifer and R. W. Vishny. "Management Ownership and Market Valuation." *Journal of Financial Economics*, 20 (1988):293.

_____. "Alternative Mechanisms for Corporate Control." *American Economic Review*, 79 (1989):842.

Pagano, M., F. Panetta and L. Zingales "Why do Companies Go Public: An Empirical Analysis." (Unpublished Manuscript, 1994).

Rosenstein, S. and J. Wyatt. "Outside Directors, Board Independence, and Shareholder Wealth." *Journal of Financial Economics*, 26 (1990):175.

Shleifer, A. and R. Vishny. "Corporate Governance." (Unpublished Manuscript, 1995).

Weisbach, M. S. "Outside Directors and CEO Turnover." *Journal of Financial Economics*, 20 (1988):431.

About the Contributors

Ben Amoako-Adu is Professor and Head of the Finance Area at Wilfrid Laurier University. Previously he taught Finance at York University and at the University of New Brunswick. He has published extensively in learned journals on topics related to investments, financial institutions, corporate finance, corporate governance, takeovers, restricted shares, and taxation and asset prices. He also provides consulting services to banks and multinational corporations.

Jennifer Arlen is Professor of Law at the University of Southern California Law Center, where she teaches business organizations, securities regulation and securities fraud. She holds a degree in law and a Ph.D. in Economics from New York University. Professor Arlen has written extensively on the subjects of corporate crime, deterrence and fraud.

Giovanni Barone-Adesi is Professor of Finance in the Faculty of Business at the University of Alberta and Visiting Professor of Finance at the Wharton School for 1994/95. He holds a Ph.D. from the Graduate School of Business at the University of Chicago and now teaches courses on investment issues, and options and futures at the undergraduate, master and doctoral levels. He has been a contributing author to a number of published articles on corporate financial issues.

Bruce Chapman holds both a Ph.D. and an LL.B. from the University of Toronto and now teaches at the Faculty of Law at that university. For the 1995 academic year he was the John M. Olin Visiting Professor in Law and Economics at the University of Virginia School of Law. Professor Chapman's research and teaching interests are in tort law, corporate law, legal theory, law and economics, and the theory of rational choice. He is the author of numerous articles on these subjects.

John Cragg holds a Ph.D. in economics from Princeton University and is Professor of Economics at the University of British Columbia. He has served as Director of the federal Prices and Incomes Commission and as a consultant to the B.C. Ministry of Social Services. In 1994 he gave the Innes Lecture to the Canadian Economics Association. Dr. Cragg has published widely in the areas of corporate finance, household demand behaviour, taxation, and social policy.

Ronald J. Daniels is Dean of Law at the University of Toronto. He is the author (or co-author) of numerous scholarly articles on topics as diverse as corporate and securities law, federalism and financial institution regulation, privatization in Eastern Europe, and government reform. He recently served as Chairman of the Ontario Task Force on Securities Regulation and was a member of the Toronto Stock Exchange Committee on Corporate Governance (the Dey Committee). Professor Daniels holds an LL.B. from the University of Toronto and an LL.M. from Yale University.

Jean-Claude Delorme joined the Caisse de dépot et placement du Québec as Chairman and Chief Executive Officer in July 1990 and resigned from this position on March 30, 1995. He holds an LL.B. from the Université de Montréal and was admitted to the Québec Bar in 1960. Mr. Delorme is an Officer of the Order of Canada and a member of the Board of Directors of several major Canadian corporations. He is Chairman of the Board of Directors of the National Gallery of Canada and Vice-Chairman of the Board of the Conference Board of Canada.

Ramy Elitzur is Associate Professor in the Faculty of Management at the University of Toronto. Much of his work has been in the area of agency problems in the firm and their effects on performance and reporting; his research has been published in numerous academic journals. In addition, he has written Management Accounting Guidelines on the design of executive incentive compensation plans and on outsourcing information systems for the Society of Management Accountants of Canada. Dr. Elitzur holds a Ph.D. from the Stern School of Business, New York University.

Stephen Foerster holds a Ph.D. in Finance from the Wharton School, University of Pennsylvania and is now Associate Professor of Finance at the School of Business at the University of Western Ontario. His main teaching and research interests are in the areas of investment management and capital markets. Recent Canadian publications include studies of price momentum models, stock returns and election cycles; the foreign exposure of TSE 35 companies; and tactical asset allocation strategies. He also works closely with a major Canadian investment dealer in the design and teaching of the Retail Training Program for investment advisors; he also acts as a consultant to the Equity Department of another investment dealer.

Jean-Marie Gagnon is Professor of Financial Management at Université Laval. He holds an MSC degree from Université Laval and a Ph.D. in Business from the University of Chicago. His research interests are in corporate governance and the effects of income taxes on capital markets and he has published articles in these areas in several national and international academic journals. Dr. Gagnon is a member of the Canadian Institute of Chartered Accountants and The Royal Society of Canada.

Ronald Giammarino is Associate Professor and Chair, Finance Division, in the Faculty of Commerce and Business Administration at the University of British Columbia. His teaching and research interests are in the areas of corporate finance, bank regulation and law and economics. He has acted as a consultant to B.C. Gas and the B.C. Government, and has appeared as an expert witness before the House of Commons Subcommittee reviewing the Canada Deposit Insurance Corporation (CDIC). Professor Giammarino holds a Ph.D. in Management from Queen's University.

Lee Gill has an MA in economics from Queen's University and is a senior project leader with the Corporate Law Policy Directorate of Industry Canada. Prior to joining Industry Canada, Mr. Gill was a senior project leader with the Legislative Review Directorate of Consumer and Corporate Affairs. He has also worked as a senior policy advisor with the Policy Branch of Environment Canada and as a senior economist with the Energy Policy Branch of Energy, Mines and Resources. At present, he is leading the work on Phase II amendments to the *Canada Business Corporation Act*.

Paul Halpern is Professor of Finance at the Faculty of Management, University of Toronto, Chair of the Advisory Board of the *Canadian Investment Review*, and Chair of the Research Committee of the Financial Research Foundation of Canada. He has also served as a consultant to governments, regulatory authorities and corporations in the areas of corporate finance, capital markets and securities. Professor Halpern holds a Ph.D. in Finance from the University of Chicago and has published research and applied papers for both academic and practitioner journals. His research interests are in mergers and acquisitions, corporate restructuring and corporate governance.

Roger Heath has been a Senior Policy Analyst at the Ministry of State for Science and Technology, the Economic Council of Canada, and now Industry Canada. His research interests are in the areas of technology finance, the comparison of international technology systems and programs, and technology-based trade frictions.

Ronald Hirshhorn is an independent economic and public policy consultant, based in Ottawa. Prior to establishing his own consulting firm, Mr. Hirshhorn was a senior economist and project director at the Economic Council of Canada. Much of Mr. Hirshhorn's research is related to issues of organizational design and the general problem of identifying appropriate instruments and institutions to achieve public policy objectives.

Clifford G. Holderness is Associate Professor of Finance at the Carroll School of Management at Boston College. He has published academic and practitioner articles on topics related to corporate control, large-block shareholders in public corporations, and property rights. Professor Holderness has undergraduate and graduate degrees from Stanford University and a graduate degree from the London School of Economics.

Robert Howse is Assistant Professor in the Faculty of Law at the University of Toronto and Assistant Director of the International Business and Trade Law Programme. His teaching and research work have concentrated on international economic law, federalism, public law, social and economic regulation and conflict of laws (private international law). He is the author and co-author of numerous books and monographs on topics ranging from the regulation of international trade (with Michael Trebilcock), income tax harmonization in Canada, and industrial policy, to constitutional reform. A forthcoming journal article deals with the limitations of the economic argument in the current debate over sovereignty.

Mark Huson is Assistant Professor of Finance in the Faculty of Business at the University of Alberta. Much of his research work has been directed to the effect of just-in-time manufacturing on firm performance in the United States (with Dhananjay Nanda), the effects of stock splits on changes in transaction costs and firm value, and the effect of secondary components on offer price and underpricing in initial public offerings (with Christopher F. Noe). He has also published an article on *The Effect of Restructuring Changes on Executive Compensation* (with Patricia Dechow and Richard Sloan).

Vijay Jog is a chemical engineer with graduate degrees in management and finance from McGill University and is now Professor of Finance at the School of Business, Carleton University. He specializes in corporate finance, value creation, taxation, and business financing and has published extensively on these subjects in leading international financial journals. Professor Jog has had wide experience in business financing, capital markets and taxation issues in both the private and public sectors.

Lewis Johnson is Professor of Finance at the School of Business, Queen's University. His research interests are focused on the valuation of financial assets, the development of financial strategies, and the operation of financial markets. His book (with Bo Pazderka) on the economic efficiency of Canadian stock markets, has just been published by the Fraser Institute. Professor Johnson holds a Ph.D. from the University of Toronto.

Clifton R. Lee-Sing is an economist with the Strategic Investment Analysis Directorate of the Micro-Economic Policy Analysis Branch of Industry Canada. He has been working on the development of a micro database for the Industry Canada corporate governance paper. He has a Master of Science (Finance) degree from the College of Graduate Studies and Research at the University of Saskatchewan. His thesis included an analysis and evaluation of the implications of various option trading strategies focusing on hedging against loss in time value of an investor's portfolio.

Jeffrey MacIntosh is Associate Professor of Law at the Faculty of Law, University of Toronto. His main teaching interests are in the areas of corporate and securities law, and in law and economics, although he has also taught contract and commercial law. Professor MacIntosh has published extensively in the area of corporate and securities law on such topics as shareholders' rights, the legal relationship between majority and minority shareholders, corporate takeovers, poison pills, the statutory oppression remedy, appraisal rights, the role of institutional and retail investors in Canadian capital markets, and directors' fiduciary duties. His current research deals with the special problems of financing high-technology enterprise in Canada.

Vikas Mehrotra holds a Ph.D. from the University of Oregon and is now Assistant Professor, Finance, in the Faculty of Business at the University of Alberta. His research interests have focused on empirical issues in corporate finance and on corporate restructuring and governance. Current work in progress includes an examination of firm performance and holding period returns around seasoned equity offerings (with Ken Shah), and an analysis of debt offerings and changes in the investment opportunity set facing issuing firms (with Mark Huson). He is also examining the subsequent performance of firms that spin-off assets.

Randall K. Morck obtained a Ph.D. in economics from Harvard University and currently holds the Stephen A. Jarislowsky Distinguished Chair in Finance at the University of Alberta's Faculty of Business. His research and teaching interests are in corporate finance and economics. His published works include a textbook on Managerial Finance (with P. Lusztig and B. Schwab); numerous articles in scholarly publications, – most recently on the economics of concentrated ownership and on corporate ownership and management – and several working papers, including one on banks and corporate control in Japan (with Masao Nakamura) and another on large shareholders and corporate performance (with David Stangeland).

Alice Nakamura holds a Ph.D. in Economics from Johns Hopkins University and is currently the Winspear Professor of Business in the Faculty of Business at the University of Alberta. She was the 1994/95 President of the Canadian Economics Association and is on the Executive and Board of the Canadian Employment Research Forum (CERF). Professor Nakamura was a member of the Axworthy Task Force on Social Security Reform. Her research interests lie in the areas of labour economics, firm behaviour, micro-analytic simulation, econometric methodology, price and productivity measurement, and social policy. Two of her recent publications deal with social security reform and the roles of insurance and income assistance related to Unemployment Insurance.

Masao Nakamura holds a joint appointment in the Faculty of Commerce and Business Administration and the Faculty of Applied Science at the University of British Columbia, where he teaches international business, technology management, Japanese management and new product development. He is also Japan Research Chair Professor in the UBC Institute of Asian Research. Professor Nakamura holds a Ph.D. in operations research and industrial engineering from Johns Hopkins University. His research focuses on economics and managerial decision processes underlying firm and household behaviour in North America and Japan, and in other countries. His current research topics include corporate governance and econometrics and he is the co-author of several books.

Ted Neave holds a Ph.D. from the University of California at Berkeley and is Professor of Finance at the School of Business, Queen's University. His research interests include discrete mathematics of dominance relations and derivative pricing, portfolio theory, and the economics of financial institutions. Professor Neave has been active in banking industry education, and has developed extensive simulation software for the industry. His most recent book is on the economics of financial markets.

Michel Patry is Associate Professor of Economics at the École des hautes études commerciales (HEC) and Director of the joint doctoral program in administration of Concordia University, HEC, McGill University and the Université du Québec à Montréal. He is also an associate researcher at the Centre interuniversitaire de recherche en analyse des organisations (CIRANO) and a member of the Centre d'études en administration internationale des HEC (CETAI). His research and teaching activities centre on the economic analysis of firms and industrial organization and he has published in the areas of the economic determinants of contracting out, the role of corporate takeovers and the consequences of regulation on the efficiency and productivity of Canadian firms. M. Patry holds a Ph.D. in Economics from the University of British Columbia.

Michel Poitevin holds a Ph.D. in Economics from the University of British Columbia and is currently Associate Professor in the Department of Economics at the Université de Montréal. He is also a researcher at the Centre de recherche en dévélopement économique (CRDE). As a specialist in financial and information economics at the firm level, Dr. Poitevin has conducted research in the areas of financial decision-making and production choices, information economics, financial markets and oligopolies as well as the economic consequences of asymmetric information and its effects on contracts and investment decisions. Dr. Poitevin also writes for the journal of economic analysis, *Actualité économique*.

P. Someshwar Rao is Director of the Strategic Investment Analysis Directorate in the Industry and Science Policy Sector at Industry Canada and is responsible for activities related to the Industry Canada research publications program, as well as an analysis of the effects of (domestic as well as foreign) investment, trade and technology, and Canada's corporate governance structure on the micro-growth potential of Canadian industry. Prior to joining Industry Canada, Dr. Rao was with the Economic Council of Canada, where he played a key role in the preparation of major reports on Canada's competitiveness; he also served as Acting Director of the CANDIDE model group that was responsible for the development of a disaggregated model of Canadian industry. Dr. Rao holds a Ph.D. from Queen's University.

Roberta Romano is Professor of Law at the Yale Law School and School of Management. She is the author of a recent book on American corporate law, series editor of the interdisciplinary readers in law series (published by Oxford University Press), and editor of the initial volume in that series. Professor Romano is a member of the American Academy of Arts and Science and was on the Board of Directors of the American Law and Economics Association. She has been Chair of both the Law and Economics, and the Business Associations sections of the Association of American Law Schools. Her research has focused on state competition for corporate charters, the political economy of takeover laws, shareholder litigation, and public pension funds.

Kathleen Sayers holds a Master's degree in Public Administration from the University of Southern California. She has had a long-standing involvement in adult education and skills upgrading for adult labour force participants, and has developed a series of courses and a certificate program as part of the Continuing Education Program at Simon Fraser University. An entrepreneur, she is the co-founder of Vancouver-based International Wordsmiths.

Larry Schwartz is a Toronto-based economist who is actively engaged in regulatory research and public policy analysis, with a particular interest in financial and capital markets issues. Formerly chief economist with the

Ontario Securities Commission, he worked in corporate banking and securities underwriting for many years and, since establishing his own consulting practice, he has provided economic and statistical research and policy development support for the federal Department of Finance, the Toronto Stock Exchange, the Investment Funds Institute of Canada, the Bureau of Competition Policy, and the Ontario Securities Commission, among others. Mr. Schwartz holds a Ph.D. from the Wharton School, University of Pennsylvania.

Brian F. Smith is Associate Professor of Finance at Wilfrid Laurier University and Director of the Mutual Group Financial Services Research Centre at that University's School of Business and Economics. Dr. Smith has researched extensively in the areas of financial institutions, mergers and acquisitions, and corporate governance. His research has been widely published. He is co-editor, with Michael Robinson, of a recent book on Canadian capital markets, and co-authored (with Lucy Ackert) a paper on stock prices, ordinary dividends and cash flows to shareholders. The Financial Services Research Centre, of which Dr. Smith is Director, was recently founded to promote applied research on Canadian financial institutions and markets. The Centre's main sponsor is the Mutual Group of Waterloo, Ontario, one of Canada's largest insurance companies.

David A. Stangeland is Assistant Professor of Finance in the Faculty of Management at the University of Manitoba and teaches all levels of corporate finance. His research concentrates on corporate control, shareholders' rights, and mergers and acquisitions. Dr. Stangeland has published articles in the *Journal of Financial and Quantitative Analysis, Business Quarterly* and the *Canadian Journal of Economics.* His article on antitakeover devices received the Irwin Distinguished Paper Award at the 1995 meeting of the Southwestern Finance Association. He holds a Ph.D. in Finance from the University of Alberta and is a member of the American Finance Association, the Financial Management Association and the Southwestern Finance Association.

Josée St-Pierre holds a Ph.D. from Laval University and is Professor of Finance at the Université de Québec à Trois-Rivières. Her current research focuses on corporate governance mechanisms, problems related to initial public offerings, the financial management of SMEs and project financing, while her teaching interests also include project management, and working capital managements. In 1990 Professor St-Pierre was the first recipient of the Harvey Rorke Memorial Prize, presented by the Financial Research Foundation of Canada for the best Ph.D. dissertation addressing a Canadian investment topic.

Michael J. Trebilcock is Professor of Law, Director of the Law and Economics Programme, and Chairman of the International Business and Trade Law

Programme at the University of Toronto Law School. His book, *The Common Law of Restraint of Trade* (1986), was awarded the Walter Owen Prize in 1988 for the best legal text in English published in Canada in the previous two years. Professor Trebilcock has been associated with various studies on Canadian competition policy, public enterprise in Canada, business bail-outs in Canada, misleading advertising and unfair business practice laws, regulatory reform, trade-related adjustment assistance policies and trade remedy laws. He has also been an expert witness or consultant for private law firms and the Competition Policy Bureau in a number of competition law matters.

Adrian Tschoegl currently teaches Multinational Management at the Wharton School at the University of Pennsylvania. He has published numerous monographs and articles in scholarly journals on international banking, Japanese finance, gold prices, and international trade and business. Prior to his appointment at Wharton, he worked for the Tokyo branch of a subsidiary of the Swiss Bank Corporation. In Tokyo, he was associated with SBCI Securities (Asia) Ltd. as a macro-economist following the Japanese economy for SBCI's equity clients in the United Kingdom, Europe, the United States and Japan, and the Swiss economy for SBC's clients in Japan. Dr. Tschoegl has a Ph.D. in International Business from the Sloan School at MIT.

Ajit Tulpule is Manager of Financial Applications with the Corporate Renaissance Group, Ottawa. A member of the Institute of Chartered Accountants of India, Mr. Tulpule came to Canada in 1990 and is a graduate of the Masters in Management Studies program at the School of Business, Carleton University.

Michael S. Weisbach holds a Ph.D. in Economics from the Massachusetts Institute of Technology and is Associate Professor in the College of Business and Public Administration at the University of Arizona. His research and teaching interests include corporate finance, the economics of organizations and corporate governance and control. Dr. Weisbach has published on the subjects of CEO turnover and the firm's investment decisions; corporate governance and hostile takeovers; and the effects of board composition on firm performance (with B. E. Hermalin). He is currently carrying out research on the design of corporate governance systems.

Bernard Yeung is Associate Professor in International Business at the School of Business Administration, University of Michigan, and is also a faculty member of the University's Tax Policy Research Centre. His research interest is in multinational enterprise economics and empirical international trade. He has collaborated with Randall Morck, among others, on articles in economics and management for several scholarly journals. Professor Yeung holds an MBA and a Ph.D. from the Graduate School of Business at the University of Chicago.

INDUSTRY CANADA UNDERTAKES MICRO-ECONOMIC STUDIES on a wide range of subjects to provide a solid analytical foundation for the Department's policies and programs. Many of these studies are made available through the Industry Canada Publications Program, which consists of a Research Volume Series; a Working and Occasional Paper Series; Policy Discussion Papers; and a quarterly newsletter.

The research volumes draw together work by several authors on diverse aspects of a given micro-economic theme. Industry Canada appoints distinguished academics to act as general editors; they, in turn, select experts in their fields to prepare draft papers on identified issues. The papers are presented and subjected to peer review at a conference attended by representatives invited from the business, legal, and academic communities as well as government organizations. The proceedings of the conferences are subsequently published.

The working and occasional papers have a more concentrated focus and provide a vehicle for new research. The discussion papers provide the department with important background information on micro-economic policy issues of strategic importance. All documents are reviewed by outside experts.

All of these important research and policy efforts are disseminated directly to key organizations throughout Canada. Summaries of major research findings and their policy implications are disseminated more broadly through the Department's quarterly newsletter, *MICRO*.

THE INDUSTRY CANADA RESEARCH SERIES

- FOREIGN INVESTMENT, TECHNOLOGY AND ECONOMIC GROWTH

- CORPORATE GLOBALIZATION THROUGH MERGERS AND ACQUISITIONS

- MULTINATIONALS IN NORTH AMERICA

- CANADIAN-BASED MULTINATIONALS

- CORPORATE DECISION-MAKING IN CANADA